WILLIAM HAZLITT
By William Bewick
The National Portrait Gallery

William Hazlitt

HERSCHEL BAKER

THE BELKNAP PRESS OF

HARVARD UNIVERSITY PRESS

Cambridge, Massachusetts

1 9 6 2

This book is for
Ann and Bill and Pam,
who grew up with it

PREFACE

Any effort to deal compendiously with a man like Hazlitt, whose work is so vast and varied and disorderly, is, if not presumptuous, at any rate imprudent. But a generation has passed since the late P. P. Howe produced his standard *Life* and then his great edition of the *Works*, during which time new manuscript sources have become available and new information has been published on Hazlitt and his contemporaries; and so a further effort to deal with this important and exasperating writer would seem to be in order.

My intention has been to place Hazlitt in his literary, political, and philosophical milieu, and to trace the development and expression of his main ideas, relating them to the facts of his career in so far as these are known or can be ascertained. Despite Howe's splendid and devoted labors, which have put all students of the period deeply in his debt, ideas as such did not greatly interest him, and his comparative neglect of the aspect of Hazlitt's work that Hazlitt himself regarded as the most important has long been recognized. The ideas, to be sure, are inseparable from the man, and are expressed in the battles he engaged in, the causes he championed, the friends and enemies he made.

To regard Hazlitt merely as an essayist, or as a journalist and pamphleteer, or as a lecturer and critic, is to ignore the scope and contour of his whole immense production. Because that production, which embraces so many kinds of work that it seems to lack a single focus, is itself almost an index of the period, and because it all bears the stamp of his tenacious individualism and his obstinate convictions, this effort to assess it as a whole will, I hope, enable us to see why Hazlitt is important, and why he retains our affection and respect.

In the course of my researches I have incurred many pleasant obligations. Professor Willard Pope abetted me in plundering Benjamin Robert Haydon's journal, which is now in his possession. Professor Lewis Patton put at my disposal his transcript of William Godwin's diary, as well as photostats of many other items from the Abinger Collection in Duke University Library. Professor H. M. Sikes generously permitted me to appropriate anything I wanted from his forthcoming edition of Hazlitt's correspondence. Sir Geoffrey Keynes and Mr. and Mrs. Donald F. Hyde let me use unpublished Hazlitt letters that they own. Officials of the British Museum, the Forster Collection of Victoria and Albert Museum, the National Library of Scotland, Dr. Williams's Library, the

PREFACE

John Rylands Library, the Carl and Lily Pforzheimer Foundation, Inc., the Henry W. and Albert A. Berg Collection of the New York Public Library, the Historical Society of Pennsylvania, the Wordsworth Collection of Cornell University Library, Yale University, and the library of my own institution have been unfailingly cooperative. For permission to reproduce the illustrations in this book I am indebted to the National Portrait Gallery of London, the Harvard Theatre Collection, the Houghton Library of Harvard University, and Professor Willard Pope. I am grateful to the John Simon Guggenheim Memorial Foundation for a fellowship permitting time for travel and research in the early stages of this work, to the editorial board of the *Keats-Shelley Journal* for allowing me to use, in a slightly different form, some things that I had written for that publication, to the Clark Fund of the Harvard Foundation for aid in the preparation of a complicated manuscript, and to Miss Constance Nelson, the most patient and adroit of typists, for her struggles with my Coptic script. My wife's contribution to this book, as to all my undertakings, scholarly and other, has been so great that she would not wish to have it told.

H. B.

Harvard University
May 1961

CONTENTS

CONTENTS

CONTENTS

PART THREE
THE LATER YEARS

ILLUSTRATIONS

PORTRAITS

HOLOGRAPHS

xiii

ILLUSTRATIONS

PART ONE

BEGINNINGS

I

Prologue

❖◇◆❖

THE TRADITION OF DISSENT

Although only a few names and dates make up the scanty record, what little we know of Hazlitt's early years tends to prove that the child is father to the man. The second son and third child of an expatriate Irishman with no money and unfashionably liberal notions about civil and religious liberty, he was born 10 April 1778 at Maidstone, Kent, where his father led the Unitarian congregation.* After various moves in England and Ireland, most of them prompted by the elder Hazlitt's inability to accommodate his thinking to the received prejudices about seditious American colonists, the family sailed in 1783 for New York, perhaps hoping, as their friends surmised, to "emancipate" America from the yoke of Calvinism,[1] and surely expecting to find the freedom and security they had failed to find at home. As their daughter's diary shows,[2] bad luck plagued them up and down New England. After four years of trial sermons, temporary appointments, illness, and frustration, the elder Hazlitt took his family back to England and to a safe, if dull, anchorage with the Unitarian flock at Wem, a few miles north of Shrewsbury.[3]

Between his ninth and fifteenth years this little market town on the border of Wales was Hazlitt's home, but in 1793, aided by a fund for needy preachers' sons,[4] he was sent to the new Unitarian academy at Hackney to study for the ministry. Although the next two or three years as a student undermined his faith and so dashed his father's hopes for

---

* The Hazlitts, though a close-knit family, were not greatly given to expressions of affection. To be sure, Hazlitt's veneration of his father (1737–1820) irradiates his later works (see pages 19–22), but there seems to be only one clear reference (10.63) to his mother, Grace Loftus Hazlitt (1746–1842/43). His brother John (1767–1837), a professional miniaturist in London after 1787, provided him a home, or at any rate a base of operations, between 1799 and about 1807. His sister Margaret (1770–1844) — "who took some notice of us when children, and who augured, perhaps, better of us than we deserved" (4.97) — remained a spinster all her life and did not long survive her aged mother.

3

him, they put him in the way of books and ideas whose influence was to be decisive in confirming the libertarian ideals that he had learned at home and would carry like a banner all his life. Leaving Hackney with a spotty education and no means of livelihood, he went limping back to Wem, there to read and brood and deplore his sorry lot. For the next couple of years, when, as he said later, he did "nothing but think," [5] he tried, but tried in vain, to finish an ambitious essay on ethical theory that he had begun at school. His difficulties were immense: having made, as he thought then and later, a "metaphysical discovery" of real importance, he felt he "owed something to truth" by setting it in prose; but the words refused to come. An older and more verbal Hazlitt remembered that in eight years he wrote eight pages, "under circumstances of inconceivable and ridiculous discouragement." [6]

Finally, in the spring of 1798, when he lay "crushed" and "bleeding" under the weight of his disappointments and disabilities, he met Coleridge, and for the first time the boy who had "passed for an idiot" [7] began to find a language for his thoughts. [8] This event, one of the pivots on which his life turned, he would one day describe with the finality of art, but its only immediate result was that he made one more effort — his twentieth — to finish the essay on ethics. Halfway down the second page, having tried in vain to "pump up" words and images from the "gulph of abstraction" in which he had been buried, he threw away his pen and "shed tears of helpless despondency on the blank unfinished paper." [9] It was then, when he had failed at everything he tried, that he went out into the world to become a painter like his elder brother John. The awkward, inarticulate boy, without friends or money or connections, could hardly hope for quick success, nor did he find it.

His early struggles, like those of other men, were private and obscure, but they were framed by public events of spectacular importance. Although it is easy for us, like him, to exaggerate his woes, it is hard to overestimate the effect of these events upon his life and work. A few months after he went to Hackney, France and England were at war; and between then and 1803, when the uneasy Peace of Amiens yielded to the struggle that would end at Waterloo, he acquired the stock of emotions and ideas that served him all his life. It was in this decade, when he was "bewildered in a shadow, lost in a dream," [10] that he turned from boy to man. For such an incorrigible egotist, he says little of his childhood, and what he says is reticent, [11] but the ten years after 1793 afforded him a theme for boundless introspection. Then he read the books, looked at the pictures, and met the men who formed his mind and taste; then his configuration of character assumed the shape it kept;

then he laid up that emotional capital that became his treasure trove. "If what I write at present is worth nothing," he said in 1823, "at least it costs me nothing. But it cost me a great deal twenty years ago. I have added little to my stock since then, and taken little from it." [12] Such comments — and Hazlitt made them often toward the end — oblige us to examine the dim years of his youth with care, to explore the sources of his "stock," to record his private responses to public events, and to trace his progress, if we can, through that late eighteenth-century dawn when it was bliss to be alive and very heaven to be young.

⋄ ⋄ ⋄

One of the first and sturdiest of Hazlitt's intellectual legacies was the tradition of English nonconformity. He was bred to the moral and political ideals of what Carlyle, with gruff condescension, called the "Dissenterage," and despite the erosion of his own religious faith he continued to revere the motives of those who thought that political and social opprobrium was not too high a price to pay for intellectual independence. To be sure, Dissenters had been "tolerated" since 1689, but in what Joseph Priestley called the "capital branches" of civil liberty [13] — religion and education — they, like Roman Catholics, were an oppressed minority throughout the eighteenth century. They were barred from holding public office under the Crown or from attending either university; they could be neither married nor buried except with Anglican rites in which they disbelieved; and they were compelled to contribute financially to a church whose articles they abjured. Although the curious, and curiously English, evasion known as the Indemnity Acts had afforded some relief,* the Church of England, while no longer a persecuting body after 1689, took care to guard its vested interests. Until 1828 Dissenters continued to groan under a "tyranny of incapacitation" which retained its legal status [14] and to resist, as best they could, that "absurd and odious test" that Macaulay later described as a scandal to the pious and a laughing-stock to the profane. [15] By Hazlitt's time, moreover, the Dissenters' notorious advocacy of two great revolutions had added fear and anger to the contempt and easy ridicule that they had borne for generations. Sydney Smith said that when a country squire

---

* Although a statute of Charles II's early reign required that every official under the Crown should receive the Anglican sacrament within three months of assuming office, in its almost annual Indemnity Acts after 1727 Parliament extended the time for those who "through ignorance of the law, absence, and unavoidable accident" had failed to qualify. See William Lecky, *A History of England in the Eighteenth Century,* I (1878), 280 f.

heard about an ape he wished to give it nuts and apples; when he smelled a Dissenter his first impulse was to have him whipped and jailed.[16]

For Hazlitt, such opprobrium was a badge of honor. He thought that Dissenters had met the forces of superstition and legal imposture with a responsible commitment to their own convictions, and if their long habit of resistance made them obnoxious to the vested interests it also constituted their peculiar glory. "Our sciolists would persuade us that the different sects are hot-beds of sedition," he wrote in 1818,

> because they are nurseries of public spirit, and independence, and sincerity of opinion in all other respects. They are so necessarily, and by the supposition. They are Dissenters from the Established Church: they submit voluntarily to certain privations, they incur a certain portion of obloquy and ill-will, for the sake of what they believe to be the truth: they are not time-servers on the face of the evidence, and that is sufficient to expose them to the instinctive hatred and ready ribaldry of those who think venality the first of virtues, and prostitution of principle the best sacrifice a man can make to the Graces or his Country. . . . On the contrary, the different sects in this country are, or have been, the steadiest supporters of its liberties and laws: they are checks and barriers against the insidious or avowed encroachments of arbitrary power, as effectual and indispensable as any others in the Constitution: they are depositaries of a principle as sacred and somewhat rarer than a devotion to Court-influence — we mean the love of truth.[17]

The dissidence of dissent and the Protestantism of the Protestant religion, as Burke had called it, was for the elder Hazlitt and his friends the first and last responsibility of anyone attentive to the claims of self-respect, and when, near the end of his life, Hazlitt cited "republicanism and puritanism" [18] as the indelible marks of his early training he underscored a major motif in his work.

Coleridge, himself a nonconformist in his salad days, traced the "generation" of Dissent as Presbyterian, Arian, Socinian, and finally Unitarian,[19] and his remark reminds us that the various nonconformist sects represented not so much a unified minority as a certain state of mind. Historically and temperamentally Dissenters were committed to assert the "rights" that continued to elude them, and from the days of the Clarendon Code in the early Restoration to the repeal of the Test and Corporation Acts in 1828 they were agreed only in objecting to the *status quo.* Such resistance was anchored in the conviction that since questions of conscience and religion were beyond the reach of any institution, any law that penalized religious individualism must be wrong. As the early history of Protestantism makes regrettably clear, the leaders of the Reformation (whom Hazlitt sentimentalized) were less concerned with real religious freedom than with their own alleged prerogatives; but their successors advanced to a kind of religious *laissez faire,* and on this principle they built the demands for civil and religious freedom that loom so large in later English history. Whereas a bishop's speculations were bounded by the Thirty-nine Articles, Dissenters recognized no such statutory restraint. If Anglican theology was a kind of Gothic shrine in the Palladian basilica of eighteenth-century thought, as once was said, Dissenters refused to seek its shelter: they were scornful of convention and hostile to control. It is not surprising that Samuel Johnson deplored the work of Joseph Priestley (who scrapped Trinitarian theology and expounded the doctrine of a corporeal soul), for he thought it "tended to unsettle every thing, and yet settled nothing." [20] None the less, the unceasing search for "truth" was for Priestley and his coreligionists a moral obligation, and freedom of opinion a right invulnerable to any regulation. Priestley spoke for all Dissenters when he told Pitt that honest religion required neither a politician's aid nor protective legislation. "It wants no support that you, Sir, as a statesman, can give it, and it will prevail in spite of any obstruction that you can throw in its way." [21]

The political implications of such an attitude are clear. Dissent, which began as a protest against ecclesiastical authority, became an affirmation of both civil and religious freedom. In Hazlitt's boyhood we hear little of the ancient claims for "Christian liberty" as the prerogative of the regenerated man under the New Law of the Gospel, but much about political "rights" that are as natural and inexorable as the force of gravitation. Although an age of scientific progress and expanding capitalism no longer cared for the arguments of a Tyndale or a Cartwright, it was enchanted by the slogans and procedures that could demonstrate, as it seemed, the truth of nature; and the resulting effort to establish moral value on the same foundation as, say, Newton's second law of motion is too much like our own mistakes to afford surprise. After the Restoration the energies of Protestant individualism tended to find expression in demands that, if not new, were given new emphasis by changes in the social structure, in economic behavior, and in political action. Natural liberties, common to all men, dislodged the Christian liberties that Luther and Calvin had assigned to the elect, and promises of future felicity for regenerated sinners were converted into the immediate political and financial advantages of life, liberty, and property for every solvent citizen.

In the course of this long and complicated secularization of English thought no man looms larger than that loyal Whig and Anglican, John Locke. As almost all Dissenters thought, he had nailed down the philosophical foundations of civil and religious freedom. Calvin had about as much interest in toleration as Henry VIII or Pope Paul III, and his

PROLOGUE

Genevan theocracy reminds us that Protestantism and liberty were not initially convertible terms. Even a century later Milton secured his republicanism, such as it was, in theology, and his stirring defense of religious individualism rested ultimately on theological sanctions. But Locke freed politics from theology, and so it fell to him to philosophize the *status quo* of Restoration politics. Laying forever the ghost of divine right, he not only refuted the claims of Stuart absolutism, as the triumphant Whigs believed; he also undermined the foundations of a hierarchical society and proclaimed the principles of freedom and equality that Dissenters thought were, or ought to be, the boast of English-speaking people. No English monarch after Charles II was in any doubt that he owed his crown to Parliament, and any who defied its sovereignty learned, like James II, the price of his temerity. Locke provided the philosophical sanctions for political behavior that the Tudors would have thought incredible, and therefore his work, as Hazlitt said, should be regarded as the great "text-book" of liberty.[22]

Locke's achievement was to justify political aspirations as natural rights. Responding to the social and economic pressures of a new age, he formulated the great principle of government by consent, and then secured it by secular sanctions that almost everyone endorsed, at least in theory. In seeking to rationalize assaults on the obsolete restraints of church and state he converted the ancient concept of natural law from a restrictive code for curbing sinful man into a franchise for his expanded freedoms. Despite the creaky machinery of the social contract with which Locke shored up the doctrine of consent, it is significant that he looked for a juridical, rather than a theological, basis of government and that he did not resort to supernatural sanctions. He believed that man has a natural and inalienable right to life, liberty, and property, and that the great — indeed, the only — end of government is the protection of these rights. It follows, of course, that when a government does not fulfill its function, the people who have delegated to it their authority may recall it once again.

Almost all Dissenters held Locke in special veneration. In his theory they could find the sanctions they required for toleration, civil liberty, and a healthy respect for solvency; and throughout the eighteenth century — when the Whig and then the Tory oligarchs sat upon their vested interests — they admiringly reworked and expanded Locke's doctrine of natural rights to support demands that they never quite secured.

8

THE TRADITION OF DISSENT

Happily we need not survey the huge literature of Dissent (for Dissenters were incorrigibly prone to publication), but in the work of the two most noted nonconformists of Hazlitt's youth we may sample it.

Richard Price (1732–1791), once famed for his skill in public finance and now remembered, if at all, for his defense of two great revolutions, was a preacher of such luminous piety that he seemed almost saintly to his coreligionists.[23] To his piety was added a genuinely philosophical mind and a zeal for constitutional reform. Although the ten big volumes of his collected works attest to the scope and vigor of his thought, compared to Joseph Priestley (1733–1804) he was something of a sluggard. The Voltaire of the Unitarians, as Hazlitt called him,[24] and a man whom young Charles Lamb loved and honored "almost profanely,"[25] Priestley was on many counts remarkable. A distinguished scientist who discovered oxygen and won membership in the Royal Society for the treatise on electricity that Benjamin Franklin encouraged him to write, he moved easily from chemistry to metaphysics, from metaphysics to theology, from theology to political theory, from political theory to history, revealing a dilettante enthusiasm and a professional competence in everything he touched. He probably wrote more books on more subjects, said Francis Jeffrey, than any other English author,[26] and certainly more, as he himself admitted, than he would wish to read again.[27] But he was first and last a man of God, and young Coleridge expressed a view that no doubt many shared when he said that Priestley's experiments in science gave "*wings* to his more sublime theological works."[28] He not only tried to reconcile Christianity with philosophical materialism and to dislodge the doctrine of predestination with his own variety of determinism, but as a pioneer in the historical method of Biblical exegesis he attacked such "corruptions" as Trinitarian theology and the plenary inspiration of the Scriptures in order to show that Unitarianism alone was compatible with primitive Christianity and the new-found facts of science.

Price and Priestley (both of whom were friends of Hazlitt's father) did not agree on everything — otherwise they would not have been Dissenters — but both were committed to the proposition that, as Price put it, liberty "is the foundation of all honour, and the chief privilege and glory of our nature."[29] There are various kinds of freedom, Price explained, but whether physical, moral, religious, or civil it rests upon "the universal law of rectitude." This moral law, like other natural laws, is "coeval with eternity; as unalterable as necessary, everlasting truth; as independent as the existence of God; and as sacred, venerable, and awful as his nature and perfections."[30] It is the source and sanction of all freedom and, because freedom is the necessary condition of virtue, of all our moral choices too. In his *Observations on the Nature of Civil Liberty* (1776) — next to Paine's *Common Sense* the most influential defense of the American Revolution — Price insisted that the colonists' cause was to be determined not by citing *"Precedents, Statutes and Charters"* but by invoking the eternal truths of "reason and equity, and the rights of humanity" that the universal law of rectitude subsumes;[31] and at the end of his life he welcomed the French Revolution as exemplifying the same great principle. Genuine patriotism, he said to Burke's dismay, is based on virtue, truth, and liberty; and no government that denies the fact is worthy of support. Moreover, since the moral law of nature requires, among other things, popular sovereignty, even a king must remember that he is merely "the first servant of the public, created by it, maintained by it, and responsible to it."[32] Tactfully, Price did not mention George III by name.

Like Price, Priestley sought no more than a practical application of the principles by which England had nominally been governed since 1689. It was reported that when these two champions of constitutional reform — one a kind of belated Cambridge Platonist, the other a militant empiricist — argued philosophically they seemed like fencers in a test of skill, but when they attacked the enemies of civil and religious liberty they leaped upon their prey together.[33] Preaching his old friend's funeral sermon, Priestley, while skirting their philosophical disagreements, spoke for all Dissenters when he said that Price had made the axioms of good government as "indisputable" as those of geometry.[34] It was the kind of eulogy that Priestley himself tried to earn. His sharp, eclectic mind worked with zeal (and sometimes originality) on a staggering array of subjects, but in his many political tracts he was content to restate the principles of consent and toleration on which Dissenters pinned their hopes throughout the eighteenth century.

Thus his famous *Essay on the First Principles of Government* (1768), a defense of natural rights, equality, and social progress, expounds in lucid, easy prose the republican ideals that Locke had adumbrated but that were yet to be converted to reality. Certain "political" liberties like high office, he concedes, perhaps should be reserved for men of substance, but in defending personal rights against restrictions that the general good requires he goes far beyond the *status quo*. On the prerogatives of a free conscience he is adamant. They are sacred, Priestley says, and if the countrymen of Milton and Algernon Sidney should ever sink into despotism it will be "by means of the seeming necessity of having recourse to illegal methods, in order to come at opinions or persons generally obnoxious." [35] Because "the business of religion, and every thing fairly connected with it" is a "personal" matter "altogether foreign to the nature, object, and use of civil magistry," all arguments for conformity must infallibly yield to "the authority of God and conscience." [36] Against any appeal to the collective wisdom or the mystical solidarity of the community or to the expedients of practical politics, Priestley opposes a flinty individualism; [37] and even though his object is religious toleration he supports it by invoking natural rights that epitomize the aggressive secularism of the age which he adorned.

As Price and Priestley realized, the Dissenters' disabilities were rooted in an electoral system that enabled a few powerful families and their agents to control Parliament. An exchange between Johnson and Boswell as they were touring Scotland in 1773 puts the problem tersely. "Consider, sir," said Boswell, "what is the House of Commons? Is not a great part of it chosen by peers? Do you think, sir, they ought to have such an influence?" Mindful of Wilkes and the unruly Middlesex elections, Johnson had no doubts at all: "Yes, sir. Influence must ever be in proportion to property, and it is right it should." "But is there not reason to fear that the common people may be oppressed," asked Boswell. "No sir. Our great fear is from want of power in government. Such a storm of vulgar force has broke in." [38] Since no group ever willingly relinquishes power, we need not be surprised that the Whig and Tory oligarchs did not rush to extend the franchise to those whom they regarded as socially undesirable and politically unstable. Drawing their strength mainly from the lower and middle classes, the Dissenters comprised the tradesmen, small landowners, and laborers who were "the bones, and muscles, and sinews of civil society," [39] but despite their social status they were not content with toleration. As a Quaker stay-maker from Thetford told Burke, toleration itself was an insult to freeborn Britons, for it was the counterfeit, and not the opposite, of "intoleration," and both were despotisms. "The one assumes to itself the right of withholding liberty of conscience, and the other of granting it." [40] Conservatives found it possible to resist such arguments and still sleep soundly, for they knew that real religious freedom would mean political reform. When the Dissenters pointed to their rising economic strength and cited their part in the bloodless triumph of 1688, their adversaries, ensconced behind hereditary privileges, remembered the regicides of 1649 and did nothing to correct the absurdities of a parliamentary system that insured their power. "Of all ingenious instruments of despotism," said Sydney Smith not long before the First Reform Bill, "I must commend a popular Assembly, where the majority are paid and hired, and a few bold and able men by their brave Speeches make the people believe they are free." [41]

❖ ❖ ❖

From the Establishment itself, of course, Dissenters — and Catholics — could look for no concession. Elizabeth's creation of the Anglican Church had been an act of political expedience, and its clergy had never forgotten (or been permitted to forget) their dependence on the Crown. The extent of that dependence had been underscored in the early eighteenth century by two influential men: by Benjamin Hoadly, Bishop of Bangor and protagonist in the so-called Bangorian controversy that disturbed the reign of George I, and by William Warburton in *The Alliance between Church and State* (1736), a classic statement of Erastianism. Hoadly's famous sermon (1717) on the text "My kingdom is not of this world" elaborately construed the church as a kind of civil service without divine authority or political independence, and when the dust of more than two hundred pamphlets settled and Hoadly had gathered his rewards at Hereford and Salisbury and Winchester, Warburton came forward with his urbane assertion that all was well in the Establishment. [42] Invoking the "united reason of the whole community" as vested in the government, Warburton justified the "restraints" — sometimes miscalled "punishments" — that the state decrees to curb "mischievous" opinion. Whatever "small casual *Harm*" may result from such restraints, he smoothly says, is "abundantly compensated by those vast Advantages accruing to the State therefrom," for like all Erastians, and unlike all Dissenters, he assumed that the whole is greater than the sum of all its parts. Whatever its cost in terms of the individual's rights, an established church is justified, in his view as in Hooker's or in Burke's, on the same ground that the state itself is justified: as a bulwark against the chaos of private opinion and as the embodiment of the general good. To be sure, he conceded, each man has a natural (Lockean) right to hold his own beliefs, but not the right to act upon them; and however shrill the objections to compulsory tests and legal disabilities, the good citizen will remember that "THE TRUE END FOR WHICH RELIGION IS ESTABLISHED IS, NOT TO PROVIDE FOR THE TRUE FAITH, BUT FOR CIVIL UTILITY." [43]

Throughout the eighteenth century the Establishment reposed on its protective legislation, and by Hazlitt's time its nadir had been reached. Stripped of everything but legal power, it used that power only to maintain itself. As the Jacobite attempts of 1715 and 1745 had shown, Catholicism could no longer endanger its existence; but even in the face of the Methodist revival, the Dissenters' agitation, and the gains of natural science it was content with mere survival. The spiritual needs that Wesley had recognized and the social problems that the Industrial Revolution had created were ignored by bishops blind to everything but the threat of innovation. On Warburton's high authority they held that the clergy should be regarded as a group of civil servants, and on even higher authority that the laborer is worthy of his hire; and their leaders, by luck or cunning, made sure that they were well rewarded. Of twenty-seven bishoprics — some of them, like Durham, Ely, and Winchester, worth twenty or thirty thousand pounds a year — eleven were at one point held by noble houses and fourteen by former tutors or friends of politicians.[44] The powerful Manners family occupied eight English and twelve Irish sees; one of its eminent pluralists enjoyed an estimated income of £650,000 from the Establishment;[45] and its most distinguished cleric, who held the see of Canterbury from 1805 to 1828, parceled out sixteen livings and various cathedral appointments among seven of his kinsmen. Watson of Llandaff, to whom young Wordsworth addressed one of the angriest republican manifestos of the age, retained his hold on sixteen livings, but he found his estate on the shores of Windermere so beguiling that he visited his diocese only once in thirty-four years.[46]

While the clergy grimly held their pluralities and sinecures as the praying section of the Tory party, their opponents' protests mounted. Mary Wollstonecraft, answering Burke's defense of Anglican privilege, tartly pointed out that when an English family had a son for whom there was nothing else to do they made a clergyman of him,[47] and Wordsworth called such drones the natural advocates of "slavery civil and religious." [48] As a young man Coleridge denounced "the eighteen-thousand-pound-a-year religion of episcopacy," [49] and even as a defender of the Church in his old age he conceded that it was blighted by "prudence" and servility.[50] In all the venerable hierarchy, asked Godwin, is there one man who "can lay his hand upon his heart, and declare, upon his honour and conscience, that the emoluments of his profession have no effect in influencing his judgment? The supposition is absurd." [51] Hazlitt thought the venality of the Anglican clergy a scandal and their politics obscene, but the very head and front of their offending was their surrender of conscience to authority. An aspiring young clergyman, with "day-dreams of lawn-sleeves, and nightly beatific visions of episcopal mitres," acknowledges to the world that ease means more to him than principle. His profession is not to tell his version of the truth but to repeat the formulas that other men prescribe.

He expects one day to be a Court-divine, a dignitary of the Church, an ornament to the State; and he knows all the texts of Scripture, which, tacked to a visitation, an assize, or corporation-dinner sermon, will float him gently, "like little wanton boys that swim on bladders," up to the palace at Lambeth.[52]

For Hazlitt, the casuistry and cynicism of the Establishment were epitomized by William Paley, the high priest of theological utilitarianism and the prince of Anglican apologists. In Coleridge's republican days he and Hazlitt agreed that for Paley's *Principles of Morals and Political Philosophy* to be a required text at Cambridge was "a disgrace to the national character,"[53] and in 1818, thirteen years after Paley's death, Hazlitt ended a withering essay "On the Clerical Character" by describing that "shuffling Divine" as the hero of the Establishment. He was a man who had employed all his second-hand abilities "in tampering with religion, morality, and politics, — in trimming between his convenience and his conscience, — in crawling between heaven and earth, and trying to cajole both." That his famous book on moral philosophy should have been a sacred text for Anglicans was entirely natural, he ironically observed, for to the defense of "existing abuses of every description" he had contrived "a very elaborate and consolatory elucidation of the text, *that men should not quarrel with their bread and butter.*" *

Hazlitt summarized one of the cardinal precepts of Dissent when he said that "religion cannot take on itself the character of law without ceasing to be religion; nor can law recognise the obligations of religion for its principles, nor become the pretended guardian and protector of the faith, without degenerating into inquisitorial tyranny."[54] That the Anglican policy of exclusion would eventually collapse was the hope of all Dissenters, and confidence in the inevitable triumph of reform was one of the major motifs in the propaganda of Dissent. When Hazlitt admiringly cites man's slow progress from the Cave of Bigotry, through "one dark passage after another," to enlightenment,[55] he strikes the note that Price and Priestley had so often struck, and even in the age of Metternich and Castlereagh he did not despair. Although skeptical of inevitable and accelerating progress, he shared the Dissenters' disrespect for political obsolescence, and in the dark night of reaction that clouded his adult life he saw, or professed to see, glimmerings of the dawn. Long acquaintance with their disabilities had not unnaturally made Dissenters

* 7.252. As early as 1807, in his *Reply* to Malthus (1.246n), Hazlitt expressed his "slender opinion" of Paley's intellect, and later in the same work (1.346n) he stated his objections to Paley's theology in terms that anticipate "On the Clerical Character" (7.242–253).

wary of precedents and prescriptive rights and sentimental talk about the beauty of the past. Appeals to tradition, they had learned, generally served to protect offensive vested interests, and what they sought was change. The past as a register of the crimes, follies, and misfortunes of despots had no charms for them, and so they lacked a sense of history. Their gaze was on the future; their hopes were fixed on the triumph of justice and liberty. They looked upon government — which, after all, men had made and which men could change — not as a *mystique* but as an instrument for securing certain rights, and so they held progressive reform to be its main objective. When society is out of order, said Hazlitt, it is like a broken clock; and when "the interests of the many are regularly and outrageously sacrificed to those of the few," reform becomes not a grudging concession but a necessity.[56] Institutions cannot "for ever exist at war" with public opinion, and public opinion, however slow to challenge prescriptive rights, is bound to make its power felt.[57]

This is a somewhat muted statement of the theme that runs so briskly through the work of Priestley and his friends. Dissenters of their vintage were nothing if not cheerful in the knowledge that what was past was prologue to the swelling triumph of reform. This is the burden of Priestley's notorious *Doctrine of Philosophical Necessity Illustrated* (1777) and, almost a generation later, of his *Lectures on History and General Policy* (1793); and it also binds together the rather desultory *Letters* with which he answered Burke's *Reflections*. The men who brought in William III, he warns the champion of prescriptive rights, had merely cauterized a wound, and had graver measures been required they surely would have taken them. "Had they apprehended *government by kings* in general to be as great a grievance as that by *Popish kings,* they would have abolished kingly government altogether, and this country would now have been a republic." [58] As he had long since said, progress is the only law of history, and its general movement, under God's protective providence, has to be from bad to better.[59] William Godwin (an obscure Dissenter turned eminent radical) agreed, and so did Richard Price,[60] as well as many other men. "I seem to myself to see the commencement of a new aera," wrote a happy Unitarian in 1790, "in which rational Christianity united with zeal and fervent piety shall prevail in the world." [61] Despite their elation when the Bastille fell, such men required a sturdy optimism, together with a certain innocence of the political realities of England, to think that the millennium was at hand, but they had lived on hope for years, and they were slow to recognize defeat. As a young man Priestley had predicted that the triumph of reform would be a consummation "glorious and paradisical, beyond what our imaginations can now conceive"; [62] and in his old age, still waiting for the dawn he did not live to see, he told Burke that even if his optimism rested on a dream, it was at least a "pleasing" hope, with nothing in it "malignant, or unfriendly to any." [63]

This is the theme of Price's *Discourse on the Love of Our Country,* the famous sermon, preached before the Revolutionary Society at the Old Jewry Meeting House on 4 November 1789, that prompted Burke's crushing counterattack in *Reflections on the Revolution in France.* At the end of a long life dedicated to reform, Price says that he has lived to see the slow decay of "superstition and error" and the ascent of human rights, with thirty million people "spurning at slavery, and demanding liberty with an irresistible voice." He sees a future bright with promise, with "the ardour for liberty catching and spreading; a general amendment beginning in human affairs; the dominion of kings changed for the dominion of laws, and the dominion of priests given way to the dominion of reason and conscience." In these happy circumstances, he warns the agents of reaction, it is too late to sneer at good men's aspirations. "You cannot now hold the world in darkness. Struggle no longer against increasing light and liberality. Restore to mankind their rights; and consent to the correction of abuses, before they and you are destroyed together." [64]

◇   ◇   ◇

These consoling nonconformist commonplaces are the principal ingredients of Hazlitt's view of history. In the "roar and dashing of opinions, loosened from their accustomed hold," he said, the sixteenth century saw the moral qualities of Protestantism working like an angry sea, and that sea had "never yet subsided." [65] A tireless "contention with evil" was for the great reformers their reason for existence, [66] and their struggles are instructive: building their creeds upon the claims of conscience, they "loved their religion in proportion as they paid dear for it," for a thing that costs nothing is worth nothing. [67] That stalwart breed who had defied Rome and formed "the first school of political liberty in Europe," [68] inspired the heores of a later age to oust "Popery and slavery" under the Stuarts, and when "the tiara and the crown lost their magnetic charm together" the English stepped into the modern age. [69] It was in the Dissenters' refusal "to subscribe to bigotted dogmas for conscience-sake and in matters of faith" that lay the "germ and root" of English freedom. [70] Their "stern and sullen opposition to church dogmas and arbitrary sway" [71] thwarted Charles II, a treacherous voluptary, and destroyed his brother James, "a blind, narrow, gloomy bigot"; [72] and it remained the spur of English liberty in the days of George III.*

However partisan and inadequate as an account of English history, these orthodoxies of Dissent bring us close to one of Hazlitt's major themes, for they underlie his ethics. Nonconformists, he admits, were sometimes crude and tedious in their doctrinal disputes, but they command respect because they were so earnest. For them, belief and action were reciprocal, and prudence was a sign of moral cowardice. Tireless in their "contention with evil," as evil seemed to them, they had the habit of resistance. When Hazlitt says that "the mind strikes out truth by collision, as steel strikes fire from the flint," [73] the remark suggests what another eminent nonconformist called the trial of virtue and the exercise of truth, for, like Milton, he thought that we are purified by trial, and that trial is by what is contrary." [74] "There appears to be no natural necessity for evil, but that there is a perfect indifference to good without it." [75] To take up arms in a good cause, and against great odds, gives a man the arrogance that, as Hazlitt told his son, was the stigma of Dissenters, [76] but it was also their distinction. "The incessant wrangling and collision of sects and parties" is, in this imperfect world, essential to the endless search for truth, and even though the truth may lie beyond our grasp, the struggle to achieve it is itself our guerdon. We may smile to see the moldy tomes of old polemics weighed up by the pound and sold for waste paper, Hazlitt grants, but he warns us not to smile in condescension.

Many a drop of blood flowed in the field or on the scaffold, from these tangled briars and thorns of controversy; many a man marched to a stake to bear testimony to the most frivolous and incomprehensible of their dogmas. This was an untoward consequence; but if it was an evil to be burnt at a stake, it was well and becoming to have an opinion (whether right or wrong) for which a man was willing to be burnt at a stake. [77]

Lethargy and a fashionable detachment may serve the uses of the shallow-hearted, but an honest man seeks truth, and he knows the search means moral struggle, valor, and commitments. Therefore it is "essential to the triumph of reform" that it should not succeed. [78]

This strenuous nonconformist morality never lost its hold on Hazlitt. In his recoil, in his later teens, from all forms of organized religion, he damned the Dissenters' "exclusiveness" and self-righteousness, the Catholics' superstition, and the Anglicans' complacency with impartial dis-

---

* For a statement of the same view by Hazlitt's father see his *Human Authority, in Matters of Faith, Repugnant to Christianity* (1774), pp. 45–49. Hazlitt's last important comment on the subject (16.364–393), in the last year of his life, is his *Edinburgh* review of Walter Wilson's biography of Defoe.

respect, but he himself exemplified the nonconformist temper, and he recognized the fact. The Dissenters' "captious hostility to the prevailing system" flows from self-esteem, suspicion, and a perverse delight in opposition, he admits. "They feel themselves invulnerable behind the double fence of sympathy with themselves, and antipathy to the rest of the world." A doctrinaire commitment to one set of ideas — for example, the staggering notion "that one was not three, or that the same body could not be in two places at once" — leads them into labyrinths of controversy. But their faults are outweighed by their courage, and their "principle of strong fidelity" is one that Hazlitt venerated. The "safest partisans, and the steadiest friends," they are "almost the only people who have any idea of an abstract attachment either to a cause or to individuals, from a sense of duty, independently of prosperous or adverse circumstances, and in spite of opposition." [79]

Hazlitt was repelled by Calvin's libels on the human race and bored by doctrinal dispute, but he remained a kind of puritan: he had a compulsion to resist whatever he thought wrong. His world was no longer menaced by the dark satanic powers that had haunted the Tudor and Stuart divines whose prose and probity he so much admired, but it was still a world beleaguered, where the ogres of tyranny, prescriptive rights, and conformity lay in wait for the timid and unwary. In his opposition to these evils he showed the moral vigor of Dissent in an age when Dissent itself had ceased to count for very much. De Quincey, who detested him as an ignorant malcontent, deplored his bad manners as "the peevishness of a disappointed man" and thought his habit of keeping one hand in his waistcoat gave him the look of a villain searching for a hidden dagger. "*Whatever is* — so much I conceive to have been a fundamental lemma for Hazlitt — *is wrong.*" [80] The comment is not without a certain justice, but it ignores the fact that his bad manners were more than just a pose. At least in part they reflected his aversion to the *status quo,* and that aversion was an act of moral judgment. In the era of Lord Liverpool and Castlereagh, Hazlitt, after his fashion, sustained the contention with evil to which he had been bred.

For the struggle had no end. We need not trace the Dissenters' efforts to remove their disabilities and achieve the golden age which they naively thought could be legislated into being, but we should remember that they failed, contrary to the dictates of logic, the movement of history, and even Price's law of universal rectitude. In 1790, after almost a century of intermittent agitation, a major campaign to repeal the Test and Corporation Acts was lost in Commons by a big majority, and the event was hailed by all conservatives as a victory of the Crown and church over the republican heresies of France that most Dissenters were thought to favor. That same year, when Hazlitt was a boy of twelve, Burke published his great defense of political privilege, and the success of his *Reflections* showed how effectively a man of genius could exploit the Briton's fear of rapid social change. For a generation — and it was Hazlitt's generation — reform was dead in England, and reaction went from bad to worse. Answering Burke's attack on the Dissenters, young James Mackintosh had jeered at laws "which reward falsehood and punish probity," [81] but the laws remained in force while other bitter, futile protests rose. "Shall we never serve out our apprenticeship to liberty," Hazlitt asked. "Must our indentures to slavery bind us for life?" [82] In an age when panic yielded to reaction and reaction to triumphant complacency, such questions went unanswered. At the repeal of the Text and Corporation Acts in 1828, two years before he died, Hazlitt wondered what the victory would have meant to his father and to his "old friends" Price and Priestley, and he grieved that the English had finally given "as a boon to indifference what they so long refused to justice." [83] But when the great bill of 1832 announced reforms that he and many others had hoped for all their lives, he had been for two years in his grave.*

THE YOUNG DISSENTER

If, as Hazlitt thought, the "bias" of character is determined at the age of two,[1] he must have been a formidable young Dissenter before he reached his teens. On a visit to Liverpool in 1790 he wrote home that he had spent a "very agreeable" Sunday in reading one hundred sixty pages of Priestley and hearing "two good sermons," and his father replied that such piety must have been a "great refreshment." The boy told his mother of dining with a certain rich man who, like many Liverpudlians, had prospered in the slave trade, and whose wealth was therefore contemptible: "The man who is a well-wisher to slavery, is always a slave himself." Reporting acidly on his first visit to an Anglican service he made it clear that the experiment would not be repeated. He ex-

---

* Even though their political disabilities were removed in 1828, Dissenters continued to be barred from the universities until 1871, when compulsory subscription to the Thirty-nine Articles was finally ended by the University Test Act. See George Macaulay Trevelyan, *British History in the Nineteenth Century and After* (1782–1919) (1937), pp. 284, 356. On the events leading to the repeal of Dissenters' disabilities in 1828 see Henry W. Clark, *History of English Nonconformity*, II (1913), 287–353.

patiated — before he had begun to shave — on the "unspeakably happy" lot of those who, when they come to die, can say, "I have done with this world, I shall now have no more of its temptations to struggle with, and praise be to God I have overcome them." Prim and proud, he told of demolishing a playmate's defense of the Test Act: "At last, when I had overpowered him with my arguments, he said he wished he understood it as well as I did, for I was too high learned for him." His father duly congratulated him on the victory, explaining that "if we only think justly, we shall always easily foil all the advocates of tyranny." A year later, when rioters had destroyed Priestley's house and driven him from Birmingham — "a regular, systematic scene of High-church villainy," as a friend of the elder Hazlitt said * — the future journalist for the first time achieved the dignity of print with a long, stern letter to the Shrewsbury *Chronicle,* where, with a rhetoric that does not conceal his deep emotion, he denounces persecution as "the bane of all religion" and defends Priestley as a champion of the emancipated mind. If that great man's works are, as his enemies charge, nothing but sedition and heresy, then sedition and heresy are honorable, "for all their sedition is that fortitude that becomes the dignity of a man and the character of a Christian; and their heresy, Christianity." These early letters, whatever their stylistic affectations, tell us much about the boy who became the man we know.[2]

You must, his father had insisted, "fixedly resolve never, through any possible motives, to do anything which you believe to be wrong," and there is no reason to doubt that for the elder Hazlitt the precept was a rule of action. "Who is there indeed," he once asked,

has the least right to take offense, at the undisguised declarations of an honest man, who has truth alone for his object, and who recommends what he believes to be truth, not with the view of insulting any individual, but only in the discharge of what he thinks his duty?[3]

The clergyman would have been a wretched schoolmaster, an admiring friend of his remarked, for by teaching his students invariably to tell the truth and align their actions and beliefs he would have disqualified them for making their way in the world.[4] As we see him in his son's

---

* *Christian Reformer,* V (1838), 702. Sparked by a dinner at which the Constitutional Society celebrated the second anniversary of the fall of the Bastille, a mob destroyed Priestley's house and scientific equipment (although he did not attend the dinner and had already fled the city), and then, warming to the task, burned a nonconformist chapel. Beginning on Thursday, 14 July 1791, the disturbance may have been encouraged by the municipal authorities, as Priestley's friends said later; at any rate it was not ended until a company of dragoons from Nottingham appeared on Saturday night. Priestley's first act on reaching London the following Monday was to begin work on a discourse about the forgiveness of enemies.

affectionate reminiscences, in his daughter's diary, and in his own stiff prose, he is a man of piety and valor without an ounce of prudence. Born in Ireland and educated at Glasgow, he early changed from Presbyterian to Unitarian, and thereafter labored in his ministerial vocation for almost half a century. As the world regards success, he did not succeed. When almost penniless with a large family in America, he rejected a safe clerical berth that would have required his making an orthodox profession, because, according to his daughter, he would "sooner die in a ditch than submit to human authority in matters of faith." [5] Even "the most distant attempt" to secure religious conformity, he once wrote, was "a most abominable despotism, repugnant to the very nature of religion itself, to the genius and groundwork of the christian religion, to the dignity of reason, to the genuine principles of freedom, to the best interests of humanity, to the common Protestant cause, and to our avowed principles as Protestant Dissenters." [6] Through a long life of obscurity often sharpened with misfortune, he retained his cheerful zeal for social progress. Writing to Price about a certain rigidity in American religious thought, he ventured the hope that in another generation there would be as much "freedom of thinking" in the new country as "at present among the Dissenters in England," [7] and in a Thanksgiving sermon preached during the American visit he congratulated his hearers on their "happy constitution" that, subject to progressive changes, would continue to improve their lot "until the end of time." [8]

His father's piety, his integrity, and his benign confidence in the triumph of reform stayed in Hazlitt's memory. His recollections of family Scriptures glow in his famous opening lecture on the Elizabethan age, with its stirring testimonial to the united force of Protestantism and liberty, [9] but there are homelier memories too: of his father fingering his watch, of his pride in the beans and broccoli from his garden, of the formidable folios in his library — Fox and Neale and Calamy for the children, Pripscovius, Crellius, and Cracovius (any one of which would "outlast a winter") for his own devoted study. [10] Such study was dry and dusty toil, but it was prompted by the zeal that had prompted great reformers: "no flippancy, no indifference, no compromising, no pert shallow scepticism, but truth was supposed indissolubly knit to good, knowledge to usefulness, and the temporal and eternal welfare of mankind to hang in the balance." [11] Hazlitt wrote of his father always with affection, and sometimes with veneration, as the very incarnation of Dissent, a humble minister who, "tossed about from congregation to congregation," at last found refuge in a little village "far from the only converse that he loved, the talk about disputed texts of Scripture and the cause of civil and religious liberty." * Once, when visiting Wem, Hazlitt painted a portrait of his father in his "green old age, with strong-marked features and scarred with the small pox," and finished it on the glorious day that brought the news of Austerlitz. "I walked out in the afternoon, and, as I returned, saw the evening star set over a poor man's cottage with other thoughts and feelings than I shall ever have again. . . . The picture is left: the table, the chair, the window where I learned to construe Livy, the chapel where my father preached, remain where they were; but he himself is gone to rest, full of years, of faith, of hope, and charity." [12]

In the "neglect and supercilious regards of the world," as Hazlitt realized, men like his father did not amount to very much. "Half-learned, half-witted, half-paid, half-starved," as Robert Southey said,[13] most nonconformist preachers were generally looked upon as public pests, for they were usually poor and pious, and they fomented discontent. But Hazlitt remembered them as men of principle whose principles cost them dear, and in the squat, heavy figure of his father — a man of "solidity" rather than "stolidity," a friend of his reported [14] — he found the embodiment of the patriot-priest. Such men, he thought, were venerable. "They set up an image in their own minds, it was truth; they worshipped an idol there, it was justice." Their creed was compounded of reverence to God and good will to all men, and to this creed, "fixed as the stars, deep as the firmament," they held fast. "This covenant they kept, as the stars keep their courses: this principle they stuck by, for want of knowing better, as it sticks by them to the last. It grew with their growth, it does not wither in their decay. It lives when the almond-tree flourishes, and is not bowed down with the tottering knees. It glimmers with the last feeble eyesight, smiles in the faded cheek like infancy, and lights a path before them to the grave!" [15] Hazlitt's essay, said a critic in the *London Magazine,* shows that he "feels where the fountain-head of lofty thoughts really lies." [16] It also makes clear his great respect for the ethos of Dissent. The life of men like his father may have been a "dream" built of such implausible components as human liberty, Moses with the burning bush, the twelve tribes of Israel, "types, shadows, glosses on the law and the prophets," and the shape of Noah's ark; but it was "a dream of infinity and eternity, of death, the resurrection, and a judgment to come," and unlike most dreams it did not fade away.[17]

❖ ❖ ❖

* 17.110. We get an oblique but none the less revealing view of the elder Hazlitt in a group of letters from various friends, mainly Unitarians like Lindsey and Kippis and Price, that are brought together as "The Hazlitt Papers," *Christian Reformer,* V (1838), 505–512, 697–705, 756–764.

THE YOUNG DISSENTER

When Hazlitt was fourteen, as he remembered not long before he died, he overheard an argument between his father and an old lady of his congregation about the Test Act and the limits of religious toleration. Although such a conversation could hardly have burst upon him with surprise, it did prompt him to scrutinize his own ideas, and thereafter he regarded this, the "first time" he attempted to think for himself, as the "circumstance that decided the fate of my future life." Some of the consequences became apparent a year later, when he was sent to Hackney (then a pleasant village on the northeastern edge of London) to study for the ministry. His father hoped that he would be a man of God, but the boy himself, as he said later, wanted only "to be satisfied of the reason of things." [18] The resulting debacle was a grievous disappointment to the elder Hazlitt, a questionable loss for the Unitarian ministry, and a triumph for literary journalism.

The Unitarian New College at Hackney, to give its full resounding name, was a late, precarious addition to the many Dissenting academies that had dotted England throughout the eighteenth century. Some of them, at least, were better than the universities from which the Dissenters were excluded. A galaxy of notables — among them, Wesley, Adam Smith, Gibbon, and Bentham — have certified the scandalous decay of Oxford and Cambridge in Hanoverian England; and if we tend to think of Thomas Warton's college as a sleepy hollow where the fellows drank good port and sneered at Methodists, as one historian has put it, we may wonder why the nonconformists complained so bitterly about the "thorn hedge of oaths and subscriptions and regulations" contrived to block their entry.[19] But there was a principle at stake, and it was vital to Dissenters. "Is it not very hard," said one of them to Johnson, "that I should not be allowed to teach my children what I really believe to be the truth?" [20] It was an affront to Christianity and a denial of their natural rights, they thought, to make education an Anglican prerogative, and their answer to exclusion, therefore, was to found their own academies. Guarded by compulsory subscription to the Thirty-nine Articles, Priestley told Pitt, the universities were "pools of *stagnant water* secured by dams and mounds, and offensive to the neighborhood," whereas the nonconformist schools were *"rivers,* which, taking their natural course, fertilize a whole country." As a consequence, he said, the absurd and wicked policy of exclusion works a greater harm on the universities than on its intended victims.[21] Groaning over his collegiate dissipations, young Coleridge put the matter differently: "The Education, which Dissenters receive among Dissenters, generates Conscientiousness & a scrupulous Turn / will this be gained at the Wine Parties in Cambridge?" [22]

PROLOGUE

The first academies, founded in the early Restoration, were generally conducted by a single ejected minister, and when he retired or died they ended. An example is provided by the well-known establishment at Newington Green — the alma mater of the elder Wesley and Defoe — which Charles Morton presided over until he emigrated to New England, where he eventually became vice-president of Harvard. Although primarily concerned with training an educated ministry, the late Stuart and early Hanoverian academies gradually broadened their curricula and their clientele, and often the results were bad; but the great academies like those at Northampton, Daventry, Hoxton, Taunton, and Warrington were solid and formidably respectable, a tonic force in eighteenth-century England.[23] Thus Philip Doddridge, a renowned pedagogue whose memory was green for generations, made Northampton a famous seat of learning; and Daventry, where Joseph Priestley went in 1751, was an exhilarating place for a boy who was already a junior polymath. Since, as he recalled, nobody there agreed on anything, topics like "Liberty and Necessity, the sleep of the soul, and all the articles of theological orthodoxy and heresy" were the common themes of conversation; the lectures were "friendly conversations" on disputed questions; and the curriculum, which had been modeled on Doddridge's at Northampton, made "free inquiry" and wide reading imperative.* After the middle of the century the academy at Warrington was as noted for preparing boys for business and commerce as for training ministers. Its staff, a gallery of once-famous men, included John Taylor (an eminent Hebraist), John Aikin (the learned father of the learned Anna Letitia Barbauld), Priestley, the great Latinist Gilbert Wakefield (one of whose favorite students was Thomas Malthus), and William Enfield (whose *Speaker* was a text for Hazlitt and countless other schoolboys).

In happier times Hackney College might have become equally distinguished. Designed to serve the clientele that the defunct academies at Exeter, Warrington, and Hoxton had earlier served, it was promoted by a group of London businessmen (including the wealthy father of Sam Rogers, the banker-poet) and opened, in 1786, under the patronage of such Unitarian stalwarts as Price, Priestley, and Theophilus Lindsey. Its main function, of course, was to train a learned ministry, but it was also designed "to supersede the necessity of sending the sons of Dissenting parents to the English universities, where they are under an obligation

---

* Priestley, *Memoirs* (1806), I, 15–18. Doddridge's plan of study included, in the first year, logic, rhetoric, geography, metaphysics, geometry, and algebra; worked up through such subjects as conic sections, natural and experimental philosophy, civil history, and Jewish antiquities; and finally reached civil law, English history, preaching, and pastoral care. See Irene Parker, *Dissenting Academies in England* (1914), p. 86.

of subscribing to articles which they do not believe, and of attending upon forms of worship which they do not approve." [24] The new academy quickly became a center of liberal Dissent and therefore of political heterodoxy.

The faculty, though transient like all faculties, included at one time or another men of great eminence and ability, the very elite of late eighteenth-century Dissent. Andrew Kippis, famed for the erudition of his massive *Biographia Britannica* (1778–1795), had studied with Doddridge at Northampton and then for almost twenty years had taught at Hoxton (where one of his students was William Godwin); a prime mover in the affairs of Hackney College, he maintained his interest in the school even after he retired in 1791. [25] Andrew Rees, who had served as head of the academy at Hoxton, was long famed as a preacher at the Old Jewry. Thomas Belsham, Hazlitt's tutor in divinity, had made his reputation as a teacher at Daventry, and later he was famous, at least among Dissenters, as an indefatigable and somewhat cantankerous expositor of Unitarian theology.* The ill-tempered Gilbert Wakefield, a brilliant undergraduate at Jesus College, Cambridge, who had gone on to become a vigorous Unitarian, was to win applause as editor of Vergil and Lucretius and notoriety as an implacable critic of Pitt's foreign policy. And the great Priestley himself came to Hackney to lecture on history and chemistry after the debacle at Birmingham. Thirty-five years later Hazlitt still remembered his sharp nose, keen glance, quivering lip, and placid but indifferent countenance; and although he did not assess him in the highest terms — Priestley's controversy with Price about materialism was, he said, both a "masterpiece" of intellectual gymnastics and an "artful evasion of difficulties" — he admired his versatility in "history, grammar, law, politics, divinity, metaphysics, and natural philosophy." For boldness and "elasticity" of mind and for a lucid expository style, said his former student, Priestley "had no superior." †

---

* John Williams, *Memoirs of the Late Reverend Thomas Belsham* (1833), pp. 422–462, quotes liberally from Belsham's letters to give an informative but depressing account of Hackney in its decline.

† 20.236–239. Elsewhere (4.49n) Hazlitt brackets Priestley and Jonathan Edwards as the "only two remarkable men," apart from the founders of sects, that the Dissenters had produced, but in *Lectures on English Philosophy* (2.261) he contrasts unfavorably Priestley's "easy, cavalier, verbal fluency" to Edwards' "plodding, persevering, scrupulous accuracy." In *Biographia Literaria* (I, 91) Coleridge speaks slightingly of Priestley, and even as a young man he was troubled by his views (Griggs, I, 192f.; II, 821). In 1804 he expressed relief at having extricated not only himself but also Wordsworth and Southey from the "labyrinth-Den" of Priestley's necessitarianism, for Wordsworth had professed the wicked doctrine "even to Extravagance," and Southey, although abhorring it, had regarded it "unanswerable by human Reason" (Griggs, II, 1037).

PROLOGUE

But whatever academic distinction the new school may have gained was lost in mounting complaints about its politics. Ten members of its directing committee were members of the Revolutionary Society before which Price preached his notorious sermon in 1789, and it is a fair guess that they were all warm friends of liberty. Of the forty-nine boys enrolled at Hackney in 1790 only nineteen were preparing for the ministry, but the whole student body, as one alumnus recalled, was hot in the cause of reform, pouring "hearty execration" on kings, priests, and aristocrats, and bellowing out *Ça Ira* and the *Marseillaise* at "College symposia." [26] Not unnaturally, Tom Paine was the idol of the students (who gave a breakfast in his honor) and Priestley the sage whom they revered — a martyr to that "spirit of inquiry," as they told him, that no violence could destroy. The old man had responded by pointing out that the Anglican Church, "equally the bane of Christianity and of rational liberty," must reform itself or fall to ruin; and he urged his students to take heart from recent events in America, France, and Poland to dedicate themselves to the "universal toleration" that would soon, and inexorably, "illuminate" the world. [27]

Remembering these old scandals, Coleridge later attributed to such flamboyant radicalism the "Infidelity" into which Hackney College lured the young Dissenters. But how could it have been otherwise, he asked, when "the Tutors, the *whole* plan of Education, the place itself, were all wrong?" [28] That such an institution could have long survived the rising hostility to all kinds of nonconformity and reform would have been surprising. One of Hazlitt's tutors later decided that the academy, though founded on a "generous and noble" design and conducted as a "grand experiment," had fallen victim to "the spirit of the times."

The mania of the French Revolution, which began so well and ended so ill, pervaded all ranks of society, and produced a general spirit of insubordination. The ferment of the times gave birth to insidious and even to daring attacks upon natural and revealed religion, which produced mischievous effects upon uninformed and undisciplined minds. [29]

Moreover, financial problems were increasingly severe. In 1793 — the year that Hazlitt went to Hackney — there was doubt whether the academy could carry on at all; [30] during the next three years it staggered from one crisis to another; and in 1796 it fell. As some thought, Priestley's advent had been the final blow, many solid but cautious Dissenters withdrawing their support when he assumed the "principal professorship." [31] But almost from the start Hackney College had been denounced as a hotbed of heresy and sedition, and at its collapse a correspondent of the *Gentleman's Magazine* rejoiced that Babylon had fallen, presumably through the anger of an offended deity whose sympathies were

26

Anglican and monarchical.[32] More temperately, an editorial in the same publication (which had long marked the college for destruction) [33] cited the event as proof that Englishmen were disinclined to support "modern philosophers in their attempts to undermine the constitution." [34] After the building itself had been knocked down at auction in June 1796, a "late Student" explained sadly that although the academy had started well it soon made itself offensive to decent folk, including "respectable" Dissenters. "When such seminaries become the volcanos of sedition, and nurseries of riot, they cannot, and should not, long remain established." [35]

When Hazlitt went to Hackney in 1793 the academy that had feted Paine and adopted Priestley was entering its decline, and the two or three years he spent there were anything but tranquil. In any event, he had troubles of his own: the pious and dutiful youth of twelve had at fifteen become truculent and discontented in his "craving to be satisfied of the reason of things," and in the letters he wrote home, only five of which survive,[36] we may trace a situation both commonplace and painful. The first, containing dark allusions to his "past behaviour" and to the "nervous disorders to which, you well know, I was so much subject," shows that he was in trouble from the start. His tutor, one Thomas Currie, having imprudently set for a weekly theme a subject not "suited" to his "genius," Hazlitt asked and received permission to write on a more congenial topic; and then, with swollen eyes and a "sullen" countenance, he announced that he had failed to do the work. Thinking the time had come for a serious talk, Currie told him to stay after class, "mildly" asked if he had ever written any essays, and finally persuaded him to bring out a draft of a piece on laws — presumably the first fruit of those speculations on the Test Act and the limits of religious toleration that he had begun the year before. Impressed by what he saw, the tutor must also have been relieved when his intractable student agreed to "inlarge and improve" the essay in lieu of the routine assignments. Almost forty years later Hazlitt recalled and gratefully acknowledged his sympathetic interest.[37]

With Currie's endorsement, the project was soon expanded from an analysis of toleration to a discussion of man's "natural" and "artificial" rights and duties as a citizen. "This I think an excellent plan," Hazlitt wrote his father, but it would be "a terrible labour, and I shall rejoice most heartily when I have finished it." Meanwhile he was toiling from seven in the morning to nine-thirty at night on a course of studies that included Greek, Hebrew, algebra, geometry, shorthand, and geography. When the day's work was finished, he added, he read David Hartley from nine-thirty to eleven.* It was a formidable routine for a boy of fifteen afflicted with "nervous disorders," and not unnaturally he soon began to hint at further trouble in his letters. The elder Hazlitt had been made uneasy at the turn his son's studies were taking, for the boy was at Hackney to prepare for the ministry, and not to addle his brains with metaphysics and psychology. "I was sorry to hear from your last two letters that you wish me to discontinue my essay," Hazlitt wrote, "as I am very desirous of finishing it, and as I think it almost necessary to do so." Hard work is necessary, he explained, for one should ground his politics securely; "moreover, by comparing my own system with those of others, and with particular facts, I shall have it in my power to correct and improve it continually." He was neither "gloomy" nor "low-spirited," he assured his father, for he was contemplating an essay on providence ("a very good subject") and making "it my study to acquire as much politeness as I can."

And there the record of his schooling stops. Although the circumstances of Hazlitt's departure from Hackney are obscure, the last letter of the series, perhaps written from his brother's house in Long Acre, near Drury Lane, implies that they were catastrophic.† He writes as one whose boyish days were done, of the "repeated disappointment" and the "long dejection, which have served to overcast & throw into deep obscurity some of the best years of my life." But he finds it soothing to his wounded spirit that "there are one or two persons in the world who are [not] quite indifferent towards me, nor altogether unanxious for my welfare." He reports that he is working on a book — the first mention of the *Essay on the Principles of Human Action,* which did not appear until almost a decade later — but that it was going slowly. "I know not whether I can augur certainly of ultimate success. I write more easily than I did. I

---

* Teaching loads, as well as students' assignments, were heavy at Hackney. According to Kippis (Lyson, *Environs of London,* III, 632), in the early years of the academy the "general course of lectures" in pneumatology, ethics, divinity, Jewish antiquities, and church history were given by Andrew Rees, who "had some concern likewise in the mathematical and philosophical department." Kippis himself taught universal grammar, rhetoric, chronology, and history, "to which were occasionally added other subjects connected with Belles Lettres." See Williams, *Belsham,* pp. 434, 444.

† Even the date of Hazlitt's departure from Hackney is uncertain. His son (*Literary Remains,* I, xxxv) says he "left College, and returned home in the year 1795," but Hazlitt's last known letter of this period, which is dated "Sunday, Oct. 23d.," must be ascribed to 1796, when October 23 fell on Sunday. Moreover, it was in 1796 that he first read Burke in the *St. James's Chronicle* (12.228), a fact which strongly suggests, if it does not prove, his presence in London at the time. It is possible that the "affliction" for which Kippis consoled the elder Hazlitt in 1795 (see page 29) was the boy's decision to forsake the ministry, and that he lingered on at Hackney as a lay student during the winter of 1795–96. On the other hand, the letter of "Sunday, Oct. 23d" may have been written during a visit to his brother. Whatever the date of his departure, he obviously had left Hackney in despair.

hope for good. I have ventured to look at high things. I have toiled long and painfully to attain to some stand of eminence. It were hard to be thrown back from the mid-way of the steep to the lowest humiliation."

Presently, however, he was back at Wem. Hackney had not made a clergyman of him, or even given him an education, but it had prompted his "first perilous and staggering searches after truth," [38] and it had brought him close to the swirling currents of reform at a period when reform, it seemed, might finally be achieved. Returning home an "avowed infidel" — or so Crabb Robinson was given to believe [39] — he had not only jettisoned his clerical career but had failed to prepare for any other. Moreover, his intellectual independence, perhaps the one achievement of his schooling, had darkened his relations with his father, so that their "unreserved communication" was ended. It was the kind of estrangement, as Hazlitt realized later, that is all too common. His own Presbyterian grandfather had failed to recover from the shock of his son's apostasy to Unitarianism, and when Hazlitt blasted his own father's hopes it made three generations "set at variance, by a veering point of theology, and the officious meddling biblical critics!" [40] Perhaps the allusion is to Andrew Kippis, who had served as sponsor to the boy,* and who, as a friend and benefactor of his father, was prompt with his condolences. "What can I say to you," he wrote,

I can only say that I sincerely sympathize with you in your affliction. I deeply feel for your distress and disappointment, and wish that I could impart to you any sufficient thoughts or words of consolation.

However regrettable the boy's behavior, Kippis told his father, "at any rate you have the consciousness of your own integrity to support you"; and he ventured the hope, not very warmly, that Hazlitt would perhaps become "a wise and useful man" in some other walk of life. What that walk might be, he said he did not know, but he made it clear that from him no further aid would be forthcoming.[41]

WINDS OF DOCTRINE

A few months before Hackney College closed its doors forever, Thomas Belsham, Hazlitt's tutor in divinity, suggested darkly that the academy,

---

* *Christian Reformer*, V (1838), 508, 763. Another of the elder Hazlitt's ministerial friends, one John Ralph, had written in 1791 (*ibid.*, V, 703), to ask what plans had been made for the young *"scholar"* of the family and to offer aid in getting help for him if he wished to study for the ministry ("though there is but poor encouragement for a young man in that *'line'* at present").

a monument to free thought and speculation, perhaps had fostered irreligion in its students. "There is an unaccountable tendency in the young men, in this part of the world, to infidelity, and the studious and virtuous part of our family have very generally given up Christianity."[1] Could he have been thinking of the troubled boy from Wem? In his later years Hazlitt was not noted for his piety, and neither were his friends. In 1822 Alaric Watts, buzzing with the ugly gossip that Byron and Shelley had thrown dice for the dubious honor of having sired Clara Clairmont's child, reported to William Blackwood in Edinburgh that all the literary crew in London — Lamb, Procter, Hazlitt, Hunt, Peacock, Talfourd, and Reynolds — boasted of their "freedom from the shackles of religious sentiment of every kind."[2] Such venomous remarks may be discounted, but Benjamin Robert Haydon more reliably testifies to the same effect;[3] and according to Talfourd, Leigh Hunt's sporadic outbursts of religion were a jest among his friends. "Damn it," Hazlitt is reported to have said, "it's like a rash that comes out every year on him. Why doesn't he write a book and get rid of it?"[4]

Although Haydon, whose ejaculatory Christianity perhaps made him wary of those less vocal than himself, regarded Hazlitt as the only "sceptic" of the group willing to discuss religion "with the gravity such a question demanded," [*] it is clear that the one-time student of divinity was hostile to theology. Smiting Calvinists, Methodists, and Anglicans alike, he implied that all of them were guilty of arrogance and fraud, and in the old tradition of anticlericalism (but without Erasmus' erudition or Voltaire's icy wit) he tended to regard all ministers as professional equivocators. "There is no dogma, however fierce or foolish, to which these persons have not set their seals, and tried to impose on the understandings of their followers, as the will of Heaven, clothed with all the terrors and sanctions of religion."[5] Theology, which should make men "wise and virtuous," generally teaches them to gloss over their own failings and to "hoodwink the Almighty,"[6] and in the long history of crimes and follies there has not been one, he said, that clergymen have failed to deck out and accredit "in the garb of sanctity."[7] Credulity, despotism, and murder have found their spurious sanctions in religion, and even persecution has been urged as the will of God upon the followers of the Prince of Peace.[8]

We might expect Hazlitt, as a relapsed Dissenter, to assail the Roman Catholic Church as an engine of tyranny and superstition, but

---

[*] *Autobiography*, I, 255. Hazlitt was perhaps remembering Shelley when he told Northcote (11.246) that he had once defended the literary merits of the Bible against the criticism of a "young poet."

he usually writes of it with the nostalgia reserved for fictions of antiquity. For that reason, perhaps, he preferred the ruins of Melrose Abbey to St. Peter's as a memorial to the power of Rome.[9] Organized religion serves its only purpose, he declared, when it is the unchallenged repository of a faith in which imagination finds a stimulus and an object. In that respect Rome was once supreme. Although it "engrafted" the morality of the Gospels upon superstition and priestcraft to become a "dreadful engine of power,"[10] in its days of glory it made Europe a shrine of art and a temple of the imagination. If faith is the evidence of things unseen, "Popery furnished this evidence in the highest degree — a trust and conviction in sacred things, strengthened and exalted beyond the reach of doubt, of guilt, or passion by time, by numbers, by all that could appal or allure the imagination."[11] Although its rites were "childish mummeries" and its doctrines "the wildest absurdities," Hazlitt remembered that its rulers were "architects of human happiness and builders of the loftiest fiction," and he was unconvinced that Protestantism (with its "dry, meagre, penurious imagination")[12] or modern philosophy (with its gifts of reason and corrosive skepticism) constituted a gain.[13] For Catholicism was a work of art:

It strikes upon the senses studiously, and in every way; it appeals to the imagination; it enthrals the passions; it infects by sympathy; has age, has authority, has numbers on its side; and exacts implicit faith in its inscrutable mysteries and its gaudy symbols.[14]

When that faith is gone, however, the symbols lose their meaning. Therefore, although he supported Catholic emancipation[15] on the same principle that he supported civil rights for Jews and Dissenters, he knew that Rome would never be what it had been, and that Napoleon could not, through the diplomatic juggling of his Concordat, bring back "the times of Popery in their full power and splendour, when the Catholic faith was like one entire chrysolite without flaw or seeming spot."[16] A religion of beads and "maudlin superstition" that required, he thought, nothing in moral obligation, self-control, and self-respect, latter-day Catholicism was adjusted to "the pride and weakness of man's intellect, the indolence of his will, the cowardliness of his fears, the vanity of his hopes."[17] It was once a religion built on faith and absurdity; but the faith had drained away, and man cannot revere an absurdity after he knows that it is one.[18]

If Hazlitt could condone Catholicism because it was "enriched" with the "dust and cobwebs of antiquity,"[19] however, he had no patience with the Anglican establishment. Time-serving, venal, and reactionary, it appeared to him to be the proper butt of every honest man's contempt. Its spruce and well-fed clientele, lacking the Dissenters' valor and the Catholics' rich tradition, went to church merely to beguile the time; [20] its ceremonies and vestments, shabby imitations of Rome, could neither warm the heart nor inspire the head; the intellectual eunuchs comprising its clergy, men "hired to maintain certain opinions, not to inquire into them," [21] were "servants of God by profession, and sycophants of power from necessity"; [22] and its alleged prerogatives, shored up by outdated theology and outrageous statutes, were bitter proof of the affinity between priestcraft and despotism. Defending the Establishment as "a sacred temple, purged from all the impurities of fraud and violence and injustice and tyranny," Burke had rejoiced in the benign and princely ease of the Bishop of Winchester with ten thousand pounds a year; [23] but the very sight of a "well-pinched clerical hat on a prim expectant pair of shoulders" disgusted Hazlitt. "Stand off," they seem to say, "for I am holier than you." [24] He regarded a "full-dressed ecclesiastic" as "a sort of go-cart of divinity," [25] and when he contrasted the sumptuous garb with the meager piety of an English bishop he echoed countless puritan divines: "Vestments and chalices have been multiplied for the reception of the Holy Spirit; the tagged points of controversy and lackered varnish of hypocrisy have eaten into the solid substance and texture of piety." [26]

Although Anglican formalism and reaction were the natural prey of a man bred up in the traditions of Dissent, they did not exhaust his arsenal of complaint against organized religion. For Hazlitt, the means by which a man makes peace with his conscience are lonely, dark, and secret, and in the old tradition of Protestant individualism he bridled at any effort to formalize and mechanize one's relationship with God. Dr. Price, sneered Burke, had urged that if one could find nothing to satisfy his "pious fancies" in either the established church or in the "well-assorted warehouses of the Dissenting congregations" he should set up "a separate meeting-house after his own particular principles." [27] Hazlitt would not have sneered at the proposal. If incapable of religious belief himself, he understood the struggle by which people like his father had achieved their faith, and he would not profane, through the codification of ritual and doctrine, the process of salvation. In his view, the intellectual arrogance of a rational theologian, no less than the vulgar spectacle of a Methodist luxuriating in his sense of sin, did violence to the elemental decencies. Although he admired the celebrated Thomas Chalmers' *Astronomical Discourses* because he thought that "whatever appeals to the pride of the human understanding, has a subtle charm in it," [28] he was offended by the attempt to reconcile Christ's teachings with Newtonian physics. It was an exercise betraying more solicitude for the writer's reputation than for the believer's purity of conscience. It was an effort to vindicate the ways of God to the head instead of to the heart, and by "carving out excuses or defences of doctrinal points from the dry parchment of the understanding or the cobwebs of the brain" Chalmers had merely gratified his own sharp intellect. [29]

The nonconformist sects were also open to objection. Those Dissenters who called themselves "rational," like the Unitarians, confused their "exclusive pretensions to reason with the absolute possession of it" and thus revealed the prejudice that they deplored in others. [30] Those, like the Quakers, whose prim austerity barred them from the alleged deceits of poetry, art, and music, pretended to ignore the world; yet their solvency was notorious, and by converting monastic cells into counting-houses and beads into ledgers they had kept "a regular debtor and creditor account between this world and the next." [*] But it was the Methodists whose frailties Hazlitt most delighted to expose. Like Sydney Smith, for whom they were a pet aversion, he wrote about them with irresistible *élan*. He did not recognize, or at any rate would not concede, that Wesley had inspired his followers — "melancholy tailors, consumptive hair-dressers, squinting coblers, women with child or in the ague" [31] — with fresh religious fervor. He looked upon the new proletariat of the Industrial Revolution bawling forth their hymns and indulging in orgies of emotion as vulgar hypocrites, and their religion as one of the "slobbering-bib and go-cart." [32] Demanding nothing in the way of intelligence or purity or fortitude, Methodism loosed understanding from reason and conscience from morality; [33] its appeal to "vicarious righteousness" was fortified with rant and sex; and its "vital Christianity" was merely an attempt "to lower all religion to the level of the capacities of the lowest of the people." [34] Like Catholicism, it was a religion by proxy. "What the one did by auricular confession, absolution, penance, pictures, and crucifixes, the other does, even more compendiously, by grace, election, faith without works, and words without meaning." [35]

But however crude the Methodist effort to turn "morality into a sinecure," [36] it was the Calvinists whom Hazlitt hated most. Theirs was

---

[*] 4.50f. Elsewhere (19.254f.) Hazlitt warmly praises Quakers for their campaign against the slave trade, and he eulogizes Thomas Clarkson (whose portrait he had painted) as "the true Apostle of human Redemption" (11.149).

an offense not against candor and decorum but against the dignity of man. Their doctrine, a slander on human decency and divine goodness, was fatal to any hope of virtue. On the assumption that man has "no natural disposition to good" they refused him any chance to "improve, refine, and cultivate" himself, and with lurid threats of punishment they built a "*negative* system of virtue" that leads to the lowest "style of moral sentiment." [37] Not unnaturally, the celebrated Edward Irving both repelled and fascinated Hazlitt. That remarkable Scot, Jane Welsh's teacher and suitor and the subject of a famous chapter in her husband's *Reminiscences,* achieved such success in London as a prophet of damnation that he was inspired to found his own Holy Catholic Apostolic Church. In the 1820's all the world flocked to see him rekindle "the old, original, almost exploded hell-fire in the aisles of the Caledonian Chapel" in Hatton Garden, where, like a titan, grim and swarthy, he handled fire and brimstone and forged new tortures for countless reprobates. [38] Celebrities like Brougham and Mackintosh, Peel and Lord Liverpool, Canning and Hone, Lord Landsdown and Coleridge pushed and shoved among the "lords, ladies, sceptics, fanatics" met to join in approbation of the new Savonarola; [39] and while some admired his doctrine, others his vibrant voice, and others his superb theatricality, Hazlitt marveled at the triumph of such a "blear-eyed demon of vulgar dogmatism and intolerance." [40]

His assaults on "the great Goliath of modern Calvinism" [41] were more than journalistic bravado. He charged that Irving wished to be regarded as the "*thaumaturgos,* or wonder-worker," of vicarious salvation, [42] setting himself up as "the right-hand and privy-counsellor of Providence" in order to bully nervous people. [43] "His speculative malice asks eternity to wreak its infinite spite in, and calls on the Almighty to execute its relentless doom!" [44] Impatient with (and ill-informed about) theology, Hazlitt was repelled by Calvin's modern advocate just as he was repelled by any threat of licentious and despotic power. Although slenderly equipped with a knowledge of history, he stumbled on the theory, common among modern historians, that Calvin's religion of terror was a form of sixteenth-century absolutism: a God of limitless and irresponsible power is rooted in corruption, and a dogma of damnation for all except the privileged few restates the political ideal of despotism. In either its political or its theological form such an ideal violated Hazlitt's conviction of man's essential dignity. [45]

Although a late and bitter epigram records the opinion that "vice is man's nature: virtue is a habit — or a mask," [46] Hazlitt's moral and political values are built upon belief in man's essential goodness. Even the intricacies of Calvin's theology, he thought, "admit of a moral and natural solution." Humanity may appear in a den of robbers, modesty in a brothel, for "nature prevails, and vindicates its rights to the last." [47] Whatever Locke's weakness as the apostle of modern mechanical philosophy, he was right, Hazlitt thought, in rejecting the ancient Augustinian assertion that men are innately and incorrigibly prone to evil. Without the mumbo-jumbo of theology, he had justified the natural man. Unitarianism was an eighteenth-century version of this humanistic creed, and whether or not Hazlitt, by his own "profession," was a Unitarian in his later years (as at least one friend of his asserted),[48] he praised the sect as one of "sense and honesty" [49] and in his moral theory he tended to exemplify its values.

At a party where Hazlitt, then a schoolboy at Hackney, heard two persons "of remarkable candour and ingenuity" assert that all prayer was "a mode of dictating to the Almighty, and an arrogant assumption of superiority," somebody — was it he? — suggested that the Samaritan's "Lord, be merciful to me a sinner" might be an exception, whereupon the two sophisticates preened themselves on having shocked his naive prejudices. "This did not appear to me at that time quite the thing," said Hazlitt in his middle age, "and this happened in the year 1794." * The cryptic anecdote, buried in a footnote, permits the generalization that although Hazlitt writes much about the follies and vulgarities of organized religion he has almost nothing to say about what he himself believed, and the reticence of a man not given to reticence is always puzzling. In a passage from the lectures on Elizabethan literature that the *Examiner* praised as touching "the common humanity of his audience, whether Christians or Deists," † he comes as close as he ever came to giving his own creed. "Leaving religious faith quite out of the question," he writes glowingly of Christ as the prototype of "sublime humanity" and the most notable advocate of "abstract benevolence." In terms indistinguishable from those with which he elsewhere sets forth the aspirations of reform he describes Christianity as "the religion of the

---

* 8.152n. See 1.77, where Hazlitt cites the Good Samaritan in a discussion of benevolence. In 1818, in his lectures on the English comic writers, he mentioned (6.103f.) as proof of Johnson's greatness his carrying an "unfortunate victim of disease and dissipation on his back up through Fleet Street," and when his audience tittered at such impropriety "he paused for an instant, and then added, in his sturdiest and most impressive manner, — 'an act which realizes the parable of the Good Samaritan;' at which his moral and delicate hearers shrunk, rebuked, into deep silence" (Talfourd, II, 176).

† 7 November 1819, p. 714. On November 21 the *Examiner* (pp. 747f.) printed a long excerpt from this lecture, and a few months later (16 January 1820, p. 46) one of its correspondents called Hazlitt's comments on Christ a "complete *proof of the truth of Christianity*."

heart," and he makes it clear that its strength lies not in supernatural sanctions but in its moral energy.

The gospel was first preached to the poor, for it consulted their wants and interests, not its own pride and arrogance. It first promulgated the equality of mankind in the community of duties and benefits. It denounced the iniquities of the chief Priests and Pharisees, and declared itself at variance with principalities and powers, for it sympathizes not with the oppressor, but the oppressed. It first abolished slavery, for it did not consider the power of the will to inflict injury, as clothing it with a right to do so. Its law is good, not power.[50]

Nowhere does Hazlitt attack the faith that sustained his father, and his customary attitude toward real belief, as toward the other tarnished ideals of his youth, is a blend of nostalgia and respect. The beautiful essay "On the Fear of Death" has nothing about personal immortality but much about the "repose" that crowns "the troubled dream of life," and as he reaches for support he cannot grasp he feels "emptiness and desolation" in thinking of the King of Terrors.[51] The ancients, he says elsewhere, could at least meet death with equanimity, but "the modern believer, or even infidel," feels only "horror and repugnance." Taught to expect eternal felicity for the good, he is dismayed when his belief is shattered, for it is "the indulgence of hope that embitters disappointment." [52]

If Hazlitt's reticence implies disapproval of the militant atheism that some of his acquaintances espoused — "as to that detestable religion, the Christian," Shelley once casually remarked, to Haydon's horror [53] — his memories of a boyhood spent in the presence of his father and his easy familiarity with the Bible do not prove that he maintained his early faith. Deploring the vile habit of applauding religious sentiments on the stage, he argued that England had lost the kind of piety that had helped to make it great, and he comments on the fact with a terseness that speaks volumes: "religion, except where it is considered as a beautiful fiction which ought to be treated with lenity, does not depend upon our suffrages." * If he lost the "dream of infinity and eternity, of death, the resurrection, and a judgment to come," [54] he honored, and maybe even envied, the faith that anchored such a dream in the realities of life. Scornful of partisan theology and its rancors, he none the less revered the moral strength that could bring a good man to the stake. In everything except theology, it seems, he sustained the tradition of Dissent.

* 9.205. We are all remarkably well disposed at a play, Hazlitt says elsewhere (9.209), for we can all applaud the right and condemn the wrong "when it costs us nothing but the sentiment."

II

The Currents of Reform

❖◇

THE PRESENT DISCONTENTS

For Hazlitt and his generation the towering event of the nineties was the cataclysm in France. After the Bastille fell in 1789, there was of course a mixed reaction: some Englishmen watched with complacency if not elation the misfortunes of an ancient foe, and some were terrified; but Dr. Price was not alone in calling it an apotheosis. His famous sermon, epitomizing a century of reformers' hopes, celebrated the apparent victory of such ideals as popular sovereignty and the right of resistance to oppression, as well as the establishment of civil and religious freedom, and his delight was widely shared. When, as an old man, Southey explained his enthusiasm for reform as a boyish aberration, he remarked that in the early nineties such opinions were as unpopular "as they deserved to be,"[1] but in forty years he had let himself forget the hopes that had swept the England of his youth. The Dissenters, a group with some influence, had hailed events in France with "peculiar ardor," and as their ardor waned they were solaced by the hope that the French — who had perhaps been rash and weak and wicked — would win the liberty and justice desired by all good men.[2] As bellwether of the Unitarians, Priestley hailed the transition "from darkness to light, from superstition to sound knowledge, and from a most debasing servitude to a state of the most exalted freedom";[3] and a friend of Hazlitt's father said that, in view of what the French had done, the English too would quickly win reforms that had for generations been delayed.[4] It was true, as a writer for the *New Annual Register* observed, that most Tories viewed the Revolution with "sullen doubts" and that some extreme "republicans" had viewed it with "malignant pleasure," but almost every "moderate" man had watched its progress with "increasing satisfaction."[5]

THE CURRENTS OF REFORM

There was reason for such cheer. As Tom Moore remembered many years later, even those who had scoffed at the wilder doctrines of perfectibility saw in the early triumphs of the Revolution "almost enough to sanction the indulgence of that splendid dream." [6] It was as Joel Barlow said in his ironical *Advice to the Privileged Orders* in 1792: since the Revolution was at last "not only accomplished, but its accomplishment universally acknowledged, beyond contradiction abroad, or the power of retraction at home," it remained only for men of good will to consolidate their gains and "to comfort those who are afflicted at the prospect." [7] The horrors of the Revolution lay ahead; its achievements were secured. After a century of oppression and misrule the French, through orderly processes, had substituted constitutional monarchy for despotism, and in doing so they had guaranteed the civil rights of every creed and party. Returning from France in 1793, Wordsworth, although troubled by the recent drift toward terror, was convinced

> That, if France prospered, good men would not long
> Pay fruitless worship to humanity,
> And this most rotten branch of human shame,
> Object, so seemed it, of superfluous pains,
> Would fall together with its parent tree. [8]

Is it any wonder that in England, the cradle of constitutional government, the liberals were elated, the Dissenters filled with admiration, the advocates of Parliamentary reform inspired with hope, and the radicals dizzy with anticipation? "Hey for the New Jerusalem!" Holcroft wrote to Godwin. "The millennium! And peace and eternal beatitude unto the soul of Thomas Paine." [9] Twenty years later, Hazlitt tried to explain the thrill, of joy or fear, that swept through England in the early nineties. "The pillars of oppression and tyranny," he recalled, "seemed to have been overthrown: man was about to shake off the fetters which had bound him in wretchedness and ignorance; and the blessings that were yet in store for him were unforeseen and incalculable. Hope smiled upon him, and pointed to futurity." [10]

They were indeed tumultuous times, and made more so by the electrifying effect of the French Revolution on the old and steady impulse for reform that for generations had been contained within or submerged by parliamentary processes. Not only had the Dissenters deplored their disabilities for a hundred years and more, but ever since the early reign of George III social unrest, a perplexed foreign policy, and recurrent constitutional crises had afforded many motives for complaint. Although the American debacle had finally ended the king's attempt to make the Crown and government synonymous, many of the other evils that Burke had pointed to in *Thoughts on the Causes of the Present Discontents* (1770) had not yielded to his rhetoric: for decades before 1789 a series of foreign and domestic calamities, from the Wilkes and Gordon riots at home to the disasters in India and America, had stirred political discussion.

Closer to the average man's concern, of course, was money. Cowper might melodiously lament the "penury" that claimed the thoughts, lessened the comforts, and curtailed the "colloquial pleasures" of the English yeoman, and Goldsmith deplore the hastening ills of an unbalanced agrarian system; but toward the end of the century many new forces — notably the problems raised by the Industrial Revolution — converged to emphasize the need for prompt reform. The fact that out of more than half a million Londoners 20,000 rose each morning without knowing how they would survive the day or where they would sleep the following night, while 150,000 supported themselves by pursuits that were criminal, illegal, or immoral,[11] was not ignored by those who advocated change, and neither was a savage penal system that had no mercy on the poor. Godwin, for instance, suggested that since the rich are "directly or indirectly" the legislators of the state, it is obviously their purpose to reduce oppression to a system,[12] and Joel Barlow denounced the "Draconian codes of criminal jurisprudence which enshrine the idol property in a bloody sanctuary, and teach the modern European, that his life is of less value than the shoes on his feet."[13] Such friends of liberty could not endorse a social system that in fifty years had almost doubled those offenses thought to merit death, that penalized both Catholic and Protestant nonconformity, that condoned the trade in slaves, that permitted a staggering rise in prices while keeping wages down. Moreover, a half-mad king and a Parliament representing only an entrenched minority did nothing to ease their discontent.

◇ ◇ ◇

Discontent was one thing, however, and revolution was another; and it required only one extraordinary man to show how thin this crust of disaffection was. There can be no doubt that Burke was truly terrified at the specter of an English revolution. He remembered, with a shudder, the Gordon Riots of 1780, when "wild and savage insurrection quitted the woods, and prowled about our streets in the name of Reform," and a decade later he saw an even more appalling form of danger, with "the portentous comet of the Rights of Man" hurling England "into all the vices, crimes, horrors, and miseries of the French Revolution."[14] Calling on all Britons to save their threatened way of life, he seemed to think, as one of his opponents charged, no contumely "too debasing, — no invective too intemperate, — no imputation too foul" in denouncing the proponents of reform.[15] Regarding, or pretending to regard, Dr. Price's sermon as the prelude to moral chaos and civil insurrection, he sprang to the attack, and his success was overwhelming. Reformers were thrown first into a posture of defense and then into utter disarray. Those who answered him — mainly liberal Whigs and nonconformists — were fighting to preserve a losing cause, for however consoling or inspiring they were to one another, they could not allay the average Briton's fear of rapid social change or prevent that hardening of opinion which indefinitely postponed the triumph of reform.

Burke's campaign against the French Revolution and the kind of social change that it was thought, at first, to herald must be accounted one of the most remarkable accomplishments in English political history. Barricading the Tories behind Magna Carta, Crown, and church, he gave a voice to their conservatism, and to his countrymen of all parties he provided the slogans for resisting change at home and revolution abroad as aspects of a single peril. He made them the champions of English tradition against French arms and French ideas, against Parliamentary reform, against popery, against nonconformity, and against any concession to the social and industrial changes that had already destroyed the England they were bent on saving. For four decades his counsels, forged in desperate haste to meet a present danger, enabled the Tories to suppress or ignore the pent-up forces of the age. No one would claim that Burke alone effected a shift in public opinion to bring England forward as the paladin of orthodoxy and legitimacy, but he profoundly understood the slow processes of political action and the *mystique* of English conservatism, and to their defense he brought the strength of genius. In recoiling from what seemed to him the pernicious folly of accelerated change, he sometimes sank to shrill abuse, he quarreled with Fox, and he left the Whigs whose councils he had long adorned; but he also raised a banner to which Englishmen of almost every class could rally, and when Pitt and the Tories translated his principles into a policy of foreign war and domestic inertia the doom of liberal thought was sealed.

Burke's apostasy, as it seemed to many routed friends of liberty, was a staggering blow. As the conscience of the Whigs, the advocate of the unruly American colonists, and the most formidable foe of George III's attempt to extend the Crown's prerogatives, he had for almost thirty years been the champion of advanced opinion. The man who had proclaimed, in defense of America, that he knew not the method of drawing up an indictment against a whole people [16] had also led his party in seeking to relieve the Irish Catholics. In the charge that he had "pushed the principles of general justice and benevolence too far" he exulted: "In every accident which may happen through life," he had said, "in pain, in sorrow, in depression, and distress, I will call to mind this accusation, and be comforted." [17] He had told Parliament, standing obstinately on its abstract rights, that nobody could be argued into slavery, [18] reminding it that the question is "not whether you have a right to render your people miserable, but whether it is not your interest to make them happy." [19] In hammering at the arrogance of Lord Bute and his royal master he had insisted upon a monarch's responsibility to his subjects. "In all disputes between them and their rulers, the presumption is at least upon a par in favor of the people," he observed, for experience infallibly teaches that they have no interest in disorder. "When they do wrong, it is their error, and not their crime." [20] In his great Economic Reform Bill of 1782 he had checked if not destroyed the ancient scandal of Parliamentary corruption. He had pointed out the folly of oppression — after a century of persecution, Ireland was still "full of penalties and full of Papists" [21] — and in a score of splendid speeches he had nailed down the proposition that "the coercive authority of the state is limited to what is necessary for its existence." [22]

This same man, the hero of many a lost but valiant battle, had then come forward, as many thought, to attack his own ideals. "The loud assertor of American independence," Hazlitt later said, "appeared first the cautious calumniator, and afterwards, inflamed by opposition and encouraged by patronage, the infuriated denouncer of the French Revolution." [23] Actually, Burke's motives were more complex and honorable. That part of the *Reflections* in which he is the chronicler of French atrocities, although matchless in its rhetoric, is weakened by his failure to link effect with cause. Denying that the *ancien régime* sustained any faults not amenable to gradual alteration from above, he was incapable of realizing that the Revolution from below was a popular eruption against evils that were insupportable. However, when he turned from cataloguing the alleged crimes of the National Assembly to exploring the larger problem of reform, he was on more solid ground, or at least in an area when he could make the classic English defense of social stability.

He viewed society as an organism of slow, autonomous growth, not as a Lockean and mechanistic contraption that men devise and then may tinker with. It is not an association of individuals bound together by a quasi-legal contract, he asserted, but a majestic edifice sprung from a people's deepest moral and emotional needs. Its purposes are fulfilled by growth, tradition, and cohesion; and its moral strength is shown in institutions and commitments which, though inexplicable by shallow creeds and slogans, are essential to its proper function. Believing these things, and appalled by the advance of French reform, Burke could say, to the dismay of all reformers, that he would bear with infirmities "until they fester into crimes," [24] and he could palliate the grossest political anachronisms with sonorous appeals to the sanctity of tradition. If loyal to their ancient ways, he intoned, the victims of Bourbon tyranny and incompetence would rely upon "the balmy compassion of mankind to assuage the smart of their wrongs." [25] Against those who would destroy the *ancien régime,* rickety as it was, his sentence was for open war. In his younger days he had said that "when bad men combine, the good must associate," [26] and when he came to denounce the *philosophes* and theorists of the Revolution he merely wrote a set of splendid variations on the theme.

"There is no safety for honest men, but by believing all possible evil of evil men, and by acting with promptitude, decision, and steadiness on that belief." [27] Burke derided the "delusive plausibilities" of political theorists who, loud in their defense of man's so-called "natural" rights, could not distinguish benevolence from imbecility; [28] he lashed Dissenters like Price as pious frauds; he urged upon his countrymen a "sullen resistance to innovation," [29] boasting of England's prescriptive rights and prejudices and ridiculing the "coarseness and vulgarity" of French reformers. "Their liberty is not liberal. Their science is presumptuous ignorance. Their humanity is savage and brutal." [30] The English, as he thought, are wiser.

We are not the converts of Rousseau; we are not the disciples of Voltaire; Helvetius has made no progress amongst us. Atheists are not our preachers; madmen are not our lawgivers. We know that *we* have made no discoveries, and we think that no discoveries are to be made, in morality, — nor many in the great principles of government, nor in the ideas of liberty, which were understood long before we were born altogether as well as they will be after the grave has heaped its mould upon our presumption, and the silent tomb shall have imposed its law on our pert loquacity.*

Although the heat of partisan strife does not generally make for objective judgments, it is regrettable that so great a man and so great a writer as Burke deserved at least a part of the abuse he got. But what the reformers of the nineties failed to see was his consistency. Burke's defense of the American colonists and his rage at the French National

---

* III, 345. Hazlitt repeatedly charged (for example, 4.105n, 7.146, 9.31, 13.50) that Burke opposed the Revolution because he was jealous of Rousseau.

Assembly sprang from the same conviction that political questions relate not to truth or falsity but to good and evil.[31] All the schemes of all the theorists count for nothing unless they work, and they work only if they are grounded in the "stable and eternal rules of justice and reason."[32] It was Burke's profound belief that such rules are valid only in a hierarchical society. The prudent legislators of 1689 understood these matters; the irresponsible visionaries and "metaphysicians" of France did not. Wise men know that a people's strength resides in customs, institutions, and "prejudices" far more binding than the pronouncements of "declaratory" law, hence their contempt for paper constitutions, philosophical sanctions, and the jargon of reform. "I feel an insuperable reluctance in giving my hand to destroy any established institution of government, upon a theory, however plausible it may be."[33]

Burke was a professional politician who had toiled to reform administrative and budgetary procedures, but he refused to tamper with the social system. In this as in so many other matters this Irishman profoundly understood the English temperament. Like most other eighteenth-century statesmen, he was content to repose upon established fact. With James's abdication certain basic doctrines were secured: the obsolete notions of divine right and nonresistance were decently interred, a degree of toleration was conceded, and sovereignty was firmly lodged in Parliament. But these blows to the pretensions of Stuart absolutism, although duly decked out with philosophical sanctions by Locke and his disciples, did not mean that democracy burst upon England when William III landed at Brixham. Until 1832 the country was ruled, whether Whigs or Tories occupied the seats of power in Westminster, by a few great families or their delegates in Parliament. That such an aristocracy was generally acceptable to the English is shown by the thin quantity and quality of political speculation in the eighteenth century. On the tacit assumption that the anchor of the social structure had already been secured, Hanoverian politicians urbanely refined and clarified the doctrines of 1689 but rarely ventured to assess them critically; consequently their achievement was administrative, not formal or theoretical. It was one thing for a Walpole and a Newcastle to work out the machinery (and the patronage) of the party system, and for like-minded men to resolve such questions as the Crown's prerogatives, the relation of church and state, or the heavy duties of administering an empire. It was a different and possibly a very dangerous thing to raise issues that might destroy the delicate equilibrium holding Parliament, Crown, and people in harmonious relation.

Thus Burke was expressing the national sentiment when he said that "it is always to be lamented, when men are driven to search into the foundations of the commonwealth." [34] Detesting theory and doctrine — notably the doctrine of natural rights and vaporings about a mythical social contract — he affirmed the claims of experience, expedience, and utility. "Those things which are not practicable are not desirable," he proclaimed. "If we cry, like children, for the moon, like children we must cry on." [35] What is old has survived because it has worked under the conflicting but adjustable pressures of human conduct, and it should not be lightly changed or cast aside. Recalling those years big with ominous change, Wordsworth depicted Burke as a mighty oak with "stag-horn branches" and as a sage who

> forewarns, denounces, launches forth,
> Against all systems built on abstract rights,
> Keen ridicule; the majesty proclaims
> Of Institutes and Laws, hallowed by time;
> Declares the vital power of social ties
> Endeared by Custom; and with high disdain,
> Exploding upstart Theory, insists
> Upon the allegiance to which men are born. [36]

Burke could conceive nothing harder than "the heart of a thorough-bred metaphysician," [37] under which opprobrious rubric he classed all men seeking to accelerate the processes of reform at the cost of ancient prejudices, or invoking the chimeras of natural rights and natural sanctions to justify assaults on precedent and tradition. As John Morley put it, he belonged preeminently to that class of people who prefer that which has grown to that which is made. "No lines can be laid down for civil or political wisdom. They are a matter incapable of exact definition. But, though no man can draw a stroke between the confines of day and night, yet light and darkness are upon the whole tolerably distinguishable." [38] It cannot be too often repeated, Burke said in his magnificent *apologia* to the Duke of Bedford, "line upon line, precept upon precept, until it comes into the currency of a proverb, — *To innovate is not to reform.*" [39] It is true that a state without the means of change is without the means of conservation, [40] but English reform, unlike the upheaval in France, is always based on an appraisal of political possibilities. "In what we improve we are never wholly new, in what we retain we are never wholly obsolete." [41] Burke's immense respect for the English constitution derived from his respect for the slow accretions and deliberate rhythms of life itself, for to him it was a living and a sacred thing — a "spirit" which, "infused through the mighty mass, pervades, feeds, unites, invigorates, vivifies every part of the empire, even down to the minutest member." [42] To "rub off a particle of the venerable rust that rather adorns

and preserves than destroys" the ancient metal of constitutional precedent was infamous, he thought. It was to be guilty of "tampering, —
the odious vice of restless and unstable minds. I put my foot in the tracts
of our forefathers, where I can neither wander nor stumble." [43]

An advocate of representative government so long as only the proper
minority is represented, Burke opposed a thorough electoral reform because he feared a real democracy. Such persons as hair-dressers and
tallow-chandlers ought not to suffer oppression from the state, he conceded, but neither should the state endure what happens when they,
"either individually or collectively, are permitted to rule." [44] His gravest
charge against the French republicans was their shameless desire to
make a mathematical majority "the perpetual, natural, unceasing, in-
defeasible sovereign," and to reduce their "magistrates, under whatever
names they are called," to the status of "functionaries." [45] His thinking
was based on a deep response to the lumbering utility of the English
constitution, which enshrined the power of property, as he said, and
therefore sanctioned inequality. At the outset of his Parliamentary career
he had proclaimed his allegiance to "rank, and office and title, and all
the solemn plausibilities of the world." [46] At its end, still convinced that
nobility is the Corinthian capital of polished society,[47] but fearful of the
storm to come, he intoned a *nunc dimittis* for the death of political
privilege. A thousand repetitions have not staled its gorgeous rhetoric:

The age of chivalry is gone. That of sophisters, economists, and calculators has
succeeded; and the glory of Europe is extinguished forever. Never, never more,
shall we behold that generous loyalty to rank and sex, that proud submission,
that dignified obedience, that subordination of the heart, which kept alive, even
in servitude itself, the spirit of an exalted freedom! The unbought grace of life,
the cheap defence of nations, the nurse of manly sentiment and heroic enterprise,
is gone! It is gone, that sensibility of principle, that chastity of honor, which felt
a stain like a wound, which inspired courage whilst it mitigated ferocity, which
ennobled whatever it touched, and under which vice itself lost half its evil by
losing all its grossness! *

As far as England was concerned, this lament might have been postponed. The products of Burke's final phase — the *Reflections, An Appeal from the New to the Old Whigs, Remarks on the Policy of the
Allies, Letters on a Regicide Peace,* and the incomparable *Letter to a
Noble Lord* — are in a sense the last great effort to defend political

* III, 331f. Hazlitt quotes or alludes to the invocation to the age of chivalry many
times (for example, 4.26, 295, 7.260, 8.163, 10.14, 17.47), but almost always ironically. Thus his comment (14.58) on the Austrians' execution of French envoys bearing
a safe-conduct pass to the Congress of Radstadt: "Such was their 'unbought grace of
life,' their 'cheap defense of nations!' Yet these are the people, they who authorized,
who repeated, and who applauded outrages like this, who were the professed supporters
of religion, morality, and social order."

privilege, but they were powerful enough to save it for a generation. Confronting revolutionary and Napoleonic France, England turned to men who found in Burke all the sanctions they required for sustaining war abroad and the *status quo* at home. The era of an aging George III and his portly son, of Pitt, Perceval, Sidmouth, Castlereagh, and Canning, may not have been an age of chivalry, but such men ruled the kind of England Burke had wanted. Although they preserved beyond its normal span a political ideal that would one day have to yield, they checked the spread of French reform. In short, they succeeded, and Burke would have regarded the fearful cost in human values as not too high a price for their unquestioned triumph.

THE ADVOCATES OF CHANGE

Despite Burke's success among the most influential segments of the public, the reformers carried on their agitation throughout the early nineties, and much of it, of course, was aimed at him.

> Oh Burke, degenerate slave! with grief and shame
> The Muse indignant must repeat thy name,

Joel Barlow sang,* while Coleridge also versified his betrayal of reform †
and Wordsworth, in prose, assigned to his malign influence all of England's woes. By riveting his countrymen's freedom to the "dead parchment" of 1689 and thus compelling them to "cherish a corse at the bosom when reason might call aloud that it should be entombed," Burke, said Wordsworth with much more heat than accuracy, had aroused almost universal "indignation." [1] The *Reflections* prompted many such sporadic comments and also many formal answers, some of them still readable and one, at least, still read; but none burns with fiercer passion than Mary Wollstonecraft's *Vindication of the Rights of Man* (1790). Disdaining the "equivocal idiom of politeness," its embattled author attacks Burke hip and thigh, impugning his principles, his "mortal antipathy to reason," his probity, and his sense of common decency. Whatever she lacks in lucidity and poise she provides in feeling. Her sympathy for

---

* *The Conspiracy of Kings* (1792), in *Political Writings* (1796), p. 245. Barlow explains his indignation in a "Note on Mr. Burke" (pp. 252–258), which closes by assigning the apostate to "the execration of posterity."

† *Poems*, pp. 80 f. In addition to his harsh review of the *Letter to a Noble Lord* (*Essays*, I, 107–119), which was printed in the *Watchman*, Coleridge told Tom Poole (Griggs, I, 195) that he thought Burke's work "as contemptible in style as in matter — it is sad stuff." When he came to write *Biographia Literaria*, however, he regarded Burke as an oracle of political sagacity and a man who related politics to principles (I, 125).

46

the oppressed is matched only by her fury at Burke's lofty disregard. When he cites "the moral constitution of the heart" in defense of hierarchy and property she, invoking Locke, chides him like an angry schoolmarm: "What do you mean by inbred sentiments? From whence do they come? How are they bred?"[2] When Burke charges that the reformers with their pernicious nonsense have deprived the poor of the only consolation they can have — felicity in "the final proportions of eternal justice" — she retorts with a jibe at his "contemptible hard-hearted sophistry" in referring social evil to the will of God. "It is, Sir, *possible* to render the poor happier in this world, without depriving them of the consolation which you gratuitously grant them in the next."[3] Burke's errors in logic and in fact are bad enough, she says, but his indifference to the miseries of the common man and his horror at the inconvenience of the great are worse. He might "mourn for the idle tapestry that decorated a gothic pile, and the dronish bell that summoned the fat priest to prayer," but she remembers the sick wretch who "steals to a ditch to bid the world a long good night."[*] As a statement of reformers' aspirations the *Vindication* is merely an able piece of work, but as a cry from the heart at what man has made of man it is deeply moving.

Compared to Mary Wollstonecraft's outburst, most of the other replies to Burke seem a little pallid. Speaking for the nonconformists, the indefatigable Priestley was prompt with a series of sweetly reasonable *Letters,* and many other men — among them Capel Lofft, Sir Brooke Boothby, Thomas Christie, and Henry Mackenzie — wrote with varying degrees of heat and logic against the great apostate. Except for Tom Paine, none was more successful than a brilliant but impecunious young Scot named James Mackintosh. When older he was described by an admiring fellow-Whig as one who did not wish for the best in politics or morals, merely "for the best which can be obtained."[4] In his palmy youth, however, he knew no such reservations. Dr. Samuel Parr, whose pomposity if not his talents justified his soubriquet as the Johnson of the Whigs, wrote to compliment the author of *Vindiciae Gallicae* (1791) on his "dreadful severity of expostulation";[5] Fox praised him in the House of Commons; and the National Assembly rewarded him with honorary citizenship. Though written from the same convictions, his book is not another *Vindication of the Rights of Man.* Where Mary Wollstonecraft glows with indignation, as she herself admits, he urbanely

---

[*] *A Vindication of the Rights of Man,* pp. 152f. In 1798 Hazlitt told Coleridge (17.111) that he had met Mary Wollstonecraft "for only a few minutes." His only comment on her work, many years later, is a tart allusion (12.234) to her feminism.

tries to prove Burke's book "false in its principles, absurd in its con-clusions, and contradicted by the avowed sense of mankind." [6] Con-ceding that his adversary could escape from an untenable position by his declamation, cover his ignominious retreat with an allusion, sap the most impregnable truth with pathos, and "put to flight a host of syllogisms with a sneer," [7] Mackintosh arraigns him as "an advocate against fellow-citizens." [8] It is not foolish, he asserts, to hold that by taking thought and acting upon principle, men can repair the disorders of society. The champions of democracy in France are not rogues and foolish theorists, but responsible citizens who, in drawing up a consti-tution, had only "to affix the stamp of laws to what had been prepared by the research of philosophy." Mackintosh profoundly respects the work of "legislative intellect," and he prefers "a government of *art*" to Burke's "moral constitution of the heart," that blind, mysterious force that can justify the worst of despotisms. If government is to serve its purpose, he says, men must learn to "tolerate nothing ancient that reason does not respect, and to shrink from no novelty to which reason may conduct." [9]

Mackintosh insists upon a longer view than Burke's. To denounce the Revolution because its leaders make mistakes is like stopping a sur-geon about to amputate a gangrenous limb or a judge about to sign the sentence of a parricide. [10] He thought that the upheaval in France was a national response to evils that long familiarity could not make tolerable, and that to call it the criminal effort of one clique to dislodge another was to deny the fact of popular sovereignty. Mackintosh regarded the National Assembly, on which Burke had lavished his horror and con-tempt, as an authentic organ of popular opinion, and he urged England to profit by its timely warning that reform cannot be indefinitely post-poned. It is a fact, not theory, he asserts, that the subjects of George III resent expensive wars, persecuting statutes, a savage penal code, ex-orbitant taxes, and Parliaments controlled by the delegates of a few important families; but as such evils yield to the irresistible forces of reform, all "friends of freedom" may rejoice that "in the long cata-logue of calamities and crimes which blacken human annals, the year 1789 presents one spot on which the eye of humanity may with com-placence dwell." [11]

Since Mary Wollstonecraft and Mackintosh show the range of the reaction to Burke, we need not lose ourselves in the thicket of replies to the *Reflections*. But one of them still stands tall and strong, and can-not be ignored. Tom Paine's *Rights of Man*, dashed off in angry haste, is a monument to the republican commonplaces that had inspired the age.* Burke's success in alerting the hereditary rulers of England to the threat of rapid social change was very great indeed, but he met his match in Paine, who supplied a very different clientele with slogans and aspirations for a program still to be achieved. It was one thing for Pitt to have made a futile, graceful effort at electoral reform; it was another for a malcontent like Paine to demand, in the name of a disfranchised laboring class, rights that would wreck the social system. His book, as Hazlitt said, was the "only really powerful reply" to Burke — so powerful, in fact, that it could be met only by the government's exiling its author and declaring war on France.[12]

Between Burke and Paine there could be no common ground except the field of battle. The one might talk loftily of prescriptive rights and proclaim the use of ancient prejudices, but the other denounced hereditary privilege as an imposition on mankind. When Burke, ignoring the miseries of the French peasantry, described Marie Antoinette in terms to make a nation weep, Paine jeered that he pitied the plumage but forgot the dying bird. Burke, superbly contemptuous of what, in an evil hour, he had called "the swinish multitude," [13] asserted that only those with a stake in the country were eligible for Parliamentary representation; Paine, insisting that government is the property of the whole community, cited embarrassing statistics about the bizarre electoral system. "The town of Old Sarum, which contains not three houses, sends two members" to Parliament, he observed, "and the town of Manchester, which contains upwards of sixty thousand souls, is not admitted to send any. Is there any principle in these things?" [14] Burke might hymn the glories of the British constitution, but Paine talked instead about a graduated income tax, old-age pensions, and maternity benefits. Burke, convinced that the settlement of 1689 had set the social structure, thought that for alleged reformers to demand perquisites undreamed of by their fathers was to violate a sacred trust: between the living and the dead and generations yet unborn, he believed, there was a mystic bond that defined the classes of society, preserved its values, and prescribed the duties by which its members live. Paine scouted such quasi-moral notions with the assertion that "man has no authority over posterity in matters of personal right." [15]

Not content with mere reform, Paine called for the reconstruction

---

* Part I, a point-by-point reply to Burke, was published in February 1791 by Joseph Johnson (who also issued books by Hazlitt and his father). When Johnson timorously withdrew the edition after only a few copies had been sold, Paine, by then in Paris, asked Godwin, Holcroft, and Thomas Hollis to arrange a new edition, and it duly appeared on 13 March 1791. A French translation with a second (and inflammatory) preface was published in May 1791.

of society, and therein lay his great mistake. Long before, in stiffening the resolve of the American revolutionists, he had said that a king is nothing but the heir of "the principal ruffian of some restless gang," who had come to power by chance, election, or usurpation,[16] and that the "much boasted" British constitution was a shabby thing, much subject to "convulsions" and shattered, since the Conquest, by eight civil wars and nineteen insurrections.[17] The success of French reformers had confirmed him in these disrespectful views. Although any government is bad, he said, because it means constraints (like dress, "it is the badge of our lost innocence," and "the palaces of kings are built upon the ruins of the bowers of paradise"),[18] when it rests upon consent and preserves man's "natural and imprescriptable" rights it serves a useful purpose.[19] When it flaunts these rights, however, it should be set aside and replaced by something better. Monarchy is a glaring case in point:

> It is time that nations should be rational and not be governed like animals for the pleasure of their riders. To read the history of kings a man would be almost inclined to suppose that government consisted in stag-hunting, and that every nation paid a million a year to the huntsman. Man ought to have pride or shame enough to blush at being thus imposed upon, and when he feels his proper character, he will.[20]

Paine's allusion to "that weak and witless person, the Elector of Hanover, sometimes called the King of England"[21] and Burke's to "the unbought grace of life" suggest how far apart they were. It is unfortunate that two such able men could not have reached an understanding, for there was justice on both sides. But it was Burke, of course, who won. In identifying social progress with extreme republicanism Paine assured his own defeat: his book, whose success had terrified the government, was proscribed, and he was named a traitor. Perhaps the seat in the National Assembly with which the grateful French rewarded him afforded consolation, but the cause for which he fought lay crushed for more than forty years. Appalled by his attack upon tradition, the English chose to follow Burke; and when they rallied to support the Crown and church whose destruction Paine had asked they proved how deeply Burke had understood their wants and needs.

BURKE AND HAZLITT

That Hazlitt, like Paine, tended to ignore the people's wants and needs is shown by his response to Burke. As a boy at school he of course was not involved in the struggles of the early nineties, but when he later came to know and worship Burke the artist, it was despite his contempt for Burke the politician. Like many friends of liberty he was often less than fair to Burke's ideas, but for his style he had unbounded admiration. In 1796, when he first read the *Letter to a Noble Lord* in newspaper excerpts, he was enchanted by its prose, "forked and playful as the lightning, crested like the serpent"; * and two years later, when he bought the *Reflections,* his admiration was confirmed. It was the year of his memorable meeting with Coleridge, to whom his first remark was a bold defense of Burke,[1] and thereafter it became for him a perennial and unsolved problem to explain how a man who wrote so well could think so badly. "If there are greater prose-writers than Burke," he said in 1821, "they either lie out of my course of study, or are beyond my sphere of comprehension." Both as man and boy, he remarked with obvious restraint, he "did not care" for Burke's pernicious doctrine, and yet the mystery of that noble style remained — a style that made all others, even Johnson's and Junius', seem "pedantic and impertinent,"[2] and that retained its secret strength because "first-rate powers" can be defined only by themselves. "They are *sui generis,* and make the class to which they belong."[3]

Hazlitt's first systematic effort to explain a great writer whose opinions he abhorred was a sketch of Burke in *The Eloquence of the British Senate* (1807), which, though not wholly to his liking, as he told his father,[4] he thought worthy of inclusion in *Political Essays* twelve years later. In spite of many subsequent attempts to deal with Burke — some petulant, some abusive, but all admiring of his style — this early piece remains the best, perhaps because, as Hazlitt later said, it "was written in a fit of extravagant candour, at a time when I thought I could do justice, or more than justice, to an enemy, without betraying a cause."[5]

Politics aside, there were marked affinities between the old conservative and the young radical. For one thing, both distrusted the trim constructions of theorists undisciplined by feeling and experience. Speculative systems and logical deductions are very well, Hazlitt said later, but "fact, concrete existences, are stubborn things" that cannot be juggled like abstractions.[6] Collectively, men have a wisdom and a common sense that speculative thinkers lack, and such ideas as liberty, morality, and humanity are the residue of many men's experience, not the inventions of reform.[7] They are "truths as old as the creation."[8] Even Sir Francis Burdett, a forward-looking politician, seemed to Hazlitt to be always searching for "the principles of law and liberty" instead of re-

---

* 12.228. Thirty years after first reading this *Letter* Hazlitt was still puzzling (12.115n) over the knotty syntax of a favorite sentence and analyzing (12.11f.) the rhythm of its famous invocation to "the proud keep of Windsor," which he had long since decided (7.312n) was Burke's "most splendid passage."

lying on his feelings;[9] and Brougham, whose eccentricities could not conceal his good intentions, was a slave to logic and statistics. People cannot be "*calculated into* contempt or indignation on abstract grounds," Hazlitt warned, and all Brougham's facts and figures, "ticketed and labelled," could never "save a nation or an individual from perdition."[10] Such opinions, drawn at random from Hazlitt's later work, are cognate with the theme of his *Reply* to Malthus at the start of his career, and they show how close his thinking was to Burke's. Though they were poles apart politically, he, like Burke, was mindful of the force of time and habitual association in shaping human values; he insisted that man was not a purely rational creature who calculated every action, but one of sympathy and feeling, and of ancient, dimly understood allegiances; he detested all brisk accounts of human motives that ignored the promptings of the heart.[11]

Some of these affinities with Burke the youthful Hazlitt must have recognized. He would one day snarl at bigots who, recoiling from the threat of change, invoke the sanctions of antiquity to condone "any knavery, or any folly";[12] and he would ironically compliment the author of the *Reflections* for having taught England to cast its anchor "through time and eternity in the harbour of passive obedience and non-resistance."[13] His first essay on Burke, however, was inspired by an immense respect. That great man's understanding of mankind, he said there, was "inexhaustible as the human heart, and various as the sources of nature,"[14] and his strength of intellect, together with his intuition, made him tower over all his rivals. To speak contemptuously of Burke, he had said in 1798, showed a "vulgar democratical mind,"[15] and nine years later his opinion was unchanged: "It has always been with me a test of the sense and candour of any one belonging to the opposite party, whether he allowed Burke to be a great man."[16] In his broad and comprehensive view, said Hazlitt, Burke believed

that the interests of men in society should be consulted, and their several stations and employments assigned, with a view to their nature, not as physical, but as moral beings, so as to nourish their hopes, to lift their imagination, to enliven their fancy, to rouse their activity, to strengthen their virtue, and to furnish the greatest number of objects of pursuit and means of enjoyment to beings constituted as man is, consistently with the order and stability of the whole.[17]

Burke's arguments for political privilege may not be decisive, but they are true within their limits; and, "fatal" as the application of his notions proved to be, he was none the less without a peer. "He presents to you one view or face of society. Let him, who thinks he can, give the reverse side with equal force, beauty, and clearness."[18]

BURKE AND HAZLITT

Apart from his role as spokesman for the *ancien régime,* however, Burke the artist challenged speculation, and the rest of Hazlitt's early essay is a hard-breathing attempt to account for the glory of his style. For all his wealth of diction and surge of movement, he observes, Burke is one of the "severest" of all writers because "his words are the most like things; his style is the most strictly suited to the subject." [19] A man of boundless power, he used his power not to dazzle or beguile the reader but to state the truth of things. With his "untameable vigour and originality" he did not have to seek grace or beauty, because they came unsought from the "furnace" of imagination. [20] He was never verbose, for when he multiplied words it was not because he lacked ideas but because language was too thin and pallid for his needs. In a "formal" style like Johnson's the "words are not fitted to the things, but the thing to the words," [21] and consequently truth and nature are betrayed; but Burke, who sought nothing but precision, found expression in a style of overwhelming amplitude and power. Compared to him, other political writers must take a lesser rank. Cicero's forte is seen to be "artful regularity," Chatham's simply feeling. And even though Junius may be at the head of his own class, "that class is not the highest"; Burke yields to him only "if the stalk of a giant is less dignified than the strut of a *petit-maître.*" [22]

Never again was Hazlitt so generous to the man whom he worshiped as a writer and detested as a politician. To compare the tribute of 1807 with an annihilating attack of 1816 (which also found its way into *Political Essays*) * is to observe how his style has gained and his prejudice hardened. An older Hazlitt, wounded by the defeat of a cause that Burke had worked to overthrow, charges "the apologist of all courtly abuses" with chicanery, cruelty, and lunacy. A man of "fine fancy and subtle reflection," he was inadequate to the demands of "abstract reasoning" or even practical politics. [23] "Facts or consequences never stood in the way of this speculative politician." He could defend the shameless French clergy as ardently as he falsified the Glorious Revolution; and his thrilling valediction to the age of chivalry showed that by a principle of false refinement "there is no abuse, nor system of abuses, that does not admit of an easy and triumphant defence." [24] Burke's example demonstrates that once the restraints of common sense and honesty are scrapped "we may easily prove, by plausible words, that liberty and slavery, peace and war, plenty and famine, are matters of perfect in-

* 7.226–229. First published as part of the review of Coleridge's *Biographia Literaria* in the *Edinburgh* of August 1817 (16.130–134), this sketch of Burke was reprinted two months later in the *Champion* and two years after that in *Political Essays.*

difference." [25] But despite his rancor Hazlitt could not impugn Burke's style, which showed imagination matched only by control of language. "As long as the one or the other has any resources in store to make the reader feel and see the thing as he has conceived it, in its nicest shades of difference, in its utmost degree of force and splendour, he never disdains, and never fails to employ them." [26]

These two pieces fairly represent the scope and depth of Hazlitt's response to Burke. At various times he portrayed him as a "pensioned sophist"; [27] an Irishman incapable of discovering truth but competent to palliate a lie; [28] a court lackey whose powerful, wicked book, bound up in morocco and recommended by the king himself as one that every gentleman should read, was admired by lords of the bedchamber, simpered over by peeresses, praised by bishops, and imitated by scholars trying to write themselves into a bishopric. [29] Burke was the "most accomplished rhetorician" that the world had ever seen, said Hazlitt, and he did his work so well that he changed the course of English history: he persuaded the people of England that "Liberty was an illiberal, hollow sound; that humanity was a barbarous modern invention, that prejudices were the test of truth; that reason was a strumpet, and right a fiction." [30]

No Romantic writer is more prone to lose himself in the colonnade of time than Hazlitt, and none is more sensitive to the magic that distance gives to recollection and association. But when Burke invokes the past to justify his stand, as he does so often and with such extraordinary success, Hazlitt always bridles. A disrespect for antiquity was common with Dissenters, and in jeering at the sentimental Toryism that converted political privileges into sacred relics he was on familiar ground. "There is nothing of hereditary growth but pride and prejudice," he said. [31] His wrath was always sparked when Burke and such latter-day disciples as Coleridge and Southey relied upon tradition to justify contemporary abuses. It was through Burke's good offices, he remarked, that a "crazy, obsolete government" was transfigured into "an object of fancied awe and veneration, like a mouldering Gothic ruin, which, however delightful to look at or read of, is not at all pleasant to live under." [32] To the disenchanted Hazlitt, as to Paine, history seemed a "royal hunt, in which what is sport to the few, is death to the many." [33] Conversely, the misfortune of a royal line always gave him pleasure. The so-called martyrdom of Charles I, he said, was really nothing but an act of simple justice, for "in him that monstrous fiction, the *jure divino* doctrine, first tottered and fell headless to the ground." *

---

* 19.140. Hazlitt repeats this phrase elsewhere (19.180), and in one of his last essays (19.329–334), on the expulsion of the Bourbons, he takes it as his theme.

Therefore Hazlitt thought that Burke's talk about vice when privileged as losing half its evil was sentimental cant. Burke's assertion of the "indissoluble connection between learning and nobility" and of "the respect universally paid by wealth to piety and morals" would impress him more, he said, if he could only forget Parson Adams drinking his ale in Sir Thomas Booby's kitchen.[34] His own attitude is illustrated in his "Sketch of the History of the Good Old Times," an angry piece he wrote for the *Examiner* in the depths of his despair about Napoleon's fall.[35] It is a caustic analysis of the chivalric ideal that Burke had eulogized. Surveying the long history of royal crime and folly in France, Hazlitt moves from Hugh Capet (who waded to the throne through blood) to Charles V (called "the Wise" because his father was a fool and his son a madman) to Louis XI ("a bad son, a bad father, a barbarous brother, an ungrateful master, a dangerous friend, an implacable and perfidious enemy") to Charles IX ("an infernal monster" who "executed, in childhood, what Caligula had only wished"). Ending his tour with their newly crowned legatee Louis XVIII, he shudders to think what the future holds, but the inference is clear: anyone who drivels the "slavering" Tory cant about the "mild paternal sway, and the blessings of Legitimacy" is either a consummate hypocrite or fool.[36] The same repugnance to one of Burke's great themes made him leave unfinished Sully's *Memoirs* because "the pages seemed slippery with blood," [37] and he recoiled from Buckingham's enormities in *Peveril of the Peak* as relics of a past that only wicked men revere.[38]

Reviving the political morality of the past, Burke had changed the course of modern history, for it was he, said Hazlitt in almost his final word on the subject, who at a decisive moment "stood at the prow of the vessel of the state, and with his glittering, pointed spear *harpooned* the Leviathan of the French Revolution." [39] Despite this sin against humanity, however, he remained "the most powerful, the most dazzling, the most daring" master of English prose.[40] When Hazlitt blasts with furious energy the objects of his wrath, we wish for him, as he wished for Burke, that such power were directed toward a nobler end. But if he was never false to his convictions, he never failed to pay the tribute owed to genius. To praise Burke, he told Northcote, was a task he could not weary of.[41] When he lashes Burke or Scott or Wordsworth for his politics we sigh and turn aside; but when, with priestly adoration, he celebrates the mysteries of their art we marvel and are still. He is most triumphant when he salutes his mighty adversaries. "Anger may sharpen our insight into men's defects," he said, "but nothing should make us blind to their excellences." [42] His last sustained effort to account for

THE CURRENTS OF REFORM

Burke's supreme command of language does not significantly add to the essay of 1807, but it is written with the ease and force that Burke himself exemplified, and it proclaims, with undiminished admiration, the allegiance of a lifetime: "the principle which guides his pen is truth, not beauty — not pleasure, but power." [43]

FRIENDS OF LIBERTY

The last decade of the eighteenth century was a time, as an older, disenchanted Hazlitt said, when schemes "of motives and actions, of causes and consequences, of knowledge and virtue, of virtue and happiness" were "spoken on the house-tops, were whispered in secret, were published in quarto and duodecimo, in political treatises, in plays, poems, songs, and romances"; [1] and the literature of discontent was staggering in bulk and energy, if not in quality. Such veterans of reform as Price and Paine and Priestley were dead or in exile after 1794, but other men were pressing forward and other voices being raised, some of them with programs that would have shocked an older generation. In 1793, for example, the hard-pressed reviewer of contemporary literature for the *New Annual Register* found something good to say about a dozen sober tomes on politics, and he noted that one of them — a work called *Political Justice* — had "greatly excited the public attention." [2]

In the mounting public debate of the mid-nineties the line between reformers and radicals was not always clearly drawn. Many so-called friends of liberty gathered around Joseph Johnson, the publisher of much radical literature as well as of Cowper's *Task* (from which he made ten thousand pounds), [3] Wordsworth's *Evening Walk* and *Descriptive Sketches,* and the sermons of the elder Hazlitt. [4] At the weekly luncheons in a "little quaintly shaped upstairs room" [5] above his shop in St. Paul's churchyard, there congregated artists like Fuseli, reformers like Price and Priestley, radicals like Godwin and Holcroft, celebrities like Paine and Mary Wollstonecraft, and nobodies like William Blake (whom Johnson occasionally employed). To call them members of a coterie would be misleading, because they stood for different things: Price and Priestley wanted nothing that the settlement of 1689 had not guaranteed, but Paine was willing to demolish church and Crown, and Godwin was as thoroughgoing a philosophical anarchist as England had produced. However sharp the differences between, say, the godless Holcroft (who "absolutely infests you with *Atheism,*" as Coleridge later wrote to Southey) [6] and the staid Dissenting ministers, or between Price and

Godwin on the question of taxation, all these men could subscribe to a set of consoling commonplaces. A like-minded minority confronting rising hostility and derision, they could at least agree upon the axioms that had been laid down in 1689 and were being proved, they thought, by the progress of reform in France. As Price had tersely put the matter, they all believed that a people had three unalienable rights: to choose their governors, to cashier them for misconduct, and to frame a government responsive to their needs. Although sometimes lost or weakened through oppression and neglect, these were natural rights; their preservation was the end of government, and their restoration was the goal of all reform.*

In addition to men of the caliber of Godwin, Price, and Paine, there were many friends of liberty who took up politics, it seems, as they might have taken up whist or Roman coinage or shooting with the longbow. Ardent and self-conscious, they fashionably vilified Pitt, venerated Godwin and Rousseau, and wasted much ink and paper in their sentimental advocacy of natural rights and primitive virtues. Among them was "Perdita" Robinson, once Garrick's protégée and mistress of the Prince of Wales (her "Florizel"), who, crippled and impoverished, was appallingly prolific in both verse and prose. Although Coleridge praised and pitied her,⁷ William Gifford made fun of her affliction and denounced her as a "wretched woman" who "in the wane of her beauty fell into merited poverty, exchanged poetry for politics, and wrote abusive trash against the government at the rate of two guineas a week, for the Morning Post." † Helen Maria Williams, to whom Wordsworth addressed his first published poem, also wrote unfortunate novels, but she lived long in France and interestingly described the Revolution in the *Letters* which Hazlitt, thirty years later, used in writing of Napoleon.‡ Mary Hays, author of *The Victim of Prejudice* and other things,

---

* It was mainly on these three principles as enunciated in Price's famous sermon that Burke (III, 251) and Paine (p. 60) conducted their debate about reform.

† *The Baviad, and Maeviad* (8th ed., 1811), p. 56. Gifford's "unmanly" jibe, as Hazlitt called it later (11.125) prompted Leigh Hunt's retaliation in *The Feast of the Poets* (1814) and *Ultra-Crepidarius* (1823). It was this attack on Mrs. Robinson, Hunt recalled as an old man (*Autobiography*, p. 263), "which put all the gall into anything which I said, then or afterwards, of Gifford, till he attacked myself and my friends [in the *Quarterly Review*]." See Hunt's comments on Gifford in the preface to *Ultra-Crepidarius, Poetical Works*, p. 711, and below, page 367.

‡ Because of her alleged connection with Wordsworth Helen Maria Williams has received a good deal of scholarly attention. See Mary Moorman, *William Wordsworth . . . The Early Years, 1770–1803* (1957), pp. 59f.; F. W. Bateson, *Wordsworth* (2d ed., 1956), p. 82n; F. M. Todd, "Wordsworth, Helen Maria Williams and France," *MLR*, XLIII (1948), 456–464. On her *Letters* see M. Ray Adams, "Helen Maria Williams and the French Revolution," *Wordsworth and Coleridge: Studies in Honor of George McLean Harper* (ed. Earl Leslie Griggs, 1939), pp. 87–117.

was one of Godwin's disciples whom Coleridge regarded as an "ugly & petticoated" atheist trying "to run Religion thro' the body with an Icicle." [8] Even though her republicanism owed much to Rousseau, Paine, and Godwin, the author of *Political Justice* cannily refused her offer of marriage, whereupon she pushed his match with Mary Wollstonecraft and later wrote a thinly disguised autobiography, on the theme of female emancipation, in *The Memoirs of Emma Courtney* (1796). With "some reputation as a novel of passion," Crabb Robinson recalled, the book "was thought to be heretical on the great question of marriage." [9]

Although it would not do to take Mary Hays very seriously, there were other disaffected persons who deserved a more respectful hearing than they got. We tend to think of late eighteenth-century radicalism in Godwin's terms, and in this book he will stand as its main advocate, partly because he is so useful as a specimen and partly because Hazlitt had so much to say about his work. But he was only one of many, and mention should be made of men like Thomas Spence (who proposed land nationalization as the key to reform), Joseph Gerrald (who sought the abolition of war and for his pains was sent to Botany Bay), and John Thelwall (who saw more clearly than most the relation between poverty and social disorder). Another reformer, and one with many literary connections, was George Dyer. Although depicted as a lovable buffoon in Charles Lamb's letters, he was a learned man and a dedicated supporter of reform. Turned publishers' hack after a stint as nonconformist preacher, he became a poetaster of astonishing ineptitude, a valued friend of Holcroft, Priestley, and many other men (including Hazlitt), [10] and an indefatigable advocate of civil and religious freedom. His *Complaints of the Poor People of England* (1793) cannot qualify as a monument of political theory, but its humanitarian sympathies are a credit to the author and a reproach to the evils he attacked.

Joseph Fawcett, another forgotten friend of liberty, deserves a longer notice because of his effect on Hazlitt. A school friend of Godwin's who had impressed that unimpressionable man as one of the few persons of original genius he had ever known (Coleridge was to be another), [11] he was for many years the Unitarian minister at Walthamstow. After 1785, when he became evening preacher at the Old Jewry meeting house, the basilica of London Dissenters, his sermons made him one of the most popular pulpit speakers of the day. Moving intimately among reformers * and preaching weekly to great crowds of the "most genteel people" (including the celebrated Sarah Siddons), Fawcett was something of a personage. As one of his listeners recalled, he united a stately Johnsonian rhetoric and the "Action" of a player, but with no taint of vulgarity or of the "Cant of Methodism." [12] The Old Jewry sermons that he published in 1795, which combine reform and Christian ethics, make his attractions clear. As he expounds such topics as the "moral services" that a good man owes his fellows, [13] the injurious effects of wealth on character, [14] and the nature of "disinterested goodness" or benevolence, [15] he shows that politics have, or should have, moral implications. Irradiated with the Dissenter's confidence in the power of truth and reason, these sermons are built upon the theme of toleration. Perhaps those who worship God "with pomp and tapers, and with clouds of incense" are right, and perhaps those with simpler rites offend the deity; but such questions do not really matter. It is the search for truth that counts, says Fawcett, and no man who conducts the search with candor "shall ever lose the smile of celestial approbation." †

Similar in theme but inferior in style is a poem called *The Art of War* (1795), a tumid Godwinian plea, filled with personifications and marks of exclamation, for reason and justice to replace Pitt's destructive foreign policy.

> Afflicted Wisdom weeps that forms erect,
> Which might be men, should be no more than brutes;
> But, being what they are, she marvels not
> That furious thus each other they devour.
> The scene she gazes with a wild amaze,
> O'er which she shivers agued and aghast,
> Doubting her sense! incredulous she lives!
> Is the cold carnage of the cultur'd world!

And so on until, many pages later, he salutes Reason as the agent of reform and the savior of the world:

> Haste, royal infant, to thy manhood spring!
> Almighty, when mature, to rule mankind.‡

* Godwin's diary records scores of meetings with Fawcett and also lists the topics that the two old friends discussed. On 21 September 1791, for example, the talk was about "genius and virtue, and of Christianity," on 22 July 1793 about the "future state," and on 6 September 1793 about "poetry and God." After Fawcett retired to Hedge Grove in Hertfordshire in 1795, he and Godwin often exchanged visits — eight times in the spring of 1797, for example — and their intimacy continued until Fawcett died in 1804.

† *Sermons Delivered at the Sunday-Evening Lecture, for the Winter Season, at the Old Jewry* (2d ed., 1801), I, 171. Fawcett was probably the "old friend" who, said Hazlitt (17.65), had Burke's *Reflections* and Paine's *Right of Man* bound as one volume because he thought that "both together, they made a very good book."

‡ Pages 20, 51f. Hazlitt not only quotes from *The Art of War* as late as 1827 (17.191), but even names the poem, which is rare for him.

Although an older Hazlitt found this "laboured and artificial to a fault," [16] as a boy he idolized its author. In 1795 Fawcett — obviously an "eccentric character," as a writer in the *Gentleman's Magazine* observed [17] — resigned his ministry and moved to Hertfordshire to spend his last nine years in a Horatian pursuit of small farming and literature. Hazlitt must have heard him preach in London, but it probably was after Fawcett had retired that he came to know him well and, as he later testified, to develop a sound literary taste under his benign influence.[18] It is regrettable that a projected biography of "the friend of my early youth" and "the first person of literary eminence, whom I had then known" was never written.[19] Their talk was of literature and philosophy — "Sterne, Fielding, Cervantes, Richardson, Rousseau, Godwin, Goethe, &c." — and the display of Fawcett's "profound and subtle" taste afforded the younger man "a delight, such as I can never feel again," for Fawcett was a man with "no flaw or mist in the clear mirror of his mind." Whatever his merits as a writer, his critical responses to the style of others, from Milton to Shenstone, from Bishop Butler to Smollett, were impeccable. He was "the person of the most refined and least contracted taste I ever knew," [20] said Hazlitt in his middle age. From a friend of Coleridge, Lamb, and Keats this is praise indeed.

Fawcett's charm for Hazlitt was no doubt doubled by his interest in reform. To literature he added politics, and after he died Hazlitt revered him as an unselfish friend of liberty and in a sense a martyr to a noble cause that failed.

Of all the persons I have ever known, he was the most perfectly free from every taint of jealousy or narrowness. Never did a mean or sinister motive come near his heart. He was one of the most enthusiastic admirers of the French Revolution; and I believe that the disappointment of the hopes he had cherished of the freedom and happiness of mankind, preyed upon his mind, and hastened his death.*

Since it was on this very ground that Wordsworth later censured Fawcett, the praise of one great man and the strictures of another have earned for him a niche in history. In his republican days Wordsworth had admired Fawcett's sermons at the Old Jewry, but later, when he drew upon him for the portrait of the Solitary in *The Excursion*, he described him as a reader of *Candide* (that "dull product of a scoffer's pen"), a renegade Christian, and a victim of the "mortal taint" of French philosophy. Once, he said, Fawcett had preached

* 3.171n. Could Hazlitt have been thinking of Fawcett when he said (20.126) that he had known only one man "who had a passion for truth — and only one who had the same regard to the distinction between right and wrong, that others have to their own interest"?

FRIENDS OF LIBERTY

> The cause of Christ and civil liberty,
> As one, and moving to one glorious end,

but in his later years he changed:

> His sacred function was at length renounced;
> And every day and every place enjoyed
> The unshackled layman's natural liberty;
> Speech, manners, morals, all without disguise.[21]

As Wordsworth told Isabella Fenwick near the end of his life, Fawcett came to typify for him that blend of shallow Christianity and sentimental republicanism that had made so many unstable men helpless against "wild and lax opinions" in an age of revolutionary turmoil;[22] but in the preface to his *War Elegies* (1801) Fawcett himself had put the matter differently. "In these days of fashionable despair of the final amendment of human manners," he said there, "I am not ashamed to own myself of the number of those reputed enthusiasts who look forward to fairer times."[23]

It is on this point that Hazlitt defends one former friend and chides another in his great review of *The Excursion*, which appeared in 1814. Pointing out that *dull* is an epithet grotesquely inappropriate for *Candide*, he warns Wordsworth that "a speculative bigot is a solecism in the intellectual world," and he then restates the aspirations of reform that Fawcett had espoused and the poet had forsworn. "Confidence in social man" may be an illusion, Hazlitt says, but it is surely better than the use of naked power, in which Wordsworth had come to acquiesce. In the Armageddon of 1814 one can hardly keep the hopes of fifteen years before, he grants,

yet we will never cease, nor be prevented from returning on the wings of imagination to that bright dream of our youth; that glad dawn of the day-star of liberty; that spring-time of the world, in which the hopes and expectations of the human race seemed opening in the same gay career with our own; when France called her children to partake her equal blessings beneath her laughing skies. . . . To those hopes eternal regrets are due; to those who maliciously and wilfully blasted them, in the fear that they might be accomplished, we feel no less what we owe — hatred and scorn as lasting.[24]

STRIPLING BARDS

Among the hot reformers, cranks, and zealots who qualified as friends of liberty when Hazlitt was a boy there were two whom we remember as great men. Wordsworth and Coleridge have a special place in the story not only because of their renown but because they epitomized for

Hazlitt the failure of his age. In their progress — or decline — from reform to acquiescence in the *status quo* he read an allegory that haunted him for more than twenty years, and to understand its meaning we must try to relate it to the facts.

In 1793 when Hazlitt, at fifteen, entered Hackney College, Wordsworth, at twenty-three, had just returned from France aflame with ardor for the Revolution; Coleridge, two years younger, was an unruly undergraduate at Jesus College, Cambridge; Southey, hard at work on *Joan of Arc*, was chafing at the restraints of Balliol. All three poets were fascinated by what De Quincey later called "the gorgeous festival era of the Revolution — that era when the sleeping snakes which afterwards stung the national felicity were yet covered with flowers." [1] When Coleridge, bruised by his disappointed love for Mary Ann Evans and his silly escapade in the King's Light Dragoons as "Silas Tomkin Comberbach," visited Oxford in the summer of 1794 and there met Southey, their friendship, "hastened by the similarity of the views they then held, both on the subjects of religion and politics," [2] made them ripe for folly. Both professed to be Godwinians, but having read Voltaire and briefly "sported infidel," [3] Coleridge was veering toward Priestley and the Unitarians, as was Southey. It was the very nature of such religious views, as Coleridge put it in the *Watchman* in 1796, to generate "habits precursive to the love of freedom. Man begins to be free when he begins to examine." [4] At seventeen he had celebrated the fall of the Bastille in an ode swarming with capital letters and prophesying the quick demise of despotism —

> Heard'st thou yon universal cry,
> And dost thou linger still on Gallia's shore?
> Go, Tyranny! — [5]

and five years later his convulsive sentimentality struck a responsive chord in his new friend. Southey "is truly a man of *perpendicular Virtue*," Dyer was informed, "a *downright upright Republican!* [6] Reared with strenuous freedom by a maiden aunt who fortified herself by studying *Emile*,* Southey had been expelled from Westminster for an article in a school paper against flogging, and he went on to Balliol, as he later

---

* Elizabeth Tyler, Southey's aunt, was, like her nephew, a person given to extreme opinions. Among her other quirks was a passion for cleanliness that kept both her and her servants in an uproar. She once buried a cup for six weeks, Southey recalled (*Life and Correspondence*, p. 50) to "purify it from the lips of one whom she accounted unclean; all who were not her favorites were included in that class. A chair in which an unclean person had sat was put out in the garden to be aired; and I never saw her more annoyed than on one occasion, when a man, who called upon business, seated himself in her own chair: how the cushion was ever again to be rendered fit for use, she knew not!"

said, "in a perilous state — a heart full of feeling and poetry, a head full of Rousseau and Werter, and my religious principles shaken by Gibbon." [7] Furiously impatient with Pitt's reactionary policies, and harboring an "invincible repugnance" to the Church of England, he was then the victim of opinions which his cautious son was probably safe in calling "somewhat unsettled." [8]

When Coleridge reported his discovery of *The Robbers* to his new friend, he confessed that he had stopped at the scene in which the Moor cocks a pistol at the sleeping brigands. "I could read no more — My God! Southey! Who is this Schiller? This Convulser of the Heart?" [9] The same tremor of elation marked their response to the catchwords of reform, and in feverish excitement both Pantisocracy and, as a by-product, Coleridge's bizarre engagement with Sara Fricker (the sister of Southey's fiancée) were quickly hatched. In its author's view Pantisocracy was simplicity itself: it undertook to "make men *necessarily* virtuous by removing all Motives to Evil — all possible Temptations," [10] and since property was demonstrably the most fertile source of wrong the Pantisocrats required its *"Abolition."* [11] It was, in fact, and despite Coleridge's subsequent disclaimers,* a communistic scheme, but it was bathed in poetry.

> O'er the ocean swell
> Sublime of Hope, I seek the cottag'd dell
> Where Virtue calm with careless step may stray. [12]

"My God! how tumultuous are the movements of my Heart," blurted Coleridge in the fall of 1794. "America! Southey! Miss Fricker. . . . Pantisocracy — O I shall have such a scheme of it! My head, my heart are all alive." [13] Perhaps Joseph Cottle was right in saying that if the Susquehanna (a region of "excessive Beauty" and also safe from "hostile Indians," reported Coleridge) [14] had been called the Miramichi or the Irrawaddy it would have lost its charm for the Pantisocrats, [15] but in those heady days when reform was in the air their amatory and social aspirations blended into one Utopia. "I hail thee *Brother*," Coleridge wrote in salutation to an ass,

> spite of the fool's scorn!
> And fain would take thee with me, in the Dell
> Of Peace and mild Equality to dwell,
> Where Toil shall call the charmer Health his bride,
> And Laughter tickle Plenty's ribless side! [16]

* For example, see *The Friend*, p. 140: "From my earliest manhood, it was an axiom in politics with me, that in every country where property prevailed, property must be the grand basis of the government; and that that government was the best, in which the power or political influence of the individual was in proportion to his property, etc."

THE CURRENTS OF REFORM

Bombarding the *Courier* in the winter of 1794–95 with a set of sonnets on "Eminent Characters," Coleridge reveals his state of mind with painful rhetoric. He writes on Burke, the "Great Son of Genius" who had been seduced by Error; on Priestley, the martyr driven by "Vizir Riot" and "Superstition and her wolfish brood" across the sea; on Pitt, the "dark Scowler" who had betrayed his country with Iscariot's kiss; on Godwin, the godlike prophet of reform.[17] "Owls I respect & Jack Asses I love," he told a college friend about this time, but

for Aldermen & Hogs, Bishops and Royston Crows I have not particular partiality —; they are my Cousins however, at least by Courtesy. But Kings, Wolves, Tygers, Generals, Ministers, and Hyaenas, I renounce them all — or if they *must* be my kinsmen, it shall be in the 50th Remove — May the Almighty Pantisocratizer of Souls pantisocratize the Earth.[18]

Although both were "shamefully hot with Democratic rage," [19] Southey's attitude toward church and state was, if anything, sterner than his friend's. Cautioned by a priest that "Nature only teaches man to sin," his Joan of Arc ("a Tom Paine in Petticoats," as Coleridge later said) [20] replies, in terms made common by Rousseau, that

> Nature is all benevolence, all love,
> All beauty,[21]

and she dies a victim to evil institutions. Philosophic anarchism also marks *Wat Tyler,* that youthful indiscretion that rose to haunt its author in the heyday of his Toryism. Written in 1794 but not exhumed and published — much to Southey's indignation — until 1817,[22] this crude republican play is vigorous to the point of violence. "Oh, 't is of vast importance," Tyler ironically explains, that the poor should venerate "royal pests" and "legal robbers," for without their killing taxes "the luxuries and riots of the court" would be impossible. And when John Ball is condemned to die for his "insolent and contumacious" defense of English freedom, he smilingly predicts the "destined hour" of man's release from tyranny.

> Flattery's incense
> No more shall shadow round the gore-dyed throne;
> That altar of oppression, fed with rites,
> More savage than the priests of Moloch taught,
> Shall be consumed amid the fire of Justice;
> The rays of truth shall emanate around,
> And the whole world be lighted.[23]

Inevitably Southey and Coleridge found much to talk about. Having joined forces to write *The Fall of Robespierre,* they abandoned university life and, full of love and Pantisocracy, repaired to Bristol. There they courted the Fricker girls — one because he loved his Edith and the other because he thought it was his duty — and lectured on a wide variety of subversive topics, Southey sticking to history and Coleridge characteristically taking everything from the slave trade to Pitt's unjust tax on hair powder.[24] As a consequence, said Coleridge with proud exaggeration, they were savagely opposed by "Mobs and Mayors, Blockheads and Brickbats, Placards and Press gangs." [25] Although their plan to issue *Joan of Arc* by subscription failed, the hand of providence reached down when Joseph Cottle agreed to publish that inflammatory epic and, incredibly, pay fifty guineas for the privilege. "It can rarely happen," said an older and a wiser Southey, "that a young author should meet with a bookseller as inexperienced and as ardent as himself." [26] Coleridge helped to prepare it for the press — the work that had been dashed off in six weeks in 1793 requiring six months for revision — but he and Southey, each of whom had married his Miss Fricker in the fall of 1795, were already in a sense estranged. Coleridge admitted to Southey that he had lost some cherished friends of whom he never spoke without affection and of whom he never thought without respect. "Not 'to this Catalogue', Southey! have I 'added *your* name'. You are *lost* to *me*, because you are lost to Virtue." [27] In short, Pantisocracy had failed before it fairly started, and by the time *Joan of Arc* had burst upon the world early in 1796 its leaders had gone their separate ways — Southey, leaving his bride at the church door, to Portugal and the Coleridges to that cottage at Clevedon so tenderly described in "The Eolian Harp."

⬦   ⬦   ⬦

Entering Coleridge's life just as Southey left it, Wordsworth, though "a Republican, & at least a *Semi*-atheist," [28] was on the same path from reform to disenchantment. Neither had yet achieved that repudiation of reform which, as Hazlitt thought, stained their later years, but both had suffered the erosion of their young ideals, both were appalled when France invaded Switzerland in 1798, and both had begun to swing toward the patriotic Toryism that, a decade later, found expression in *The Friend* and *The Convention of Cintra*. Coleridge's diagnosis in *Biographia Literaria* may be taken as substantially correct:

The youthful enthusiasts who, flattered by the morning rainbow of the French revolution, had made a boast of *expatriating* their hopes and fears, now, disciplined by the succeeding storms and sobered by the increase of years, had been taught to prize and honour the spirit of nationality as the best safeguard of national independence, and this again as the absolute prerequisite and necessary basis of popular rights.[29]

THE CURRENTS OF REFORM

When in the labyrinthine reaches of *The Prelude* Wordsworth described
with beauty and precision his progress toward maturity, he recorded
not only the events of his career but also, in a sense, the spiritual biography of his generation. Some of the details — the North Country boyhood, Cambridge, London, Switzerland, France, and England once
more — are his own, but the emotional and intellectual pressures that
he had felt were felt by many men; and in retracing his own course he
transformed the political forces of a momentous decade into the permanence of art.

In the beginning was his deep response to nature — those "Pres-
ences" of earth and sky that haunted him among his boyish sports and
made

> The surface of the universal earth
> With triumph and delight, with hope and fear,
> Work like a sea.

Later, when he read into the lovely forms of nature "a moral life" and
"inward meaning," it was to add a new dimension to experience, for he
came to worship not only the winds and cataracts and mountains, but
also man himself, "Ennobled outwardly before my sight" and worthy of
a dedicated spirit's "love and reverence." To the youth at Hawkshead the
Lancashire peasant, stationed in his native hills, "working for himself,
with choice / Of time, and object," was an image of "inevitable grace."
It is the ideal that finds its noblest form in *Michael.* Later, though
stunned by the human swarm in London,

> Living amid the same perpetual whirl
> Of trivial objects, melted and reduced
> To one identity,

Wordsworth retained his awe of man's essential dignity, and when
the French Revolution seemed to topple ancient tyrannies he hoped
that Europe would achieve the freedom that is a natural right. The
great events in France, where he quickly went, led him to predict that
he would one day see

> All institutes forever blotted out
> That legalized exclusion, empty pomp
> Abolished, sensual state and cruel power,
> Whether by edict of the one or few;
> And finally, as sum and crown of all,
> Should see the people having a strong hand
> In framing their own laws; whence better days
> To all mankind.

Though deeply disturbing, the September massacres of 1792 could not cool his ardor for reform. Enraptured with the love of Annette Vallon, the friendship of Michel-Armand Beaupuy, and the apparent triumph of social justice, he reached the summit of his early hopes. Even in retrospect his memories of that period glowed:

> Bliss was it in that dawn to be alive,
> But to be young was very Heaven! O times,
> In which the meagre, stale, forbidding ways
> Of custom, law, and statute, took at once
> The attraction of a country in romance!
> When Reason seemed the most to assert her rights
> When most intent on making of herself
> A prime enchantress — to assist the work
> Which then was going forward in her name! *

Wordsworth's response to social wrong and his hopes for the reconstruction of society are most clearly marked in the works of 1793, the year of his return to England. In *Descriptive Sketches* he embodies his rational ideal in the man who, as "Nature's child,"

> all superior but his God disdained,
> Walked none restraining, and by none restrained;
> Confessed no law but what his reason taught,
> Did all he wished, and wished but what he ought.[30]

The memory of this ideal is reflected in that famous passage in *The Prelude* which "makes our Reason's naked self / The object of its fervour."

> What delight!
> How glorious! in self-knowledge and self-rule,
> To look through all the frailties of the world,
> And, with a resolute mastery shaking off
> Infirmities of nature, time, and place,
> Build social upon personal Liberty,
> Which, to the blind restraints of general laws
> Superior, magisterially adopts
> One guide, the light of circumstances, flashed
> Upon an independent intellect.[31]

(It was on these "Infirmities of nature, time, and place" that Burke had built his politics, and it was to save them that he defied the Revolution.) On a lonely walk across Salisbury Plain Wordsworth composed "Guilt and Sorrow," in which the "Heroes of Truth" are exhorted to

---

* *The Prelude*, i.464–475; iii.129–132; vii.725ff.; viii.275ff.; ix.525–532; xi.108–116. Almost none of this found its way into the autobiographical sketch that Wordsworth dictated near the end of his life (Christopher Wordsworth, *Memoirs of William Wordsworth* [1851], I, 15), but his brother none the less apologized (*ibid.*, I, 74) for the political mistakes of "an orphan, young, inexperienced, impetuous, enthusiastic."

THE CURRENTS OF REFORM

> uptear
> The oppressors' dungeon from its deepest base;
> High o'er the towers of Pride undaunted rear
> Resistless in your might th' Herculean mace
> Of Reason

until every trace of "Superstition's reign" is razed except "that eternal pile which frowns on Sarum's plain." [32]

Both motifs — dismay at what man has made of man and confidence in the power of reform — mark the angry protest of *A Letter to the Bishop of Llandaff*. Prompted by Richard Watson's complacent defense of English institutions, Wordsworth's attack on church and state and everything that Burke held dear was so strong that he himself, presumably, decided not to publish it. When finally printed in 1876, it gave a vivid proof that men are prone to change their minds. Drawing much on Paine, it is notable mainly for its fury. Wordsworth berates Burke (an "infatuated Moralist") and his Tory sycophants for mouthing platitudes about wicked and obsolete conventions instead of serving human needs, and although he does not minimize the excesses of the Revolution, he condones them as regrettable necessities. One should lament not the death of Louis XVI, he observes, but the "monstrous situation which rendered him unaccountable before a human tribunal," and one should trust the French to attain a social balance. "The animal just released from its stall will exhaust the overflow of its spirits in a round of wanton vagaries; but it will soon return to itself, and enjoy its freedom in moderate and regular delight." The horrors that appall Wordsworth are those the Tories overlook: "the scourge of labour, of cold, of hunger" resulting from a useless war with France; a penal code so barbaric that a conscientious man can neither condone nor execute English laws without surrendering his humanity, his honor, and the esteem of his fellow citizens; Parliamentary elections that burlesque the ideal of representative government. But the Bishop of Llandaff is warned that "acquiescence is not choice," obedience not freedom, and that reform is close at hand. The hereditary rulers of England have drunk too deep of Burke's intoxicating bowl to satisfy the people's needs. Lost to shame and hysterical in their fear of changes that cannot be deferred, they have survived their usefulness.* But meanwhile the friends of

* *Prose Works*, I, 9, 5, 13, 12, 15, 23, 7. The occasion of the *Letter* was the publication of Bishop Watson's sermon *The Wisdom and Goodness of God in Having Made Both Rich and Poor*, to which was affixed a comment on the unhappy state of French affairs (see Emile Legouis, *Early Life of Wordsworth 1770–1798* [trans. J. W. Matthews, 1921], pp. 226f.). Mrs. Moorman (*Wordsworth . . . The Early Years*, p. 226) thinks that Joseph Johnson declined to publish it for fear of prosecution. Despite the alleged Godwinian influence (C. W. Roberts, "The Influence of Godwin on Wordsworth's Letter to the Bishop of Llandaff," *SP*, XXIX [1932], 588–606) it is by

liberty are true and steady, strengthened by their knowledge that the French "convulsion" is the prelude to a golden age.

GODWIN

Although Wordsworth's *Letter* served its author as a vent, perhaps, and helps us measure the depth of his commitment to reform when he was young and green, it was of no importance to anyone except himself. The publication of Godwin's *Political Justice* in the same year, however, was a significant event. It marked the apogee of reformist propaganda in the early nineties. It summarized and codified one of the persistent elements of eighteenth-century thought, and it survives as the boldest and most thoughtful statement of the angers and desires that flowed together in the era of the Revolution. For that reason Godwin exemplifies for us, as he exemplified for Hazlitt, both the force and the futility of the attempt to prescribe a Utopia that, however sweetly reasonable, ignores men's motives and behavior. The poets' flirtation with reform was a youthful aberration; Price and Priestley sought merely to adjust political realities to the principles of 1689; Paine was a brilliant pamphleteer; but Godwin, the philosopher of anarchism, was a truly speculative and subversive thinker. No other reformer of Hazlitt's youth approached his fame, and when the inevitable reaction set in no other felt its strength so hard. Thrust into a "sultry and unwholesome" notoriety when his book appeared, he "blazed as a sun in the firmament of reputation; no one was more talked of, more looked up to, more sought after," Hazlitt later said, "and wherever liberty, truth, justice was the theme, his name was not far off." [1] And then, like Lucifer, he fell, and thereafter lived "obscure, retired" for almost forty years amid the ruins of a reputation that had shared the fate of his ideals. [2]

Godwin began life not only as a nonconformist preacher, like so many other friends of liberty, but as a Sandemanian. It was said of the founder of that small and flinty sect that "when with the eye of a lynx, he detects faults, he tears them to pieces with the rage of a tyger," [3] and, except that he did not resort to violence, his disciple may be said to have applied the same technique to politics. He was, said Hazlitt, "the metaphysician engrafted on the Dissenting Minister." [4] Progressing from

---

no means certain that Wordsworth had read *Political Justice* when he wrote the *Letter*. On the other hand, Paine's influence is apparent. See Edward N. Hooker, "Wordsworth's Letter to the Bishop of Llandaff," *SP,* XXVIII (1931), 522–531; Moorman, p. 255; F. E. L. Priestley's discussion in his edition of *Political Justice* (1946), III, 102f.

Calvinism to deism to Socinianism and then to utter disbelief, Godwin deserted the ministry for literary hack work,[5] but he retained the Dissenter's moral bias, and his wide reading in reformist literature in the eighties convinced him that social institutions were in need of drastic change. Although his diary (for the most part still unpublished) shows him moving intimately among nonconformists and reformers like Priestley, Rees, Kippis, Paine, and Holcroft, he was one who elicited respect rather than affection. When *Political Justice* flung him briefly into fame there had been nothing in his drab career to foreshadow such success, and there would be nothing in his later life to match it. While some of his subsequent works in drama, scholarship, and fiction — notably the powerful *Caleb Williams* (1794) — achieved and held a certain popularity, they could not support his lurid reputation as the theorist of reform. His liaison and marriage with Mary Wollstonecraft was his one surrender to emotion, and if that brave and generous woman had lived she might have softened the professor (as Lamb and others called him); but after the formidable Widow Clairmont had won him with her flattery and cooking[6] he entered into the neglect, obscurity, and chronic insolvency that marked his later years. He lived by his writing and his borrowing, a biographer has said, but mainly by his borrowing,[7] and there is no reason to think that the aging parasite who preyed on Shelley and his other friends was significantly different from the reformer of the nineties.

It was in the nineties that he and Hazlitt met — one the laureled hero of reform, the other a boy at Hackney College. Having dined with Holcroft on 17 September 1794, Godwin recorded in his diary, he then took tea with John Hazlitt and his wife, and there the younger brother ("Hazlitt junr.") was presented to him. The two families had probably had a long connection. The elder Hazlitt had succeeded Godwin's father as a Dissenting minister at Wisbeach, Cambridgeshire (where he wooed and won his wife), and a generation later the John Hazlitts were moving freely in the group that regarded Godwin as a lion.* For obvious reasons of age, however, "Hazlitt junr." was not at once admitted to the inner circle. Not until 1799 does he reappear in Godwin's diary, but thereafter the two men maintained a friendship that lasted, off and on, until the younger died. As we shall see, Godwin was of aid to Hazlitt at the

---

* As Godwin's dairy shows, on 5 December 1794 the John Hazlitts were among the well-wishers who celebrated John Thelwall's acquittal at his trial for treason, and they were twice again with Godwin and Thelwall within the next two weeks. A typical run of entries in the diary for the following year puts them with Godwin at Holcroft's on February 22 and April 8, and at Thelwall's on March 5. Other meetings are recorded on April 19 and June 16.

start of his career, and later they were collaborators of a sort. Godwin did not greatly like his work,* but he respected his intentions; and for his part Hazlitt, though never a Godwinian, stuck with Godwin to the end, praising his novels when he could and seizing every chance to prop his sagging reputation. When Northcote said in 1829 that Godwin had always been "a profligate in theory, and a bigot in conduct," Hazlitt could not, with candor, disagree:

"Yes," I said, "he writes, against himself. He has written against matrimony, and has been twice married. He has scouted all the common-place duties, and yet is a good husband and a kind father. He is a strange composition of contrary qualities. He is a cold formalist, and full of ardour and enthusiasm of mind; dealing in magnificent projects and petty cavils; naturally dull, and brilliant by dint of study; pedantic and playful; a dry logician and a writer of romances." [8]

Despite this series of antitheses, however, Hazlitt valued Godwin as a writer and a man, and as one whose life epitomized England's betrayal of reform. It was hard, he said, that a person of his intellect and power, whose motives were so good and whose fame had been so great, could be so soon forgotten, and in his famous sketch of Godwin in *The Spirit of the Age* he tried to balance the account. There he paid the debt that, as he believed, his generation owed to one of its great figures.

Godwin was not an easy man to like. "Bold and adventurous in opinions," as he himself admitted, but "not in life," [9] he was timid and reserved and also very cold. Writing as both a "father, and a philosopher" in reply to Mary Shelley's letter about his little grandson's death, he was sternly disapproving: "I cannot but consider it as lowering your character in a memorable degree." [10] When he refused to visit Thelwall, waiting in the Tower to be tried for treason, it was on the ground that the "mere gratification" of having done a friendly office should not sway a man of reason. [11] He reproved the dying Mary Wollstonecraft for an "unscientific expression" when she murmured of the joys of heaven.† Even those who admired his mind could say little for his manners. Speaking as one with much experience, Crabb Robinson called him "most ungracious in demanding and receiving favours"; [12] Charles Cowden Clarke, a gentle man himself, deplored the "snarling tone of voice" in which he sneered at people; [13] Hazlitt, who himself was not effusive, said that in conversation Godwin had "not a word to throw at a dog"; ‡ even the faithful Lamb was

---

* According to Hazlitt himself (8.285) Godwin thought that his disrespectful letters to "Vetus" of the *Times* in 1813–14 (7.33–73) were the only thing he ever did that was "worth a farthing."

† Procter, p. 203. In his *Memoirs* (1798) of Mary Wollstonecraft Godwin recorded, with obvious satisfaction, that during his wife's last illness "not one word of a religious cast fell from her lips" (p. 195).

‡ 12.198. This comment in *The Plain Speaker* (1826) must have angered Godwin,

obliged to explain that on occasion the professor's dullness was relieved by a "dash of affection." [14] It is depressing to follow the author of *Political Justice* through his later years as hack writer, antiquary, disgruntled playwright, and publisher (under an antiseptic pseudonym) of books designed for children, and one should make allowance for a man bowed by his domestic and financial blows; but that the apostle of reform was himself so cold and dry and hard of heart is not without its irony.

Godwin's preface to *Political Justice* conveys something of his sedate enthusiasm for reason as a tool of social progress. Mindful of the "general interest of the species" (and no doubt prompted by events in France), he began in September 1791 to set down the principles which for several years, he said, had been "the almost constant topic of conversation" between Holcroft and himself. He made it clear that reform, not insurrection, was his goal, and that this reform would come when truth — which always conquers error — asserted its sovereign power.[15] The initial success of his book was almost great enough to justify his confidence. The work which Pitt decided not to ban because he thought it cost too much to do the poor much harm made its author famous overnight and went through three editions. A year after its publication, when Godwin went to Warwickshire to visit Dr. Samuel Parr (who had earnestly sought his "acquaintance and intimacy"), he was able to report that everybody knew, or knew about, his book and that he was "nowhere a stranger." [16] Having written to strengthen the "habits of sincerity, fortitude and justice" in his readers, he was gratified by his success, but being Godwin he would not permit himself the vulgar pleasure of elation. That there had been "aspersions" on the "seditious and inflammatory nature" of his book, he admitted when he launched a new edition, but he urged his adversaries to remember that if false his principles would surely fall, and if true they would just as surely triumph.* These are the customary slogans of reform, of course, but Godwin seems almost to convert them into facts.

---

for in the Abinger Collection there is a draft of a rebuttal that runs to four pages in his shaky hand. Admitting his deficiency "in what is called chat," Godwin defends his skill at serious conversation and cites for proof his talks with various celebrities, including Wordsworth (whom in the course of one evening he converted from "the doctrine of self-love, to that of benevolence"). He says that without such conversations with his friends *Political Justice* would never have been written, for "Many of the best passages of my books were talk at first." If he sent this rejoinder to Hazlitt it presumably went unanswered.

* *Political Justice*, I, xvii. Godwin explained (I, xiii ff.) that the popularity of his book imposed on him "the duty of a severe and assiduous revisal" for the new edition. These revisions are fully treated by his most authoritative editor, F. E. L. Priestley. My citations are from Godwin's third edition, which contains all three prefaces and also the useful "Summary of Principles" — the tersest (if not the most inflammatory) statement of his views.

GODWIN

A large and sober book, *Political Justice* does not enchant the modern reader, yet it has the virtue of simplicity. Almost all it has to offer is contained in three sentences from the prospectus for a "seminary" that its author had once tried (and failed) to organize at Epsom:

The state of society is incontestably artificial; the power of one man over another must be always derived from convention, or from conquest; by nature we are equal. The necessary consequence is, that government must always depend upon the opinion of the governed. Let the most oppressed people under heaven once change their mode of thinking, and they are free.[17]

In *Political Justice* Godwin develops these axioms, to the length of almost a thousand pages, with the imperturbable gravity of a nonconformist preacher and the pedantry of a village schoolmaster. Without raising his voice or relapsing into either wit or anger he undermines — at least in theory — the religious, economic, and political bases of European culture. His cold and cheerless vision of Utopia is of a world where the "pleasures" of intellectual feeling, of benevolence, and of self-approbation will infallibly produce the "varied and uninterrupted" bliss compatible only with "a state of high civilization." Government, an evil "forced on mankind by their vices," will wither, and so will its devilish brood of oppression, war, and inequality; but its one benefit, security, will be guaranteed by the universal sway of justice — the principle "which proposes to itself the production of the greatest sum of pleasure or happiness." Justice will prevail because when men realize that their "voluntary actions" are under the control of reason they will make reason, rather than passion or emotion, the mainspring of their actions. Since reason "depends for its clearness and strength upon the cultivation of knowledge," which is itself capable of "unlimited" expansion, it follows that "the modes of social existence" will perpetually improve. Godwin builds his New Jerusalem, then, on the reciprocal relationship between man's knowledge and his pleasure, and on the triumph of reason over passion.[18]

Despite its repudiation of emotion, however, his book rests upon the premise, unverified by reason, that man's desire to promote the general good is fundamental. The doctrine of benevolence or of man's essential goodness was, of course, essential to reform, and Godwin had to build upon it, but it is curious that he erected such a cold, forbidding structure. As he described his method in the *Enquirer* (1797), a set of essays on political and philosophical topics, he said that he had laid down one or two principles beyond "the hazard of refutation" and then derived their inferences to form a system "consentaneous to itself" and "conformable to truth." [19] He was proud of his achievement, and so, briefly, were many other men; but since few books are more consistently logical or more desperately impractical than his, *Political Justice* is a monitory monument to the futility of prescribing for human behavior in terms of naked reason. Man interests him, and serves the uses of his theory, only in so far as he is a logical machine, clicking along from stimulus to response to judgment to action; and if reason fails, says Godwin, then he is doomed to vice and folly.

> In that case the salutary prejudices and useful delusions (as they have been called) of aristocracy, the glittering diadem, the magnificent canopy, the ribbands, stars and titles of an illustrious rank, may at last be found the fittest instruments for guiding and alluring to his proper ends the savage, man.[20]

Abhorring the kind of "prejudice" and sentiment that Burke had called the very essence of political morality, Godwin tried to prove that surrender to emotion means misery, crime, and squalor. Therefore he made reason the only test of virtue, and virtue the only guide to action.

Like all reformers, Godwin begins by recoiling from the *status quo*. When he examines man as he is and things as they are his moral indignation almost overpowers his self-control, and he admits to "grief" when he contemplates the cost in human happiness of church and state and accumulated wealth.[21] Seeing man enchained by the solemn frauds and evils that appear to be "the unalterable allotment of our nature," he writes almost like Calvin,[22] and like Calvin he is concerned with reformation — or rather with reform. Because the fallen world that he describes is the consequence not of sin but of error, its reconstruction must be the work of intellect. Not man as he is but man as he will be is Godwin's main concern, and the salvation that he brings will depend not on the "blind submission and abject hypocrisy" of organized religion (which always links itself with evil power)[23] but on the liberated mind. Godwin's hope, like Bacon's long before, is for the indefinite improvement of man's secular "commodity," and his theme is man's inevitable triumph over error, fraud, and prejudice. His reformist credo marks a peak of eighteenth-century optimism:

> Sound reason and truth, when adequately communicated, must always be victorious over error: Sound reason and truth are capable of being so communicated: Truth is omnipotent: The vices and moral weakness of men are not invincible: Man is perfectible, or in other words susceptible of perpetual improvement.[24]

By taking thought, therefore, man can win his earthly paradise. Since "voluntary" actions, which "flow from intention, and are directed by foresight," are grounded in "opinion,"[25] to change a man's opinion is to change the way he acts; and to change many men's opinion is to secure the most massive social gains. Hence the cardinal maxim of *Political Justice*: "the perfection of the human character consists in approaching as nearly as possible to the perfectly voluntary state." [26]

In pushing home the implications of this ethic Godwin remorselessly decrees the extinction of European culture. Since virtue is a function of intelligence — a "true estimate" of motives for voluntary action [27] — reason and goodness will one day coalesce, he says, and benevolence will triumph over self. "The man, who vigilantly conforms his affections to the standards of justice, who loses the view of personal regards in the greater objects that engross his attention, who, from motives of benevolence, sits loose to life and all its pleasures, and is ready, without a sigh, to sacrifice them to the public good, has an uncommonly exquisite source of happiness." [28] The church, the state, the family all must go, and even law itself will wither when, "in proportion as weakness and ignorance shall diminish, the basis of government will also decay." [29] Not only monarchy (a folly founded in imposture) [30] but government itself (the "perpetual enemy to change" [31] and "an usurpation upon the private judgment and individual conscience of mankind") [32] will be scrapped. Marriages, by which a man secures a woman through "despotic and artificial means," [33] will yield to an elevated "species of friendship"; [34] private property, with its avarice and oppression, will not be tolerated; [35] vulgar sentiments like gratitude (which has in it "no part either of justice or virtue") [36] and family affection will be discarded with the other trash that foolish men once valued. Needless to say, war and violence and even revolution in a righteous cause will be unthinkable.*

As things now stand, says Godwin, it is "visionary" indeed to look for such reforms, [37] but to deny that they can ever come to pass is to forget the power of education. While at birth the differences between two children are "arithmetically speaking something," Locke had proved that actually they are "almost nothing," [38] and therefore all our vice and inequalities must be charged up against "preceptors." It is they — parents, teachers, and the upholders of the *status quo* — who preserve society and its wretched institutions. "Like the barbarous directors of the Eastern seraglios, they deprive us of our virility, and fit us only for their despi-

---

* I, 263–284; II, 148f. In 1795, during the Parliamentary debate on the Treason and Sedition Bills, Godwin wrote his *Considerations on Lord Grenville's and Mr. Pitt's Bills* to discredit both the government's policy of repression and the radicals' threat of violence. The qualified success of the French Revolution, he said, would induce no sensible man to attempt such an experiment in England, for even though everyone except the stupid, the bigoted, and the selfish thought that reform was necessary, the methods of achieving it posed a "delicate and awful" problem. "No sacrilegious hand must be put forth to this sacred work. It must be carried on by slow, almost insensible steps, and by just degrees" (Brown, *Godwin*, pp. 100 f.).

cable employment from the cradle." [39] Used for better ends, however, education will be the means of our salvation. "Speak the language of truth and reason to your child," Godwin says, "and be under no apprehension for the result." [40] Opinion is the mistress of the world, and once we learn to relate opinions with the truth we will usher in the golden age.

THE NATURAL MAN

Burke and Pitt to the contrary notwithstanding, it was not a wicked hope that inspired the friends of liberty. Politically naive, they were powerless themselves and without the means of gaining power; they belonged to that class of persons who, as Scott said later, live and die "in the heresy that the world is ruled by little pamphlets and speeches" and think that as soon as men are shown the evil of their ways, they will promptly change.[1] They talked of social progress, and some spoke with familiarity of the millennium, while more dull-witted men were arming for a war with France. Generally poor and inexperienced, they were quick to say that bad things could be bettered on the model of the Revolution, but they were slow to see that French reform was sinking from terror to aggression. By and large their motives were impeccable. Many years later, after Southey had derided Holcroft as an atheistical Jacobin, Lamb defined him as "one of the most candid, most upright, and single-meaning men" whom he had ever known;[2] and whereas Hazlitt came to think, reluctantly, that Godwin and his friends were guilty of confusing hopes with facts, he never questioned their intentions. All that they attempted, he said at the end of his life, was a "sympathetic interpretation" of the text — "itself pretty old and good authority" — that one should love his neighbor as himself.[*] Although the men and women who appear in Holcroft's diary and Godwin's *Memoirs* of Mary Wollstonecraft may have lacked elegance and charm, they were not without valor. Sensitive to man's inhumanity to man, they thought that oppression, vice, and error were evil accidents; and in an effort to remove them they resolved

> to exercise their skill,
> Not in Utopia, — subterranean fields, —
> Or some secreted island, Heaven knows where!
> But in the very world, which is the world
> Of all of us, — the place where, in the end,
> We find our happiness, or not at all![3]

[*] 3.134. See 11.19f. and the discussion of Christianity in Hazlitt's lecture on Elizabethan literature (6.183ff.). In later life Coleridge remarked (*Unpublished Letters*, II, 452) that he had built his own reformist hopes upon the Gospels.

THE NATURAL MAN

Although Southey's *Wat Tyler* is a very different thing from "Perdita" Robinson's *Walsingham, or the Pupil of Nature*, both of them, like other works of more solid fame and merit, are built upon a set of common notions. The chief of them is an optimistic view of man, and for our purposes in tracing Hazlitt's thought this cheerful commonplace is more important than the literature that it inspired. It is the assumption, as Godwin phrased it, that social wrongs, from war through juridical and administrative malfeasance to inequality, are "not the inseparable condition of our existence, but admit of removal and remedy." Whips, axes and gibbets, dungeons, chains, and racks have been "the most approved and established methods" of regulating human action, the reformer drily adds, but the resources of reason and benevolence are still untried.[4] This is matched by young Coleridge's assertion that "vice originates not in the man, but in the surrounding circumstances; not in the heart, but in the understanding,"[5] and when Hazlitt came to write about the reformers of the nineties he invoked the same great principle: "Men do not become what by nature they are meant to be, but what society makes them."[6] Godwin, Coleridge, and Hazlitt disagreed on many things, but in these comments each reveals a major theme of eighteenth-century optimism.

It had had a complicated history. Working from premises diametrically opposed, Calvin and Hobbes had argued that man is a creature marked by sin and egotism and that the world he occupies is either wicked or amoral. A line of thinkers best exemplified by Locke and Newton, however, had changed these views to suit an age whose tastes were not for gloom. If, as science seemed to prove, nature was sustained by certain "laws" that man could understand and use, and if man himself was part of nature, then disorder, sin, and error were not intrinsic to the scheme of things. The implications for political behavior were great, as Locke was quick to show. He defined a set of natural "rights" that had the force, almost, of Newton's laws of motion, and he insisted that they were normative in all political arrangements. Meanwhile Shaftesbury declared that a natural "Scheme of Moral Arithmetick" — and the metaphor is not without significance — revealed itself in our capacity for benevolence, love, and pity: he found planted in man's heart an instinctive moral sense which, though sometimes stifled by custom or by faulty education, was his distinctive attribute.

Throughout the eighteenth century this assumption of man's essential goodness — or of his capacity for goodness if he were unimpeded — found many varied statements. It informed the subtle moral theory of Butler, Hutcheson, and Hume, and it even reached the boards of Drury

Lane. No reader of *The Conscious Lovers* or *The London Merchant* can fail to learn that men are mainly good and kind, and that when they err the fault is not their own. Although circumstances (which, as Locke had shown, have a decisive force on character) are sometimes evil and corrupting, man's intrinsic merit is never totally obscured; it is his defining characteristic, and if the promptings of his nature are allowed free play his goodness is bound to find expression. Richardson's Mr. B. and Fielding's Tom Jones exemplify this consoling view of human nature, and when we pass from these great writers to smaller fry like Henry Mackenzie and Charlotte Smith and Holcroft we see that the theme of natural goodness was, for the sentimental novelist, as useful as the invention of movable type.

But not merely for the artificers of fiction. The many advocates (including Price and Priestley) of a "refined" Christianity compatible with the new-found truths of science urged man to "follow nature" and slough off the superstitions and deceits that have dimmed his native luster. Their theology of natural goodness and their politics of natural rights were expressions of the same ideal that Rousseau's work exemplifies in other ways. *Discours sur l'inégalité, Le Contrat social,* and *Emile* hardly qualify as nonconformist tracts, of course, but they defend the feelings of the natural man against the checks of privilege, rank, and institutions; and that Priestley borrowed from their author is no more surprising than that Johnson considered him a "rascal." [7] As Hazlitt (who admired Rousseau prodigiously when young) came to understand, his political theory was an extension of his extreme subjectivism, and his celebration of the uncorrupted natural man, like his attack on institutions, was a form of self-assertion. "Insensés qui vous plaignez sans cesse de la nature," Rousseau told the victims of prejudice and error, "apprenez que tous vos maux viennent de vous." His great myth of the emancipated individual therefore had immense appeal. His "acute and even morbid feeling of all that related to his own impressions" not only inspired a generation of Romantic poets to think that self-expression was the only moral absolute; it also gave a focus to reform. "He did more towards the French Revolution than any other man," said Hazlitt.

Voltaire, by his wit and penetration, had rendered superstition contemptible, and tyranny odious: but it was Rousseau who brought the feeling of irreconcilable enmity to rank and privileges, *above humanity,* home to the bosom of every man, — identified it with all the pride of intellect, and with the deepest yearnings of the human heart.[8]

In various ways these diverse currents of eighteenth-century thought tended to flow from a pained response to present ills and to converge upon a hope for future bliss. If men are by nature created good and equal, with certain rights that guarantee their happiness and freedom, is it not clear that the effort to enjoy these rights is good and that the effort to inhibit or cancel them is bad? Behind much social protest of the period was the urge to find natural sanctions for aspirations which, if gratified, would disturb, if not destroy, the *status quo*. Generally speaking, however, the task of analyzing current evils attracted better minds than the more demanding task of defining the required reforms. Although it is easy to see how the clerical and political abuses of the *ancien régime* might stir a critical intelligence, it is hard to share the apocalyptic raptures of the reformers' social vision. For Montesquieu (of the *Lettres Persanes*), Diderot, Voltaire, Paine, Priestley, and the rest to expose established error was a tonic exercise; but for Rousseau — who said that iron and corn, by civilizing man, had ruined humanity — to advocate a return to noble savagery was sentimental nonsense; and for Condorcet and Godwin to herald the millennium was to convict themselves of folly. For Godwin to proclaim that man is capable of "being continually made better and receiving perpetual improvement" if only he applies to everything the test of reason and then acts upon his findings[9] was, as Hazlitt said, to think "too nobly of his fellows."[10] For Condorcet to predict an egalitarian state so flawless that even death itself would cease to be a problem was to lose himself in fantasy.

Combien ce tableau de l'espece humaine, affranchie de toutes ses chaînes, soustraite à l'empire du hasard, comme à celui des ennemis de ses progrès, & marchant d'un pas ferme & sûr dans la route de la vérité, de la vertu & du bonheur, présente au philosophe un spectacle qui le console des erreurs, des crimes, des injustices dont la terre est encore souillée, & dont il est souvent la victime? C'est dans la contemplation de ce tableau qu'il reçoit le prix de ses efforts pour les progrès de la raison, pour la défense de la liberté.*

Remembering the exhilaration of reformist propaganda, Hazlitt, not long before his death, wrote of it with cold detachment:

it was agreed that the world had hitherto been in its dotage or its infancy; and that Mr. Godwin, Condorcet, and others were to begin a new race of men — a new epoch in society. Every thing up to that period was to be set aside as puerile or barbarous; or, if there were any traces of thought and manliness now and then discoverable, they were to be regarded with wonder as prodigies — as irregular and fitful starts in that long sleep of reason and night of philosophy.[11]

Had he been writing in 1793 he would not have written thus. When he "set out in life with the French Revolution," youth was "doubly such,"

* *Esquisse d'un tableau historique des progrès de l'esprit humain* (1798), pp. 389f. Although both Howe (*Life,* p. 24) and Miss Maclean (p. 78) assert that Hazlitt read Condorcet, he himself disclaimed any first-hand knowledge of his work as late as 1807 (1.286), and it does not appear that he repaired the oversight.

he said: "the sun of Liberty rose upon the sun of Life in the same day, and both were proud to run their race together. Little did I dream, while my first hopes and wishes went hand in hand with those of the human race, that long before my eyes should close, that dawn would be overcast, and set once more in the night of despotism — 'total eclipse!' " [12] This eclipse provided him a major theme, and as he writes its endless variations he reveals, when old, the depth of his commitment to the ideals of his youth.

Unlike the wilder prophets of reform, he came to realize that the restraints of civilization, obnoxious though they be, serve to check man's retrogression to the cave; and although he deplored the fact that custom and convention, as codified in law and institutions, are always inhibitory and often obsolete, he knew that such restraints are needed. But he did not forget the major premise of reform — that men do not become what by nature they are meant to be, but what society makes them — and the pathos or the anger with which, in later life, he recalled a vanished dream is an index of its power. His remarks on Holcroft, for example, might stand as a motto for the age. Deprecating force and tumult, Holcroft was, he said in 1816, "a purely speculative politician" convinced that man's political and moral improvement would be "gradual, calm, and rational." Locke had freed the mind, as some men thought, from privileged fraud and superstition; and the subsequent advance in all the arts and sciences, as well as the mounting pressure for reform, compelled the inference that error, though sanctioned by authority and preserved by vested interest, could not long survive a confrontation with the truth. "That this inference was profound or just," said an older and a wiser Hazlitt, "I do not affirm: but it was natural, and strengthened not only by the hopes of the good, but by the sentiments of the most thinking men." One great revolution had proved the triumph of man's natural rights, and another, not yet perverted by the hostility of despots and the servility of the French people, promised such victories for humanity that "there were few real friends of liberty who did not augur well of it."

The emancipation of thirty millions of people (so I remember it was considered at the time) was a change for the better, as great as it was unexpected: the pillars of oppression and tyranny seemed to have been overthrown: man was about to shake off the fetters which had bound him in wretchedness and ignorance; and the blessings that were yet in store for him were unforeseen and incalculable. Hope smiled upon him, and pointed to futurity.[13]

III

The Assault upon Reform

<><><><><><><><><><><><><><><><><><><><><><><><><><><><><>

THE CONSERVATIVE REACTION

When, in response to mounting public pressure and to the logic of events, England finally went to war with France in 1793, the reformers' hopes for inexorable and accelerating change were of course destroyed. It was a collapse that any realistic student of affairs might have easily foreseen, for Godwin and the other friends of liberty were, like Thomas Holcroft, "purely speculative" politicians confronting men of power and action, and the contest was bound to be uneven. When what had started as a debate about reform became a struggle for survival, the little knot of nonconformists and reformers were easily dispersed, and the cause which they had thought invincible was ruthlessly suppressed. Though only an episode in England's long campaign against the Revolution, this was to be one of the formative events in Hazlitt's life, and it is important that we try to understand the meaning he ascribed to it.

If Burke had been the prophet of reaction, Pitt became its strong right arm. Unfortunately for their adversaries, both were men of genius. Named the king's first minister in 1783 (when he was twenty-four) Pitt had not only begun the restoration of a shattered empire and rebuilt its tottering finance, he had even advocated a degree of Parliamentary reform. But when, finally, he resolved to check the course of French aggression he framed a policy that left no place for such luxuries as Dissent, reformist agitation, or even civil liberties; and to Hazlitt and his like, therefore, he became the very symbol of oppression. Scott, whose Toryism flowed from both instinct and conviction, eulogized him as one

> Who, when the frantic crowd amain
> Strain'd at subjection's bursting rein,
> O'er their wild mood full conquest gain'd,
> The pride, he would not crush, restrain'd,
> Show'd their fierce zeal a worthier cause,
> And brought the freeman's arm to aid the freeman's laws.[1]

But historians have generally assessed his motives and achievements otherwise: he may have decided on a strategy of terror in order to incite hysteria and thus maintain himself in power; misled by poor intelligence, he may have made an honest error in overestimating the danger of revolt; he may have thought that terror was a necessary response to the threat of French ideas. Whatever his motives, however, there can be no doubt that he exploited panic as an instrument of state, and his depredations on the freedom of his countrymen are a stain upon his memory.[2]

They were so regarded by almost every major writer of Hazlitt's generation. When Coleridge, far advanced in Toryism, described himself when young as "a vehement anti-ministerialist,"[3] he invoked a title and an attitude appropriate to all varieties of Whigs, reformers, and Dissenters. His repugnance to Pitt's "wild and priestly war against reason, against freedom, against human nature"[4] inspired the Bristol lectures of 1795, the sulphurous "Fire, Famine, and Slaughter" (which, in reprinting it nineteen years later, he felt obliged to sterilize with an "Apologetic Preface"),* a famous character of the prime minister written for the *Morning Post* in 1800,† and countless tirades in his letters.[5] To the end of his life he regarded Pitt as having cynically exploited the "panic of property" for political ends,[6] and he continued to abominate him "in a degree" which De Quincey (who had never flirted with reform) found "difficult" to understand.[7] There must have been many young men like John Rickman, who told Southey in 1799 that Pitt ("a sorry drunkard") used "pillage" to maintain himself in power,[8] but there were others who, though less impassioned, were no less bitter about ministerial abuses. Within a year of his return from France Wordsworth had come to recoil from "the bare idea of a Revolution," but none the less he feared such a "dreadful event" if Pitt went on unchecked;[9] and fifteen years later, in *The Convention of Cintra,* he again denounced the government whose "transgressions" could be neither forgotten nor forgiven.[10] Sydney Smith, who regarded Pitt as "one of the most luminous eloquent blunderers with which any people was ever afflicted," agreed with Francis Jeffrey that he could have done nothing without hypocrisy, folly, and fraud.[11] Southey, than whom nobody could be less like Sydney Smith, embellished the same rich theme as late as the eve of Waterloo.‡

* See *Poems,* pp. 595–606. Clarke (p. 34) thought that this preface was a "triumphant specimen" of Coleridge's "talent for special pleading and ingenuity in sophistication."

† *Essays,* II, 319–329. This was one of young Hazlitt's favorite pieces (1.112n), and after he had quarreled with Coleridge over politics he reprinted it in *Political Essays* (7.326–332) as a memento of its author's early views.

‡ *The Life of Horatio Lord Nelson,* pp. 44, 134. For an earlier and equally un-

THE CONSERVATIVE REACTION

It would seem, then, that Godwin, in 1806, expressed a widely shared opinion when he said that Pitt's achievements, such as they had been, were bought with bloody and unnecessary war, "formidable innovations on the liberties of Englishmen," duplicity, dexterity, and treachery.[12] That this was Hazlitt's view is clear. *Free Thoughts on Public Affairs* (1806), his first excursion into political analysis and therefore the first index to his thinking on the problems of the day, is more temperate than his later comments on the subject, but it is marked by the sternest disapproval of Pitt's career and policy. The reformers of the nineties had been perhaps extravagant in their demands, he says, but Pitt, in his response to them, was desperately misguided.

Perhaps it was then necessary that we should be told, *ex cathedrâ,* that the people had nothing to do with the laws but to *obey* them: perhaps it was right that we should be amused with apologies for the corrupt influence of the crown; that integrity, honour, the love of justice, public spirit, or a zeal for the interests of the community should be laughed at as absurd chimeras, and that an ardent love of liberty, or determined resistance to powerful oppression should be treated as madness and folly.[13]

At the start of his career Hazlitt implied that England's rulers were in error; at the end, having lived for thirty years in the shadow of reaction, he was convinced that they were evil. He said near the close of his life that when Pitt and his royal master resolved that war abroad and tyranny at home were essential to the preservation of the state they destroyed the Briton's moral fiber; when, in 1800, they rebuffed Napoleon's overtures for peace, England "lost her liberties, her strength, herself and the world."[14]

No one could say, however, that Pitt had been hurtled into action. Despite the swirling agitation for reform after Burke had opened the debate in 1790, the prime minister, watching events in France with mounting concern, had preserved an ostensible neutrality while many of his party called for sterner measures. As early as May 1792 the king himself noted the ominous spread of "wicked and seditious writings" and called for prompt reprisal,* and in December he warned Parliament that "the destruction of our happy constitution, and the subversion of all order and government" were a real and present danger.[15] Meanwhile, France was whirling from reform to revolution. Although the massacres of September 1792 profoundly shocked the English people, Pitt did not

---

flattering view see Southey's *Letters from England* (ed. Jack Simmons, 1951), pp. 71–75.

New Annual Register . . . for the Year 1792 (1793), "Public Papers," pp. 52f. Hazlitt (3.141) regarded this famous proclamation as the beginning of a reign of terror.

join the coalition that Austria and Prussia had formed to chasten France, nor did he intervene when the French astonished themselves and terrified every royal house in Europe by turning back the monarchs ranged against them at Valmy. It was becoming clear, however, that England would be obliged to take a part in the war that was spreading over Europe. The abolition of the French monarchy and the execution of Louis XVI showed how far reform might go, and the tricolor flying in the Savoy, the Rhineland, and the Austrian Netherlands confirmed the boast that France stood willing to support with armed assistance any nation desirous of a change in government. When, at the start of 1793, France declared that she and England were at war it was an acknowledgement of the inevitable.

In 1805 Francis Jeffrey said that the direst consequence of the war with France had been the repudiation of reform. "The bad success of an attempt to make government perfect, has reconciled us to imperfections that might easily be removed." [16] A generation later, however, Macaulay could take a longer view. "Was there one honest friend of liberty," he asked,

whose faith in the high destinies of mankind had not been shaken? Was there one observer to whom the French Revolution, or revolutions in general, appeared in exactly the same light on the day when the Bastile fell, and on the day when the Girondists were dragged to the scaffold, the day when the Directory shipped off their principal opponents for Guiana, or the day when the Legislative Body was driven from its hall at the point of a bayonet? [17]

In any event, the later years of Hazlitt's youth were a time of troubles for all but noisy patriots. For more than a century it had been the Briton's patriotic duty to look asquint at France, and the war intensified his prejudice. Boswell, as so often, merely uttered commonplaces when in 1793 he denounced the "detestable sophistry which has lately been imported from France, under the false name of *Philosophy*, and with a malignant industry has been employed against the peace, good order, and happiness of society, in our free and prosperous country"; [18] and even better thinkers, as Hazlitt bitterly recalled, thought it "heroical" to scrutinize the actions of their friends, goad them to seditious utterance, and then "turn informers against the intemperance they had provoked." [19] Pitt's spies apparently never slept, and judges and juries, swept away by panic, were ready with grotesque convictions. As Coleridge said, the prime minister was a "State-Nimrod" who led his "motley pack" along the trail of "rancid plots and false insurrections." [20] These were the years, Godwin pointed out, when a man unwilling "to sign the Shibboleth of the constitution" was marked down as a traitor, and when one who dared "to promulgate heretical opinions" was prosecuted with money raised by "voluntary subscription." *

Although the author of *Political Justice,* next to Paine the most notorious of all the friends of liberty, managed to escape, others were less fortunate, for after Paine himself, late in 1792, had fled to France just before his conviction for high treason, the government launched its reign of terror. Its first victims were certain journalists and Dissenting ministers who naively thought their liberties secure. For preaching his annual sermon on the Glorious Revolution, one William Winterbotham, a Baptist minister of Plymouth, was convicted of sedition, imprisoned for four years, and fined two hundred pounds. Richard Phillips, an eccentric Leicester publisher who questioned the theory of gravitation but advocated Parliamentary reform, spent eighteen months in jail for distributing *The Rights of Man.* In 1792 James Perry, editor of the *Morning Chronicle,* had narrowly escaped conviction for seditious libel when he printed a political advertisement offensive to the government, but six years later he was sentenced to Newgate for three months and fined fifty pounds on a charge of libel against the House of Lords. The year before, Joseph Johnson, the publisher-general of nonconformists and reformers, paid with fifty pounds and nine months in jail for printing a pamphlet by Gilbert Wakefield. Wakefield himself, a cantankerous man "particularly obnoxious" to the government, said Southey,[21] because he stood so high with the Dissenters, was shortly convicted of seditious libel for his *Reply* to the Bishop of Llandaff's *Address to the People of Great Britain.* "What rulers we had in those days!" said Samuel Rogers when he remembered Wakefield's persecution,[22] and how "atrocious," Sydney Smith recalled in 1811, was Pitt's campaign against anyone who tried to "think and reason."[23] Not even poets were safe. In Felpham, William Blake was charged with seditious remarks about the king on the perjured testimony of a soldier whom he had ejected from his garden, and the fracas caused such "consternation thro' all the Villages round," reported the alleged incendiary, that "every man is now afraid of speaking to, or looking at, a Soldier."[24] Far off on the Bristol Channel, presumably safe from the contagion of London Jacobins, a "titled Dogberry" suspected the worst of Coleridge and Wordsworth (then busy with *Lyrical Ballads*) and fetched in a government spy *"pour surveillance."* As Coleridge later told the story, the poets were tracked for three weeks with "truly Indian perseverance," but despite

---

* *Political Justice,* I, x. Since "terror was the order of the day" in 1794, said Godwin (*Caleb Williams* [3d ed., 1797], I, vii), he withdrew the original preface to *Caleb Williams* lest even a "humble" novelist "might be shown to be constructively a traitor."

their dark talk of one Spy Nozy (Spinoza) they were finally absolved. It is a fact for which all admirers of English poetry may be duly grateful.*

❖   ❖   ❖

The Tories used poets as well as spies to denounce unorthodox opinion, and the fact that such a tedious thing as Thomas Mathias' *Pursuits of Literature* could go through sixteen editions says little for their taste. Although an able Italianist, Mathias was heavy-footed and pedantic as a satirist; he feared reform too strongly to write about it wittily. *The Pursuit of Literature* is a silly book, buttressed by long and fearful disquisitions on political and literary theory, and revealing on each page a thin trickle of text embellished with gigantic polylingual notes. Ignoring the "war-whoop of Jacobins, and democratic writers," Mathias declares his purpose of exposing the atheists and republicans of France, "the vulgar illiterate blasphemy of Thomas Paine, and the contemptible nonsense of William Godwin." But the villain of his book is that compound of immorality and sedition called "French philosophy":

> Treason, the pile; the basis, blasphemy.
> Free from dull order, decency, and rule,
> With dogmas fresh from the Sans Souci-school.[25]

Mathias' work was indeed small beer compared with the vintage champagne of the *Anti-Jacobin*. Appearing each Monday from November 1797 to June 1798 under the editorship of William Gifford, this sprightly publication, marked by intelligence and wit, showed that even Toryism could be gay.

> Thy sophist veil, dread Goddess, wear,
>   Falsehood insidiously impart;
> Thy philosophic train be there,
>   To taint the mind, corrupt the heart;
>
> The gen'rous Virtues of our Isle,
>   Teach us to hate and to revile;
> Our glorious Charter's fault to scan,
>   Time-sanction'd Truths despise, and
>   preach THE RIGHTS OF MAN.[26]

* *Biographia Literaria*, I, 126–129. For a fuller account of this episode, one of the funniest in a book not noted for hilarity, see *Letters of Samuel Taylor Coleridge* (ed. Ernest Hartley Coleridge, 1895), I, 232n; De Quincey, II, 274f.; A. J. Eagleston, "Wordsworth, Coleridge, and the Spy," in *Coleridge: Studies by Several Hands* (ed. Edmund Blunden and E. L. Griggs, 1934), pp. 73–87. That Hazlitt was not amused by it is clear from his *Edinburgh* review of *Biographia Literaria* (16.129).

THE CONSERVATIVE REACTION

Declaring themselves to be the "avowed, determined, and irreconcileable enemies" of Jacobinism in all its forms,[27] Gifford and his contributors (Ellis, Canning, and Frere, and perhaps occasionally Pitt himself) were sometimes brutal in their prose, but their verse is a marvel of urbane malice. To say that the *Courier* "was written by Madmen for the use of Fools" or that Benjamin Flower's *Cambridge Intelligencer* was "a mass of loathsome ingredients"[28] may have proved their Tory principles but it hardly added to the gaiety of the nation; on the other hand, the haughty wit of the poetical satires and parodies is so adroit that it raises journalism into literature. From Southey (whose *Joan of Arc* and *The Fall of Robespierre* made him suspect) to Erasmus Darwin, no reformer who wrote badly or thought foolishly was exempt. The famous "New Morality," expressing the contempt of many clever men for the slogans of reform, remains one of the few really good political poems in the language. From the languid apostrophe to Rousseau, "Sweet child of sickly Fancy," to the clattering roll call of Britons sympathetic to reform (including Coleridge and the apolitical "Lambe") it conveys not only disciplined disgust but also the strength of the conservatives' resolve to protect

> 'Gainst Learning's, Virtue's, Truth's, Religion's foes,
> A kingdom's safety, and the world's repose.[29]

When some of its choicer pieces, including "New Morality," were re-printed in *Poetry of the Anti-Jacobin* in 1799, Coleridge was mentioned in a note as having abandoned his country, turned citizen of the world, and left *"his poor children fatherless and his wife destitute. Ex his disce his friends* LAMB *and* SOUTHEY."[30] Coleridge was so much incensed that he contemplated legal action, for which, he told Southey, his attorneys assured him he had "a clear Case,"[31] but characteristically he did not press charges. In any event, as one of his biographers has said, the accusation was merely "premature."[32]

THE TREASON TRIALS

Coleridge, Southey, and the like were indeed small fry, and proper butts of witty verse, but the various political clubs of the nineties were, in Pitt's view, a danger to the government. Although Burke estimated one-fifth of the 400,000 "political citizens" of England to be "pure Jacobins, utterly incapable of amendment, objects of eternal vigilance, and, when they break out, of legal restraint,"[1] it is now apparent that he — and the ministers — exaggerated their numbers and their power. What we know of the so-called radical clubs, dedicated mainly to conviviality and reformist propaganda, scarcely permits the inference that their existence was incompatible with the safety of the state. For example, the Society for Commemorating the Revolution in Great Britain, before which Price had preached his famous sermon, was a covey of prosperous Dissenters who met annually for a banquet and a speech along sound Whig lines. Their nominal purpose was to celebrate the Glorious Revolution; and for seven and six, said their steward, patriots could "get as good a dinner and as much sherry, punch and port as they liked, and leave, well contented with their country."[2] Of the one hundred thirty-seven members of the fashionable Society of the Friends of the People, twenty-two were in Parliament, and presumably all were able to pay their heavy dues. Somewhat less expensive and probably more radical was the London Constitutional Society, which met to expound Tom Paine's doctrines and see that *The Rights of Man* had a proper distribution. Although Paine had handed over to the Society a thousand pounds in profits from his *succès fou,* the club received no aid from such Whig magnates as Fox and Grey, and after Paine's precipitous flight and subsequent conviction (*in absentia*) for treason it declined in membership and zeal.

The most notorious of all these clubs was the London Corresponding Society. Founded in 1792 by one Thomas Hardy, a Scottish bootmaker whose friends were mainly among "the lower and middle classes of Dissenters," it was designed for the small shopkeepers and workingmen who would have been distinctly out of place at the dinners of the Revolutionary Society and the Friends of the People. Hardy's *Memoirs,* written almost forty years after his hour of lurid fame, show the exhilaration and the danger of agitating for reform. Although the dues were modestly set at one penny, only nine persons were mustered for the first meeting at the Sign of the Bell in Exeter Street. As Hardy remembered it, they partook of bread and cheese and porter, and as they smoked their pipes they deplored "the hardness of the times and the dearness of all the necessaries of life" and exhorted one another on the need of Parliamentary reform.[3] Sheridan may have had this sort of club in mind when he ironically announced in Parliament that the lord mayor had ferreted out a debating society in Cornhill where a traitorous person could "buy treason at six-pence a head" and, by the glimmering light of a candle, speak for five minutes "to perform his part in overturning the State."[4]

But Hardy and his little band soon broadened their activities. The nine persons at the first meeting were joined at the second by nine new members; at the third there were twenty-four, and thereafter their numbers quickly mounted. Organizing its cells or "divisions" into groups of thirty (each represented by a delegate to a central committee) and maintaining at least a loose epistolary connection with similar clubs in Edinburgh, Sheffield, Leeds, Bristol, Norwich, and elsewhere, the society may have eventually enrolled some thirty thousand members, with perhaps a tenth of them in London.[5] Convinced, as Hardy said, that all the ills of England could be traced to "a comparatively few influential individuals" who dominated Parliament,[6] they framed a constitution (in March 1793) that showed electoral reform, not sedition, to be their goal;[7] and by means of correspondence, circulation of reformist tracts, and public meetings they did more, their leader said, "to diffuse political knowledge among the people of Great Britain and Ireland than all that had ever been done before."[8] As secretary of the London committee, Hardy addressed his first communication to a clergyman of Sheffield, pointing to the need for electoral reform, his second (a "Congratulatory Address") to the National Convention in Paris, deploring the loss of English liberties to a "restless, all consuming aristocracy."[9] Other communications followed, as well as large public meetings in various parts of London.

The war with France brought matters to a head, and Pitt, fearing or pretending to fear an insurrection, resolved to crush reformist agitation at a stroke. After a "convention" — odious word — of delegates from some forty corresponding clubs had begun its deliberations in Edinburgh in November 1793, the government abruptly halted the proceedings and charged the leaders with sedition. Their trial before the notorious Lord Braxfield (whom Stevenson would one day draw as the hanging judge in *Weir of Hermiston*) at once became a *cause célèbre*, although most reformers seemed to think that no Briton could be punished for having exercised the ancient right of peaceful assembly. As Godwin wrote to one of the defendants, strength and candor would surely win acquittal: "Depend upon it, that if you can establish to their full conviction the one great point — the lawfulness of your meeting — you will obtain a verdict."[10] The event proved him wrong. Incredibly, five of the alleged conspirators, including two delegates from London, were found guilty and sentenced to deportation under conditions that staggered their friends and shocked some, at least, of their opponents.

In later, calmer times the Martyrs' Memorial on Calton Hill in Edinburgh was raised as a kind of public penance,[11] but in 1794 only a few had the courage or folly to resist the government. Among these few were Hardy and his friends. When, ignoring the monitory verdict, they pushed ahead with plans for a convention of their own in London in the spring of 1794, Pitt took decisive action. Already armed with a bill against "traitorous correspondence," he decided, in effect, to make public discussion of public affairs a capital offense. On 12 May 1794 he moved against the London Corresponding Society, and within a week Hardy and ten of his colleagues were in Newgate or the Tower. To make sure they stayed there without a formal charge, he secured, against the opposition of the Whigs, a suspension of habeas corpus. In September the prisoners were finally charged with treason, the address to the jury being so patently biased that Dr. Parr told Godwin his "bosom glowed with honest rage." [12] When the jury returned with an indictment including Holcroft's name, Holcroft himself dramatically appeared in court, although he had not been previously arrested. "Surely," he had said on first hearing of the charge, "either there have been practices of which I am totally ignorant, or men are running mad." [13]

On October 25 the twelve alleged traitors — including not only dissidents like Hardy and Thelwall and Holcroft but also Horne Tooke, that elegant Whig relic of Wilkes's and Junius' age * — were formally arraigned, and three days later Hardy's trial began. It was, said Holcroft later, a "portentous" moment. "The hearts and countenances of men seemed pregnant with doubt and terror. They waited, in something like a stupor of amazement, for the fearful sentence on which their deliverance, or their destruction, seemed to depend." [†] If, as one historian has said, the trials of 1794 constituted the gravest threat to English liberties in modern times, Holcroft did not exaggerate. The heart of the Crown's case was not evidence of treason as treason had been statutorily defined since the reign of Edward III, but an attack upon the defendants' right to discuss political questions and seek redress for grievances. Although the attorney-general could adduce no proof that they had sought to take the king's life or levy war against his people, he could charge them with entertaining opinions obnoxious to the government, and so he asked an English jury for their lives. Moreover, if we may believe Hardy, he was so certain of success that he had prepared eight hundred

* Tooke had already won a niche in history. In 1778 he had been fined and jailed for raising a subscription for the widows and orphans and aged parents of "our beloved American fellow-subjects, who, faithful to the character of *Englishmen,* preferring death to slavery, were for that reason only, inhumanely murdered, by the king's troops at or near Lexington and Concord" (Alexander Stephens, *Memoirs of John Horne Tooke* [1813], I, 435n). Tooke's inclusion among the alleged traitors of 1794 was bizarre, as Hazlitt later said (11.52f.).

† 3.150. Holcroft's *Narrative of Facts Relating to a Prosecution for High Treason* (1795) forms the basis of Hazlitt's account in his life of that strange man (3.139–154), and this, in turn, has been usefully expanded from contemporary documents by Elbridge Colby in his edition (1925) of that work (II, 26–80).

warrants, almost half of them already signed, to serve when the test case had been won. Hanging would have been the order of the day, Sam Rogers said, if Pitt had not been checked.[14]

The fact that he was checked was due in no small part to Godwin. Rushing back to London from Warwickshire, where he was visiting Parr, in two days he composed and sent to the *Morning Chronicle* a letter on the government's case. Reprinted as *Cursory Strictures on the Charge of Chief-Justice Eyre* (1794), it was, said Hazlitt, one of the most "acute and seasonable" political pamphlets ever written,* for it showed with deadly accuracy what Pitt's intentions were. Are we to infer, asks Godwin, that henceforth men may be doomed to a barbaric death "for a crime, that no law describes, that no precedent or adjudged case ascertains, at the arbitrary pleasure of the administration for the time being?" Should an English jury be required to sanction the destruction of "twelve private and untitled men" as the price of an "atrocious and inexplicable despotism?"[15] It was Hazlitt's opinion that Godwin, the architect of philosophical anarchism, saved the day for constitutional liberty and preserved the lives of "twelve innocent individuals, marked out as political victims to the Moloch of Legitimacy."[16] Even though the attorney-general burst into tears and pleaded for a judgment that would vindicate "his character and fame,"[17] the jury, on whose "awful voice," said Hardy, "depended the liberty of eleven millions of their fellow citizens,"[18] returned a verdict of acquittal on November 5. To settle Hardy's fate they had deliberated for three hours, but it required only eight minutes for them to free Horne Tooke; and when Thelwall was acquitted too the government dropped its case against the others. Not without justice did Tooke kiss Godwin's hand for having saved his life.[19]

One eminent historian has said that this "timely check" on Pitt's expanding reign of terror saved England from a bath of blood and perhaps a retributive revolution.[20] It did not, however, end Pitt's campaign against reform. Although he failed to make disaffection treasonable, he resolved to make it painful. When the Duke of Norfolk, at a birthday dinner for Fox in 1798, proposed a toast to "our Sovereign's health — the Majesty of the People," he was deprived of his colonelcy in the militia and the lord-lieutenancy of the West Riding, and when Fox in-

---

* 16.408. Although William Taylor of Norwich later quarreled with Godwin, he continued to revere him for the *Cursory Strictures,* and, as he told Southey, he could not forgive the detractors of the man who had "rendered such critical service" to his country in such a perilous hour. See Brown, *Godwin,* p. 209n. For Mary Godwin Shelley's vivid account of her father's hasty composition of the work see Paul, I, 128–135.

dignantly repeated the toast he was banished from the privy council —
although Pitt himself thought he should be sent to the Tower.[21] "Giants
in their impiety alone," said Wordsworth later in reference to these
years, the ministers were "in their weapons and their warfare base / As
vermin working out of reach." * While Parliament, reflecting that "panic
of property" which Coleridge regarded as the motive of the terror, oblig-
ingly voted the suspension of habeas corpus from year to year, the prime
minister and his home secretary, Henry Dundas, took care to make
reform impossible. It was on Pitt's aristocratic nose, said Hazlitt, that
he "suspended the decisions of the House of Commons, and dangled
the Opposition as he pleased."[22] In 1795, the year that Burke retired
from public life, the Treasonable Practices Bill decreed it a high mis-
demeanor to publish or say anything tending to incite hatred or contempt for the king, the government, or the constitution; concurrently
the Seditious Meetings Bill spelled the doom of reformist agitation by
prohibiting assemblies of more than fifty persons, as well as all political
debates and lectures, except under governmental supervision. At the
urging of William Wilberforce, whose solicitude for the blacks in Jamaica
did not extend to the textile workers in Lancashire, Pitt five years later
endorsed the Combination Acts which outlawed trade unionism among
the "labouring poor." In short, with the Tories united behind Pitt, the
Whigs rendered impotent by the defection of the conservative Duke of
Portland and his faction in 1794, and public sentiment rising to support
the war, England was committed to reaction. In 1798 the *Anti-Jacobin*
reported that *"Menial Servants of Families"* were "voluntarily" con-
tributing a large part of their modest wages "for the defence of a Cause
in which all Ranks are interested,"[23] and three years later Godwin acknowledged the success of Pitt's campaign against reform when he admitted that "even the starving labourer in the alehouse is become a
champion of aristocracy."[24]

THE POETICAL APOSTATES

Godwin's wry comment comes from 1801, when he tried to show that
his own reputation had fallen "in one common grave with the cause and
the love of liberty."[1] It would seem that he was right, for his brief
and lurid fame was strongest with a few obscure associates and with

---

* *The Prelude* (1805), x.653–657. In the 1850 version the language was con-
siderably softened. On the changes in Wordsworth's political opinions as expressed in
his rewriting of this poem see *The Prelude* (ed. Ernest de Selincourt, 2d ed., revised by
Helen Darbishire, 1959), pp. lxv–lxviii.

disaffected youths who, when older, deplored their early indiscretions. Among others, Coleridge, Southey, Wordsworth, Mackintosh, Basil Montagu, John Stoddart, and Crabb Robinson had briefly been bewitched, and since they all recanted, Hazlitt's remark that Godwin at the peak of his renown had "carried with him all the most sanguine and fearless understandings of the time" is at once factual and ironic.[2] It must be said that the author of *Political Justice* had drawn his share of freaks. No one who has dipped into the reformist literature of the nineties can fail to rejoice in Miss Letitia Sourby's letter to the *Anti-Jacobin*, where she grimly records her father's devotion to Godwin's book: once "a respectable Manufacturer in the Calico line," he became so hot for social justice that he scandalized his wife by denouncing matrimony, jeered at gratitude as a "bad passion," abandoned the church of his fathers, and even named his little boy Buonaparte.[3] Remembering that he and Mackintosh had in their youth subscribed to Godwin's folly, an older Basil Montagu could only marvel at their naiveté.[4]

Political Justice is a shocking book, and its shock may have constituted a part of its appeal. De Quincey likened its effect to that of an "accursed submarine harrow" that for one dreadful moment scrapes against a majestic ship in mid-ocean, and even allowing for his blind conservatism we may accept the simile.[5] Although many foolish, ponderous works have attained the dignity of print, the renown of most has not reached beyond the author's loyal kin. *Political Justice* enjoyed a brief acclaim, however, because it reflected and seemed to justify the needs of a generation eager for reform, and when reform acquired the stigma of the Revolution, its reputation fell. Stiffened in their patriotism by the threat of France, men who had applauded Godwin's courage in prescribing the end of English institutions began to look upon reform as the embodiment of the abstractions that the success of French arms had converted into menacing realities. Atheism, disrespect for marriage, and denial of the sacred rights of property were not the essence of his creed, but they were strongly recommended; and even men without the brains to read the book were quick to damn it as obscene. By the end of the decade, Godwin himself admitted, his name was so opprobrious that "not even a petty novel for boarding-school misses" could aspire for popularity unless it vilified his views.[6]

His more perceptive followers came to see that their master's schemes were built upon a bizarre appraisal of the way people really think and feel and act. When Southey first encountered *Political Justice* in 1793 he "all but worshiped" Godwin,* and it was at his "recommendation"

---

* *Life and Correspondence*, p. 81. Southey borrowed the first volume of *Political*

that Coleridge, who had not read the book,* saluted its author in a eulogistic sonnet as one "form'd t' illumine a sunless world forlorn." [7] Not to be outdone, Southey also wrote a poem to Godwin:

What tho' Oppression's blood-cemented fane
    Stands proudly threat'ning arrogant in state,
    Not thine his savage priests to immolate
Or hurl the fabric on the encumber'd plain
As with a whirlwind's fury. It is thine
    When dark Revenge mask'd in the form ador'd
    Of Justice, lifts on high the murderous sword
To save the erring victim from her shrine. [8]

Meanwhile, however, France was descending into terror, and the execution of Brissot — an event which shocked most friends of liberty [9] — so much "harrowed" Southey's faculties that he was moved to re-examine his position. "There is no place for virtue," he informed a college friend. "Here are you and I theorizing upon principles we can never practice, and wasting our time and youth — you in scribbling parchments, and I in spoiling quires with poetry." [10] Consequently we find him presently analyzing Godwin's "fundamental error" in misjudging human motives [11] and, a few years later, comparing him "to a close Stool pan, most often empty, & better empty than when full." [12] He had "just looked enough into your books to believe you taught republicanism and stoicism," Coleridge explained to Godwin in 1811; "ergo, that he was of your opinion and you of his, and that was all." †

As for the chief Pantisocrat himself, his enthusiasm for *Political Justice* could not survive a reading of the book. *Conciones ad Populum,* his Bristol lectures of 1795, records his dismay at the excesses of the French, and a year later, in the *Watchman,* he turned his fire on Godwin. [13] When a correspondent protested his remarks he returned to the attack: "O this enlightened age! when it can be seriously charged against an essayist, that he is prejudiced in favour of gratitude, conjugal fidelity, filial affection, and the belief of God and a hereafter!!" [14] His intention to write a series of articles to demolish Godwin's system came to nothing, and so did a projected "six shilling Octavo" in which he planned to expose not only Godwin's "absurdities and wickedness" but also those of

Justice from the Bristol Library between 25 and 28 November 1793, the second between 9 and 18 December 1793. See Paul Kaufman, "The Reading of Southey and Coleridge: The Record of Their Borrowings from the Bristol Library, 1793–1798," *MP,* XXI (1924), 318.

    * Paul, II, 224. But see Griggs, I, 115, where Coleridge tells Southey (21 October 1794) that he had read Godwin "with the greatest attention" and was not altogether satisfied.

    † Paul, II, 225. I assume that it is Southey to whom Coleridge alludes when he explains, in this important letter, the rise and fall of Godwin's reputation.

every system-monger "before & since Christ." [15] Meanwhile, moreover, he and Godwin had met and had failed to get along. [16] Not only did the philosopher speak "futile sophisms in jejune language," he complained, [17] but his irreligion was a frightful bore. What could be done with a man who apologized for the vulgarity of saying "God bless you"? [18] It was not that atheism turned him against Godwin, he told Thelwall in 1796, but that Godwin turned him against atheism, [19] and a year later he could thank heaven that he abominated "Godwinism." *

Coleridge's discontent with Godwin was sharpened by his conviction that reform itself had failed. As an old man he said, and perhaps believed, that even before 1793 he had "clearly" seen and publicly exposed the "horrid delusion" of the Revolution, [20] and the assertion, though questionable, is in part compatible with the verse that he was writing at the time. In "Religious Musings," that exceedingly "desultory" poem on the state of things in 1794, he excoriated the war with France and wrote luridly of Europe as a "sun-scorched waste" where

> by night
> Fast by each precious fountain on green herbs
> The lion crouches: or hyaena dips
> Deep in the lucid stream his bloody jaws;
> Or serpent plants his vast moon-glittering bulk,
> Caught in whose monstrous twine Behemoth yells,
> His bones loud-crashing!
> O ye numberless,
> Whom foul Oppression's ruffian gluttony
> Drives from Life's plenteous feast! [21]

He still thought, however, that reform would eventually succeed, and by comparing the fall of tyranny and political privilege to that of "untimely fruit / Shook from the fig-tree by a sudden storm," his "young anticipating heart" predicted an apocalypse of peace and universal love. [22] Two years later, in the direful "Ode to the Departing Year," he was full of grim misgivings, and in a later comment on this piece he said that "the name of Liberty" had been "both the occasion and the pretext of unnumbered crimes and horrors." † Two events, one personal and the other public, made 1797–98 a crucial time for him, for it was then that his intimacy with Wordsworth started to bear fruit and that the

* Griggs, I, 306. For some of Coleridge's unexecuted plans to combat "Godwinism" see *Notebooks*, nos. 161, 174. The latter entry concerns a "hymn" against Godwinian atheism and "particularly the Godwinian System of Pride Proud of what? An outcast of blind Nature ruled by a fatal Necessity — Slave of an ideot Nature!"

† *Poems*, p. 161n. According to Hartley Coleridge (*Letters* [ed. Grace Evelyn Griggs and Earl Leslie Griggs, 1937], pp. 189f.) his father, who spoke "harshly of the political subserviency of W. — and S. —," was sympathetic to the French Revolution "long after its true character appeared."

French invaded Switzerland. The great ode on France (which at first was called "The Recantation") not only marks a turning point for Coleridge; it epitomizes the revulsion of many former friends of liberty who felt themselves betrayed.

> O France, that mockest Heaven, adulterous, blind
> And patriot only in pernicious toils!
> Are these thy boast, Champion of human kind?
> To mix with Kings in the low lust of sway,
> Yell in the hunt, and share the murderous prey;
> To insult the shrine of Liberty with spoils
> From freemen torn; to tempt and to betray? *

In his progress from revolution to reaction Wordsworth too had dallied briefly with the Godwinian ideal. With his doctrine of progressive education Godwin seemed to offer refuge to reformers who were sickened by Frenchmen's use of terror; and for a year or so following his return to England in 1793 (when he professed himself eternally a democrat) [23] Wordsworth probably regarded *Political Justice* with respect and admiration. But although Hazlitt reports him as telling a young student to throw away his chemistry book and "read Godwin on Necessity," [24] his Godwinian phrase was brief. As he, at least, believed, it was Michel-Armand Beaupuy, not the author of *Political Justice*, who shaped his social thinking, [25] and when his ideals began to crumble, Godwin's ethical rationalism could do no more than briefly check their fall. England's decision to challenge French reform with arms had given him a shock such as he had never known "Down to that very moment," [26] and thereafter, in a series of long, reflective letters written to a college friend, he set forth the claims of pacifism, reason, and education as the only means of social justice. "Freedom of inquiry is all that I wish for," he wrote in 1794; "let nothing be deemed too sacred for investigation. Rather than restrain the liberty of the press I would suffer the most

* *Poems*, p. 246. Curiously, as Coleridge drifted further from reform his and Godwin's friendship grew. Although he does not appear prominently in Godwin's diary until November 1799, thereafter many meetings are recorded. For example, in the winter of 1799–1800 the two men were together on at least fifteen occasions, and on March 29 he paid a call which did not end till two days later. There were moments of strain, to be sure, and at least one *opéra bouffe* quarrel when Godwin, "cool and civil" as always, ridiculed Coleridge's journalistic efforts while his friend, betrayed by a "Plusquam sufficit of Punch," railed drunkenly at the "grossness & vulgar Insanocaecity of this dim-headed Prig of a Philosophicide" (Griggs, II, 1058f.; II, 1071–1074). But it was Coleridge, said Godwin later (Paul, I, 357f.) who led him from atheism to theism; and Coleridge himself, once "a warm and boisterous anti-Godwinist," came to a far "juster appreciation" of the man who had lost so many "admirers and disciples" (Paul, II, 224f.).

atrocious doctrines to be recommended: let the field be open and un-encumbered, and truth must be victorious." [27] With this ideal before him he even toyed with the notion of a "Monthly Miscellany" (to be called the *Philanthropist*) as a way of propagating his opinions among "dispassionate advocates of liberty and discussion." [28] Convinced that "hereditary distinctions, and privileged orders of every species" were in-compatible with "the progress of human improvement," he of course disliked the British constitution, but he was dismayed at the "bare idea" of violence. [29] Understandably, then, his heart leapt up when he heard of Robespierre's fall in July 1794:

> They who with clumsy desperation brought
> A river of Blood, and preached that nothing else
> Could cleanse the Augean stable, by the might
> Of their own helper have been swept away;
> Their madness stands declared and visible;
> Elsewhere will safety now be sought, and earth
> March firmly towards righteousness and peace. [30]

It was in this calm, Godwinian mood that he met Godwin a few months later, and for a while, at least, they were on very cordial terms. Many years later the philosopher recorded that in the course of one evening he converted the poet "from the doctrine of self-love, to that of benevolence." * The character of the Sailor in "Salisbury Plain" (re-vised from "Guilt and Sorrow") no doubt reveals the influence of their conversations, and such lyrics as "Simon Lee" and "Goody Blake and Harry Gill" are also built on one of Godwin's favorite themes: the withering effect of social evil on man's essential goodness. [31] This high Godwinian phase, however, was not of long duration, and when it passed, Wordsworth reached the crisis recorded in the eleventh book of *The Prelude*. There we see a man who had exchanged revolution for ethical rationalism as the anchor of his humanitarian ideals, and then, dismayed, had watched the anchor slip. It was bad enough that the Revolution, running wild in terror, had mocked the dream of its sup-porters; it was even worse that reason, justice, and equality — those con-soling absolutes — were also shown to be mere words.

---

* See page 71n. As Godwin's diary shows, he and Wordsworth met on 27 February 1795, and for a time thereafter they saw much of one another. Indeed, their friend-ship long survived Wordsworth's admiration for Godwin's social views, and when the poet was in London in 1805 he and Godwin were together at least fifteen times be-tween January and June. However, when Godwin stayed the night with Wordsworth at Grasmere in April 1816 the two men parted, says Crabb Robinson (I, 183) with "very bitter and hostile feelings" because of their political estrangement. Earlier, Robinson himself had "all but quarrelled" with Godwin about politics: "He was very rude, I very vehement, both a little angry, and equally offensive to each other" (I, 171). See Ben Ross Schneider, Jr., *Wordsworth's Cambridge Education* (1957), pp. 210–229.

THE ASSAULT UPON REFORM

> I summoned all my best skill, and toiled, intent
> To anatomize the frame of social life;
> Yea, the whole body of society
> Searched to its heart.[32]

But all was vain. "Misguided, and misguiding," he stumbled on in error,

> Dragging all precepts, judgments, maxims, creeds,
> Like culprits to the bar,[33]

and seeking the "formal *proof*" that reason, despite its high pretensions, was unable to afford. The result was chaos. His early faith was shattered, and he could find no substitute. It was then, "sick, wearied out with contrarieties," that he yielded up moral questions in despair.[34]

The process of Wordsworth's regeneration, aided by his sister, by Coleridge, and by the new-found strength of nature, is another story, and one with immense consequences for English poetry, but we need not linger over it. *The Borderers* deserves a glance, however, for it suggests the first stirrings of the healing and restorative morality which for Wordsworth took the place of politics.* Whatever its merits as a drama — and they are negligible — the play is important because it shows a thoughtful, troubled man working away from an untenable position. The fact that *Political Justice* is not even mentioned in *The Prelude* is significant, and so is the almost complete neglect of Godwin in Wordsworth's letters of the period; † and when, in his one attempt at drama, he dealt with the ethical rationalism of which Godwin was the spokesman, it was to register revulsion. Since *The Borderers* at least inferentially endorses Godwin's cardinal precept of benevolence by presenting a monster devoid of that essential virtue, it can hardly be said to attack Godwinian ethics; but the evil Oswald is a horrid travesty of Godwin's intellectual man, and the play as a whole expresses a recoil from reason as the only norm of action. Moving far beyond the anger and arrogance of his letter to Bishop Watson, Wordsworth does not indict the social system; instead, he deals with human values. Oswald's crimes are not against society, but

---

* Wordsworth completed *The Borderers* in 1796, and sometime before 1800, it would seem, Mary Hutchinson made a fair copy of the preface that has only recently been exhumed and published. See Ernest de Selincourt, "Wordsworth's Preface to 'The Borderers,'" *Oxford Lectures on Poetry* (1934), pp. 157–179. De Selincourt gives the text of the preface in the same article (pp. 165–170) and also in *Poetical Works*, I, 345–349.

† Wordsworth's comments on Godwin are anything but eulogistic. In 1796 he objected to the "barbarous writing" in the preface to the second edition of *Political Justice* (*Early Letters*, p. 156), and, a little later, revealed no more than tepid interest in Godwin's newly published *Memoirs* of his wife: "I wish to see it, though with no tormenting curiosity" (*ibid.*, pp. 188f.). F. W. Bateson (*Wordsworth* [2d ed., 1956], pp. 120–123) has analyzed *The Borderers* as Wordsworth's act of expiation for his affair with Annette Vallon.

against the promptings of charity, gratitude, and love by which all men are linked. Representing the purely rational machine, he exemplifies a code that ignores the claims of passion and emotion. It is power that Oswald seeks, not justice, and his denial of pity and remorse is, in fact, a denial of humanity.

As *The Borderers* and *Lyrical Ballads* make clear, by the end of the nineties Wordsworth had convinced himself that the affections which men feel along their pulses are the source of moral wisdom. In 1842, when he finally permitted his play to be printed, he spoke of "the hardening of the heart, and the perversion of the understanding" as sins against our nature,[35] and in another place he linked "Mr Godwyns" and — of all people — William Paley's books as those from which no good could ever come. "I know no book or system of moral philosophy written with sufficient power to melt into our affections, to incorporate itself with the blood & vital juices of our minds, & thence to have any influence worth our notice in forming those habits of which I am speaking." [36] It was no doubt Godwin and his kind whom Wordsworth and Hazlitt discussed at Nether Stowey in 1798, and it was this discussion that led the poet to a central statement of his creed:

> Sweet is the lore which Nature brings;
> Our meddling intellect
> Mis-shapes the beauteous forms of things: —
> We murder to dissect.[37]

MACKINTOSH AND PARR AND MALTHUS

In tracing the decline of his renown — and thus, inferentially, the failure of reform — Godwin himself singled out Mackintosh's defection as particularly significant. It was one thing for the *Anti-Jacobin* to revile the author of *Political Justice* as an atheist and adulterer whose works, "whirlpools of desolating nonsense," deserved "no refutation but that of the common hangman." [1] It was another, Godwin said, for the man who wrote *Vindiciae Gallicae* to represent him thrice weekly, before a large, admiring audience, as a "wretch unworthy to live." [2] Already there had been a "flood of ribaldry, invective and intolerance" from supporters of the church and state, and this, however painful, he could bear; but when his former friends denounced him he knew that detraction had become a vogue, and he was deeply grieved.

Appropriately, it was Burke who presided over Mackintosh's apostasy — or reclamation. In 1796, when the young Scot wrote to the old Irishman to confess his error in having defended the Revolution as a tool of social justice, Burke promptly acknowledged such a handsome letter from "the most able advocate" of a wicked cause, and he invited him to Beaconsfield. No record of their conservation survives, but as Mackintosh said later, half an hour with Burke upturned the reflections of a lifetime, and never again could he think about the French Revolution without a shudder.[3] (Hazlitt, more realistically, said the meeting showed the kind of influence exercised "by men of genius and imaginative power over those who have nothing to oppose . . . but the dry, cold, formal deductions of the understanding.")[4] There is, therefore, an ominous significance in Godwin's comment in his diary for 16 January 1797: "Call on Mackintosh, talk of Burke." Mackintosh's conversion was duly solemnized in a course of thirty-nine lectures "On the Law of Nature and Nations" at Lincoln's Inn in the spring of 1799. Although they remained unpublished, an introductory "Discourse," issued as a kind of flier, attests to the change in his opinion. Crabb Robinson, by then in a recanting mood himself, regarded it as "one of the most exquisite Morsels in both Sense and Style" that he had ever read,[5] but beyond recording in his diary that he had looked it over, Godwin himself, who must have been astonished, made no comment. Saluting Burke as "gravissimus et dicendi et intelligendi auctor et magister," Mackintosh swings from Aristotle to Cicero, from Grotius to Puffendorf, to describe the "one consistent system of universal morality" which informs political behavior. Extremely erudite, and proud to show his erudition, he levels his attack on the "shallow" and discredited doctrines of reform which produce nothing but "a brood of abominable and pestilential paradoxes."[6] The "Discourse" makes it clear, as Mackintosh said elsewhere, that he had come to abhor, adjure, and forever renounce the "abominable principles" and "execrable leaders" of the Revolution. Within half a dozen years of writing the *Vindiciae,* he wished only to "wipe off the disgrace of having been once betrayed into an approbation of that conspiracy against God and man, the greatest scourge of the world, and the chief stain upon human annals."[7]

Hazlitt heard the lectures — or some of them, at least — and was not at all impressed. He thought that ingenuity, even if "misapplied," is tolerable so long as it is honest, "but the dull, affected, pompous repetition of nonsense is not to be endured with patience. . . . To be a hawker of worn-out paradoxes, and a pander to sophistry denotes indeed a desperate ambition."[8] So thought Hazlitt at the time, but twenty-five years later he had not forgotten how decisive was the stroke that Mackintosh had given to reform. Accomplishing his legerdemain like a "political and philosophical juggler," he did his work of destruction so well that the structure of reform, "counter-scarp, outworks, citadel, and all, fell without a blow." [9] A hollow man for all his verbal skill, Mackintosh reminded Hazlitt of an apothecary dealing in other men's ideas: in mixing the julep "that by its potent operation was to scour away the dregs and feculence and peccant humours of the body politic, he seemed to stand with his back to the drawers in a metaphysical dispensary, and to take out of them whatever ingredients suited his purpose." * As the intellectual leader of reform, Godwin was of course particularly concerned. He had gone to the lectures, said Hazlitt, "in the *bonhommie* and candour of his nature, to hear what new light had broken in upon his old friend," and he then was buried under ridicule. "The havoc was amazing, the desolation was complete." [10] In a "letter of expostulation" Godwin gravely chided his old friend, but Mackintosh, though courteous in his answer, refused to make concessions. In calling Godwin and his kind "Savage Desolators" he had intended no aspersion on their character, he said, for the phrase was a "half-pleasantry" appropriate to reformers. "You did your duty in making public your opinions," he declared. "I do mine by attempting to refute them; and one of my chief means of confutation is the display of those bad consequences which I think likely to flow from them." †

At this point the redoubtable Dr. Samuel Parr enters the story.

* 11.99. In a late paper in the *Atlas* (20.217) Hazlitt repeats the figure of Mackintosh as a "ready warehouseman" that he probably picked up thirty years before from Coleridge (see 17.111 and also Coleridge's *Table Talk*, p. 45). Coleridge always deprecated Mackintosh. He heard some of the lectures in 1799, and shortly thereafter expressed his opinion of their author in "Two Round Spaces on the Tombstone" (*Poems*, 353ff.), which was printed in the *Morning Post*. Bitter at "the Animalcula, who live on the dung of the great Dung-fly Mackintosh" (Griggs, I, 588), he assured Godwin that if the orator were so foolish as to publish his lectures, "depend on it, it will be all over with him & then the minds of men will incline strongly in favor of those who would point out in intellectual perceptions a source of moral progressiveness" (Griggs, I, 636). Later, when Mackintosh, then newly appointed recorder for Bombay, was asked by Coleridge for a post with him, he resorted to evasions that infuriated the petitioner. He assured me of his sincerity, Coleridge told Tom Poole (*ibid.*, II, 1041), "*on his Honour — on his Soul! ! !* (N.B. HIS Honor! !) (N.B. his Soul! !) that he was sincere. — Lillibullero — whoo! whoo! whoo! — Good Morning, Sir James." For Coleridge's unflattering speculations on Mackintosh's motives in abandoning reform see *Notebooks*, no. 947. In 1835 Francis Jeffrey (*Contributions*, pp. 749–752) strongly repudiated Coleridge's aspersions on Mackintosh in the newly published *Table Talk*.

† Paul, I, 328f. For Godwin's "letter of expostulation" — which Paul (I, 328) inexplicably says "is not preserved" — see his *Thoughts Occasioned by the Perusal of Dr. Parr's Spital Sermon*, pp. 13ff.

THE ASSAULT UPON REFORM

Famous for his learning, his friendship with the great, and his liberal politics, he was also famous for his wig. Resplendent in front, and scorning even Episcopal limits in back, said Sydney Smith, it swelled out "into a boundless convexity of frizz" to become a wonder to all barbers and a terror to the literary world.[11] A servant, acting as "a sort of armour-bearer," carried it in a special box when Parr went out to dine.[12] This so-called Johnson of the Whigs had long been cherished by reformers as a most ponderously respectable advocate. He was not, as De Quincey later charged, the leader of a "whole orchestra" of rebels, incendiaries, and state criminals,[13] but he was the friend of Priestley and Holcroft and others of that stripe whom Pitt would not have asked to dine, and he was also, for a time, the friend of Godwin. The two had met through Mackintosh in 1794 and at once began exchanging dinners and ideas,* and when Godwin visited Parr in Warwickshire in 1794 he was presented to all the neighboring gentry "in the highest terms of eulogium and regard."[14] Presently, however, the two warm friends began to drift apart. For one thing, the anticlerical bias of Godwin's *Enquirer* (1797) offended Parr; for another, reform itself began to lose its savor. He was gratified, as he said later, by Mackintosh's attack on opinions of which he was "accustomed to . . . disapprove"; † he maintained an ominous silence when Godwin sent to him a copy of his novel *St. Leon* in 1799; and he did not even reply to Godwin's complaint that Mackintosh had loaded reformers "with every epithet of contempt."[15] The reason was, of course, that Parr's time of public recantation was at hand.

The occasion was the annual Spital Sermon delivered before the lord mayor of London at Christ Church, Newgate Street, on 15 April 1800. In its published version, containing four pages of notes in Parr's elephantine prose to every one of text, the sermon consigns Godwin to oblivion. Since his theme was charity, Parr centers his attack on the "philanthropic system" of reason and benevolence — a system, he says, that loses itself in Utopian dreams while ignoring both the domestic ties of daily life and the precepts of religion. However dear to radicals and to speculative thinkers, he announces with awful and prolix finality, such schemes not only produce less good than their authors promise, they lead to "a long and portentous train of evils" which their "panegyrists" either evade or "insidiously" disguise.[16] Reviewing the sermon in the first number of the *Edinburgh,* Sydney Smith put the point more

* Godwin's diary swarms with references to Parr in the mid-nineties. In the fall after he and Parr and Mackintosh had dined together for the first time on 3 February 1794, for instance, he was seeing one or both of them almost daily.

† *Paul,* I, 380. Sam Rogers was almost surely wrong when he recalled (*Table-Talk,* p. 48) that Parr had chided Mackintosh for his attack on Godwin in the lectures.

tersely: to argue for universal benevolence while denying "particular affections" is like saying that "all the crew ought to have the *general* welfare of the ship so much at heart, that no sailor should ever pull any *particular* rope, or hand any *individual* sail." [17]

Despite his philosophic calm, Godwin was annoyed. He promptly wrote to Parr expressing his regret that so eminent a man and so valued a friend had joined the "pack" of apostates, and he asked him to explain "what crimes I am chargeable with now in 1800, of which I had not been guilty in 1794, when with so much kindness and zeal you sought my acquaintance." [18] In a devastating reply Parr complied with the request. He explained that Godwin's earlier letter about Mackintosh's lectures had been "laid aside" unopened because he did not "expect to find the contents of it agreeable," and that after he had glanced at the preface of *St. Leon* and heard from his wife something of its plot he "felt no anxiety" to read further in the book. Then, after paying to Mackintosh "the tribute of my thanks and my praise" for the admirable lectures, he proceeds to catalogue the reasons for his change of mind: Godwin's irreligion, his brazen *Memoirs* of Mary Wollstonecraft, the "dreadful effects" of his doctrines on several young men of virtue and talent, and the "dangerous tendency" of his moral and political opinions. Promising to return *St. Leon* ("which for obvious reasons I cannot keep without impropriety") he ventures the hope that Godwin will no longer give himself "the trouble of writing to me any more letters, or favouring me with any more visits." [19]

Wisely casting aside an unfinished reply in which he expressed his joy "that there are not many men like you," [20] Godwin then composed, as a kind of valediction to reform, *Thoughts Occasioned by the Perusal of Dr. Parr's Spital Sermon*. It is perhaps his ablest book. Marked with his customary dignity of style, but without the arrogance of *Political Justice* or the donnish affectation of the essays in the *Enquirer,* it is not only an elegy on reformist aspirations but also an admission that even Godwin's views had changed. It shows that by 1800 Godwin, like Mackintosh and Wordsworth and Coleridge and others, had ceased to be a pure Godwinian, a fact that was clear in *St. Leon* and had been acknowledged in its preface. Admitting there that readers of his "graver" works would perhaps charge him with inconsistency in making "the affections and charities of private life" topics of the "warmest eulogium" in his second novel, whereas in *Political Justice* they had been treated "with no indulgence and favour," Godwin had explained that for four years he had been "anxious for opportunity and leisure to modify" some of his austerities. "Not that I see cause to make any change respecting the principle of justice, or any thing else fundamental to the system there delivered; but that I apprehend domestic and private affections inseparable from the nature of man, and from what may be styled the culture of the heart." [21]

It is Godwin's new concern for "the culture of the heart" that makes his reply to Parr so notable. Without renouncing his faith in ethical rationalism he had come to recognize the moral power of passion — and one thinks of St. Leon's Marguerite, who was obviously inspired by Mary Wollstonecraft — for which reason finds no explanation. In Godwin's later thought reform still rests on the reciprocal claims of intellect and virtue, and he still believes that men can act in a way that is both rational and good, but he makes a large allowance for "affections." No man who has tried to think honestly about social problems "deserves to be treated like a highwayman or an assassin," he says, for reform itself, and not the quibbles of its advocates, is the main concern. Parr had emphasized the force of Christian ethics, he himself the force of reason, but they had shared — or so he thought — a common goal; and he is grieved that in the panic of the times the goal has been forgotten. In a noble and afflicted cause all support is needed, Godwin says, but some, like Parr's, is "too easily gained, and too easily forfeited" to be of lasting value.*

Neither Mackintosh with his cadenced prose nor Parr with his heavy piety was as dangerous to the apostles of reform as an unassuming young clergyman from Albury in Surrey. "While every body was abusing and despising Mr. Godwin," said Sydney Smith, "and while Mr. Godwin was, among a certain description of understandings, increasing every day in popularity, Mr. Malthus took the trouble of refuting him: and we

---

* *Thoughts*, pp. 13ff., 29f., 54. Despite his break with Parr, Godwin stayed on friendly terms with Mackintosh, who is often mentioned in the diary. For example, in 1813–14 Godwin records at least a dozen meetings. In 1816 Mackintosh suggested that Sam Rogers ask Byron to use his profits from *Parisina* and *The Siege of Corinth* to aid Godwin, "a man of genius, likely, for his independence of thinking, to starve at the age of sixty for want of a few hundred pounds necessary to carry on his laborious occupation." Byron promptly agreed, but the plan fell through when John Murray, who then was Byron's publisher, "demurred." See P. W. Clayden, *Rogers and His Contemporaries* (1889), I, 212f.; Brown, *Godwin*, pp. 306f.; Leslie Marchand, *Byron* (1957), II, 567f. In 1823, when Godwin was evicted from his house in Skinner Street, Mackintosh joined Lamb, Crabb Robinson, and others in raising funds for him (Paul, II, 283); and nine years later, when the Whigs at last returned to power, he strongly urged a sinecure for the old radical who, forty years before, had done so much to save the English constitution with his *Cursory Strictures*. As a result Godwin was enabled to spend his last days as a Yeoman Usher of the Exchequer in a snug little house in New Palace Yard.

hear no more of Mr. Godwin." [22] Not without reason did the author of *Political Justice* regard "the Author of an Essay on Population" with Mackintosh and Parr as an opponent to be answered, for against the reformers' hopes for Utopia, once the triumph of reason and benevolence was achieved, Malthus had raised a formidable objection. The son of a bookish and indulgent father who knew Rousseau and was fashionably ardent about Condorcet and Godwin, he early (and perhaps understandably) became skeptical of the imminent millennium. In particular, Godwin's essay "Of Avarice and Profusion" in the *Enquirer,* where "a state of cultivated equality" is described as being "most consonant to the nature of man, and most conducive to the extensive diffusion of felicity," [23] led to family arguments which in turn led to the anonymous publication, in 1798, of a short book with a long title: *An Essay on the Principle of Population As It Affects the Future Improvement of Society, with Remarks on the Speculations of Mr. Godwin, M. Condorcet, and Other Writers.* It was destined to be one of the most admired and hated works of the age, for, although Malthus himself, a modest and engaging man, disclaimed originality, his views were so embarrassing for reformers and so consoling for their adversaries that he came to challenge Burke's bad eminence as the symbol of reaction.*

Malthus says that he began his speculations prompted only by the desire to learn

whether man shall henceforth start forwards with accelerated velocity towards illimitable, and higherto unconceived improvement; or be condemned to a perpetual oscillation between happiness and misery, and after every effort remain still at an immeasurable distance from the wished-for goal. [24]

Caught between conservatives who despised reformers as either "artful and designing knaves" or "mad-headed enthusiasts" and reformers who despised conservatives as slaves of prejudice, he was convinced that in such an "unamicable contest, the cause of truth cannot but suffer." Therefore he resolved to reach his own conclusions by testing fact and

* The first edition of Malthus' book was expanded and in part rewritten in 1803 to accommodate the illustrative material that he had gathered in his reading and his travels. There was further but not very important tinkering in each of the four subsequent editions published before his death in 1834. Although the response to his *Essay* is indicated by the scope of the bibliography (pp. 84–112) in D. V. Glass's *Introduction to Malthus* (1953), a few modern titles of particular utility may be cited. The most authoritative work is James Bonar's *Malthus and His Work* (2d ed., 1924), a more recent (and very sympathetic) study being G. F. MacCleary's *Malthusian Population Theory* (1953). On the history of his theory Harold A. Boner's *Hungry Generations* (1955) is good, and on Hazlitt's objections to Malthus William P. Albrecht's *William Hazlitt and the Malthusian Controversy* (1950) is excellent. The same author's "Hazlitt and Malthus," *MLN,* XL (1945), 215–226, treats the subject on a smaller scale.

theory and by ignoring mere conjecture, "the realization of which cannot be inferred upon any just philosophical grounds." As a result, he shook the hopes of many men. By treating the proposals of Condorcet and Godwin as a problem in demography rather than an exercise in ethical theory, Malthus reduced the impulse toward reform to strictly natural terms. Whereas Burke had denounced it as a plot to destroy the English constitution, Mackintosh as a threat to the moral structure of the universe, and Parr as a program incompatible with the needs of Christian ethics, Malthus checked it against what he called the "imperious, all pervading law of nature," and he found it to be impracticable.

His conclusions are so famous that we may summarize them quickly. Beginning only with the postulate that food and sex are essential human needs, he derives the proposition "that the power of population is indefinitely greater than the power in the earth to produce subsistence for man." Because population, when unchecked, increases in no less than a geometrical and subsistence in no more than an arithmetical ratio, it is clear that if the effects of these two unequal powers are to be balanced — as required by that "law of our nature which makes food necessary to the life of man" — there must be "a strong and constantly operating check on population from the difficulty of subsistence." Since nature scatters the seeds of life with a "most profuse and liberal hand" while scanting the means of maintaining life, her "great, restrictive law" demands that many must perish if some are to survive. For plants and animals the inexorable law of survival leads to "waste of seed, sickness, and premature death"; for man it leads to misery and vice. These are the harsh but thrifty checks by which nature adjusts the energies of production to the limits of subsistence, and since man cannot "escape from the weight of this law which pervades all animated nature" we should cease to hope for a condition of life that we never can attain. "Consequently, if the premises are just, the argument is conclusive against the perfectibility of the mass of mankind." [25]

Briefly stated, this is the theory that served to discredit reformers for a generation and that has agitated the problems of social planning to this day. Malthus explored the implications of his "incontrovertible truths" with the chill precision of a surgeon and the clarity of a geometer. One need not rehearse his mountainous statistics and close analyses of economic data to realize that he transposed the question of reform into terms that his critics found it hard to juggle. Those fearful ratios and the "laws" that they reveal acquired a providential status, and the conservatives, to their astonishment and delight, discovered that indifference to misery, injustice, and inequality was not, as the reformers had charged, a mark of moral apathy but an inevitable and even commendable response to the brutal facts of life. Existence can be maintained comfortably for a lucky few and wretchedly for most, said Malthus, only through such "positive" checks as hunger, hard work, "unwholesome habitations," pestilence, and war — in short, by the inevitable miseries and vices that mark the struggle of too many people for too little food. Poets and reformers may dream their dreams, but an honest observer must admit that the sons and daughters of peasants are not "such rosy cherubs in real life, as they are described to be in romances." [26] Malthus grants that nature's harsh measures may be softened when men exert their own "preventive" or prudential check by abstaining from marriage (or sexual intercourse), but by a secular redaction of the doctrine of original sin he sees the condition of most people as poor, nasty, brutish, and short, and wisdom as a kind of acquiescence. Such palliatives as the poor-law or pumped-up wages, even though prompted by benevolence, are worthless because they have "the great and radical defect" of weakening the preventive check: by increasing population without increasing the means for its support they merely "create more poor." Although it is hard, Malthus admits, not to admire Godwin's plan to make men perfect "merely by reason and conviction," no sensible person could subscribe to conjectures that "far outstrip the modesty of nature."

> The great error under which Mr. Godwin labours throughout his whole work, is, the attributing almost all the vices and misery that are seen in civil society to human institutions. Political regulations, and the established administration of property, are with him the fruitful sources of all evil, the hotbeds of all the crimes that degrade mankind. Were this really a true state of the case, it would not seem a hopeless task to remove evil completely from the world; and reason seems to be the proper and adequate instrument for effecting so great a purpose. But the truth is, that though human institutions appear to be the obvious and obtrusive causes of much mischief to mankind; yet, in reality, they are light and superficial, they are mere feathers that float on the surface, in comparison with those deeper seated causes of impurity that corrupt the springs, and render turbid the whole stream of human life. [27]

✧ ✧ ✧

In answer to these charges Godwin could do little more than recognize the strength of Malthus' case and reassert his confidence in man's capacity for rational self-control. Admitting the "grand propositions and outline" of the *Essay* to be "not less conclusive and certain, than they are new," and the "general doctrine" so "irresistible" and the ratios so "unassailable" that they drain away one's "power of expostulation and distinction," [28] he even hints at abortion and infanticide as preferable to the horrors Malthus had described. "I had rather . . . a child should perish in the first hour of its existence," he said, "than that a man should spend seventy years of life in a state of misery and vice." * But is it not possible to hope that a prudential restraint may serve to avert catastrophe? Not every mind will "meet its mate," and in England, at any rate, prudence and pride often delay marriage so long that large families do not constitute a problem. (Godwin himself was one of thirteen children.) Moreover, he suggests, as men move toward social justice they will come to "understand the interests of the community." Everyone will love his brother. "He will conceive of the whole society as one extensive household." [29] And so on. To propose a larger role for the prudential check was, of course, Godwin's only hope of escaping Malthus' logic, but it was one that Malthus had anticipated. In replying to one of Godwin's letters † he had pointed out that prudence and an eye to the main chance are hardly compatible with the ethical and economic ideals of *Political Justice*. "Can you give me an adequate reason," he had asked, why a desire to evade economic ills would not lead to "such a competition as would destroy all chance of an equal division of the necessary labour of society, and produce such a state of things as I have described?" [30]

Impaled upon the "general doctrine" of the *Essay*, Malthus' adversaries, though unable to refute him, were convinced that he had slandered human nature. Coleridge made this point when he scribbled in his copy of the book that "Lust and Hunger" are not "both alike Passions of physical Necessity, and the one equally with the other independent of the Reason, and the Will"; and he thought it shameful for the race that "there lives the individual" who dares to say they are. [31] It is possible that Southey used Coleridge's notes in writing for the *Annual Review* of 1803 a bitter article that he hoped would give Malthus "a mortal wound." [32] In any event he had the benefit of his friend's advice — "be exceedingly temperate & courteous & guarded in your Language" [33] — and he restated the common complaint against the notion that man deserves his vice and misery because he cannot rule

---

* *Thoughts*, p. 65. "Good God! and so you heard me gravely represented in a large company yesterday as an advocate of infanticide," wrote Godwin (Paul, II, 72ff.) to an unnamed correspondent in 1801. He goes on to deny the accusation with unwonted fervor. It is probably to this passage in the *Thoughts* that Coleridge referred (Griggs, II, 761) when he told Godwin that he had read his book "with unmingled delight & admiration, with the exception of that one hateful Paragraph."

† As Godwin's diary shows, he and Malthus remained on friendly terms despite their public differences. On 15 August 1798 they breakfasted together, and many other meetings are recorded in the next few years.

his passions.* Malthus acknowledged this complaint when, in the second (1803) edition of the *Essay* he added "moral restraint" to the positive and preventive checks that he had earlier called the only means of restricting population; but since, as he admitted, moral restraint implies not only a prudential abstinence from marriage but also continence, it was a small concession.† This "snivelling interpolation," as Hazlitt was to call it,[34] made Malthus no more hopeful for reform. It occurs in the same edition as the notorious parable of "nature's mighty feast" that he never dared reprint:

> A man who is born into a world already possessed, if he cannot get subsistence from his parents on whom he has a just demand, and if the society do not want his labour, has no claim of *right* to the smallest portion of food, and, in fact, has no business to be where he is. At nature's mighty feast there is no vacant cover for him. She tells him to be gone, and will quickly execute her own orders, if he do not work upon the compassion of some of her guests. If these guests get up and make room for him, other intruders immediately appear demanding the same favour. . . . The guests learn too late their error, in counteracting those strict orders to all intruders, issued by the great mistress of the feast, who, wishing that all her guests should have plenty, and knowing that she could not provide for unlimited numbers, humanely refused to admit fresh comers when her table was already full.‡

Beyond this, the repudiation of reform could scarcely go.

THE FAILURE OF REFORM

Significantly, Hazlitt's arrival at maturity coincided with the formidable reaction to reform that we have just surveyed. This meant that from the start of his career he was, in a sense, committed to a losing cause and thrown into a posture of defiance. Although we shall presently look in some detail at his attempts to counter the reaction later, at this point we need only remember that the assault upon reform merely strengthened his conviction and provided him, as writer, with a theme. In 1803,

---

* *Annual Review and History of Literature; for 1803* (1804), pp. 292–301. In closing his review Southey concedes (p. 301) that "the folly and the wickedness of this book have provoked us into a tone of contemptuous indignation"; and he predicts that whatever merits Malthus as a man might have, "as a political philosopher, the farthing candle of his fame must stink and go out."

† *Essay* (1803), pp. 483f., 494–503. Shelley later said (*Complete Poetical Works* [ed. Thomas Hutchinson, 1904], p. 37n) that by conceding the principle of moral restraint Malthus had conceded everything, and so his *Essay* was reduced to "a commentary illustrative of the unanswerableness of *Political Justice.*"

‡ *Essay* (1803), pp. 531f. It is in commenting on the parable of nature's mighty feast that Hazlitt (1.313) defends the right to strike — and at a time when Pitt's Combination Laws denied to working men the right to organize.

when the second edition of Malthus' *Essay* and the reopening of the war with France seemed to prove the failure of reform, he had not yet found his voice, but two years later he opened his career with an essay on benevolence. There followed, among other things, a turbulent *Reply* to Malthus and a set of lectures on philosophy devoted, in Godwin's words, to the culture of the heart. Not until the year of Waterloo did his aspirations for reform begin to wane, and even then they found expression once again in his book on Thomas Holcroft. Even as they flickered out and died, in the post-Napoleonic era, they received a flaming valediction in the *Political Essays*; they turn up everywhere in the essays of his last decade; and *The Life of Napoleon Buonaparte,* the work with which he ended his career and by which he hoped to be remembered, was their funerary monument. From first to last Hazlitt's political thinking was built upon the notion that "men do not become by nature what they are meant to be, but what society makes them."

His hopes for the progressive reconstruction of society did not mean that he accepted all the schemes of the reformers. To the end of his life he thought, as the Dissenters of his youth had thought, that social change would come, but not along the lines that the prophets of reform predicted. He almost always reveals a strain of Burkean irony when discussing brisk and "upstart" schemes for millennial perfection. Reformers oblivious of everything but "their own sanguine, hair-brained" plans are the most "tormenting" kind of pests, he thought, because they are ignorant of the past and blind to human nature. Their visions of "imaginary and unattainable perfection" gratify, perhaps, their bent for speculation and prove their good intentions, but they ignore the slow and painful stages of "practical improvement" by which we inch along.[1] Although such visionaries may tinker with the "mechanism" of society, they can never hope to touch its "texture," nor do they really care.[2] Such "proprietors and patentees of reform"[3] as Godwin with his gospel of the emancipated intellect, the aging Coleridge with the Holy Scriptures as his guide to political behavior, Robert Owen with his plans for textile mills, and Bentham with his countless legislative plots would never bring about a fundamental change, said Hazlitt. They seem "to labour under water in the head."[4] In the "cloudy tabernacle" of his mind Shelley, for example, dreamed of universal justice and then, in verse, proclaimed the golden age — but he was none the less a bigot:

in him the rage of free inquiry and private judgment amounted to a species of madness. Whatever was new, untried, unheard of, unauthorized, exerted a kind of fascination over his mind. . . . Spurning the world of realities, he rushed into the world of noneties and contingencies, like air into a *vacuum*. . . . The weight of authority, the sanction of ages, the common consent of mankind, were vouchers only for ignorance, error, and imposture.*

Such comments, drawn mainly from the late essays, show how deeply Hazlitt's feelings were engaged with a hope that, as he thought, had been betrayed and vulgarized. A more temperate statement of his views is found in the serene, autumnal sketch of Godwin in *The Spirit of the Age*. It is the affectionate record of an old friendship and also a study in the decline and fall of an impracticable ideal; and because the ideal was one whose destruction he had watched in sorrow, his great retrospective essay is a kind of threnody on the loss of innocence. Although as late as 1820 Shelley, disregarding his father-in-law's incessant raids upon his legacy, could still speak of Godwin as a great but "fallen" man who would stand

> Among the spirits of our age and land,
> Before the dread tribunal of *to come*
> The foremost, — while Rebuke cowers pale and dumb,[5]

the old reformer himself, sunk into obscure senility, had come to look upon the "laborious trifles" of his renown as foolish toys,[6] and there were few to disagree with him. Hazlitt, however, was not of that opinion. Although he admitted, in 1825, that Godwin was "to all ordinary purposes dead and buried," he insisted that the author of *Political Justice* and *Caleb Williams* had secured his reputation: "his name is an abstraction in letters, his works are standard in the history of the intellect." Even if his once famous book was an *"experimentum crucis"* to show the limits of our vaunted reason as the "sole law of human action," it was ennobled by a "love" of truth. Godwin's temple of reason, stately and shining as the New Jerusalem, rested on a shaky base; none the less it should not have crumbled away in "the sordid styes of sensuality, and the petty huckster's shop of self-interest." He had deserved better of his contemporaries. The theme of blasted hope, always fascinating to Hazlitt, became irresistible when the hope was linked, as in Godwin's own career, with the aspirations of reform, and so his final words on *Political Justice* become a gloss upon the text *Quantum mutatus ab illo.* "Were we fools then, or are we dishonest now?"[7]

His answer was both yes and no. Of Godwin's contemporaries, none so unerringly exposed the weakness of his system, and none remained more loyal to his aims. Having spent half a lifetime in denouncing the

---

* 16.267f. For a sampling of Hazlitt's later comments on Utopian reform see, in addition to the extended discussions in "On People with One Idea" (8.59–69), "On Reason and Imagination" (12.44–55), and "The New School of Reform" (12.179–195), the following passages: 7.273, 11.11f., 19.304.

evils which Godwin had hoped to reason out of being, Hazlitt remembered the "avidity" with which, as a boy in his mid-teens, he began to read *Political Justice*. From "its title and its vast reputation" he thought that it would prove reform invincible, but he was promptly disabused. Whatever his zeal for the social and political changes that all good men desired, Godwin erred, he said, in failing to distinguish between political justice, which implies the use of force, and moral justice, which must rely on reason. In confusing what a man can be persuaded to do with what he may lawfully be compelled to do after reason and remonstrance fail, Godwin fell into the trap that catches all Utopians. Consequently his system, merging "the imperfection of the means in the grandeur of the end," shattered on the fact that men never act from purely rational motives.[8] Thinking too nobly of his fellows, Godwin raised the standard of morality so far above the reach of man that the path to social justice was made "dangerous, solitary, and impracticable." Absolved from the "gross and narrow ties of sense, custom, authority, private and local attachment" so that he might give himself to the pursuit of reason and benevolence, man was "screwed up, by mood and figure, into a logical machine"[9] — but as all experience teaches, men are not machines.

In short, despite his powerful mind and high ideals Godwin was guilty of a fundamental error, and therefore his system had everything to recommend it except any prospect of success. The bitter and instructive lesson of Godwin's failure impressed itself on Hazlitt.* We shall see its traces in his scorn for all Utopias and his impatience with all schemes and formulas — political, literary, economic, and other — that ignore man's limitations and his needs; and conversely in his reliance on "the imagination of the heart" as the source of wisdom and morality. The collapse of Godwin's reputation fed his smoldering wrath that England, in a crucial hour, had betrayed its best traditions by renouncing and then destroying the progress of reform. It confirmed his rich and devious view of man as a creature of complicated needs and motives, and it underscored his scorn for naked reason as a guide to or explanation of the way he really feels and acts. At least obliquely, the author

---

* References to Godwin abound in Hazlitt's work, and most of them revolve around a common theme. Thus he ascribes his failure as a dramatist to his dispassionate aloofness (18.307), and in a review of *Cloudsley*, written in the last year of his life, he develops (16.404ff.) the notion that Godwin's ethics were based on an improper knowledge of the human mind. He attributes to Northcote in the *Conversations* (for example, 11.231, 262) similar comments on Godwin's inability to comprehend the facts of life. When Keats (Rollins, II, 213) described Charles Dilke as a "Godwin-methodist" who "cannot feel he has a personal identity unless he has made up his Mind about every thing," he was probably echoing Hazlitt.

of *Political Justice* played a major role in Hazlitt's life and thought.

Coleridge and Wordsworth played another. For the most part the men who sought to undermine reform were, or soon became, celebrities, and their views the common topics of the age. Hazlitt thought that Burke and Mackintosh, Parr and Malthus, and the leaders of the Tory party were desperately mistaken, and he recorded his opinion with varying degrees of heat, ranging from jaunty disrespect to almost maniacal rage to a mellow but unshakable remorse. With the poets, however, he had been personally involved at a most impressionable age, and their betrayal of reform (as he regarded it) assumed a significance which to a less egocentric person would be incomprehensible. Viewing their decline — and, at a greater distance, Southey's — from republican ideals to a crusty Toryism, he had more intimate and therefore more compelling reasons to deplore the spirit of the age. Their best poetry had sprung, he said in 1818, if not from the French Revolution itself at any rate from the "sentiments and opinions which produced that revolution," and the result had been a "new school" founded "on a principle of sheer humanity, on pure nature void of art." [10] In that school, he thought, Wordsworth was supreme, for it was his distinction, and one of the "innovations of the time," that he saw "nothing loftier than human hopes; nothing deeper than the human heart": in the surging movements of reform he had found his inspiration and his theme.* As for Coleridge, he was the only person Hazlitt ever knew "who answered to the idea of a man of genius" and the only one who ever taught him anything.

His genius at that time had angelic wings, and fed on manna. He talked on for ever; and you wished him to talk on for ever. His thoughts did not seem to come with labour and effort; but as if borne on the gusts of genius, and as if the wings of his imagination lifted him from off his feet. His voice rolled on the ear like the pealing organ, and its sound alone was the music of thought. His mind was clothed with wings; and raised on them, he lifted philosophy to heaven. In his descriptions, you then saw the progress of human happiness and liberty in bright and never-ending succession, like the steps of Jacob's ladder, with airy shapes ascending and descending, and with the voice of God at the top of the ladder. And shall I, who heard him then, listen to him now? Not I! [11]

The change from what they were — or what Hazlitt thought they were — to what they subsequently became was, he said, "a thing unsightly and indecent," and one that galled him all his adult life. "The candid brow and elastic spring of youth may be exchanged for the

* 11.86f. In 1817 Hazlitt said (7.181) of Wordsworth, Coleridge, and Southey that "all the authority that they have as poets and men of genius must be thrown into the scale of Revolution and Reform."

wrinkles and crookedness of age," he said in 1827, "but at least we should retain something of the erectness and openness of our first unbiassed thoughts." [12] Such a comment helps us understand his anger and resentment with the poets, but it ignores the fact that for them, as for many other men, reform had failed because it sank to revolution and then to terror and aggression. Their greatest work derives not from the brittle slogans of the early nineties, but from the hard-bought knowledge that man's most fundamental needs could be betrayed by politicians. A month or so before Hazlitt came to visit him in 1798 Coleridge wrote his brother George that he had snapped his "squeaking baby-trumpet of Sedition & the fragments lie scattered in the lumber-room of Penitence. I wish to be a good man & a Christian — but I am no Whig, no Reformist, no Republican." [13] It was a matter of extreme regret, he began to think around this time, that "in the amiable intoxication of youthful benevolence" so many "noble and imaginative spirits" had mistaken "their own best virtues and choicest powers for the average qualities and attributes of the human character." [14] As for Wordsworth, he had convinced himself that "no perverseness equals that which is supported by system, no errors are so difficult to root out as those which the understanding has pledged its credit to uphold." [15] If, as tradition has it, "Expostulation and Reply" and its companion piece, "The Tables Turned," were prompted by young Hazlitt's kind of social theorizing, [16] and if "France: An Ode" stands as Coleridge's formal recantation of the errors of his youth, it is clear that by the time the poets met Hazlitt in 1798 they had passed a turning point that he would never reach.

Significantly, in the 1800 preface to *Lyrical Ballads* Wordsworth named contemporary politics as among the "most effective" of those interests which could blunt a poet's power and reduce his mind to "a state of almost savage toropor." [17] As the great patriotic sonnets of 1802 make clear, he could still take fire from politics, but *The Prelude* shows that the early tumults of reform had by then become for him a theme for introspection — of passion recollected in tranquillity. Like Beaupuy, he remembered them as

> an old romance, or tale
> Of Fairy, or some dream of actions wrought
> Behind the summer clouds. [18]

When, much later, he wrote again of politics, the savage vulgarities of "Ode 1815," the attacks on "monstrous theories of alien growth," [19] and the querulous denunciations of reform made it sadly clear that, as he had said in 1800, "the great national events which are daily taking place" [20] had lost their inspiration.

THE FAILURE OF REFORM

For Hazlitt, on the other hand, they retained a dreadful force. In his mature opinion the "strange terror" and the "spirit of universal rancour" which, in the late nineties, drove Holcroft into exile, demolished Godwin's reputation, and dashed the hopes of all reformers had large and sinister results. He thought that for England to have taken the "wrong side" in the French struggle between liberty and slavery, and to suppress "the natural consequences of that very example of freedom we had set," would in future ages "be considered as the greatest enormity in history, the stupidest and the most barefaced insult that ever was practised on the understandings or the rights of man." [21] (It is the same point, incidentally, that Wordsworth made in *The Convention of Cintra* in 1809 when he rehearsed the early stages of the war with France,[22] and that Southey, of all people, advanced as late as 1813, when he lamented Pitt's alliance with those "superannuated and abominable" despotisms that he had earlier shunned with "abhorrence" and "contempt.")[23] Pitt's main desire in life was to humble France, and his best energies went to building the successive, if not successful, coalitions with which he hoped to gain that end; but essential to his purpose, as he and his successors thought, was the domestic stability required to win the war and, after Waterloo, maintain the *status quo*. As a result, from Hazlitt's school days until his death England was in the grip of a formidable reaction, when even a Whig, as Henry Cockburn said, "was viewed somewhat as a Papist was in the days of Titus Oates." [24] It was, said Sydney Smith in retrospect, "an awful period for those who had the misfortune to entertain liberal opinions, and who were too honest to sell them for the ermine of the judge, or the lawn of the prelate." [25]

In 1816, commenting on Robert Owen's *New View of Society*, Hazlitt ironically remarked that any reformer who caught the public ear was doomed. Dr. Parr would preach a Spital Sermon, Mackintosh prepare another set of lectures, Malthus invoke his "checks of vice and misery," Southey vilify him in the *Quarterly,* the Tory journalists mark him as a villain, and the three estates unite to ruin his schemes.[26] Thanks to Pitt and the terror of the nineties, a whole generation had been taught "to lie by, to trim, to shuffle, to wait for events, to be severe on our own errors, just to the merits of a prosperous adversary, and not to throw away the scabbard or make reconciliation hopeless." [27] Such a comment shows how deep and lasting was his anger that England had renounced reform.

PART TWO

THE MIDDLE YEARS

IV

The Long Apprenticeship

BOOKS

Thus far we have been considering the ideas and the men that made history in the nineties. While Pitt was waging war on France and Godwin's reputation rose and fell, Hazlitt himself, young and mute and exceedingly obscure, was in his later teens, reading and thinking and trying unsuccessfully to write. It is now time to take a closer look at him and to trace, in so far as the meager record will permit, his reaction to the books and men who were shaping his ideas.

Even in his later years Hazlitt was a most unlettered man of letters whose patchy education and desultory reading, though matters of concern to his detractors, did not greatly trouble him. With much bravado, and no doubt some inverted snobbery, he remarked that "any one who has passed through the regular gradations of a classical education, and is not made a fool by it, may consider himself as having had a very narrow escape."[1] He himself had never been imperiled. Although his fond sister thought that as a child he "nearly killed himself" in learning Latin grammar,[2] and he, at ten, described his dizzy triumphs at the village school in Wem with ample self-esteem,[3] the debacle at Hackney may be taken as a symbol of his formal education. One wonders what he might have been if, like Coleridge, Lamb, and Hunt, he had learned his classics from such a pedagogue as Boyer, or, like Southey, he had built and read a library of fifteen thousand volumes. As it was, he remembered only enough Latin to cite a few tags and deplore Cicero's effect on English style;[4] of the Greek and Hebrew prescribed for him at Hackney not a trace remained. Not surprisingly, therefore, De Quincey, who had enough learning to deprecate Coleridge's Greek and question Wordsworth's Latin,[5] considered him to be an ignoramus, and even his admirers conceded that he was not a bookish man. It is ironical that he holds so high a place among the English critics. Johnson was a Tory polymath; Coleridge, by his own admission at the age of twenty-four, had read "almost every thing"; [6] Arnold's erudition was the anchor of his taste; on the other hand, Hazlitt's "want of general reading" was a fact that he himself acknowledged.[7]

There were moments when he wished he had a sounder education. He dreamed of having been a don at Oxford,[8] England's "Sacred City" where one is wise by proxy and studious by prescription; [9] he argued that a knowledge of the classics raises us above that "low and servile fear, which bows only to present power and upstart authority"; [10] he advised his son to study Latin not as the only source of wisdom but as an avenue to a "solid mass of intellect and power"; [11] he hoped to send the boy to the Charterhouse, an "old established" institution where learning was a habit; [12] he imagined that a regular education might save one from violent and volatile enthusiasms, since learned men do not mistake "an old battered hypothesis for a vestal." [13] Lest these random comments — to say nothing of such early essays as "On Classical Education" and "On Pedantry" [14] — seem to show Hazlitt in a deferential posture, we should remember that his normal stance was one of disrespect.

"Every one brought up in colleges, and drugged with Latin and Greek for a number of years," he asserted, "firmly believes *that there have been about five people in the world, and that they are dead.*" [15] He, like Priestley, described universities as cisterns rather than conduits of knowledge,[16] and he generally looked upon their products with envy and contempt. "A mediocrity of talent, with a certain slenderness of moral constitution" is the soil that produces prize-essayists and Greek epigrammatists, he said, and added, with a sneer at Canning, that "the most equivocal character among modern politicians was the cleverest boy at Eton." [17] He thought that most men of learning were either pompous or pathetic. Though expert in all the ancient tongues, Dr. Parr could neither speak nor write his own; [18] with his fingers twisted from copying Plotinus in a fine Greek hand John Taylor showed how hollow are the trophies of human pride and erudition; [19] George Dyer lived "all his life in a dream of learning" and never once had "his sleep broken by a real sense of things." [20] Even August Wilhelm von Schlegel, whose work Hazlitt generally admired, disappointed him when he wrote on ancient drama, for then an "excessive veneration" overcame his "bold and independent judgment." [21]

In short, the peccant humors of overeducated men were to him a source of constant irritation. One "got nothing" from such people except the "cant of knowledge," he told Northcote; but "go to a linen-

draper in the city, without education but with common sense and shrewd-
ness, and you pick up something new, because nature is inexhaustible,
and he sees it from his own point of view, when not cramped and
hood-winked by pedantic prejudices." [22] A hard-pressed writer who wrote
to get his daily bread, he jeered at authors who assumed rather than
acquired their reputations, thus qualifying for that aristocracy of letters
wherein birth and education are valued more than talent, and wherein
the learned languages are a "passport" to meaningless prestige. [23] In the
highly contrapuntal essays of his later years his social discontent, embellished with a scorn of mere book-learning and deepened by his dread
of bloodless theorizing, emerges as a major theme. Shuttling between
the dualities of passion and reason, nature and art, freedom and constraint, life and books, knowledge and learning, he weaves the pattern
of his values, and they comprise the credo of an anti-intellectual. "The
world itself is a volume larger than all the libraries in it," he said not
long before his death, and therefore books can never be a substitute for
life.*

Like many men — but not like many men of letters — Hazlitt did
his reading mainly in his youth. Even then the books that he liked best
concerned what he later called the "study of humanity." [24] At school
he dutifully sampled Thomson and Mrs. Barbauld and John Home's
Douglas, as well as other things thought fitting for the young, in Enfield's famous *Speaker,* [25] but at home, buried among his father's tomes
of Biblical exegesis and theology, he found Addison and Steele and
Mrs. Radcliffe, and he raced through them with joy. [26] When, at fourteen, he came upon *Tom Jones,* it was in the nature of a revelation: that
book "broke the spell" of childhood, for "it smacked of the world" he
lived in and in which he was to live. [27] It is therefore not surprising that
in his middle years he read novels when he read almost nothing else,
because he regarded them as "the most authentic as well as most accessi-
ble repositories of the natural history and philosophy of the species." [28]
Fielding led to Smollett, and Smollett to Richardson, Sterne, Cervantes,
and Le Sage; and these, no doubt, were among the "twenty or thirty
volumes" which, he said in 1821, were the only ones apart from Scott's
that he still read for pleasure. "When I take up a work that I have read
before (the oftener the better) I know what I have to expect." Whereas

---

* 12.27. "The object of books is to teach us ignorance," he wrote in 1823 (20.126);
"that is, to throw a veil over nature, and persuade us that things are not what they are,
but what the writer fancies or wishes them to be."

contemporary writers generally bored him — "I hate to read new books" — the favorites of his youth were made more dear by their associations, and they never lost their charm. "They bind together the different scattered divisions of our personal identity," he said. "They are landmarks and guides in our journey through life. They are pegs and loops on which we can hang up, or from which we can take down, at pleasure, the wardrobe of a moral imagination, the relics of our best affections, the tokens and records of our happiest hours." [29] Read the "commonest" books, he advised his son, for they are best, and they afford the kind of pleasure that a man remembers longest and least repents. "If my life had been more full of calamity than it has been (much more than I hope yours will be) I would live it over again, my poor little boy, to have read the books I did in my youth." [30]

At Hackney his reading, principally in "modern philosophy," was more unsettling and austere. Holbach and Helvetius disturbed him with their view of man as a creature of selfish, mechanistic motivation, and Thomas Chubb's deistical tracts, which he read with "particular satisfaction," [31] no doubt pushed him further from the faith which he had learned at home. Oddly enough, he did not encounter the "dry and powerful" Hobbes until later, but he worked his way through Locke (whose celebrated *Essay* he thought vastly overrated), Berkeley, Hartley, Hume, and Godwin. Such a regimen, as he said later, may have done "irreparable injury" to his health, [32] but it set him on the tack which, in 1798, made him interesting to Coleridge, and it laid the base not only for his first book in 1805 but also for a set of lectures that, in 1812, brought him at least a taste of fame.

Hartley and Helvetius, however, did not pre-empt his time. At Hackney, where liberal politics and iconoclastic books were *de rigueur,* he devoured "tooth-and-nail" Rousseau's *Nouvelle Héloïse, Confessions,* and *Contrat social* (which he had "picked up at a stall in a coarse leathern cover"), [33] and in them he found the kind of sentiment and subjectivism that he would one day make his own. The "acute and even morbid feeling of all that related to his own impressions, to the objects and events of his life" [34] that he later said was Rousseau's chief distinction struck him forcibly when young; and according to Leigh Hunt he still had that sentimentalist "by heart" when he was middle-aged. [35] The boy who sobbed at Julia's farewell letter * and endlessly reread, "with unspeakable delight and wonder," the story of her death [36] was not unnaturally "stunned" as with a blow by Schiller's *Robbers,* [37] and he

---

* 12.24. According to Patmore (III, 56), in his later years Hazlitt could weep at the very sight of *La Nouvelle Héloïse.*

thought the death scene in *Don Carlos* inspiring enough to make one "confront the King of Terrors in his grisly palace." * Inevitably, he shed "floods of tears" with Werter,[38] but for Goethe's plays,[39] even for *Faust*, later — "a mere piece of abortive perverseness" [40] — he had no taste at all. Also, it should be added, he had no German. French he had started as a little boy,[41] but he apparently knew no other modern language. However giddy his delight in Cervantes and Boccaccio,[42] it was a delight derived from those "paltry and somewhat worn" translations which a "poor student" might have "picked up at a stall, standing out of a shower of rain." [43] Many years later, when, as he confessed to Landor, he tried to teach himself Italian, he "made out" only one page before abandoning the effort.[44] But since he computed that a lifetime was required to read "a thousandth part" of one's own literature, he decided that it was futile to seek "the *dialect* of truth and nature" in a language not his own.[45]

Oddly, Hazlitt never speaks about his introduction to the writer who meant the most to him, but he had Shakespeare's works by heart,[46] and according to Keats he thought that the greatest of all writers was enough for any man.[47] He wandered through Spenser "with a sort of voluptuous indolence," liked Chaucer "even better," [48] and found his true repose in the poets, novelists, and playwrights of the Restoration and the eighteenth century. For any "insight into the mysteries of poetry" he was indebted, as he said later, to the authors of *Lyrical Ballads*,† but long before he heard their heady talk in 1798 he had read and reread Pope and Goldsmith, Farquhar and Congreve, Richardson and Sterne, and with them and their contemporaries he was affectionately at home. "In forming an estimate of passages relating to common life and manners," he said, "I cannot think I am a plagiarist from any man." [49] It was mainly upon his long familiarity with eighteenth-century literature that he built the lectures of his middle years; and the infectious enthusiasm of his comments on the English poets and the English comic writers are our safest guide to the critical responses of the boy at Wem. On a trip to Shrewsbury in 1798 he bought copies of Milton and Burke's *Reflections*, "both of which I have still," he wrote almost a quarter of a century later, "and I still recollect, when I see the covers, the pleasure with which I dipped into them as I returned with my double prize. I was set up for one while." [50] In trying to achieve a style in prose he

---

* 17.197. Elsewhere (8.325n) Hazlitt said that this passage "almost choaked" him when he read it.

† 12.226. Elsewhere (5.146) Hazlitt said that Coleridge and Wordsworth taught him little of the major English poets because "they were always talking of themselves and one another."

pored over Johnson, Burke, and Junius — but mainly Burke — with the admiration appropriate to youth, pausing only to marvel at "the secret of so much strength and beauty" and reading on so he could admire the more. "So I passed whole days, months, and I may add, years; and have only this to say now, that as my life began, so I could wish that it may end." [51]

THE MEETING WITH THE POETS

In a sense that phase of Hazlitt's life did end in 1798, when he and Coleridge met. He himself has told the story so well in "My First Acquaintance with Poets" * that it is now the common property of the race; but because it records a crucial moment in his life it deserves our close attention. In July 1797, after a series of adventures and misadventures not unconnected with their ardor for reform, Coleridge and the two Wordsworths, William and Dorothy, had met and come together as neighbors in the west of England. The events and literary consequences of the *annus mirabilis* that followed are too familiar to repeat. Thanks to a providential legacy, the Wordsworths were, in a small way, solvent; but with a family and a bevy of in-laws to support — "five mouths opening & shutting as I pull the string" [1] — Coleridge needed money, and since he was still a Unitarian of sorts he thought that preaching might be a safer thing than verse or journalism. Thus he went, early in January 1798, to Shrewsbury to give a trial sermon before the congregation there; and thus young Hazlitt, having risen before day and walked ten miles through the mud from Wem, came to hear him preach. It was one of the decisive moments of his life. Coleridge himself reported that one "shrewd" member of the congregation, having heard the sermon, said that he would rather hear him talk than preach, [2] but young Hazlitt was stricken dumb with admiration. Giving out his text, "And he went up into the mountain to pray, HIMSELF, ALONE," Coleridge launched into his subject "like an eagle dallying with the wind"; and although the sermon embraced such threadbare topics as the separation of church and state and the iniquity of war, Hazlitt thought that he was hearing the music of the spheres.

Poetry and Philosophy had met together. Truth and Genius had embraced, under the eye and with the sanction of Religion. This was even beyond my hopes. I

* 17.106–122. This famous essay, so dear to all anthologists, was worked up for the *Liberal* in 1823 from "Mr. Coleridge's Lay-Sermon," a letter contributed to the *Examiner* in 1817 and reprinted in *Political Essays* (7.128f.) two years later.

returned home well satisfied. The sun that was still labouring pale and wan through the sky, obscured by thick mists, seemed an emblem of the *good cause*; and the cold rank drops of dew that hung half melted on the beard of the thistle, had something genial and refreshing in them; for there was a spirit of hope and youth in all nature, that turned every thing into good.

When Coleridge came to Wem the following day to call upon the elder Hazlitt the boy at first said nothing. He was content to listen, and as Coleridge talked — of Mary Wollstonecraft and Mackintosh and Burke — it seemed "that Truth had found a new ally in Fancy." When, finally, he ventured a remark — that to speak of Burke contemptuously was the "test of a vulgar democratic mind" — the visitor allowed that it was a very "just and striking observation." In later years the scene retained for Hazlitt the clarity of direct perception: the little wainscoted parlor, the guest's "gross, voluptuous, open, eloquent" mouth, the leg of Welsh mutton and the flavor of the turnips, the talk about reformers and reform. It was the very next morning * that Coleridge received from Tom Wedgwood the offer of an annuity which would free him for the "study of poetry and philosophy," and when, in the process of tying his shoelaces, he decided to accept it,† Hazlitt was dismayed: "instead of living at ten miles distance, of being the pastor of a Dissenting congregation at Shrewsbury, he was henceforth to inhabit the Hill of Parnassus, to be a shepherd on the Delectable Mountains. Alas! I knew not the way thither, and felt very little gratitude for Mr. Wedgwood's bounty." Before setting forth on his return, however, Coleridge advanced toward Hazlitt with "undulating step" and invited him to visit Nether Stowey in the spring, and in stammering out his thanks the boy felt that a thunderbolt had struck.

As he walked with the departing guest along the road to Shrewsbury he drank in his monologue like nectar. "In digression, in dilating, in passing from subject to subject, he appeared to me to float in air, to slide on ice." [3] Coleridge's strange habit of shifting from one side of the footpath to the other (which Hazlitt did not then associate with "any instability of purpose or involuntary change of principle") had no effect

* I follow Hazlitt's recollection of the sequence of events, but perhaps he was in error. On Tuesday 16 January 1798 Coleridge wrote a long letter, postmarked Shrewsbury, to a friend in Bristol to announce the glad tidings of the Wedgwoods' annuity and to solicit his advice (Griggs, I, 370-373), and the next day he informed Tom Poole that he had decided to accept the offer (*ibid.*, I, 374f.). Perhaps he had squeezed in an overnight visit to Wem, but he says nothing of it in the extant correspondence.

† Joshua Toulmin, one of the elder Hazlitt's correspondents (*Christian Reformer*, V [1838], 763), regarded Coleridge's decision as providential for Dissent. "I still think that Mr. Coleridge's settlement at Shrewsbury would have been very injurious," he wrote in 1802. "He is too eccentric and volatile and changeable to become a fixed Dissenting minister: a *genius* is not to be kept with the trammels of rules, customs and habits."

upon his flow of words: he spoke of theology, of Berkeley * and Hume, Johnson and Tom Paine, Paley and Butler, and the talk, of course, was mainly his. Hazlitt did say that he had "written a few remarks" on ethical theory, which he bungled in trying to explain; none the less Coleridge listened to him with "great willingness," and when they parted at the six-mile stone Hazlitt turned again to Wem "pensive but much pleased," with the voice of Fancy ringing in his ears and the face of Poetry shining like a light before him.

◇ ◇ ◇

One result of this encounter was Hazlitt's renewed attempt — his twentieth — to complete his essay on benevolence. After a "few meagre sentences in the skeleton-style of a mathematical demonstration," however, he stopped halfway down the second page; "and, after trying in vain to pump up any words, images, notions, apprehensions, facts, or observations, from that gulph of abstraction in which I had plunged myself for four or five years preceding, gave up the attempt as labour in vain, and shed tears of helpless despondency on the blank unfinished paper." But as the winter turned to spring he consoled himself in thinking of Coleridge's invitation, and when the visit was postponed † the delay increased his ardor. In April he tramped to Llangollen Vale to initiate himself "in the mysteries of natural scenery," reading on the way *La Nouvelle Héloïse* and applying Coleridge's "Ode to the Departing Year" *con amore* to the objects which he saw. When, late in May,‡ he finally set forth for Nether Stowey by way of Worcester, Tewksbury, Gloucester, and Bristol, he approached his goal as if it were a shrine. He was "well received," and the very first afternoon he and Coleridge walked over to Alfoxden to call on Wordsworth. The poet was away from home, but Dorothy made them welcome, and Hazlitt leafed through the manuscript of *Lyrical Ballads* "with the faith of a novice." That night he slept "in an old room with blue hangings, and covered with the round-faced family-portraits of the age of George I," and the next morning, as Coleridge, sitting on the trunk of a fallen ash tree, read "The Thorn" and "The Mad Mother," Hazlitt for the first time felt the power of Wordsworth's poetry. "It had to me something of the effect

---

* According to Cottle (p. 21), in 1795 Coleridge's main topics of conversation were Pantisocracy (his "everlasting theme"), Berkeley, Hartley, and Bowles's sonnets.

† On 9 March 1798 Coleridge, writing to a friend in Wem (Griggs, I, 394), was specific in sending his compliments to "young Mr. Haseloed" and in renewing his invitation.

‡ Among other things, the birth of Berkeley Coleridge in May might have put off Hazlitt's visit. For conjectures on its actual date see Abbie Findlay Potts, "The Date of Wordsworth's First Meeting with Hazlitt," *MLN*, XLIV (1929), 296–299.

that arises from the turning up of the fresh soil, or the first welcome breath of Spring, 'While yet the trembling year is unconfirmed.' "

When Wordsworth, who had been at Bristol, appeared the following day, dressed in a brown fustian jacket and striped pantaloons, he had a "roll" and a "lounge" in his gait that reminded one of his own Peter Bell. "There was a severe, worn pressure of thought about his temples, a fire in his eye (as if he saw something in objects more than the outward appearance), an intense high narrow forehead, a Roman nose, cheeks furrowed by strong purpose and feeling, and a convulsive inclination to laughter about the mouth, a good deal at variance with the solemn, stately expression of the rest of his face." Devouring half a Cheshire cheese and reporting acidly on *The Castle Specter* (which he had seen at Bristol), he did not cut a very poetical figure; but his comment on the sunset through a latticed window made Hazlitt marvel at his powers of perception, and ever after, when he saw the sunset stream in golden splendor, he was grateful for the memory. There were other memories not so golden. On one occasion he and Wentworth got in a "metaphysical argument" in which neither of the disputants could make the other understand his views. In a sense, however, Wordsworth was the victor, for this was probably the conversation, mentioned in the "Advertisement" to *Lyrical Ballads,* which prompted the composition of "Expostulation and Reply" and "The Tables Turned" as rebuttals to "a friend who was somewhat unreasonably attached to modern books of moral philosophy." * Years later, after the two had become acknowledged enemies, Hazlitt said that when he once tried to explain his theory of benevolence to Wordsworth — "and it is a hard matter to explain any thing to him" — he was told that he might have had a point but that "it was what every shoemaker must have thought of." Coleridge, on the other hand, was impressed by Hazlitt's "discovery," and said that he had "the most metaphysical head he ever met with." *

The passing days brought more walking and talking and poetry, and finally, after three weeks at Nether Stowey, an expedition down the Bristol Channel with Coleridge and his mute, mysterious friend John Chester, who kept up a kind of trot "like a running footman by a state coach, that he might not lose a syllable or sound that fell from Coleridge's lips." On this tour the talk and scenery were superb. In the parlor of a little inn they found a dog-eared copy of Thomson's *Seasons* in the

* 9.3; cf. 17.312. After Hazlitt's death Wordsworth wrote to the essayist's son about the "acuteness and originality of mind" that he had shown at Nether Stowey (*Four Generations,* I, 233), and to another correspondent about the same time (*Later Years,* I, 511) he recalled that during their "short" period of intimacy Hazlitt seemed to be "a man of extraordinary acuteness, but perverse as Lord Byron himself."

window seat, and Coleridge explained it as an example of "true fame."
Being Coleridge, he also explained many other things: Vergil's *Georgics*
("but not well"), the diction of *Lyrical Ballads,* the difference between
Shakespeare and Milton. He had read everything, and about everything
he had his own opinions — "profound and discriminating" about the
authors whom he liked, but "capricious, perverse, and prejudiced in his
antipathies and distastes." Contemptuous of Gray, intolerant of Pope,
condescending about Junius and Johnson, he was fond of Burke (whom,
however, he ranked below Jeremy Taylor "in richness of style and
imagery") and preferred Richardson to Fielding. Hazlitt later said that
in whatever company Coleridge found himself he promptly established
a division of labor with himself as speaker and all the rest as listeners,[5]
but perhaps it was different in 1798. Their companion said nothing, or
almost nothing, but Coleridge and Hazlitt ranged freely through prose
fiction, ethical theory, and associationist psychology, Chester all the
while listening closely "not from any interest in the subject, but because
he was astonished that I should be able to suggest any thing to Coleridge
that he did not already know." In three days they were back at Nether
Stowey, and the following Sunday Hazlitt left for Wem. Coleridge, who
had preached that day at Taunton, rejoined him at Bridgewater for the
walk to Bristol, on the way reciting some lines of his which, in retrospect, must have seemed ironical:

> Oh memory! shield me from the world's poor strife,
> And give those scenes thine everlasting life.

At Bristol they parted, Hazlitt turning north to Wem and Coleridge east
to London. They would not meet again for several years, and never with
the full rapport that they had shared at Nether Stowey.

PICTURES

Capping the book-filled years at Hackney and at Wem, Hazlitt's meeting
with Coleridge in 1798 was a kind of initiatory rite into those "mysteries" of literature which as a boy he knew nothing of.[1] Although exhilarating, the conversation seems to have skirted two subjects which,
then and later, were much in Hazlitt's mind: one, oddly enough, was
politics; the other, not so oddly because it was the one thing that Coleridge did not know about,[2] was art. Both were to occupy much of Hazlitt's time for the next five years or so.

When, at the age of ten, he told his brother that he wanted to learn

PICTURES

as much Greek and Latin as possible, he added that he would "not paint the worse for knowing everything else."[3] Nineteen years later, after he had published two books and was preparing two more for the press, he explained to his father that he had done what he wanted to in writing, "and I hope I may in painting."[4] Long after he had made his mark in letters he thought that to paint a great picture was a felicity and a triumph from which mere writers were excluded — "no absurd opinions to combat, no point to strain, no adversary to crush, no fool to annoy[5] — and there can be no doubt that he would have traded all the prose he wrote for the joy of having painted a single masterpiece. Encouraged by his brother John's success, as a little boy he had hoped to be a painter, and it was a hope which he relinquished, with characteristically deep sighs, only in his middle thirties. "Industry alone can only produce mediocrity," he at last admitted, "but mediocrity in art is not worth the trouble of industry."[6] Although his devotion to painting vastly exceeded his modest talent as a painter, the devotion remained to inspire some of his most vivid criticism, and such famous essays as "On the Pleasure of Painting," "English Students at Rome," and "The Letter-Bell" record his minor triumphs and major failure in the art that he admired above all others.

To the end of his life he visited picture galleries as the pious go on pilgrimages, and there "the solitude, the silence, the speaking looks, the unfading forms" of his favorite masters filled him with an awe that in other men is called religious.[7] To admire a great picture was for him "an act of devotion performed at the shrine of art," and even to have felt the power of something so superb as Guido Reni's *Annunciation* in the Luxembourg was, he thought, enough to justify the pains of life.[8] Although such "glittering waste of laborious idleness" as William Beckford's Fonthill Abbey filled him with disgust,† he regarded a collection with only one authentic masterpiece — an "heir-loom of the

---

* 10.111. Customarily a diffident man, Hazlitt boasted of his "importunity" in gaining access to collections. It was a trait, he said (8.112n), that would have taken him far in politics.

† 18.173. Hazlitt's excoriating piece on Fonthill Abbey (18.173–180), which appeared in the *London Magazine* in 1822, lends credence to Benjamin Robert Haydon's report (*Correspondence and Table-Talk*, II, 79) in September 1823 that the auctioneer in charge of selling Beckford's things had hired Hazlitt "to write up, for fifty guineas, what he wrote down from his conscience last year." Another version of the story is that which Edward Irving, the celebrated preacher, told Carlyle (*Reminiscences* [Everyman's Library, 1932], p. 239) — that Hazlitt had attended the auction at Fonthill Abbey in 1823 as a "false bidder merely appointed to raise prices." At his financial and emotional nadir in 1823 Hazlitt may have stooped to this, but his published views on Fonthill Abbey, both before and after the alleged event, show that he did not change his mind about William Beckford's taste. See 12.292, 17.279; Patmore, III, 60–68.

imagination" that "haunts us with an uneasy sense of joy for twenty miles of road, that may cheer us at intervals for twenty years of life to come" — well worth a three-day hike.⁸ Hoping that his son might succeed where he had failed, he urged him to consider art as a means of livelihood;⁹ he was insatiably curious about the lives of painters; and he sought the friendship of contemporary artists with a zeal entirely out of character. The endless chitchat of his *Conversations of James Northcote* (1830) reflects his curiosity and knowledge about the work of men like Reynolds, Nollekens, Fuseli, West, and Conway; and a big body of criticism, including *Sketches of the Principal Picture-Galleries in England* (1824) and *Notes of a Journey through France and Italy* (1826), shows that his enthusiasm lasted to the end. Less enthusiastic but no less revealing about his taste and knowledge are the comments on current exhibitions which he wrote for the *Champion* and the *Examiner* during his early years of journalism.

But this is to anticipate. When he left Wem and set out to make his way in life at the age of twenty-one he hoped to be a painter, and between then and 1804 or thereabout painting was his livelihood. It goes without saying that the record of these years is spotty, and that most of what we know about him in this period must be pieced together from the cryptic and discreet allusions in his later work, but here and there a solid fact appears. In mid-December 1799, for instance, he had just returned to London from a visit to his family when he wrote this touching and revealing letter home: *

> Monday morning
> London
>
> My dear Father,
>   I arrived here yesterday evening a little after five. I got to Shiffnal the day I left you in very good time, & without any fatigue. The next morning, I set off on foot about nine, & had walked seven miles, when the mail overtook me. I rode on the outside the rest of the way to Oxford, where I slept that night. I only stopt there to breakfast the next day, as I was too cold, & uncomfortable to have had any pleasure in looking at the buildings. I proceeded that day to Henley, which is 23 miles from Oxford, & I left Henley yesterday morning at half past 7. I walked 35 miles in 10 hours. My travelling expences in all amounted to 2 guineas, & a shilling. I paid 22 shillings for coach hire. I dined the first day on my hard egg, & wigs. I did not eat the pudding till the day after. I was very much shook on the coach box; & I wore out my gloves, & bruised my hands by the rubbing of the iron rail, which I was obliged to keep fast hold of, to prevent my being thrown from my seat. I rode inside from Woodstock to Oxford. I just now began Godwin's new novel, which I do not at present admire very much. It is called

---

* That Hazlitt was in London during most of 1799 is clear from Godwin's diary, where about a dozen "calls" or chance encounters are recorded between February 12 and September 8. Thereafter Hazlitt's absence from the diary suggests that he was out of town, and this letter shows where he had been. See page 131n.

SAMUEL TAYLOR COLERIDGE
By Peter Van Dyke (1795)
The National Portrait Gallery

WILLIAM WORDSWORTH
By Robert Hancock (1798)
The National Portrait Gallery

PICTURES

The Travels of St Leon, a tale of the 16th century. I do not know, whether I shall begin any thing this week as I have neither paints, nor brushes here. The little box with the clothes came yesterday. You will let us know, when you write, if you have not already, where to inquire for the other boxes, & when they are to arrive in London. John tells me, that he wrote on Friday, & gave you a letter full of all the news. I am in pretty good spirits. The weather is colder than it was, when I left Wem, & quite as dark. I shall give you another letter when the pictures come, & I have begun to paint again. I saw two, or three little views on the road, which I shall endeavour to sketch out in some way, or other from memory. The dinner is just coming up, & I can hardly see to write. You must give my love to my mother, & Peggy. I shall send the things I talked of as soon as I can. When I looked back on the road to the Lea Hills, & saw how dim, & low they grew, & how small the objects upon them appeared, & recollected, that you were still farther off, I wondered at the distinct idea I had of you all: and yet I still recollect you as I saw you last in the parlour at breakfast. I am.

your affec. son
W. Hazlitt *

Although his movements for the next few years are extremely hard to trace, we get a glimpse of him from time to time. It was in 1799, apparently, that he had met Crabb Robinson, who thought him bashful, inarticulate, and slovenly, but none the less "extraordinary." He was ardent in the cause of liberty as Godwin and Holcroft understood the word, and so enthusiastic about the poetry of Coleridge and Wordsworth that Robinson ever afterward regarded him as the "director" of his taste.† Still coursing through the English novel [10] and still hoping some day to finish (or perhaps begin) the philosophical essay which he had repeatedly given over in despair, Hazlitt had not entirely abandoned politics and books for painting. Not only did he renew his acquaintance with Wordsworth (who, with Dorothy, had just returned from Germany, where Coleridge lingered on) [11] but he met Southey [12] and also became a friend of Godwin, to whom, it will be recalled, his brother John had introduced him five years earlier.‡

But painting, not literature, was his obsession then, and the event that stood out in his memory of these years was the Pall Mall exhibition, in the spring of 1799, of Italian masters from the collection of the Duc

* *Shelley and His Circle, 1773–1822* (ed. Kenneth Neill Cameron), I (1961), 219f. This letter, postmarked 16 December 1799, and no doubt written from John Hazlitt's house in Rathbone Place, is quoted with the permission of The Carl and Lily Pforzheimer Foundation, Inc.

† Robinson, I, 6. On 12 August 1799 Godwin recorded in his diary that Robinson and Hazlitt had paid a call on him.

‡ Beginning with the call on February 12, Godwin and Hazlitt saw much of one another for a while. The diary records meetings, or attempted meetings, on March 31, April 1, 2, 28, 29, June 17, 26, July 25, August 5, 12, 25, September 8, December 28, and then, in 1800, on January 3 (at Coleridge's), 16, 27, February 25, April 7, May 29, and June 15. Thereafter the diary is silent about Hazlitt until 12 May 1802, when he "sups & sleeps" at Godwin's.

d'Orléans. Seeing the works of Titian, Raphael, Guido Reni, and Domenichino for the first time, he was "staggered." A mist passed away from his sight, he said later of this episode, and the scales fell from his eyes. "A new sense came upon me, a new heaven and a new earth stood before me." [13] During the next two years, for all we know to the contrary, he lived upon the memory, sometimes working at copies of Rembrandt and Jan van Goyen "in a little *back* painting-room" at John's house in Rathbone Place,* sometimes tramping the provinces to visit private collections and pick up commissions for portraits. The allusions to this period are sprinkled liberally through the later essays. For example, once in Manchester he lived on coffee for a fortnight while painting a half-length portrait of a manufacturer who, incredibly, paid him five guineas when the job was done; † and once, when going for the third time to Burleigh House, in Leicestershire, to see the pictures there, he trudged on in a "dreaming mood" to Peterborough and then to Wisbeach to look upon his mother's girlhood home.

I had at this time, simple as I seemed, many resources. I could in some sort "play at bowls with the sun and moon;" or, at any rate, there was no question in metaphysics that I could not bandy to and fro, as one might play at cup-and-ball, for twenty, thirty, forty miles of the great North Road, and at it again, the next day, as fresh as ever. . . . I knew Tom Jones by heart, and was deep in Peregrine Pickle. I was intimately acquainted with all the heroes and heroines of Richardson's romances, and could turn from one to the other as I pleased. I could con over that single passage in Pamela about "her lumpish heart," and never have done admiring the skill of the author and the truth of nature. [14]

* 17.379. It was owing to his brother John's good offices, perhaps, that one of Hazlitt's portraits of his father was shown in 1802 at the Royal Academy exhibition at Somerset House. See 8.13.

† 17.180. Hazlitt's visits to Manchester and Liverpool, where, "when I was young, I spent a good deal of my time" (8.204n), are poorly documented. During one of them, perhaps, he had the love affair alluded to in his *Reply* to Malthus (1.283) and mentioned in a letter to his fiancée (*Memoirs*, I, 154). Years later, when they were quarreling over their divorce, his wife recalled (Bonner, pp. 247f.) his "frenzy about Sally Shepherd," but she dismissed it as a "flea-bite." As Howe has shown (*Life*, p. 99), it is unlikely that the Sally Shepherd who stirred Mrs. Hazlitt's jealousy was the daughter of the Dr. Shepherd of Gateacre, near Liverpool, whose portrait was one of Hazlitt's few successes (*Literary Remains*, I, li).

At Manchester, "of all places in the world," he first read Mrs. Inchbald's *Simple Story* and was duly "transported" (12.303f.), perhaps about the time that he offended a potential client by challenging his taste in literature: as a consequence, he said many years later (8.204n), "here I am writing *Table-talks*." A correspondent of the elder Hazlitt, writing in March 1802 (*Christian Reformer*, V [1838], 562) establishes the fact of Hazlitt's presence in Manchester at the time and also implies that he was short of money. The two long hiatuses between Hazlitt's appearances in Godwin's diary in these years — from 15 June 1800 to 12 May 1802 and from 22 March 1803 to 25 July 1804 — permit the inference that he was not in London, and we know that during part of 1803 he was painting at the Lakes (see pages 134–139).

PICTURES

The great event in Hazlitt's brief career as painter — as great, almost, as the trip to Nether Stowey in his literary development — was a four-month visit to Paris in the fall and winter of 1802. His letters to his father at the time [15] and the allusions scattered through his later work illuminate it vividly. Joining the streams of English tourists who visited the Continent during the short-lived Peace of Amiens, he reached Paris in the middle of October.* Such money as he had was provided by a Mr. Railton, of Liverpool, who had commissioned him to make some copies in the Louvre. Although he did not greatly care for Paris, which he thought "very dirty and disagreeable, except along the river side," he was enchanted by its art. Once he had worked his way past "the purgatory of the modern French gallery" in the Louvre and was admitted, for a gratuity, to the Italian masters, his rapture was unbounded. "I marched delighted through a quarter of a mile of the proudest efforts of the mind of man, a whole creation of genius, a universe of art!" [16] Thanks to Napoleon's tactic of acquisition through conquest, the Louvre was in its glory, and except for the frescoes of Raphael and Michelangelo ("which could not be transported, without taking the walls of the building across the Alps"), [17] it sheltered, "heaped, massed together to a gorgeous height," [18] all the priceless jewels of Europe. "Art lifted up her head and was seated on her throne. . . . There she had gathered together all her pomp, and there was her shrine, and there her votaries came and worshipped as in a temple." [19] In later years Hazlitt often sang again his paean to the glory of the Louvre in 1802, for in the shining spoils of revolution he saw objectified his ideal in both politics and art. [20] Returning to the desolated "temple" in 1824, he said that in the giddy rapture of his youth he had gazed himself "almost blind." Why should he not, therefore, weep himself blind in finding the spoils of human genius gone, "and with them gone all that I had once believed and hoped of human kind"? [21] For Napoleon's rape of foreign treasure was not "robbery and sacrilege," but

the crowning and consecration of art; there was a dream and a glory, like the coming of the Millennium. These works, instead of being taken from their respective countries, were given to the world, and to the mind and heart of man, from whence they sprung. . . . All that it had entered into his mind to conceive, his thought in tangled forests, his vision of the night, was here perfected and accomplished, was acknowledged for the fair and good, honoured with the epithet of *divine,* spoke an intelligible language, thundered over Europe, and received the bended knee of the universe.†

* Hazlitt's absence from Godwin's diary between 14 October 1802 and 1 March 1803 suggests the length of his visit to the Continent.

† 13.212. In 1814, when, said Hazlitt (19.126), the victorious Allies were so hot for vengeance that they "would, if they could, blot the Sun out of heaven, because it

THE LONG APPRENTICESHIP

To his sorrow, he had to leave the Louvre at closing time, but there were other things to do in Paris. He improved his French, went to the theater, and even met a few people, including Southey's friend Richard Duppa, the painter Richard Cosway, and a former "fellow-student" from Hackney whom, twenty-two years later, he saw again on his second trip to France.[22] His happiest hours, however, were spent in making copies of the Italian masters, some designed for Railton and some for his own satisfaction. In later years, although he cared nothing for possessions, he clung to these with a tenacity that certain of his friends found moving and others merely irritating.[23] Charles Cowden Clarke and his bride were deeply touched by his affection, at the end of his life, for a copy of Titian's *Ippolito de' Medici* that he had made in 1802. Told by Northcote (one of the artists whom his brother John had introduced him to) that it was "one of the finest pictures in the whole world,"[24] he had resolved to make a copy. When he first saw it in the Louvre it seemed " 'a thing of life,' with supernatural force and grandeur,"[25] and it remained for him one of the few unquestioned triumphs of art. When the Clarkes visited him not long before his death they were shown his copy of this famous picture, lying unframed on a sofa, while he

stood by holding the candle high up so as to throw the light well on to the picture, descanting enthusiastically on the merits of the original. The beam from the candle falling on his own finely intellectual head, with its iron-grey hair, its square potential forehead, its massive mouth and chin, and eyes full of earnest fire, formed a glorious picture in itself, and remains a luminous vision for ever upon our memory.[26]

Somewhat less luminous in 1803, Hazlitt, "brow-hanging, shoe-contemplative, *strange*,"[27] returned from France to resume his trade of painting portraits, and it was in that capacity that he turned up at the Lakes the following summer. Although the poets had, for one reason or another, seen little of him since the Nether Stowey visit, they apparently made him welcome. Announcing his arrival to Godwin, Coleridge spoke of his "profound Genius and original mind," and even planned to write a piece on Hartley ("entirely defecated from all the corpuscular hypotheses") by way of preface to an abridgment of Abraham Tucker's *Light of Nature* that Hazlitt then was contemplating.[28] With Wordsworth, newly established at Grasmere with his wife — a lady whose intellect, said De Quincey delicately, was "not of an active order" —[29] his infant

---

shines upon France," he bitterly protested the dispersal, or return, of the treasures that Napoleon had gathered in the Louvre.

son, and Dorothy, Hazlitt's relations were also very cordial. The poet read to him from his unpublished work; * the two sailed on Grasmere Lake [30] and tramped the hills together; [31] and if we may believe De Quincey [32] (who was not there) the visitor even asked Dorothy to marry him — which would have been an interesting if implausible match. But painting was what had brought him to the Lakes, and he worked hard at it, with the poets and their children as his subjects and Titian as his model. [33] According to Southey, who arrived at Keswick in the early fall, [34] the results were anything but gratifying. About the portraits of the children he says nothing, † but although at first he liked the one of Coleridge ("said to be in Titian's manner") which Sir George Beaumont had commissioned, [35] he eventually decided that it made the poet look as if he were on trial "and certainly had stolen the horse." [36] Conceding that Coleridge's face was "absolutely impracticable" for a painter, Wordsworth none the less thought that Hazlitt's portrait was too "dolorous and funereal," [37] and Dorothy concurred. "I thought of Coleridge dying," she told Lady Beaumont, "and not merely dying, but dying of sorrow and raised up upon his bed to take a last farewell of his Friends." [38] As for the portrait of Wordsworth — which, said Southey, seemed to show the subject "At the gallows — deeply affected by his deserved fate — yet determined to die like a man" [39] — it was so unsatisfactory that Hazlitt himself destroyed it.‡

If his second (and last) visit with the poets was a dubious professional success, it was a disaster otherwise. Significantly, it is Coleridge who tells us most about its failure. "Hazlitt to feelings of Anger & Hatred Phosphorous," he confided to his notebook, "—it is but to open the Cork, & it flames — but to Love & serviceable Friendship, let them, like Nebuchadnezzer, heat the Furnace with a 7 fold Heat, this Triune Shadrach, Meshach, Abednego, will shiver in the midst of it." [40] By the fall, after the poets had returned from a tragi-comic tour of Scotland and Hazlitt from a trip to Manchester, [41] the bonds of friendship had worn

* Including a passage from *The Borderers* (ll. 1539–1544) which, to Wordsworth's astonishment (*Poetical Works*, p. 719), Hazlitt remembered well enough to misquote (11.92) almost twenty-five years later.

† Hazlitt was still tinkering with Hartley Coleridge's portrait in October (Griggs, II, 1004) and with the Wordsworth infant's — of which Howe (*Life*, p. 395) was apparently unaware — the following spring. See Wordsworth, *Later Years*, III, 1349.

‡ *Memoirs*, I, 103n; cf. Frances Blanshard, *Portraits of Wordsworth* (1959), pp. 43–46, 142. The present whereabouts of these pictures painted at the Lakes in 1803 is unknown. Apart from the famous portrait of Lamb now in the National Portrait Gallery presumably all of Hazlitt's extant pictures — some of them in a very dilapidated state — are preserved in the Maidstone Museum. The "lying landscapes, filched from old rusty Titians," that Lamb made jokes about in 1806 (Lucas, II, 5) have apparently disappeared. See *Memoirs*, I, xvi; *Life*, p. 395.

very thin indeed. By then Coleridge had come to think of the visitor as a bright but sinister freak with "singularly repulsive" manners and a vicious code of morals. To Tom Wedgwood, who had asked about Hazlitt's qualifications as a companion on a projected Continental junket, he wrote that despite the painter's intellectual and artistic gifts and his endearing ways with children he was

jealous, gloomy & of an irritable Pride — & addicted to women, as objects of sexual Indulgence. With all this, there is much good in him — he is disinterested, an enthusiastic Lover of the great men, who have been before us — he says things that are his own in a way of his own — & tho' from habitual Shyness & the Outside & bearskin at least of misanthropy, he is strangely confused & dark in his conversation & delivers himself of almost all his conceptions with a Forceps, yet he says more than any man, I ever knew, yourself only excepted, that is his own in a way of his own — & oftentimes when he has warmed his mind, & the synovial juice has come out & spread over his joints, he will gallop for half an hour together with real Eloquence. He sends well-headed & well-feathered Thoughts straight forwards to the mark with a Twang of the Bow-string. — If you could recommend him, as a Portrait-painter, I should be glad. To be your Companion he is, in my opinion, utterly unfit. His own Health is fitful.[42]

As the event proved, these harsh remarks, delivered "most freely *imo ex corde*," were justified, for by the time that Hazlitt left the Lakes a few weeks later * he had not only offended Sir George Beaumont (a potential benefactor) and quarreled again with Wordsworth "in Rage & Hatred, self-projected," [43] but he had also got himself into a scrape that, in retrospect at least, the poets looked upon as shameful. What they thought about it at the time is not known; and since Hazlitt's only allusion to the episode is a jocular description, written many years later, of a certain kind of low-bred woman who misconstrues her swain's advances,† it is hard to say just how culpable he was. When, in 1815, Wordsworth was so much vexed by Hazlitt's comments on *The Excursion* that he saw fit to resurrect the story, he made it sound as bad as possible. Characteristically, Lamb used Wordsworth's gossip as the occasion for a pun,‡ but Crabb Robinson, also characteristically, embalmed it in his diary, and for want of something better we must follow his account:

* As certain dated entries (nos. 1610, 1619) in Coleridge's *Notebooks* show, Hazlitt was still at Keswick in late October, but when Southey wrote to Richard Duppa on December 14 (*Life and Correspondence,* p. 167) he implies that he had gone.
† 8.288. Hazlitt's various unflattering comments on the morals of country people, most notably those in his review of *The Excursion* (19.21-24), perhaps also derive from his escapade at Keswick. In his *Reply* to Malthus (1.237) he contrasts the "extreme licentiousness" of Lancashire rustics with the purity of those in Westmorland. See "Character of Country People," 17.66-71.
‡ Lucas, II, 146. From the date of this letter (28 December 1814) in which Lamb comments on Hazlitt's escapade it is clear that Wordsworth had begun to spread the story even before he came down to London in the spring of 1815.

PICTURES

It appears that Hazlitt, when at Keswick, narrowly escaped being ducked by the populace, and probably sent to prison for some gross attacks on women. (He even whipped one woman, *more puerorum,* for not yielding to his wishes.) The populace were incensed against him and pursued him, but he escaped to Wordsworth, who took him into his house at midnight, gave him clothes and money (from three to five pounds). Since that time Wordsworth, though he never refused to meet Hazlitt when by accident they came together, did not choose that with his knowledge he should be invited.*

Having launched the story on its rounds, Wordsworth went home again to Grasmere, but a year later — Hazlitt having meanwhile mounted his campaign against the poets for their political apostasy — Coleridge came forward with his version of the episode. Since he had befriended Hazlitt "for several years with the most improvident kindness when he was utterly friendless," he had been dismayed by the "loathsome" episode at Keswick, he said; but rather than expose himself to fresh slanders by his former friend, he would "submit to the annoyance as the appropriate punishment of that weak good nature and that disposition to overvalue Talent, which put it in the power of such a Wretch to sign and seal all his other vices with ingratitude." [44] A few months later, however, he was moved to embellish this account with new details for Francis Wrangham's benefit: not only had he given Hazlitt all the money he had in the world, he said, but even "the very Shoes off my feet to enable him to escape over the mountains." [45] Meanwhile, back in Keswick, Sara Coleridge was reporting to Tom Poole that "some person has taken up this tale" and that Wordsworth was annoyed to find his name "connected with the thing in any way." [46] He was not sufficiently annoyed to let the matter drop, however, for in 1824 he provided Benjamin Robert Haydon with a fresh account of Hazlitt's "licentious conduct" of some twenty years before: "No woman could walk after dark, for 'his Satyr & *beastly* appetites,' " he recalled. "Some girl called him a black-faced rascal, when Hazlitt enraged pushed her down, '& because, Sir,' said Wordsworth, 'she refused to gratify his abominable & devilish propensities,' he lifted up her petticoats & *smote* her on *the bottom.*" [47]

Although Hazlitt was so "excessively shy" when Crabb Robinson met him in 1799 that all the women teased him, [48] even then the violent sexual passion one day to be revealed in *Liber Amoris* was probably gathering force. Four years later, as we have seen, Coleridge found his

---

* I, 169f. That Hazlitt's escapade was a topic of discussion in the Wordsworth household before the poet publicized it is shown by an allusion in a letter from Mary Wordsworth to her sister-in-law Dorothy on 29 October 1814 (*Letters of Mary Wordsworth* [ed. Mary E. Burton, 1958], p. 24): speaking of Hazlitt's acid remarks about country people in his review of *The Excursion* (19.21–24) she says that "a pretty comment upon these opinions would be to relate the story of the critics departure for [?from] this unaccommodating country."

Wordsworth's Account of Hazlitt's Escapade at Keswick in 1803
From Haydon's Diary, 29 March 1824

morals shocking. It is altogether probable that a man so passionate and maladroit as he would have cut a sorry figure as a suitor, and that his conduct at the Lakes was odd. In retrospect, however, it perhaps seemed odder than it was, and although the poets' stories were clearly based on fact, they just as clearly lost nothing in the telling. Coleridge, the compulsive letter-writer who had no secrets from his correspondents, said nothing at the time of Hazlitt's misadventures; * and although neither Southey (to whom Coleridge later ascribed a big part in rescuing the "Wretch" from the angry rustics) [49] nor Wordsworth (who wrote to Hazlitt a very friendly letter shortly after he had left the Lakes) [50] even mentioned the affair, with the passing years their opinions no doubt changed. As early as 1807 Hazlitt told Godwin that he had "committed four or five riots" in Wordsworth's and Coleridge's behalf, and all the thanks he ever got for his "zeal in their favour was some of the last indignities that can be put upon any person. In my list of friends it has always been my good luck to come in like the tail of an etc. & to subsist only upon sufferance." [51] A year later Wordsworth was intensely

* There is possibly a veiled allusion to Hazlitt's escapade in a letter that Coleridge wrote to his wife in January 1804 (Griggs, II, 1024): "perhaps dear Southey will be so kind as to overlook the man, & to satisfy himself that the Pictures will receive no harm, as far as the Packing goes."

vexed to encounter Hazlitt at the Lambs,[52] and since it was presumably about this time that his former friend began to seem to him a "fiend"[53] it is hardly surprising that after 1810, so far as we know, the two men never met again.*

Hazlitt's inglorious departure from the Lakes in 1803 may be said to stand as a kind of coda to his youth. By then he must have known that he would never rival Titian, and even if he did not promptly fling away his pencil in despair at having failed "to engraft Italian art on English nature,"[54] he none the less began to recognize the limits of his modest talent and to cast about for other ways to make a living. When we hear of him again he is trying once again to write and so, at the age of twenty-six, stumbling toward his real vocation.

THE *ESSAY*

Writing is a lonely trade, and apart from Hazlitt's new intimacy with the Lambs and his marriage to their friend Sarah Stoddart his life from 1804 to 1812 was punctuated mainly by the books that mark his progress as a hack. "Generally," he told his fiancée in 1808, he just sat by the fire and thought.[1] After a decade of gestation, *An Essay on the Principles of Human Action* came to birth in 1805, and in 1806 Pitt's death and Fox's brief return to power provided the occasion for *Free Thoughts on Public Affairs,* an earnest, unread pamphlet urging peace with France. Stepping up his pace, he produced three books in 1807: an abridgment of Abraham Tucker's *Light of Nature* (the project that Coleridge had endorsed four years before),[2] then a big anthology, with elaborate notes, of Parliamentary speeches since the time of Charles I, and finally an angry counterblast to Malthus. Thereafter courtship and marriage provided a hiatus, but at the end of 1809 Godwin published his *New and Improved Grammar of the English Tongue* and helped secure for him the commission to put together a book on Holcroft that, though completed by the start of 1810, was not published until six years later. Such drudgery having failed to make him rich or famous or even solvent, he turned again to painting, and when that too failed he tried another tack with a set of lectures on English philosophy at the Russell Institution in the early months of 1812. Although a qualified success at best, these

---

* Although Howe (*Life,* p. 102) is probably right in suggesting that Wordsworth's and Hazlitt's unexpected meeting in April 1808 was their last (*Middle Years,* I, 196f.), Godwin's diary records a large supper-party at the Lambs' on 9 October 1810 when both Hazlitt and Dorothy Wordsworth were present.

lectures proved to be the "one more push" [3] that closed his years of random, fruitless effort. Six months later he declined into a journalist, and thus, having failed at everything that he had ever tried, at thirty-five he found his true vocation.

In Hazlitt's own mature opinion the most significant event of these uneventful years was the anonymous publication, in the summer of 1805, of his first and favorite book, the essay on benevolence that he had tried and failed at least a dozen times to finish. A hitherto unpublished letter shows that the fiasco at the Lakes in the fall of 1803 had forced him back to Wem, and that he was eager to escape:

> Wem in Shropshire
> December 29

Dear Sir,

> I should think it an essential service if you could procure me 3, or 4 pictures to do at 5 guineas each among any of your friends, or acquaintance in London. I am merely anxious about such a number as would clear my expences for board, & lodging for a month, or six weeks' stay in town. If you think there is any chance of this, & would let me know, I would send a picture of my father which I was to send to my brother to town immediately, which you might either see there, or it could be left at your house. I remain your obliged friend, & servant

> W. Hazlitt *

What came of this request we do not know, but it is certain that the *Essay* was completed in the months that followed. When Hazlitt did turn up in London in July 1804 it was to find a publisher, and since he promptly called on Godwin for help that Godwin promptly gave we may suppose that Joseph Johnson's decision to print the "dry, tough, metaphysical *choke-pear*" [4] was based at least in part on Godwin's intercession.†

Although copies were dispatched to Coleridge at the Lakes,[5] to Mackintosh in Bombay,[6] and no doubt to others thought strong enough to digest such hardy fare, the book, as its author later said, "fell still-born

* ALS, Abinger Collection. Although not dated as to year, this letter may be confidently assigned to 1803. The recipient, who is not named, was almost surely Godwin. Hazlitt's picture of his father — and he painted several — was probably the one shown at the 1802 Royal Academy exhibition at Somerset House (8.13).

† Here as elsewhere Godwin's diary is extremely useful. Having dined with the philosopher on 22 March 1803, before going to the Lakes, Hazlitt disappears from the diary for sixteen months. His son said (*Literary Remains*, I, lii) that the *Essay* was completed in 1804, and the fact that Hazlitt's first two calls on Godwin in more than a year (25 and 28 July 1804) were followed three days later by Godwin's "Call on Johnson (Hazlit)" shows the sequence of events. In October 1805 the *Edinburgh Review* (VII, 255) listed the *Essay* among the "New Publications" that had appeared since July. Many years later Crabb Robinson (I, 6) recalled that his brother Anthony "procured" for Hazlitt "his first job by inducing Johnson to publish his first work — *The Eloquence of the British Senate*," but the imprecision may perhaps be attributed to an old man's failing memory. Elsewhere (I, 386f.) Robinson claims that he himself "assisted" Hazlitt to "find a publisher for his first book."

from the press." * Mackintosh, "even amid the enervating heat of Hindostan," found strength to read the work, or at any rate to acknowledge its receipt,† but from Coleridge came no word, it seems, and his silence must have been disturbing. At Nether Stowey he had applauded Hazlitt's views on ethics and urged their publication, for he then thought that the boy had "guts" in his brains and would surely make his name if he ever found a "language" for his thoughts."⁷ For such encouragement at such a time Hazlitt's debt was large, and Coleridge's great and supple mind, as he never tired of saying, was a major influence in his life. None the less, there is no reason to doubt that he regarded his "discovery" as his own, and therefore for Coleridge to claim, as De Quincey says he claimed,‡ that he had suggested everything "important" in the book was bound to nettle Hazlitt. The two would meet from time to time in later years, but after Coleridge had become an ardent Tory friendship was no longer possible and even civility was something of a strain. Twelve years after the publication of the *Essay* Coleridge at long last alluded, in his second *Lay Sermon,* to its author's "ability and originality," ⁸ whereupon Hazlitt scorned the comment as a "hard-earned, extorted, unlooked for, despaired of, thankless acknowledgement, in a fag-end note of an unreadable performance." ⁹ As he said in 1820, Coleridge did not rejoice in the success of his disciples.

> He looks upon what he nicknames *a man of genius,* but as the breath of his nostrils, and the clay in the potter's hands. If any such inert, unconscious mass, under the fostering care of the modern Prometheus, is kindled into life, — begins to see, speak, and move, so as to attract the notice of other people, — our jealous patroniser of latent worth in that case throws aside, scorns, and hates his own handy-work; and deserts his intellectual offspring from the moment they can go alone and shift for themselves.¹⁰

Although Hazlitt later realized that "from speculative pursuits we must be satisfied with speculative benefits," ¹¹ the publication of his book in 1805 must have been a lift for his morale. For the first time he had done what he set out to do, and thereafter he felt "a certain weight and tightness" taken from his heart.¹² He had taught himself that "the spirit of philosophy consists in having the power to think, and patience to

---

* 17.312. A writer for the *Annual Review* (IV [1805], 657–664), although respectful of its author's "acuteness, discrimination, and *analytical* talent," suggested delicately that the *Essay* offered nothing new. A critic for the *Critical Review* (IX [1806], 413–416) apparently read only enough of Hazlitt's book to take exception to his style.

† 11.102; cf. George Gilfillan, *Sketches of Modern Literature (A Gallery of Literary Portraits),* I (1846), 63. In view of Hazlitt's comments on the Lincoln's Inn lectures (1.63f., 67n, 76) it is remarkable that Mackintosh wrote to him at all.

‡ XI, 351f.; cf. II, 344; III, 82. In 1816 Coleridge told Crabb Robinson (I, 200) that Hazlitt had pilfered from Lamb all the good things in his journalism, and in his later years he made the charge again (*Table Talk,* p. 194).

wait for the result," [13] and consequently he rejoiced, though with few or none for company, at having won his spurs with a "metaphysical discovery, supported by a continuous and severe train of reasoning, nearly as subtle and original as anything in Hume or Berkeley." [14] It is well that he admired the contents of the book, for there was nothing in its style that could give him satisfaction. Apart from one passage [15] later praised by Southey as "something between the manner of Milton's prose-works and Jeremy Taylor" [16] the *Essay* is so dry and husky that it could have led its author nowhere as a writer. Acknowledging this fact after he had made his reputation, Hazlitt still insisted that it was his most important book, and he lost no chance to publicize its doctrines. He dredged them up again for his preface to *The Light of Nature* in 1807 [17] and for the lectures on philosophy five years later; [18] thereafter he recast them twice for more popular consumption, first in an impassioned *apologia* addressed to William Gifford in 1819 [19] and again in a long piece that the *New Monthly Magazine* printed not long before his death. [20] His first awkward little book does not contain all he had to say about politics and art and morals, but its affinity with his later and more accomplished work is, as we shall see, apparent everywhere. Naturally, therefore, he always held it in esteem.

In one sense the *Essay* is an occasional book, prompted by a set of special circumstances and contrived to serve a special need. Committed to certain ethical and political ideals that by 1800 had become objects of derision, Hazlitt wrote not to argue politics but to raise an old debate to a new and higher plane. Pitt and the Tories had proscribed reform as a luxury in a time of peril, but men of a more speculative turn had found other reasons for rejecting the various innovations that reformers wanted. Mackintosh, the metaphysician, had cited Locke and Hartley to prove disinterested social action chimerical; Parr, the Christian moralist, had balked at Godwin's morals and denounced his ethics as hostile to revealed religion; Malthus, the man of social science, had shown that by nature's stern decree a concern for other people's hunger and disease brings on a fearful retribution. Representing different things and working from different motives, these men tended to agree that any thorough-going change of British institutions would be both dangerous and unwise.

Although in his *Essay* Hazlitt does not deal with politics directly he tries to make a new and better case for man's essential goodness and thus, inferentially, to counter such objections to reform. In arguing that a disinterested attachment to things outside ourselves is the primary source of human action he takes an inconspicuous place — despite his assertions of originality — at the end of a distinguished line of eighteenth-century moralists committed to benevolence. Thus his *Essay* may be read as the beginning of his long campaign against the arrogant deceits of the "modern philosophy" that, as he thought, flouts common sense, ignores our complex mental operations, and presents a sterile, mechanistic view of man and nature. Although it is regrettable that we have no fuller records of his "metaphysical argument" with Wordsworth, in 1798, about "modern books of moral philosophy" [21] and of their renewed discussion at the Lakes in 1803,[22] Hazlitt's published work compels the inference that he had been a kind of vitalist from the start. The philosophical doctrine that was derived from Hobbes and exemplified in Locke's epistemology, Hartley's psychology of association, Helvetius' mechanism, and Godwin's austere rationalism had repelled him, it would seem, ever since his youth. Priestley's brisk necessitarian theology, Locke and Hartley, Godwin and Helvetius, had been the intellectual fare at Hackney, and the *Essay* — which had its origins there — shows that he must have found it hard to swallow. No philosophy that turned thought into sensation, morality into pleasure, and action into mechanical impulse [23] could engage his dark and moody sensibility. The aridities of eighteenth-century materialism held no charm for a boy who spent two delicious years in weeping with Rousseau [24] and throbbing at the sorrows of Werther; and therefore it is not surprising that his first attempt at systematic thought was to justify his notion of how people really feel and think and act.

Later, in his lectures on philosophy and then more variously in the essays of his last decade, Hazlitt broadened his attack on mechanism, but in his first book he centered on its ethics. Even that required a certain valor, for it meant that he had to deal with Hobbes, the most formidable of the moderns and a man whose strength of mind he respected deeply. As he conceded later, "there is an air of grandeur in the stern confidence with which he stands alone in the world of his own opinions, regardless of his contemporaries, and conscious that he is the founder of a new race of thinkers." [25] To the dismay of conventional moralists, Hobbes had jeopardized almost all of man's alleged distinctions. If, as he had tried to prove, our conduct follows natural "laws" which are a set of mechanistic forces devoid of moral purpose, then virtue is a concept without meaning and ethics is a name for self-deception. Knowing nothing but his own sensations, dominated by a lust for power, and governed by a sense of fear, man, said Hobbes, is a creature so incapable of any action not centered on himself that even when he seems to think of others he merely gratifies himself and feeds his self-esteem.

The success with which these views were urged may be gauged by both the disciples whom Hobbes won and the consternation that he caused: for if Mandeville, La Rochefoucauld, Condillac, and others built their work upon his doctrine, there were also able men who challenged him. Dismay, defiance, and finally intelligent reconstruction became the order of the day; and if the timid and the merely orthodox were filled with indignation at Hobbes's view of man, better thinkers — Shaftesbury, Butler, and the rest — began to reconstruct their moral theory. Abandoning the Cambridge Platonists' notion of universal reason as the source and test of human action (for the sensationalists, led by Locke, had reduced reason to a mere reflective power), they advocated "moral sense" or feeling as the sign of man's humanity, and their ethic, with its implication for reform, grew to be a potent force in eighteenth-century thought. It also left its mark on Hazlitt, whose *Essay* is, among other things, yet another contribution to the debate on self-love and benevolence that Hobbes had started a century and a half before.

Hazlitt was sure that Hobbes was wrong, but except perhaps in Bishop Butler's sermons (which he discussed with Coleridge in 1798) * he had found no satisfactory effort to challenge his bad eminence; and since, as he thought, the advocates of both intuitional ethics and revealed religion had proved to be unequal to the task, he himself took on the job. Shaftesbury's soothing talk about man's moral sense was not enough to answer Hobbes, he said, because it was only a flattering hypothesis.[26] In his influential *Theory of Moral Sentiments* (1759) Adam Smith (once the elder Hazlitt's teacher at Glasgow) had argued that the sight of others' pain prompts us to associate it with troubles of our own, and so compels our sympathy; but all this tells us nothing about self-love or benevolence or anything else, said Hazlitt, except the "unending game of battledore and shuttle-cock kept up between the nerves and muscles." † When Joseph Fawcett explained that we should sympathize with others because the Bible tells us to, the "vigorous and

* 17.113f. As a boy Hazlitt had read (and disliked) Butler's famed *Analogy*, but he was unacquainted with the sermons; and when he heard of them from Coleridge he had already made the "discovery" that even then he was eager but unable to explain (9.3f., 11.32, 17.114). Not until thirty years had passed did he grant (20.163) that Butler was the first to give a "satisfactory" answer to the Hobbesians by proving that when one feels affection or desire or love he need not feel it only toward himself. For a sampling of Hazlitt's many respectful allusions to Butler see 1,50 n, 2.24f., 17.121.

† 1.80. See 1.86: "It is absurd to say that in compassionating the distress of others we are only affected by our own pain or uneasiness, since their very pain arises from our compassion. It is putting the effect before the cause."

invincible benevolence" that he urged upon Dissenters was *au fond* authoritarian.[27] Although Godwin, convinced like all reformers that man should act disinterestedly, devoted an entire chapter in *Political Justice* [28] to adjudicating the claims of self-love and benevolence, his ethic, however rarefied and rational, was a kind of hedonism. He who "loses the view of personal regards in the greater objects that engross his attention," Godwin had intoned, "who, from motives of benevolence, sits loose to life and all its pleasures, and is ready, without a sigh, to sacrifice them to the public good, has an uncommonly exquisite source of happiness." [29] Such pronouncements mark no advance whatever on Abraham Tucker's notion that benevolence, conceived as "a diffused love to the whole species," works to man's advantage because it provides a superior kind of "satisfaction." [30] In short, concluded Hazlitt, to think kindly of one's fellows and hope that they would thrive, as shoals of eighteenth-century moralists had urged, was not enough to shake Hobbes's steely logic.

Therefore he refuses aid from intuitional, Christian, or hedonistic morals. Accepting the psychology of the sensationalists (the only philosophers whose work he really knew) and conceding that the mind, with no innate ideas, works only on the data of sensation, he sets out to prove that our alleged capacity for disinterested behavior is neither a sentimental fraud nor a "moral feeling" different from other kinds of intellection, but a "natural" mode of action. The proof of this conviction — the "discovery" which he called his most memorable achievement — may be quickly summarized. Professing himself "utterly unable" to comprehend the nature of perception or the source of our ideas,[31] he none the less was certain that our responses to things outside the mind, which prompt aversion or desire, may be analyzed. If they concern the past they are objects of memory; if the present, of sensation; if the future, of imagination. The first two faculties (like reason, by means of which, as Locke had proved, we merely "reflect upon and compare our ideas") [32] cater to our own wants and needs, and, centering on ourselves, they constitute our "personal identity"; but the third, pointing to the future, has no subjective reference. Through it we are disengaged and liberated, as it were, and because we have no "distinct faculty" giving us "a direct present interest in future sensations" we are enabled to transcend our own identities and escape the ties of self.

The imagination, by means of which alone I can anticipate future objects, or be interested in them, must carry me out of myself into the feelings of others by one and the same process by which I am thrown forward as it were into my future being, and interested in it. I could not love myself, if I were not capable of loving others. Self-love, used in this sense, is in it's [*sic*] fundamental principle the same with disinterested benevolence.[33]

It may seem odd that Hazlitt, for whom subjectivism was a creed, was so eager to escape from self. A man's commitment to his own beliefs and even prejudices ought to be inviolable, he thought; and he himself exemplified the valor, egotism, and indifference to the world's opinion that his tough Dissenter's code comprised. But it was, perhaps, because of this obsession with the claims of self that he required some sort of counterbalance, and in his great "discovery," as he regarded it, he showed that one's duty to oneself might be reconciled with larger human interests. Although the residue of what a man has known and done and suffered — in other words, that which links him with the past — constitutes, he thought, his identity and character, that which lies ahead or that which he has not assimilated by experience cannot be anchored to his private needs and fears. Such things are the objects of his sympathetic intuition; he perceives them by imagination, and imagination is the bridge by which he surmounts habit and self-interest to identify himself with others. "Thrown forward," as it were, into another form of being, he enlarges and expands his range of feeling, and thus, ultimately, he attains the freest and most inclusive form of knowledge. "I do not *will* that to be which already exists as an object of sense, nor that to have been which has already existed, and is become an object of memory. . . . The only proper objects of voluntary action are (by necessity) future events: these can excite no possible interest in the mind but by means of the imagination; and these make the same direct appeal to that faculty whether they relate to ourselves, or others." [34]

❖　❖　❖

This doctrine of the sympathetic imagination, which goes back, in embryo, at least to Shaftesbury's implied connection between taste and morality as both depending on "internal" sense, was a commonplace in eighteenth-century thought.[35] Not only had reformers found it useful, but by Hazlitt's time it had been captured by the aestheticians. Man's alleged ability to put himself in another's situation and to feel as others feel was named by Adam Smith the foundation of his ethics, and the same faculty that he cited as the source of moral action was said by other Scottish theorists to be the poet's chief distinction. In such influential works as Alexander Gerard's *Essay on Genius* (1774) and Hugh Blair's *Lectures on Rhetoric and Belles Lettres* (1783) the poet is endowed with an instinctive "sensibility" by means of which he throws himself into his subject and identifies himself with it, thus rising over mere description to achieve a fuller and more "natural" truth. Shakespeare, it was said, was the supreme example of such imaginative power. He wrote his plays not by viewing life as a spectator or by relying solely on the facts of observation, but by projecting himself into the minds of other men; consequently his triumph was one of passion and sympathetic interest rather than of reason, art, or calculation.

If, then, the doctrine of the sympathetic imagination was not original with Hazlitt, it was none the less the anchor of his later thought on politics and art and morals, and in the history of critical theory he stands as its most imposing advocate. In 1805, when his main concern was politics and his purpose as a writer was expository, he did not press the application of his theory, but its significance was clear. The imagination, conceived as intuition, is seen to be the faculty by which we rise to a level of "disinterested benevolence" essential to reform, and thus reform itself acquires a new prestige. When our concern for something or somebody beyond our selfish interests is regarded as a "natural" mode of intellection rather than a sentimental aberration from common sense and prudence, and when this concern finds expression in political behavior, the results are very large. Similarly in moral and aesthetic theory: knowledge that is cold, discursive, and prudential has a certain value, Hazlitt says, but art and moral action work through sympathy, and "the boundary of our sympathy is a circle which enlarges itself according to its propulsion from the centre — the heart." [36] Reason and other kinds of "formal" cerebration show us how to make distinctions, to measure and divide, and to murder in order to dissect; but imagination, the faculty that "accumulates" and aggrandizes,[37] is "an *associating* principle" [38] that obliterates our sense of self and leads us to a larger knowledge. "To relinquish a profitable delusion, and embrace the dowerless truth" requires the moral tact that imagination generates, and so does the ability to recognize the power of nature as nature is revealed in art.[39]

For Hazlitt, as for most Romantic critics, imagination was a crucial word. Sometimes he seems to mean by it a molding and creative power by which the artist, eschewing mere representation, constructs another nature (as Sir Philip Sidney said) to satisfy his own desires — a Freudian *Wunschbild* to objectify his secret longings.[40] Sometimes he defines it as association, through which we discover "something similar in things generally alike, or with like feelings attached to them." [41] Sometimes it appears to be a conveying power, which permits the man of genius (like Dante or Milton) to carry over "a given feeling into other situations" and thus to stamp his "strength and depth of feeling" on unrelated things.[42]

But most consistently and characteristically Hazlitt speaks of imagination as the "sympathetic" and intuitive faculty by which we are linked with other things or people, with the result that our perceptions are deepened and enlarged. There is, therefore, a necessary relation between art and morals. "The largest hearts have the soundest understandings: and he is the truest philosopher who can forget himself." [43] Hazlitt himself had learned in trying to paint an old woman's wrinkled face that the artist is, or should be, captured by his subject,[44] and when he turned to criticism he made this commitment to what lies outside the artist's self the test of all great art. Raphael and Scott and Shakespeare not only soar beyond their own "petty, narrow, and bigotted prejudices," [45] but they enable us to do the same. They expand our spectrum of experience and teach us, not by precept but example, to share their passion for the truth of things. "Shakespear was in one sense the least moral of all writers; for morality (commonly so called) is made up of antipathies; and his talent consisted in sympathy with human nature, in all its shapes, degrees, depressions, and elevations. . . . He was a moralist in the same sense in which nature is one. He taught what he had learnt from her. He shewed the greatest knowledge of humanity with the greatest fellow-feeling for it." [46]

This conviction, variously expressed, underlies many of Hazlitt's critical pronouncements. What Keats called "the wordsworthian or egotistical sublime" — as distinguished from his Hazlittian conception of the "camelion Poet" who has no "Identity" or "self" [47] — is one of Hazlitt's recurrent themes: Wordsworth's "intellectual egotism," he said, was "the bane of his talents and of his public principles," [48] and his incapacity for a "venturous magnanimity" confined him, despite his extraordinary power, to the second rank of genius.[49] Enraptured by his subjects, the great artist — pictorial or literary — knows that whatever checks "the genial expansion of the moral sentiments and social affections, must lead to a cold and dry abstraction," [50] whereas art means passion and involvement. Thus Scott's *absence of egotism* [51] is the secret of his strength, and Shakespeare, "the Proteus of human intellect," shows that the "test and triumph" of the highest genius is the ability to transcend his own identity.[52] Since imagination is "another name for an interest in things out of ourselves, which must naturally run counter to our own," [53] both the "homage" that we pay to art and the concern we have for others are tokens of its power. "The excellence that we feel, we participate in as if it were our own — it becomes ours by transfusion of mind — it is instilled into our hearts — it mingles with our blood." [54] (When Hazlitt writes like this one tends to think of Keats: "If a Sparrow come before my Window," he told Bailey, "I take part in its existince and pick about the Gravel.") [55]

❖   ❖   ❖

Such comments, gleaned mainly from Hazlitt's later work, express in various ways his discontent with the "modern philosophy" that had dominated later eighteenth-century thought; but that they mark no radical change from his opinions as a youth is made clear by the "Remarks on the Systems of Hartley and Helvetius" appended to the *Essay* as a kind of coda. Dealing there with the psychology of association and the ethics of self-interest, two cardinal points of *avant-garde* philosophy, he shows, at the start of his career, how deeply he distrusted any mechanistic explanation of human thought and action. The workings of the human mind were a subject about which, as many people seemed to think, David Hartley's *Observations on Man* (1749) had been the final word. In 1775 Priestley's abridgment of that famous book had ensured its popularity among the Unitarians, and as Wordsworth's early poems and Coleridge's early letters show, its prestige continued very high. In 1794, announcing to his new friend Southey that thought itself was corporeal and that it worked through motion, Coleridge explained that he understood these matters "as well almost as Hartley himself," [56] and two years later he named his first-born after the great philosopher whom he had already saluted poetically for marking "the ideal tribes / Up to the fine fibres through the sentient brain." [57] Although at Hackney Hazlitt had stayed up after hours to read Hartley [58] (probably in Priestley's version), we may infer that his response was muted. As early as 1798 he was voicing doubts about the doctrine of association, [59] and by 1803 he had presumably persuaded Coleridge — whose early views had meanwhile changed * — to analyze Hartley's theory by way of preface to his abridgment of Tucker's *Light of Nature*. [60] Although this project was postponed (and Coleridge's contribution abandoned altogether), two years later, in the appendix to his *Essay*, Hazlitt finally found a way to express his views on Hartley.

---

* As late as February 1801 Coleridge still ranked Berkeley, Butler, and Hartley as the "only three *great* Metaphysicians which this Country *has* produced" (Griggs, II, 703), but a month later he told Tom Poole that he had "overthrown the doctrine of Association, as taught by Hartley, and with it all the irreligious metaphysics of modern Infidels" (*ibid.*, II, 706). On Coleridge's escape, in the spring of 1801, from what he regarded as the impasse of mechanism see his important letters to Poole and Josiah Wade in Griggs, II, 704–713; John Shawcross' introduction to *Biographia Literaria*, I, xxix ff.; J. H. Muirhead, *Coleridge as Philosopher* (1930), pp. 40–59; R. J. White (ed.), *The Political Thought of S. T. Coleridge* (1938), p. 21. Coleridge himself devoted three whole chapters (V–VII) to the subject in *Biographia Literaria*.

They were anything but cordial. The associationists, he said, were convinced that

> if any given sensation, idea, or motion be for a number of times either accompanied, or immediately followed by any other sensation, idea, or muscular motion, the recurrence of the one will afterwards mechanically give rise to that of the other.[61]

The operative word here is "mechanically," which implies that the workings of the mind are governed by the laws of matter. The notion that the primary and most general principles of thought and action were "vibrations" caused by the similarity and contiguity of external stimuli was, said Hazlitt, "absolutely false," [62] and he devoted almost fifty tortuous pages to explaining his objections. He did not deny the mind's associative or amalgamative power — indeed, his later work exemplifies it brilliantly — but he could not regard it as mechanistic in its operations. To be sure, if A is followed by B and B by C, and if B later "lapses" from the chain of linked associations, then A may either recall C directly or coalesce with it. But the "feeling" we associate with B remains, and even contributes to the final rich amalgamation. Even though we forget certain facts and things, they leave reverberations in the mind, and these, in various combinations, constitute that "series of unpremeditated conclusions" which are fused and marshaled by imagination, and which therefore defy the laws of matter.[63]

Although he was certain, then, that Hartley's mechanistic theory, which related the communication of "ideas" to "particular places in the brain" corresponding with the physical and temporal relations of things in nature, was built upon a "gratuitous supposition," [64] he himself had no final system to propose. "I stand merely on the defensive," he said. "I have no positive inferences to make, nor any novelties to bring forward, and I have only to defend a common-sense feeling against the refinements of a false philosophy." [65] This "common-sense feeling" was the conviction that if all our complex mental operations were reduced to the matter of one "vibration" setting off another there could be "no reasoning, no abstraction, no regular contrivance, no wisdom, no general sense of right and wrong, no sympathy, no foresight of any thing, in short nothing that is essential, or honourable to the human mind would be left to it." [66] To regard our thoughts and feelings as a set of linked associations deriving from "the naked impression of material objects" [67] is to deny the freedom of the mind from matter, Hazlitt said, for it ignores the fact that our ideas — whatever they are and however we acquire them — differ in degree of complexity and in kind from their constituent sensations. The fact that they are more than the sum of all their parts means that their texture and configuration somehow depend upon the operations of the mind.

If from the top of a long cold barren hill I hear the distant whistle of a thrush which seems to come up from some warm woody shelter beyond the edge of the hill, this sound coming faint over the rocks with a mingled feeling of strangeness and joy, the idea of the place about me, and the imaginary one beyond will all be combined together in such a manner in my mind as to become inseparable.[68]

Such fusion, Hazlitt says, is the work of mind, not of mechanically related "vibrations" in our sensory apparatus.

Our mental operations are too rich and dense to be charted by the quasi-scientific, quasi-mathematical jargon of a "sharpened intellect" like Hartley's.[69] Even if we could understand the "real relations" of things in nature — and it is unlikely that we ever will — we may be sure that the ideas prompted by these things are otherwise, for even though they are generated by sensation they are shaped and unified by intellection: they are not the copies of external stimuli but creations of the mind itself. The mind is more than a recording apparatus; it is a plastic, organizing power that produces new configurations from the data of experience. It works by an "inward conscious principle" that is not only the central fact of intellection but also the source of moral choice and voluntary action. Thus psychology broadens into ethics.[70]

Turning from Hartley to Helvetius, then, he restates his doctrine of benevolence as the product of imagination — that projective faculty by which we transcend the limits of sensation, time, and personality. Whereas Mackintosh, in his Lincoln's Inn lectures, "used to deny the existence of such a feeling as general benevolence or humanity, on the ground that all our affections necessarily owe their rise to particular previous associations, and [say] that they cannot exist at all unless they have been excited before in the same manner by the same objects," [71] Hazlitt refuses to concede the limitation. There is no "essential difference" in our response to the misery of a hungry child who is our own and to one we never saw before, he says, and any attempt "to reason us out of a sense of right and wrong and make men believe that they can only feel for themselves, or their immediate connections is not only an indecent but a very bungling piece of sophistry." [72] If the mechanists were right, then man would truly be a selfish animal, incapable of entertaining any idea relating to himself or others except as it is sanctioned by association and rooted in his past experience. But they are wrong, and therefore when Adam Smith argues that compassion is the memory of our old pains prompted by the sight of others in distress he tries to explain morality as a thing of nerves and muscles.[73] Similarly, when Hobbes and his descendants insist that "in wishing to relieve the distresses of others we only wish to remove the uneasiness which pity creates in our own minds" [74] they ignore our capacity for disinterested behavior. All such advocates of self-interest fail to recognize the cardinal fact that man is a voluntary agent whose feelings, actions, and desires are not centered wholly in his own experience. Benevolence, says Hazlitt, means nothing more than an "immediate sympathy with the feelings of others," [75] and because sympathy — which even the mechanists concede — refers to and determines future action, it cannot be rooted in association. My compassion for another's wound is in all ways different from the pain that I would feel if I myself were wounded.

The one is an affair of sensation, the other is entirely an affair of imagination. My love of others cannot therefore be built upon the love of myself, considering this last as the effect of "physical sensibility," and the moment we resolve self-love into the rational pursuit of a remote object, it has been shewn that the same reasoning applies to both, and that the love of others has the same necessary foundation in the human mind as the love of ourselves. [76]

Although Hazlitt's labyrinthine refutation of Hartley and Helvetius accounts for some of the dullest pages in his badly written book, it presents in different terms the conviction that underlies his most mature and artful work. His repudiation of mechanistic ethics was for him, as for many others of his generation, a mark of intellectual independence. "There are moments in the life of a solitary thinker which are to him what the evening of some great victory is to the conqueror and hero," he wrote in 1805, [77] and it is clear that he regarded the completion of the *Essay* as such a moment in his own career. Although a book that no one reads with pleasure and that few would care to read at all, it enabled him to define his intellectual position, and it provided him a reservoir for the ideas, or at any rate the emotions and convictions, that would serve him to the end. However desiccated, dull, and hard, it therefore retains something of the value that he himself ascribed to it. As he said later of Shakespeare and *King Lear,* it is there that he is most in earnest. As he struggles to express the role of intuition and imagination, passion and feeling, in man's moral and intellectual life he converts a set of commonplaces into his own convictions, and so we get a glimpse, at least, of the kind of writer he would one day be.

THE BUSY HACK

Hazlitt's intimacy with Charles and Mary Lamb, which coincided roughly with his debut as an author, gave a new dimension to his life. Shortly before going to the Lakes in 1803 he had met them at one of Godwin's evening parties,* and on his return from that disastrous expedition a warm and lasting friendship between them soon developed. By the end of October 1804 he was at work on the portrait of Lamb that, now enshrined in the National Portrait Gallery, is his only famous picture; [1] and, as we learn from Godwin's jottings in his diary, they were frequently together in the months that followed, sometimes at tea and whist, sometimes at dinner, and occasionally at the theater.† Better than Godwin's cryptic notes, however, is the proof of their affection in the glowing pages of Hazlitt's later work, where Charles and Mary Lamb and their friends achieve the kind of fame that only literature can give. Hazlitt cherished Lamb as "the most delightful, the most provoking, the most witty and sensible of men"; [2] and Mary, even under the shadow of her great affliction of sporadic spells of madness, he thought "as good, as sensible, and in all respects as exemplary" a woman as ever lived.[3] With him Lamb shared his love of books and pictures, and he also shared his friends, his talent for holding many men's affections being one that Hazlitt was conspicuously without. Lamb knew everybody known to Hazlitt and many more besides; and although some of their common friends like Coleridge, Wordsworth, and Southey, whom Hazlitt later ranked among his chief aversions, appear briefly if at all in "On the Conversations of Authors" and "Of Persons One Would Wish to Have Seen," the nondescript regulars at Lamb's Wednesday evening parties in Mitre Court would one day inspire some of Hazlitt's most vivacious pages.‡

"When a stranger came in, it was not asked, 'Has he written any thing?' — we were above that pedantry; but we waited to see what he could do." It was a freemasonry of impecunious wit and talent, with only

---

* The date of this important event, which Hazlitt recalls in a famous passage (17.122) and which Howe (*Life*, p. 75) puts a year too late, is fixed by Godwin's diary as 22 March 1803, when Hazlitt, Coleridge, the Lambs, the Holcrofts, and James Wollstonecraft were Godwin's guests for dinner.

† See Lucas, II, 16, 18. Their best remembered evening at the theater was, of course, that of 10 December 1806, when the Lambs, together with Hazlitt and Crabb Robinson, witnessed the failure of Charles's *Mr. H.* at Drury Lane. In 1816 Hazlitt pieced out a theatrical review for the *Examiner* with memories of that melancholy evening (18.210f.), and six years later he reworked the passage for an essay in the *London Magazine* (8.232).

‡ 12.35–38, 17.122–134. In 1812, after the Lambs had moved from Mitre Court to Inner Temple Lane, their weekly Wednesday parties were shifted to Thursday, and presently they fell off to only one a month. For a lively account of these later gatherings (in which Coleridge must have had a larger part than that assigned to him by Hazlitt) see the excerpts from John Payne Collier's diary in his edition of Coleridge's *Seven Lectures on Shakespeare and Milton* (1856), pp. xx–liii; cf. E. V. Lucas, *The Life of Charles Lamb* (1907), I, 511–534.

insipidity, affectation, and fine gentlemen made unwelcome. Then and later Hazlitt detested clubs and formal groups — the candidate for a debating society, he said, is burdened with "the lowest ambition a man can have" [4] — but the camaraderie at Lamb's was precisely to his taste. There John Rickman, clerk to the Speaker of the House, hammered out hard theories "on the anvil of his brain" while Ned Phillips, his assistant, played a deadly game of cribbage. Captain James Burney, who later took offense at Hazlitt's comments on the novels of his celebrated sister, [5] "had you at a disadvantage by never understanding you," but Coleridge, "riding the high German horse" of his transcendentalism, could talk with great effect on almost anything. James White, whose *Falstaff's Letters* was a favorite book of Lamb's, wore the halo of an author. William Ayrton and Joseph Hume, a minor civil servant, were no doubt then as later always willing to take "another friendly finishing glass." The gentle, absent-minded George Dyer, who followed learning as its shadow, read the world "like a favourite volume, only to find beauties in it." [6] Among these fellows of no particular mark or likelihood Hazlitt, steeped in metaphysics,* held a special place, and after he had married and gone away from town in 1808 Mary complained that their Wednesday evenings had lost a vital spark. "All the glory of the night . . . is at an end. Phillips makes his jokes, and there is no one to applaud him; Rickman argues, and there is no one to oppose him." [7]

But if Hazlitt was "most brilliant, most ornamental, as a Wednesday-man," said Mary, he was even better on "common days, when he dropt in after a quarrel or a fit of the glooms." [8] Because he and Lamb were so unlike, they were complementary. Hazlitt's sense of humor, it would seem, was stifled in his cradle, whereas Lamb's was perhaps his crowning glory. Hazlitt's hot republicanism must have been a bore to Lamb, whose unconcern with politics was so monumental that he cared much more about Bishop Burnet than about modern "France and Frenchmen, and the Abbé Sièyes and his constitutions." [9] On the other hand, not sharing his friend's delight in quaint, forgotten authors on "the borders of oblivion," he supposed that Lamb read obsolete theology merely "to save himself the pain of thinking," [10] but he knew — and frequently said — that the caliber of Lamb's thinking in his great essays on Hogarth and Shakespeare had been a major influence on his work. [11] To be sure, there were periods of estrangement, like that in 1814 when, as Lamb told

* See 17.131, where Hazlitt recalls having told the group at Lamb's that there were only six philosophers in modern times worthy of consideration: Hobbes, Berkeley, Butler, Hartley, Hume, Leibniz — with Jonathan Edwards ("a Massachusetts man") a possible seventh.

Wordsworth, Hazlitt "blowed us up about 6 months ago, since when the union hath snapt," [12] but the "old friendship and lasting esteem" which Hazlitt cited in dedicating to Lamb his *Characters of Shakespear's Plays* in 1817 always reunited them. Although Hazlitt's manners could be, and in later years frequently were, almost beyond belief, Lamb was loyal to the end: as Wordsworth wrote in elegiac strain, "he was good, if e'er a good Man lived!" [13]

You may find better minds in Grasmere and Keswick, Lamb told De Quincey with delicate irony, "but you must allow for us poor Londoners. Hazlitt serves for *our* purposes." * De Quincey could not tell whether such astonishing remarks were made "in jest or earnest," but that Lamb was saying what he really thought is made clear by his refusal to join the chorus of detraction in 1816, when Hazlitt had offended almost everyone. Mary's explanation (to Crabb Robinson) was that she and Charles had so few friends and pleasures they "could not afford to give up" Hazlitt; [14] and her brother, although conceding the "horrible license" of their friend's campaign against the poets, admitted to a "tough" attachment that not even his vulgarity could "quite dislocate or sever asunder. I get no conversation in London that is absolutely worth attending to but his." [15] This comment occurs in a private letter to Wordsworth (then panting for revenge), but six years later in the *London Magazine* Lamb embellished the same theme for the public's benefit. Even then, after Hazlitt's irresponsible behavior over his divorce had cut him off from those few persons not already offended by his politics, Lamb said he was glad that he had "stood well with him for fifteen years (the proudest of my life)," and at that late date he saw no reason to slacken his esteem. Despite his faults and eccentricities, Hazlitt "in his natural and healthy state" was "one of the wisest and finest spirits breathing. So far from being ashamed of that intimacy, which was betwixt us, it is my boast that I was able for so many years to have preserved it entire; and I think I shall go to my grave without finding, or expecting to find, such another companion." [16] This "magnanimous" assertion, as Hazlitt rightly called it, [17] revived a friendship that nothing could destroy; and if, as he lay dying, Hazlitt saw anything at all he saw Charles Lamb standing by his bed.

But as Hazlitt's brother John once said, no young man believes that he will ever die, [18] and in those years at Mitre Court age and death must have seemed remote. Lamb's letters to Hazlitt (then visiting at Wem) in

---

* De Quincey, III, 82f. In relating this conversation, in which Lamb even suggested that Hazlitt was "another Coleridge," De Quincey achieved what is perhaps his shortest sentence: "This I could not stand."

the spring of 1806 * are in his best familiar style, chatty about their literary projects and favorite pictures and common friends, and full of warm affection. "We miss you, as we foretold we should." [19] While Hazlitt was painting and writing in Shropshire, Lamb and Godwin were scurrying around town in search of a publisher for the abridgment of Tucker's *Light of Nature* that had finally been completed; † but for *Free Thoughts on Public Affairs*, another product of his visit to the country, the author had to make his own arrangements after he returned to London in the spring. "He is, rather imprudently, I think, printing a political pamphlet on his own account," Lamb told Wordsworth late in June, adding that "the first duty of an Author, I take it, is never to pay anything." [20] The extent of his imprudence became apparent the following winter, when Hazlitt had to "settle" with the printer; but by then, as he informed his father, the abridgment of Tucker (specimens of which the publisher Joseph Johnson had received in August) ‡ had been duly published, and he was hard at work on the biographical sketches — some of them "confounded good," he said — for *The Eloquence of the British Senate*. [21] Moreover, he was about to start the three long letters against Malthus that, following their appearance in Cobbett's *Political Register* during the spring of 1807, would be expanded into a book by the middle of the summer.§ For Hazlitt, 1807 was obviously a very busy year.

Time, which, said Hazlitt, spreads a haze and glory round all things, [22] has lent no luster to these early works, and if their author had

---

* Hazlitt's absence from London is indicated by his absence from Godwin's diary between 8 October 1805 and 24 May 1806, dates which roughly coincide with Lamb's six letters between November 10 and March 15. One of these letters, that of 7 January 1806, which was unknown to Lucas, has been printed by M. A. DeWolfe Howe in the *Spectator*, 5 August 1938, pp. 237f. It was no doubt during this visit to Wem — when, as we may infer from Lamb's ironical comments, painting occupied much of Hazlitt's time — that he executed a set of landscapes, none of which survives.

† Lucas, I, 416, 423. Lamb's two letters about Godwin's calls on Johnson are dated 15 January and 19 February 1806 — days on which Godwin recorded visits to both Johnson and Lamb.

‡ *Four Generations*, I, 96. About this time Godwin's diary records a flurry of calls by Hazlitt (August 3, 16, 22, 29, September 2, 5, 10, 13), from which we may infer that he was seeking help in revising his abridgment.

§ The list of "New Publications" in successive numbers of the *Edinburgh Review* is of help in dating the appearance of Hazlitt's early work. Although for some reason the abridgment of Tucker's book was not recorded, *Free Thoughts on Public Affairs* was listed as new in the summer of 1806 (IX, 249), and both *The Eloquence of the British Senate* and the *Reply* to Malthus as new in the summer of 1807 (XI, 236, 240). A second edition of *The Eloquence of the British Senate* appeared between January and April 1808 (XII, 265) and a third in 1812. See Keynes, pp. 10 ff.

died in 1808 they would slumber in deserved oblivion. Though hardly juvenilia, they exhibit faults and virtues in such painful disproportion that nothing but Hazlitt's wiry strength of mind relieves their tedium. In style they range from gritty exposition to the most undisciplined rhetoric, and their verbal insecurity is matched by their author's chronic inability to organize the larger forms of composition. But because even the fumbles of an artist are instructive these books require attention. For one thing, they demonstrate Hazlitt's defiant loyalty to principles that Pitt, the French Revolution, and the weight of conservative opinion had rendered generally obnoxious; for another, they, like the *Essay* of 1805, reveal some major themes that he used many times again. If in a sense they constitute his votive offering to a set of obsolete ideals, they also define the ethical and political values that would reassert themselves in his later work. Following the precedent set by his contemporaries, we may quickly dismiss three of the four books, but one of them — the *Reply* to Malthus — will require a longer look.

Free Thoughts on Public Affairs, a strident pamphlet prompted by Fox's coalition with Lord Grenville in the so-called Ministry of All the Talents (February 1806), combines a withering account of Pitt's disservice to the state with a plea for peace with France. The short-lived Peace of Amiens made inoperative, as Hazlitt thought, by Tory hypocrisy and the avarice of British merchants, Pitt had returned to power in 1804 resolved to carry on the war, and when he died in 1806 Hazlitt saw a final chance for Fox to right the wrongs of his great foe. Thus *Free Thoughts* is the first of Hazlitt's many published assaults upon the Tories and also his first defense of the outmoded libertarian principles that he had entertained for years. He would expound these themes more savagely in his political journalism after Waterloo and more sedately in his life of Napoleon, but this clumsy, early tract makes clear that his allegiance to reform, like his hatred of the Tories, was full-formed, steady, and implacable at the very start of his career. Moreover, its formal character of Pitt that we have noted earlier,[23] which Hazlitt himself liked well enough to use three times again,* marks his first approach to the style that he would one day make his own.

In 1803 Hazlitt had begun, or perhaps merely conceived, his abridgment of Abraham Tucker's *Light of Nature* as a means, said Coleridge, of getting his "*Sabine* Subsistence by some Employment from the Booksellers,"[24] and although his decision, four years later, to push the project

---

* Hazlitt reprinted the character of Pitt as the introduction to his speeches in *The Eloquence of the British Senate* in 1807 (see *Four Generations,* I, 98) and thereafter inserted it in *The Round Table* of 1817 (4.125-128) and *Political Essays* of 1819 (7.322-326).

to completion was no doubt prompted by the same financial motive, he had other reasons more befitting a philosopher: he admired Tucker's merits as a speculative thinker and he thought his shapeless work would profit from compression. It is customary for an editor to say kind things about the text on which he toils, and perhaps sometimes such remarks are meant; but Hazlitt's comments on Tucker's book are cordial far beyond the call of duty. He knew no other philosophical treatise, he said, "that contains so much good sense so agreeably expressed." [25] The first four-volume installment of Tucker's gossipy soliloquies had appeared in 1778, and the second, edited by his daughter four years after his death, had swelled the total to seven. In a disarming introduction to his work Tucker admitted that although he lacked the strength for "active life" and a "sufficient fund of spirits" for scholarship, he was blessed with a habit of reflection and enough money to assure "continual leisure," and so he looked upon his endless work as a kind of public service. "I pretend, however, to no sagacity capable of striking out uncommon discoveries, my dependence must be solely on my care and vigilance in collecting such sparks of light as occur from time to time spontaneously." [26] Such care and vigilance sufficed to make an elephantine book, and had its author lived, his chef-d'oeuvre — "rather a tissue of loose essays than a regular work," as Hazlitt said [27] — might have run forever. Even as it stood, however, its digressions, "endless repetitions," and "radical" lack of structure rendered it almost inaccessible to the common reader. In his abridgment he had saved "almost everything that is worth remembering," Hazlitt wrote in submitting the first installment of his manuscript to Johnson. "I give the amusing passages almost entire. In fact I have done little more than leave out repetitions, and other things that might as well never have been in the book." [28]

His effort was to prevent a work of value from "degenerating into a mere *caput mortuum*," and his only comment on the "pains and labour" that the effort cost was to quote Reynolds' reply to someone who had asked how long he worked upon a certain picture: "All my life." [29] Crabb Robinson, who read almost all the newest books, promptly read and liked this preface,[30] and almost twenty-five years after it appeared, Sir James Mackintosh took occasion to commend it to the readers of the *Encyclopaedia Britannica*,* but otherwise it seems to have attracted slight attention. Actually it is one of the most interesting productions

---

* *Miscellaneous Works*, p. 152n. Perhaps it was in Hazlitt's preface (1.123) that Mackintosh found the source of his once-famous description of Tucker as a "metaphysical Montaigne" (*Miscellaneous Works*, p. 153).

of Hazlitt's literary nonage. Not only does it have something of the bite and vigor of his later work in point of style, but it deals with certain topics — like the nature of abstraction, the "unity of consciousness," associational psychology, and the "formative" function of the mind — that, as we have seen, were central to his philosophic thought. In the *Essay* Hazlitt's hostility to eighteenth-century mechanism had been set forth in arid, graceless prose, but here he writes with a new *élan* about the "pert" inadequacies of those "modern sophists" who think that truth "exists no where but in their experiments, demonstrations, and syllogisms." [31] An intuitionist, Tucker thought that the "instinct" by which we amalgamate experience is more certain than the "reason" which leads us to dissect and analyze, and as Hazlitt, in his preface, comments on his work we hear him speaking for the first time on his favorite topics in a voice that is his own.

Apart from certain big set pieces, like the characters of Chatham, Burke, Fox, and Pitt that Hazlitt called the "most laboured" parts of his performance [32] and that he later used again, *The Eloquence of the British Senate* may be dismissed as competent hack work. Generally the compiler of these speeches makes no effort to disguise his boredom with the task. Acknowledging the "frequent defects and chasms" in his notes, he blames his faulty works of reference,[33] and when he comes upon a speech that he himself admires he is both astonished and delighted. "To those who have to wade through the crude, undigested mass of the records of parliament, there is such a tedious monotony, such a dreary vacuity of thought, such an eternal self-complacent repetition of the same worn-out topics, which seem to descend like an inheritance from one generation to another, that it is some relief to escape now and then from the dull jargon of political controversy." [34] There are good things scattered here and there, as when he says that Cromwell talked like a man with his hand upon his sword [35] or when he describes that "modern style" of forensic architecture in which the nominative case at the top of the page and the verb at the bottom are connected by circular ladders and winding stairs of rhetoric while "the meaning drops down through the middle." [36] More impressive, however, is his disenchantment not only with political oratory but with the processes of Parliamentary government. In an age of great men confronting great constitutional problems, he remarks, the House of Commons was the "representative and depositary of the collective sense of the nation," but after Walpole's time it became a "regular debating society" — than which "nothing can be lower." [37] Thus by commenting tersely on such worthies as Coke,

Elliott, Wentworth, Pym, and Cromwell, he reveals an admiration for their style and a respect for their opinions; and as he speaks of Bulstrode Whitlocke, for example, his literary and political sympathies converge:

> What a difference between the grave, clear, solid, laborious stile of the speech here given, and the crude metaphysics, false glitter, and trifling witticism of a modern legal oration! The truth is, that the affectation of philosophy and fine taste has spoiled every thing; and instead of the honest seriousness and simplicity of old English reasoning in law, in politics, in morality, in all the grave concerns of life, we have nothing left but a mixed species of bastard sophistry, got between ignorance and vanity, and generating nothing.[38]

Hazlitt's comments on a long parade of eighteenth-century politicians exemplify the same disheartening theme, and when, in his preface, he came to summarize his findings, his words were sad and wry. Starting his task in the hope of reviving what had been forgotten, and embodying what was permanent, he had ended with the conviction that most political oratory, whatever its relevance to the topics of the day, had nothing to do with greatness of mind or utterance. "A very small volume indeed, would contain all the recorded eloquence of both houses of parliament." [39]

Such a volume would surely include the work of the four great statesmen to whom Hazlitt paid the most attention. His views on Burke and Pitt we have already had occasion to examine, and his accounts of Chatham and Fox prove that in 1807, as in 1830, he gauged a politician's worth by the zeal he showed for "liberty." The secret of Chatham's well-earned place in history, he said, was not his gift of speech but his resolve to save the British constitution. Feeling "the cause of liberty as his own," he "spoke as a man should speak, because he felt as a man should feel." Great enough to ignore the petty claims of logic and Parliamentary decorum, he did not have "to dissect a doubt and halve a scruple" in order to dominate the paltry politicians of his day. He knew that liberty, truth, virtue, and justice were "good things" and that slavery and corruption were "bad things"; and as he fought for these convictions he invested common sense with the force of inspiration.[40] On the other hand, Fox was a victim of his own great talent: "his thoughts came crowding in too fast for the slow and mechanical process of speech." [41] A man not given to "self-denying ordinances," he had many failings, but his moral force was none the less so great that it obliterated all his faults. His "passions kindled into a generous flame, by a real interest in whatever related to the welfare of mankind," he combined a patriot's zeal with the enlightened knowledge of a statesman, and consequently his eloquence "warmed, expanded, penetrated every bosom." [42] Although inferior to Chatham in authority, to Burke in imagination, and to Pitt in logic, he was a formidable force for good because he regarded any act of tyranny "as a stain upon the honour of his country, and as an injury to the rights of his fellow citizens." *

It was inevitable that Hazlitt should one day try to answer Malthus, and in 1807, when the opportunity came, he was obviously delighted.† The occasion was Samuel Whitbread's introduction, in February, of a poor-bill that, among other things, provided for a system of free education and for badges to distinguish deserving from undeserving paupers. Hazlitt addressed three long letters to Cobbett's *Political Register* not to push the bill (which he disliked because it made the poor the "vassals of a wealthy aristocracy") [43] but to expose the faults of Malthus' celebrated work and to gain time for thoughtful men to reflect upon the problems of reform. Then in its third edition, Malthus' *Essay*, as Hazlitt thought, had become the very emblem of reaction, and its author's name hung above the poor and wretched *in terrorem* like a "baleful meteor." Any "serious attempt" to relieve the working classes was thought to be absurd and counter to the laws of nature, for by telling those with wealth that their duty and their vices coincide Malthus had proved that "the ends of public virtue and benevolence" could best be served with "meanness, pride, and extravagance." [44]

These were the days, as Hazlitt later said, when "Mr. Malthus used to wait in the lobbies with his essay in his hand, for the instruction and compliments of Honourable Members," [45] and since Cobbett, according to the *Edinburgh Review,* was noted for his "ignorant scurrility" about the famous *Essay,* [46] he must have welcomed Hazlitt's letters to the columns of his paper. When they were expanded and published as a book

* 7.317. Stewart C. Wilcox ("A Hazlitt Borrowing from Godwin," *MLN,* LVIII [1943], 69f.) has pointed out that in this sketch of Fox the passage (7.314) beginning "If to this we add the ardour and natural impetuosity of his mind" is inaccurately quoted by memory from the character of the great Whig statesman that Godwin wrote for the *Morning Chronicle* in 1806 (Paul, II, 156). See 7.315n.

† Hazlitt addressed himself to the problem of answering Malthus on three widely separate occasions. In 1807 he analyzed his faults in three long letters (signed "A.O.") that William Cobbett printed in his *Political Register* on March 14, May 16 and 23; pieced out and expanded with two additional letters and a coda called "Extracts from the Essay on Population with a Commentary and Notes," these were published later in the year as *A Reply to the Essay on Population* (1.177-364). A decade later the sprawling materials in this book were reworked and condensed for various contributions to the *Morning Chronicle,* the *Examiner,* and other papers, and five of them were included in *Political Essays* in 1819 (7.332-361). Finally, there is the terse, compendious essay on Malthus in *The Spirit of the Age* (11.103-114). For a full discussion of the topic see William T. Albrecht, *William Hazlitt and the Malthusian Controversy,* University of New Mexico Publications in Language and Literature, No. 4, 1950.

in the fall of 1807 their author acknowledged that in style, in bad manners, and in organization they deserved the criticism they had got. To those who had objected to the "too flowery" language he promised to write as drily as they wished if only they would undertake to find him readers. As for his "severe and personal" comments on Malthus as a man, he would have preferred to expose a faulty theory without referring to its author, "but the thing was impossible. Whoever troubles himself about abstract reasonings, or calm, dispassionate inquiries after truth? The public ought not to blame me for consulting their taste." For the diffuseness, repetitions, and disorder of his argument he could think of no excuse better than the one Pascal had used for writing too long and dull a letter: it would have been shorter if he had had more time.[47]

Slogging through the wide wastes of Hazlitt's *Reply* to Malthus, a modern reader finds him guilty on each count as charged. In style he ranges from bleak statistics to lyrical autobiography, from stolid exposition to brilliant set pieces that suggest the virtuoso flights of his late essays.* Detesting Malthus' views, he assails the man himself as a slave to sex and a hireling of the moneyed class. Passionately committed to the cause that Malthus had discredited, he replies to the logic and lucidity of the *Essay* with arguments that coil upon themselves like serpents. Hazlitt was never comfortable in extended compositions, and in the *Reply* his blurting responses to Malthus are so crudely flung together that unity, order, and even syntax fall victims to his anger. Indeed, it is anger that gives to the book whatever tonality it possesses. Hazlitt does not refute his adversary: recoiling from so grim a view of man's condition, he strikes back with a set of improvised variations on the theme of human dignity; and consequently, as Crabb Robinson remarked, the *Reply* is full of good things without being a good thing itself.[48] Near the end of his life Hazlitt said that Malthus' offense had been to stifle "the voice of humanity," [49] and it is as a plea for humanity that his rebuttal should be read. A confused and confusing book, it none the less generates real power as it asserts the great theme of reform: human misery is rooted not in the laws of nature but in institutions that men must learn to change.

The *Reply* is easier to summarize than read. Hazlitt repeats, dilates,

---

* The stylistic variety of the *Reply* is notable. The lyrical passage (1.283) beginning "I never fell in love but once" remains a biographical puzzle (see page 132 n). One of the bravura pieces (on women's clothes, 1.281f.) turns up in both *The Round Table* (4.13) and *Lectures on the English Comic Writers* (6.153f.). Another favorite passage, which Crabb Robinson (III, 844) considered "a piece of masterly eloquence," was the conclusion to Letter V (1.284). Hazlitt used it for an essay in the *Examiner* in 1815 (20.52f.) and again in the *Yellow Dwarf* three years later, but for some reason he did not include it in reprinting parts of Letter V in *Political Essays* in 1819. See 7.398.

CHARLES LAMB
By William Hazlitt
The National Portrait Gallery

WILLIAM GODWIN
By James Northcote
The National Portrait Gallery

and doubles back upon himself, but his central points are clear. Thus in one letter he concedes and expatiates upon Malthus' malign influence; in another he elaborately if implausibly tries to prove that his principle of population is unoriginal and therefore irrelevant to the problems of reform. The *Essay*, "in which the little, low, rankling malice of a parish-beadle, or the overseer of a workhouse is disguised in the garb of philosophy," [50] is not an invincible answer to men's aspirations for a better way of life, he asserts, but a perversion of the view that Robert Wallace had expressed, in 1761, in *Various Prospects of Mankind, Nature, and Providence*. When Wallace pointed out that a limited earth and a limited fertility determine the growth of population he said all that needs to be said, for until the earth is full and its fertility exhausted, the tricky ratios with which Malthus had doomed the poor to vice and misery would not even start to operate. Until that day comes, says Hazlitt, population can be controlled, if control is needed, by the will of man. "Till then, Mr. Malthus has no right to set up his arithmetical and geometrical ratios upon the face of the earth, and say they are the work of nature." [51] Although the earth could and should support ten times its present population without falling into "those pits and snares, against which we are so kindly warned," [52] when it does attain its limits then man will have the means — rational, moral, and preventive — to devise relief. Meanwhile, since the growth of moral restraint will infallibly diminish the force of the positive and preventive checks so dear to all reactionaries, we should strive to "increase the influence of rational motives" in curbing excess population * — and not, like Malthus, rejoice that a kindly providence has arranged for the poor to exterminate themselves.

Hazlitt's opposition to Malthus does not spring from blind devotion to either Whig reform or Utopian panaceas; rather, it is prompted by his anger at complacent Toryism. Rejecting Whitbread's bill as patently absurd, and distrusting all "imaginary schemes of improvement" because

---

* 1.231. Hazlitt reverted frequently to the question of the earth's fertility. In Dieppe, in 1824, he saw a girl sitting in the sun, some gnarled old women gossiping in the corner, and a group of children tugging a fishing boat from the water and shouting with delight. It was, he says (10.93), "a sight to make Mr. Malthus shudder," for "life here glows, or spins carelessly round on its soft axle." Likewise the smiling plains of Lombardy reminded him (10.276) that in spite of Malthus' doctrine "plenty and comfort" are not invariably "accompanied by an appearance of proportionable want and misery, tracking them at the heels." Even overcrowded Corsica, he says in his life of Napoleon (13.34), is "one instance, among so many others that history and geography afford, to shew that the earth is not full, or that population is not necessarily and wisely kept back by its having reached the utmost possible limits of the means of subsistence, but that various political and accidental causes constantly conspire to depress it much below the level of the means of subsistence or natural resources of the country."

they ignore "the real capacities of our nature,"[53] he admits to being "as little sanguine in my expectations of any great improvement to be made in the condition of human life either by the visions of philosophy, or by downright, practical, parliamentary projects, as Mr. Malthus himself can be."[54] But any fixed decree — though buttressed by mathematical tables and expounded as the law of nature — that dooms the mass of men to vice and misery he refuses to accept. If Malthus' "law" is valid, he asserts, then we are "to consider all human institutions, good, bad, and indifferent, all folly, vice, wisdom, virtue, knowledge, ignorance, liberty and slavery, poverty and riches, monarchy, aristocracy, democracy, polygamy, celibacy, all forms and modes of life, all arts, manufactures, and science, as resulting mechanically from this one principle."[55] It is a principle that, however consoling to the proponents of the *status quo,* sacrifices human dignity to political privilege. Hazlitt thought that it was shameless for a rich man to tell a pauper that his case was hopeless, and ironical for "a red-faced swag-bellied" bishop who "could drink his two bottles of wine without being affected" to "belch out a severe reprimand against a poor labouring man, who was staggering home after drinking a quart of small beer."[56]

In *The Spirit of the Age* he would ironically congratulate Malthus for having won "a *scientific* reputation in questions of moral and political philosophy."[57] This is a major theme that underlies the angry rhetoric of the *Reply*. The ratios may be all very well, he concedes, but they are not infallible, and in any event they merely tell us what we know already.* Moreover, Malthus manipulates them to support inferences that only the vicious and the foolish could applaud. We are not obliged to believe that all the "passions, follies, imperfections, or perversities of human nature" are rooted in the laws of mathematics; we are not obliged to ignore history and repudiate humanity in order to substantiate a theory.

If it can be shewn . . . that there is some connection between the form of government and the state of morals, and that the better the government, the better the morals, the evils of population instead of forming an excuse for bad governments will only aggravate their mischief, and increase the necessity of getting rid of them.[58]

Godwin's Utopia is probably unreal, Hazlitt thinks, but "theoretically or practically, generally, or particularly" Malthus has failed to prove it

---

* A terse statement of Hazlitt's principal objections to Malthus' use of science in treating moral problems is provided by the "Questions Relating to the Essay on Population" (7.357–361) that he wrote in 1810 in answer to the unfavorable *Edinburgh* review of the *Reply*. See 7.408–411.

so. To exaggerate the evils of reform while denying that reform can ever be achieved is illogical; to abandon the poor to vice and misery while admitting the force of moral restraint is cruel. Men are weak and vain and often desperate, Hazlitt says, but they are better than Malthus will allow. Imperfect as we are, we do in some manner contrive to make both ends meet and to cut our coat according to the cloth: we are not "carried away, neck or nothing, by this high-mettled courser, Population, over all the fences and barriers of common sense." [59] Having conceded that man has enough wit and prudence to control his fate, Malthus had conceded everything: trying to save his conclusion after giving up his principle — like a bad poet who, to get rid of a false concord, alters the ending of the first line and forgets that he has spoiled the rhyme [60] — he himself had exposed the fatal weakness of his theory. And thus, concludes Hazlitt somewhat prematurely, whereas Malthus stands convicted by his contradictions and his "principle" lies in ruins, better men continue in the quest for social justice.*

A hitherto unnoticed consequence of Hazlitt's work on Malthus was a spat with Godwin. As one with something of a vested interest in all

---

* The critical response to the *Reply* was thin and largely negative. In May 1808 Horace Twiss wrote a flippant notice of the book for the *London Review* (see 1.377), and two years later it was castigated by the *Edinburgh* — which was consistently favorable to Malthus — in a review that Malthus himself may have written (James Bonar, *Malthus and His Work* [1924], p. 329n). It would have been a "cruel preventive check," the *Edinburgh* reviewer says (XVI [1810], 465) if men like Hazlitt were compelled to undergo the "drudgery" of reading a book before they answered it. Hazlitt replied to this jocose attack in a letter that Cobbett promptly printed (7.408–411), and although Lamb told him that his rebuttal was "complete" (Lucas, II, 112), the *Edinburgh* refused to notice it. In 1815 Hazlitt resurrected this rebuttal for a Round Table paper in the *Examiner*, and four years later he reprinted parts of it in *Political Essays* (7.357–361). Thereafter the *Reply* seems to have been ignored until Godwin reread it in preparing his *Of Population*, a long-delayed retort to Malthus that appeared in 1820. Although a writer in the *Examiner* (1 April 1821, p. 206) thought that this was an "altogether triumphant" piece of work, he regretted the fact that Godwin had not acknowledged his reliance on those letters in which Malthus had long before been crushed by "a man of first-rate powers, since well-known to the literary world." In 1823, when De Quincey treated Malthus in "Notes from the Pocket-Book of an Opium Eater" in the *London Magazine*, Hazlitt, in a letter to the editor (VIII [1823], 459f.), promptly pointed out the "rather striking coincidence" between his and De Quincey's arguments. "I do not wish to bring any charge of plagiarism in this case," he said; "I only beg to put in my own claim of priority." Commenting on the episode to his partner, John Hessey, coeditor of the *London Magazine*, conceded that, since Hazlitt "has been a good deal abused for his differing from Malthus, he may as well claim the credit of priority in publishing his Opinions" (*Keats Circle*, II, 450). When De Quincey replied to Hazlitt in the next issue of the *London* he slyly derogated the *Reply* (which he dimly remembered glancing through at Southey's house many years before), but he admitted that "in substance" he was obligated to the work (IX, 27).

theories of reform, Godwin, as his diary shows, began reading the *Reply* as soon as it appeared. When he finished the book four days later he wrote about it to the author, and the fact that Hazlitt promptly favored him with calls on two successive days (August 5 and 6) and also with a letter (August 6) that Godwin answered one day later suggests that the two old friends had found themselves in disagreement. What the contention was about may be inferred from Hazlitt's previously unpublished letter:

Dear Sir,
I am sorry I inserted the passage you object to. For my own part I looked upon it as a joke, & thought you would do the same. As to any serious offence, it was so far from my thoughts, that I brought the manuscript one day in my pocket to read, but was prevented by somebody's being there. I think if you recollect all circumstances, you will find that the passage in question clenches the attack upon Malthus, & that I could not taken [*sic*] the advantage I have done of his expressions, without glancing at you. You stood a little in my way, but I was determined not to lose my blow at him. This was the vow I made when I began the work, & I have performed it as well as I could. When you recollect that the whole book is written on your side of the question as far as the present controversy was concerned, & when I add farther that my spleen against Malthus, & the bitterness with which I have treated him arose originally from the unfair & uncandid use which was made of some unguarded expressions you let fall on this very subject, you will perhaps find that a single sentence may be passed over as no very great matter. It was not in my power to remove an unjust aspersion; except in the very way that I have done it, & with which you find so much fault, viz. by bringing Malthus into the same scrape. This is the best excuse I can make, & as you will see a very sincere one.
I am, Dear Sir, yours very truly,
W. Hazlitt.
P.S. No one has ever been more ready than I have to take part with my friends on all occasions. I have committed four or five riots in my zeal for the reputation of Coleridge & Wordsworth: & all the thanks I ever got for this my zeal in their favour was some of the last indignities that can be put upon any person. In my list of friends it has always been my good luck to come in like the tail of an etc. & to subsist only upon sufferance. — I called this morning, but you were out.*

The offensive "single sentence" in the *Reply* was probably that in which Hazlitt — in a footnote — compared Malthus' unfeeling comment about abandoned children to "Mr. Godwin's saying, he does not regard a new-born infant with any peculiar complacency," [61] and in view of their continued good relations it would seem that his explanation was accepted. On the other hand, the allusion to the poets suggests that by 1807 the breach between them and their one-time protégé was already wide. It also suggests that Hazlitt was beginning to assume the manner for which he later came to be notorious. Certainly the critical response to his *Reply* would not have made him mild. In 1809 he asserted, with

---

* ALS, postmark 6 August 1807, Abinger Collection. This must be the letter recorded by Godwin in his diary.

some exaggeration, that three books of his had been "suppressed,"[62] and as his string of failures lengthened his temper grew no softer.

THE EARLY YEARS OF MARRIAGE

The toil required for writing three big books might be presumed to have taken most of Hazlitt's time in 1807, but, as we learn from Mary Lamb, he was also busy courting Sarah Stoddart. That lady, recently returned from Malta, where her brother John had been king's advocate since 1803, had come home to claim a modest legacy and find herself a husband; * and since both she and Hazlitt were friendly with the Lambs it was fated that they should one day meet. At Wem, in 1806, he had heard good things of her from Charles,[1] and later Mary wrote to her of his return from Shropshire as an event very beneficial to her brother, for Thomas Manning's recent departure for China had left Lamb "very dull, and he likes Hazlitt better than any body, except Manning."[2] But if Hazlitt was "a great acquisition" to Lamb's small store of domestic comforts, as Wordsworth was informed, his attractions for "Girlery" were sparse,[3] and it is not likely that his first meeting with Miss Stoddart, whenever it occurred, gave hint of future bliss. In any event, Mary's letters of 1806, full of an old maid's good advice about matrimony, make it clear that Sarah, though already in her thirties, had a choice of suitors, for if she had lost the bloom of youth she was not without her charms, including a modest property at Winterslow, near Salisbury. These charms should be remembered as we read Mary's letter of October 1807 — the first after a long hiatus — in which Hazlitt's "comical love affair" usurps all other topics. Writing to Sarah at Winterslow, Mary disclaims any intention of meddling, but she confesses to "a mighty solicitude about the event of love stories," and in her role as confidante she asks for further news. "I learn from the Lover that he has not been so remiss in his duty as you supposed. His Effusion, and your complaints on his inconstancy, crossed each other on the road." And so on, until she closes with the wish that their lovers' quarrel be composed, "for if I were sure you would not be quite starved to death, nor beaten to a mummy, I should like to see Hazlitt and you come together, if (as Charles observes) it were only for the joke sake."[4]

Somehow, then, this strange pair reached an understanding. Before

---

* Working mainly through the Pinney Papers at the University of Bristol, John R. Barker ("Some Early Correspondence of Sarah Stoddart and the Lambs," *Huntington Library Quarterly*, XXIV [1960], 59–69) has thrown new light on Sarah Stoddart's strong but futile efforts to attract a husband in the years before her match with Hazlitt.

the year was out, Mary Lamb was urging that Hazlitt make a formal declaration in order to have John Stoddart (who himself had just come home from Malta) "friendly in the business," [5] and by the start of 1808 Hazlitt was writing to Sarah, in bantering style, as her accepted lover, dreaming of sitting down with her to "a boiled scrag-end of mutton, and hot potatoes," promising to call *"in form"* upon her pompous brother, and suggesting that by her selling some property and his borrowing a hundred pounds they might "set off merrily in spite of all the prudence of Edinburgh." [6] In view of the suitor's prospects and political opinions the call "in form" upon the lady's brother no doubt presented certain problems, for John Stoddart, once a good Godwinian who "went all lengths in Radicalism, and wore the Phrygian cap," [7] had already begun his progress toward a Toryism so profound that it would one day earn for him a knighthood and the soubriquet of "Dr. Slop." Lamb had thought him "cold hearted well bred conceited" even as a young radical in 1796, [8] and for Stoddart, as for Lady Wishfort, the passing years had confirmed the apprehension of offending against decorums. With a contempt bred of long familiarity Hazlitt later spoke his mind about him — "he will yield, in absurdity, to no man" [9] — but in 1808, with a modest legacy at stake, he behaved himself.*

Even after Stoddart, no doubt with grave reluctance, had assented to the match, and after Hazlitt had visited Winterslow to inspect (and paint pictures of) his future home,[10] the marriage was delayed by "something about settlements." For although Sarah's eighty pounds a year would be a third more when her aged mother died, said Lamb, her betrothed had nothing "except what he can claim from the Parish. *Pauper est Cinna, sed tamen amat.* The thing is therefore in abeyance." † If John Stoddart could have looked into the future he would have acted on his doubts, but as it was he made difficulties enough about the "settlements" to keep the lovers waiting through the spring. When, at long last, they were married at St. Andrew's, Holborn, on 1 May 1808, Lamb's antics almost disrupted the ceremony. "Any thing awful makes me laugh," he explained to Southey. "I misbehaved once at a funeral." ‡

⬦ ⬦ ⬦

* Thus on 8 December 1807, we learn from Godwin's diary, Hazlitt had Stoddart, Godwin, the Lambs, and Joseph Hume for dinner at his rooms in Southampton Building (where he had moved not long before from his brother's house in Great Russell Street); and on March 18 Stoddart, Northcote, Lamb, Hume, George Dyer, Crabb Robinson, Godwin, and the Holcrofts were his guests at tea.

† Lucas, II, 48. For an account of Lamb's tedious and tasteless joke in reporting Hazlitt's alleged suicide, presumably in a fit of amatory despair, see W. C. Hazlitt, *Lamb and Hazlitt* (1899), pp. 63–79; Lucas, II, 41–44.

‡ Lucas, II, 167. In 1816 Hazlitt (7.96n), without mentioning Lamb by name, called him a "mad wag" who "would laugh at a funeral and weep at a wedding."

EARLY YEARS OF MARRIAGE

Even though he had wooed and won a lady possessed of Wiltshire property and eighty pounds a year Hazlitt could hardly qualify as landed gentry, and after marriage, as before, hack writing was his trade. Partly for that reason, no doubt, and partly because he, like Lamb, liked the feel of paving stones beneath his feet, he often went to London. Despite his biographers' assumption that in his early years of marriage he stayed almost constantly at Winterslow,[11] it is clear from Godwin's diary that this was not the case. He supped with Godwin on 20 May 1808, less than three weeks after marriage, and the two saw each other often during the months that followed. Some of their meetings probably occurred on Hazlitt's hurried trips from Winterslow, but the sequence of the others suggests extended stays in London. It was no doubt to acknowledge the Lambs' hospitality on such long visits that he sent them suckling pigs from Winterslow.[12] Except for a hiatus between 16 November 1808 and 10 February 1809 — when the final weeks of Sarah's pregnancy and the birth of their first child on January 15 no doubt kept him close to home — he saw Godwin at least once and usually several times each month between his marriage in May and the following April.*

Despite these frequent trips to London, however, Winterslow was nominally his home from 1808 to 1812. With the nearby picture galleries of Stourhead, Wilton House, and Longford Castle[13] and with Salisbury Plain at hand, that Wiltshire village was not without attractions; and in later years, when a little inn called the Hut was almost his only haven, he was genuinely fond of it. Among other things, he thought that the beauty of the Wiltshire countryside made his style more gentle and "excursive."[14] In town he heard the clocks, but in the country he could listen to the silence, and as he said in one of his last essays he liked "to lie whole mornings on a sunny bank on Salisbury Plain, without any object before me, neither knowing nor caring how time passes, and thus 'with light-winged toys of feathered Idleness' to melt down hours to moments."[15] However, Hazlitt was not a professional votary of rural delights. From Wordsworth he had learned that nature herself shows "neither hypocrisy, caprice, nor mental reservation in her favours,"[16] but he found nothing ennobling or even very pleasant about rustics who had been "taken out of a state of nature, without being put in possession of the refinements of art,"[17] and as for nature in its grander forms, he thought it "more adapted for occasional visits than for con-

* Some of these meetings were so frequent — like those on March 15, 16, 17, 21, and 23 — that we can only suppose business to have been the motive. Hazlitt was apparently away from London during April and early May in 1809, but he resumed his calls on May 26, and between then and June 18 he and Godwin were together on at least nine occasions.

stant residence." [18] Like all sensible men, he was dismayed by bands of tourists who, as Keats said later, came "hunting after the picturesque like beagles"; [19] he hated to hear the sea "roaring and raging like a wild beast in its den"; [20] and even in Switzerland, a visitor reported, he complained that one range of Alps was very like another.* In short, Hazlitt would agree with Coleridge's dictum that not every man "is likely to be improved by a country life or by country labors," [21] and therefore the fact that posterity has linked his name with Winterslow is not without its irony.

None the less he remembered these years at Winterslow with pleasure, for then he found time to paint and think — his favorite occupations — and then the Lambs paid visits (once in the fall of 1809 and again the following summer) that neither he nor they forgot. [22] But these years were also full of problems, some of them domestic and others of a more accustomed kind. All but one of Sarah's many pregnancies ended in disaster,† and Hazlitt's own attempts in literature and art were hardly more successful. We learn about his painting in a long, affectionate letter that he wrote to Sarah when she was staying with the Lambs in the spring of 1810. "I go on something like Satan, through moist & dry," he reports from Wiltshire, "something [sic] glazing & sometimes scumbling, as it happens, now on the wrong side of the canvas & now on the right, but still persuading myself that I have at last found out the true secret of Titian's golden hue & the oleaginous touches of Claude Lorraine." [23] Although our knowledge of his writing is not quite so circumstantial, the hints we have show that he was hard at work. His ambition was to write a critical history of English philosophy, and to that end he printed a prospectus with which he hoped to lure subscribers. If, as he said there, the "long and patient habit of thinking" which had been the "business" of his life [24] could fit him for the task, he was fit indeed, and all that he required was cash. "I have no other excuse to make for this intrusion," he explained to the celebrated William Windham in sending him the prospectus in February 1809, "than that I believe the design of the work is such as may meet with your approbation, — & the

* Medwin, p. 278. Hazlitt said (10.272f.) that we would rather see Titian's *St. Peter Martyr* than the grandest peak in Switzerland.

† A memorandum apparently in Sarah Hazlitt's hand (British Museum Add. MS. 38,898) gives the grim details: following the loss of her first child (a son who was born 15 January and died 5 July 1809), she had two miscarriages (6 March and 6 September 1810) before producing young William on 26 September 1811, an event that was duly pleasing to the Lambs (Lucas, II, 117f.). Another miscarriage occurred on 15 October 1813, after the Hazlitts had moved back to London, and the last child, John, who was born 28 September 1815, "died in the measles" on 19 June 1816. It is no doubt to John's funeral that Hazlitt alludes poignantly in "On the Fear of Death" (8.326), a passage on which Howe's note requires correction.

natural wish of every one that what has employed many years of his life & many anxious thoughts may not be entirely lost. My principal view in it would be to chastise the presumption of modern philosophy." *
That the author of *Free Thoughts on Public Affairs* (which Windham probably never heard of) should have sought support from a panjandrum of the Tories who had been a valued friend of Pitt's betrays either naiveté or cynicism; at any rate, since neither Windham nor presumably anybody else was stirred to generosity, the project had to be abandoned for something that would make some money.

◇   ◇   ◇

From no other motive, surely, did Hazlitt grind out *A New and Improved Grammar of the English Tongue*, a schoolbook to which Godwin, under his pseudonym of "Edward Baldwin," affixed a "Guide" to the language,† and which he and his formidable second wife — a "damn'd infernal bitch," as Lamb explained to Hazlitt [25] — published in their "Juvenile Library" late in 1809. An undated (and hitherto unprinted) note to Godwin toward the end of the previous June suggests that Hazlitt's *Grammar*, like every book before or since, attained the dignity of print in spite of certain differences between the author and the publisher. "Dear Sir," it opens coldly,

I was not at all offended, but a good deal vexed at the contents of your former letter, having had three books which I have written suppressed, & as I had taken some trouble with the grammar, I thought it might answer the purpose, & as you seemed to approve of what I had done to it, I was sorry to be dashed in pieces against the dulness of schoolmasters. I do not much like the style & title of *Mr. W. Hazlitt* it looks like one of a firm of ushers; otherwise I can have no objection to the matter. I send you Crombie, & the revised grammar, & remain, Dear Sir,
yours truly,
W. Hazlitt.

The Lambs will be down here in the beginning of July. I can only say that the woods & walks will be then green, & that the sherry is not all drank up. Friday ‡

* ALS, British Museum Add. MS. 37,916. Windham's copy of this *Prospectus*, which is preserved among his papers in the British Museum, is apparently unique, but Geoffrey Carnall (*TLS*, 19 June 1953, p. 397) has pointed out that it appeared in an earlier and somewhat different form in the February 1909 issue of the *Monthly Magazine* (pp. 15–19) as a letter entitled "Proposals for the Basis of a new System of Metaphysical Philosophy" and signed by "W.H."

† This "Guide" had first appeared in the second (1809) edition of W. F. Mylius' *School Dictionary of the English Language*, another of the Godwins' publications and one reprinted many times. At the end of Hazlitt's *Grammar* are advertisements for other works in the "Juvenile Library," including the second edition of Mylius' *Dictionary* (the first "having been sold in two months"), Godwin's own *Fables Ancient and Modern*, Charles and Mary Lamb's *Mrs. Leicester's School* and *Tales from Shakespear* and Charles Lamb's *Adventures of Ulysses*.

‡ ALS, [?June 1809], Abinger Collection. Late June 1809 would seem a likely date for this letter because Godwin's diary shows Hazlitt to have been in London at

THE LONG APPRENTICESHIP

Although the reference to Alexander Crombie (whose influential *Etymology and Syntax of the English Language* had already gone through several printings) and the tart allusion to schoolmasters and ushers make it clear that Hazlitt did not share his publisher's deference toward pedagogues and their approach to grammar, he made the necessary revisions, and so the work went forward.* In later years he did not try to mask his scorn for Lindley Murray's prestigious *English Grammar,* which he thought to be a work of grotesquely greater fame than merit,† but in 1809 he bowed to Godwin's prudent counsel. Remarking in a letter to his publisher that "whenever there is a question of a blunder" Murray's "name is not far off," he none the less concedes that "perhaps it would look like jealousy to make a formal set at him." Moreover, since he was already "noted" (perhaps by the critics of his *Reply* to Malthus) "for want of liberality, & an undisplined [*sic*] moral sense," he grants it might be well to moderate his language. In this unwonted yielding mood he expresses his polite dismay at Godwin's pseudonym ("for assuredly the works of William Godwin do not stand in need of those of E. Baldwin for vouchers or supporters") and commends the "very simple & ingenious" arrangement of the little "Guide." "But the truth is," he adds wearily, "I know very little about the matter, & I am besides sick of the subject of Grammar." [26] On the other hand, Godwin kept, or seemed to keep, his interest in the book, and in his role as businessman he tried to drum up trade for it. The author was an "inward" friend of his, he told Archibald Constable (who owned the mighty *Edinburgh Review*), and a man of "singular acuteness and sound understanding." [27] So far as we know, however, the author himself was so "sick" of grammar that he never even alluded to the book again except as one of Godwin's own productions. [28]

---

least through the eighteenth of that month. Owing to the death of the Hazlitts' baby on July 5 the visit mentioned here by Hazlitt and by Mary Lamb in a letter at the start of June (Lucas, II, 72f.) was postponed until October (*ibid.*, II, 85).

* On November 23 Godwin wrote to Archibald Constable that he had just "forwarded to the proprietors of the *Edinburgh Review*" a copy of the *Grammar* (see note 27); a string of letters that he wrote to Hazlitt (and recorded in his diary) between October 11 and November 23 suggests that the two were exchanging views about revisions; and by 2 January 1810 Lamb (Lucas, II, 91) had seen the printed *Grammar* and expressed his approbation. Thus although the book must have been printed late in 1809 it was postdated 1810, as a copy now at Harvard shows and as Keynes (pp. 13f.) conjectured. Many years later De Quincey (XI, 353) said he "was once told" that Hazlitt's book had been "suppressed," adding that "this suppression must have been purchased by some powerful publisher interested in keeping up the current reputation of [Lindley] Murray." However, at least one copy of a second and revised edition, also dated 1810, survives (16.444).

† In *The Spirit of the Age* (11.57) Hazlitt arraigns Murray for incompetence, and in a short paper contributed to the *Atlas* the year before his death he comments (20.213f.) on the fact that his bad book had reached its thirty-eighth edition.

EARLY YEARS OF MARRIAGE

Hazlitt's aversion to his work is not hard to understand. Beginning at the beginning — with the alphabet and spelling — he trudges on to parts of speech, and then to syntax, prosody, and punctuation. The examples and exercises comprised in the appendix underscore his — or, more probably, his publisher's — pedagogical intentions. Not even Hazlitt's brisk and serviceable expository style, which marks a real advance upon the *Essay,* can save the little book from dullness. Godwin told Constable that he had never seen the parts of speech so well defined before — "I could almost say at all defined" — and it is true that Hazlitt neatly cuts through jargon when he calls a noun the name of "any idea or thing considered as standing by itself," or says that "verbs, as well as adjectives, denote the attributes of nouns," the one implying a connection and the other expressing it directly.[29] But in his preface he explains that such unorthodox opinions were not original with him, and that in his approach to language he had merely followed John Horne Tooke. Whereas conventional grammarians like Lowth and Murray and the rest were guilty "of mistaking words for things" and therefore "of admitting a distinction without a difference," he said, Tooke's *Diversions of Purley* (1786, 1805) exemplified a fresh and realistic way of treating language, and in his own "compilation," he had merely tried "to take advantage of the discoveries contained in that work, without adopting its errors." [30]

Hazlitt had dealt with Tooke before (in the preface to *The Light of Nature*) [31] and he would deal with him again (in his lectures on philosophy [32] and, much later, *The Spirit of the Age*),[33] for as a champion of liberal politics, an amateur philologist, and a vigorous advocate of Lockean metaphysics that remarkable man had won a varied fame. An old-fashioned radical who had been the friend of Wilkes, he had gone to jail in 1778 for supporting the American revolutionists and, as one of the "Twelve Traitors," had stood trial for treason in 1794. Meanwhile his sardonic wit and his philological "discoveries" brought him fresh renown, and long before his death in 1812 he became almost an institution. Hazlitt's memories of his estate at Wimbledon — where Godwin, Holcroft, and their friends were always welcome — are of an old man whose mind was like "a bow of polished steel" and whose malice was as sharp as poisoned arrows. A relic of the former generation who could not share the ardors or accept the slogans at a later day, he was, said Hazlitt later, a political anachronism,

a mere pettifogger, full of chicane, and captious objections, and unmeaning discontent; but he had none of the grand whirling movements of the French Revolution, nor of the tumultuous glow of rebellion in his head or in his heart. His politics were cast in a different mould, or confined to the party distinctions and court intrigues and pittances of popular right, that made a noise in the time of Junius and Wilkes — and even if his understanding had gone along with more modern and unqualified principles, his cautious temper would have prevented his risking them in practice.[34]

Whatever his opinion of Tooke as politician or, as we shall see, as a speculative thinker, Hazlitt regarded his "discoveries" in philology as basic contributions to our knowledge of how language operates. Tooke himself was no doubt gratified that *The Diversions of Purley* had earned five thousand pounds for him,[35] but Hazlitt, always quick to challenge privileged error, thought that it had been neglected by the pedants, and in his little *Grammar,* therefore, he undertook to publicize its merits.

Tooke's linguistic theories, based on his shaky but enthusiastic etymologies, have not stood the test of time. First in *A Letter to John Dunning, Esq.* (1778), then more elaborately in *The Diversions of Purley,* he argued that most words are not the immediate signs of ideas or of things, but are instead abbreviations of fundamental nouns and verbs. Only these basic words, which either name things or give directions for joining them together, correspond precisely to their referents, and all the other parts of speech are derived from them. Thus the so-called conjunction *if* is an ossified imperative of *gifan* ("to give"), and all the rest — *still, unless, but, since, and* — are abbreviations of their parent verbs.[36] According to conventional grammarians *that* may be an article or a pronoun or a conjunction, but according to Tooke it is merely a particle of the verb, and therefore it always has the same significance. Similarly the other indeclinable parts of speech may be reduced in rank and nomenclature: *before, behind, below,* for instance, are not prepositions, but combinations of an imperative and a noun — and the nouns (*fore, hind, low*), with no orthographic change, can be converted into adjectives.[37] Arguing from these and such examples Tooke concluded that the "farrago of senseless distinctions" so dear to most grammarians has no reference to the facts of language.[38]

One reason Hazlitt found this theory so appealing was, as he said later, that it "clears away the rubbish of school-boy technicalities" and penetrates to "the naked truth of things." [39] Another, which he expounded in the preface to his *Grammar,* was that it enables us to see how language is connected with our mental operations. Tooke had shown, he thought, that "the grammatical distinctions of words do not relate to the nature of the things or ideas spoken of, but to our manner of speaking of them." For example, a substantive is not "the name of a thing really subsisting by itself" but of a thing, idea, or quality *"considered"* by the speaker as subsisting by itself. As doublets such as *white* and *whiteness* show, nouns and adjectives do not represent absolute distinctions, but shifting and subjective points of view. "The things themselves do not change, but it is we who view them in a different connection with other things, and who accordingly use different sorts of words to show the difference of the situation which they occupy in our thoughts and discourse." Convinced that there is no necessary connection between old-fashioned terms of grammar and the linguistic activity they are said to represent, Hazlitt thought that Tooke had merely tried to simplify a subject which the pedagogues had hopelessly obscured, and thus had made a contribution so "essential" it could not be "overlooked or forgotten." [40]

✧ ✧ ✧

On the other hand, Tooke's "errors" in philosophy, though scarcely mentioned in the *Grammar*,[41] gave him great concern. Since he had glanced at them already in his preface to *The Light of Nature* and, a few years later, would discuss them fully in his lectures, we might pause upon them here. Not content with tying all the other parts of speech to nouns and verbs, Tooke had also tried to show that nouns and verbs themselves are tied to concrete objects of perception; and since this effort to reduce "all our ideas to points and solid substances" was, in fact, an effort to prove that mind is governed by the laws of matter, Hazlitt was bound to disagree with it. Tooke's "etymological system" was, he thought, a clue to the "actual history of language," but the "superficial gloss of philosophy which is spread over it" did violence to his most fundamental views, and therefore his comments on these "errors" are important.[42] In a gigantic chapter of the second part (1805) of *The Diversions of Purley* Tooke had maintained that all abstractions, when etymologically explored, point to things in nature. Thus since the word *right* is derived from *rect-um,* the participle of *regere,* which itself is linked with *rex,* a man who insists upon his right "asks only that which it is *Ordered* he shall have." [43] Similarly, such imposing words as *fate, heaven, providence, innocence, spirit, true,* and *merit* — and they "compose the bulk of every language" — are nothing but participles and adjectives that, invested with a spurious distinction, lead to "metaphysical jargon and a false morality." [44] To suppose that the "imagined *operation of the mind,* which has been termed *Abstraction,*" conveys a kind of truth higher, broader, and more general than that which rests upon sensation is, said Tooke, fallacious. These nouns, like others, rest ultimately on our response to things, and, as Locke had proved to the "inestimable benefit" of mankind,[45] things are essential to all forms of intellection.

Hazlitt's first published comment on Tooke, in his preface to *The Light of Nature,* was in opposition to these mechanistic views. Hartley having done his best "to prove the human soul to consist of a white curd," he remarked, Tooke then proceeded to deny that our thoughts have any "life or motion" except as "they are dragged about mechanically by words." In 1807 he professed to being made "a little uneasy" by Tooke's excursions into metaphysics,[46] but five years later, in his lectures on philosophy, he described the effort to apply etymology "to the illustration of moral and metaphysical truth" as "downright, unqualified, unredeemed nonsense."[47]

Like all these lectures, the one on Tooke was in protest to that "modern philosophy" that denied the creative power of mind. The second part of *The Diversions of Purley,* he remarks ironically,

consists chiefly of about two thousand instances of the etymology of words, to prove that there can be no abstract ideas: scarcely one of which two thousand meanings is anything else but a more abstract idea than the word was in general supposed to convey: for example, the word *loaf* commonly stands for a pretty substantial, solid, tangible kind of an idea, and is not suspected of any latent, very refined, abstracted meaning. The author shews, on the contrary, that the word has no such palpable, positive meaning, as the particular object to which we apply it, but merely signifies something, any thing, raised or *lifted* up. A singular method, surely, of reducing all general and abstract signs to individual, physical objects![48]

Hazlitt's real concern in this lecture, however, is not Tooke's jejune attempts at metaphysics — in which the "new-invented patent-lamp of etymology goes out just as it is beginning to grow dark, and as the path becomes intricate"[49] — but the deficiencies of mechanistic psychology. He attempts to prove, against Hobbes and Locke and all their latter-day descendants, that the mind is not passive and inert, but an instrument of life and power. It is not a mechanism for recording sensory impression — "a lazy Looker-on on an external World," as Coleridge had called it in deriding Locke and Newton[50] — but the very source of all our intellection.

We do not arrive at general notions by accumulating "facts" of sense and then arranging them in groups to which we give class-names, says Hazlitt. Intellection does not begin with "absolutely simple and individual" ideas, each related to its corresponding "thing" in nature and subsequently parceled out and labeled; it begins with general notions which the mind itself supplies and by means of which we order our sensations even as they come to us. The simplest natural object — a table, chair, or blade of grass — presents to us a "configuration" of simple sensory data such as color, hardness, odor, and extension, and these must be "put together by the understanding" before we form the least complex "idea." "Without the cementing power of the mind, all our ideas would be necessarily decomposed and crumbled down into their original elements and flexional parts." In short, abstraction is not a matter of adjectives and participles, as Tooke had held; it is the primary act of intellection, and the vital function of the mind. As Hazlitt said in paraphrasing Kant, the mind alone is formative: "it is that alone which by its pervading and elastic energy unfolds and expands our ideas, that gives order and consistency to them, that assigns to every part its proper place, and that constructs the idea of the whole. Ideas are the offspring of the understanding, not of the senses." [51]

It is odd, says Hazlitt in conclusion, that although the mechanists cannot explain such basic things as motion and extension, their obsession with the "facts" of nature leads them to deny the power of mind. Locke and Hartley and Tooke to the contrary notwithstanding, we need not regard its generalizing power "as a sort of artificial refinement upon our other ideas, as an excrescence, no ways contained in the common impressions of things, nor scarcely necessary to the common purposes of life." [52] Man's mind, with its "pervading and elastic energy," is his unique distinction, and although the little system-makers cannot hope to penetrate its mystery, they should at least concede its power.

Matter alone seems to have the privilege of presenting difficulties and contradictions at any time, which pass current under the name of *facts*; but the moment any thing of this kind is observed in the understanding, all the petulance of logicians is up in arms. The mind is made the mark on which they vent all the modes and figures of their impertinence; and metaphysical truth has in this respect fared like the milk-white hind, the emblem of pure faith, in Dryden's fable, which

<blockquote>
Has oft been chased
With Scythian shafts and many winged wounds
Aimed at her heart, was often forced to fly,
And doomed to death, though fated not to die.[53]
</blockquote>

THE HOLCROFT *MEMOIRS*

When Thomas Holcroft died in March 1809, leaving both his large family and his uncompleted memoirs unprovided for, a committee of his friends including Godwin, William Nicholson, and George Tuthil promptly went to work to settle his affairs.[1] The result, astonishingly, was a thousand-pound subscription for the widow and her children [2] and a commission (no doubt arranged by Godwin) for Hazlitt to piece the memoirs out with letters and prepare the manuscript for publication. This was the assignment that Mary Lamb first mentioned in November,[3] that Hazlitt said a month later he was "tired to death of" but "pushing hard" to finish,⁴ and that, as the dated preface shows, was ready for the press a few weeks later. Even though Hazlitt's job of arranging Holcroft's papers was largely editorial, as it neared an end, he told Robinson, he worked at it "unceasingly."⁵ A history of his early life that Holcroft had dictated during his last illness served for Hazlitt's opening chapters, and a diary that he kept in 1798–99, together with his *Narrative of Facts* about the treason trials of 1794 and a big batch of "Letters to and from the Author," accounted for more than half the rest. For what remained, however, Hazlitt was responsible, and it is fortunate that his reputation does not rest upon the work. As he points out in his preface, he had known the old reformer only in his later years, and therefore on many points he had drawn his information, such as it was, from Holcroft's "early and most intimate friends" and from the autobiographical hints scattered through his works.* When he could, Hazlitt presumably tried to ascertain the facts of his subject's extraordinary career as stable boy, shoemaker, actor, playwright, translator, novelist, and radical; † but he was working on consignment, and his conscience did not smite him when he had to improvise or rely upon conjecture.⁶ For example, he gives a very close account of young William Holcroft's suicide on the ground that the event had been "sometimes misrepresented," ⁷ but he is vague about the elder Holcroft's complicated family life and reticent to the point of obscurity about other parts of his career. Thus we learn, not greatly to our edification, that "after wandering for seven years as an itinerant actor, with no very brilliant success," Holcroft "resolved upon trying his fortune in London, and arrived there early in the latter end of 1777." ⁸ Similarly, for the fifteen years between Holcroft's trial for treason and his death Hazlitt's information is both patchy and confused.⁹ When all else failed, he was content to summarize the plots of endless novels.

With all its errors and omissions, however, the *Life* retains a certain interest, partly because it provides the text of Holcroft's diary and partly because it contains Hazlitt's first extended comment on the reformist agitation of the nineties. He writes like something of a hack when he deals with Holcroft's own hack work, and he fails, or does not try, to catch the anger, pride, and vanity for which his man became a legend.

* 3.ix–x. In "My First Acquaintance with Poets" (17.112) Hazlitt implies that he had known (and rather disliked) Holcroft before 1798. They had no doubt met through Godwin.

† In one of his letters to Godwin about preparations for the *Grammar* (see page 172) Hazlitt included several questions about Holcroft's early life, from which we may infer that he was working, or was preparing to work, on the *Memoirs* in the summer of 1809.

But Holcroft as a friend of liberty was a subject to his taste, and in those chapters where he describes the creed and motives of the "purely speculative politician" he rises to great power.[10] In this section Holcroft emerges — somewhat plausibly — as the champion of a noble, hopeless cause, and his *Narrative of Facts* as a modern *Areopagitica*. It is here that Hazlitt's dedication to reform, a theme that underlies much of his late work, emerges bold and strong.

Although the sponsors of the book were apparently untroubled by Hazlitt's errors and omissions they were quick to pounce on his use of Holcroft's private papers. He had already told Robinson that an appendix containing the unexpurgated diary, with its unflattering comments on some of Holcroft's friends, might involve him in a "scrape," and when, early in January 1810, he took the completed manuscript to London his prediction was fulfilled. Godwin was particularly upset. Losing his philosophic calm, he told Holcroft's widow that since Hazlitt's assignment had been to put together a biography and a selection from the letters there was "not the least imagination" that he would use the diary except as a source for facts and dates. To print it verbatim was unthinkable. "It is one thing for a man to write a journal," he asserted, "and another for that journal to be given to the public." Many eminent persons (like Dr. Parr and Mrs. Siddons) would surely take offense; others might regard its publication as actionable; and as for Godwin himself, he would not care to have Mary Wollstonecraft's "private transactions" with her first lover (Gilbert Imlay) aired. If I had known, he added tartly, that

every time I dined with or called upon Mr. H. I was to be recorded in a Quarto book, well printed, and and [sic] with an ornamental frontispiece in the ridiculous way of coming in to go out again fifty times I would not on that penalty have called upon, or dined with him at all.

To such a publication, he concluded, he would be "no part or party." * But all was not yet lost, as we learn from William Nicholson's letter to Mrs. Holcroft on January 22.[11] It was clear, he said, that Hazlitt's manuscript should not be printed as it stood, but since Godwin himself had volunteered to edit it, the situation could be saved.

I am very much pleased to hear that he is disposed to take the trouble of doing what may be proper, with regard to the manuscript, to render it what it ought to be, in justice to the deceased, who if he had a right to keep such a Journal, can

* Godwin's diary shows that Hazlitt came for tea on January 6 and called again three days later. Godwin spent the fourteenth and fifteenth going through the manuscript Hazlitt left with him, and shortly thereafter, it would seem, he drafted the undated letter (now in the Abinger Collection) from which I quote. There is an inaccurate transcript in Paul, II, 176f.

never be supposed to have contemplated its entire publication; and to yourself, upon whom the discretionary power of publishing has devolved. . . . I think it absolutely necessary that what Mr. Godwin proposes to do should be done and I rejoice for your sake, that a friend so capable of doing it as it ought to be done, is willing to undertake the task.

This comedy of errors sputtered out in anger and confusion. Presumably Godwin's threat of redoing Hazlitt's work was never executed, but a string of calls and letters recorded in his diary suggests that the two men arranged a sort of truce and tried to salvage something from the manuscript.* Some two months after Mrs. Holcroft had reclaimed her husband's papers she was still trudging from Nicholson to Tuthil, from Tuthil to Godwin, from Godwin to Tuthil, and again from Tuthil to Godwin "to consult on the publication, or no publication." Meanwhile the Lambs had dubbed Hazlitt's book the Life Everlasting.[12] In this state of suspended animation the matter rested, for all we know, until the late summer of 1816,† when Longman's finally published, in three small volumes, *Memoirs of the Late Thomas Holcroft, Written by Himself, and Continued to the Time of His Death, from His Diary, Notes, and Other Papers.* It will be noticed that no editor is named. The fact that the offensive diary was included suggests that Godwin, after all, had not revised the manuscript himself; but since certain racy spots that he had singled out for disapproval were apparently deleted it would seem that Hazlitt had yielded to at least some of his objections. "There are some personalities in the original which are omitted," reads the introduction to the diary as the text was finally printed, "and others which may still be thought improper." [13] For want of more specific information we may suppose that these omissions, together with the deletion of certain of the letters, represented Hazlitt's effort to placate Mrs. Holcroft and her friends.‡ To assume that he made these changes to

---

* Letters from Godwin on February 8 and 20 were followed by calls by Hazlitt on the twenty-third and twenty-fourth, and Godwin wrote to him again on March 15, May 29, and June 4. In addition, Sarah Hazlitt saw Godwin several times while she was staying with the Lambs in April (Lucas, II, 97). After 4 June 1810 Hazlitt disappears from Godwin's diary until October 4, when he made another call on him. It was during this stay in London in October that he replied to the *Edinburgh* review of the *Reply* to Malthus (see page 164 n), about which Lamb wrote to him on November 28 (Lucas, II, 111f.).

† The date is fixed by Godwin's diary, which records his reading the three volumes of the *Memoirs* between August 21 and 23.

‡ While this book was going through the press Ernest J. Moyne's discovery, in the Massachusetts Historical Society, of a letter of 5 November [1809] from Hazlitt to his father has provided welcome confirmation of my conjectures about the picayune revisions in the Holcroft *Memoirs*. The *Grammar*, already printed, would be published very soon, he said, and his work on Holcroft was proceeding briskly. Before the Lambs came down to Winterslow he had transcribed almost a hundred pages from Holcroft's own account of his career, he told his father, and by working hard each evening —

soothe his employers' ruffled feelings does no violence to the facts we have; moreover, it enables us to scotch the rumor of an alleged fourth volume of the *Memoirs* that Hazlitt's grandson said was written and suppressed [14] but that no one has ever seen. The mystery of the missing volume fades when we recall what Hazlitt must have cut from the first draft. The fact that the work, after such vicissitudes, was finally cleared for publication permits the hope that Mrs. Holcroft and her friends at last were made content.*

THE LECTURES ON PHILOSOPHY

The two bleak years following the fiasco over Holcroft's *Memoirs* need not detain us long. In February 1810, telling Crabb Robinson that none of the "many plots & projects" running through his head seemed to promise much, Hazlitt said that with "one more push" he hoped "to be afloat, at least for a good while to come"; [1] but since the year slipped by with no new work begun we may assume that his decision, early in 1811, to return to London for another stab at painting was born of desperation. Misfortune dogged him still, and as we see him in the pages of Crabb Robinson's newly started diary he cuts a sorry figure. For one thing, Coleridge, having quarreled with Wordsworth and left the Lakes forever, was living as his neighbor in the Southampton Buildings, [2] moving briskly in the Lamb and Godwin circle, and proving to be a source of constant irritation. Not only did he impose upon the Lambs and keep them in "a perpetual fever" that was very bad for Mary, [3] but his politics had stiffened in a way that Hazlitt must have found infuriating. The recent Tory vaporings in *The Friend,* he said later, were proof that even "the finest intellects" could not escape the contagion of the time. [4] For his part, Coleridge, whose addiction made him strangely unctuous about other people's faults, was convinced that through his intimacy with Hazlitt Lamb had jeopardized his health and character. [5] It was about this time, moreover, that he began telling all and sundry that Hazlitt had stolen all his good ideas from him. [6] I do not know how intimate you

---

for his days were spent in painting — he had done another thirty-five. Since his task was mainly one of compilation, he hoped that the manuscript would be done by Christmas. As the plan then stood, of the projected 450 pages eighty would be filled with Holcroft's reminiscences, fifty with his diary for 1798–99, 170 with Hazlitt's comments and reflections, and 150 with the subject's correspondence. Mr. Moyne's transcription of this letter is scheduled for early publication in *PMLA.*

* For an able discussion of this and other problems connected with the Holcroft *Memoirs* see Virgil R. Stallbaumer, "Hazlitt's *Life of Thomas Holcroft,*" *American Benedictine Review,* V (1954), 27–44.

are with Coleridge, Mrs. Thomas Clarkson wrote to Robinson about the recent row with Wordsworth, "but he is apt to make any one who listens to him the confident of his gloomy fancies or wild dreams of injuries — his best friends are not exempted from his accusations upon these occasions — let me caution you therefore against believing any thing to the prejudice of W[illiam]. W[ordsworth]. I mean with regard to his conduct as a friend to C. It has been affectionate & forbearing throughout." [7]

To add to these vexations Hazlitt's work was going badly. Despite the several commissions for portraits that Robinson got for him, his painting, as always, led only to frustration. A portrait of Thomas Clarkson turned out fairly well,* but the others (including one of Crabb Robinson's brother) gave him so much trouble that finally, about mid-April, he abruptly left for Winterslow. As Godwin told the story, one of the pictures had been rejected with such an "abusive letter" that Hazlitt "left town in great agony" without even completing the work upon his easel. "He has not sent my brother's picture," Crabb Robinson confided to his diary, "and I fear does not mean to let it go out of his hands; perhaps he has already destroyed it. And I fear he had not the money to refund. I saw also to-day Mr. Howel's portrait. It is a good caricature likeness, but a coarse painting. I fear poor Hazlitt will never succeed. With very great talents and with uncommon powers of mind I fear he is doomed to pass a life of poverty and unavailing repinings against society and his evil destiny." [†]

A month later, in May, Robinson learned that Hazlitt had neither sent the uncompleted portrait nor offered any explanation. "Let me know his address," his brother asked, "in order that I may write to him again." [8] Finally, after another month had passed, Hazlitt made a "lame," belated explanation to his disgruntled patron. "I was quite ashamed to receive your letter, & know not what to answer." Attributing the delay in part to his "unfortunate habit" of procrastination and in part to his fear of botching the assignment, he promised to "do what I can to it before I come to town in October, & will then leave it with your brother. Till then I do not forget that I am your debtor." Crabb Robinson's terse endorse-

---

* "I think the face of Mr Clarksons picture most beautifully painted & there is a freedom in the whole Picture very creditable to Hazlitt" (ALS, Mrs. Thomas Clarkson to Crabb Robinson, 21 July 1811, Dr. Williams's Library).

† I, 30. Hazlitt is mentioned eight times in Godwin's diary between February 4 and March 23, whereupon he disappears until the fall. We may assume, therefore, that he fled to Winterslow in early April. In May he wrote to Thomas Hardy, the bootmaker who had been the hero of the treason trials of 1794, about an unpaid bill (The Hazlitts, pp. 448f.): "I was obliged to leave London without discharging my promise," he explained, "the reason of which was that I was myself disappointed in not receiving £20 which was due to me, £10 for a picture, & £10 for revising a manuscript. I am at present actually without money in the house."

ment on this letter tells the ending of the story: "To T[homas] R[obinson] ab[ou]t his portrait So bad a one that it was never finished — and what was done was destroyed." *

❖ ❖ ❖

In September 1811 Sarah Hazlitt finally bore a child who lived[9] — an event that prompted charming letters from the Lambs[10] — and within a week or so her husband was in London once again, this time to seek subscriptions for a set of lectures on philosophy. Having got thirty names at two guineas each, he told Crabb Robinson in late October, he needed only "ten or a dozen more" in order to justify the venture. "If therefore you could assist me by picking up one or two names, I can only say I shall be much obliged to you, & that the lectures will be as good as I can make them." Of the ten projected lectures, he explained, six had been completed and the topics of the other four were set. Although he did not say so, we may infer that they had been designed as a critique of that "modern philosophy" that had occupied his thoughts for the last ten years or so, and that, earlier, he had hoped to write a book about. The topics were as follows: Hobbes's metaphysics, Locke's epistemology, Berkeley, self-love and benevolence, Helvetius and Hartley, Butler, Price and Priestley's controversy on materialism (two lectures), Horne Tooke's theory of abstraction, and natural religion.[11]

Although Robinson, characteristically, was sympathetic with a man in trouble, he was also filled with gloomy doubts. Not only did he question Hazlitt's ability to bring the lectures "to effect," as he told his brother,[12] but also he was offended by the way the man preyed upon his friends. "C. and M. Lamb feel as I do," he wrote to Mrs. Clarkson, "& express themselves strongly on the *indelicacy* (to use a *delicate* word) of Hazlitt's application to Mr. Clarkson — he is also [like Coleridge] an instance of great powers of intellect rendered worthless to their possessor from constitutional infirmities & moral obliquities!!!"[13] By mid-December Robinson was convinced that Hazlitt's latest scheme would fail, just as all his other schemes had failed. "The truth is," he informed his brother, "that poor H. is so poor & so unhappy that I can't but feel more pity than displeasure [at his evasions about the uncompleted portrait]. He an-

---

* ALS, 18 July 1811, Dr. Williams's Library. A year later, still "operating on Thomas," Hazlitt had given to the portrait "the fierceness of the Saracen," Crabb Robinson recorded (I, 104), but even then he was not prepared to let it go. Finally, on the day before Christmas of 1812, by which time Hazlitt had become a journalist, Crabb "ventured to ask" again about his brother's portrait and received a promising reply; "I believe I shall get it," he remarked in triumph (I, 116). When and by whom the picture was "destroyed" does not appear.

nounced you know lectures on the history of philosophy & wrote to me to procure him Subscrip^s. I informed him J Buck & J Collier would subscribe. He first sent me three tickets & then wrote to beg I would pay for them. J.B. & J.C. consented And I left him the Six Guineas.* When the lectures will be delivered I can not tell. He means to deliver them as he does to deliver y^r picture, And will probably do both sooner or later, but we must wait his time — I feel real compassion for the poverty into which a man of great powers of mind is cast; And I can find a number of excuses in the affliction of a situation I should sink under." [14] Despite such misgivings — which were no doubt widely shared — by Christmas 1811 Hazlitt had completed his arrangements,† and three weeks later, at the Russell Institution, a subscription library and reading room in Great Coram Street, he delivered his first lecture.

Lectures were such a rage in early nineteenth-century London that Lamb cited "ten thousand institutions" where culture could be bought and sold.[15] Since Coleridge got a hundred guineas for a series that he gave (or failed to give) in 1808 [16] and Thomas Campbell the same sum for his debut three years later,[17] it is clear that for men with reputations lecturing paid very well indeed and that even for nobodies like Hazlitt, who had to scramble up subscriptions from their friends, it was a source of ready cash. Badly as he needed money, however, he must have trembled at the prospect of talking on his feet, and according to Robinson his fears were not without foundation. His first performance, a knotty piece on Hobbes, was read so fast, and in such a low, monotonous voice, that it was hardly understood; and the post-mortem by certain of his friends (including John Stoddart, who kindly wrote a letter setting forth his faults) was so unflattering that he almost gave the project up. But he improved, and the series that opened in disaster proceeded fairly well. At his second appearance he was several times "interrupted by applauses," by the fourth his manner had become "very respectable," by the eighth he was "interesting and animated." Then, in March, his "debts" grew so oppressive that he could not "proceed." "I wish I could afford him assistance," said

* John Buck (whose sister Catherine married Thomas Clarkson, the noted abolitionist) and John Dyer Collier (father of John Payne Collier, the scholar and forger) were early friends of Robinson (I, 2f.) as well as of Godwin, Coleridge, and the Lambs. See Edith J. Morley, *The Life and Times of Henry Crabb Robinson* (1935), p. 5, and below, page 192.

† On December 19 the committee of the Russell Institution voted to accept Hazlitt's proposal for a set of lectures, and a week later they approved the topics he proposed. The minutes of these committee meetings are preserved in British Museum Add. MS. 38,899; cf. *Memoirs*, I, 192f.

THE LECTURES ON PHILOSOPHY

Robinson, "for I know no state of suffering more dreadful than that of indigent genius. Nor is my pity less for Hazlitt, because my esteem for him is not great." By the end of the month, however, he resumed the series, and when, on April 27, he gave his final lecture it was so "very well delivered and full of shrewd observation" that it seemed a minor triumph. The conclusion, said Robinson, was especially attractive: Hazlitt told about a Brahman who was so much addicted to philosophy that he forgot his moral duties and neglected his religion, and was consequently turned into a monkey. Even then, however, he shunned the other monkeys, and delighted only in eating coconuts and pondering metaphysics. " 'I, too,' said Hazlitt, 'should be very well contented to pass my life like this monkey, did I but know how to provide myself with a substitute for coconuts.' " *

It is by no means certain that the lectures that survive are the ones Hazlitt gave. The ten topics he outlined for Robinson in October 1811 correspond to those the committee of the Russell Institution voted to approve, and the manuscripts exhumed by Hazlitt's son from an old forgotten hamper and first printed in 1836 † may be plausibly identified as units of this group. On the other hand, the lectures Robinson reported in his diary [18] differ in all kinds of ways from those the speaker had announced. Instead of ten there were eleven lectures, and the subjects were as follows: the first on Hobbes (January 14), the second, third, and fourth on Locke (January 21 and 28 and February 4), the fifth and sixth on benevolence (February 11 and 18), the seventh on Hartley (February 25), the eighth on Helvetius (March 3), the ninth (March 17) on a topic not named (Robinson having skipped the lecture for a game of whist), the tenth on free will and necessity (March 31), and the eleventh (April 27) apparently on the use of metaphysics. Although Hazlitt's son assumed that some of the manuscripts written for this series were "altogether missing, burnt probably, by the ignorant people of the house" where they had been abandoned,[19] it is possible that those he found and printed were all his father wrote.‡ Having begun the series by reading — very badly — from manuscript,[20] Hazlitt may have decided to speak from notes or im-

---

* Robinson, I, 58, 60, 62, 63, 65f., 69f. In 1815 Hazlitt used this anecdote (20.52) in a Round Table paper for the *Examiner*. Howe (20.402) suggests that the essay (a two-part piece called "Mind and Motive") may have been derived from his final lecture on philosophy.

† Four appeared in *Literary Remains*, I, 115–362, and another (on abstract ideas) in the second (1836) edition of the *Essay*, pp. 139–176. See Keynes, p. 103. Both Howe (2.289f.) and Schneider (p. 12) assume that the extant lectures are those that Hazlitt gave in 1812.

‡ On the other hand, the eight "articles" on modern philosophy that Hazlitt tried to sell in 1821 to Robert Baldwin, proprietor of the *London Magazine* (*Life*, p. 280) may have been the texts of these old lectures.

provise the later lectures so that he could cut, adapt, and rearrange the ones that he had written; and if so, the lectures that survive are not the ones his audience at the Russell Institution heard.

None the less, it is certain that they express the same convictions. Lecturing at the Philosophical Society in Fleet Street in the winter of 1811–12, Coleridge touched on "every subject that ever entered the head of man," * but Hazlitt, perhaps because he knew so little else, stuck to the subject he announced. It was one that he had thought about for ten or fifteen years. As we have seen, the *Essay* had been generated by his discontent with the ethics of "modern philosophy," and his preface to *The Light of Nature* and his *Reply* to Malthus had broadened the attack. A hostility to sensationalism had inspired his prospectus for the book that he had wished to write in 1809, and although a year later, as he told Crabb Robinson, he was still toying with the notion of "turning the History of E[nglish] Philosophy into a volume of Essays on the subjects mentioned in the prospectus," this was one of his many "plots & projects" that were never executed.[21] Thus when he finally had the chance to do an extended piece of work on a topic of his choice, his subject was at hand.

The subject, which might be compendiously described as the inadequacies of English empiricism, is outlined in the 1809 prospectus, where Hazlitt summarizes his objections to the philosophy that resolves all "thought into *sensation*, all morality into the *love of pleasure*, and all action into *mechanical* impulse." It was a philosophy, he said, in which "the mind itself is nothing, and external impressions everything." [22] When Bacon, recoiling from the pretensions of the Schoolmen, construed "experience" as nothing more than "a knowledge of things without us," [23] he began the mischief that Hobbes, the real "father of the modern philosophy," † transformed into a system. Popularized by Locke (whose only talent was for using, and sometimes vulgarizing, other men's ideas), and applied by Hartley, Condillac, and others, Hobbes's notion that the "downright blows of matter" [24] are the source of all our mental operations had hardened into dogma. It was a dogma that Hazlitt, as a "metaphysician," spent ten years or more in trying to dislodge and that in his later years he continued to attack in more oblique and artful ways. In his lectures of 1812 he did not presume to expound a system of his own, for

* L'Estrange, I, 162; cf. Robinson, I, 53, 55. Godwin's diary shows that whereas he attended many of Coleridge's lectures he went to only one of Hazlitt's (on February 4).

† 2.116. This was one of Hazlitt's favorite notions. In 1816 he wrote two papers for the *Examiner* on Locke as a plagiarist from Hobbes (20.69–83), and he frequently reverted to the subject later (for example, 11.191, 16.123, 258).

he was skeptical of philosophic systems and of men who manufactured them; but he did try to show that mechanism evaded or suppressed the claims of "mind," or conscience, and of common sense. If we attribute to sensation "the form, the substance, the colour, the very life and being of whatever exists in our own minds," he said, or if we cite the "laws" of matter to explain the subtleties of intellection, then we "confound two things essentially distinct." [25] "The Mind has laws, powers, and principles of its own, and is not the mere puppet of matter." [26]

The ten "principles" of the 1809 prospectus, a kind of gloss upon this text, present the topics that in the lectures are worked out in great detail.* Since understanding is a primary mental operation rather than a means by which we generalize upon and synthesize the concrete data of sensation, Hazlitt says, it is the source of all our "after-knowledge," and therefore a distinct "inlet of truth, over and above *experience*." [27] It follows that just as Hartley's rigid associationism cannot explain all our mental functions, an ethics built upon the proposition that mind is subject to the laws of matter cannot explain all our moral promptings. Neither hedonism nor utility exhausts the reservoir of human motives, for action has its source in "the moral and rational nature of man, or in that principle — call it reason, conscience, moral sense, what you will — which, without any reference to our own interests, passions, and pursuits, approves of certain actions and sentiments as right, and condemns others as wrong. To act right is to act in conformity to this standard." [28] Therefore mind is not enslaved by matter. We are moved, not, like billiard balls, by external pressures as recorded through sensation, but only by the will, and will is guided by the "mind."

It is *free*, in as far as it is not the slave of external impressions, physical impulses, or blind senseless motives. It is free, as the body is free, when it is not subject to a power out of itself, though its operations still depend on certain powers and principles within itself. It is not thrust upon any actions without its own consent and concurrence. This does not imply that actions are without a cause, but that *that* cause is not a mechanical one. [29]

Except for the debonair assault on Horne Tooke's theory of abstraction (which we have noted earlier) all the so-called lectures that Hazlitt gave in 1812 are based upon these "principles" that he drew up in 1809. As his first big effort to evaluate the books and theories that had dominated eighteenth-century thought, they are his assessment of the empirical tradition, and so, whatever charms they lack, they are not without importance. Consisting of mainly derogatory comments threaded on a string

* At the end of his first lecture (2.144f.) Hazlitt formulates the "leading principles" of the "School" of Hobbes under ten headings and then announces his intention of opposing them "to the utmost of my ability."

of long quotations, they are anything but brisk to read, and if delivered as they stand today they would have been almost intolerable to hear. Now and then we meet emphatic comments on Hobbes's "air or grandeur," [30] Locke's timidity in tackling fundamental problems, [31] Berkeley's incomparable "subtilty" of thought and ease of style, [32] Condillac's skill at "substituting words for things," [33] Helvetius' shaky defense of utilitarian morals, [34] and the like; but in the main the lectures are chunky and expository, and they make us work for what we get.

From these ungainly lectures a central theme of Hazlitt's later work emerges: the conviction that although mind works only on the data of sensation, it does so with a power and freedom of its own. In asserting that our mental operations are subject to the so-called natural laws that govern things in motion, Hobbes, he thought, had made a basic error. He had held that our responses to external stimuli are single, and that we have no "comprehensive power" by which we fuse the data of sensation into genuine ideas. Despite their refinements and evasions, Hobbes's disciples had merely compounded this mistake. Making a bad simile — the *tabula rasa* — the basis of his metaphysics, Locke, the most admired of modern thinkers, had written a highly influential book on the human understanding without saying anything at all about the subject; and his followers — Hartley, Helvetius, Condillac, and the rest — had elaborately refined upon established error.

The unifying theme of Hazlitt's lectures is his opposition to this doctrine. Surely it is not enough, he says, to regard the mind as "a sort of empty room into which ideas are conveyed from without through the doors of the senses, as you would carry goods into an unfurnished lodging." [35] Over and beyond sensation there is a "superintending faculty, which alone perceives the relations of things, and enables us to comprehend their connexions, forms, and masses"; [36] and this faculty, which the Hobbesians had deprecated, is man's unique distinction. Refusing to refine on Locke as Locke refined on Hobbes, Hazlitt bluntly contradicts him. As we have seen in his remarks on Tooke, he holds that to deal in general notions, rather than in sharp, concrete sensations, is the fundamental operation of the mind. "The smallest division of which our notions are susceptible is a general idea. In the progress of the understanding, we never begin from absolute unity but always from something that is more." [37] Owing to the limitations of our sensory apparatus we do not perceive simple entities and later put them into groups and clusters; instead, "aggregates" themselves are the primary objects of sensation, and these the mind creates from data provided by the senses. To be sure, "consciousness" is a process that baffles comprehension, but whatever it it, or whatever relation exists between external objects and the notions that we have of them, it is clear, says Hazlitt, that mind is not a mere sensorium. It is an activity or "power" by which we organize and, in a sense, create our impressions of the outer world. This theory of abstraction underlies his conviction that "the mind alone is formative." * Perhaps first prompted by his attempts at painting — which had taught him that our responses to individual things are "vague broken and imperfect" [38] — it came to occupy the center of his philosophic thought. Whether exposing Locke's mistakes about the role of understanding,[39] or attacking utilitarian ethics,[40] or contending for the freedom of the will,[41] he cites the power of mind by which we construe the realm of matter in terms that are moral and intelligible.

Despite this idealistic strain in Hazlitt's philosophic thought we should not forget — as he sometimes tended to forget — how much he owed to the empiricists. Ignorant of Plato,[42] mistaken about Kant (whose language was unknown to him),[43] and dissatisfied with Berkeley,[44] he was obliged to rest on Hobbes. He rebelled against sensationalism, especially in its ethics, but he was fastened to the system; and as his later work in art and literature makes clear, it served him very well. He had a deep respect for "fact" and "common sense," and as a critic he did not need the jargon of philosophy to realize that "experience" is the source and test of knowledge. That there are no innate ideas, he said, is a truth so "obvious" that it needs no formal demonstration,[45] and his crude attack on Kant's a priori notions as the "forms of *nothing*" makes his own position clear: "the business of the mind," he said, "is twofold — to receive impressions and to perceive their relations; without which there can be no ideas." [46] All his work is grounded on this proposition, for the power that he ascribed to mind was, *au fond*, the power to organize and in a sense transform the data of sensation.

His doctrine of imagination, as developed in his later work, was a doctrine of cognition, and it was built on concrete objects of perception — not on general and abstract ideas — as the source of knowledge, the base of all deep feeling, and the stimulus of art. It is not through "reason," with its artificial constructs and abstractions, that we attain our highest truths, but through "passion" and involvement with what is felt along the

---

* 2.153, 280. Hazlitt first used this Kantian tag, which he perhaps picked up from Coleridge, in his preface to *The Light of Nature* (1.130), and there he cites it to oppose the "mechanical ignorance" of Locke and his successors. His subsequent hostility to "notions a priori" is recorded in a series of articles on Madame de Staël in 1814 (20.12–36 and especially pp. 18–22) and three years later in his *Edinburgh* review of *Biographia Literaria* (16.123f.). It was a hostility born of ignorance and nurtured by his growing discontent with Coleridge. See Schneider, pp. 29ff.; René Wellek, *Immanuel Kant in England 1793–1838* (1931), pp. 164–171.

pulses. This is truth not merely of perception, but of good and evil too, for "in art, in taste, in life, in speech, you decide from feeling, and not from reason." [47] "With respect to moral truth (as distinct from mathematical)," he said not long before he died,

whether a thing is good or evil, depends on the quantity of passion, of feeling, of pleasure and pain connected with it, and with which we must be made acquainted in order to come to a sound conclusion, and not on the inquiry, whether it is round or square. Passion, in short, is the essence, the chief ingredient in moral truth; and the warmth of passion is sure to kindle the light of imagination on the objects around it. The "words that glow" are almost inseparable from the "thoughts that burn." Hence logical reason and practical truth are *disparates.*[48]

Whereas French dramatic dialogue, he said in 1825, is "frothy verbiage or a mucilage of sentiment without natural bones or substance," English drama "clings to the concrete, and has a *purchase* upon matter." [49] Without such anchorage in fact, thought is loose and vapid and art is drained of meaning. Hazlitt's greatness as a critic derives at least in part from his conviction that "facts, concrete existences, are stubborn things" that no great art ignores.[50] "Truth does not lie *in vacuo,*" he said, "any more than in a well. We must improve our concrete experience of persons and things into the contemplation of general rules and principles; but without being grounded in individual facts and feelings, we shall end as we began, in ignorance." [51]

❖ ❖ ❖

The lectures mark an end to Hazlitt's years of preparation and to the ragged hack work of his youth. His discontent with eighteenth-century mechanism, his doctrine of the shaping mind, and his respect for "common sense" and the facts of observation do not receive their fullest statement there, of course, but these themes served to unify his lectures, and they show that he stood poised for his more important work. Not impelled by Coleridge's quest for absolutes, hostile to Wordsworth's pantheistic urges, incapable of Blake's or Shelley's mystic exaltation, he was none the less a product of his age. His decade of philosophizing, from the *Essay* to the lectures at the Russell Institution, made no lasting contribution to European thought: the works are hard and badly written, he has no system to propound, and his most intense convictions are among the commonplaces of the day. But it is in these works that he takes his mental bearings and asserts his own position, and if the conclusions that he reached were, *mutatis mutandis*, much like those that other men were reaching, still they were his own, earned with much hard thought and shaped by his own needs and temperament. At long last he was ready for the work that he was born to do.

V

The Trade of Letters

◇◇

THE RISING JOURNALIST

That Hazlitt should have stumbled into journalism might be cited as a sign of special providence, but he himself provided a more prosaic explanation. Any man so poor that he is avoided by those who recognize his merit, regarded as a burden to his family, and plagued by thoughts of suicide has a hard decision, he remarked: he may become a law-stationer, a scrivener, a scavenger, or a reporter.[1] Coleridge, in looking back upon his own career, lamented that he had wasted the "prime and manhood" of his intellect in scribbling for the press,[2] but when Hazlitt, a failure on the verge of middle age, began writing for the London papers, he finally found his métier.

His lectures in early 1812 having led to nothing, for six months or so he lingered on in London, tinkering with Thomas Robinson's still unfinished portrait,[3] trying to borrow money from his friends,* and looking for a job. At last, prodded by Crabb Robinson and Stoddart (both of whom had journalistic contacts), and no doubt by Hazlitt's own solicitations, James Perry of the *Morning Chronicle* gave a "conditional promise" of employment to the disgruntled painter and philosopher, and

---

* Robinson, I, 110. It was about this time, presumably, that Hazlitt wrote for the Society for the Diffusion of Knowledge on the Punishment of Death a little piece on capital punishment (19.324–329) that was not printed until 1831, when it appeared in *Fraser's Magazine*. There (II, 666) it is described as "part of an essay which was written, a few years ago, by the late Mr. Hazlitt, at the request of a Society then existing in London, for obtaining a repeal of this formidable law [of capital punishment]. . . . It has never yet been published." According to an entry of 8 September 1812 in Crabb Robinson's diary (which Miss Morley does not print), Hazlitt had borrowed thirty pounds from Anthony Robinson with the promise of repayment in a fortnight, when he would get his fee from the Society. "However, several fortnights have elapsed," the diarist reported, "and he [Anthony] has never heard from or seen H. since. Such are the difficulties from which great talents alone, without discretion, will never relieve a man." See Howe's note, 19.368.

John Walter of the *Times* undertook to "do something" for him too. Although Robinson fretted over Hazlitt's "injudicious conduct" in seeming to play one against the other, by late September he decided that the "prospect of his finding the means of subsistence" were brighter than before.[4] It is pleasant to think that the scales were tipped by a note from Lamb to John Dyer Collier, who was Perry's foreign editor. Hoping that a "reporter's situation" might be found for an able, desperate man, Lamb said, he recommended Hazlitt highly. "I am sure I shall *myself* be obliged to you for your exertions, having a great regard for him." * As a consequence of these exertions, no doubt, in the fall of 1812 Hazlitt went to work as a Parliamentary reporter, at four guineas a week,[5] for the *Morning Chronicle*, the noted Whig organ whose contributors included, at one time or another, Sheridan, Lamb, Mackintosh, Brougham, and even young Charles Dickens, and which Hazlitt himself regarded as the best of all the London dailies.[6] In the same fall he rented from Jeremy Bentham a house at 19 York Street, Westminster — a house that Milton once had occupied and that James Mill had just vacated because it was "unhealthy" [7] — and so, at thirty-four, he at last began to enjoy solvency and even a modest measure of success. Dropping by a few months later to find him with the Lambs and Burneys at supper, Crabb Robinson rejoiced at the change in Hazlitt's fortune.†

Although he was by no means hurtled into wealth and fame, his next six years as journalist, compared with what had gone before, were giddy with success. His first assignment — and a lowly one it proved to be — was to report on Parliamentary speeches, a type of oratory that his work on *The Eloquence of the British Senate* had made him wary of and that his duties in the press gallery led him to despise. To speak the truth in the House of Commons, he said later, was the "greatest test of courage" that he knew,[8] and when, on rare occasions (like Mackintosh's maiden speech in 1813), one of the honorable members did show candor and intelligence, it was an event to be cherished in the memory.‡ Even though

* Lucas, II, 124. Although Howe (*Life*, pp. 133f.) assumes that Mrs. Collier prompted Lamb's letter to her husband, Robinson (I, 116) makes it clear that Mrs. Thomas Clarkson was responsible. It will be recalled (see page 182n) that she had liked Hazlitt's portrait of her husband.

† I, 116. Although Sarah Hazlitt appears twice in Godwin's diary (May 15 and July 12) during the summer of 1812, it would seem that she and her infant son were generally at Winterslow until her husband found a job. For Hazlitt's later allusions to the York Street house and to his famous landlord see 10.283, 11.6; cf. Patmore, II, 260 ff.; Landseer, I, 109f.; George Ticknor, *Life, Letters, and Journals* (1909), I, 293f.; below, pages 257f.

‡ 11.97. Hazlitt's memories of the press gallery inspired two essays written for the *London Magazine* in 1820: "On the Difference between Writing and Speaking" (12.262–279) and "On the Present State of Parliamentary Eloquence" (17.5–21). Another relic of this period was a notebook, containing Sarah Hazlitt's transcription of

Hazlitt's "best faculties" were not needed for the job, Robinson confided to his diary, they at least were kept awake, and it was certain that with any encouragement his "most powerful intellect" would soon reveal itself.[9] Perhaps Hazlitt hoped that the chance to review Coleridge's *Remorse*, which, rewritten from *Osorio*, was produced at Drury Lane in January 1813, would lead to something better; but apart from the poet's irritation at what he took to be the reviewer's condescension * the piece had no effect, and Hazlitt went back to reporting Parliamentary speeches. Not until the following fall, in fact, did he escape from the drudgery of the press gallery. It was then, toward the end of 1813, that Perry — a man of "strong natural sense, some acquired knowledge, a quick tact"[10] — took a fancy to some trifles he had written and printed them as "Common-Places." †

These little essays on such genteel topics as education and the love of life marked a turning point, for Perry was impressed by them. Having "despaired" at his failure in philosophy and being no doubt restive as a mere "reporter," Hazlitt was quick to push his advantage. "I resolved to

---

Christabel (as well as excerpts from Campbell, Holcroft, Lamb, and others), in which Hazlitt jotted notes on Parliamentary speeches. Sarah's transcription of *Christabel* no doubt derived from her brother's visit to Keswick in 1800 (Griggs, I, 643), and it must have been to this version that Scott was indebted, as he implies (*Poetical Works* [ed. J. Logie Robertson, 1916], p. 52), for the prosody of *The Lay of the Last Minstrel.* From the same source Hazlitt probably got the 253d line, which, though omitted from the printed version of the poem, he remembered (and misquoted) in the *Examiner* review of 2 June 1816 (19.33). On this review see pages 346f. See Coleridge's *Seven Lectures on Shakespeare and Milton* (ed. John Payne Collier, 1856), note to p. xxxix; Coleridge's *Poems*, p. 213n; W. C. Hazlitt, *Lamb and Hazlitt* (1899), pp. xxiii f.

* Although Hazlitt spoke of a certain "sentimental whine and affectation of fine feeling" in *Remorse*, he said that the piece was "fraught with beauty and interest," and his long review (18.463ff.) was generally favorable. Coleridge was not pleased, however, and complained to John Rickman (Williams, p. 166) that Hazlitt had "sneered" at him for trying to compete with Shakespeare. For Hazlitt's later comments on the play see 5.247, 368, 11.35, 17.122, 18.304.

† In August 1813 Hazlitt submitted to Perry a sheaf of his unpublished work with the explanation (ALS in the possession of Mr. and Mrs. Donald F. Hyde) that he had "several papers of this kind by me, if they can be made of any use, such as — on classical education — on advantages & disadvantages of education in general — on love of posthumous fame — on taste and seeing — on love of nature — on patriotism — causes of methodism — on envy among artists — characters of writers, painters, actors, &c." Perry printed two of these, "On the Love of Life" (4.1–4) and "On Classical Education" (4.4ff.), which, together with others that subsequently appeared in the *Examiner* — "On the Love of the Country" (4.17–21), "On Posthumous Fame" (4.21–24), "On the Causes of Methodism" (4.57–61), and "On Patriotism — a Fragment" (4.67f.) — were included in *The Round Table* in 1817. Even earlier than these, however, was an amusing paragraph on the Marquis Wellesley's oratorical style that the stoutly Tory *Courier* inexplicably printed on 13 April 1813 and that six years later found its way into *Political Essays* (7.23). Professor H. M. Sikes has suggested to me that Hazlitt probably wrote the long letter on Napoleon's military and political situation (incidentally highly critical of the *Courier*) that the *Morning Chronicle* printed as the work of "Philalethes" on 28 October 1813.

turn over a new leaf — to take the public at its word, to muster all the tropes and figures I could lay hands on, and, though I am a plain man, never to appear abroad but in an embroidered dress . . . Having got my clue, I had no difficulty in stringing pearls upon it." [11] Though lacking both the practice and the fluency for the daily grind of journalism, as he told Northcote later, he "perceived that with the necessity, the fluency came. Something I did, *took*; and I was called upon to do a number of things all at once. I was in the middle of the stream, and must sink or swim." [12] In September a wickedly ironic account of Southey's new laureateship — "his flaming patriotism will easily subside into the gentle glow of grateful loyalty" * — inaugurated Hazlitt's long assault on the poetical apostates, and in November he began a series of letters against the bellicose editorials of "Vetus" (Edward Sterling) in the *Times*, a paper whose anti-Gallican policy was being hotly fanned by Stoddart.† Meanwhile, on September 25 and October 13, two letters prompted by William Mudford's rhetorical query about the dearth of modern comedy had seemed so "masterly" that Coleridge was sure he remembered having "*conversed* the greater part" of one of them at Lamb's. [13] Perry, however, expressed his admiration in a different way: he promoted Hazlitt to Mudford's former post as drama critic of the paper.‡

During his last six months on the *Morning Chronicle* — that is, until the late spring of 1814 — Hazlitt not only reported on the London stage (including, most notably, Kean's dazzling debut at Drury Lane) [14] but also reviewed books, [15] wrote on politics [16] and art, [17] and even refurbished parts of the lectures on philosophy for popular consumption. [18] It was a shock, therefore, when, according to Mary Russell Mitford, Perry "turned him off" the following May just as he might have fired a footman. [19] A man who "wished to be head and chief of his own paper, and would not have any thing behind the editor's desk, greater than the desk itself," § Perry was perhaps offended by Hazlitt's remarks on the "smug,

---

* 7.25. To the "pretended contradiction" of this article, in the *Courier,* Hazlitt printed a reply on 20 September 1813 (19.115ff.).

† Most of these inflammatory letters were reprinted in *Political Essays* (7.33f., 39–72). According to Hazlitt himself (8.285) they were the only work of his that Godwin considered "worth a farthing."

‡ Hazlitt included most of the first letter in *The Round Table* (4.10–14), and in 1819 he used it and part of the second in the eighth lecture on the English comic writers (6.148–151). For the full text of the second see 20.1–12. Mudford moved on to the *Courier,* of which he ultimately became the editor. When Hazlitt later (8.293n) attributed the ugly things the *Courier* said about his style to his rival's pique, Mudford replied in kind. See 8.111 for Hazlitt's comments on Mudford's *Historical Account* (1817) of Wellington's campaigns, and 19.214f. for his low opinion of his merits as an editor.

§ 16.224. As an intimate friend of Holcroft, Perry had figured largely in the *Memoirs.* Hazlitt's longest comment on him there (3.92ff.) is mainly factual.

smart, upstart, haberdasher look" in Sir Thomas Lawrence's new portrait of Castlereagh,[20] and he was certainly made uneasy by his advocacy of a lenient peace with France.[21] On the other hand, Hazlitt thought that Perry had mistreated him, and a few months later, when he "bitterly" explained the details of his dismissal, Crabb Robinson accepted his version of the fracas — for he was "too proud and high-minded to lie" — and agreed that Perry's conduct had been both insolent and evasive.[22] Some years later Hazlitt cited a certain writer, well known to him, who, having written "upwards of sixty columns of original matter on politics, criticism, belles-lettres, and *virtù* in a respectable Morning Paper, in a single half-year, was, at the end of that period, on applying for a renewal of his engagement, told by the Editor 'he might give in a specimen of what he could do! ' "[23] Not without reason did Perry's "over-weening pretension" stick in Hazlitt's memory.[24]

It was none the less a most instructive apprenticeship, and despite Robinson's laments that "the highest powers of intellect" were going unrewarded, Hazlitt landed on his feet.[25] His eighteen months with Perry had given him a trade. Moving from the *Morning Chronicle* to the *Champion*, then to the *Examiner*, and finally to the *Times*, in the next four years he worked for nearly all the leading London papers, sometimes as a member of the staff, sometimes as a free-lance writer; and except that he was loath to tell "the secrets of the prison-house," he said later, an account of his career would make "rather an amusing story."[26] Even before his contretemps with Perry he had printed in John Scott's newly founded *Champion* an attack on politicians of "the Pitt-school" that had been "originally" written for (and no doubt rejected by) the *Morning Chronicle*,[27] and for almost a year thereafter — until Scott, too, took umbrage at his politics — he supplied the *Champion* with art[28] and drama[29] criticism. In addition, early in 1814 he made an important new connection with John and Leigh Hunt's *Examiner*, the best-known liberal weekly in the kingdom. He had no doubt met the Hunts through Lamb, and after they had been convicted (in February 1813) of libeling the Regent, Hazlitt — like Byron, Bentham, Lamb, and many others — paid Leigh Hunt "the honour of a visit" in Surrey Gaol.[30] This, the real beginning of a long and somewhat ragged friendship, led, in the spring of 1814, to the appearance in the *Examiner* of pieces in the style of Perry's "Common-Places" and then to formal criticism of the arts and drama.*

* For example, "On Posthumous Fame," 22 May 1814 (4.21–24), "On the Love of the Country," 27 November 1814 (4.17–21); "On Hogarth's Marriage a-la-Mode," 5 and 19 June 1814 (4.25–31), "The Elgin Marbles," 16 June 1814 (18.100–103); "Mr. Kean's Iago," 24 July and 7 August 1814 (5.211–221) and 11 September 1814 (18.200–204).

THE TRADE OF LETTERS

By the end of 1814 Leigh Hunt, about to be released from jail and full
of sanguine plans, announced that the "occasional articles on Literary
and Philosophical Subjects . . . under the signature W.H." would be
continued in his paper.[31]

The row with Perry, then, had only broadened Hazlitt's scope, and
for about a year thereafter — until the spring of 1815 — he led a
double journalistic life, reviewing art and drama for the *Champion* and
occasionally writing on more varied topics for its rival.[32] This arrangement, like others of more public interest, did not survive the year of
Waterloo. Never one to mask his own opinions, Hazlitt was a pugnacious
bore where his hero Napoleon was concerned, and the months before and
after Waterloo, when he drank too much and talked too wildly, found
him at his worst.[33] Wordsworth, who had come to London in the spring,
was so much outraged by his politics — to say nothing of his review, the
fall before, of *The Excursion*[34] — that he not only avoided Hazlitt's
company but dredged up the old story about his misconduct at the Lakes
in 1803 to prove that all his friends should drop the "miscreant" too;[35]
Crabb Robinson found both his manners and his views "offensive";[36]
even the gentle-minded, loyal Lamb was driven to complain.[37] Whether,
in these circumstances, Hazlitt was fired or resigned from the *Champion*
is not entirely clear, but at any rate John Scott's disinclination to hail
Napoleon's return from Elba in March 1815 as "the triumph of popular
right over usurped power"[38] meant that between him and his hot-headed
subordinate there was something less than full rapport. It was probably
a relief to both when the Hunts in the spring of 1815 came forward with
a full-time job for Hazlitt on the *Examiner*.*

They were no doubt glad to hire a man of Hazlitt's demonstrated
skill. Seasoned by a lot of hard hack work, yet fresh enough to write with
zest, he not only had survived in the journalistic jungle but by the spring
of 1815 had even won a kind of sultry fame. The previous year had
marked a steady gain, for all his work was able and some of it — like his
long review of *The Excursion*, his accolades of Kean's successive triumphs, and his broadsides against academic art[39] — of extraordinary
merit. Moreover, toward the end of 1814 his new prestige had been confirmed, as it were, when Francis Jeffrey invited him to contribute to the
mighty *Edinburgh Review* — and to be a writer for the *Edinburgh*,

* Despite Howe's implication to the contrary (*Life*, p. 163) it may have taken
several months for Hazlitt to establish his position with the Hunts. Two weeks after
his last identifiable contribution to the *Champion* on March 5 (18.96–100), he reviewed Kean's Richard II for the *Examiner* (5.221–224), but through the spring his
appearances were, to say the least, sporadic (5.224–228). Not until June did his work
appear with any regularity; and thereafter, first as drama critic and then, in August,
as director of the Round Table, he wrote for almost every issue.

Hazlitt ironically observed a few years later, was to occupy "the highest rank in modern literary society." * By 1815, then, he had at last arrived.

THE *EXAMINER*

Given Hazlitt's unfashionable politics and the state of public opinion in the year of Waterloo, he could hardly have found a better berth than that provided by the Hunts. In 1815 the *Examiner* was at its peak of notoriety. Founded in 1808 to promote Parliamentary reform, "liberality of opinion," and the "fusion of literary taste into all subjects whatsoever," [1] it was a sprightly, sometimes raffish weekly crammed with news of politics, "amusements," executions, art exhibits, legal actions, market reports, births, deaths, and many other things in addition to the poems and essays that the editor and his friends supplied. The fact that Leigh Hunt regarded it as his "tavern-room" for talk of politics and art [2] meant that the paper sometimes had a pert and flippant tone; but it also served a serious purpose, for John Hunt was a coproprietor, and he was not a man of antic disposition. "With the exception of a little egotism and twaddle," Hazlitt said a few years later, "and flippancy and dogmatism about religion or morals, and mawkishness about firesides and furious Buonapartism, and a vein of sickly sonnet-writing, we suspect the Examiner must be . . . allowed to be the ablest and most respectable of the publications that issue from the weekly press." [3]

Though printed in horrid type on sleazy paper, it was almost always entertaining, and it had found an eager audience. Within a year of its debut its sale had risen "gloriously" to 2,200, Leigh Hunt told his fiancée; [4] according to Jeremy Bentham this figure was almost trebled three years later; [5] and even in 1820, when financial problems mounted as the circulation dropped, each proprietor made more than four hundred pounds after all the bills were paid. [6] By 1821, however, with Leigh Hunt ill and John Hunt in prison for libeling the House of Commons, the *Examiner* fell to "so low a pitch" that its future was in doubt. [7] Happily it survived Leigh's departure for Italy and the brothers' squabbles over money to attain new strength under the long editorship (1830–1847) of Albany Fonblanque. John Forster and Henry Morley followed him, and not until 1880 did the *Examiner* finally run its course.

* 12.365. According to Robinson (I, 153), Jeffrey acted on the recommendation of Lady Mackintosh, who had been so much impressed by the *Champion* articles on the British Institution that she found out the author's name. A letter from Crabb Robinson to his brother Thomas of 29 November 1814 (ALS, Dr. Williams's Library) contains a similar explanation of Hazlitt's unexpected honor.

THE TRADE OF LETTERS

In its early years it was an exhilarating paper to readers who were young, politically disaffected, and inclined to things artistic. To his son's delight John Clarke bought it from the start,[8] and his one-time pupil Keats was such a constant reader that when he went out of town he had his friend Dilke save and send him the latest numbers, which he devoured and then relayed to his brother in America.[9] Burning to become an artist, young William Bewick read the *Examiner* to learn the names and styles of all the leading painters.[10] When Shelley first came upon the paper he naively thought that the editor wrote it all "right through — 'Money Market,' 'Price of Coals,' and all," [11] and he was so much stirred by Leigh Hunt's attack on military flogging that he expressed his admiration in a letter, thus inaugurating one of the most famous friendships of the period.* Even as late as 1821 Leigh Hunt's presence in Plymouth, during his ill-starred trip to Italy, stirred the local "Examinerions" to propose a public dinner in his honor.[12]

With its Whiggish coloration, the *Examiner* was always quick to denounce maladministration and royal impropriety, but it was by no means antimonarchist;[13] none the less, men who revered church and state and the sacred rights of property viewed it with alarm and sometimes even horror. There were perhaps a few like Lamb who, though above the strife of party, were made unhappy by the Hunts' strong language;[14] but others took a graver view, and consequently, as Hazlitt later said, the *Examiner* succeeded to the "abuse and obloquy" that had once been heaped upon the pope, the devil, and the agents of the Inquisition.[15] Alarmed by the influence of the paper on the discontented lower classes, Coleridge complained in 1812 that its seditious editorials were being hawked as broadsides in the Midland manufacturing towns,† and five years later, when the Hunts' disgust at the Holy Alliance became apparent, Wordsworth grew wrathful that "such injurious writings" were allowed.[16] About the same time, Southey was insisting that all such rags be suppressed and their editors sent to penal servitude — preferably by due process of law, he explained to the prime minister, but if necessary with a "vigour beyond the law which the exigence requires." [17] If men like Cobbett and the Hunts were permitted to spread their poison, he told Crabb Robinson, a "convulsion" would destroy the country.[18]

Such views were not confined to former Pantisocrats. Four times in five years the government had moved against the Hunts with charges of

---

* *Letters*, I, 49f. Later, in Italy, Shelley asked Peacock to send him copies of the *Examiner* "clipped" in order to economize on postage (*ibid.*, II, 602, 710, 720, 761).

† Griggs, III, 410. Southey, to whom Coleridge had made this allegation, repeated it a few months later in an article on industrial conditions in the *Quarterly Review* (VIII [1812], 342).

seditious libel,[19] and although the first three suits were unsuccessful, on 3 February 1813 the proprietors were fined a thousand pounds and sentenced to two-year terms in jail for having called the Regent a licensed libertine "without one single claim on the gratitude of his country, or the respect of posterity." [20] Bracing himself for another term in prison, eight years later, John Hunt conceded that although these and similar remarks about army scandals and Parliamentary corruption, which had also prompted libel actions by the Crown, may have been "scandalous, seditious, malignant, and so forth," they at least were true.* If he and his brother, the *enfants terribles* of the British press, were on occasion jocose and impolite, Leigh Hunt later said, they were also fearless and sincere.[21] Uncowed by their imprisonment, they retained their ardor for reform, and they were still determined that the *Examiner* should make each man "feel and assert his own political value, as an individual." [22] Although such "knight errantry," as Leigh Hunt called it later,[23] sometimes seemed to be a substitute for policy,[24] it defined their editorial creed. Consequently when they offered Hazlitt a job in the year of Waterloo he was delighted to accept.

❖ ❖ ❖

For about a year, until the spring of 1816, his main duties were to comment on the London stage and provide essays for the Round Table, a feature launched by Leigh Hunt just before his release from jail. It had been Hunt's plan to call on certain of his "friends" for little essays on "subjects of Miscellaneous Interest, Literature, Manners, &c.," [25] one of his "knights" (Thomas Barnes) being "deep in the learned languages," another (Hazlitt) steeped in metaphysics, and the third (Hunt himself) very fond of poetry.[26] It was their hope, the editor explained, "to recommend an independent simplicity in Manners, a love of nature in Taste, and truth, generosity, and self-knowledge in Morals." [27] At the start the Round Table was a collaborative effort, and in its first two months Hazlitt twice appeared with pieces rewritten from the *Morning Chronicle*;[28] but in the spring events conspired to thrust a larger role upon him. Because of "unexpected avocations" Barnes had been unable to assist at all;[29] Hunt was giving almost all his time to politics; and Hazlitt, having quarreled with the editor of the *Champion*, was looking for a steady job. "Our plan had been no sooner arranged and entered upon," he recalled, "than Buonaparte landed at Frejus, *et voila la Table Ronde*

---

* *Examiner*, 3 June 1821, p. 338. "Whatever are the faults of the Examiner," said Haydon (*Diary*, II, 397), "it is consistent. When you read an opinion there, you feel it is a sincere one, unbiased for a love of lucre, or a paltry motive."

dissoûte. Our little congress was broken up as well as the great one [at Vienna]; Politics called off the attention of the Editor from *Belles Lettres*; and the task of continuing the work fell chiefly upon the person who was least able to give life and spirit to the original design." *

Despite such self-deprecation Hazlitt stamped his contributions with distinction, and the forty pieces that he reprinted (with twelve of Hunt's) two years later show his new-found power.† Tighter, shorter, more genteel and disciplined than the essays of his later years, they are written with a wiry strength. Though working in the form that Addison's great prestige had canonized, he could not, and did not try to, imitate his predecessors. In lecturing on the essay as a literary form, a few years later, he made his likings clear. He thought that Cowley and Temple were learned and attractive but that Shaftesbury offended by his "flirting" condescension; that Addison, despite the "gravity" of his pretensions, was a lesser man than Steele; that Johnson's sententious pomp could not conceal the limitations of his mind, and that the great Cham's docile imitators "are, and deserve to be, little read at present." [30] None of them approached Montaigne, that "most magnanimous and undisguised egotist" who first dared "to say as an author what he felt as a man": learned without pedantry, sprightly without affectation, he wrote as every honest man would wish to write — not to make "converts" but to seek and state the truth of things. [31]

Hazlitt himself said later that his Round Table papers often gave offense because he "preferred the true to the agreeable, which I find to be an unpardonable fault." [32] Certainly his essays have a strong, forensic thrust that spurns equivocation. Whether explaining the secret of Rousseau's power [33] or deriding the pretensions of the British Institution, [34]

---

* "Advertisement" to *The Round Table* (1817). Following the fourteenth number, on 16 April 1815, the series was abandoned until Hazlitt revived it on August 6 with a piece on "Lycidas" (4.31–36). Thereafter he sustained the feature virtually unassisted until it ended with No. 48 ("On Actors and Acting" [4.153–160]) on 5 January 1817.
† Although Hazlitt was reading proof on *The Round Table* as early as April 1816 (see P. P. Howe, "Unpublished Letters of William Hazlitt," *Athenaeum*, 8 August 1919, p. 712), the book did not appear until the following year, when the *Examiner* (16 February 1817, p. 107) announced its recent publication. Of Hazlitt's forty contributions, twenty-two had been printed as Round Table papers in the *Examiner* and the rest were culled from various places: from *Free Thoughts on Public Affairs* (1806) he chose the character of Pitt (4.125–128) that he had used already in *The Eloquence of the British Senate* (1807); from his early contributions to the *Examiner* he selected essays on Kean's Iago (4.14–17), Hogarth (4.25–31), Wordsworth's *Excursion* (4.111–125), and the British Institution (4.140–151), as well as some on more discursive topics (4.17–25, 128–131); from the *Morning Chronicle* he reprinted some little "Common Places" (4.1–6), a letter on modern comedy (4.10–14), a scrap from one of his attacks on "Vetus" of the *Times* (4.67f.), an essay "On the Literary Character" (4.131–136), and "Why the Arts Are Not Progressive" (5.160–164). The Round Table papers not included in the 1817 volume are brought together by Howe, 20.43–89.

he tries to change men's minds. He writes for effect, and his effects are calculated. Johnson had said that about things on which the public thinks long it commonly attains to think right, but Hazlitt did not respect received opinions. Declaring war on "certain vulgar errors" — for example, that pedantry is always bad, or that erudition can convert a fool into a sage [35] — he tried to build his essays on his own hard thinking. Consequently his conclusions are sometimes fresh and bold, sometimes merely truculent; but even when misguided and perverse (as in his praise of Thomas Amory's tedious *Life of John Buncle* [36] or his petulant attack on even-tempered men),[37] he reveals a mind at work.

On everything he has his own opinion, and he expounds it with the blunt authority that became the touchstone of his style. With a sidelong glance at Southey and Wordsworth, he argues that poets have no moral strength because their function is to please: is it therefore odd that they "exchange their principles for a pension" and woo the muse in comfort at "romantic situations in the country"? [38] When he discusses Milton's metrics [39] or pillories religious hypocrites [40] or proclaims that "gusto" is the source and test of all great art,[41] he shows the jaunty ease of one who knows his strength. "The first Methodist on record was David," he announces.

He was the first eminent person we read of, who made a regular compromise between religion and morality, between faith and good works. After any trifling peccadillo in point of conduct, as a murder, adultery, perjury, or the like, he ascended with his harp into some high tower of his palace; and having chaunted, in a solemn strain of poetical inspiration, the praises of piety and virtue, made his peace with heaven and his own conscience.[42]

Johnson really had no style, we learn; he merely translated his ideas into Latin words with English terminations.[43] "*Prospero* and his world of spirits are a set of moralists: but with *Oberon* and his fairies we are launched at once into the empire of the butterflies." [44] Vandyke's flesh color lacks "gusto," but when Correggio paints a woman's hand we always want to touch it, and Milton shows the same degree of "passion" because his imagination "has a double relish of its objects, an inveterate attachment to the things he describes, and to the words describing them." [45] A "common-place critic," who never lacks for words, "tells you either what is not true, or what you knew before, or what is not worth knowing": that Shakespeare was "a great but irregular genius," that Milton's work is blemished by its pedantry, that Locke was "a very original and profound thinker," that Gibbon's style is "vigorous but florid," that "there is a great deal of grossness in the old comedies," that Richardson is "very minute and tedious," that the French Revolution has hurt the cause of freedom, that Buonaparte was too ambitious, that Horne Tooke's account of the conjunction *that* is most "ingenious," that poetry should be pleasing, that astronomy is a useful study. "He thinks all this, and a great deal more, that amounts to nothing"; for the "best company," of which he talks perpetually, are persons "who live on their own estates, and other people's ideas." *

Having hired a man with such a mind and style, the Hunts did well to give him all the freedom that he liked. As a result, Hazlitt's years with the *Examiner* (1815–1817) were perhaps the most febrile and productive of his whole career. By then he could turn his hand to almost any journalistic chore, and since his employers, despite their liberalism, knew nothing of the rights of labor, his output was immense. In the fall of 1815, while reporting almost weekly on the drama and supplying the Round Table with essays on a wide variety of topics, he branched out into political journalism with a set of articles on Napoleon and the Duc d'Enghien.† This proved to be a kind of preliminary barrage for the heavy artillery of the so-called "Literary Notices" that he launched the following summer.‡ These disrespectful pieces, dealing mainly with the political behavior of Southey, Coleridge, and Wordsworth as symptomatic of the sins of Toryism, provoked the *Quarterly Review* and then *Blackwood's Magazine* to a savage counterattack, the brutality of which Hazlitt promptly matched in his rebuttals. Meanwhile, however, the embattled champion of radicalism had begun to build his reputation as a critic. Between 1815 and 1817 he somehow found time to turn out a string of major pieces for the *Edinburgh Review*,[46] initiate a series of essays for Constable's *Edinburgh Magazine*,§ write a pair of articles on art for the *Encyclopaedia Britannica*,‖ stitch

---

* 4.137ff. Both Robinson (I, 198) and Keats (Rollins, I, 173) were impressed by this essay.

† 19.129–150. If Howe is correct in attributing to Hazlitt another political article called "Chateaubriand — the Quack" (19.128f.), then we should probably expand the canon further to include "M. Chateaubriand's Opinion of Shakespear" (*Examiner*, 27 October 1816, pp. 681f.), which is markedly similar.

‡ Some thirty-one "Literary Notices" appeared at irregular intervals between 2 June 1816 and 13 July 1817. Hazlitt launched the series with a review of *Christabel* (19.32ff.), and his final contribution was a strenuous three-part analysis of Southey's *Letter to William Smith* on 4, 11, 18 May 1817 (7.186–208). Following his departure from the *Examiner* Leigh Hunt carried on the feature with a three-part review of Keats's *Poems* (1 June, 6 and 13 July 1817), after which it disappeared.

§ Beginning in December 1817 with a piece on Benjamin West (18.135–140), Hazlitt progressed to essays in the manner of his later work for the *London Magazine*. Perhaps the most notable item of the group is "On the Ignorance of the Learned" (8.70–77), which he subsequently included in *Table-Talk* in 1821. See pages 254f.

‖ 18.111–134. For Hazlitt's correspondence with Macvey Napier about these articles, which were written for the serially published supplements to various editions of the *Encyclopaedia Britannica*, see P. P. Howe, "Unpublished Letters of William Hazlitt," *Athenaeum*, 8 August 1919, pp. 711ff. His connection with this important

together forty pieces from the *Examiner* and elsewhere for *The Round Table*, and compose the famous *Characters of Shakespear's Plays*.

In the early summer of 1817, shortly after these two books appeared,* he parted from the Hunts to become the drama critic of the *Times*,† and — since Scott and Perry had relinquished their commands — to resume his sporadic contributions to the *Champion* and the *Morning Chronicle* with pieces not designed to soothe the hearts of Tories.‡ But no man could long sustain the pressures, journalistic and political, under which he worked. Although gossip had it otherwise, Hazlitt's decision to leave the *Times* and, in effect, stop writing for the papers must have been his own. Perhaps exhausted (as he himself implied) [47] and almost surely bored by six years of incessant journalistic toil, he made his exit from the *Times* at the end of 1817, not as a "discarded servant," he insisted later, but *"in spite of repeated and pressing remonstrances to the contrary."* § There is no reason to question his account, or to think that he was forced to give up writing for the lectures that would occupy him for the next two years.

Perhaps in order to escape the quick oblivion that buries journalistic prose, or perhaps — as is more likely — to make a little money, he salvaged from this mass of work almost everything that could be exhumed and put between the covers of a book. Consequently the four volumes that he published between 1817 and 1819 may be regarded as an epi-

---

undertaking, as well as his contributions to the *Edinburgh Magazine* and the appearance of *The Round Table*, must have been in part a consequence of his successful debut as an *Edinburgh* reviewer, for all of them were published by the powerful Archibald Constable, then at the height of his career.

* On 16 February 1817 the *Examiner* (p. 107) noted the publication of *The Round Table* as a recent event, and on 6 June 1817 it remarked (p. 423) that *Characters of Shakespear's Plays* had "just appeared."

† Beginning on 30 April 1817 (18.226f.) Hazlitt occasionally reviewed plays for the *Times* while still working for the Hunts. A few days earlier Crabb Robinson recorded some of the circumstances of his employment by a paper that he had called (19.356) "a patent water-closet for the dirty uses of legitimacy": "Walter has been recommended by Barnes to take H[azlitt] as Theatrical Reporter — which on account of both H[azlitt] and the paper I am glad of — I confirmed W[alter] in the project of retaining H[azlitt] as a writer, at the same time that I did not encourage him to form a personal intimacy with him." This passage, omitted by both Sadlier and Miss Morley in their excerpts from Robinson's diary, is quoted in *The History of the Times: "The Thunderer" in the Making* (1935), pp. 164f.

‡ For Hazlitt's contributions to the *Morning Chronicle* between June and August 1817 see 7.208–219. Of his vigorous political pieces in the *Champion* at this time the most notable were "On the Effects of War and Taxes" (31 August 1817; 7.219–225), "What Is the People?" (12, 19, 26 October 1817; 7.259–281), and "On the Regal Character" (28 September 1817; 7.281–287). The last two were reprinted in the *Yellow Dwarf* in the spring of 1818, all three in *Political Essays* of 1819, and the third in the Paris edition of *Table-Talk* in 1825.

§ 20.143. Although Hazlitt said that he enjoyed working for the *Times*, he afterward described it (16.225) as "the mouthpiece, oracle, and echo of the Stock Exchange." The comment prompted a reply that he answered sharply (20.142f.).

logue to this phase of his career. Following *The Round Table* and *Characters of Shakespear's Plays,* in the late spring of 1818 he brought together in *A View of the English Stage* almost all his drama criticism except that written for the *Times*; and a little over a year later he gathered into his *Political Essays* his disgruntled comments on post-Napoleonic England and its Tory rulers. This angry and uneven book, a record of the collision between his libertarian ideals and contemporary realities, was the last of his strictly journalistic works, and by the time it appeared he had already begun to give and print those lectures on the literature of England on which his reputation as a critic largely rests. Although not all his journalism found its way into these books, they fairly represent the scope and nature of his early work. For a man who had spent eight years on eight pages and then "shed tears of helpless despondency on the blank unfinished paper," [48] the output of these six years in London was an extraordinary achievement.

THE *EDINBURGH REVIEW*

About the time Francis Jeffrey added Hazlitt to the "corps" of his *Edinburgh* reviewers in 1814, he remarked with obvious satisfaction that his journal was being read by fifty thousand people.* Its beginnings were more modest. In 1802, when Jeffrey, Sydney Smith, and Francis Horner persuaded Archibald Constable to publish their proposed review, they were young and impecunious, but they were also literate and intelligent and committed to all the Whig reforms — repeal of Dissenters' disabilities, Catholic emancipation, changes in the laws for libel, poaching, and conspiracy, improvements in electoral procedures and in the Court of Chancery, abolition of the slave trade, and so on [1] — that the Tories had successfully resisted for almost twenty years. It was an audacious undertaking, said Smith in retrospect, for these were the days when anyone with less than two or three thousand pounds a year was expected to have no views on politics, and when anyone bold enough to mention the "senseless bigotry" of George III or to hint at the "abominable tyranny and persecution" of the Irish Catholics would be ostracized.[2] Although a waggish suggestion that the motto of the new review be *Tenui musam meditamur avena,* "we cultivate literature on a little oatmeal," was thought "too near the truth to be admitted," [†] its strongly belletristic tone was appar-

* Moore, II, 40. Jeffrey arrived at this figure by estimating that each of 13,000 copies would be read by an average of three or four people.

† *The Life and Times of Henry Lord Brougham Written by Himself* (1871), I, 246. The rejected motto was, of course, a play upon the opening distich of Vergil's

ent from the start. The fact that the first issue carried articles on God-win's reply to Dr. Parr and Southey's *Thalaba*, and on books about infectious fever, air pollution, public finance, foreign travel, and optics, implied that it would deal with many things; but politics and literature were to be its main concerns, and of these, said Jeffrey, politics was first.[3] Even the colors on the cover — the famous blue and buff — were those that Fox's followers had adopted from the uniform of Washington.[4]

Although young John Stuart Mill said in 1824 that the *Edinburgh* had straddled almost every public question,[5] it was shocking or exhilarating to an older generation. Despite their Whig ideals, the bright young men who founded it were not to be deceived by patriotic cant and sentiment. They defended Malthus' views on population, ridiculed the Tories, excoriated Methodists, and, as Lockhart later said, systematically deprecated whatever might appeal "to the graver and more mysterious feelings of the human heart."[6] Perhaps their finest hour came in 1808, when Jeffrey and Brougham, in their famous Don Cevallos article, jeered at British policy and predicted failure for British arms in Spain. It was then that Scott, who had already ceased his contributions to the *Edinburgh,* said that he could "no longer continue to receive or read" the publication,[7] and started enlisting Tory men of letters to organize the *Quarterly Review.* Meanwhile, from London, Smith gleefully reported general "consternation," and said that in some households even the shelves where the *Edinburgh* had lain were being fumigated.[8]

If primarily an organ of political opinion, the *Edinburgh* quickly gained attention for its literary reviews, for, as one disgruntled rival later said, the "bold and briefless barristers" who founded it seemed to be intent on ruining any writer who had, or was likely to acquire, a reputation.[9] Its predecessors in the later eighteenth century, said Hazlitt, were always simple and polite in treating recent books, and once their hacks had called a work "agreeable" and supplied a few excerpts they thought that they had done their duty.[10] The *Edinburgh* soon put an end to such gentility. "We *were* savage," Sydney Smith admitted:

I remember how Brougham and I sat trying one night how we could exasperate our cruelty to the utmost. We had got hold of a poor nervous little vegetarian [the atrabiliar Joseph Ritson], who had put out a poor silly little book; and when we had done our review of it, we sat trying to find one more chink, one more crevice, through which we might drop in one more drop of verjuice, to eat into his bones.[11]

---

first *Eclogue*: "Tityre, tu patulae recubans sub tegmine fagi / silvestrem tenui musam meditaris avena." The motto finally adopted was *Judex damnatur cum nocens absolvitur,* which was extremely apt. On the founding of the *Edinburgh Review* see John Clive, *Scotch Reviewers* (1947), pp. 186–197.

The most fearful executioner was Jeffrey, the little lawyer who in 1803 had gravitated to the post of editor. Although he professed to think that "the great boast of polished life is the delicacy, and even the generosity of its hostility," [12] he was a terror as a critic. Theoretically, at least, he distrusted all aesthetic absolutes, [13] but he was implacably opposed to whatever we would call Romantic. In his initial *Edinburgh* review — of Southey's *Thalaba* — he made it clear that the Elizabethans were the only writers to be admired, [14] and twenty-six years later, in his editorial valediction, he predicted that of all contemporary poets only Rogers and Campbell would have any hope of lasting fame. [15] Between these terminal pronouncements he had disposed of almost everyone whose work now seems likely to survive, as well as many whom we have ceased to read. He liked Crabbe and Rogers, expressed a certain fear of Byron, ignored Shelley, and abominated Wordsworth. He was so hard on *Thalaba* (and by implication on all the Lakists' poetry) that Southey forever after hated him. [16] Scott was so much wounded by his piece on *Marmion* that he would write for him no more. [17] Wordsworth, profoundly irritated by his comments on the 1807 *Poems*, threatened to kick him in the "breech," [18] and two years later, incensed by Jeffrey's allusion to "stuff about dancing daffodils" in comparing him with Burns, he talked so much of seeking satisfaction that Sydney Smith predicted bloodshed. [19] Although Tom Moore actually called him out, their duel was interrupted (moreover, the pistols were not loaded); and when Moore himself subsequently became an *Edinburgh* reviewer, a friend of Scott's complained that "there was never such a thing heard of — and not to shoot him after all, the silly fellow!" * It was not, perhaps, entirely true, as Lockhart later charged, that through his malicious laughter Jeffrey "kept Wordsworth poor, miserably poor for twenty years," [20] but he could see no merit in the greatest poet of the age, and his review of *The Excursion* remains a *locus classicus* of perverted criticism.

At the start there were ominous predictions about the new, upstart review. Southey — hardly a disinterested observer — was sure it would "not keep its ground," [21] and Coleridge thought its second number was "altogether despicable — the hum-drum of pert attorneys' Clerks, very pert & yet prolix & dull as a superannuated Judge." [22] But under Jeffrey's hand it thrived. Although contributions to the *Edinburgh* were, or were supposed to be, anonymous, the pay was very good,† and almost anyone

---

* Partington, p. 11. It was Byron's allusion to this abortive duel in *English Bards and Scotch Reviewers* that led Moore to challenge him. See Prothero, II, 59–63.

† For the first three numbers contributors were not paid at all, but thereafter they received ten guineas a sheet, and by 1811 sixteen guineas was the minimum. Jeffrey himself estimated that two-thirds of his writers made "much higher — averaging, I

except unbending Tories was glad to write for it. Endowed with what Sydney Smith called a "violent tendency" for analysis — "What's a guinea but a damned yellow circle? What's a chamber-pot but an infernal hollow sphere?"[23] — Jeffrey was born to be an editor, and like most great editors he had a very low regard for writers. Hazlitt compared his "prejudice against authors" to that of a justice of the peace confronted with a poacher,[24] and Scott (still smarting from his review of *Marmion*) remarked that in "hunting down the bards" he was like a country squire coursing after game.[25] Given the solar system to review, said Smith, he would surely damn it: "bad light — planets too distant — pestered with comets — feeble contrivance; — could make a better with great ease."[26] He occasionally wrote a favorable review, like his famous piece on Keats in 1819, but as an editor who thought that "we should make one or two examples of great delinquents in every number,"[27] he earned his fearful reputation. Naturally, as Carlyle (himself an *Edinburgh* reviewer) said, Jeffrey came to be regarded as a man of "consummate penetration" and his journal as a kind of Delphic oracle.[28] Although Shelley thought that its pretensions were grotesque,[29] De Quincey concluded sadly that in Jeffrey's prime "almost all the world had surrendered their opinions and their literary consciences . . . into the keeping of *The Edinburgh Review*."[30] It was as Byron — who had felt the lash himself — observed: to be reviewed by the *Edinburgh*, whether favorably or not, raised an author's reputation.[31]

❖ ❖ ❖

Although it was unquestionably a fillip for Hazlitt, a new arrival on the literary scene, to become a writer for this famous publication, the fact that shortly after his first piece appeared in 1815 Jeffrey asked a friend in London "for God's sake" to find him someone with "a taking style"[32] suggests that he was not an overnight sensation. It is unlikely that Jeffrey ever fully approved of anyone or anything. With a modesty entirely out of keeping with his editorial behavior he deprecated his own style and professed to write for babes and sucklings,[33] but he was noted for his ruthless way with the manuscripts of others. Whereas his biographer sedately praised the "dexterity" with which he altered contributions, and implied that writers should have thanked him for making them look better than they were,[34] his "unceremonious hashing" is known

should think, from twenty to twenty-five guineas a sheet on the whole number" (James Bain, *James Mill* [1882], p. 112). See Lockhart, *John Bull's Letter to Lord Byron* (ed. Alan Lang Strout, 1947), p. 16. According to Robinson (I, 209), Hazlitt received fifty guineas for his *Edinburgh* review (August 1817) of *Biographia Literaria*.

to have cost him more than one of his reviewers.[35] In addition to his own acknowledged contributions to the *Edinburgh,* totaling some two hundred items (about half of which he himself reprinted in 1844), he had a part in many hundreds more ostensibly the work of others, and in these his heavy overwriting often makes it hard to say where he left off and his contributors began. As a result, the canon of Hazlitt's contributions to the *Edinburgh* is by no means fixed, and even in those most authoritatively ascribed to him there are many signs of Jeffrey's hand.*

Something of Jeffrey's editorial procedure may be inferred from the letters that Hazlitt wrote to him about his first reviews. "Standard Novels and Romances" (February 1815), "Sismondi's Literature of the South" (June 1815), and "Schlegel on the Drama" (February 1816) were apprentice work, of course, and thus were supervised with care, but Hazlitt's obvious deference to Jeffrey's opinion, as revealed in this one-sided correspondence, is none the less revealing. The first surviving letter, about the revisions in his review of Fanny Burney's *Wanderer,* shows him in a grateful and accommodating mood.

Feb^ry 15, 1815

Dear Sir,

You need hardly be assured of the gratification I have felt in receiving your very obliging letter. You have however quite misunderstood what I said about *a beginning.* What I meant was a beginning for the Review, & not to write any more about the Wanderer. I meant to have done with it at once. Perhaps however in that case, it ends too abruptly & cavalierly. If so, an extract or two might be added. I return you my thanks for your obliging expressions respecting the article. As to the rest, it is entirely in your hands, if you will be at the trouble of pruning its excrescencies. I had only calculated on its making a sheet & a half. The note about the Duke of Wellington I give up beforehand, but I confess I should like to see his Majesty mounted *con amore.* But I know that I am some-

* Of the twenty-odd reviews that for one reason or another have been ascribed to Hazlitt, Howe recognizes eighteen as mostly or entirely his. Of the others, three — "Dunlop's History of Fiction" (November 1814), "Moore's Lalla Rookh" (November 1817), and "Byron's Sardanapalus" (February 1822) — may be rejected on stylistic or other grounds; but two — "Leigh Hunt's Rimini" (June 1816) and "Coleridge's Christabel" (September 1816) — pose problems. Since Hazlitt himself, in 1821, reminded Leigh Hunt that he had "praised" him in the *Edinburgh* (*Four Generations,* I, 133; cf. *Memoirs,* I, 225; P. P. Howe, "New Hazlitt Letters," *London Mercury,* VII [1923], 494f.), we may assume that he submitted a review of *The Story of Rimini* to Jeffrey; but the article was later claimed by Jeffrey as his own (Cockburn, I, 423), and since stylistically and otherwise it resembles closely his known work, Howe was probably right in denying all or most of it to Hazlitt. The notorious *Edinburgh* review of *Christabel,* the authorship of which is still unknown, was thought by Coleridge to be the work of Hazlitt, but the attribution has never been established, and there are excellent if not compelling reasons to think he had no hand in it at all (see page 356). Howe's discussions (16.419ff.; *Life,* pp. 398ff.) should be compared with that of P. L. Carver, "Hazlitt's Contributions to *The Edinburgh Review,*" *RES,* IV (1928), 385–393, who proposes somewhat different attributions. The problem of determining the authorship of articles in the *Edinburgh* is discussed by Clive, *Scotch Reviewers,* pp. 15f., who includes a useful bibliography.

what "splenetive & rash" & submit the whole to your decision. I will get Sismondi immediately. I should be glad to know whether you wish it for the next number of the review after the present one is out. I remain, Dear Sir,

very respectfully
your obliged humble serv-
ant, W. Hazlitt.

19 York Street,
Westminster.

P. S. Sir James Mackintosh is I understand in town, & I should have been happy to have conveyed your message, but I have not the honour of a personal acquaint-ance with him.*

Two months later he wrote to express his satisfaction with Jeffrey's "alterations (for I am very sensible of my want of discretion in these matters) & I am very glad to have got off so well in my first adventure." He promises that in his review of Sismondi, which would be ready "in about six weeks," he would "attend to your suggestions in manufacturing it," and he then mentions several other topics — Rousseau, Johann Spurzheim (the phrenologist), Castlereagh, and the Congress of Vienna — that he would like to write about. "I am not very well read in the modern novelists," he explains, "for in truth I hate to read new books, & my general rule is never to read a book that I have not read before. Of this practice I begin however to repent." [36] Meanwhile, bombarding Jeffrey with suggestions, he pushed his new advantage hard. Scott's edition of Swift and the recent French translation of Johann Buhle's *Geschichte der neueren Philosophie* ("a subject to which I have paid some atten-tion") would be good books for him to treat, he wrote a few days later, adding that "My friend Mr. Hunt" had expressed a certain interest in writing for the *Edinburgh*;† and then, on May 1, he renewed his offer to do a piece on Spurzheim. Jeffrey did not care for these proposals, it would seem, but Hazlitt's postscript to the letter of May 1 that "Perhaps Schlegel would make a future article" [37] apparently caught his eye, and by the next November "Schlegel on the Drama" was taking final form.

* ALS, The Yale University Library. The revisions mentioned in this letter were all embodied in the final form of the review (see below, pages 210 f.). The introduction was expanded into a notable survey of the European novel; the presumably derogatory passage on the Duke of Wellington was suppressed; and the account of George III "mounted on a great War-horse" (16.20) was retained. In February, when the review had been put into its final form, Hazlitt wrote to Jeffrey (ALS, postmark 19 February 1815, The Yale University Library) that he was "going into the country for a few days to repose on the satisfaction which your letter has given me." He no doubt went to Winterslow.

† ALS, undated, The Yale University Library. Hazlitt wrote a piece on Buhle's book, it seems, but it was never printed. He alluded to it two years later (see below, page 213), and in 1822 he asked for its return if Jeffrey still could lay his hands on it (ALS, 2 October 1822, The Yale University Library).

THE TRADE OF LETTERS

Dear Sir,

I am exceedingly sorry it has so happened that I could not get the Review of Schlegel ready in time. But circumstances absolutely prevented me. I hope to send it you in a fortnight or three weeks' time, so that it will be early for the next, if it should be approved of by you. I am afraid it will make three sheets. I received your bill for 45£. for which however you are not indebted to me. You sent me 25£. in the spring for the novels & romances. If you will let me know what it is your intention to allow for Sismondi, I will remit you the balance in your favour. I recollect nothing to add but to express my obligations to your kindness, & that I am, Dear Sir, your very respectful humble servant

W. Hazlitt.

P. S. The chief topics of the Review I am about will be the differences between the classical & modern style, & a review of the Greek & French theatres, & Shakespeare. The work has only been out a few days. I had the copy from the Translator.

Nov. 20, 1815
19 York Street, Westminster.[38]

Hazlitt's first three *Edinburgh* reviews deserved the care that he and Jeffrey gave to them, for they marked an important step in his career. It was fortunate that in his "first adventure," as he called his piece on Fanny Burney, he could draw on his wide but casual reading in the form that he preferred above all others because it was the closest to "humanity." [39] His panoramic view of European fiction, with its discussion of *Quixote, Gil Blas,* Fielding, Smollett, Richardson, and Sterne is full of excellent things, and it shows a long and affectionate familiarity with the giants of eighteenth-century fiction. Also it leads him to a meditation on the low estate of current English literature, which he attributes to the king and illustrates from Fanny Burney's latest book. "The establishment of the Protestant ascendancy, and the succession of the House of Hanover" had been good for English letters, he explains, for it showed that the people should be represented in books as well as in Parliament. "They wished to see some account of themselves in what they read, and not to be confined always to the vices, the miseries and frivolities of the great." With a security of person and property and with freedom of opinion, every man could feel "of some consequence to himself, and appear an object of some curiosity to his neighbours," and the result was the splendid growth of eighteenth-century fiction. The accession of George III, however, changed this happy state of things. "Mounted on a great War-horse," he had channeled off his people's energies, and "the glories and calamities of war" usurped all their other interests, including literature. "It is not to be wondered [at], if, amidst the tumult of events crowded into this period, our literature has partaken of the disorder of the times: if our prose has run mad, and our poetry grown childish." [40] All this Hazlitt finds exemplified in Fanny Burney's book, which represents not the decay but the perversion of her talent. It typifies contemporary frivolity. Though weak in characterization, her *Evelina, Cecilia,* and *Camilla* were full of bustle and observed reality, and they were anchored in the manners of the age. But *The Wanderer* is different: it is so refined and artificial that it seems to be an exercise. Not only are its difficulties "created out of nothing," but its delicacy is false.

Because a vulgar country Miss would answer "yes" to a proposal of marriage in the first page, Madame D'Arblay makes it a proof of an excess of refinement, and an indispensable point of etiquette in her young ladies, to postpone the answer to the end of five volumes, without the smallest reason for their doing so, and with every reason to the contrary. The reader is led every moment to expect a denouement, and is as constantly disappointed on some trifling pretext. The whole artifice of her fable consists in coming to no conclusion. Her ladies stand so upon the order of their going, that they do not go at all.*

And so on. It is hardly any wonder that this review impressed Carlyle [41] and that on reading it Captain James Burney, Madame D'Arblay's brother, announced to Hazlitt that their long friendship was ended.†

In reviewing Sismondi's *De la littérature du Midi de l'Europe* Hazlitt shows little of the verve with which he wrote about the novel. Indeed, one wonders why Jeffrey assigned this learned, massive book to him, for although it indubitably advanced his education, it was hardly suited to his taste and talents. He himself remarked that such a work as this "must contain a great deal of matter less pleasant than profitable in the perusal," [42] and as he toils behind his author from Provence to Tuscany and thence to Spain he writes like a man resolved to do his duty. For the most part he quotes and summarizes, but there are moments of relief like the notable digression on Dante (which turns up later in *Lectures on the English Poets*).[43] Dante's "power, passion, self-will" seem to be contagious, or at any rate to bring Hazlitt's prose to life. "His mind lends its own power to the objects which it contemplates," he says,

instead of borrowing it from them. He takes advantage even of the nakedness and dreary vacuity of his subject. His imagination peoples the shades of death, and broods over the barren vastnesses of illimitable space. In point of diction and style, he is the severest of all writers, the most opposite to the flowery and glittering — who relies most on his own power, and the sense of power in the reader — who leaves most to the imagination.[44]

Finally, a somewhat extraneous discussion of Chaucer and Spenser (which he would also use again) [45] leads to the conclusion that there

---

* 16.22. Hazlitt used almost all of this review for his lecture on the English novelists in *The English Comic Writers* (6.106–125) three years later.
† *Life*, pp. 166f. Hazlitt did not apologize, or change his mind about Fanny's "affectations " (8.157), but he did concede, a few years later (8.209), that she was the cleverest member of a family noted mainly for its large "pretensions."

seems to be no progress in the arts. As we shall see, this was one of his fundamental precepts as a critic.[46]

With Schlegel's *Lectures on Dramatic Literature,* a seminal work of Continental criticism, he reveals a firmer touch. It was an article of faith with him to distrust "universal undertakers, and complete encyclopedists" who fit everything into their systems,[47] but the scope of Schlegel's erudition and the uses of his kind of scholarship could not be denied. Although he himself was not a theorist and polymath, it was good for Hazlitt to read the *Lectures* at this stage of his career, for in discussing some of Schlegel's notions — like the celebrated distinction between classic and romantic art [48] — he was led to see how theory could illuminate a work and to formulate his own opinions (or at least to analyze his own experience as a reader) in ways that he had seldom tried before. Thus he concludes that imagination, instead of imitation, is the test of modern art, and that it conveys a special kind of truth. Its language "is not the less true to nature because it is false in point of fact," he says; "but so much the more true and natural, if it conveys the impression which the object under the influence of passion makes on the mind." [49] He almost groans in contemplating Schlegel's encyclopedic view of European art, which has "too much of everything, but especially of Greece"; [50] nevertheless he dutifully follows him through Greek and Latin drama and then through French, but not until he reaches Shakespeare does his pulse begin to quicken. Having announced at the start of his review that the *Lectures* contained "by far the best account" of Shakespeare that he had ever seen,[51] when he finally reaches this part of Schlegel's book it inspires his first extended treatment of the writer he admired above all others. It may be regarded as a first sketch of *Characters of Shakespear's Plays,* which appeared the following year, and despite his complaint that Schlegel praises even Shakespeare's "faults," his own account is pitched in tones of adoration.

All his faults have not prevented him from showing as much knowledge of human nature, in all possible shapes, as is to be found in all other poets put together; and that, we conceive, is quite enough for one writer. . . . Each of his characters is as much itself, and as absolutely independent of the rest, as if they were living persons, not fictions of the mind. The poet appears, for the time, to identify himself with the character he wishes to represent, and to pass from one to the other, like the same soul successively animating different bodies. By an art like that of the ventriloquist, he throws his imagination out of himself, and makes every word appear to proceed from the mouth of the person in whose name it is spoken. His plays alone are expressions of the passions, not descriptions of them.*

* 16.91. Although not an Elizabethan scholar, Hazlitt shows (16.97f.) extraordinary perception in discussing the apocryphal plays, most of which Schlegel had uncritically assigned to Shakespeare. In addition to *Titus Andronicus* and *Pericles* (which, of

With a sharp reproof to Schlegel for his superficial treatment of Restoration comedy, a refusal even to discuss his section on the Spanish drama, and a few testy remarks about his "questionable" opinions about the work of his own countrymen, Hazlitt closes his review. It was clearly one that he had labored over, but that it was labor well expended his book on Shakespeare soon would show.*

His debut safely past, Hazlitt remained a fairly steady *Edinburgh* reviewer until 1824. In addition to the three long articles just surveyed he wrote at least ten others that Jeffrey printed with only minor alterations, as well as several that were so radically revised the editor later claimed them as his own.† As the following letter shows, however, he would have written more if he had been permitted.

[*Postmark* March 4, 1817]

Dear Sir,

    I propose next week with your approbation to commence an article (taking Bühle [*sic*] or some other work, as a text) on the principles of modern philosophy. It will run above two sheets of original matter, and will contain a view (I believe somewhat novel) of most of the disputed topics in metaphysics, such as the nature of an Idea, abstraction, association, language, self-interest, the love of pleasure, of truth, &c. I hope, if you approve of it, it will be no discredit to the Review; at least no greater than what I have been already guilty of. — I would also be happy to bring down the account of novels & romances to the present time in the following number, if you have no objection. Perhaps Mr. Godwin's new novel [i.e., *Mandeville*] would be a good opportunity. If you let me know at your convenience whether the article on philosophical opinions would be acceptable, & when it would be necessary to have it ready, I would attend punctually to your wishes. I remain Dear Sir, your obliged & very faithful servant,

W. Hazlitt.

P. S. The volumes of the Round Table are out. Would you accept of a copy in my name from Mr. Constable? — If you see Mr. Napier, might I request you to tell him that I received his letter enclosing £15. & should have answered it long ago, but that I have been so ill as to be unable to do almost anything. What do you think of Wat Tyler for a flying article? — W. H.⁵²

---

course, are now regarded as canonical) he rejects *Thomas Lord Cromwell, Sir John Oldcastle,* and *The Yorkshire Tragedy*; and later, in *Characters of Shakespear's Plays* (4.356f.), he adds to these exclusions *The Puritan, Locrine, The London Prodigal,* and *Arden of Feversham.* One would like to have his views on *Edward III.*

  * Coleridge later complained (Griggs, IV, 831) that Hazlitt, who had heard his views on Shakespeare as early as 1798, failed to defend him from the charge of plagiarizing Schlegel's work because Jeffrey would have raised objections.

  † In addition to the reviews of Fanny Burney, Sismondi, and Schlegel, those of certain attribution between 1815 and 1824 are "Coleridge's Lay Sermon" (December 1816), "Coleridge's Literary Life" (August 1817), "Letters of Horace Walpole" (December 1818), "Spence's Anecdotes of Pope" (May 1820), "Farington's Life of Sir Joshua Reynolds" (August 1820), "Capital Punishments" (July 1821), "The Periodical Press" (May 1823), "Landor's Imaginary Conversations" (March 1824), "Shelley's Posthumous Poems" (July 1824), and "Lady Morgan's Life of Salvator" (July 1824). Also, Howe (16.421) assigns to Hazlitt most of "Moore and Byron" (February 1823), even though it shows very heavy signs of Jeffrey's hand. All but one of these reviews — "Capital Punishments" (19.216–255) — are in Volume XVI of the Centenary Edition.

THE TRADE OF LETTERS

Although Jeffrey vetoed all these suggestions, the two men stayed on friendly terms — a novelty perhaps not unrelated to the fact they did not meet until 1822 — and Hazlitt often called on Jeffrey for financial and other kinds of aid that, so far as we can tell, Jeffrey almost always gave. In 1817, for instance, at a crucial phase of his career, Hazlitt wrote this moving and revealing plea:

Dear Sir,

I take the liberty of troubling you with a copy of a work I have just finished relating to Shakespear. I thought perhaps if you approved of it you might take a brief notice of it in the Edinburgh Review. I should not make this abrupt proposition, but from the necessity of circumstances. My friends may praise what I write, but I do not find that the public read it, & without that, I cannot live. If I could dispose of the copyright of the Round Table & of this last work, I could find means to finish my work on Metaphysics, instead of writing for three newspapers at a time to the ruin of my health & without any progress in my finances. A single word from you would settle the question, & make what I write a marketable commodity. The book-sellers have kept me in a hole for the last ten years: do, Dear Sir, extend a friendly hand to help me out of it. I would not ask such a favour for myself, if I thought the mere notice of either of the trifles above alluded to would be any discredit to the high character of your Journal. I have had to write a new Preface to the Characters (a very bad one, as it usually happens in such cases) which has prevented me from sending the articles on modern philosophy. But I will finish & send it off as soon as possible, — I hope in time for the next number, if it is admissible in other respects. I remain, Dear Sir, with every apology for the contents of this letter, your obliged & respectful humble servant,

April 20, 1817   W. Hazlitt.[53]

Four months later, when Hazlitt sent to Jeffrey his "very long & desultory" review of *Biographia Literaria*, he raised the subject once again. His book on Shakespeare was selling well, he said, but "your notice would at once lift me from the character of a disappointed author to that of a successful one"; and he expressed the hope that Jeffrey might "*insinuate*" the review that he had promised into the next number of the *Edinburgh.*

I have to thank you for your remittance of £50. Perhaps if you like my Biographical article *very much*, I might apply in *forma pauperis* for one of 30£. in advance for the one which I meditate on modern novels. You have read the apothecary's speech in Romeo & Juliet, "My poverty," etc. & will I hope excuse these renewed applications from Dear Sir, your obliged humble servant,

W. Hazlitt.[54]

Jeffrey's review of *Characters of Shakespear's Plays,* in the August 1817 *Edinburgh,* was a big event in Hazlitt's life. The editor, whose vocation was the law, thought that a critic's function was to judge, not to lose himself in rapture, and he was no doubt made uneasy by Hazlitt's kind of veneration. In so far as he was able, however, he supplied the "helping hand" that Hazlitt had requested. The writer of this brilliant but uneven book, he observed,

continually appears acute, desultory, and capricious — with great occasional felicity of conception and expression — frequent rashness and carelessness — constant warmth of admiration for his author — and some fits of extravagance and folly, into which he seems to be hurried, either by the hasty kindling of his zeal as he proceeds, or by a selfwilled determination not to be balked or baffled in any thing he has taken it into his head he should say.[55]

Hazlitt did not, perhaps, agree with Robinson that this was a "very puffing review," [56] but he must have been delighted to be noticed by the *Edinburgh*.

The following year — not long before a rival publication announced that Hazlitt had been sacked for "want of talent" [57] — Jeffrey sent a hundred pounds to him, part of it for work already done, the rest for work that he would do when he found time; and if another hundred pounds were wanted, the generous editor said, it was ready for the asking.[58] Despite such bounty, however, Jeffrey kept a wary eye on him. He told Godwin (who had suggested that his *Mandeville* be assigned to Hazlitt for review) not only that his proposal was improper, as indeed it was, but that Hazlitt was too rash to be "a safe, exemplary reviewer." Of his "fairness and impartiality, so far as intention is concerned," he said he had no doubts, but he considered him "to be a person whose judgment is somewhat at the mercy of partialities and prejudices — and besides, the thing is of ill example, and affects the purity of our tribunal." * In view of Jeffrey's many benefactions, however, it is not surprising that his grand-seigniorial manner did not seem to trouble Hazlitt. In 1818, when the editor rejected one of his reviews because it was too "florid," he repressed his irritation,† and two years later, when he was bluntly told that another piece of his required correction because he was "too fond of paradoxes," he accepted the reproof.[59] In fact, Jeffrey seems to have been one of the few persons whose advice he sought and followed. In May 1818 he abandoned a projected lecture tour to Edinburgh when Jeffrey urged against it; [60] and he called on Jeffrey for money and advice during his shabby preparations for divorce in 1822.[61] With these benefits in mind, perhaps, in *Liber Amoris* he named his editor

* Paul, II, 253. Later Jeffrey rejected Mackintosh's suggestion that Hazlitt be permitted to review Godwin's *History of the Commonwealth of England* (Paul, II, 289), and also Hazlitt's own request that he be allowed to write on Mary Russell Mitford's *Julian* (L'Estrange, II, 161).

† 17.312. The rejected review was of Thomas Reid's *Inquiry into the Human Mind*. For Jeffrey's condescending comment on the matter see Constable, II, 217.

"the prince of critics and the king of men," * and in *The Spirit of the Age* he wrote of him and his review with perceptive admiration. The *Edinburgh* was not without its faults, he said: it was rather brisk and brittle in its judgments, it tended to treat questions of "liberty" and "humanity" like logical abstractions, it had underrated Wordsworth and overrated Malthus; [62] but for almost a quarter of a century it had been a force for good. Like its editor, it stood for "the supremacy of intellect," [63] and as the lengthened shadow of a man whose only fault, perhaps, was excessive talent, it was a tonic and invigorating organ of opinion. [64]

The *Edinburgh* review of *The Spirit of the Age* in 1825 — which shows every sign of being Jeffrey's work — was no doubt a blow to Hazlitt. His style was bright and pert, the reviewer pointed out, but marred by "paradox, error, and extravagance." His comments were arresting, but vitiated by so many "ridiculous blunders" that his sketches of the great men of the time were "fancy-pieces" instead of serious portraits. He should learn to be "more humble and diffident," and reflect upon the fact that "fine writing really cannot exist without good sense." He was urged "to think more of his subject-matter than of himself — to give up the eternal desire to strike and surprise, for the sober and rational pleasure of discovering or unfolding the truth — to say sensible things in a plain way, and be content to shine only when a great occasion arises, or when brilliancy is native to the theme, or the thought — and he has powers of thought to succeed admirably." [65] In his unpublished reply to all this good advice — his only known excursion into verse — Hazlitt ironically promised that

> From Mackintosh I'll nature learn,
> With Sidney Smith false glitter spurn;
> Lend me, oh! Brougham, thy modesty,
> Thou, Thomas Moore, simplicity;
> Mill, scorn of juggling politics;
> Thy soul of candour, Chenevix;
> And last, to make my measure full,
> Teach me, great J——y, to be dull! †

But he wrote no more for the *Edinburgh Review* during Jeffrey's time as editor. Although Jeffrey, in 1826, inquired of Procter about "our

---

* 9.126. A writer in *Blackwood's Magazine* (XIV [1823], 309) said that Jeffrey was so "tickled" and "bamboozled" by this comment that he foolishly printed Hazlitt's article on "The Periodical Press" (16.211–239) to express his gratitude. The year before, John Wilson, in one of his *Noctes Ambrosianae* (ed. R. Shelton Mackenzie, 1875, I, 262), said that "little Frank Jeffrey," in a moment of "utter silliness," permitted Hazlitt to assist him in reviewing Byron's tragedies. Every paragraph "that Billy dipped his ugly paw in," he added, could be instantly detected. The allusion was, of course, to the review of *Sardanapalus* (February 1822) that, though probably written in part by Hazlitt, was claimed by Jeffrey as his own. See page 413n.

† 20.393. The allusions are, of course, to some of Jeffrey's favorite contributors.

ancient ally, Hazlitt," [66] there is no indication that he requested further contributions, and two years later, when he resigned to become dean of the Faculty of Advocates, Hazlitt noted his departure with a tartly elegiac piece. Even if the *Edinburgh* had changed, and for the worse, he said, one should remember that it had always preferred "the clear, the polished, the manly, the intelligible" to "the puny, the affected and obscure"; and if Jeffrey too had lost his former "pith and unction" he none the less deserved a hearty valediction.

The Dean of Faculty receives the laurelled critic in his arms; and the loss of power is accompanied with an increase of honours. Those who know Mr. Jeffrey at a distance admire him: those who are better acquainted with him love and respect him; all will be glad of a distinction grateful to his feelings, and which has been merited neither by servility nor faction, but by an union of firmness with moderation. His readers alone will miss his brilliant turns and forked style.[67]

Significantly, Hazlitt resumed his contributions as soon as Macvey Napier assumed direction of the *Edinburgh*.* As editor of *The Encyclopaedia Britannica* Napier had dealt with Hazlitt's work before,† and in his new position he promptly sought him out again. In commenting on his successor's first issue, however, Jeffrey singled out a piece on Channing — which was Hazlitt's — as particularly unfortunate. Its writer, he observed, "is not a first-rate man — a clever writer enough, but not deep or judicious, or even very fair. I have no notion who he is. If he is young, he may come to good, but he should be trained to a more modest opinion of himself, and to take a little more pains, and go more patiently and thoroughly into his subject." [68] If Napier transmitted this advice Hazlitt must have been amused, for he had been getting it from Jeffrey for almost fifteen years. But whatever friction there had been between them was forgotten as Hazlitt neared his end. When, in a "sternly brief" letter, he wrote, "I am dying: can you send me £10, and so consummate your many kindnesses to me?" Jeffrey responded with a check for fifty pounds, and so, according to Carlyle, Hazlitt died "in peace from duns

---

* The reviews that Hazlitt wrote for Napier are "American Literature — Dr. Channing" (October 1829), "Flaxman's Lectures on Sculpture" (October 1829), "Wilson's Life and Times of Daniel Defoe" (January 1830), and "Mr. Godwin" (April 1830).

† Although in the early part of his career Hazlitt wrote or translated a sheaf of articles for *The Encyclopaedia Britannica*, mainly on the arts (see 20.408), it was, as he implied (8.47f.; 16.58), not the kind of work that he enjoyed. In 1818 he declined Napier's invitation to write an article on drama — an assignment that Walter Scott accepted — on the ground that he lacked the talent for systematic exposition (see page 255): where an encyclopedia leaves off, he said, "is just where I begin, that is, I might perhaps throw in an idle speculation or two of my own, not contained in former accounts of the subject, and which would have very little pretensions to rank as scientific." See Stewart C. Wilcox, "Hazlitt on Systematic in Contrast to Familiar Composition," *MLQ*, II (1941), 185ff.

at least." * His last *Edinburgh* review — an autumnal piece on God-win's *Cloudesley* — had appeared six months before.

THE RELUCTANT MAN OF LETTERS

Despite his extraordinary production, Hazlitt's life between 1812 and 1820 was not entirely one of solitary scribbling. His bad manners, a scandal that became a legend, sometimes made him seem an Ishmael, but he had a few firm friends and a host of admiring, if somewhat fearful, acquaintances who tempered his misanthropy. However isolated his early and his later years, this middle period of his life was one of journalistic bustle, when the plays and art and politics that provided him with copy also thrust him out into the world. Coleridge and Wordsworth had washed their hands of him, and Crabb Robinson eventually decided that his friendship cost too much; but Lamb, of course, was loyal, and through him he met a flock of younger men — Hunt, Haydon, Reynolds, Keats, Barnes, Talfourd, Procter, Clarke, and others — who filled, or helped to fill, his middle years. Sooner or later he quarreled with or lost sight of almost all of them, and so relapsed into his solitude, but for half a dozen years or so he had a place in literary society.

Even at the start of his career in London he was anything but debonair. The "brow-hanging, shoe-contemplative, *strange*" youth whom Coleridge described in 1803 [1] had become a sardonic, wiry man whose pallid features, as a friend of his remarked, were brightened only by his "speaking" eyes, whose conduct veered from "plain" to gauche, and whose temper was unruly.[†] Looking as if "he had no business where he happened to be," [2] he always entered a room like one brought back to it in custody; [3] but since he thought that the ability to stand erect, speak loud, and make a proper entrance "proves nothing," he studiously neglected such refinements.[4] Careless in his dress and slouching in his gait, he had an "almost painful" fear of strangers,[5] a limp handshake,[6] and a coldness of demeanor that, as he himself admitted, tended to repel those of "florid" temperament.[7] Added to his other social charms were "terrible bursts of uncontrollable rage," from which not even his

---

* *Reminiscences*, pp. 326f.; cf. p. 59; *Letters of Thomas Carlyle 1826–1836* (ed. Charles Eliot Norton, 1889), p. 171; James Anthony Froude, *Thomas Carlyle: A History of the First Forty Years of His Life* (1882), II, 72. For a discussion of the inconsistencies in Carlyle's various accounts of this transaction see *Reminiscences*, p. 327n, and for a different version altogether see Talfourd, II, 177f.

† Cyrus Redding, *Fifty Years' Recollections, Literary and Personal* (1858), II, 298f. After *Blackwood's Magazine*, in 1818, began to jeer at "pimpled Hazlitt," he explained (9.10) to his tormentors that he was "remarkably pale and sallow."

warmest friends were safe.[8] "It might sometimes have been said of him," an obituary writer observed, " 'Perhaps it was right to dissemble your love, but why did you kick us down stairs?' " *

He was no man to bandy civilities. Convinced that silence is the one great art of conversation,"[9] he found mere chitchat intolerable. Since most people, he said, "do not seem to talk for the sake of expressing their opinions, but to maintain an opinion for the sake of talking,"[10] he avoided casual social intercourse. Most high-born or highly cultivated people irked him. As he wrote in 1807, "Mr. Malthus is convinced that no young woman brought up in nastiness and vulgarity, however virtuous she may seem, can be good for any thing at twenty: I confess I have the same cynical opinion of those, who have the good fortune to be brought up in the obscene refinement of fashionable life." † The one time that he "dined at a lord's table" — in Florence in 1825 — was very dull, he said, for his host did all the talking. ‡ He enjoyed his calls on Mrs. Basil Montagu because her face was like a "coronet" and her conversation had the flavor of "fine green tea,"[11] but to learned ladies he had an absolute "aversion,"[12] and with less cultivated women he was always at a loss, so he explained, because he thought it rude to disagree with them and "not quite fair" to ask a reason for their views.[13] "If it were not for the wine and the dessert," he said, "no author in his senses would accept an invitation to a well-dressed dinner-party, except out of pure good-nature and unwillingness to disoblige by his refusal."[14] When James Perry, perhaps sorry that he had fired the man who later wrote *Characters of Shakespear's Plays,* arranged a formal dinner to introduce him to his friends, Hazlitt's reaction might have been predicted. He came and did

---

* *New Monthly Magazine,* XXX (1830), 438. It was probably in 1816 that Hazlitt had his famous fight with Charles Lamb's burly brother John, whom Talfourd (II, 121) called the Telamonian Ajax of the South Sea House. Although Hazlitt occasionally alludes to John (17.129, 20.183), he nowhere mentions their notorious argument over the relative merits of Holbein and Vandyke, or the ensuing scuffle. According to Haydon (Pope, 13 October 1828), who got the story from Talfourd, "Hazlitt burst up & swore if he [John Lamb] did not hold his tongue he would expose him in the Newspapers! 'And if you do,' Lamb's brother said, 'I'll pound you in a mortar.' Hazlitt swore he would and Lamb's Brother gave him a black eye. The Card table was overturned, & the room arose in confusion, to part the Combatants, when Hazlitt in great fright exclaimed to Talfourd, 'Be God, Sir, you need not trouble yourself. I do not *mind a blow,* Sir; nothing affects me but *an abstract Idea!*' " For other accounts of the fracas see Haydon, *Correspondence and Table-Talk,* II, 339; Talfourd, II, 6; Moore, III, 146. When Coleridge heard about the fight from Crabb Robinson (I, 200), he was "not displeased" at Hazlitt's misadventure.

† 1.283. See 20.95f. for his opinion of lords and ladies at the opera; 11.293f. for an exchange between Hazlitt and Northcote on "gentility" and fashion; 18.398 on the absurdities of the upper classes; 9.174 on the "general texture" of society; 20.143–149 on the "dandy school" of literature; 8.103 on the social nonconformist.

‡ Medwin, p. 279; cf. 17.266. The host was Henry Augustus Dillon-Lee, thirteenth Viscount Dillon. See John Forster, *Walter Savage Landor* (1869), p. 437.

the proper things, "smiled and bowed — handed Miss Bentley to the dining-room — asked Miss Perry to take wine — said once 'Yes' and twice 'No' — and never uttered another word the whole evening." [15]

One should not refer his bad behavior solely to ill breeding and dismiss him as a boor. Hazlitt was ill bred, of course, but like other ill-bred men he might have learned refinement if he had thought it worth his while. As it was, he refused to make the petty compromises that civility requires — perhaps, as Crabb Robinson concluded, because there was a "twist" about his head or heart. [16] Still he had a certain charm. Such essays as "On the Conversation of Authors" [17] and "On Coffee-House Politicians," [18] those affectionate memorials to the kind of talk he loved, reveal a side of Hazlitt's character that many people never saw. When young George Ticknor, hunting lions in 1819, called on him in York Street, he thought his conversation ("generally in short sentences, quick and pointed, dealing much in allusions, and relying a good deal on them for success") was more amusing than interesting, [19] but those who came to know him well — and it was hard to do — assessed his merits higher. Procter thought him "awkward" and "diffident" when they first met at Hunt's, but later he realized that in a group of wits and raconteurs Hazlitt said the best things of the evening,* and as their friendship ripened his conversation fairly glowed. "A great talker, when it was his cue to talk," according to Procter, he may have "uttered fewer words" than Coleridge and "expatiated less," but his talk was better organized, and it revealed as extraordinary a mind. [20] John Hamilton Reynolds was also much impressed by him. "On Thursday last Hazlitt was with me at home, and remained with us till 3 o'clock in the morning," he recorded in a letter of 1817,

full of eloquence, — Warm, lofty & communicative on every thing Imaginative & Intelligent, — breathing out with us the peculiar & favourite beauties of our best Bards, — Passing from grand & commading [sic] argument to the gaieties & graces of Wit & humour, — and the elegant and higher beauties of Poetry. He is indeed *great* company, and leaves a weight on the mind, which "it can hardly bear." He is full of what Dr Johnson terms "Good talk." His countenance is also extremely fine: — a sunken & melancholy face, — a forehead lined with thought and bearing a full & strange sorrow, but kindling & *living* at intellectual moments, — and a stream of coal-black hair dropping round all. Such a face, so silent and so sensitive, is indeed the banner of the mind. [21]

If such comments — and there are others just as warm by Hunt, [22]

---

* Procter, p. 176. When George Combe, the phrenologist, met Hazlitt in Edinburgh in 1822 — at the blackest period of his life — he was very much impressed by him. "If you pause in the conversation and reflect on what has been said during the last five minutes," he observed (Charles Gibbon, *The Life of George Combe* [1878], I, 151), "you perceive that you have been talking with an uncommon man."

Talfourd,[23] Keats,[24] Clarke,[25] and Knowles [26] — do not confirm the legend of Hazlitt as an ill-bred misanthrope, neither do they quite destroy it. The fact is that he, like most men of passion and intelligence, could exercise a power not to be confused with facile charm. He lacked Hunt's affability and Lamb's accommodating wit, but his strength was *sui generis,* and his more perceptive friends recognized the fact. In 1816 Lamb told Wordsworth (who by then was hot for Hazlitt's blood) that he got "no conversation in London that is absolutely worth attending to but his"; [27] and in 1823, when Southey and almost all the world had written Hazlitt off as mad, he nobly came to his defense. "I should belie my own conscience," Lamb told the readers of the *London Magazine,* "if I said less, than that I think W. H. to be, in his natural and healthy state, one of the wisest and finest spirits breathing. . . . I think I shall go to my grave without finding, or expecting to find, such another companion." [28]

Few men get such praise while living, and even fewer merit it, but Lamb, in the unaccustomed role of gladiator, for once was writing gravely. If Hazlitt had more faults than other men, he thought, he also had more strength. Without the benefits of wealth or breeding or a proper education, incapable of grace and afraid of affability, he may have been a crank, but he also had a touch of greatness. One did not need to share his views to admire the intelligence and valor that he used in their defense. "He was never dishonest," said Procter. "He never struck down the weak, nor trod on the prostrate. He was never treacherous, never tryannical, never cruel." [29] Also, as even his enemies conceded, he was a man without pretense. The candor that sometimes appeared as incivility and terrorized his friends also served as a kind of signature for everything he wrote. Even during the height of the scandal over his divorce in 1822, Haydon, though repelled by his behavior, was struck by his "unaffected frankness." [30] He was incapable of assuming virtues that he did not have, or of seeming other than he was. Near the end of his life, recalling that he had "glanced over" a considerable number of subjects in his time — "painting, poetry, prose, plays, politics, parliamentary speakers, metaphysical lore, books, men, and things" — he said that for all its imperfections his work at least had been sincere. "If there is haste or want of method, there is no common-place, nor a line that licks the dust; and if I do not appear to more advantage, I at least appear such as I am." [31]

Such candor — in part, perhaps, a compensation for his social gaucherie, in part bravado — was, Hazlitt told himself and others, a moral obligation. It was a form of self-assertion made essential by the shifting truths and privileged errors that usually pass for facts. He regarded self-awareness as the anchor of experience and self-expression as a duty. As the sum of all that one has known or done or suffered, personality is cumulative,[32] but at its unmoved center stands the self; and this, sacred as a chalice, a good man keeps inviolate. For Hazlitt, "personal identity" was both a psychological fact and an ethical ideal. What he called "the natural *stamina* of the mind, on which circumstances only act,"[33] was a man's unique possession and the only treasure worth preserving. Whatever organizes and compels opinion, or whatever makes for acquiescence, he considered bad because it vitiates one's independence. Hazlitt's contempt for dogma and received opinion (which, he said, makes "virtue formal and vice desperate")[34] was matched by his dislike for the formal "rules" of art; and his attack on moral absolutes, in the symphonic essays of his last decade, restates a theme that runs throughout his work. He found it puzzling that "the generality of mankind are contented to be estimated by what they possess, instead of what they are,"[35] and he could think of no advantage, social or financial, for which a good man would conceal his own conviction. To deny one's duty to one's own identity is the ultimate vulgarity, he said, for vulgarity is not ignorance or inelegance; it is affectation.[36] "We had as lief *not be* as *not be ourselves*."[37]

One sometimes passes by a gentleman's park, an old family-seat, with its moss-grown ruinous paling, its "glades mild-opening to the genial day," or embrowned with forest-trees. Here one would be glad to spend one's life, "shut up in measureless content," and to grow old beneath ancestral oaks, instead of gaining a precarious, irksome, and despised livelihood, by indulging romantic sentiments, and writing disjointed descriptions of them. The thought has scarcely risen to the lips, when we learn that the owner of so blissful a seclusion is a thorough-bred fox-hunter, a preserver of the game, a brawling electioneer, a Tory member of parliament, a "no-Popery" man! — "I'd sooner be a dog, and bay the moon!"[38]

That Hazlitt was ill equipped for drawing rooms did not matter, for drawing rooms were not common among the fledgling poets, bookish clerks and civil servants, painters, young men reading for the law, and journalists with whom he mainly found his friends; and that he was driven by a "demon," as Keats was well aware,[39] meant that he required and got a special dispensation. His friends — "all sorts of odd clever people," according to one of the oddest of them all[40] — knew that he was somber and withdrawn, that his manners were bizarre and his temper could be savage; but they also knew the thrust and vigor of his mind, and they liked the way he wrote. Living more or less on the fringes of respectability, nearly all of them were poor and some lacked even talent, yet they could recognize uncommon merit. If some were mere eccentrics, most of them had wit, and sprinkled here and there was genius. With these people, if anywhere, Hazlitt was at home. There being more interesting and intelligent men in London than anywhere else in the world, he once remarked, "it is hard if . . . you cannot find a half a dozen to your liking." [41] He himself perhaps did not exceed that figure, but at one time or another he knew most of the writers for whom his age is famous, and he generally assessed their merits well. Moreover, by some of the best of them he himself was valued as a very special man.

✧ ✧ ✧

Throughout his middle years Hazlitt moved in a set of more or less concentric circles with Charles Lamb and Leigh Hunt somewhere near the center. Stripped of his renown, Godwin had become an aging leech who preyed upon a dwindling band of friends, and with him Hazlitt's contacts were at best sporadic; * but with Lamb and his cronies, old and new, he was as intimate as ever. These "interesting and amusing people," as Crabb Robinson called them (not without a trace of condescension),[42] included not only the old familiar faces of George Dyer, the Burneys, William Ayrton, Ned Phillips, Basil Montagu, and others, but also a flock of rising younger men. John Scott, as editor of the *Champion* — for two years (1814–1816) one of the ablest weekly papers in the kingdom — printed some of Hazlitt's first reviews, and despite their quarrel over politics the two men, each so brilliant in his way, joined forces once again after Scott assumed direction of the *London Magazine* in 1820. His death in a duel in 1821 was a blow to British journalism. John Hamilton Reynolds, formerly a junior clerk in the Amicable Insurance Office, had progressed from the lush Byronic verse of *Safie, an Eastern Tale* (1814) to the post of critic for the *Champion*, in which connection he reviewed and became a valued friend of Keats, and the recipient of some of the finest letters in the language. Thomas Barnes, like Hunt and Lamb and Coleridge a former Blue-Coat Boy, had come down from Cambridge to write for the *Examiner*; in 1817 he succeeded Hazlitt's brother-in-law on the *Times* to become one of its great editors. Charles Cowden Clarke, who had not yet broken into print, was a friend of Keats and a peripheral member of the Leigh Hunt circle; he and his wife Mary, the daughter of Lamb's friend Vincent Novello, long survived as panjandrums of Victorian literature. Bryan Waller Proc-

---

* As Godwin's diary shows, on 14 March 1813 he, the Lambs, Martin Burney, the Hazlitts, and others were at Joseph Hume's for dinner; but at each of his subsequent meetings with Hazlitt before the year was out (August 24, September 2 and 28) the gregarious Lamb was host.

ter, a young solicitor who would make his name in letters as "Barry Cornwall," had just begun to write. Walter Coulson, a reporter for the *Morning Chronicle,* was already noted for his erudition about every-. thing from Indian coinage to classical prosody; * Thomas Alsager, a financial writer for the *Times,* is remembered, if at all, for having lent to Clarke the copy of Chapman's Homer that he passed on to Keats; [43] Thomas Noon Talfourd, who would one day write a famous book about these people, was then a stripling reading for the law and a neighbor to the Lambs in Inner Temple Lane.

Of all these younger friends of Lamb, Leigh Hunt was the most flamboyant. He was also in a small way famous, for through his work on the *Examiner* he had made himself the leader of an *avant garde* in politics and literature. Lamb was never stirred by politics — he was "willing to see society go on as it did, because he despaired of seeing it otherwise" [44] — but in 1810–11 he had agreed to write on belletristic topics for Hunt's *Reflector*; and when Hazlitt, looking for a job in 1812, turned up again in London, Lamb was no doubt quick to bring the two together. As we may infer from Hunt's account of Hazlitt's stilted call on him in Surrey Gaol, [45] their intimacy did not develop overnight, but by 1814 their common interest in literature and liberal politics led to Hazlitt's first appearance in the *Examiner* and ultimately to a friendship that vicissitude and even temperamental differences could never quite destroy. Older, sadder, and in some ways wiser than Hunt and the swarm of bright young men around him, Hazlitt was hardly suited to be a satellite, but he became important in this group, and there for the first time he achieved a prestige corresponding to his merits.

But if, under the "lash of necessity," [46] Hazlitt quickly made his way in letters, he never conquered his aversion to the literary profession. On the premise that to exchange admiration for knowledge is always disenchanting, [47] he held that one should read and not converse with authors, [48] for he was a critic who distrusted criticism and a writer who had a very low opinion of what Keats called "that most vulgar of all crowds the literary." [49] He found two great "defects" in most modern men of letters: they were so self-centered that they wrote only of themselves, and they lacked the kind of courage that a good man ought to have. In such early pieces as "On the Literary Character" [50] and "On Poetical Versatility," [51] as in his lectures and his late essays, he repeatedly advanced the proposition that authors were on the whole an undistin-

* Clarke, p. 26. Coulson, who stood as godfather to the Hazlitts' child, was one of Sarah's chief advisers in her negotiations for divorce in 1822. See Bonner, pp. 187n, 210, 221, 236, 260.

guished lot — not because of their frivolity and vice, but because of their "abstraction and refinement." [52] He thought that the cultivation of belles-lettres had "neutralized" the primal passions, substituting books for life and converting men of action into pallid men of letters, who mainly spent their time in drinking endless cups of tea and thinking of themselves. Although "respectable in their way," perhaps, and no doubt "suited to the mediocrity of the age," [53] they lacked the "venturous magnanimity" that marked authentic genius. [54] Things had once been different. The Elizabethans were bold and virile in their search for "truth"; [55] Milton's greatness as a poet matched his courage as a man; [56] the novelists of the eighteenth century showed a real concern for people, and drew them with unerring skill and vigor; but thereafter, when prose ran "mad" and poetry grew "childish," literature partook of the "disorder" of the reign of George III. [57] Things were far from good, he said, when prudence and self-interest became a writer's main concerns, when a man of genius had to serve as a "literary pimp" for some borough-mongering lord in order to succeed, and when an *Edinburgh* reviewer occupied the "highest rank" in letters. [58] An age whose great productions were *Political Justice*, the *Edinburgh Review, The Excursion,* and *Childe Harold's Pilgrimage* was not without distinction, he conceded, but it was an age of analysis and introspection, when "masculine boldness and creative vigour" had given way to "fastidious and effiminate delicacy," and when the critic reigned supreme. [59] The result was a literature grown arty and self-conscious and a big but lazy reading public whose notions of "mechanical refinement" had "vitiated" taste. [60]

In such a situation, he maintained, the critics, who by their "tattling and dogmatising" can make and ruin reputations, [61] are the caterpillars of the realm of letters. Their desire is not to do justice to an author but homage to themselves. Some are merely pedants, who judge by the obsolete standards of "correctness" and decorum, and treat a poem as "a piece of formal architecture." With some — the literary police who add pedantry to malice — "it is not a question of literary discussion, but of political proscription." Some are antiquarians; some are snobs who "discern no beauties but what are concealed from superficial eyes, and overlook all that are obvious to the vulgar part of mankind"; and some are mere "word-catchers," more intent upon an author's punctuation than his meaning. Nearly all are bad, however, for they forget that a disciplined self-effacement is the critic's first requirement, and that his purpose is "rather to direct attention to objects of taste, than to dictate to it." [62] It is disastrous when learning, pride, and self-assertion put the critic in competition with the author, Hazlitt said, for it means that instead of reviewers watching poets, poets watch reviewers.* Who dares to show "the colours, the light and shade, the soul and body of a work" [63] when "literary jealousy and littleness is still the motive, politics the pretext, and blackguardism the mode" of most contemporary criticism? †

❖ ❖ ❖

It is not surprising that a writer with such views of writing had no priestly sense of calling. His works were not the products of an author, he explained, but "the thoughts of a metaphysician expressed by a painter," [64] and his real ambition was to be not the best prose stylist but the best rackets player of the age. [65] Like Johnson, he wrote to make a living, and as a friend of his remarked, it was only his "necessities" that made him write at all. [66] His description of the professional writer's lot, in a review of Godwin's *Cloudesley* that he wrote not long before his death, is a poignant commentary on his own career. An "author by profession" knows nothing of serenity, he says:

If he does nothing, he is forgotten; if he attempts more than he can perform, he gets laughed at for his pains. He is impelled by circumstances to fresh sacrifices of time, of labour, and of self-respect; parts with well-earned fame for a newspaper puff, and sells his birth-right for a mess of pottage. In the meanwhile, the public may wonder why an author writes so badly and so much. With all his efforts, he builds no house, leaves no inheritance, lives from hand to mouth, and, though condemned to daily drudgery for a precarious subsistence, is expected to produce none but works of first-rate genius. No; learning unconsecrated, unincorporated, unendowed, is no match for the importunate demands and thoughtless ingratitude of the reading public. [67]

At the start, when he had just begun to "stammer out" his thoughts on paper and was "in a kind of honeymoon of authorship," [68] he took a certain satisfaction in his work, but soon he sank into the weary acquiescence that he expressed so often in his later years. To be sure, when he classified modern "men of letters" as pedants, hacks, and honest writers, he put himself into the third and highest class, and rightly so, for his candor saved him from the cowardice and cynicism that he regarded as the bane of the literary profession. [69] Sometimes he liked to think of the good things he had done — his description of Congreve's Millamant, his sketch of Dekker, certain of his Table Talks (where the ideas were

---

* 5.150. In *The Spirit of the Age* (11.95) Hazlitt applies this rule to Wordsworth, who had "thought too much of contemporary critics and criticism; and less than he ought of the award of posterity, and of the opinion, we do not say of private friends, but of those who were made so by their admiration of his genius."

† 12.323n. Bruised by the attacks of the *Quarterly Review* and *Blackwood's Magazine*, Hazlitt made many bitter comments on mixing politics and literature. One of his fullest and most measured statements of the "illiberality" of reviewers was that in his notable discussion of "The Periodical Press" in the *Edinburgh Review* in 1823 (16. 232–239). See 10.246f.

"founded as the rock, free as air, the tone like an Italian picture"), and his book of Shakespeare [70] — for he had a craftsman's pride in honest craftsmanship; [71] but he took no joy in "gaining a precarious, irksome, and despised livelihood, by indulging romantic sentiments, and writing disjointed descriptions of them," [72] and usually he could not bear to read what he had written. [73] "What abortions are these Essays!" he exclaims in "The Indian Jugglers," which is one of his unquestioned triumphs.

What errors, what ill-pieced transitions, what crooked reasons, what lame conclusions! How little is made out, and that little how ill! Yet they are the best I can do. I endeavour to recollect all I have ever observed or thought upon a subject, and to express it as nearly as I can. Instead of writing on four subjects at a time, it is as much as I can manage to keep the thread of one discourse clear and unentangled. I have also time on my hands to correct my opinions, and polish my periods: but the one I cannot, and the other I will not do. [74]

Hazlitt may have thought but little of his work, but at any rate it cost him little, as he himself admitted. [75] Partly, no doubt, because he worked only on compulsion, partly because he thought that what was "struck off at a blow" had a special vigor, [76] he spent no time in smoothing and refining what he did, but instead turned out an endless stream of manuscripts so rapidly and legibly that they almost looked like print. As someone said of Scott — who also did his best with the press "thumping, clattering, and banging" in his rear [77] — writing was for Hazlitt, as for Balzac and Tolstoi, a natural process, not, as for Turgenev and Flaubert, a ritual; and he himself named Scott and Shakespeare as proof that the best writers are usually the most "voluminous" and "indefatigable." [78] He was not surprised, he said, that Heywood wrote two hundred plays, "for the more a man writes, the more he can write," [79] and the fact that he himself produced his Elizabethan lectures in six weeks [80] or so and a volume of his *Table-Talk* in four [81] perhaps explains his disregard for the throes of other artists. "We have seen him continue writing (when we went to see him while he was pressed for time to finish an article)," recalled the Clarkes,

with wonderful ease and rapidity of pen, going on as if writing a mere ordinary letter. His usual manuscript was clear and unblotted, indicating great readiness and sureness in writing, as though requiring no erasures or interlinings. He was fond of using large pages of rough paper with ruled lines, such as those of a bought-up blank account-book — as they were.*

Such fluency of course reveals itself in Hazlitt's style, which, like all

---

* Clarke, pp. 60 f.; cf. Patmore, III, 1–5; Procter, p. 178; Medwin, p. 282n. Hazlitt's holograph manuscript of "The Fight" (17.72–86), most of which survives in the Morgan Library, shows many alterations and revisions. It has been edited by Stewart C. Wilcox as *Hazlitt in the Workshop: The Manuscript of* The Fight (1943).

great styles, can be described but not explained. Simple, clear, and strong, it appears to be so easy that when compared with, say, Gibbon's or De Quincey's it hardly seems to be a style at all; none the less it rests upon a set of principles that he worked out in some detail and that he invoked repeatedly in his comments on the prose of other men. Most of all he valued naturalness. Since he thought that style should be like conversation, and tested on the ear (as in the early eighteenth century),[82] he abhorred all signs of labor, art, and decoration. Highly wrought and sculptured prose offended him because it seemed to be dishonest. On the premise that "words are a measure of truth," [83] he hated jargon and neologisms as much as he loved solid English diction, for he thought that words acquire their strength not from novelty or color but from "the stamp of custom," and he himself was so "fastidious" in using them that he would "almost as soon coin the currency of the realm as counterfeit the King's English." [84] Consequently a natural style is hard to write, he said. It is not "vulgar" or "random," but resolutely plain and honest. Never violating idiom, it requires a "precision" and a "purity of expression" that florid, cadenced prose ignores. "How simple it is to be dignified without ease, to be pompous without meaning." [85]

But since not everyone who writes naturally writes well, it is clear that something else is needed, and that, of course, is mind. Truth, not beauty, should be a writer's goal, he said, and if one's thinking is flabby or dishonest, one's prose can not be good. Style as such is unimportant, for it is a means and not an end, and unless it serves its purpose, which is the expression of feelings and ideas, it is merely idle decoration. Of all man's tools and artifacts, words alone have "moral and intellectual perspective," and therefore they alone are sacrosanct as "a key to the affections."

They not only excite feelings, but they point to the *why* and *wherefore*. Causes march before them, and consequences follow after them. They are links in the chain of the universe, and the grappling-irons that bind us to it. . . . They alone describe things in the order and relation in which they happen in human life.[86]

A writer's first responsibility, therefore, is to state the truth of things. Prose can be cadenced and ornate and still be good, as Jeremy Taylor's proved, but generally when a stylist labors for effect he commits the primal fault of confusing ends and means: he forgets that objects should be linked to feelings, words to things,[87] and that to "impart conviction" is his only function.[88] As a critic Hazlitt disliked anything "that occupies more space than it is worth," [89] and he was merciless with those "hieroglyphical" writers who thought cadence, metaphor, and diction more important than ideas.

Personifications, capital letters, seas of sunbeams, visions of glory, shining inscriptions, the figures of a transparency, Britannia with her shield, or Hope
leaning on an anchor, make up their stock in trade. . . . Images stand out in
their minds isolated and important merely in themselves, without any ground-
work of feeling — there is no context in their imaginations. . . . The web and
texture of the universe, and of the heart of man, is a mystery to them: they have
no faculty that strikes a chord in union with it. They cannot get beyond the daub-
ings of fancy, the varnish of sentiment. . . . Scorning to imitate realities, they
are unable to invent any thing, to strike out one original idea. They are not copy-
ists of nature, it is true: but they are the poorest of all plagiarists, the plagiarists
of words.[90]

His standards for good prose were, therefore, austere and well
defined. He did not care for Johnson's famous style (in which "the words
are not fitted to the things, but the things to the words");[91] or for Bentham's "barbarous philosophical jargon" that had to be translated into
English if one would understand it;[92] or for Coleridge's tumid periods
that wind "like a patriarchal procession with camels laden, wreathed
turbans, household wealth, the whole riches of the author's mind poured
out upon the barren waste of his subject."[93] Conversely, he praised
Dryden's prose as a model of "simplicity, strength, and perspicuity";[94]
despite its occasional looseness and "caprice" he liked Leigh Hunt's for
its "tone of lively, sensible conversation";[95] and he said that Southey's
showed the traces of his strong right hand, for even when he vilified
reform or flattered George III he did so in a "straightforward, intelligible,
practical, pointed way."[96] But it was Burke whom he regarded as "the
most powerful, the most dazzling, the most daring" English stylist. Because his strength of mind was matched by his command of language
he did not need to pad or decorate his prose, for he knew that "every
word should be a blow; every thought should instantly grapple with its
fellow."[97] Hazlitt himself did not always reach this high ideal, of course,
as he was well aware. He worried over, and even made half-hearted
jokes about, his style when it was "flowery";[98] he could be prolix and obscure, and sometimes wretchedly rhetorical (especially in his sentimental
moods); but in view of his immense production he had uncommon luck
or skill in making almost every word a blow. Few writers so prolific can
be read with so much steady pleasure.

THE HUNTS

By 1815 Hazlitt had already begun to find his voice and to take his
stance as critic, but it was the Hunts who enabled him to make a reputation. Combining literature and politics, the "Sunday paper patriots,"[1]

as Byron dubbed them later, shared a "zeal for the public good,"[2] but otherwise they were ill-matched brothers, the one steady, quiet, and almost stolid, the other warm, impulsive, and gregarious. It is hardly surprising that whereas John received no notice in *The Dictionary of National Biography* Leigh's career was thought to warrant sixteen columns. But if the less vocal of the pair is to us a dim figure on the periphery of his flashy brother's orbit, some people who knew them both thought him the better man. With a modesty, or a reticence, that matched his massive strength of character, he was aggressive only in defending what he thought was right. Horace Smith said that he exemplified the best of Roman virtues;[3] Byron, who found him "a sensible, plain, sturdy, and enduring person," remarked that "he is such a one as Prynne or Pym might be";[4] Cyrus Redding concluded that he had never known "a man of sounder judgment or higher honour";[5] and Haydon (who might have served, like Leigh Hunt, as model for Horace Skimpole) called him "as noble a specimen of a human being as ever I met in my life" — adding, as if to clinch the matter, that he had borrowed thirty pounds from him.[6] Perhaps P. G. Patmore was right in thinking that John Hunt occupied a unique place in Hazlitt's affections;[7] at any rate, the dedication to *Political Essays* that he inspired stands almost alone in the depth of its esteem: "One of those few persons who are what they would be thought to be; sincere without offence, firm but temperate; uniting private worth to public principle; a friend in need, a patriot without an eye to himself; who never betrayed an individual or a cause he pretended to serve — in short, that rare character, a man of common sense and common honesty." *

Despite his easy, varied talents and his charm, Leigh Hunt commanded no such admiration. A *Wunderkind* who had published his first book at seventeen and entered journalism before reaching his majority, for more than fifty years he was facile and prolific without achieving any first-rate work. As editor and writer he revealed a wide if spotty reading, a generous interest in his friends' careers, and a zeal for liberal politics; but he was something of a fop with a mawkish strain of sentiment, and what one of his friends called "jennery-jessamy prettinesses of style and mannerism"[8] were basic to the writer and the man. His *Story of Rimini* (1816), a compound of grace and vulgarity, exposes his defects, even if it hardly deserved the drubbing that it got from *Blackwood's Magazine*. While it means nothing that Lockhart, for whom de-

---

* 7.5. John Hunt was apparently instrumental in the publication of *Political Essays*. See Frederick W. Hackwood, *William Hone: His Life and Times* (1912), p. 212, and below, pages 256f.

traction was a trade, called him "a conceited, coxcombical incendiary," [9] it is significant that so many of his friends grew weary of his affectations; for despite what Clarke regarded as his "bewitching spell of manner" [10] his charm was fragile, and often crumbled under close acquaintance. In 1813 he impressed Byron as "an extraordinary character," [11] but within five years he was demoted to the status of "a good man" whose modest talent had been spoiled, "a great coxcomb and a very vulgar person." [12] Fired with boyish admiration, Keats declared that his friendship with Hunt would mark an "Era" in his life, [13] but within a year he found his hero's "self delusions" most offensive, [14] and not long after, he had checked him off as "vain, egotistical and disgusting in matters of taste and in morals." [15] In 1813 Haydon said of Hunt, "I don't know a purer, a more virtuous character, or a more witty, funny, amusing, enlivening man," [16] but three years later he sang a different tune. "This [is] a man who can scarcely talk of a principle he has not violated, of a promise he has not broken, of a vice that he does not sophisticate into a virtue, of a virtue he has not negatived into a vice." [17] Hunt was perhaps a flower, said Haydon, but one that you seize and smell and then cast away because it "*stinks!*" [18] Against such testimony — which could be multiplied — one should weigh Hunt's quick response to talent, his kindness to his friends, and his love of literature. Not only did he bravely bear with Hazlitt and do everything he could for Shelley, but he praised and printed Keats when almost no one else was aware of his existence, he nursed him in his later illness, and he kept his name alive for almost thirty years. No one capable of inspiring the dedication to *The Cenci* and *Adonais* can have been as foolish as Hunt is sometimes shown. Perhaps his mind was "feminine," as Procter thought, [19] but it could rise to manly strength. He was warm in his affections and honest in his judgments, and therefore Lamb, not easily fooled by people, was right in calling him a "cordial-minded" man. [20]

Hazlitt must have thought so too. He recognized — and maybe even envied — Hunt's charm and generosity; he liked his politics and conversation, [21] his "bright," quick prose, [22] and his candor as a critic. [23] To be sure, there were minor irritations: he tired of Hunt's conceit and levity,* and he was puzzled by his need for adulation. "He requires not only to

---

* An entry in Haydon's *Diary* for 13 October 1817 (II, 134) bears upon this point: "Hazlitt spent Sunday evening with me, talking of our Friend's self delusion and conceit. I told him some one said 'let him be in a delusion & a sleep.' 'Yes,' said [Thomas] Barnes, 'but he *kicks* in his sleep.' 'I don't know as to his *kicking*,' said Hazlitt, 'but I know he talks & writes in his sleep.' The same Friend complained that the Quarterly Review said he preceded Bristol Hunt [the notorious demagogue and radical] as Voltaire did Marat & Danton. 'I don't know whether he *precedes* Bristol Hunt, but I am sure he comes *after* Voltaire,' said Hazlitt."

be appreciated, but to have a select circle of admirers and devotees, to feel himself quite at home." [24] Hazlitt was not a "devotee" but he was fond of Hunt, and almost alone among his friends he thought that he improved upon acquaintance. "He is the only poet or literary man we ever knew," he wrote toward the end of his life,

> who puts us in mind of Sir John Suckling or Killigrew or Carew; or who united rare intellectual acquirements with outward grace and natural gentility. Mr. Hunt ought to have been a gentleman born, and to have patronised men of letters. He might then have played, and sung, and laughed, and talked his life away; have written manly prose, elegant verse, and his *Story of Rimini* would have been praised by Mr. Blackwood. [25]

As for Hunt, he regarded Hazlitt as a man of genius whose crotchets had to be condoned. Although he himself missed greatness, he could spot the trait in others; and since envy was unknown to him, it is not surprising that he ranked Hazlitt among the master spirits of the age. [26] In his youth he was among his first admirers; in his old age, as *laudator temporis acti,* he never missed a chance to praise him.

Whatever the circumstances of Hazlitt's departure from the *Examiner* in 1817, they did not affect his friendship with the Hunts. The brothers continued to puff his books,* report and give long excerpts from his lectures,† and even print the pieces for which, presumably, he could find no other outlet.‡ In the early months of 1818 John Hunt collaborated with him in a short-lived weekly called the *Yellow Dwarf;* § four years later, when the Hazlitts had abdicated their parental duties to go to Edinburgh in search of a divorce, he kept a watchful eye upon their son; [27] and in 1823, when the events surrounding that divorce had

---

* For example, *Characters of Shakespear's Plays* on 26 October and 2 and 23 November 1817; *English Comic Writers* on 18 April 1819; *The Age of Elizabeth* on 19 March 1820; *Table-Talk* on 8 September 1822.

† For example, lectures on the English poets on 18 January, 1 February, and 8 March 1818; lectures on the English comic writers on 8, 15, and 22 November and 20 December 1818; lectures on the age of Elizabeth on 7 and 21 November, 5, 19, and 26 December 1819.

‡ For example, "The Editor of the Quarterly Review," 14 June 1818 (19.210 ff.), "Mr. Wordsworth and the Westmoreland [*sic*] Election," 5 July 1818 (19.213f.), "Illustration of a Hack-Writer," 4 June 1820 (19.214f.). Hazlitt's stirring eulogy of John Cavanagh, the famous rackets player, which he later worked into "The Indian Jugglers" (8.86–89), was first printed in the *Examiner* on 7 February 1819.

§ In 1818 Hazlitt ironically listed the *Yellow Dwarf* (7.256f.) with the *Edinburgh Review* and the *Examiner* as seditious publications that "an eminent poet and a minute philosopher of the present day" (i.e., Wordsworth) thought should be suppressed. Some of his own contributions, of a sort to make all good Tories groan, were reprinted in *Political Essays:* "On Court Influence" (7.230–242), "On the Clerical Character" (7.242–259), "What Is the People?" (7.259–281), "On the Regal Character" (7.281–287). His uncollected pieces from the *Yellow Dwarf* include a review of *Childe Harold's Pilgrimage* (19.35–43) and an essay on the opera (10.92–96). See *Memoirs,* I, 241f.

brought Hazlitt to his nadir, John and Leigh were quick to make a place for him in the newly founded *Liberal*. These continuing contacts not only reflect the Hunts' respect for Hazlitt as a writer; they also imply the real affection and esteem that, so far as we can tell, he himself returned. It meant something for Hazlitt to dedicate a book to John, but it probably meant more to present to him a picture that he had painted as a boy.[28] Surviving the frictions of an intimate collaboration, and even the embarrassment of one of Leigh Hunt's effusive poetical "Epistles" addressed to him in the *Examiner*,[29] Hazlitt invited his former editor to visit him at Winterslow [30] and even sent him a hare and a side of Wiltshire bacon.[31] Despite his deep commitment to the theory of benevolence, for him such little unremembered acts of kindness and of love were, to say the least, uncommon.

But invitations, hares, and sides of Wiltshire bacon were not enough to turn aside Leigh Hunt's wrath when, in 1821, *Table-Talk* was published. The comments there about Hunt's own "vivacious" egotism [32] and Shelley's "levity of principle" [33] were sharp enough to vex even a "cordial-minded" man. Hazlitt had no doubt disapproved of Shelley from the start. Although there are only two recorded meetings — one at Hunt's, in February 1817, where they attacked the Crown in a "very warm argument" with their host and Walter Coulson,[34] and another a few days later, when Hazlitt and his wife had dinner with the Shelleys [35] — Hazlitt's published comments on the poet, both before and after his untimely death, were always very tart,* and the attack on him in *Table-Talk* infuriated Hunt. Canceling the review that he had planned to print in the *Examiner*,† he promptly aired his indignation in a letter to the author.‡ "I think, Mr. Hazlitt," he began, "you might have found

---

* In addition to the offensive piece in *Table-Talk* ("On Paradox and Common-Place," 8.146–156), Hazlitt in 1821 wrote critically of Shelley in "On People of Sense" (12.245f.) in the *London Magazine* and again in 1824 in his *Edinburgh* review of the *Posthumous Poems* (16.265–284). One passage from this review (16.265) will serve to indicate its theme: "His Muse offers her services to clothe shadowy doubts and inscrutable difficulties in a robe of glittering words, and to turn nature into a brilliant paradox. We thank him — but we must be excused." See pages 339f. for his views on Shelley's politics.

† As George L. Barnett has pointed out ("An Unpublished Review by Charles Lamb," *MLQ*, XVII [1956], 352–356), it was perhaps when Hunt abandoned his review of *Table-Talk* that Lamb agreed to furnish one instead. Lamb's manuscript, which was apparently not published, is now in the Berg Collection of the New York Public Library. See Lucas, II, 299ff.

‡ For the texts of Hunt's and Hazlitt's letters see *Memoirs*, I, 305–312, and *Four Generations*, I, 133ff. On the somewhat stiffer first draft of Hunt's first letter (now in the Huntington Library) see George Barnett, "Leigh Hunt Revises a Letter," *Huntington Library Quarterly*, XX (1956–57), 284–291; cf. *Four Generations*, I, 131. For Hunt's comments on the episode to Shelley see his *Correspondence*, I, 166, 169, and for Shelley's weary and aggrieved reply see his *Letters*, II, 936. Newman White (*Shelley* [1940], II, 638) has suggested that Hunt was probably the author of a reply to

a better time, and place too, for assaulting me and my friends in this bitter manner," and he went on to argue that a sense of injured merit was no excuse for publicizing other people's faults. "Do you think that nobody has thought or suffered, or come to conclusions through thought or suffering, but yourself?" Hazlitt's reply — "the longest unpaid contribution which he had ever made since his boyhood to literature and to literary history," as his grandson later pointed out [36] — is a most instructive document. Denying that he could ever quarrel with Hunt — "you are one of those people that I like, do what they will" — he then itemized a long list of "small, old grievances" about the indifference and neglect of Hunt and Lamb and Godwin, as well as several others. "My God, it is enough to drive one mad," he said. "I have not a soul to stand by me, and yet I am to give up my only resource and revenge, a theory — I won't do it, that's flat." For Shelley and his ruffled feelings he said that he was not responsible, and he ended with a blurting comment that is both sad and funny: "I want to know why everybody has such a dislike to me." Hunt could have no doubt told him why, but instead he held out the olive branch. "If you do not want to quarrel with me," he wrote,

I certainly do not want to quarrel with you. . . . I have often said, I have a sort of irrepressible love for Hazlitt, on account of his sympathy with mankind, his unmercenary disinterestedness, and his suffering; and I should have a still greater and more personal affection for him if he would let one, but I declare to God I never seem to know whether he is pleased or displeased, cordial or uncordial — indeed, his manners are never cordial — and he has a way with him, when first introduced to you, and ever afterwards, as if he said, "I have no faith in anything, especially your advances: don't you flatter yourself you have any road to my credulity: we have nothing in common between us." Then you escape into a corner, and your conversation is apt to be as sarcastic and incredulous about all the world as your manner.

And so their tattered friendship was patched up again.

As Lamb had long since learned, and as Leigh Hunt never realized, Hazlitt's manners were beyond repair. In spite of his "offenses against me and mine (not to be done away with by his good word at intervals)," Hunt wrote in 1823 in the charming essay called "My Books," "I pardon the irritable patriot and metaphysician, who would give his last penny to an acquaintance, and his last pulse to the good of mankind." [37] The following year he presented Hazlitt (then visiting him in Italy) with a paper setting forth his faults, and his guest kept dinner waiting while he read it through. "By God, sir," said Hazlitt when he finished, "there's

---

Hazlitt's *Edinburgh* review of Shelley's *Posthumous Poems* in *McPhun's Glasgow Magazine* of November 1824.

a good deal of truth in it"[38] — but he did not change his ways. In 1826 he gave fresh offense by his account of Hunt's and Shelley's conflicts with Lord Byron,[39] and as a consequence Thomas Campbell, editor of the *New Monthly Magazine,* where the essay had appeared, apologized to Hunt for his "culpable negligence" in not deleting the "detestable passage" and promised to be more watchful of Hazlitt's "aspersions" in the future.[40] Hunt was sufficiently placated, it seems, to omit from *Lord Byron and Some of His Contemporaries* (1828) a section critical of Hazlitt, not because he minded speaking "disagreeable truths" about a man capable of inspiring panegyrics, he explained, but because "Mr. Hazlitt is ready enough, at all times, to save others the necessity of exhibiting his defects. Twenty such articles could not have put an end to the good understanding between us; so genuine indeed is his love of truth, violently as his passions may sometimes lead him to mistake it."[41] Replying to such double-edged remarks in "A Farewell to Essay-Writing," Hazlitt showed no rancor, but neither did he own the soft impeachment; he merely regretted his old friend's inability "to reconcile the shyness of my presentions with the inveteracy and sturdiness of my principles. . . . He finds it odd that I am a close reasoner and a loose dresser."[42] What Hunt thought of this we do not know, but he was probably more amused than mollified by Hazlitt's explanation, which he made about this time, that the "personalities" in his work had never been gratuitous, because when he "sacrificed" his friends it was always to a theory.[43]

Not long before this exchange, Hunt, who had not seen Hazlitt for "this half year," had written warmly to arrange an evening visit. "I am more at ease with you in your own house, than any where else; & have felt so comfortable there both in Florence and Down Street [where Hazlitt lived from 1824 to 1827], that I wish to please you by saying what I do, & think you should be pleased, because it is true." Is there any hope, he asked in closing, "that I might be permitted some day or other to try & bring you & Coleridge together again?" * In Hazlitt's later years such advances, if not rebuffed, were probably not encouraged, and when the two old friends did meet from time to time there were minor irritations. When Cyrus Redding, chatting in the street with Hazlitt not long before his death, inquired about their latest "difference," he was told that Hunt had probably forgotten all about it, but "if he has not, I have." † At all events, their contacts must have been infrequent,

---

* ALS, 20 June [?1826], The Houghton Library, Harvard. This letter was written from Highgate, where Hunt had found a house in 1826, shortly after his return from Italy.

† *Past Celebrities Whom I Have Known* (1866), I, 81f. Hunt's "An Earth upon Heaven," written for the *Companion* in 1828 (*Essays*, pp. 8–14), was prompted by the

for when Hazlitt died — not unexpectedly — Hunt was astounded at the news. Characteristically, he responded to the event with a grief that few men felt and even fewer cared to voice. What he then remembered was his and Hazlitt's "interchange of hopes and fears, — the talk of books, — the more than Johnsonian cups of tea, — the little quarrels, so soon appeased (the quarrels of lovers of truth are like those of other lovers) — the pleasure of welcoming and regretting on his side, and of forgiving and being instructed on ours." " However moody and irascible, he said in valediction, Hazlitt was "essentially a great man, — a master mind; and he had this characteristic of the greatest, — that his regard for human nature, and his power to love truth and loveliness in their humblest shapes, survived his subtlest detections of human pride and folly." [45] It is a tribute that Hazlitt might have smiled at wryly, but one that he surely would have liked.

HAYDON

Benjamin Robert Haydon was another member of the Leigh Hunt circle who wound in and out of Hazlitt's life for fifteen years or more. The two met in 1812 through James Northcote [1] — that perennial relic of the age of Reynolds whom Hazlitt never tired of chatting with — and until their common love of art yielded to a mutual disesteem they might have been accounted friends. Careless, boisterous, confident, gregarious,[2] Haydon was one of the sights of early nineteenth-century London, and his brawls, debts, triumphs, and ostentatious piety make his *Diary* one of the most fascinating records of the age. Beginning work on a picture of the flight into Egypt in 1806, he had asked God "to bless my career, to grant me energy to create a new era in art, and to rouse the people and patrons to a just estimate of the moral value of historical painting";[3] and until his suicide forty years later he never yielded to the rebuffs and disappointments that would have quelled a man of less heroic self-esteem. Though eight years younger than Hazlitt, by the time they met he had won a measure of success with such big and splashy pictures as *Joseph and Mary*, *The Assassination of Dentatus*, and *Macbeth*, and the fact that the officials of the Royal Society had, as he thought, spite-

---

"excellent" article "Of Persons One Would Wish to Have Seen," which, he said, "somebody" had recently contributed to the *New Monthly Magazine*. Although he did not mention Hazlitt by name, and even misquoted the title of his piece, he could hardly have failed to recognize the style. Hazlitt's essay (17.122–134), one of his warmest recollections of Lamb and the old days at Mitre Court, had appeared in the *New Monthly* in 1826.

fully hung *Dentatus* wrong at the 1809 exhibition had launched him on a subsidiary career of denouncing academic art. That this picture, the greatest ever painted by an English painter, should have been put into an anteroom and "ruined in reputation through the pernicious power of professional men, embodied by royalty for the advancement of works of this very description," [4] provided him with a grievance that stained his whole career.

Pugnacious, vain, and overbearing, Haydon was a born crusader — a hypocrite in personal relations but intensely loyal to the causes he espoused. An uneven painter but a very gifted writer who "frequently suspended the gentle labours of the pencil for the vehement use of the pen," [5] he gloried in dispute, and one of his disputes, at least, he won. When, in 1806, the Earl of Elgin brought to England, at great expense and difficulty, the sculptures he had salvaged from the Parthenon and offered to sell them to the nation, the reaction was intense. Haydon, who spent hours in gazing on and sketching the marbles, thought that Elgin's offer was "truly the greatest blessing that ever happened to this country." [6] He never approached the "divine things," he said later,

without bowing to the Great Spirit that reigns within them; I thank God daily I was in existence on their arrival, and will ever do so to the end of my life. Such a blast will Fame blow of their grandeur, that its roaring will swell out as time advances; and nations now sunk in barbarism, and ages yet unborn will in succession be roused by its thunder, and refined by its harmony; pilgrims from the remotest corners of the earth will visit their shrine, and be purified by their beauty. [7]

Others sharply disagreed. In *The Curse of Minerva* Byron excoriated Lord Elgin as a thief who "basely stole what less barbarians won," [8] and Payne Collier, a director of the British Institution and a "connoisseur" whose "judgment, taste, and feeling" were, as Haydon thought, beneath contempt, [9] strongly urged against accepting Elgin's offer. For several years the argument continued, and in 1816, when a select committee of the House of Commons was named to report upon the matter, Haydon girded on his armor and sallied forth to war. Unfortunately the committee did not invite his testimony, but when both the *Examiner* and the *Champion* printed his defense of Lord Elgin and the marbles, the effect, as Haydon said, was overwhelming. "The public voice so completely and enthusiastically responded to my letters that the patrons were afraid to let me see their hatred. . . . In a week my painting-room was again crowded with rank, beauty and fashion, to such excess that I ordered the front doors to be left open." [10] Haydon was not a man to minimize his triumphs, but when Parliament voted to buy Lord Elgin's sculptures he had reason to rejoice: as Sir Thomas Lawrence said, it was he who "saved the Marbles." [11]

There was excess in everything he did. "I always filled my painting-room to its full extent," he recalled; "and had I possessed a room 400 feet long, and 200 feet high, and 400 feet wide, I would have ordered a canvas 399-6 long by 199-6 high." [12] His egotism, like his hatred of the Royal Society and his battle for the Elgin Marbles, stamped itself upon the age, and he was hailed in certain quarters as a genius. Although Coleridge thought "Mr. Haydon's immortality dear at two shillings" when he had to pay the postage on a letter in which the painter assured him of undying fame, [13] Hunt and Keats and others were glad to worship at his shrine, at least until they came to know him better. The prospect of an evening with "this glorious Haydon" made young Keats tremble with elation, [14] and one of their subsequent encounters so "wrought me up," he informed the artist, that he had to seek release in verse — and so we have "Great spirits now on earth are sojourning." [15] A few months later Haydon told "dear Keats" that only he, of all his many friends, "reflected" his enthusiasm with a proper "burning ripeness of soul": you "add fire," he said, "when I am exhausted, & excite fury afresh — I offer my heart & intellect & experience." [16] Haydon was on such febrile terms with, and borrowed money from, some of the master spirits of the age; but he could also be a boon companion, and his account of the "immortal dinner" where Lamb got drunk and called Wordsworth a rascally old Poet is worth more than acres of his painting.*

Occasionally Haydon hired a hall and rewarded his admirers with a spectacular one-man exhibition. *The Judgment of Solomon* created a sensation in 1814, and six years later *Christ's Triumphal Entry into Jerusalem* (which required a frame that weighed six hundred pounds) [17] was, if we may believe the painter, an event that almost crowded out George IV's accession to the throne. "All the ministers and their ladies, all the foreign ambassadors, all the bishops, all the beauties in high life, the officers on guard at the palace, all the geniuses in town, and everybody of any note, were invited and came"; [18] but it was not until the majestic and superannuated Sarah Siddons appeared, stood rapt in contemplation, and "then ejaculated, in her deep, low, thrilling voice, 'It is perfect!'" that success was doubly sure. [19] From the corner of the room, "really rejoicing," Keats and Hazlitt surveyed the glittering scene,† and

---

* Haydon, *Autobiography*, I, 269ff.; cf. *Diary*, II, 173–176; *Correspondence and Table-Talk*, II, 54f.; Rollins, I, 197f. One wishes Hazlitt had attended — and written an account of — this celebrated gathering.

† *Autobiography*, I, 282. This was Keats's and Hazlitt's last recorded meeting (25 March 1820). See Rollins, II, 284n.

the fact that old Sam Rogers spitefully called the ass on which Christ rode the savior of the picture could not diminish Haydon's exultation.[20] Despite such triumphs, however, his financial problems were incessant. All his life, he told Mary Russell Mitford, he had been "seeking for a butcher whose respect for genius predominated over his love of gain." [21] He was intimately familiar with the debtors' prison, and not long before his suicide in 1846 he observed that of the thirty-nine years that he had devoted to uplifting English art, thirty-two had been "without an order of any kind." [22]

Despite their feverish love of art, their intimacy with Hunt and Keats, and their shared contempt for academic painting, two such irascible and self-centered men as Hazlitt and Haydon were bound to disagree. The record of their friendship — if that is not too strong a word — is one of recurrent irritations. As Hazlitt himself said, he was nothing if not critical; and Haydon, even more than most of us, resented criticism: he lived on adulation. In 1814 he professed to be relieved at Hazlitt's "capital" review of *The Judgment of Solomon* in the *Morning Chronicle,* knowing that the critic had "abused" the picture in conversation with a friend; [23] but since the review both praised the artist's "bold and aspiring mind" and also underscored the disproportion between effort and success, it is altogether probable that Haydon was annoyed.[24] As the diary entry reproduced on the next page indicates, however, he was resolved to bear with Hazlitt's crotchets, for he thought that if properly instructed he could "do great good" for English painting.

All his sneers & attacks at times at my views I take as nothing. My object is to manage such an intellect for the great purposes of art; and if he was to write against me for six months, still would I be patient. He is a sincere good fellow at Bottom, with fierce passions & appetites. Appeal to him & he is always conquered & yields, & before long I'll venture to predict he shall assist the good cause [of establishing an English school of "historical painting" with Haydon as its leader], instead of sneering at it.[25]

And as evidence of his effect on Hazlitt he cites the critic's excoriating comments on the Catalogue Raisonné of the British Institution and on academic hucksters.[26]

Hazlitt was no mere ventriloquist, but he and Haydon did see eye to eye on certain things — for example, the pernicious influence of the British Institution, Sir Joshua Reynolds' inflated reputation, and the merits of the Elgin Marbles — and for a few years, at least, they united in a set of common causes. As Hazlitt's first reviews make clear,[27] he did not need Haydon's help to recognize the errors of academic painting; but he himself admitted that he had never "cared for" sculpture until

Haydon's Report of a Visit from Hazlitt
From Haydon's Diary, 3 November 1816

he saw the Elgin Marbles,[28] and when, in 1816, he announced the glad discovery, it was in terms that strongly echoed Haydon's views.[29] On the other hand, Haydon thought that Hazlitt underrated David Wilkie's work,[30] and he copiously recorded his dissent from the critic's favorite theory that the arts are not "progressive":

Futile, vain, imbecile assertion, the product of disappointed irritability, of morbid vanity, & of conscious weakness, of deep rooted indolence, of that blurred & envious wretchedness the result of disappointed failure, of just aimlessness enough to know what ought to be done of that, & just perseverance enough to attempt and relinquish it.[31]

Although these are hardly the words that one friend would use about another, we must not infer that Haydon always quarreled with Hazlitt. With a large voice in the newly founded *Annals of Fine Arts,* he arranged for some of the critic's most effective pieces to be reprinted there; * he preached to him, without success, the glories of his style of art;[32] he wined and dined with him;[33] as a mark of special favor he included him — along with Keats, Wordsworth, Sir Isaac Newton, and Voltaire — in *Christ's Triumphal Entry into Jerusalem.*[34]

There was camaraderie, perhaps, but little real rapport. Whereas Hazlitt regarded Haydon, as he told Northcote later, as a man who tried to "bully" the public into thinking him a genius,† Haydon marveled at Hazlitt's "singular compound" of "malice, candour, cowardice, genius, purity, vice, democracy and conceit."[35] He looked upon him as a cynic who, disgruntled by his failures, turned derision into habit.[36] As early as 1817, when Haydon was still thick with Hunt and Hazlitt and the rest of the *Examiner* group, he berated them to Wordsworth, calling Hunt a fool who "perplexes himself, and pains his friends" and Hazlitt a critic of such "malignant morbidity" that in his article on fine art in the *Encyclopaedia Britannica* he "mentioned every living painter now eminent, but me!"[37] Although by 1824 Haydon had persuaded himself that Hazlitt had "all along been my furious defender,"[38] the evidence does not support his claim. In 1814 Hazlitt's review of *The Judgment of*

* Among others, part of "The Catalogue Raisonné of the British Institution," "On the Character of Sir Joshua Reynolds," and "Fine Arts. Whether They Are Promoted by Academies and Public Institutions." See Clark Olney, "William Hazlitt and Benjamin Robert Haydon," *Notes & Queries,* CLXIX (1935), 237ff., 256ff.; cf. Olney's *Benjamin Robert Haydon* (1952), pp. 96–99.

† 11.252. Elsewhere (20.392) Hazlitt said that Haydon "should have been the boatswain of a man of war: he has no other ideas of glory than those which belong to a naval victory, or to vulgar noise and insolence." It is altogether likely that a passage in the Table Talk "On Patronage and Puffing" was inspired by Haydon. "Do not think to bully posterity," Hazlitt says (8.297) "or to cozen your contemporaries. Be not always anticipating the effect of your picture on the town — think more about deserving success than commanding it. In issuing so many promissory notes upon the bank of fame, do not forget you have to pay in sterling gold."

Solomon was anything but eulogistic, and six years later, in the *Edinburgh,* he was still restrained. Haydon, "a young artist of great promise," he remarked, should not rest upon the somewhat sultry fame of *Christ's Triumphal Entry into Jerusalem,* for that picture was "the foundation, not the superstructure of a first-rate work of art," and if the painter wished to earn his reputation he should discipline himself. "We wish to see this artist paint a picture (he has now every motive for exertion and improvement) which shall not only have a striking and imposing effect in the aggregate, but where the impression of the whole shall be the joint and irresistible effect of the value of every part." [39] A year later, in the *London Magazine,* he was even more explicit. The commercial exploitation of *Christ's Triumphal Entry* — involving tours to Edinburgh and Glasgow and mountains of contrived publicity — had been both vulgar and successful, and when *Christ's Agony in the Garden* was launched with equal fanfare Hazlitt did not conceal his disapproval. Instead of trying to swim to popularity "with borrowed bloated bladders, and flimsy newspaper paragraphs," he wrote, an artist should learn to wait and work for fame. Smaller than his other things but just as slapdash, *Christ's Agony* was "a comparative failure, both in execution and probable effect." Haydon was the sort of painter who did better with a group than with a single figure, and better with ten groups than with one: "reduce him within narrow limits, and you cut off half his resources." *

Such remarks might well offend a man who, in his more euphoric moments, thought he had "air-balloons under his armpits, and ether in his soul"; [40] but Haydon had other — and better — reasons for disliking Hazlitt. In 1819 he received the following note from him:

Dear Haydon,
    Esau sold his birth-right. My copies in the Louvre and the recollections associated with them are all I have left that I care about. You shall have them if you feel inclined for a forty pound bill at a twelve-month's date. Would you call tomorrow morning before twelve?

W. H. [41]

According to his own account, Haydon promptly called on Hazlitt, found him "in great distress," and pressed a note for fifty pounds on him, in return for which he took the copies from the Louvre — not because of their "artistic" merit but because they had been made "by a literary man with great feeling for the beauties of High Art." [42] The

---

* 18.141f. It is curious that after Hazlitt's death Haydon remembered this review with pleasure. It was enough, he told the critic's son (*Four Generations,* I, 234) "to make a man forgive a host of faults, and overlook the age of malice. I forgive him all that, and consider accounts are balanced."

Dear Haydon,

Esau sold his birth-right. My copies in the Louvre and the recollections associated with them are all I have left that I care about. You then, have them, if you feel inclined, for a forty pound bill at a twelvemonth's date. Would you call tomorrow morning before twelve?

✕

W. H.

✕. I gave him fifty to relieve his wants — all my misfortunes — by telling Mary he should get them again cheap — (at least, I knew) they got them again cheap — He bought for 5 or 6 pounds. I now chuckles at having got *them again* — This is the meanest thing Hazlitt ever did —

Hazlitt's Maltreatment of Haydon
Letter from Hazlitt to Haydon, and Haydon's comment on it in his Diary

sequel is a sorry story: a year later, when Haydon, despite the success of *Christ's Triumphal Entry*, was himself in need of money, Hazlitt — who had paid off only half his debt — bought back the pictures for "5 or 6 pounds" and then chuckled at his bargain. One can hardly wonder at Haydon's angry scribble in his diary, "This is the meanest thing Hazlitt ever did." *

Not even this shabby piece of business severed their relations. In 1820 Hazlitt requested Haydon's help in finding outlets for his work,† and throughout the next few years their contacts were much as they had been before — prickly and sporadic. Like almost everybody else, Haydon, then newly married and a devoted family man, was outraged by Hazlitt's treatment of his wife and his affair with Sarah Walker; and although he continued to receive his visits because he liked his "unaffected frankness," [43] in his *Diary* he paraphrased *King Lear* to call his friend a "hog in sloth, fox in stealth, wolf in greediness, dog in madness, lion in prey, 'one that sleeps in the contriving of lust & wakes to do it.' " [44] In 1823 Hazlitt drank tea with Haydon in King's Bench Prison (where his debts had landed him), [45] and two years later, on an afternoon so "impenetrably dark" that the artist could not paint, he dropped in on Hazlitt, "as being all in character with the day, and had a regular groan." [46] Their disputes about art went on, of course, [47] and Haydon found, or thought he found,

---

* This comment occurs in the marginal note to Hazlitt's letter shown on page 243. Writing to Sir Walter Scott in 1828 (Partington, p. 174), the painter tells a slightly different story. There he says that Hazlitt regained possession of the pictures for £2 16s. — "or some sum of that sort" — and then kept them "as a triumph to gratify his *spite*, that I had the power to [assist] him!" At least twice later in his *Diary* (II, 495, and Pope, 3 August 1826) he alludes to Hazlitt's bad behavior about his copies from the Louvre. Patmore's version of the episode (III, 105–110) should be accepted with reserve.

† Haydon pasted the following letter (ALS in the possession of Professor Willard Pope) in his diary:

Winterslow Hut
Aug. 11
1820

My dear Haydon,
    I have a letter from Jeffrey in these words. "I shall print your Farington with some corrections — You are too fond of paradoxes." Can't you upon the strength of this raise the wind for me with some great man? Have you settled with Allatt, the little man? I liked your painting *versus* sculpture. Have you seen any more of the historic model, or of a very different person, J. Scott? I suspect he is at me again. Yours truly

W. H.

Hazlitt's review of Joseph Farington's *Memoirs of the Life of Sir Joshua Reynolds* appeared in the *Edinburgh* in August 1820 (16.181–211). "Allatt, the little man" was perhaps John Allnutt, a resident of Clapham who collected pictures, befriended John Constable, and later quarreled with Haydon. See Haydon, *Diary*, II, 441; M. Sturge Henderson, *Constable* (1905), p. 38.

new evidence of Hazlitt's malice and conceit.[48] His disloyalty was "painfully cutting," the artist said in 1824:

Here's a man whom my generosity saved from starvation by purchasing his heathen [?] copies from the louvre Titians, whose necessities I have again and again assisted, to my own ruin, whose habits & ways I have ever consulted at my own table, whom I have introduced to genteel Society, for which he was totally unfit, when first I knew him, but whose heart is so innately fiendish, nothing can soften or tame him. He, as Gifford said, "wishes an Autocracy of Malediction." He is disappointed in Politicks, disappointed in Art, always in the wrong. England, of course, can never produce Painters because Mr. Hazlitt had not talent enough to be one.[49]

And yet, in spite of everything, Haydon retained a certain admiration for the rogue.

Poor old Hazlitt, with his fine candour, his consciousness of never shaving and of a soiled shirt, his frank avowal of his vices and follies, his anti-Bourbon thoroughbred hatred, his Napoleon adhesiveness, his paradoxical puttings forth at so much a sheet, his believing himself the fine, metaphysical, caustic philosopher, going about like Diogenes with a lantern impaling all his acquaintance, while he is the most impaled of the whole, is worth ten thousand poets, and has more real virtue too.[50]

Haydon's opinion of Hazlitt continued to oscillate from wrath to condescension. In 1827 he agreed with Talfourd that one should "overlook" in him "every thing villainous, treacherous, mean, dirty, & contemptible, from the apparent candour of his nature," [51] and yet a few months later he assured Sir Walter Scott that his former intimacy with Hunt and Hazlitt had almost ruined him. "Pleased with Hunt's wit and Hazlitt's entertaining conversation," he wrote in memory of his heedless youth (when he was only thirty), "I did not sufficiently foresee that I should be mingled up with their opinions on Politicks, Religion and Morality — though I never in the whole course of all my life agreed with them in one single opinion on such subjects." [52] Toward the end of Hazlitt's life, it seems, he and Haydon no longer met — a circumstance no doubt pleasing to them both — but when Hazlitt died in 1830 Haydon had the final word. "A very formidable enemy to English Art" was gone, he recorded in his diary.

Immoral in principle, treacherous in Friendship, a fiend in heart, & coward in personal feelings, yet he was a consistent, determined, heroic upholder of the rights of Nations, and the noble principles of political and constitutional liberty. For this I honor him. He died poor, nor do I believe he would have sacrificed one iota of his political creed to have possessed millions. B. R. Haydon.
    Poor Hazlitt! — entertaining, inconsistent, fiendish, cowardly, saturnine & treacherous, yet heroical on one great point, sufficient to compensate for crimes. Farewell.[53]

_18_

William Hazlitt is dead — a very formidable enemy to English [art?], with the sophism of a metaphysician and the practical knowledge of a disappointed artist he added the malignity that ever accompanies failure in Hazlitt — He did great harm, and I really feel happy that I did in my answer to his article in the Westminster, completely refute him in the Spectator as I always said I would —

Immoral in principle, treacherous in Friendship, a fiend in heart, & coward in personal feeling. Yet he was a consistent, determined heroic upholder of the rights of Nations, and the noble principles of political and constitutional liberty —

For this I honour him — he died poor, nor do I believe he would have sacrificed one iota of his political creed, to have possessed millions...

B. R Haydon

Poor Hazlitt! — entertaining — inconsistent — prejudiced — cowardly — saturnine Theartism, well deserved in one [who?] had sufficient talents, to compensate for crimes.

Farewell.

Haydon's Final Assessment of Hazlitt
From Haydon's Diary, 18 September 1830

HAYDON

Although a man is not upon his oath in lapidary inscriptions, as Johnson said, we may none the less rejoice that Haydon was not called upon for composing Hazlitt's epitaph.

KEATS

Most of the *Examiner* group, even Hunt and Haydon, are of interest mainly to students of the period, but the greatest of them all is remembered, as he hoped that he would be, among the English poets, and therefore his friendship with Hazlitt is particularly important. Shy, austere, and evil-tempered, Hazlitt had no gift for keeping friends, and Keats, in his dizzy rise to splendor, quickly grew beyond the men who once had seemed to him to be great spirits; but so far as we can tell, the affection and respect these two felt for one another suffered no attrition. Always rather captious about contemporary writers, Hazlitt no doubt undervalued Keats (as Haydon charged),[1] but he was the first to anthologize his work and to proclaim that he had shown "the greatest promise of genius of any poet of his day." * It is clear, moreover, that Keats held Hazlitt in extraordinary esteem. He had second thoughts about many of his friends, and, as his letters show, he came in time to recognize Leigh Hunt's "self delusion," Haydon's affectations, Wordsworth's egotistic moralizing, and Shelley's bent for rhetoric, but for Hazlitt, alone among his eminent contemporaries, he maintained a steady admiration. He praised and quoted him, adopted his opinions, and turned them into art. He knew that Hazlitt was sometimes coarse and cruel, but he also knew how much he owed to him, and the debt is plain throughout his work.†

They probably met toward the end of 1816, when Hazlitt was preparing *The Round Table* and *Characters of Shakespear's Plays* and Keats his *Poems* for the press. The young poet had just been taken up by Hunt and Haydon and pronounced in the *Examiner* (along with

---

* 9.244. In *Select British Poets, or New Elegant Extracts from Chaucer to the Present Time* (1824) Hazlitt printed portions of *Endymion*, "The Eve of St. Agnes," "Ode to a Nightingale," "Hyperion," and other things.

† The relationship of Keats and Hazlitt has been so extensively investigated by Garrod, De Selincourt, Finney, and others that there is a small library on the subject, but two fairly recent articles may be cited as representing our current state of knowledge: Clarence Thorpe ("Keats and Hazlitt: A Record of Personal Relationship and Critical Estimate," *PMLA*, LXII (1947), 487–502) has collected most of the biographical data, and Kenneth Muir ("Keats and Hazlitt" in *John Keats: A Reassessment* [ed. Kenneth Muir, 1958], pp. 139–158) has treated Keats's use of some of Hazlitt's main ideas. Bertram L. Woodruff's unpublished Harvard dissertation, "Keats and Hazlitt: A Study of the Development of Keats" (1956), is encyclopedic.

Shelley and Reynolds) worthy of attention.[2] It was a heady time for him, and in a string of famous poems — "Great spirits now on earth are sojourning," "Sleep and Poetry," the Chapman's Homer sonnet, and "I stood tiptoe" — he recorded his elation. Whereas Hazlitt made no public comment on Keats at this stage of his career — although he of course had heard about his work from Hunt[3] — Keats's praise of Hazlitt runs strong throughout his letters. He read his books and journalism, and most, at least, of what he read he liked; moreover, his scribbling in his copy of *Characters of Shakespear's Plays* that he could not "help seeing Hazlitt like Ferdinand — 'in an odd angle of the Isle sitting — his arms in this sad Knot' "[4] implies an intimacy that is confirmed by certain imitated mannerisms in the letters.* Not even Hazlitt's attack on the poetical apostates, which reached its peak about this time, could stifle Keats's admiration. Superbly sane and generous, he of course regretted some of Hazlitt's jibes — as when he ridiculed Southey's grey hair[5] and scolded Wordsworth for his feeble poem about the gypsies[6] — but he thought his prose was matchless[7] and his judgment almost always sound.[8] "I know he thinks himself not estimated by ten People in the world," he wrote in 1817; "I wishe he knew he is."[9]

Unfortunately there survives no correspondence between these two great men (for Hazlitt hated writing letters and did not even save the ones he got); but, moving in the same small circle, they were often thrown together, and there is ample evidence of a close relationship.[10] Keats thought nothing, apparently, of walking seven miles from Hampstead to hear Hazlitt lecture on the English poets,[11] and once, at least, Hazlitt let him have the manuscript of a lecture he had missed, so that he might read and copy excerpts from it.† Keats sought advice from him,‡ quoted from and paraphrased his works,[12] and even wrote like him when he attempted journalistic prose.§ He admired "the force and innate power"

* "It's the finest thing by God — as Hazlitt wo^d say," Keats wrote to Reynolds in March 1817 (Rollins, I, 123). Two months later he remarked (I, 143) that he was "very near Agreeing with Hazlitt that Shakespeare is enough for us"; and the following year he implied (I, 280) that Shakespeare and Hazlitt were always associated in his thinking. Writing from Italy in 1823, Leigh Hunt imagined Hazlitt as saying, "By God, Sir, I think it will do, — eh?" (William H. Marshall, "Three New Leigh Hunt Letters," *Keats-Shelley Journal*, IX [1960], 122). See Patmore, III, 85.

† Rollins, II, 24; cf. I, 217n. Hazlitt apparently lent this manuscript (of Lecture VI in his series on the English comic writers [6.106–132]) to Reynolds, who used it for a eulogistic piece in the *Edinburgh Magazine* (III [1818], 540–548) and then passed it on to Keats. See Leonidas M. Jones, "New Letters, Articles, and Poems by John Hamilton Reynolds," *Keats-Shelley Journal*, VI (1957), 102.

‡ Rollins, I, 274, II, 174, 177. In the "Chest of Books" that Keats asked John Taylor to divide among his friends (*Keats Circle*, I, 260 n.) was a copy of Hazlitt's *Essay on the Principles of Human Action* (ibid., I, 254).

§ On Keats's theatrical criticism, which he wrote for the *Champion* in January 1818 in the absence of his friend Reynolds, the regular drama critic for the paper, see Rollins,

of his style,[13] with its "fiery laconiscism,"[14] and he thought that his invective was superb. Hazlitt "hath a demon," he decided:[15] "He is your only good damner and if ever I am damn'd — damn me if I shoul'nt like him to damn me."[16] But it was Hazlitt's "depth of taste" that he found most impressive,[17] and after 1817 the implications of this famous phrase are everywhere apparent in his work. Not only does he often echo Hazlitt's comments — as when he said that the followers of Pope "sway'd about upon a rocking horse, / And thought it Pegasus,"[18] that "Philosophy will clip an Angel's wings,"[19] that Wordsworth's egotism hurt his poetry,[20] that Coleridge was "incapable of remaining content with half knowledge"[21] — but many of his fundamental views on literature may be traced to Hazlitt's work. His conviction that "the excellence of every Art is its intensity"[22] no doubt had its source in Hazlitt's Round Table paper "On Gusto" and in his comments on King Lear,[23] and his assertion that "Men of Genius" have no "determined Character"[24] and poets no "identity"[25] restates (and refines upon) the theory that imagination is a liberating faculty and that Shakespeare, the great ventriloquist, is the Proteus of the human intellect.[26]

It would be pleasant to record that Hazlitt saw in Keats a major poet, but his attitude was at best equivocal. Although we may assume that he liked him as a man, and we know that he respected his opinions and praised him after his death for what he might have done, we can not be certain that he fully recognized his merits. To be sure, when Keats, in 1818, was "very disappointed"[27] by his remarks on Chatterton in his lectures on the English poets, he expressed regret at having "given dissatisfaction to some persons, with whom I would willingly agree on all such matters," and tried to justify and clarify his views.[28] But other than to quote (or misquote) occasionally from his work[29] he did not do much, publicly at least, to secure his reputation while he lived. The two men were together for the last time, so far as we know, at the exhibition of *Christ's Triumphal Entry into Jerusalem* in March 1820,[30] and there is no evidence that Hazlitt came to Keats's aid during his last sad months in London or wrote to him in Italy. In December 1820 he finally made a testy comment on his work — to compare Keats and Shakespeare was absurd, he said, although he at any rate was better than his tormentors in the Tory press[31] — but this could not have given satisfaction to the dying poet or to his many loyal friends.

A month later Hazlitt prematurely spoke of Keats as one already dead, a victim of the harsh reviewers.

I, 195f., 199; Lowell, *John Keats*, I, 537–541; Leonidas M. Jones, "Keats's Theatrical Reviews in the *Champion*," *Keats-Shelley Journal*, III (1954), 55–65.

249

Poor Keats! What was sport to the town was death to him. Young, sensitive, delicate, he was like

> A bud bit by an envious worm,
> Ere he could spread his sweet leaves to the air,
> Or dedicate his beauty to the sun —

and unable to endure the miscreant cry and idiot laugh, withdrew to sigh his last breath in foreign climes.[32]

Keats's death a few weeks later put Hazlitt in an elegiac mood. Mixing pathos with invective, he shows us a beleaguered poet hounded by his critics, and in place of criticism, therefore, we get sentiment and rancor.

He lay bare to weather — the serpent stung him, and the poison-tree dropped upon this little western flower: — when the mercenary servile crew approached him, he had no pedigree to show them, no rent-roll to hold out in reversion for their praise: he was not in any great man's train, nor the butt and puppet of a lord — he could only offer them "the fairest flowers of the season, carnations and streaked gilliflowers," — "rue for remembrance and pansies for thoughts" — they recked not of his gift, but tore him with hideous shouts and laughter,
> Nor could the Muse protect her son! [33]

Although this sort of thing grows tedious, Hazlitt never tired of it. Thereafter when he wrote of Keats it was almost always to denounce those writers of the *Quarterly Review* and *Blackwood's Magazine* who had damned them both as the Cockney friends of Hunt. "To be a Reformer, the friend of a Reformer, or the friend's friend of a Reformer, is as much as a man's peace, reputation, or even life is worth. Answer, if it is not so, pale shade of Keats, or living mummy of William Gifford!" [34] The poet's "fine fancy and powerful invention" were not enough, he said in 1823, to excuse his having won the praise of the *Examiner*,[35] and consequently, as he remarked a few years later, he had paid the forfeit of his health and life.[36]

Hazlitt's strictly literary comments on the greatest of all his friends are few and disappointing. The longest, which he wrote in 1822, occurs at the end of his essay "On Effeminacy of Character" in *Table-Talk,* and it merits full quotation because it contains, regrettably, almost everything he had to say of Keats.

I cannot help thinking that the fault of Mr. Keats's poems was a deficiency in masculine energy of style. He had beauty, tenderness, delicacy, in an uncommon degree, but there was a want of strength and substance. His Endymion is a very delightful description of the illusions of a youthful imagination, given up to airy dreams — we have flowers, clouds, rainbows, moonlight, all sweet sounds and smells, and Oreads and Dryads flitting by — but there is nothing tangible in it, nothing marked or palpable — we have none of the hardy spirit or rigid forms of antiquity. He painted his own thoughts and character; and did not transport himself into the fabulous and heroic ages. There is a want of action, of character, and so far, of imagination, but there is exquisite fancy. All is soft and fleshy, without bone or muscle. We see in him the youth, without the manhood of poetry. His genius breathed "vernal delight and joy." — "Like Maia's son he stood and shook his plumes," with fragrance filled. His mind was redolent of spring. He had not the fierceness of summer, nor the richness of autumn, and winter he seemed not to have known, till he felt the icy hand of death! [37]

However appropriate to *Endymion*, these remarks seem so irrelevant to the author of "Hyperion" and the odes that if one did not know otherwise one might think that Hazlitt had not read beyond the early poems. Even his generous praise of Keats in *Select British Poets* is tempered by the same reserve.[38] Significantly, his most moving words on Keats, which he wrote in 1821, tell us more about his own emotional fatigue than about his dying friend. Books had lost their "power" over him, he said, but a rereading of "The Eve of St. Agnes" had made him sorry that he was not young again.

The beautiful and tender images there conjured up, "come like shadows — so depart." The "tiger-moth's wings," which he has spread over his rich poetic blazonry, just flit across my fancy; the gorgeous twilight window which he has painted over again in his verse, to me "blushes" almost in vain "with blood of queens and kings." I know how I should have felt at one time in reading such passages; and that is all. The sharp luscious flavour, the fine *aroma* is fled, and nothing but the stalk, the bran, the husk of literature is left.[39]

With this autumnal valediction Hazlitt dismissed the only one of his contemporaries who, if he had lived, might have reached his own ideal of greatness.

THE LECTURER

When, after six years of journalism, Hazlitt left the *Times* in December 1817, it was not to rest upon his tattered laurels. To be sure, he had won a slender fame with the clientele of the *Examiner*; his contributions to the *Edinburgh Review* had attracted some attention; and his book on Shakespeare had enjoyed — or so he later said [1] — a brief but real success before William Gifford and other Tory critics decided to destroy his reputation. That the great Jeffrey himself, after his fashion, had publicly commended him [2] and that a writer in the *Edinburgh Magazine* had proclaimed him to be the best essayist since Goldsmith [3] tells us less, perhaps, about his growing fame than that the *New Monthly* saw fit to libel him as "a manufacturer of essays for a jacobinical Sunday newspaper," a "green-eyed critic of an infidel review," and a slovenly hack who had "been recently gaining more ground with a certain gossiping class of readers, than his merits in any degree warrant." * Even more indicative of his ominous success was the first of a series of attacks in the April 1817 *Quarterly*, the very voice of Toryism,⁴ and then, six months later, the beginning of the celebrated blows at him and all his so-called Cockney friends in *Blackwood's Magazine*.⁵ The force of these attacks, together with fatigue from his extraordinary exertions as a writer, may have prompted him to take another tack with a new attempt at lecturing. Although he did not abandon journalism altogether (as his contributions to the *Edinburgh Magazine* and John Hunt's *Yellow Dwarf* make clear),⁶ he was no doubt glad to move from politics to literature and, from the serenity of the lecture-desk, to talk about the books that he had known and loved for years.

The lectures on the English poets, like everything else he did, were drummed up in a hurry. After Thomas Alsager, his colleague on the *Times* and an "influential member" of the Surrey Institution, had endorsed (and perhaps conceived) the project, Hazlitt called on P. G. Patmore, the secretary of the governing committee, to work out the details. It was not an exhilarating interview. On entering the room where Hazlitt was awaiting him Patmore saw

a pale anatomy of a man, sitting uneasily, half on half off a chair, with his legs tucked awkwardly underneath the rail, his hands folded listlessly on his knees, his head drooping on one side, and one of his elbows leaning (not resting) on the edge of the table by which he sat, as if in fear of its having no right to be there. His hat had taken an odd position on the floor beside him, as if that, too, felt itself as much out of its element as the owner.

He half rose at my entrance, and, without speaking a word, or looking at me, except with a momentary and furtive glance, he sat down again, in a more uneasy position than before, and seemed to wait the result of what I might have to say to him, with the same sort of desperate indifference with which a culprit may be supposed to wait the sentence of his judge, after conviction.

The fact, as Patmore learned to his surprise, that the lectures had been "merely *thought of*" but not yet written was hardly reassuring, but somehow the arrangements were concluded and the series was announced.⁷

Despite the heavy competition — for in the opening months of 1818 other lectures were in progress at the Royal Academy and the Royal

* X (1818), 198f., 304. This brutal two-part article of October and November 1818 (X, 198–202, 299–304), no doubt inspired in part by Hazlitt's lectures earlier in the year and strongly reminiscent of the language used in *Blackwood's Magazine*, calls Hazlitt the "most contemptible" of all recent "pretenders to the chair of critical supremacy," "the shabby petit maitre — the dirty dandy of literature," a "pimpled coxcomb," and a "cankered Cockney." A few months earlier the *Literary Gazette* (3 May 1817, pp. 228ff.) had printed a long letter (signed "A New Examiner") in which *The Round Table* was denounced for its "cruel personalities, defamation, gross indecency, libertine principles and a spirit of irreligion and scepticism."

THE LECTURER

Institution, Coleridge was holding forth on "the *Belles-Lettres* somewhere in Fleet-street," John Thelwall had just completed "three or four courses on Poetry, the Drama, Elocution, &c.," and a Mr. Webster (aided by a "beautiful apparatus") was discussing steam [8] — Hazlitt's talks were well attended. Unfortunately the audience, as Talfourd said, was hardly sympathetic, for it consisted mainly of Dissenters (who, like Hazlitt, hated Castlereagh but who also "loved no plays"), Quakers (who "heard no music"), citizens bent on self-improvement (which they badly needed), enemies who came to sneer, and a few friends "eager to learn, and to admire"; [9] and at the first lecture, on January 13, the speaker was so nervous that he bolted from the platform and was forced back by his friends.[10] But he gained courage as he went along, and, according to the *Examiner,* at the last lecture on March 3 the audience, which had steadily increased in size, was "crowded to the very cieling [*sic*]" and shouted "Bravo!" at the end.*

Crabb Robinson, whose attendance was sporadic because he was also following Coleridge's course of lectures, was duly shocked from time to time. He thought Hazlitt "almost obscene" in quoting Prior, "indiscreet and reckless" in his comments on Voltaire, and so "contemptuous" about Wordsworth's *Letter to a Friend of Robert Burns* that he felt obliged to hiss (even though he was "on the outside of the room"). Inevitably, he was outraged by the final lecture "On the Living Poets" (which he read as soon as it was printed) because it so "flippantly and cavalierly" attacked some writers whom he liked.† On the other hand, young William Bewick, then studying with Haydon, was goggle-eyed with admiration. They were "said to be the finest lectures that ever were delivered," he reported to his family, and Hazlitt was "the Shakespeare prose writer of our glorious country." [11] Keats, after an unfortunate beginning — for he walked seven miles from Hampstead to find the audience coming out [12] — heard the lectures "regularly," together with "many" of his friends.[13] For the most part he was pleased with what he heard, it seems, but he disliked the tart comments on Chatterton, and when Hazlitt was informed of his objections he acknowledged them and tried to justify his views.[14] As for Lamb, whose opinion we would like

---

* 8 March 1818, p. 154. Perhaps the *Examiner* reports were written *in absentia.* A few years later Hazlitt complained (*Four Generations,* I, 133) that after he had "praised" Leigh Hunt in the *Edinburgh* — an allusion to the mysterious review of *The Story of Rimini* (see above, page 207n) — Hunt himself had not come to hear him lecture, "saying it would seem a collusion, if you said any thing in my favour after what I had said of you." See page 407.

† Robinson, I, 218, 219, 220, 222. Earlier (I, 182) Robinson had said that Wordsworth's *Letter* proved his "indulgence for the irregularities of Burns" to be most "amiable."

to have, he wisely never went to lectures because, as he explained, he thought them "dismal flat" when read and he was made uneasy when they were improvised.[15]

Almost before he finished giving them Hazlitt was busy with the publication of his lectures. He was reading proof on March 6,[16] and by May 20, when Benjamin Bailey, Keats's friend at Oxford, wrote that he burned to read the book,[17] *Lectures on the English Poets* was in print, together with a second edition of *Characters of Shakespear's Plays* and *A View of the English Stage,* a potboiler that Hazlitt had assembled from his theatrical reviews.* Meanwhile he had been repeating the lectures at the Crown and Anchor Tavern in the Strand (which, despite the money it would bring, Keats thought was "letting his talents down a little"),† and it was only a discouraging letter from Jeffrey,[18] apparently, that prevented him from giving them again in Edinburgh. In their printed form they sold well enough to justify a new edition in a year.‡ The *Examiner,* of course, had praised them highly from the start, and so, surprisingly, had *Blackwood's Magazine* (in a series of reports by Patmore);[19] but the triumph was short-lived, for a withering attack in the July 1818 *Quarterly Review* — which Hazlitt bitterly resented[20] — so gravely injured sales that in 1820 the publishers, conceding that they had "overprinted" the edition, were wondering what to do with all the unsold stock.[21]

With his lectures polished off and two new books in print Hazlitt might have thought to take a rest, but the summer of 1818 found him busy making plans for future work. Already committed to preparing another set of lectures — on the English comic writers — for the Surrey Institution in the fall, he also hoped to do some writing, and thus, on July 28, he sent a note to Archibald Constable of the *Edinburgh*

---

* Although *A View of the English Stage* attracted little notice, Mary Russell Mitford was enchanted by it. Perhaps it was "rather dangerous to one's taste," she said (L'Estrange, II, 47), "— rather like dining on sweetmeats and supping on pickles. So poignant is he, and so rich, everything seems insipid after him." For her other comments on Hazlitt, all of them admiring, see L'Estrange, II, 79; *Letters* (2d Series, ed. Henry Chorley, 1872), I, 39, 122.

† Rollins, I, 259. Hazlitt's finances about this time were obviously a matter of concern to him and to his friends (*Four Generations,* I, 134; Patmore, II, 251; *Life,* pp. 255, 257), hence Keats's delight at "Moore's present" to him, which he mentions in a letter to Reynolds on May 3 (Rollins, I, 282). Although Howe (*Life,* p. 227) took this present to be an inscribed copy of Tom Moore's *Fudge Family in Paris,* which Hazlitt had reviewed in April 1818 for the *Yellow Dwarf* (7.287–297), Rollins (I, 282n) has plausibly supported Louis A. Holman's suggestion that it was a gift of money from Peter Moore, one of the managers of Drury Lane and a man well known for his interest in the arts.

‡ Keynes, pp. 35f. On 12 May 1818 Hazlitt wrote to Jeffrey (ALS, The Yale University Library) that with "Lectures & copyright included" he had made two hundred guineas on the series, "which is very well for ten weeks work."

Magazine. "Could you by any possibility let me have on account the sum of fifty pounds," he asked.

If you could, I would send you articles to that amount for the Magazine within the next two months on the subjects of which I have given in a list, & which the Editors would then have ready by them for the next year. The occasion of my making this abrupt application is that I am going in the country for the rest of the summer, & I wish to leave all accounts clear behind me.[22]

In August, then, he was back in Winterslow, at the Hut, a little inn about a mile outside the village, and so busy with his work that he had to turn down Macvey Napier's invitation to write an article on drama for the *Encyclopaedia Britannica.*

> Winterslow Hut, near Salisbury
> August 26, 1818
>
> My Dear Sir, — I am sorry to be obliged, from want of health and a number of other engagements, which I am little able to perform, to decline the flattering offer you make me. I have got to write, between this and the end of October, an octavo volume of a set of lectures on the Comic Drama of this country for the Surrey Institution, which I am anxious not to slur over, and it will be as much as I can do to get it ready in time. I am also afraid that I should not be able to do the article in question, or yourself, justice, for I am not only without books, but without knowledge of what books are necessary to be consulted on the subject. To get up an article in a Review on any subject of general literature, is quite as much as I can do without exposing myself. The object of an Encyclopaedia is, I take it, to condense and combine all the facts relating to a subject, and all the theories of any consequence already known or advanced. Now, where the business of such a work ends, is just where I begin, that is, I might perhaps throw in an idle speculation or two of my own, not contained in former accounts of the subject, and which would have very little pretensions to rank as scientific. I know something about Congreve, but nothing at all of Aristophanes, and yet I conceive that the writer of an article on the *Drama* ought to be as well acquainted with the one as the other. If you should see Mr. Constable, will you tell him I am writing *nonsense* for him as fast as I can? — Your very humble servant,
>
> W. Hazlitt.*

Meanwhile there was trouble brewing. Before going down to Winterslow Hazlitt had incisively acknowledged the *Quarterly* review of *Characters of Shakespear's Plays* with a piece in the *Examiner,*[23] and as the summer ended he had to meet a new and more insidious attack; for in its August issue *Blackwood's,* which had been making wicked fun of

---

* Napier, p. 21. The "nonsense" for Constable — all of which was duly printed in the *Edinburgh Magazine* — consisted of a string of pieces — "On the Ignorance of the Learned" (8.70–77), "On Nicknames" (17.44–51), "On Fashion" (17.51–56), and "Thoughts on Taste" (17.57–67) — that anticipate the form and manner of his later essays for the *London Magazine.* It was perhaps in this same busy summer that he began to write his introductions to William Oxberry's reprints of items from the standard repertory in the series (1818–1825) called *The New English Drama.* The eighteen essays that Howe (9.63–94) ascribes to him were published in 1818–19. See page 298.

Hunt and other Cockney writers since the previous fall, finally got around to him. "Hazlitt Cross-Questioned" brought him back to London breathing fire and talking of a suit for libel. As a result, the next few months were marked by journalistic war, the main results of which were the payment of a hundred pounds in damages by *Blackwood's Magazine* and the publication, in February 1819, of his *Letter to William Gifford, Esq.,* an authentic triumph of invective.[24]

In the course of these forays and rebuttals the lectures on the English comic writers were tossed off with his customary ease. On October 23, when he called on Hessey to ask "of course" for money, he had finished only half of them,* but the series duly opened on November 3 and apparently all went well. Unfortunately Keats attended none of them (although he read at least one in manuscript and copied excerpts from it for his brother in America),[25] and Crabb Robinson disliked the few he heard;[26] but the *Examiner* was, as always, loyal and admiring in reporting them,† and Reynolds wrote a eulogistic series of reports for the *Edinburgh Magazine.*[27] When the lectures ended the *Morning Chronicle* announced that by "universal assent" Hazlitt was established as "one of the ablest and most eloquent critics of our nation." ‡ This, if perhaps somewhat overstated, was no doubt closer to the truth than the spiteful comment in *Blackwood's,* about the time *Lectures on the English Comic Writers* appeared the following April, that the audience at the Surrey Institution had consisted only of "aspiring apprentices and critical clerks."[28] Like so much else in *Blackwood's,* this may be regarded as an extraliterary opinion.

◇ ◇ ◇

The new year brought domestic and financial woes. In February 1819 Hazlitt arranged with William Hone, at a dinner with John Hunt, for the

---

* *Keats Circle,* I, 53. In September 1818 Hazlitt told Archibald Constable ("Three Hazlitt Letters," *TLS,* 21 March 1936, p. 244) that he had arranged to "sell" the new lectures for £200 instead of £100, and this, as he remarked, was an "improvement."

† Despite efforts "by certain anonymous slanderers" to deprecate the speaker's talents, the *Examiner* reported (8 November 1818, p. 713) of the first lecture, Hazlitt had treated his material with "equal solidity and sprightliness." On November 15 it commented (p. 726) on the gratifying size of the "assembly" at the second lecture, but the following week it announced (p. 744) the suspension of the series "for a while" owing to the death of Queen Caroline. On December 20 it expressed regret (p. 806) at having missed the last two lectures (one of which, on Johnson, had been acclaimed as "masterly"), and on December 27 it printed (pp. 825f.) a long excerpt on Godwin from the lecture of the previous week.

‡ I quote from the *Examiner* reprint (10 January 1819, pp. 25f.) of the review in the *Morning Chronicle.* In its own review of the published *Lectures* the *Examiner* (18 April 1819, pp. 250 f.) predicted that in popularity it would be second only to his book on Shakespeare.

publication of his *Political Essays*,[29] a collection of his journalistic pieces that appeared the following August, and he also wrote a bit for the *Examiner*, including a stirring epitaph on Cavanagh, the noted rackets player; [30] but if he did anything else except play fives — a form of handball that he doted on [31] — and quarrel with his wife, it has left no record. Almost from the start, it seems, his life with Sarah and their son had been wretchedly unhappy. Perhaps he did not regard his wife, as Coleridge regarded Sara Fricker, as her husband's inferior "in sex, acquirements, and in the quantity and quality of natural endowments, whether of Feeling, or of Intellect," [32] but from all their years in London there survives not one word of affection or endearment. Moreover, Hazlitt's published views on women, both before and after his divorce in 1822, were not contrived to gladden Sarah Stoddart's heart. "Women in general have no ideas, except personal ones," he said. "They are mere egotists. They have no passion for truth, nor any love of what is purely ideal. They hate to think, and they hate every one who seems to think of any thing but themselves." [33] For such a man to take a wife was obviously grotesque, and the marriage that had sent Lamb into paroxysms of laughter was one of quiet and then of noisy desperation. Even in 1808 Sarah, as a bride, was not a vision of delight; ten years later — after six pregnancies, three miscarriages, and two funerals — all her meager charms had vanished, including, it would seem, her money, which, though probably a prime consideration in her suitor's calculations, had been put beyond his reach.

After Hazlitt came to London, began to make his name, and "got into Society," he found the manner of his wife "unpleasant," said Haydon, and "the poor woman, irritated by neglect, irritated him in return." [34] The few glimpses we have of them as man and wife are bleak. Except for his copies of pictures from the Louvre Hazlitt cared nothing for possessions,* and since he objected strongly to women's *"magpie faculty"* of rearranging and disturbing things,[35] Sarah was not burdened with domestic chores.

* Although Patmore (III, 105), Procter (p. 171), and Leigh Hunt (*Essays*, p. 186) all remark with evident surprise that Hazlitt did not even own a book, he himself recorded (12.227) that he had kept the tattered copies of *Paradise Lost* and Burke's *Reflections* that he had bought in Shrewsbury as a boy. On his visit to the Continent with his second wife in 1824–25 he apparently bought some books (10.186f.) that he asked Charles Armitage Brown, in Florence, to send to him in England; but five years later Brown was still fussing over the arrangements (Jack C. Stillinger, "The Letters of Charles Armitage Brown" [Harvard dissertation, 1958], II, 197), and it seems that the books were never sent. It was no doubt these books "of no value" that Robinson (I, 387) said Hazlitt had bequeathed to Brown. One of them was the copiously annotated copy of Bacon's *Advancement of Learning* that eventually came to Dilke and is now in the Keats House at Hampstead (Payson G. Gates, "Bacon, Keats, and Hazlitt," *South Atlantic Quarterly*, XLVI [1947], 238–251; cf. "By Whom?" *TLS*, 28 June 1947, p. 323). According to Elbridge Colby (*The Life of Thomas Holcroft* [1925], I, 301n) Hazlitt also owned a copy of Holcroft's *Road to Ruin*; cf. *Memoirs*, II, 272.

Their house in York Street, notoriously untidy, was defaced with Hazlitt's scribbles on the walls, for there he kept his notes and memoranda.[36] One visitor in their early years in London found him caressing his son — whom Keats called, cryptically, "little Nero" [37] — like an "ardent loving mother," [38] and another caught him "acting the great horse with a boy on his shoulder"; * but in general it was a strange household — loveless, cheerless, and disordered. Haydon's account of young William Hazlitt's christening there in 1813 is vivid and depressing. When he arrived, by invitation, to find the house in utter disarray, his hostess in a dirty bed-gown by the fire, and his host out looking for a "parson," he prudently decided to go in search of Hazlitt. Presently he found him coming down the street "in a rage" because the parsons were all "out."

"What will you do?" "Nothing." So in we walked, Hazlitt growling at all the parsons and the church. When we came in we sat down — nobody was come — no table laid — no appearance of dinner.

On my life there is nothing so heartless as going out to dinner and finding no dinner ready.

I sat down; the company began to drop in — Charles Lamb and his poor sister — all sorts of odd clever people. Still no dinner. At last came in a maid who laid a cloth and put down knives and forks in a heap. Then followed a dish of potatoes, cold, waxy and yellow. Then came a great bit of beef with a bone like a battering ram, toppling on all its corners. Neither Hazlitt nor Lamb seemed at all disturbed, but set to work helping each other; while the boy, half-clean and obstinate, kept squalling to put his fingers into the gravy.

Even Lamb's wit and Hazlitt's disquisitions, in a large room, wainscotted and ancient, where Milton had meditated, could not reconcile me to such violation of all the decencies of life. I returned weary, and placing a candle on the floor of my room soon recovered under the imposing look of my picture and retired to bed filled with thought.†

By 1819 the Hazlitts had reached a stage of crisis. For one thing they were always out of money, and for another Hazlitt apparently made no effort to conceal his promiscuity. His playing fives all day with low-bred friends looked odd, as Sarah told him later in discussing their divorce, but when he took his son along, and even included him in his scouting expeditions for "the girls" around the town, she was not unnaturally annoyed. It was "likely to corrupt and vitiate" the little boy, she said, whereupon he growled that a child should not be raised in ignorance of

* Thus Leigh Hunt (*Examiner*, 1 January 1815, p. 12) in speaking of an unnamed colleague, but the allusion is almost certainly to Hazlitt.

† *Autobiography*, I, 161. See the page opposite for Haydon's original account of the episode (cf. *Diary*, I, 303), which has a few details that should not be lost. Among the guests was a "young mathematician, who whenever he spoke, jerked up one side of his mouth, and closed an eye as if seized with a paralytic affection, thus [*sketch*]; an old Lady of Genius with torn ruffles; his [Hazlitt's] Wife in an influenza, thin, pale & spitty; and his chubby child, squalling, obstinate, & half-cleaned." For William Bewick's account of the christening, which he no doubt got from Haydon, see Landseer, I, 120 f.

I dined on Friday last with ᵐⁱⁿᵉ a ___ of Genius ᵂⁱˡˡⁱᵃᵐ ᴴᵃᶻˡⁱᵗᵗ — his children were to be christened and I was desired to be there punctually at four — at four I came but he was out! his wife ill by the fire, nothing ready, and all wearing the appearance of neglect & indifference — at last home he came, the cloth began to cover the table — and then followed a feast with a dozen large, waxen, cold, clayey, slaty potatoes — down they were set — and down we sat also — a young mathematician who whenever he spoke, pushed out one side of his mouth, and closed an eye as if seized with a paralytic affection thus — ___ — an old Lady of Genius with torn ruffles his wife in an influenza, thin, pale, & spitting; and his chubby child, equally destinate, & half-cleaned — after watching a little while cooking forlornly at the potatoes for fear they might the the chief dish — in issued a bit of overdone beef — burnt, an toppling about on four — c seven or eight corners — with a great bone sticking out like a battering ram — the great difficulty was to make it stand upright! but the greater to even discover a <u>cuttable</u> place for all was jagged, & jutting & irregular — like a true Genius — he forgot to go for a parson to christen his child — till it was late — about every Parson was out or occupied so the child was not christened — he seemed so good heartedly & indifferent to the common comforts of life, may annoy those who were attentive & cleanliness —

the world. "He said I had always despised him, and his abilities," she recorded in her journal.

I asked him if the women with whom he associated, were any better judges of them. and told him, that in spite of his assertion, that he did not wish them to know or understand that he had abilities; nobody was more sore on that point: but, I added, that all recrimination was now useless, as probably all intercourse between us had for ever ended.*

No one whom the Lambs thought well of could have been entirely dull, but Sarah Hazlitt was obviously not a fascinating creature. As we see her in the journal where, in 1822, she recorded the ugly story of her divorce from a man she never should have married, she is shrewd and unpretentious, annoyed but not heartbroken by her husband's scandalous behavior, concerned about her bowels, indefatigable in taking exercise, frugal, sensible, and blunt. That she neither could nor would exemplify the feminine ideal that Hazlitt later thought he found in the sluttish Sarah Walker is not surprising, but that she endured her husband's indifference and abuse for so many years provides a theme for speculation. Her life with him must have been a model of what Johnson called connubial infelicity.

❖ ❖ ❖

By midsummer 1819 Hazlitt had fled again to Winterslow, and there, for the next two months or so, he was busy with his fourth and final set of lectures, which he had outlined for Patmore in early February [39] and which were scheduled for the following fall. This time his subject was Elizabethan literature, and since, apart from Spenser and Shakespeare, it was largely new to him, he had to work it up from the "few odd volumes of old plays and novels" that he had brought from town.[†] He of course had asked advice from Lamb,[‡] whose lore in "ancient authors" was profound, and from Procter he had borrowed "about a dozen volumes" of

---

* Bonner, p. 196. "Good God, Sir," Haydon asked Northcote later (Pope, 3 August 1826), "is it true that he brought London strumpets into his Lodgings when his boy of 10 years old was reading, & that the boy was so shocked, he either kicked or abused them away?" Northcote said that it was true.

† 17.68. "Character of the Country People," the essay from which these words are taken, appeared in the *Examiner* on July 18, and so we are able to date, at least approximately, Hazlitt's return to Winterslow.

‡ In a mock obituary that he prepared in anticipation of his own demise, Lamb (*Works*, I, 420) recorded that he had been "the first to draw Public attention to the old English Dramatists." His famous *Specimens of English Dramatic Poets, Who Lived about the Time of Shakespeare* had appeared in 1808, and although Hazlitt later joked about Lamb's antiquarian enthusiasms (11.179f.) he respected his knowledge and opinion. Even when he disagreed with him — as about John Ford, for instance — he did so deferentially (6.268).

old plays to equip him for the task. "He then went down to Winterslow Hut, in Wiltshire," Procter wrote in his old age, "and after a stay of six weeks came back to London, fully impregnated with the subject, and with his thoughts fully made up upon it, and with all his lectures written. And he then appeared to comprehend the character and merits of the old writers more thoroughly than any other person, although he had so lately entered upon the subject." [40] Hazlitt wrote these lectures *con amore*. "There are neither picture-galleries nor theatres-royal on Salisbury-plain," he said, but

> here, even here, with a few old authors, I can manage to get through the summer or the winter months, without ever knowing what it is to feel *ennui*. They sit with me at breakfast; they walk out with me before dinner. After a long walk through unfrequented tracks, after starting the hare from the fern, or hearing the wing of the raven rustling above my head, or being greeted by the woodman's "stern good-night," as he strikes into his narrow homeward path, I can "take mine ease at mine inn," beside the blazing hearth, and shake hands with Signor Orlando Friscobaldo [in Dekker's *Honest Whore*], as the oldest acquaintance I have. Ben Jonson, learned Chapman, Master Webster, and Master Heywood, are there; and seated round, discourse the silent hours away. Shakespear is there himself, not in Cibber's manager's coat. Spenser is hardly yet returned from a ramble through the woods, or is concealed behind a group of nymphs, fawns, and satyrs. Milton lies on the table, as on an altar, never taken up or laid down without reverence. . . . I should have no objection to pass my life in this manner out of the world, not thinking of it, nor it of me; neither abused by my enemies, nor defended by my friends; careless of the future, but sometimes dreaming of the past, which might as well be forgotten! [41]

In September John Hunt, who had lately moved to Devon, wrote to him about an unpaid bill for fifty pounds for which he, as guarantor, was being threatened with "immediate" legal action. He also extended a cordial invitation for a visit, but as we learn from one of Leigh Hunt's chatty notes a few days later Hazlitt's financial affairs were in such a parlous state that he probably returned at once to London. [42] A bleak appeal to Jeffrey at this time shows how grave the crisis was:

> Winterslow Hut, near Salisbury,
> Septr 25. [1819]
>
> Dear Sir,
> I blush when I sit down to write this letter. But you some time ago said if I wanted it & would send to you for *another* 100£. you would let me have it. It would at this present moment interpose between me & almost ruin. I do not know that since that time I have done any thing to deserve your less favourable opinion. I shall receive 150£. for my next Lectures (on the age of Elizabeth) at Christmas, but I shall be prevented from completing them in time to deliver [them] (next month) to the utter discomfiture of all my hopes, if I am not enabled to parry an immediate blow (a bill for 66£) with which I am threatened down here, which I see no means of meeting but through your often experienced liberality. Mr. Thomas Moore interested himself with the Longmans a week or

two ago about a literary project in my behalf, but in vain — *tan tum potuit ira* Blackwood. Permit me to add, I have a good 50£ note of hand which has six months to run & which I would transmit you immediately, & my own note of hand for 50£ at 3 months, which I could be certain of honouring, when I receive my money from the Surry [*sic*] Institution. The 100£. which I am in your debt I hope still to write out in Edinburgh Reviews! Hoping you will excuse the ungraceful importunity of this application, I remain, Dear Sir, your obliged, humble servant, W. Hazlitt.[43]

Whatever answer Jeffrey made to this appeal, Hazlitt's troubles mounted through the fall until finally, as he remarked in bitterness of spirit, his landlord Bentham "philosophically" put an execution in his house.[*] Meanwhile, he began his lectures on November 5 and finished them, as scheduled, six weeks later.[†] Although Lamb, for a wonder, went "regularly," [44] he made no comments in his extant correspondence; Crabb Robinson apparently did not go at all; and if Keats attended them, as he implies,[45] his attendance was sporadic.[46] Both Talfourd in the *Edinburgh Review* and John Scott in the newly founded *London Magazine* praised the *Lectures* later in their published form — one for the skill with which the author made the beauties of his favorite books so "palpable" to sense, the other for his extraordinary taste — but both had reservations about the disorder of his work.[47] Leigh Hunt contented himself with a rather gasping piece in which he noted, with approval, Hazlitt's "usual relish of pithy sentences, apposite similes, and sharp detections of poor sophisticated human nature." [48]

Not knowing, or perhaps not caring, how much he had enriched the literature of criticism, Hazlitt merely felt profound fatigue. Forming as they did a kind of coda for these busy middle years, the Elizabethan lectures also coincided with the breakup of his marriage, and about the time they ended he and Sarah left the York Street house to go their separate ways. Hazlitt had no reason for elation. With his domestic life in ruins, no steady work in view, and himself the object of vituperative abuse from the influential Tory press, he had reached the turning-point,

---

* *Four Generations*, I, 134. Later, when Hazlitt came to write the sketch of Bentham in *The Spirit of the Age*, he said (11.6) that this great apostle of utility would tear up Milton's garden and turn his house — "the cradle of Paradise Lost" — into a thoroughfare, "like a three-stalled stable, for the idle rabble of Westminster to pass backwards and forwards to it with their cloven hoofs." According to his son (*Literary Remains*, I, lix) Hazlitt himself had put into the wall of the house a commemorative stone to Milton in veneration "for the Poet and the Patriot."

† The *Examiner* (7 November 1819, p. 714) carried a eulogistic notice of the opening lecture, gave a schedule for the series the following week (p. 728), and thereafter printed three long excerpts from Hazlitt's comments on Christ (November 21, pp. 747f.), Jeremy Taylor (December 19, pp. 814f.), and Bacon (December 26, pp. 830 f.). The lecturer's "portraits" of John Webster and his fellow dramatists, it reported on November 21 (p. 745), were "worthy of the deep-toned colouring and deeper eyes of the old Italian heads."

or, as it must have seemed to him, the collapse of his career. The peroration of his final lecture has a sere, autumnal tone that no doubt matched his mood. "I have done," he said, "and if I have done no better, the fault has been in me, not in the subject." He had learned that a writer's life is hard, his studies "painful" and "obscure," his success "fleeting as a shadow, hollow as a sound." When young, we have hope and courage to sustain us, but life is so abrasive and its struggle so unceasing that soon these props begin to fail, and the effort "to be what we are not, and to do what we cannot" leads finally to despair. At last we come to know that there is nothing worth obtaining. "We stagger on the few remaining paces to the end of our journey; make perhaps one final effort; and are glad when our task is done!" [49] At the age of forty-one, and on the threshold of his greatest work, apparently Hazlitt thought his life a failure, and except perhaps for Lamb and Hunt and Keats few who knew him would have disagreed.

The Making of a Critic

THE LURE OF ART

Hazlitt's conviction that artists have no "exclusive right and power" to judge of art [1] was perhaps related to the fact that he became a critic only after he had failed at painting. Although he would rather have produced one great picture, he said, than be the finest writer of the age, [2] the gap between his talents and desires, which might amuse an ironist, shows that the creative and critical faculties rarely coincide. Perhaps he would have been a happier man if, like his mute, inglorious brother John, he could have made his living as an artist; but if he was nothing, or almost nothing, as a painter he never lost his love of art, and his knowledge of the painter's craft was, as he believed, essential to his function as a critic. He thought that no one who has not "contended with the difficulties of art" could know its beauties or be "intoxicated with a passion" for them. [3] "He practiced Painting long enough to know it," said Haydon, "and he has carried into Literature a stock which no literary man ever did before him." [4] He haunted galleries and exhibitions, lounged and gossiped with old Northcote and his cronies, and occasionally, returning to his easel, endured "the tormenting struggle to do what I could not"; [5] and he also wrote on art with a feeling and perception fortified by knowledge. In 1814 his art reviews first brought him into notice as a writer; in 1830 his *Conversations of James Northcote* provided proof, if proof were needed, that art retained its fascination for him to the end.

Hazlitt began writing about art as soon as Perry freed him from the grind of reporting Parliamentary speeches, and some of his first efforts for the *Morning Chronicle* — notably a discussion of "Why the Arts Are Not Progressive" and his salty comments on current exhibitions [6] — must have caught John Scott's eye, for within six months that astute editor relinquished to him the art department of the *Champion*. His subsequent reviews[7] — which, said Crabb Robinson, were "excellent," if "bitter and severe"[8] — promptly gained attention, and his articles on Sir Joshua Reynolds and the regrettable prestige of academic art[9] provided him an entrée to the *Edinburgh Review*. Although it was as drama critic that he joined the *Examiner* in 1815, Leigh Hunt's brother Robert having been assigned to art, he had already contributed a piece on Hogarth to the paper,[10] and he soon found ways, via the Round Table and otherwise, to treat his favorite subject. The result was a string of fervent essays — "On *Gusto*,"[11] "The Catalogue Raisonné of the British Institution,"[12] "The Elgin Marbles,"[13] and others — that reflect his progress as a critic and his intimacy with Haydon. His growing reputation was signalized, about this time, by an important article, "Fine Arts," for *The Encyclopaedia Britannica*[14] (which attracted young Carlyle's attention)[15] and by a long, disrespectful piece on Benjamin West for the *Edinburgh Magazine*.[16]

Between 1818 and 1820 politics and lecturing mainly occupied his time, but in the great essays of his last decade he reverted to the subject that haunted his imagination. For the *London Magazine* he wrote such famous pieces as "On the Pleasure of Painting"[17] and "On a Landscape of Nicolas Poussin,"[18] as well as most of the articles brought together in 1824 as *Sketches of the Principal Picture-Galleries in England*. Three of his later *Edinburgh* reviews * are studded with his own aesthetic theories, and his *Notes on a Journey through France and Italy* (1826), a series commissioned by the *Morning Chronicle*, deals extensively with art. Such essays as "On Genius and Common Sense,"[19] "On Certain Inconsistencies in Sir Joshua Reynolds's Discourses,"[20] "On Reason and Imagination,"[21] and "Whether Genius Is Conscious of its Powers"[22] provide the last and most accomplished statement of the ideas that had underlain his first reviews; and finally, certain of his later pieces like "On the Old Age of Artists,"[23] "On Sitting for One's Picture,"[24] and "English Students at Rome"[25] afforded him the theme and manner for the alleged "conversations" with Northcote that were written in his last four years and published as a book just before he died. As either painter or critic, then, he was intimately concerned with art for more than thirty years.†

⋄ ⋄ ⋄

* "Farington's Life of Sir Joshua Reynolds" (August 1820, 16.181–211), "Lady Morgan's Life of Salvator" (July 1824, 16.284–318), "Flaxman's Lectures on Sculpture" (October 1829, 16.338–363).

† Apart from certain pieces in *The Round Table* like the essays on Hogarth, gusto, and imitation, Hazlitt himself reprinted little of his early work on art. In 1838 his son published *Painting, and the Fine Arts: Being the Articles under Those Heads Contributed to the Seventh Edition of the Encyclopaedia Britannica, by B. R. Haydon, Esq*

THE MAKING OF A CRITIC

From his boyhood the Dissenter's awkward son, hard-bitten and pugnacious, found in pictures a sensuous charm that made him tremble with emotion,[26] and consequently we hear a great deal, later, about the brimming eyes and breathless adoration with which he gazed upon his favorites.[27] "It is now seventeen years since I was studying in the Louvre," he wrote in *Table-Talk*, "(and I have long since given up all thoughts of the art as a profession), but long after I returned, and even still, I sometimes dream of being there again — of asking for the old pictures — and not finding them, or finding them changed or faded from what they were, I cry myself awake!"[28] Sometimes his style grows soft and languorous to match the work that he describes,[29] and sometimes he glides into trancelike recollection to recapture, if he can, the mood of dreamy introspection that a picture had provoked when he was young and filled with inspiration.[30]

Indeed, introspection was for him a tool of criticism, for he was more concerned with the psychological effects of art than with art itself. When he revisited Burleigh House and found a Rembrandt there less good than he had thought it twenty years before, he made the only inference that a man like him could make: "The picture was nothing to me: it was the idea it had suggested. The one hung on the wall at Burleigh; the other was an heir-loom in my mind."[31] Hazlitt's most characteristic criticism consists of evocation. As he reflects upon the heirlooms of his mind, gliding from one association to another and investing pictures with a web of memory and desire, he himself creates, as it were, another work of art. "On a Landscape of Nicolas Poussin" tells us more, perhaps, about the critic than about the picture that inspired his composition; but if criticism is, among other things, a record of responses, then this famous essay may be said to deserve its reputation.

When his emotions were involved, as they always were with things he liked, he indulged them with a self-intoxicating joy. Moreover, if he was deeply stirred he thought his reader should be too. Words like *truth* and *beauty, genius* and *nature,* turn up everywhere, but they are rarely well defined, or indeed defined at all; they serve as symbols for a euphoric state of mind that, as he thought, art alone induces. He regarded rapture as the only legitimate response to the kind of painting he admired. When we walk into a great gallery, he said, "we are abstracted to another

---

and William Hazlitt, Esq., and in 1843 he brought together a big collection of his father's work under the title *Criticisms on Art: and Sketches of the Picture-Galleries of England*, a book reprinted in 1854 and (under the supervision of W. C. Hazlitt) in 1873. Not until the eighteenth volume (1933) of Howe's Centenary Edition were all of Hazlitt's scattered comments on art — or all that could be plausibly attributed to him — finally reprinted.

sphere: we breathe empyrean air; we enter into the minds of Raphael, of Titian, of Poussin, of the Caracci, and look at nature with their eyes. . . . Here is the mind's true home. The contemplation of truth and beauty is the proper object for which we were created, which calls forth the most intense desires of the soul, and of which it never tires." [32] His own effort to produce great art was a memory to be fondled and caressed,[33] and his failure was a cue for self-indulgent pity.[34]

But cutting through the pity, of which one quickly tires, is the exhilaration that is Hazlitt's signature as critic. "I have seen a whole-length portrait by Velasquez," he has Northcote say, "that seemed done while the colours were yet wet; every thing was touched in, as it were, by a wish; there was such a power that it thrilled through your whole frame, and you felt as if you could take up the brush and do any thing." [35] Hazlitt's ardor sought repose in strength; his Romantic *Sehnsucht* found its goal in power; and in art as in other things his ideal was effortless control. "What we imagine of the Gods," he said in one of his last essays, "is pleasure without pain — power without effort," [36] and his private pantheon was reserved for heroes like Shakespeare, Titian, and Napoleon who exemplified such strength. "Gusto" or intensity, which he called the "power or passion defining any object" and which he made the test of art, was his measure of perfection. "We judge of science by the number of effects produced," he said, "of art by the energy which produces them. The one is knowledge — the other power." * Therefore for him to say that a picture was "bursting with expression" was the highest accolade. He venerated Hogarth's work because it was so full of "life and motion." "Not only does the business of the scene never stand still, but every feature and muscle is put into full play; the exact feeling of the moment is brought out, and carried to its utmost height, and then instantly seized and stamped on the canvass for ever." [37] Because he worshiped Titian as the apotheosis of might, or of genius conscious of its power, he treats him not in terms of rhythm, line, and composition but of disciplined vitality. Not only do that painter's heads seem to think, he said, but his bodies seem to feel; his figures have not merely "the look and texture of flesh, but the feeling in itself." [38]

To recognize such power and describe the impact that it had on him was Hazlitt's aim as critic. Titian's *Hippolito de' Medici*, with its "keen glance bent upon me," seemed " 'a thing of life,' with supernatural force and grandeur," [39] and his *Man in Black* struck him like a blow. [40] When he first saw the prints of Raphael's great cartoons in the parlor of a little

---

* 18.8. Even as a boy copying masterpieces in the Louvre Hazlitt preferred pictures to which a "principle of motion" gave energy and force (12.288).

country inn, "How were we then uplifted!" he recalled.* And later, when the originals burst upon him in their glory at Hampton Court it was "a sort of *revelation*." Although the heroic figures "fill, raise, and satisfy the mind," he said, "they seem to have cost the painter nothing." In Raphael's work "the sense of power supersedes the appearance of effort," [41] and in a sense, therefore, it defies the critic's explanation. [42]

In art as in literature Hazlitt found his "mind's true home" in that small body of supreme masterpieces that formed his taste and provided him a norm. "There have been only four or five painters," he thought, "who could ever produce a copy of the human countenance really fit to be seen." [43] The Renaissance Italians, Vandyke and Rubens, Rembrandt and Hogarth, were the artists whom he loved, and together with the Elgin Marbles their works were the ones he turned to time and time again. "Who cares any thing about such frippery," he remarked of Beckford's collection at Fonthill Abbey, "time out of mind the stale ornaments of a pawnbroker's shop; or about old Breughel, or Stella, or Franks, or Lucas Cranach, or Netecher, or Cosway?" [44] He tediously deprecated most French art as glossy, cold, and superficial; [45] and on the principle that "no one ever felt a longing, a sickness of the heart, to see a Dutch landscape twice" [46] he ignored the minor Flemish masters. With the exception of one authentic genius in Hogarth, he said, England had produced only academic hucksters — painters "more tenacious of their profits as chapmen and dealers, than of the honour of the Art." [47] He thought that not one of them, including the highly touted (and pecunious) Reynolds, had "made even a faint approach to the excellence of the great Italian painters." [48]

According to Haydon, whose messianic vision of himself as the greatest English painter was one not widely shared, Hazlitt's long campaign against English art and artists revealed the malice of a disappointed man. "Mortified at his own failure," said Haydon, "he resolved as he had not succeeded no one else should, and he spent the whole of his after life in damping the ardour, chilling the hopes and dimming the prospects of patrons and painters." [49] There is probably an element of truth in this, but Hazlitt had another explanation: he thought the English had no gift for art. Perhaps because of climate, [50] perhaps because their genius was for words, [51] perhaps because they subordinated means to ends, [52] they were incapable of a "high and heroic pursuit of art for its own sake." [53] Their portraits, he said, were manufactured for the trade, and their "historical"

---

* 4.144f. Hazlitt repeated this passage in his lecture on Hogarth in *The English Comic Writers* (6.148), and in the famous "On Going a Journey" (8.185) he identified the scene as St. Neot's in Huntingtonshire.

pictures — which Reynolds had defined as characters in action [54] — mistook size for grandeur with calamitous results. "There was not, in all probability, a single head in an acre of canvas, that, taken by itself, was more than a worthless daub, scarcely fit to be hung up as a sign at an alehouse door: but a hundred of these bad portraits or wretched caricatures, made, by numerical addition, an admirable historical picture." [55] Thus John Martin, once famous for his lurid *Fall of Babylon* and *Belshazzar's Feast*, was not content with truth, said Hazlitt; he tried to "outdo" nature. "He reckons that if one range of lofty square hills is good, another range above that with clouds between must be better." [56] If you tell people who admire such works that Murillo's *Two Beggar Boys* is one of the finest pictures in the world, they will answer that the subject is too low." [57] Not unnaturally, men like these made Benjamin West president of the Royal Society — that "hospital and infirmary for the obliquities of taste and ingenuity" [58] — and agreed that his insipid *Christ Rejected* was a triumph. Hazlitt, however, assessed this famous picture at a somewhat lower rate. He thought that it made Joseph of Arimathea look like

a respectable elderly country gentleman in the gallery of the House of Commons, listening to a speech of Lord Castlereagh's; — James the Less is a pert yeoman's son, thrusting himself forward to see a trial at Guildhall, or the humours of an election dinner; — St. Peter is a poor old man, who has had his goods distrained for rent; — Mary Magdalen would do for one of the sprawling figures, Ceres, or Juno, or Minerva, that we see at the head of ships of war.*

Much of Hazlitt's criticism is in this pert and strident style, and much of it is dull. He was of the opinion that most contemporary English painting, turned out by the yard, might do for gaudy decoration but was not to be confused with art. A perennial young Turk, he had a disregard for "the ambiguous quackery of rules." [59] a contempt for those who paint by them, and a yelping discontent with "corporate bodies" like the Royal Academy and the British Institution, which, he said, were merely trade associations. In 1816 his three-part article on the Catalogue Raisonné of exhibitions sponsored by the British Institution developed angry variations on the theme that art had fallen prey to hucksters, and the theme had been apparent in his criticism from the start. For example, in alluding to West's studio as a "hardware manufactory," [60] in calling Turner's drawing an example of "impudent and obtrusive vulgarity," † and in

* 18.32. Hazlitt not only wrote long, damaging reviews of West's two most celebrated pictures — *Christ Rejected* (18.28–34) and *Death on a Pale Horse* (18.135–140) — but he often used him later (for example, 12.94f.) to illustrate the difference between artisan and artist.

† 18.14; cf. 18.110. Later (4.76n) he grudgingly called Turner "the ablest landscape painter now living."

reporting that Lawrence made Castlereagh look like an upstart haber-dasher * he had indulged in uncouth journalese; and its effect, as John-son said of the work of a critic given to detraction, was to make its author public but not to make him known. But he could also yield to melting moods. He found William Collins' sentimental picture of a lamb being led to a butcher's cart so full of feeling that it made one weep; [61] and Margaret Sarah Geddes' *Favourite Kitten* was so "exquisitely painted," he said, that "you may almost hear it *purring*." [62] He thought that art should either stir or soothe the viewer, and that painting that does not "lay open the fine network of the heart and brain of man, that does not make us see deeper into the soul, is but the apparatus and machinery of history-painting, and no more to it than the frame is to the picture." [63]

Although these highly charged opinions sound like Delphic utter-ances, they rest upon a set of principles that Hazlitt had laid down, in a rough and ready fashion, at the start of his career. The "metaphysician" who, though an empiricist in the Lockean tradition, had rejected "modern philosophy" because it was so cold and dry became the critic who con-strued both art and criticism in terms of passion, feeling, and imagina-tion. The *Essay*, the lectures on philosophy, and the early journalism all lay along an axis where, later, his more famous criticism fell, and there-fore his early work on art, which constitutes a kind of scrappy manifesto against neoclassic doctrine, assumes a large importance. It was there that he first applied, as critic, the principles that inform his metaphysics. When he began to think about the aims and methods of the artist or the poet, and to expound such topics as genius, style, and imitation, he first set forth the themes on which he built his later, more accomplished work; and therefore, whatever the inadequacies of this apprentice journalism, it served for him a very useful purpose.†

In this respect the significance of a little essay called "Why the

---

* 18.18. It was this remark, perhaps, that cost Hazlitt his job on the *Morning Chronicle*. See pages 194f.
† The relevant documents are "Why the Arts Are Not Progressive" — a little piece that Hazlitt wrote for the *Morning Chronicle* in 1814 (18.5–10), then expanded for the *Champion* (18.37–51), and finally telescoped for *The Round Table* (4.160–164) — and five articles on Reynolds (18.51–84) that were printed in the *Champion* in 1814–15. The opinions adumbrated there are more vehemently developed in his later essays on the Elgin Marbles (18.100–103, 145–166), his attack on the Catalogue Raisonné of the British Institution (18.104–111, 4.140–151), and his article on fine art in *The Encyclopaedia Britannica* (18.111–124). In *Table-Talk* he devoted two more essays (8.122–145) to Reynolds' "inconsistencies," and in "Originality" and "The Ideal" (20. 296–306), a brace of articles written for the *Atlas* in the last year of his life, he traversed the same terrain more swiftly.

THE LURE OF ART

Arts Are Not Progressive" is out of all proportion to its length. Ostensibly a challenge to the notion that art, like science, inexorably "advances," it is also Hazlitt's first attack on the authoritarian dogma that had dominated much of neoclassic theory. Lying within the terrain already staked out by Warton's *Observations on the Faery Queen,* Young's *Conjectures on Original Composition,* and Hurd's *Letters on Chivalry and Romance,* it may be read as yet another plea for fresh, untrammeled genius mounting high above the "rules"; but if it tells us nothing really new, it provides an energetic statement of a theme that Hazlitt made his own. That theme, which Longinus had announced almost two thousand years before, is the identification of art with power and power with genius. Hazlitt says that art conveys a special kind of truth by means that are unique, and that it is therefore superior to all other kinds of knowledge. Whereas science is mechanical and "reducible to rule," the arts cannot be codified: they "hold immediate communication with nature" and depend on intuition. To be sure, since the "mechanic parts of painting" — perspective, for example — require a mere "discursive" faculty, they can be taught and therefore learned, but no method can convey the secrets of that "intensive" power which glows in Titian's color or Raphael's expression. Even though art is imitation and derives its "soul" from nature, its triumphs have an elemental and exhilarating truth that makes them new creations. A chemist or astronomer builds upon his predecessors' work and starts where they left off; but an artist must begin *ab ovo* and hope for "inspiration." It follows not only that art is irreducible to rule but that it tends to reach its peak in the early stages of a culture, before formulas and the weight of precedent begin to stifle it. As Homer, Shakespeare, Raphael, and Titian show, it is produced by "individual and incommunicable power"; the greatest artists are the first, and their successors are epigoni.

There is in the old poets and painters a vigour and grasp of mind, a full possession of their subject, a confidence and firm faith, a sublime simplicity, an elevation of thought, proportioned to their depth of feeling, an increasing force and impetus, which moves, penetrates, and kindles all that comes in contact with it, which seems, not theirs, but given to them.*

❖ ❖ ❖

* 18.5–10. For some of Hazlitt's many other statements of this theme see 8.127, 13.210 f., 16.199, 20.4. He also builds upon it in "Pope, Lord Byron, and Mr. Bowles" (19.62–84), which he wrote for the *London Magazine* in 1821. "Art" is unlike "nature," he says there, for "art" refers to "those objects and feelings which depend for their subsistence and perfection on the will and arbitrary conventions of man and society," and "nature" to "those objects which exist in the universe at large, without, or in spite of, the interference of human power and contrivance, and those interests and affections which are not amenable to the human will" (19.74). Thus poetry yields to art as natural feeling yields to fashion and convention.

THE MAKING OF A CRITIC

Hazlitt began to work out the implications of these views in a series of articles on Sir Joshua Reynolds written for the *Champion* during 1814–15. In a sense it is odd that he chose the celebrated leader of the English school as the object to attack. Although he himself could not have known the painter (who died in 1792), his brother John had studied under him,[64] and his old friend Northcote, Reynolds' one-time assistant and the custodian of his fame, had eulogized his master in a more or less official *Memoir*. Moreover, for an itinerant portrait painter to impugn the merits of the most successful artist of the age, and for a nameless hack to challenge the aesthetic doctrines that the president of the Royal Society had set forth ex cathedra, was not without a certain irony. The irony was compounded by the critic's refusal or inability to deal quite fairly with his subject. In a sense, however, Reynolds was the victim of his own prestige, and it is not hard to see why Hazlitt regarded him as the high priest of neoclassic theory. Although Reynolds had preached the moral and didactic use of art, shown profound respect for precedent and discipline, and, like Johnson, named "general nature" as the only proper subject for great art, he was not the pedant Hazlitt thought, and no one who reads only Hazlitt's attempted refutation of his views will understand how varied, rich, and forward-looking his *Discourses* are. His early lectures are, as Hazlitt charged, donnish and austere, and read out of context some of his pronouncements on the value of tradition and the necessity for rules are what one might expect in a presidential speech. But his annual lectures cover a span of more than twenty years, and in the later ones, where he maintains that the "great end" of art is "to make an impression on the imagination and the feeling,"[65] he emerges almost as a prophet of the new Romanticism.

This is by no means apparent in Hazlitt's hostile comment on his work. In a preliminary essay on Reynolds' merits as a painter he recognizes the gap between certain aspects of his theory and his practice; but he argues that although his grasp of "individual nature" had brought the art of portraiture far beyond the reach of Lely, Kneller, and their undistinguished fellows, he was none the less a man made rich by borrowed wealth, "an industrious compiler" rather than "an original inventor in art." An indifferent colorist and a poor draftsman, he succeeded only when, in defiance of his foolish theory, he kept his subject straight before his eyes and painted what he saw. Consequently he was best in portraying those he knew (like Johnson and Baretti), less good with women because he almost always flattered them, and poor with children because he tried, without success, to imitate Correggio. Moreover, as the famous *Count Ugolino* showed, his historical pictures were generally disastrous: the difference between what the picture is and what it ought to be, said Hazlitt tartly, is as great as that between Crabbe and Dante. "Shall we speak the truth at once? In our opinion, Sir Joshua did not possess either that high imagination, or those strong feelings, without which no painter can become a poet in his art." [66]

But if Reynolds' pictures were at best a qualified success, said Hazlitt, his aesthetic theory was almost wholly bad, and his presidential lectures were marked by such "systematic" error and fuzzy metaphysics that they must have stifled all the "zeal" and "ardour" in the students they were meant to edify. The dean of English painters had told young artists that genius is produced by imitation, that a "great style" requires the suppression of details, that portraiture should emphasize the general at the cost of the concrete and specific, that beauty or ideal perfection consists in a "central form" rather than in sharp details, and that "to imitate nature is a very inferior object in art." It was in an effort to expose the fundamental error of these views that Hazlitt launched his career as critic. [67]

◇ ◇ ◇

He first takes up the notion that, as he put it in paraphrasing Reynolds, "genius and invention are principally shown in borrowing the ideas and imitating the excellence of others." This formulation of the doctrine that is at the heart of neoclassic theory is not altogether fair, but it indicates the grounds for Hazlitt's discontent. Even the most capacious neoclassic view of genius — which, of course, is Johnson's — did not present the artist as an agent of transcendental truth who worked through means that no one else could understand. Johnson assumed that the genius is a man like other men except that he has the "energy" to collect, combine, amplify, and animate whatever he acquires through study and experience. [68] His distinction rests ultimately upon his "knowledge" of the world and of his craft. Even his "imagination," that faculty upon which a new generation of critics would erect a new aesthetic, is worthless, Johnson said, without a hard-bought knowledge, for "nature gives in vain the power of combination, unless study and observation supply materials to be combined." [69] Indeed, as he lay dying he told Fanny Burney that genius "is nothing more than knowing the use of tools," adding, characteristically, that one must know which tools to use: "A man who has spent all his life in this room will give a very poor account of what is contained in the next." [70] As any reader of *The Lives of the English Poets* knows, Johnson did not judge art by a mechanistic creed, but none the less he would have agreed with Reynolds that "even works of genius, like every other effect, as they must have their cause, must likewise have their rules," [71] and his distinction between that which is established because it is right and that which is right only because it is established is central in his work. His respect for form and style rests upon a base of neoclassic doctrine about the imitation of the ancients as exemplars of universal truth, about decorum as a due regard for probability in depicting types instead of individuals, about the value of discipline and training, and about judgment as the guide of fancy, feeling, and enthusiasm. These ideas, of course, could be and on occasion had been pushed to silly lengths, but they had solid merit, and when Reynolds said that "our minds should be habituated to the contemplation of excellence" [72] he evoked a rich tradition, the force of which, one hopes, will never be entirely spent.

However, there is another side to neoclassic theory. Even though Hobbes, in 1650, derided the enthusiast who speaks by inspiration ("like a Bagpipe"), [73] and Reynolds, in 1770, proclaimed that "every thing which is wrought with certainty . . . is wrought upon some principle," [74] the long history of what we now call Preromanticism shows that few eighteenth-century critics were completely shackled by the rules. Boileau, of all people, translated Longinus as early as 1674, and the influence of *Peri Hypsos* on Dennis, Lowth, and many others has long been recognized. Addison described the pleasures of the imagination and distinguished the "natural Genius's that were never disciplined and broken by Rules of Art" from those who "submitted the Greatness of their natural Talents to the Corrections and Restraints of Art." [75] Pope made large allowance for the "nameless graces which no methods teach" and praised Shakespeare as an "original" whose poetry flowed from inspiration. [76] Johnson, who said that there is always an appeal from criticism to nature, told Mrs. Thrale not to set up Edward Young (who "froths, and foams, and bubbles" with propriety) against Shakespeare, or to compare the noise made by her tea-kettle with the roaring of the ocean; [77] and when he heard Young himself read from his *Conjectures on Original Composition* he expressed surprise that such "very common thoughts" should be received as "novelties." [78] Maurice Morgann said that if a legalist like Rymer should lift up his constable's staff and charge the great magician Shakespeare ("the daring *practicer of arts inhibited*") to surrender in the name of Aristotle, the Stagyrite himself, "disowning his wretched Officer, would fall prostrate at his feet and acknowledge his supremacy." [79] In almost Longinian terms Reynolds warned against "an unfounded distrust of the imagination and feeling, in favour of narrow, partial, confined, argumentative theories." [80] Such substantial books as William Duff's *Essay on Original Genius* (1767) and Alexander Gerard's *Essay on Genius* (1774) significantly expanded the limits of neoclassic theory. And finally — although one could cite examples by the score — Johnson's noble Preface to his edition of Shakespeare (which Adam Smith called the most manly piece of criticism ever written) still stands, in monumental strength, as the work of a literary intelligence both supple and profound.

Therefore when Hazlitt proclaimed the prerogatives of genius he was hardly venturing into strange seas of thought alone. By the early nineteenth century, critical attention had shifted from the relation between a work of art and certain pre-established "rules" to the way in which a work of art is created and to its effect upon the viewer. Hazlitt's focus upon art as a means of self-expression and illumination helps us understand his objections to neoclassic theory, but it does not entirely justify his crude attack on Reynolds. On the other hand, Reynolds, especially in the early discourses, had overstated his position. "There is one precept," he said,

in which I shall only be opposed by the vain, the ignorant, and the idle. I am not afraid that I shall repeat it too often. You must have no dependence on your own genius. If you have great talents, industry will improve them: if you have but moderate abilities, industry will supply their deficiency. Nothing is denied to well-directed labour: nothing is to be obtained without it.[81]

Such cautionary precepts might do for a "well-bred drawing-master," Hazlitt said, but they had no bearing on fine art.[82]

The principles thus laid down may be very proper to conduct the machinery of a royal academy, or to precede the distribution of prizes to the students, or to be the topics of assent and congratulation among the members themselves at their annual exhibition dinner: but they are so far from being calculated to foster genius or to direct its course, that they can only blight or mislead it, wherever it exists.[83]

To counter the neoclassic emphasis on tradition, discipline, and rules, Hazlitt, at the start of his career, laid down the proposition that genius is the power to do what no one else has done,[84] and in all his later comments on art and books and drama the theme is fundamental — as applicable to Titian as to Shakespeare or to Kean. For those, like Reynolds, who belong to "the laborious and *climbing* class," he said later, study, precept, and example have a certain use — he himself, it will be recalled, had copied pictures in the Louvre * — but the really great creative minds do not depend upon such labor. Truth, and not

---

* "It requires more talent to copy a fine portrait than to paint an original picture of a table or a chair," said Hazlitt (12.288), "for the picture has a soul in it, and the table has not."

refinement, is their goal. Driven by a force that even they do not comprehend — for, as Hazlitt argued in a famous essay and as Blake and Shelley and Carlyle agreed, genius is never conscious of its power [85] — they generate their own techniques. "An intimate acquaintance with the works of the celebrated masters may, indeed, add to the indolent refinements of taste," he said, "but never will produce one work of original genius, — one great artist.[86] Degrees of capacity, which range from that of an oyster to that of a Newton, may sometimes be enlarged, because they relate to the quantity of knowledge; but genius, which relates to quality, is a "power" that no one can acquire by taking thought.[87] "Those who have produced immortal works, have done so without knowing how or why," [88] and if Correggio, for example, had been asked why he painted thus and so he would have answered, "Because he could not help it." [89] What Hazlitt later called "the bold licentious hand of genius" [90] seizes what it wants, immune to precedent or rule, and its prescriptive rights are sanctioned by its triumphs. "A man of genius is *sui generis* — to be known, he need only to be seen — you can no more dispute whether he is one, than you can dispute whether it is a panther that is shewn you in a cage." [91] Although some of these remarks are drawn from Hazlitt's later work, they merely underscore and amplify what he had said in 1814: genius is "a power at all times to do or to invent what has not before been done or invented." [92]

If his notion of what an artist is exemplifies the new Romantic theory, however, his notion of what an artist does appears to be old-fashioned. The representational function of art, an honored commonplace in European thought from Aristotle on, had been essential to neoclassic theory, and it was fundamental in Hazlitt's thinking too. In 1814 he declared, without equivocation, that "the imitation of nature is the great object of art"; [93] two years later he devoted a Round Table paper to analyzing the kinds of pleasure that imitation gives; [94] and in 1817 he organized his important article for *The Encyclopaedia Britannica* on the "ruling principle" that "*the immediate imitation of nature*" is the end of art.[95] Although such pronouncements would seem to leave no room for dissent from Reynolds, who had said many times and in many ways that art is "intrinsically imitative," [96] Hazlitt thought that neoclassic critics had failed to understand the artist's primary function, and he devotes much time, therefore, to discussing their mistakes.

Whatever imitation means, he said, it does not mean the attempt to do what other men have done, and therefore the pedagogical fallacy that students should build their style on that of others seemed to him a source of endless trouble. In his sixth discourse Reynolds had embellished Pope's advice —

> You then whose judgment the right course would steer,
> Know well each ancient's proper character —

to urge that the discipline of imitation opens the mind, shortens labor, and provides "the result of the selection made by those great minds of what is grand or beautiful in nature." [97] In its best and sanest advocates this doctrine stood for a tonic conservatism; it gave distance, depth, and space to judgment; it provided norms; and it showed that tradition could be an energizing force. But Hazlitt thought that such "servile" imitation could lead to nothing but "mediocrity and imbecility," [98] for it reduced creation to making a copy of a copy. The only thing a man excels in, he asserted, "is his own and incommunicable; what he borrows from others he has in an inferior degree, and it is never what his fame rests on." [99] Whereas originality is the defining mark of genius, the "habitual study and imitation" of one's predecessors kills creative power. "It is the necessity for exertion that makes us conscious of our strength; but this necessity and this impulse once removed, the tide of fancy and enthusiasm, which is at first a running stream, soon settles and crusts into the standing pool of dulness, criticism, and *virtù*." [100]

An artist, then, should copy only nature — but in a special way. When neoclassic critics talked of art and nature it was usually to argue that art is the instrument by which nature, which seems so wild and helter-skelter, is ordered, raised, and somehow purified. Most of them shared the notion that if "truth" resides in general types or forms that may be rationally perceived, it is these — and not the concrete or accidental — that should concern the artist. Johnson, who thought that "nothing can please many, and please long, but just representations of general nature," [101] has Imlac say that "the business of a poet . . . is to examine, not the individual, but the species; to remark general properties and large appearances: he does not number the streaks of the tulip, or describe the different shades in the verdure of the forest." [102] Shakespeare does not need to make his Romans thoroughly Roman or his kings extremely royal, Johnson replied to the cavils of Rymer and Voltaire, for he "always makes nature predominate over accident; and, if he preserves the essential character, is not very careful of distinctions superinduced and adventitious. His story requires Romans or kings, but he thinks only on men." [103] Reynolds, too, thought that for an artist to record "minute particularies, and accidental discriminations," was to deviate from "the invariable and general ideas of Nature" and "pollute his canvas with deformity." * The "whole beauty and grandeur" of art, he told the young academicians, consists in depicting general truth,[104] and his long and subtle efforts to define such truth provided him a basic theme. Even Wordsworth, whose famous preface reveals the lasting strength of eighteenth-century thought as well as the impact of the new aesthetic, warned the poet against "transitory and accidental ornaments," urged him to convey the "knowledge which all men carry about with them," and prescribed "general nature" as his only proper subject.[105]

Against this theory, which "limits nature and paralyses art,"[106] Hazlitt registers a vigorous dissent, and he does so in terms that relate aesthetics to his moral theory and his metaphysics. Whereas art, he said in 1821, deals only with "those objects and feelings which depend for their subsistence and perfection on the will and arbitrary conventions of man and society," nature lies beyond man's reach: it is "those objects which exist in the universe at large, without, or in spite of, the interference of human power and contrivance, and those interests and affections which are not amenable to the human will."[107] He was a pluralist who thought nature so multiform and varied that it transcends not only our rules and categories and formulas but even our perceptive faculties. Anything we know, or think we know, is but an aspect of a whole that we can never comprehend. Modern theorists to the contrary, our minds are not machines that transform perceptions into general truths; for nature is so subtle, and our perceptions are so gross, that even our simplest ideas cannot be said to correspond precisely to things as they exist outside the mind, much less to any "types" or "central forms" that underlie the surface of experience. "Nature is stronger than reason: for nature is, after all, the text, reason but the comment. He is indeed a poor creature who does not *feel* the truth of more than he *knows* or can explain satisfactorily to others."[108] In short, Hazlitt was a man who recoiled from absolutes, and his remark, made just before he died, that the mind is a prism "which untwists the various rays of truth"[109] may stand as summary for one of the most fundamental motifs in his work.

Even in politics, where he seems so hard and doctrinaire, his main concern was the freedom of the individual; and his comments on art and literature and morals are also predicated on the notion that "truth is not one, but many."[110] The secret of his power as critic was his plastic, supple mind that, as it were, went out to meet experience. He thought

* *The Idler*, no. 82 (*Discourses* [ed. Zimmern], p. 283). Reynolds told Boswell (p. 234) that this sentence was Johnson's own addition to the text.

that a sympathetic identification with the objects of perception was the ripest kind of knowledge, and that "feeling," rather than the constructs of discursive reason, was the highest kind of truth. Hence the unique importance of the artist: whereas most men, with their blunt, dull minds, repose on fuzzy generalities and received opinions, the artist looks at things afresh, and then records, in sensuous, concrete terms, the wonders he has seen. He cuts through, refines, and clarifies the crude abstractions by which we tend to organize experience; and he enables us to see, as he has seen, that nature is "deep, obscure, and infinite." [111] Most of us imagine that we see "the whole of nature, because we are aware of no more than we see of it," [112] but the man of genius has perceptions of a different sort: he sees nature "differently from others, and yet as it is in itself." [113] He is of all men least a mannerist (who copies himself) or an imitator (who copies others), [114] for his eye is fixed on nature. He will not, of course, attain to any final truth, for "nature is consistent, unaffected, powerful, subtle: art is forgetful, apish, feeble, coarse," [115] and "a feeble and imperfect transcript" must be regarded as the summit of an artist's skill. [116] None the less, he who "seizes forcibly and happily" on any part of nature "does enough for fame," [117] for he brings himself and us nearer to the truth. Whereas a man of mere mechanic skill, whose actions terminate in themselves, leaves the world as he found it, an artist changes other people's lives, and since "greatness is great power, producing great effects," [118] his ultimate distinction is that he expands and clarifies our knowledge.

To argue that he does so by concentrating on what De Quincey, almost a century after Reynolds, called the grand catholic feelings that belong to the grand catholic situations of life through all its stages * was, thought Hazlitt, to authorize the pretentious and the imprecise. To think of art in terms like these, he said, is to regard Dr. Johnson's *Irene* as a better play than *Hamlet*. [119] An artist should express as much truth as is given him to know, but he has no sanction to rearrange or simplify, suppress or elevate, any aspect of his subject. His job is simply to show us what he sees, and his presentation is of value because it excites "a more intense perception of truth." [120] There is a "gross" style that consists in giving no details, a "finical" style that consists in nothing but detail; but a man of genius like Correggio will be bound by neither. [121] To seek a statistical average or a composite ideal is to ignore a thousand shades of truth; to convert what is dark, obscure, and infinite into something that

---

* II, 251. Speaking of his own work in 1823, Wordsworth used almost the same language (*Later Years*, I, 127): "I have endeavoured to dwell with truth upon those points of human nature in which all men resemble each other, rather than on those accidents of manners and character produced by times and circumstances."

might — or might not — answer to our notions of elegance and style is to falsify experience.

It was one of Hazlitt's main complaints against Reynolds that he had urged such stylization. Even if occasional "circumstances of minuteness" are allowable because they "tend to give an air of truth," Sir Joshua had told his students, details are hard to reconcile with grandeur, and grandeur is the aim of art. "The general idea constitutes real excellence. All smaller things, however perfect in their way, are to be sacrificed without mercy to the greater." [122] Hazlitt, however, insisted that "nature is more liberal, art is wider than Sir Joshua's theory." [123] On the principle that grandeur consists in leaving out details, a house-painter could equal Michelangelo. [124] The real grand style, he said, is marked by intensity of perception, not by size or indistinctness. To spurn details in order to achieve a "neutral" or a "central" form is to supplant nature with an idea, which, "existing solely in the mind," was "never yet embodied in an individual instance." [125] For example, Reynolds was dismayed by Hogarth's "low and vulgar" characters and embarrassed by his fondness for details; [126] but Hazlitt praised that painter as a "true and terrific historian of the human heart" [127] and agreed with Lamb that those who deprecate him "confound the painting of subjects in common or vulgar life with the being a vulgar artist." * On the other hand, when Reynolds reached for elevation in depicting Sarah Siddons as the tragic muse he produced what Hazlitt called a bastard style of art. "It is not Mrs. Siddons, nor is it the tragic muse, but something between both, and neither." [128] Conversely, when he forgot about his foolish theory and showed Dr. Johnson blinking at a book he achieved great portraiture.†

* *Works*, I, 95. Hazlitt's debt to Lamb's "On the Genius and Character of Hogarth," which had appeared in Leigh Hunt's *Reflector* in 1811 (*Works*, I, 91–112), was very great, as he himself acknowledged (4.31, 6.138, 18.22). Not only does his early *Examiner* essay on Hogarth (5 June 1814) — which was subsequently reprinted in *The Round Table* (4.25–31) and then reworked for a lecture in *The English Comic Writers* (6.133–138) — reflect Lamb's views, but so do most of the countless allusions to the painter that are scattered through his work. The extent of Hazlitt's indebtedness might be gauged by comparing a passage from his lecture beginning "What distinguishes his compositions" (6.138) with Lamb's "The faces of Hogarth have not a mere momentary interest" (*Works*, I, 100). Lamb's remark that we look at other painters' work but read Hogarth's (*Works*, I, 92) was one that Hazlitt quoted many times (for example, 6.133, 18.22).

† 18.75. In calling portrait-painting "the biography of the pencil" and citing Boswell as "the prince of biographers" (10.75) Hazlitt may have remembered Boswell's defense (p. 343) for describing Johnson's tics and twitches: "I am fully aware of how very obvious an occasion I here give for the sneering jocularity of such as have no relish of an exact likeness; which to render complete, he who draws it must not disdain the slightest stroke."

THE LURE OF ART

In "On the Ideal," the concluding essay in this early series on Sir Joshua's aesthetic, Hazlitt raises questions that plagued him through his whole career. Resting on the views of genius and imitation that he had previously advanced, he again rejects the great neoclassic doctrine that art must deal in "general nature" in order to arrive at "ideal" beauty, but none the less he finds it hard to say what his conception of the "ideal" is. Convinced that the "shadowy middle forms" that Sir Joshua sought are meaningless — for art, "like all the works of imagination," must be rooted in the "concrete" data of sensation — he says that by "stripping" nature of "substance and accident" Reynolds was left with only a "decompounded, disembodied, vague" abstraction. But all great art, says Hazlitt, finds its subject in "a common or general character" as "defined and modified by individual peculiarities." An ideal that eschews significant details is a pure abstraction, and pure abstraction is a solecism in both art and nature. The ideal must correspond to the idea of something, rather than "to the idea of any thing, or of nothing"; otherwise it melts away into "effeminate, unmeaning insipidity." In Shakespeare, Chaucer, Raphael, and the Elgin Marbles — and characteristically he swings from literature to painting to sculpture in seeking his examples — the same great principle is clear: "individuality" is the secret of artistic power. Although ideal beauty does not mean "fastidious refinement," or "flimsy abstraction," it may mean many other things, says Hazlitt in floundering for an explanation: "a preference for what is fine in nature to what is less so," expression, consistency, and "a certain symmetry of form." Indeed, if it were not for "the censure of an eminent critic" — no doubt Jeffrey — he says he might become a mystic and talk of "universal harmony." *

This is a lame conclusion for such a truculent assault on Reynolds, but it shows at least that Hazlitt resisted convenient orthodoxies. In 1815 as in 1830 he was sure of only this: that the true grand style is not attained by calculation or built upon a theory. Because it takes the shape of things in nature, its main concomitant is truth, and an artist reaches grandeur through the knowledge that truth and splendor

---

* 18.77–84. Like most writers on the subject, Hazlitt never succeeded in defining beauty. In his early Round Table paper on the question he said (4.68) that it consists of "a certain conformity of objects to themselves, a symmetry of parts, a principle of proportion, gradation, harmony (call it what you will)"; and although he refined upon this later — as when he distinguished beauty from elegance, which gives "*the pleasurable in little things*" (12.357), and from grandeur, which "elevates and expands" the mind instead of soothing it (8.137) — a satisfactory explanation of the term eluded him. He of course knew and cited (4.72, 12.112f., 269, 19.307, 310) Burke's *Philosophical Inquiry into the Origins of Our Ideas on the Sublime and Beautiful,* but not with any special admiration.

are the same.[129] A work is not ennobled by its subject, but by the way in which it makes the subject felt: by gusto (which conveys to the mind "the impressions of the soul"), by use of the picturesque (those objects or "accidents" of objects "most striking to the mind"), and by an imitation so "exact and laborious" that the pencil serves as microscope.[130] Above all else, great art exemplifies intensity. It requires from both the artist and the viewer a passionate involvement, and it makes the abstract and the coldly formal seem impertinent. As the Elgin Marbles show — and they became Hazlitt's stock example of the true ideal — "the utmost freedom and grandeur of style is compatible with the minutest details."[131] Just as Raphael's models seem to have walked off the streets of Rome into his pictures in the Vatican,[132] the figures in the Elgin Marbles are "immediate, entire, palpable."

Let any one, for instance, look at the leg of the Ilissus or River-God, which is bent under him — let him observe the swell and undulation of the calf, the inter-texture of the muscles, the distinction and union of all the parts, and the effect of action every where impressed on the external form, as if the very marble were a flexible substance, and contained the various springs of life and motion within itself, and he will own that art and nature are here the same thing.*

A style that rests on restraint or understatement, on refinement or abstraction, says Hazlitt, may exemplify the "rules" or show the artist's knowledge of anatomy, but it is bound to lack "expression," and expression is the final strength of art. It is the passionately conveyed response to the "concrete and individual" object,[133] and where it is, there also are "grandeur and refinement."[134] There was one of Titian's portraits in the Louvre, he recalled, that

draws itself up, as if to say, "Well, what do you think of me?" and exercises a discretionary power over you. It has "an eye to threaten and command," not to be lost in idle thought, or in ruminating over some abstruse, speculative propo-sition. It is this intense personal character which, I think, gives the superiority to Titian's portraits over all others, and stamps them with a living and permanent interest. Of other pictures you tire, if you have them constantly before you; of his, never.[135]

Whereas Sir Joshua would "neutralise" expression,[136] the greatest masters show that it resides only in extremes. A thing is not perfected by be-coming something else, "but by *being more itself*."[137] Refinement, grace, and even beauty are inferior to the fully felt and intensely stated truth

---

* 18.145f. One of Hazlitt's fullest and most systematic efforts to codify the aesthetic theory adumbrated in his first essays on Reynolds is in the second of two articles on the Elgin Marbles that he wrote for the *London Magazine* in 1822 (18.150–166). The ten points he develops there — all of them, as he admits, things that he had said before in one form or another (18.150) — are a useful summary of his Romantic theory.

of things, for in art, as in life, all depends on feeling.[138] The language of imagination is "not the less true to nature because it is false in point of fact," said Hazlitt; "but so much the more true and natural, if it conveys the impression which the object under the influence of passion makes on the mind." [139] Keats's statement of this theme reveals how much he learned from Hazlitt: Sir Benjamin West's *Death on the Pale Horse* has "nothing to be intense upon," he reported to his brothers, "no women one feels mad to kiss; no face swelling into reality. the excellence of every Art is its intensity, capable of making all disagreeables evaporate, from their being in close relationship with Beauty & Truth." And then he cites *King Lear*.[140]

King Lear intrudes itself because for Keats as for Hazlitt it epitomized that "o'er informing power" wherein the secret of great art resides. Had Hazlitt been content to regard the artist merely as a kind of microscope he could not have chided Cooper for describing an Indian chief "down to his tobacco-stopper and button-holes" [141] or complained that Crabbe, whose muse was "an old toothless mumbling dame . . . doling out the gossip and scandal of the neighbourhood," gives us only part of nature — "the mean, the little, the disgusting, the distressing." [142] Nor could he have said that whereas Hogarth was "absolute lord and master" of the "gross, material, stirring, noisy world of common life and selfish passion," he was alien to the other "mightier world, that which exists only in conception and in power, the universe of thought and sentiment." [143] In his pictures you see "only the faces which you yourself have seen, or others like them," and because his characters are so "personal and local" they do not expand our feelings. "The Master of the Industrious and Idle Apprentice is a good citizen and a virtuous man; but his benevolence is mechanical and confined: it extends only to his shop, or, at most, to his ward." On the other hand, in one of Raphael's or Leonardo's Madonnas the tenderness and piety appear under an aspect of eternity, and thus exemplify the true ideal: "passion blended with thought and pointing to distant objects, not debased by grossness, not thwarted by accident, nor weakened by familiarity, but connected with forms and circumstances that give the utmost possible expansion and refinement to the general sentiment." Their truth and beauty exist "only in *idea*," which is the true domain of art. It is here that our needs and aspirations are fulfilled, and it is these that genius serves.*

* 6.146ff.; cf. 10.45. Hazlitt makes a similar point on contrasting Scott and Godwin (11.25): in a book like *Caleb Williams* "we see the genuine ore melted in the furnace of fervid feeling, and moulded into stately and *ideal* forms; and this is so far better than peeping into an old iron shop, or pilfering from a dealer in marine stores!" One of Hazlitt's fullest statements of this theme is the *Plain Speaker* essay "Madame

As such a passage shows, in his later work Hazlitt emphasized the role of discipline and mind (and thus moved closer to Sir Joshua), but he did not give up the notion that art should tell the truth about the "things" it imitates. His remarks on Shelley illustrate both principles. On the one hand he found such poems as *The Witch of Atlas* and *The Triumph of Life* so loose in form and structure that "it is impossible, in most instances, to guess the drift or the moral"; [144] on the other, he said that no one is ever "happier, better, or wiser" for having read *Prometheus Unbound*, for its author "gives us, for representation of things, rhapsodies of words." [145] The man of genius must do more than copy or transcribe, he finally decided: he must supply a contribution of his own, "a reflection of the artist's mind — an emanation from his character," which if it does not obscure the facts of nature at any rate transforms and orders them. [146] In his last decade — and perhaps instructed by the Elgin Marbles — Hazlitt spoke more and more of form, and by defining "grandeur" as the "principle of connexion between different parts" of a work of art [147] he implied that the function of the artist, with his "presiding mind," [148] is to unite and harmonize the things he finds in nature. He is, therefore, both imitative and creative. In showing the "idea" behind the things, he records what other men have missed, and in a sense creates it. Poussin's "triumph," like Milton's, was in portraying nature as "we have never seen, but have often wished to see it." [149] The enlargement of the artist's purpose, he says, produces a "corresponding enlargement of form" and so ultimately art becomes a moral statement, with the grandeur of its composition a function of its meaning. In such a process the role of "mind" is paramount. "The actions in Raphael are like a branch of a tree swept by the surging blast," he says; "those in Hogarth like straws whirled and twitched about in the gusts and eddies of passion. I do not mean to say that goodness alone constitutes greatness, but mental power does." [150]

In a sense, then, Hazlitt ends as he began, with the conviction that "the mind alone is formative." Contrasting Scott and Shakespeare, he says that although the Waverley novels are wonderfully veracious, they are only compilations; the author of *King Lear,* however, is a true creator. He does not rely on costume, geography, architecture, or dialect; "but there is an old tradition, human nature — an old temple, the human mind — and Shakespear walks into it and looks about him with a lordly eye, and seizes on the sacred spoils as his own." When he has

---

Pasta and Mademoiselle Mars" (12.324–335), where he attacks artists exhibiting a "perverse fidelity" to details: "in invention, they do not get beyond models; in imitation, beyond details. Their microscopic vision hinders them from seeing nature" (12.332f.).

Lear talk about his little dogs he does not draw on a stock of poetical commodities or use materials "surcharged with a prescriptive influence over the imagination," but the passage has a "weight of passion" that produces power — and this, says Hazlitt, "is the poet's own doing. This is not a trick, but genius." [151] Coleridge, in the great ode that virtually closes his career as poet, laments the loss of "this beautiful and beauty-making power" that he called imagination,[152] and in the preface to his 1815 *Poems* Wordsworth alludes to "the process of creation or of composition, governed by certain fixed laws," as essential to great art.[153] Much of Hazlitt's later criticism might be regarded as a gloss upon these texts. That "*strong quality in the mind, answering to and bringing out some new and striking quality in nature*" [154] which stamps the man of genius was for him the final test of greatness. Without it, the artist is at best a craftsman; with it, he becomes almost a god.

PLAYS AND PLAYERS

Stage-struck since the age of twelve, when he saw Kemble act in Liverpool,* Hazlitt always loved the theater. Reviewing plays was one of his steady jobs in journalism, and despite his irritation at clumsy authors, venal managers, and actors who had missed their true vocation, he usually found the task a grateful one. Consequently it is an important segment of his work that secures his reputation as a critic of the drama.

Between October 1813, when, in a "kind of honey-moon of authorship," [1] he turned in his first review to Perry, and the end of 1817, when he retired as drama critic for the *Times*, he wrote so copiously on the theater that he could furnish two substantial books — *A View of the English Stage* and *Characters of Shakespear's Plays* — with the gleanings of his work. In 1820 he contributed eleven brilliant essays on the stage to the *London Magazine*, and in the spring of 1828 he resumed, briefly and for the last time, the post of drama critic for the *Examiner.*†

---

* The plays were Kemble's expurgated version of Aphra Behn's *The Rover* (on which see my *Kemble* [1942], pp. 164ff.) and, as Hazlitt recalled almost forty years later (11.270), Prince Hoare's *No Song, No Supper*. For his boyish account of the performance, and incidentally his first theatrical review, see the letter to his father in *Literary Remains*, I, xx. The strolling players of his youth in Wem are vividly recalled in an essay written for the *London Magazine* in 1820 (18.294–297). Hazlitt said that he enjoyed composing this "very pretty little kaleidoscope" (18.343), and he subsequently defended it (8.160) against the fastidious complaints of Thomas Griffiths Wainewright, the forger and poisoner who, as "Janus Weathercock," was then his colleague on the *London Magazine*.

† Most of Hazlitt's occasional reviews in the *Morning Chronicle* (from October 1813 to May 1814), the *Champion* (from August 1814 to January 1815), and the

THE MAKING OF A CRITIC

Even after all this compulsory playgoing he still drew upon his "golden" memories of the stage for some of his last and most affecting essays,[2] for when he thought about his "beloved corner" in Covent Garden, he said he wished he might surround that "throne of felicity" with "a balustrade of gold"; to him it had been "a palace of delight."[3]

> Ill will it fare with us, when we do not cast a sidelong glance at those pregnant abridgements, the play-bills, and when their flaunting contents, that unfold to us the map of our life, no longer excite a smile or a sigh. Any one who pleases may then write our epitaph, though it will not be worth writing.[4]

Although Hazlitt assessed the "peculiar charm" of a good, well-acted play as one of life's real joys,[5] he rarely had the chance to relish such delight. As almost everyone agreed, drama in the early nineteenth century had reached a very low estate. The sort of play that Keats made fun of — one "made up of a virtuous young woman, an indignant brother, a suspecting lover, a libertine prince, a gratuitous villain, a street in Naples, a Cypress grove, lillies & roses, virtue & vice, a bloody sword, a spangled jacket"[6] — was painfully familiar. Girding himself to review the latest products of the stage in 1811, Leigh Hunt said that only those whose job required their attendance at the theater could understand the "horrors" of the task,[7] and seventeen years later another hard-pressed critic declared Melpomene to be "in the last stage of a consumption, with strong hectic symptoms; and Thalia in a tabes, inclining to the dropsical."[8] Though couched in different terms, Hazlitt's diagnosis was the same — "the age we live in is critical, didactic, paradoxical, romantic, but it is not dramatic"[9] — and consequently his comments on most new plays run from exasperation to contempt, with here and there a hint of weary resignation. If theatrical criticisms were written only when there is something worth writing about, he said, "it would be hard upon us who live by them."[10] Thus he thought *Love and Toothache* not misnamed, for it was "as disagreeable as the one and as foolish as the other."[11] When Hannah More's *Percy* was at long last over he was "heartily glad," its construction being such that all the characters had to die, "and when this catastrophe took place, the audience seemed perfectly satisfied."[12] He explained that *The Conquest of Taranto* ex-

Examiner (during the latter part of 1814) were reprinted in *A View of the English Stage* (5.179–221), but the bulk of that volume is made up of his regular contributions to the *Examiner* from May 1815 to June 1817. The *Times* reviews (April–December 1817) not included in that book, as well as a few uncollected pieces, the 1820 essays on "The Drama" for the *London Magazine*, and his 1828 reviews in the *Examiner* are brought together by Howe, 18.191–417. The best account of the subject is Alvin Whitley's "Hazlitt and the Theater," University of Texas *Studies in English*, XXXIV (1955), 67–100; cf. William Archer's introduction to *Hazlitt on Theatre* (ed. William Archer and Robert Lowe, 1957).

emplified the whole art of the romantic dramatist by putting ordinary characters in extraordinary situations and blending commonplace sentiments with picturesque scenery.[13] It would be a compliment to say that the author of *The Unknown Guest* had "failed in wit, character, incident, or sentiment," he wrote, "for he has not attempted any thing of the kind."[14] A short-lived piece called *A Man in Mourning for Himself* he found impossible to classify, "but — *de mortuis nil nisi bonum*. So let it pass."[15]

In addition to shabby stuff like this, one had to reckon with the managers. Despite their monopolistic charters, these businessmen, obliged to fill such gigantic houses as Covent Garden and Drury Lane, were saddled with some heavy problems, but Hazlitt thought that their offenses against good taste and even "ordinary decency"[16] were too rank to be endured. Like most critics before and since, he was tireless in instructing them. For six years he scolded and admonished, and his guerilla war against managerial arrogance,[17] deceit,[18] and incompetence[19] enlivened almost all of his reviews. Toward the end of his career as a journalistic critic, however, he was ready to concede defeat, and as his articles for the *London Magazine* in 1820 show, his sense of disenchantment deepened month by month. Convinced that modern playwrights were good for nothing but turning out pretentious "trash,"[20] that most critics dealt in cowardice and fraud,[21] that in the dearth of actors both the patent houses combined could scarcely assemble a decent cast,[22] he concluded that drama was a dying art: "the theatres in general seem to totter, and feel the hand of decay."[23]

Chief among his irritations, perhaps, was the cheap theatricality that managers relied upon to woo the public. As theaters grew larger, he said in 1828,

the scene travels, and our scene-shifters, scene-painters, mechanists, and the whole theatrical *commissariat* go along with it. The variety, the gaudiness, the expense is endless: to pay for the getting up such an immense apparatus, the houses must be enlarged to hold a proportionable rabble of "barren spectators:" the farther off they are thrown, the stronger must be the glare, the more astonishing the effect, and the play and the players (with all relish for wit or nature) dwindle into insignificance, and are lost in the blaze of a huge chandelier or the grin of a baboon.[24]

Although the assumption that, when all else fails, people will pay for noise and color and easy titillation is probably correct, Hazlitt argued that managers should lead and raise, instead of yielding to, the public taste.[25] The proprietors of Covent Garden should remember, he said, that they are not the Society of Antiquaries, for whatever the faults of *The Distressed Mother* (in which "a Mr. Macready" made his debut in

1816), they are not to be relieved by spurious and expensive costumes.[26] In reviewing *John du Bart* he described with heavy irony the climax of the piece, when, "to the amazement and confusion of the audience," a ship was brought upon the stage.[27] A gaudy production of *A Midsummer Night's Dream* at Covent Garden led him to admit that even Shakespeare could be vanquished by bad taste.

> All that is fine in the play, was lost in the representation. The spirit was evaporated, the genius was fled; but the spectacle was fine: it was that which saved the play — Oh, ye scene-shifters, ye scene-painters, ye machinists and dressmakers, ye manufacturers of moon and stars that give no light, ye musical composers, ye men in the orchestra, fiddlers and trumpeters and players on the double drum and loud bassoon, rejoice! This is your triumph; it is not ours.[28]

❖ ❖ ❖

Like Lamb, who loved the theater despite its imperfections, Hazlitt centered his delight upon the players. Though not prone to theorizing on the art of acting, he seemed to regard a great actor as one stamped with the same quality of imagination as the painter and the poet. The essence of his art, he said, is "passion," and unless he can lose his own identity to *become* the role he plays, his craft and study lead to nothing. "To say that the intellect alone can determine or supply the movements or the language of passion," he wrote in 1825, "is little short of a contradiction in terms. Substituting the head for the heart is like saying that the eye is a judge of sounds or the ear of colours." [29] He wrote about Kean and Mrs. Siddons in a strain of exaltation, and even about bad actors with a warmth that is often sentimental. If superannuated, old, and poor they always moved his pity,[30] and the memory of their former triumphs led him to extravagant regret. He disliked to see his favorites off the stage and out of costume — for then they shed their aura [31] — and he loved to reminisce about the pleasure they had given. There was "Gentleman" Lewis (who "made your heart light and your head giddy"), Munden and Fawcett, Suett ("the delighted old croaker"), the incomparable Jack Bannister (whose retirement brought Hazlitt to the verge of tears),[32] and the delightful Mrs. Jordan (who was "Cleopatra turned into an oyster-wench, without knowing that she was Cleopatra, or caring that she was an oyster-wench").[33]

Towering over all these relics of a former day, stately as a shrine, was Sarah Siddons. Incomparably the greatest actress of her age, as Hazlitt thought, she inspired in him a kind of awe. "For *her* to be, was to be sublime!" [34] Like the French Revolution, she was an emblem of his youth. He no doubt first saw her in the nineties, when she was at the peak of her majestic art and he a boy in school, and although she had nominally retired before he began reviewing plays he feasted on the memory of her glory. He said that time, which destroys so many things, could not erase the impression that she made. "Her voice was power: her form was grandeur." [35] He wept throughout her Isabella; [36] her greater roles left him "stunned and torpid"; and even in such a third-rate piece as *Tamerlane* she invested everything with magic:

I was in a trance, and my dreams were of mighty empires fallen, of vast burning zones, of waning time, of Persian thrones and them that sat on them, of sovereign beauty, and of victors vanquished by love. . . . No wonder that the huge, dim, disjointed vision should enchant and startle me. One reason why our first impressions are so strong and lasting is that they are *whole-length* ones. We afterwards divide and compare, and judge of things only as they differ from other things. At first we measure them from the ground, take in only the groups and masses, and are struck with the entire contrast to our former ignorance and inexperience. [37]

When, later, he came to evaluate her style he realized that she was not without faults of tempo, recitation, and delivery; [38] none the less she remained the only person who ever embodied his ideal of tragedy. [39] "Power was seated on her brow, passion emanated from her breast as from a shrine; she was tragedy personified." [40] He would no more "cross-examine" her about her art, he said, than try to trap one of the Elgin Marbles into an argument. [41] Inevitably — for the ideal should not be made too common — he thought it cruel for Kemble to bring his sister from retirement to decorate his own farewell. "To have seen Mrs. Siddons, was an event in every one's life; and does she think we have forgot her? Or would she remind us of herself by shewing us what *she was not*?" [42] Hazlitt had no wish to witness or record "the progress of her decay." [43]

Though far beneath his sister in the scale of art, John Philip Kemble was for Hazlitt another fallen giant. Despite his managerial prowess and his long prestige he was no match for Edmund Kean, and as his rival's reputation rose, he himself declined. Always stirred by old affections, Hazlitt tended to resent this fact, [44] for Kemble had dominated tragic drama for a generation, and his eclipse was a lesson in mortality. "Our associations of admiration and delight with theatrical performers, are among our earliest recollections — among our last regrets. They are links that connect the beginning and the end of life together; *their* bright and giddy career of popularity measures the arch that spans our brief existence." [45] Apart from such sentimental ties, Hazlitt's attitude toward Kemble is hard to understand, for he was a stiff and formal actor, and his haughty style, though effective for roles like Cato and Macbeth, [46] was generally cold, inert, and hard. Leigh Hunt sneered at his "majestic dryness and deliberate nothings" as a monumental fraud,[47] but Hazlitt praised him for his merits and tended to forgive his faults. If incapable of "sudden and irresistible bursts of passion," he said, Kemble stood unrivaled in roles "where all the passions move round a central point, and have one master key." [48] Where the part was right, his hauteur was invincible. Although he played Coriolanus with "the abstracted air, the contracted eyebrows and suspended chin of a man who is just going to sneeze," said Hazlitt, he played it with a real patrician force.[49] Because he was the only great actor whose art had come with study,[50] he sometimes appeared not to feel a part, but rather "to be considering how he ought to feel it." [51] In his great roles, however, he himself was great, and Hazlitt's valedictory comments on his farewell season in 1817 constitute an accolade that would gladden any actor's heart. In *The Stranger,* as in his other famous parts, he had come to be "a sentiment embodied":

a long habit of patient suffering, not seen but felt, appears to have subdued his mind, and moulded his whole form. We could look at Mr. Kemble in this character and listen to him, till we could fancy that every other actor is but a harlequin, and that no tones but his have true pathos, sense, or meaning in them. "So fare thee well, old Jack!" We ought to say so. You are a very, very old friend.*

If Kemble and his stately sister had fallen prey to time, the fiery Edmund Kean was at his peak during Hazlitt's years as drama critic, and it was he who inspired his best reviews.[52] That their careers converged was fortunate, for in Hazlitt the actor found an astute but ardent critic, and in Kean the critic found an ideal subject; as a result, they assisted one another's fame. Warned by his editor to be as kindly as he could, Hazlitt had gone to Drury Lane for Kean's debut on 26 January 1814 with some misgivings, and when he found the house half empty he prepared himself for trouble.[53] Kean's first entrance, however, electrified the audience, and the performance, "giving perpetually fresh shocks of delight and surprise," proved to be a triumph. In "voice, eye, action, and expression," Hazlitt reported next day in the *Morning Chronicle,* the new Shylock was stunning and unrivaled,[54] and on that "proud" night, he said not long before he died, there began an era in the English stage.[55]

As the spring wore on and Kean's successes mounted Hazlitt's string of rave reviews lent credence to the rumor that he himself was being paid by Drury Lane to inflate the actor's reputation.[56] The new star's

* 18.233f. The résumé of Kemble's career that Hazlitt contributed to the *Times* on 25 June 1817 (5.374–379) is one of the peaks of English drama criticism. For Haydon's waspish account of the banquet in Kemble's honor on 27 June 1817 see the *Diary,* II, 122ff. One would like to know if Hazlitt too attended it.

SARAH SIDDONS
After a portrait by William Hamilton
The Harvard Theatre Collection

EDMUND KEAN
By George Cruikshank
The Harvard Theatre Collection

Shylock, he told his readers, had no peer,[57] his Richard III revealed an "animation" that had never been excelled,[58] his Hamlet was "extraordinary," [59] his Othello was "a master-piece of profound pathos and exquisite conception," [60] and even after all these triumphs Iago proved to be "the most faultless" of his roles.[61] In an age of easy journalistic morals, when, as Leigh Hunt recalled, "what the public took for a criticism on a play, was a draft upon the box-office, or reminiscences of last Thursday's salmon and lobster-sauce," * such comments might well have generated gossip, but Hazlitt had a forthright explanation: "I am not one of those who, when they see the sun breaking from behind a cloud, stop to ask others whether it is the moon." [62] Later, in alluding to the charge that he had manufactured Kean's acclaim, he denied that any actor could be "written up or down" by journalists,† and there can be no doubt that his admiration was sincere. No man to trim or to tailor his opinions, he found in Kean not a perfect artist but one whose genius was almost great enough to conceal his imperfections,[63] and he proclaimed the fact with joy. "My opinions have been sometimes called singular: they are merely sincere. I say what I think: I think what I feel." [64]

Though in person small, misshapen, and ungraceful,[65] Kean acted with a power that obliterated almost all his disadvantages. A virtuoso fascinated by his own technique, he was, suggested Hazlitt, perhaps unable to surrender to his roles completely, "but why do we try this actor by an ideal theory? Who is there that will stand the same test? It is, in fact, the last forlorn hope of criticism, for it shews that we have nothing else to compare him with." [66] Kean's Othello, for example, was "the finest piece of acting in the world," [67] and even in such a thing of "cant and rant" as *Tamerlane* his Bajazet redeemed the worthless play: "his eyeballs glare, his teeth gnash together, his hands are clenched. In describing his defeat, his voice is choked with passion; he curses, and the blood curdles in his veins." [68]

From these and many other feverish comments about Kean's "terrible energy," "electrical shocks," and "violence of action" we must infer

---

* *Autobiography*, p. 191. The *Examiner* was so fiercely independent that when Kemble once complained of harsh reviews John Hunt returned his pass and thereafter bought his tickets to the theater (Cyrus Redding, *Fifty Years' Recollections, Literary and Personal* [1858], I, 277f.). When William Cobbett, in his *Political Register*, called the editor of the *Examiner* a "paid-for paragraph monger," Leigh Hunt asserted that "not one sixpence" had ever been accepted by his paper for anything it printed, and he demanded an unqualified retraction. Characteristically, Cobbett did not apologize, whereupon Hunt, in a rare signed piece, denounced him as a knave. See the *Examiner*, 3 March 1816, p. 140; 21 March 1816, pp. 201f.

† 8.293. William Macready (*Diaries* [ed. William Toynbee, 1912], I, 90), was told many years later that when Hazlitt once tried to borrow fifty pounds from Kean the actor turned him down.

not only that a furious theatricality was his stock in trade but that Hazlitt, like so many other men of letters, was enraptured by his grunts and groans and writhings. Byron called Kean's Richard III "Life-nature-truth without exaggeration or diminution"; [69] Keats declared that his "intense power" of "anatomizing" passion had wrought a revolution in the style of acting; [70] Haydon predicted that "his purity, his truth, his energy" would stifle opposition; [71] even Godwin's philosophic calm was shattered when he saw Kean upon the stage. [72] But Hazlitt led the loud hosannas. Kean's Othello, he said, was such "a masterpiece of natural passion" that even his contortions were essential to the role. "The convulsed motion of the hands, and the involuntary swellings of the veins of his forehead in some of the most painful situations, should not only suggest topics of critical panegyric, but might furnish studies to the painter or anatomist." * His originality was his most "radical" and astonishing gift, [73] and because it was rooted in his own instinctive knowledge of the human heart it defied attempts at imitation. [74] Subordinating all his art to nature, he stood on his own ground, because he was a natural genius. [75] "A Kemble school we can understand," said Hazlitt: "a Kean school is, we suspect, a contradiction in terms. Art may be taught, because it is learnt: Nature can neither be taught nor learnt." [76]

None the less the critic lost no chance to instruct the actor in things that he neglected. Like a proud parent with a bright, unruly child, he watched his progress with almost proprietary concern, salting praise with blame and sprinkling his most eulogistic comments with reproofs and adjurations. He even defended him — unwisely, as it seems — against the charge of drunkenness. [77] Successful as Kean's Richard III had been — "more refined than Cooke; more bold, varied, and original than Kemble" — Hazlitt said that it had a few rough spots: he should not have dropped his voice in commanding Hastings' execution, and he should not have put his hands behind him in receiving Buckingham's account of his reception by the citizens. [78] On the whole, Hazlitt thought his Hamlet "wrong" because it was "too strong and pointed," but certain scenes were stunning, and his business of coming back from the edge of the stage after the rejection of Ophelia was so "electrical" that it could be regarded as "the finest commentary that was ever made on Shakespear." [79] Although Kean's Iago, at the end of his first London season, was beyond reproach, [80] his exaggerated mannerisms after a summer tour of Ireland called forth the tart reminder that he had a reputation to maintain. [81] Certain parts of his Macbeth were "deficient in the

---

* 18.263. Hazlitt liked this passage well enough to use it twice again (18.302, 393f.).

poetry of the character," but other parts — for example, the scene after Duncan's murder — took one's breath away:

The hesitation, the bewildered look, the coming to himself when he sees his hands bloody; the manner in which his voice clung to his throat, and choked his utterance; his agony and tears, the force of nature overcome by passion — beggared description. It was a scene, which no one who saw it can ever efface from his recollection.[82]

Despite the force of Kean's bravura passages, however, the defects of his florid operatic style became more and more apparent as he enlarged his repertory. For such rubbish as the role of Zanga (in Young's *Revenge*) his limitations did not matter, Hazlitt said, for there his very "vices" — "his cruel eye, his quivering visage, his violent gestures, his hollow pauses, his abrupt transitions" — were enough to guarantee success.[83] But for better plays, and especially for Shakespeare, the critic thought that something more was needed. To hint a fault and hesitate dislike was not in Hazlitt's character, and from the very night of Kean's debut he was troubled by the actor's failure to adjust his flashes of technique to the general coloration of the role. "The fault of his acting was (if we may hazard the objection), an over-display of the resources of the art, which gave too much relief to the hard, impenetrable, dark ground-work of the character of Shylock."[84] This admonitory and corrective note was struck with greater force as Kean's list of triumphs grew. Although his Hamlet was a tumultuous popular success, Hazlitt questioned the "severity, approaching to virulence," with which he played a role of "undulating lines." * His Richard III revealed a boundless energy, but it was only the "energy of action," and in consequence he "gesticulated, or at best vociferated the part." [85] Failing to realize that Macbeth is a good man made cruel by circumstances, whereas blood is Richard's "pastime," he played both of them alike.[86] With "nothing of the lover in it," his Romeo was neither ardent nor voluptuous.[87] Despite its "electrical shocks" his Richard II, at the end of his second London season, seemed to Hazlitt almost entirely bad. "Mr. Kean made it a character of *passion*, that is, of feeling combined with energy; whereas it is a character of *pathos*, that is to say, of feeling combined with weakness. This, we conceive, is the general fault of Mr. Kean's acting, that it is always energetic or nothing."[88]

The fact was, of course, that Kean, although unmatched for thrilling moments, was an actor who relied on "points" or "hits," [89] hurling himself from one big passage to the next but neglecting almost every-

* 5.187. From Haydon's analysis of Kean's Hamlet, which he saw the following fall (*Diary*, I, 397), we may infer that the actor had redesigned the role.

thing between. His titanic bursts of passion were superb, but they were merely bursts. His portrayals lacked a steady, throbbing power that flowed from first to last and related cause to consequence. In his performances the parts were greater than the whole, and therefore, as Coleridge remarked, to see him act was like reading Shakespeare by flashes of lightning.[90] Gripping as his big scenes were — for example, the third act of *Othello*,[91] Hamlet's rejection of Ophelia,[92] and Duncan's murder in *Macbeth* [93] — Hazlitt thought they rose too high above the level of the play because they were not anchored in a sense of character. In expressing certain passions, like anger or revenge, Kean made criticism futile; but joy and hope and love were not suited to his style, and because he knew nothing of "repose" he was incapable of the "deep, sustained, internal sentiment" that had no vent in frenzy or despair. Thus, although he could move from violence to pathos, he seldom rose to pathos "from the power of thought and feeling." [94] In gesture, style, and voice he could often be superb, and the "bye-play" with which he pointed certain scenes was so illuminating that one might think it was Shakespeare's stage direction.[95] None the less, to provide a string of "shocks" was not to build a round, plastic character, and as Kean's defects hardened into mannerisms Hazlitt's dissatisfaction grew.

Changing from panegyric to analysis during 1815, his reviews became longer, darker, and more thoughtful. As if to explain his roles to Kean — for example, Romeo [96] and Richard II [97] — he expounded the meaning of the play, traced motivation, and showed how conduct must be tied to character. Although the effect of these reviews was no doubt lost on Kean, they were essential to the man who, even then, was probably contemplating *Characters of Shakespear's Plays*. Sometimes brusque but more often patient and expository, Hazlitt ticked off Kean's mistakes, praising bits of action here and there, but mainly finding fault with his conception of a role. Early in 1816 the gathering gloom was briefly broken by a masterful Sir Giles Overreach that Hazlitt welcomed with relief,* but two months later he pronounced Kean's Sforza (in Massinger's *Duke of Milan*) to be a failure because the actor's customary vigor seemed to lack a steady drive and object.[98] His long review of Maturin's *Bertram* the following May contained only one tepid sentence on Kean's performance in the title role,[99] and in reporting on another new play two years later — George Colman's *Surrender of Calais* — he could only wonder why the actor had agreed to play a part so unsuited to his

---

* 5.272ff. A few weeks after writing this review Hazlitt watched *A New Way to Pay Old Debts* from an unaccustomed seat in the boxes and decided (5.284) that from such a vantage Kean appeared to be no more than "a little man in a great passion."

talents.[100] In 1820 Hazlitt's return to writing on the drama, in the *London Magazine,* coincided with two of Kean's most celebrated efforts in *Coriolanus* and *King Lear*. Despite their popular success Hazlitt was disappointed in them both. The first had been one of Kemble's greatest roles, he recalled, but as Kean swaggered through the play it became a patchy, vulgar thing.[101] And as for his Lear, it was both "feeble" and "perverse," as if the actor lacked the "comprehension" to portray the "gigantic, outspread sorrows" of Shakespeare's greatest role. Too violent and too tame by turns, he yielded to his old defects, and although he "chipped off a bit of the character here and there" he failed "to pierce the solid substance" of that ancient granite.[102] This, almost the last of Hazlitt's judgments on the greatest actor of the age, may serve as epilogue to the general view that he expressed a few months earlier: although Kean was never able to achieve a "broad and massy" sense of character,[103] he was none the less without a peer — "an *experimentum crucis,* to shew the triumph of genius over physical defects, of nature over art, of passion over affectation, and of originality over common-place monotony."[104]

Next to Kean in Hazlitt's admiration was Eliza O'Neill, whose brief career was one of the most splendid of the age. In 1814 her debut as Juliet prompted a review notable for its comparison of her with Mrs. Siddons, as two women whose "fine play and undulation of natural sensibility" enabled them to "become" whatever part they played.[105] There could never really be another Sarah Siddons, though, decided Hazlitt, and Miss O'Neill's defects, especially in comedy, became painfully apparent as she moved from role to role. Her Lady Teazle, lacking elegance, ease, dignity, and playfulness, "was not any thing that it ought to be,"[106] and on occasion even her Belvidera failed because by exhibiting some of Kean's mannerisms it showed that "the excellences of genius are not communicable."[107] Generally, however, he thought she was enchanting. "Her correctness did not seem the effect of art or study, but of instinctive sympathy, of a conformity of mind and disposition to the character she was playing, as if she had unconsciously become the very person."[108] He accorded her a lonely eminence among all modern actresses, and to mark her marriage and retirement in 1820, at the height of her career, he wrote one of his most eulogistic essays for the *London Magazine*.[109] With his cold, declamatory style Macready was less to Hazlitt's taste,[110] yet at his debut in 1816 he conceded that except for Kean he was "by far the best tragic actor that has come out in our remembrance." [111] As Othello — a role that challenged even Kean, who unfortunately tended to play it like a gypsy rather than "a majestic serpent wounded" — if he failed at all it was because he attempted to excel; [112] but he was a poor Macbeth because, for all his gloss and finish, he lacked a sense of grandeur. [113]

If such comments seem to damn with faint praise, they are warm in comparison with his more systematic studies in detraction, for when displeased he could express himself with cruel precision. A "respectable" actor, he said, was one "who never disappoints us, because we do not expect any thing from him," [114] and he had little patience with the "successful mediocrity" [115] or mere incompetence with which he seemed to think the theater had been plagued ever since Thespis climbed upon a wagon. One of his recurrent complaints was the star system, which, despite its Keans and Kembles, meant that most parts of a performance were bungled or neglected. [116] Thus of Kean's production of *Richard II* in 1815 he reported wearily that it was unnecessary to dwell upon the cast: Gaunt was "respectable," York "lamentable," and Bolingbroke "indifferent." [117] It was when a hapless actor strayed or was pushed beyond his range that Hazlitt loosed his lightning. As long as Charles Mayne Young was content with modest parts, the critic promised to avert his gaze, "but whenever he plays Shakespear, we must be excused if we take unequal revenge for the martyrdom which our feelings suffer. His Prospero was good for nothing; and consequently, was indescribably bad." [118] When George Bentley played Ben (in Congreve's *Love for Love*) Hazlitt declared that Miss Prue's distaste for him was very natural. [119] "A Lady by the name of Alsop" proved to be "a very nice little woman," but desperately ill-advised to attempt Rosalind. [120] When Alexander Rae, as Romeo, described the apothecary, he sounded like a man hired to make a speech after riding ten miles on a high-trotting horse. [121] As Richard III, Thomas Cobham "raved, whined, grinned, stared, stamped, and rolled his eyes with incredible velocity" — but all to no avail. [122] There was no more reason for Stephen Kemble to act Falstaff than for Louis XVIII to be given the French throne merely "because he is fat, and belongs to a particular family." [123] In the preface to his collected reviews Hazlitt tried to justify these and other harsh opinions. Since any actor puts himself on "trial" and must accept the "verdict," he explained, the critic has a duty, both as judge and executioner, to "prevent a lingering death, by anticipating, or putting in immediate force, the sentence of the public." [124] He must have been a terror to the actors, for although his reviews were sometimes merely witty and derisive, they were sometimes brutal. At least once, in denouncing William Conway's "monstrous burlesque" of Romeo, he was so tasteless and offensive that he was forced to make apology.[*]

❖ ❖ ❖

Like all professional critics, Hazlitt was obliged to watch and write about an appalling lot of trash, and from some of his reviews — which were as trivial as their subjects — it would seem that on occasion he wearied of the job. Especially in the summer season, when opera and farce were standard fare, he thought that the poor critic was like a mouse in an air pump, "gasping for breath, subsisting on a sort of theatrical half-allowance."[125] Thus, although he dutifully and dully reported on the opera, it was a form that he almost always deprecated. For one thing — and despite his protestations to the contrary[126] — he really had no taste for music. Perhaps agreeing with Lamb's assumption that oratorios profane "the cheerful playhouse,"[127] he was glad when their annual presentations ended.[128] He was bored by the interpolated songs in Shakespeare[129] — Ophelia does not go mad because she can sing, he said, but she sings because she has gone mad[130] — and he thought that even the best music fails to satisfy the mind because as the "pure effusion of sentiment" it gives us neither "objects" nor "ideas."[131] Similarly, opera, in seeking to gratify all the senses at once, affords us nothing to engage the mind.[132] As the apotheosis of art — or rather artifice — it defies the truth of nature,[133] and like all "perverted" forms its only purpose is display.[134] It is like "a tawdry courtesan," he said, "who, when her paint and patches, her rings and jewels are stripped off, can excite only disgust and ridicule."[135] When "light" it is merely pert and flippant,[136] when "tragic" it is so patently unreal that the audience responds with a "sleek and sordid apathy."[137] In short, he thought that opera had no meaningful relation to life, and he was too earnest to enjoy it for its style alone. Music, scenery, and dancing are not without a certain charm, he said, but only words have the "moral and intellectual perspective" that the highest art requires.[138]

Reviewing oratorios and operas was at most a peripheral part of Hazlitt's job as critic, but with legitimate drama he was intimately concerned, and therefore his comments on the comedies and tragedies he saw from week to week — comments which eventually take the configuration of a theory — merit more attention. Owing to the repertory system

---

[*] 5.404f.; cf. 5.177. To be sure, Conway's sins were grievous, said Hazlitt later (18.386) in a retrospective mood, but he was also something of a sacrificial lamb: the guilt should have fallen on the shameless, greedy managers who "pushed him forward" when he could not "stand the trial, or meet the consequences."

current in his day he saw a lot of old stock pieces, and despite his sentimental attachment to plays that he had known and loved for years —
"why can we not always be young, and seeing the School for Scandal?" [139]
— he thought that mere longevity was not enough to justify a shabby
work. To retain upon the stage such "a piece of wretched cant" as *George
Barnwell* was, he said, an anachronistic folly, [140] and to revive Colley
Cibber's *Refusal* was an attempt to raise the dead. [141] Still he generally
admired, or at least felt affection for, almost any play that had pleased
many and had pleased long. His reviews are studded with tender comments on his boyhood favorites from the standard repertory, and his prefatory notes for William Oxberry's reprints of the old stock pieces are
compounded of nostalgia and commercialism: not only do such plays
glow with the patina that only time confers, but they have "held possession of the stage" through successive generations, and there is no better
test of merit. Even if Nicholas Rowe was a middling man of letters, he
said, it was his "rare felicity" to write two plays that had survived a century, and whatever the defects of *Jane Shore*, its reputation was "embalmed in the tears it has drawn from numberless eyes." [142] John Home
had "dared little" in his famous *Douglas*, but it was the only tragedy in
a hundred years that had outlived its author, and therefore "it is like a
green spot in the desert, which, though its verdure may be scanty, and
its recesses soon explored, we hail with gladness and turn from with regret, from its contrast to the dearth and barrenness around." [143]

◇ ◇ ◇

The remark about death and barrenness points to one of Hazlitt's
fundamental notions — that for various reasons his age could not produce great drama. He studiously disparaged modern comedy, in part because he, like Hobbes, regarded comedy as a form of wit and malice and
therefore not a product of "imagination," in part because he shared the
wide Romantic view that tragedy is a nobler kind of literature, [144] and in
part, of course, because there were so few good comedies produced in the
early nineteenth century. Both comedy and tragedy, he said, are based
upon the felt distinction between "what things are, and what they ought
to be," [145] but the comic writer, and his audience, view this distinction
with detachment. Tragedy stirs the sympathetic imagination by which we
identify ourselves with the objects of our passion and so expand our
spectrum of response: we lose ourselves in Lear and feel his sorrows as
our own. But comedy has a restrictive and segregating force: we keep our
distance from Miss Prue, and her rebuffs stir only condescending laugh-

ter. Comedy loosens the "habitual stress" of expectation by which we organize experience into pattern, form, and sequence.[146] It effects a "decomposition and recomposition of our ideas."[147] The comic writer searches out the unexpected. He deals in broken sequence and uncompleted pattern, but because he touches only fops and fools and monsters he exonerates the audience (which is, presumably, made up of normal people), and the audience, aloof and disengaged, and relieved to learn that it is so much better or more knowing than the dupes upon the stage, expresses its relief in laughter. "It is like taking a grain of sand out of the eye, a thorn out of the foot. We have discharged our mental reckoning, and had our revenge."[148]

There is also a kind of gentle comedy, best exemplified by Shakespeare, in which "our follies, turning round against themselves in support of our affections, retain nothing but their humanity."[149] Falstaff and Bottom are "natural" comic types who make us laugh at folly rather than despise it,[150] and for that very reason Shakespeare's comedy lacks the cutting edge of Congreve and Molière: he is so "good-natured and magnanimous" that he mounts above his quarry, and when he laughs at Justice Shallow his laughter is "social and humane."[151] Critical comedy, however, is not "an affair of the heart or the imagination,"[152] for it relies on wit, and by means of wit the "proud, obstinate, sacred tumours" of the world are punctured and reduced to their "native insignificance."[153] It is the product of a later age, when man becomes "a truly contemptible animal" by learning to ape the folly of his fellows,[154] and when there are writers sharp enough to comment on the fact. Between what Lady Wishfort is and what she thinks she is lies the comic writer's province, which his wit enables him to cross. He underscores distinctions, contrasts, compares, discriminates — and he does so with a cold and calculating eye. Although, as Locke had said, wit sometimes enables us to make "unexpected resemblances," it mainly works to separate and disentangle things that merely seem to be alike,[155] and therefore it ultimately derives from reason, the faculty by which we measure and divide.[156]

This, then, is the province of wit; to penetrate through the disguise or crust with which indolence and custom 'skin and slur over' our ideas, to move this slough of prejudice, and to resolve these aggregates or bundles of things into their component parts by a more lively and unshackled conception of their distinctions, and the possible combinations of these, so as to throw a glancing and fortuitous light upon the whole.[157]

Imagination, on the other hand, is the "associating principle" and the "monopolizing faculty"[158] that fuses things and overleaps distinctions. As we learn from Jonson's "laborious caution" and Shakespeare's "heedless magnanimity," one of them narrows and refines, the other enlarges and unites.[159]

If, then, the comic writer works best upon perceived distinctions, usually in etiquette and manners, an age that has leveled such distinctions affords him no material. His purpose is to smooth and polish eccentricities through the abrasive force of ridicule. He preys upon the socially abnormal, and since his criticism is, or ought to be, corrective, he eventually uses up his subject. "Comedy naturally wears itself out — destroys the very food on which it lives; and by constantly and successfully exposing the follies and weaknesses of mankind to ridicule, in the end leaves itself nothing worth laughing at." [160] Hazlitt thought that by his time conversation, like dress, had become so dull and uniform that even Congreve would find nothing left to write about. Remembering such great comic creations as Lovelace, Lothario, Lord Foppington, Squire Western, Uncle Toby, Don Quixote and his squire, Count Fathom, and Joseph Surface, he concluded that they had left no heirs.[161] "Lost in a kind of intellectual *hermaphroditism*," he explained, we are rendered "tame, correct, and spiritless," and "drilled into a sort of stupid decorum." [162] In an age of political reaction and social conformity we have lost the priceless gift of individuality, and so we "toil slowly on to the Temple of Science, seen a long way off upon a level, and end in one dull compound of politics, criticism, chemistry, and metaphysics!" [163] The Restoration, when "individual infirmities" passed into "general manners," was the golden age of English comedy, for then the court put its stamp on folly and gave vice a "meretricious lustre." [164] After Farquhar, however, a decline set in. Wycherley's exacerbated sense of folly and Congreve's glittering malice gave way to complacency, propriety, and sentiment, and the result was that species of *"do-me-good*, lack-a-daisical, whining, make-believe comedies" that Steele and his posterity produced.[165] To be sure, Sheridan, a comic genius who "could imitate with the spirit of an inventor," [166] wrote as Congreve and Vanbrugh would have written if they had lived in the later eighteenth century, but no one followed him, and by Hazlitt's day the kind of "cautious purity" that marked the boldest reach of comic writing showed that the disaster was complete.

✧ ✧ ✧

Tragedy, too, had slackened, Hazlitt thought, in an age when passions were "remote" and "sentimental." [167] The most stirring kind of drama, because it is kindled by and in turn produces passion, feeling, and involvement, it is killed by reason and restraint. To be objective and judicious and arrive at nice distinctions is not the tragic writer's style.

Although he gratifies that primordial lust for blood which draws us to an execution, knowing that "there is a natural tendency in the mind to strong excitement, a desire to have its faculties roused and stimulated to the utmost," [168] he does not rely merely on action and sensation, for he "resolves the sense of pain or suffering into the sense of *power* by the aid of imagination, and by grandeur of conception and character." [169] He does not study or soliloquize upon his subject, but reveals its force in action. His element is passion, that heightened and exhilarated state in which imagination, like a fiery furnace, melts and renders malleable "the most contradictory materials." [170] Words that glow, said Hazlitt, spring from thoughts that burn, [171] and in the crucible of the dramatist's imagination, character, plot, and language are fused to make a living principle. [172] Thus Maturin's *Bertram* (1816) was a failure — despite its popular success — because it lacked such consolidating power: instead of surrendering to his subject the writer used it as a text on which to drape his own reflections, and consequently the "biting edge" of passion was "blunted, sheathed, and lost." * In *Virginius,* on the other hand, Knowles, almost alone among the moderns, had achieved "real tragedy." Like Shakespeare, he understood what "true imagination" is: "to put yourself in the place of others, and to feel and speak for them!" [173]

This view of tragic drama as, par excellence, the literature of power and passion reflects Hazlitt's doctrine of imagination. Analysis and introspection are useful modes of thought, he says, but they rise too far above the level of experience to convey the force of things directly felt. On the other hand, imagination is always fired by passion, and passion is always stirred by "facts, concrete existences" felt along the pulses.† That is why Euripides retains his power, whereas the "fatal composure" of the other Greek tragedians fails to move the reader: in their plays "the mind is not shaken to its centre; the whole being is not crushed or broken down." [174] In his *Edinburgh* review of Schlegel [175] Hazlitt tried to do justice to the kind of pleasure that classic art affords, but restraint and order and repose were virtues that he failed to understand. As a literary historian he knew that there were various types of drama — the "antique or classical," the Gothic or "romantic," the French or "common-place rhetorical," and the German or "paradoxical" — but as a critic and a man

---

* 5.305. *Bertram* was the play that the Drury Lane Committee, in 1816, chose instead of Coleridge's *Zapolya*, and Coleridge's subsequent attack on a successful rival's work — first in the *Courier* and then in *Biographia Literaria* (II, 180–207) — was duly marked by Hazlitt (16.138, 19.208). See Prothero, IV, 172.

† 12.52. One of the general principles that Hazlitt derived from his study of *King Lear* (4.271) was that the "greatest strength of genius is shown in describing the strongest passions: for the power of the imagination, in works of invention, must be in proportion to the force of the natural impressions, which are the subject of them."

he looked for "power" and "richness," and these he found in the Eliza-bethans.[176] An art built on reason and control has a certain austere beauty, he conceded, but it lacks the throb of passion. Reason tends to freeze the ceaseless ebb and flow of feeling, but through imagination we trace the subtle lines of life and draw the shape of truth. This is perhaps the process that Keats, who so often paraphrases and develops Hazlitt's notions, described as "the innumerable compositions and decompositions which take place between the intellect and its thousand materials be-fore it arrives at that trembling delicate and snail-horn perception of Beauty." [177]

Of all poetic forms drama is the most securely anchored in experience, for it must deal with character in action, not with speculative theory. It portrays opposing wills, each regarded as a "centre of repulsion to the rest," and therefore it concerns the "individual and concrete" as they are apprehended through imagination.[178] It is the truest form of poetry be-cause imagination requires the complete submission of the writer to his subject; it is the noblest form of poetry because imagination leads the spectator, as it led the artist, to soar beyond himself and reach the liberal-izing truth of nature.[179] Is it any wonder then, asked Hazlitt, that the age whose characteristic products were the *Edinburgh Review, Political Jus-tice, The Excursion*, and *Childe Harold's Pilgrimage* should lack a real dramatic poet? In *Marino Faliero* the superbly egocentric Byron, unable to "wind into the march of human affairs upon the earth, or mingle in the throng and daily conflict of human passions," makes drama "a resting-place for his own pride and irritability." [180] Godwin's characters in *Antonio* are only speculative studies; Wordsworth, though unmatched in power of introspection, lacks the "venturous magnanimity" by which imagina-tion annihilates the dramatic poet's sense of self; Coleridge's *Remorse* is a "spurious tragedy" because its author mistakes "scholastic speculations for the intricate windings of the passions"; and Scott's diffuse, romantic themes could not be focused for the stage.[181] As a result, tragedy, once "tossed about by the winds and waves of passion," had become, in Haz-litt's time, a rickety machine "moved by the sole expansive power of words." [182]

SHAKESPEARE

Although we have ranged through Hazlitt's later work to illustrate his views, almost everything he had to say about the art of drama found its first authoritative statement in *Characters of Shakespear's Plays* in

1817. If somewhat out of style today, and also overshadowed by the work of Coleridge, this once-famous book retains a certain luster. The advance of scholarship, resulting in a firmer knowledge of Elizabethan life and language, has made us wary of Hazlitt's high-pitched adulation, and our concern with metaphor and symbol and archetypal patterns and the like has opened up a whole new set of problems with which he was unconcerned. He lacks Johnson's elephantine common sense and Coleridge's supple, generalizing mind, but he exemplifies an attitude that will never be passé. He strikes a note of almost priestly adoration as he celebrates the fact of genius. His book on Shakespeare is rough, uneven, ill-informed, and tediously exclamatory, but it conveys a real exuberance. It stands as a monument not only to Shakespeare's lasting power but also to the kind of critical response that we have come to call Romantic.

Because this work was built upon — and indeed reprints in part — the reviews that he had scribbled for the press, it has a rather jerky pace; but it was conceived and put together as a book, and therefore it has more scope and structure than his other writings on the stage. It presents the seasoned critic freed from the pressures of the quick review to speculate upon the principles of art. Upon the premise, which he taught Keats to share, that "Shakespeare is enough for us" [1] he asserted that "our admiration cannot easily surpass his genius." [2] He sought and found in the god of his idolatry all he most admired in drama, and consequently his book is both a commentary upon specific plays and a treatise on the art that they exemplify.

Although Hazlitt knew the plays almost by heart (and could quote — and misquote — them with a freedom that De Quincey found offensive,) [3] his scholarship was shaky. As his title indicates and as the preface underscores, his main concern is character, and such value as his work retains lies in his analysis of motive, action, and response. This kind of criticism was anything but new in 1817. A generation earlier Whately, Richardson, and Morgann had initiated it, and in a sense Hazlitt, like Coleridge, merely carried on their work. None the less he somewhat disingenuously claims originality. [4] He shows acquaintance with the major eighteenth-century critics, and especially with the newly translated Schlegel (whose *Lectures on Dramatic Literature* he had enthusiastically reviewed for the *Edinburgh* the year before), [5] but he is silent about the important contributions of Reed and Steevens and Malone, and he attacks Johnson's noble work as the labored product of a "didactic reasoner" temperamentally unable to understand "how the nature of man was modified by the workings of passion." [6] As he remarked a few years later, "if we wish to know the force of human genius, we should read Shakespear. If we wish to see the insignificance of human learning, we may study his commentators." [7]

Even though Hazlitt reads Shakespeare *con amore*, his defects are glaring. He tends to slight the comedies, and about some of them, like *Two Gentlemen* and *Love's Labour's Lost*, he is skimpy and jejune; he spends so long on Romeo and Juliet that he has no space for Mercutio; and since his "idolatry," not to say his "admiration," ceases with the plays, [8] he is superficial on the nondramatic poems and downright banal on the sonnets. Moreover, there are many kinds of problems that he altogether skirts. He ignores all textual questions (which, in any event, he lacked the knowledge to resolve); he shows no interest in Shakespeare's use of language or in the texture of his poetry; * like Coleridge, he makes bizarre mistakes in facts and dates that the scholars might have saved him from; and he pays almost no attention to the structure of the plays. Despite such errors and omissions — or perhaps because of them — his book is a trophy of Romantic criticism. Surely no one would trade *Characters of Shakespear's Plays* for Johnson's splendid Preface, but as Hazlitt leads us through the pieces that he loved he infects us with his own enthusiasm, and some of his perceptions are so fresh and bold that they burst upon us like our own.

Not inappropriately he dedicates his book to Lamb, for although he expresses discontent with "a celebrated person" — obviously Coleridge — who valued Shakespeare chiefly for his metaphysics, [9] he tends to hold Lamb's paradox that the greatest of all playwrights wrote works not suited for the stage, or at least for the stage of early nineteenth-century England. He would not, perhaps, endorse Lamb's assertion that Shakespeare's characters are "the objects of meditation rather than of interest or curiosity as to their actions," [10] but by hard experience he had learned that almost all productions of the plays were bad, and like most perceptive readers he preferred his own interpretations to a vulgar mishmash on the stage. [11] Even the best production, he said, abused "the genius of the poet." [12] Some were "mortifying," [13] and the really bad ones, like the "vile jumble" of *Richard III* at Drury Lane or the absurd *Tempest* at Covent Garden, were such scandals that he wished he never had to see Shakespeare played again. [14] He occasionally saw something that reminded him "a little" of Shakespeare — if Miss O'Neill's Juliet, for example, did

---

* One of Hazlitt's few comments on the language of the plays is a remark (4.236n) quoted from "a friend" — probably Lamb — on *Hamlet*, IV.vii.167f.

not correspond to his idea, she at least did not "degrade" the role [15] —
but he generally seemed to think, and on occasion said, that writing
about plays would be a pleasant line of work if one were not obliged to
see them acted.[16]

In Shakespeare Hazlitt found an ideal subject for his kind of hiero-
phantic reading. Probing motives, testing the force of circumstance on
character, quoting endlessly, and exclaiming with delight at the wonders
thus revealed, he shows in his responses an extraordinary ardor. To be
sure, some of the pieces, like the one on *Troilus and Cressida*, are thin and
dry because he did not admire all the plays alike; but when he himself is
enraptured by his subjects, as in *Macbeth* and *Lear*, he tries to make us
share the thrill. The mind of Lear, he says,

is like a tall ship driven about by the winds, buffetted by the furious waves, but
that still rides above the storm, having its anchor fixed in the bottom of the sea;
or it is like the sharp rock circled by the eddying whirlpool that foams and beats
against it, or like the solid promontory pushed from its basis by the force of an
earthquake.[17]

Johnson does not surrender to his subject in this way. He has more poise
and self-control, and he keeps himself (and us) a certain distance from
the text while he formulates his judgment; moreover, when he hands it
down it is in the nature of decree. "The language of *Shakespeare* is very
licentious," he says coldly of Lear's mad scenes, "and his words have often
meanings remote from the proper and original use." [18] Hazlitt, on the
other hand, presents himself as advocate and herald. He proclaims his
author's power, and tells us to submit. The results are not uniformly
good, for one tires of exclamation points and rapture; but when he is
able to convey his own exhilaration he writes with stunning force. As he
winds around his subject his style grows rich and dark, and criticism
seems to merge with incantation. Thus, he says, in *Macbeth*

the action is desperate and the reaction is dreadful. It is a huddling together of
fierce extremes, a war of opposite natures which of them shall destroy the other.
There is nothing but what has a violent end or violent beginnings. The lights and
shades are laid on with a determined hand; the transitions from triumph to
despair, from the height of terror to the repose of death, are sudden and startling;
every passion brings in its fellow-contrary, and the thoughts pitch and jostle
against each other as in the dark. The whole play is an unruly chaos of strange
and forbidden things, where the ground rocks under our feet. Shakespear's genius
here took its full swing, and trod upon the farthest bounds of nature and passion.*

* 4.191. Hazlitt's Shakespearean criticism often exemplifies the creed that he elsewhere tried to formulate abstractly. In "Thoughts on Taste" (17.57–66), which he contributed to the *Edinburgh Magazine* in 1818, he defines genius as "the power of
producing excellence" and taste as "the power of perceiving the excellence thus produced." To proportion "admiration to power, pleasure to beauty," he explains, requires not knowledge, judgment, and detachment but sympathy and intuitive percep-

THE MAKING OF A CRITIC

Because he *feels* the force of Shakespeare's characters he responds to them as he would to living people. He tells us that Lady Macbeth is "a great bad woman, whom we hate, but whom we fear more than we hate"; [19] that Goneril and Regan are so detestable he does not even like to say their names; [20] that he cannot "forgive" Hal's rejection of Falstaff; [21] that Portia and Nerissa do not appeal to him as women, [22] whereas his affection for Imogen is as great as hers for Posthumus; [23] that Richard II's sufferings as a man "make us forget that he ever was a king"; [24] that Henry V is a "very amiable monster" [25] and Richard III a man not striving "to be great, but to be greater than he is." [26] Whatever the merits of such subjective criticism, its defects are clear. Hazlitt's own involvement with the characters is so deep and intimate that on occasion it almost stifles judgment. He is attracted or repelled, and tries to tell us why; but he often seems oblivious of the plays as works of art. He refuses to stay outside the action or to assume a critic's stance. It had been a commonplace of eighteenth-century critics to say that Shakespeare rose above the "rules," and so Hazlitt's refusal to invoke them hardly calls for explanation; but we sometimes wish for less subjective commentary and more objective judgment. We can hardly disagree when he remarks that to clamp the so-called unities of time and place on *Antony and Cleopatra* would kill its passion and "perspective," and convert a play of surging force into "a smartly contested, three hours' inaugural disputation"; [27] but as we pant after Hazlitt we lack the solid footing that rule and precept could provide. With him, as with certain modern critics, the need to explore his own reaction seems more important than the duty of expounding works of art. Sometimes his idolatrous response intrudes itself between the reader and the play.

Despite his gift for observations that illuminate the text as with a lightning flash, he does not try to frame a systematic view of Shakespeare's art. The plays move him not to analysis, but to a series of ejaculations. Some of his peripheral comments are so good that one wishes he had been able, or willing, to pause and work them out; but they come to him as *aperçus* rather than as principles of explanation. It is splendid when he says that *Antony and Cleopatra* is full of a "pervading comprehensive power," [28] that Romeo is Hamlet in love, [29] that to read *A Midsummer Night's Dream* is "like wandering in a grove by moonlight," [30] that *Lear* is the greatest of the plays because Shakespeare was "most in earnest" when he wrote it; [31] but it would be better if he, like Coleridge,

---

tion. It requires intense involvement in a work of art, and therefore the "ultimate and only conclusive proof of taste" is enthusiasm. For other, later statements of this theme see 8.224, 11.161f., 12.102, 158, 20.386–391.

had tried to expand and generalize upon such sharp but scattered insights. An occasional sputtering digression on politics is an unsatisfactory substitute.[32]

      ✦ ✦ ✦

Hazlitt's attitude toward Shakespeare is essentially emotional, and his emotion is the gauge by which he tests the plays. Thus, unlike Johnson, he preferred the tragedies because he thought "that the greatest strength of genius is shewn in describing the strongest passions"; [33] and unlike Coleridge he refused to treat the playwright as a systematic thinker, or even as an artist who took thought about his art, because he regarded drama as a heightened and impassioned kind of "truth" rather than a mode of exposition. He held that the "perfect" artistic imagination is, like nature, "unconscious" of its power,[34] and that because Shakespeare "saw every thing by intuition" he was the sublimest type of genius.[35] Some poets, like Chaucer, keep their ideas "labelled, ticketed and parcelled out in a set form, in pews and compartments by themselves," and bring them out when needed; but Shakespeare's mind, he says, worked otherwise. It illuminated even the deepest truths of nature with a "radiant light" that transcends the normal modes of intellection.[36] In *Hamlet*, for example, "there is no attempt to force an interest: every thing is left for time and circumstances to unfold. The attention is excited without effort, the incidents succeed each other as matters of course, the characters think and speak and act just as they might do, if left entirely to themselves." Unlike lesser men, Shakespeare did not paraphrase, describe, or comment on the truth of nature; instead, he gave "the original text, that we may judge for ourselves." [37] Because his creations have "the force of things upon the mind" [38] they do not stand for this or that; they simply *are*, and they require the same response that life itself requires. Our reaction to his work is not as to an artifact but as to elemental things. In the crucible of his imaginative power he fused himself with what he wrote about, so that he "appears to have been all the characters, and in all the situations he describes," [39] and we, in reading him, are subject to the same mutations. Hamlet, therefore, is astonishingly real because he stamps himself upon our minds: "it is *we* who are Hamlet." [40] On the other hand, *Measure for Measure* baffles us because, despite its strength, there is "in general a want of passion; the affections are at a stand; our sympathies are repulsed and defeated in all directions.[41]

Such an aesthetic does not encourage one to expound the moral meaning of a work of art. Although Johnson charged that Shakespeare is "so much more careful to please than to instruct, that he seems to write without any moral purpose," [42] Hazlitt turned this alleged defect into a virtue. Shakespeare, he said, has nothing to do with morality, "for morality (commonly so called) is made up of antipathies, and his talent consisted in sympathy with human nature, in all its shapes, degrees, depressions, and elevations." [43] Even his disreputable characters, like Pistol, Nym, and Bardolph, are drawn with such consummate tact and truth that they mock our moral judgments. "Shakespeare takes up the meanest subjects with the same tenderness that we do an insect's wing, and would not kill a fly." [44] Only one of his works, *The Taming of the Shrew*, may be said to have a "downright moral"; [45] the other, greater plays have no designs upon the reader, and they do not formulate a doctrine: they merely tell the truth. Although Juliet's speech of longing for her lover might offend the hypocrites, it is, says Hazlitt, a "pure effusion of nature," which the feelings of the heart can sanctify without disguise. [46] For like nature itself, Shakespeare's art transcends our little categories. "We confess we are a little shocked at the want of refinement in those who are shocked at the want of refinement in Hamlet." [47] Macbeth and Richard III are both ambitious, Hotspur and Prince Hal both gallant, Falstaff and Parolles both cowardly, but none is like the other. Shakespeare "produced a world of men and women as distinct, as true and as various as those that exist in nature," and when all is said and done it is his supreme distinction to be able to convey such "truth." [48]

Within the limits of his rather sprawling book Hazlitt finds room to state (or restate) his theories of comedy and tragedy, his prejudices about politics, his doctrine of poetic power, his high opinion of Boccaccio, his objections to a psychology of mechanism, and his opinion of Mrs. Siddons, Kemble, Kean, and other famous actors of the day: but it is in exploring Shakespeare's characters that he writes the best. Then he exemplifies the gusto, power, and passion that he regards as the unique effect of art. [49] His chief distinction as a critic lies precisely here, in his ability to perceive the imaginative truth of art and to convey the rapture that he feels. At the very start of his career in journalism, in a striking essay on "Mr. Kean's Iago," [50] he had offended Leigh Hunt and others by his audacious comments on Iago as a "genius" of "diseased intellectual activity" and on Desdemona as a woman not immune to sexual desire; and this early piece epitomizes the critical temper that informs his riper work. He tried to "read" a character as one might "read" a page of print. He regarded art as the most certain source of truth, and Shakespeare as the greatest of all artists because he cut through cant, parochial morality, and received opinion to show how people really act, and why. Hazlitt does not expound or analyze; he merely gives his own response, and as he whirls along he sweeps the reader up with him. In reading *Hamlet*, he said, "we catch the passions living as they rise." [51]

His effort is to feel with Shakespeare's characters, not to test them by a theory. He identifies himself with them and says what they would say if they could talk about themselves. He tells us, for example, that Shylock is not the object of a maudlin pity, but a man whose pride almost ennobles him; [52] that in Romeo and Juliet the lovers' passion is based on pleasure they had not experienced, for "all that was to come of life was theirs"; [53] that "the sense of weakness leaning on the strength of its affections for support" gives to Imogen a woman's "true perfection." [54] In his accommodating way Hazlitt seems to merge with the character he describes, and to look out upon the world through another pair of eyes. He is particularly good at discriminating characters only superficially alike. Although Richard III and Macbeth are both "courageous, cruel, treacherous," he says, one of them is a hardened knave, coarse-grained and unperceptive, the other an uncommon man racked by a kind of double vision. Macbeth "stands in doubt between the world of reality and the world of fancy. He sees sights not shown to mortal eye, and hears unearthly music. All is tumult and disorder within and without his mind; his purposes recoil upon himself, are broken and disjointed; he is the double thrall of his passions and his evil destiny." [55]

If *Characters of Shakespear's Plays* is rich in such moments of illumination it is also often banal. To read this famous book is to understand why Hazlitt is the most uneven of our major critics, for he writes well only when his cue is admiration. A man who defines the highest art in terms of power and passion is not likely to be stirred by formal grace or artifice. Obsessed with Lear's titanic force, he himself is galvanized, but the dainty arabesques of *Love's Labour's Lost* offend him: "it is as if the hand of Titian had been employed to give grace to the curls of a full-bottomed periwig." [56] Although Hazlitt, unlike Johnson and Arnold, does not succeed with things that fail to energize his own emotions, at any rate he knew his tastes and limitations. [57] Work that he regards as bad or mediocre seems to blunt his mind, and to make him querulous or dull, but when his "sympathy" is aroused "in an extraordinary degree" [58] he rises to a height that his rivals almost never reach. When he wearily dismisses Mercutio as "spirited" [59] or describes Cressida and Pandarus as "amusing and instructive" [60] he is clearly writing from a sense of duty, but when he describes Cleopatra as "the triumph of the voluptuous" [61] we understand Keats's comment on his "fiery laconiscism." [62] Johnson pointed out that we tend to rate a living writer by his worst production, a dead one by his best. On that principle, and mindful of the stirring essays on *Othello* and *Macbeth*, we can find a place for Hazlitt near the top of those who have written greatly on the greatest of all writers.

THE LITERATURE OF ENGLAND

Hazlitt's three sets of lectures in 1818–19 on the English poets, the English comic writers, and Elizabethan literature may be said to have completed his education as a critic and to have secured his reputation. If prompted by his urgent need for money, like almost everything he wrote, they also served a larger end, for they enabled him, for the first and only time in his career, to deal extensively with literature as an object of delight and contemplation. Released from the journalistic mill, he read, reread, and thought about the literature of England, and moved beyond the bustle and the rancor of contemporary affairs to what he himself regarded as the timeless realm of art. Books were his great solace, as he said in working up his Elizabethan lectures, and with them he never felt ennui.[1] He had a poignant sense of change and evanescence,[2] and in a world where envious and calumniating time laid its blight on almost everything, he, like Keats in meditating on the Grecian urn, found permanence in those "eternal forms of truth and beauty" that sustain us all through life.[3] Words are "the only things that last for ever," he remarked,[4] and when hammered to the shape of truth they can suffer no attrition or decay. "The poet's verse slides into the current of our blood. We read them when young, we remember them when old."[5] When Griselda shows her "patient sorrow," when Lear invokes the heavens that, like him, are old, and when Titian's haughty young Venetian glares at us from the canvas, we know that art can have no date, because its power never fails.

And what have we left to console us for all this? Why, we have Mr. Rogers's "Pleasures of Memory," and Mr. Campbell's "Pleasures of Hope"; Mr. Westall's pictures, and all West's; Miss Burney's new novel (which is, however, some comfort), Miss Edgeworth's Fashionable Tales, Madame de Staël's next work, whatever it may be, and the praise of it in the *Edinburgh Review*, and Sir James Macintosh's *History*.[6]

Turning from the present, with its busy little men trying to seem greater than they are, he sought the mighty, tranquil dead, and with them he found repose. They took one from time into eternity. Since death itself, which "cancels everything but truth," is "a sort of natural canonization," as he said when Byron died,[7] it is not until a man is dead that we are able to assess his merits. For a writer to complain that he is not enough esteemed is to forget that glory is the residue of time, and that the judgment of posterity can be neither bargained for nor hurried.[8]

Genius is the heir of fame; but the hard condition on which the bright reversion must be earned is the loss of life. Fame is the recompense not of the living, but of the dead. The temple of fame stands upon the grave: the flame that burns upon its altars is kindled from the ashes of great men. Fame itself is immortal, but it is not begot till the breath of genius is extinguished. For fame is not popularity, the shout of the multitude, the idle buzz of fashion, the venal puff, the soothing flattery of favour or of friendship; but it is the spirit of a man surviving himself in the minds and thoughts of other men, undying and imperishable.[9]

Although composed as independent units, each with a title and a subject of its own, the three sets of lectures are really one long disquisition on the literature of England. Each consists of a general introduction and seven other lectures, in roughly chronological order, on books and writers germane to the subject, but within their sprawling limits Hazlitt ranges very freely. There were four great categories of English literature that were excellent, he said: Elizabethan and Jacobean tragedy, Restoration comedy, the periodical essay, and the eighteenth-century novel;[10] and it is these, together with Chaucer, Spenser, and Milton, that he writes about with the greatest ardor and effect. Even when he dutifully tries to cover other things he seems to be impatient or fatigued, and there are many things, of course, that he does not treat at all. Thus in his lecture on the minor eighteenth-century poets he gives short shrift to Shenstone, Akenside, Goldsmith, and Warton; refuses even to discuss their fellows on the ground that "it will be hard to persuade so many respectable persons that they are dull writers, and if we give them any praise, they will send others"; and dismisses Chatterton in a condescending coda that gave offense to Keats.[11] The intrusion of Sidney's *Arcadia* into a lecture nominally concerned with eighteenth-century poetry [12] and a long digression on Voltaire and Rabelais in a piece on Swift [13] shows that he was not burdened by chronology, and the fact that he adopted or reused scores of things that he had printed in *The Round Table*, the *Edinburgh Review*, and elsewhere suggests that the lectures were, in part at least, an exercise in carpentry.*

* Sometimes he lifts short passages from his earlier work, like the comments on Joseph Munden (5.278) and John Liston (18.251f.) that reappear in his lecture on Restoration comedy (6.71, 159) and those on Molière (20.10 f.) that recur in his account of wit and humor (6.27f.). Often, however, his borrowings from himself are more extensive, like that hardy perennial "Why the Arts Are Not Progressive" (5.44f.) which had already gone through various transformations (see pages 270 f.). His early letters to the *Morning Chronicle* on the decline of modern comedy (see page 194n), one

They were also celebrations of the fact of genius. As always, he was sparse with dates and unconcerned with mere details, for he had small respect for scholars and none at all for the kind of scholarship that demanded systematic exposition. Although he no doubt knew such standard works as Warton's *History of English Poetry* and occasionally alludes to Johnson's famous *Lives*, it is clear that no one who cites "Mother Hubberds Tale" as one of the best parts of *The Shepheardes Calender* [14] and dusts off Drayton in half a dozen lines [15] can be regarded as a slave to secondary material or devoted to the minutiae of literary investigation. Since the "obscure and trivial researches of antiquarianism" did not interest him, [16] he said, he did not try "to adjust the spelling, or restore the pointing" of the authors whom he treated. To "draw the curtain of Time, and shew the picture of Genius" was all that he desired to do. [17]

I do not come to the task with a pair of compasses or a ruler in my pocket, to see whether a poem is round or square, or to measure its mechanical dimensions, like a meter and alnager of poetry: it is not in my bond to look after excisable articles or contraband wares, or to exact severe penalties and forfeitures for trifling oversights, or to give formal notice of violent breaches of the three unities, of geography and chronology; or to distribute printed stamps and poetical licences (with blanks to be filled up) on Mount Parnassus.

Instead, he proposed to treat his audience as he would treat a friend in talking of his favorite books, "to feel what was good, and to 'give a reason for the faith that was in me' when necessary, and when in my power." [18]

Consequently his lectures tend to be a record of his admirations. He is at his best not when spying faults but when unfolding beauties, and if they are beauties that have been neglected or denied his delight is all the greater. When he discusses Congreve's Millamant, [19] for instance, or Tristram Shandy's Uncle Toby ("one of the finest compliments ever paid to human nature"), [20] or the *terrible graces of the obscure, forgotten Webster*," [21] he creates literature even as he writes about it. With a prodigal expense of talent, as he skims along he throws off flashing phrases that illuminate his pages. He says that almost all of Crabbe's characters "are tired of their lives, and you heartily wish them dead"; [22] that Tom

---

of which had already been reprinted in *The Round Table* (4.10–14), turn up in his lectures on the comic writers (6.149–154); his Round Table papers "On the Tatler" (4.7–10) and on Milton (4.31–41) are altered slightly for reuse (6.95–99, 5.61ff.); and "On Hogarth's Marriage a-la-Mode" (4.25–31) inevitably finds its way into his lecture on Hogarth in *The English Comic Writers* (6.133–138). He also made heavy use of his early *Edinburgh* reviews: the long passage on classic and romantic drama in the final Elizabethan lecture (6.348–354) was drawn from his review of Schlegel (16.60–66), much of his lecture on the eighteenth-century novel (6.106–132) from "Standard Novels and Romances" (16.5–24), and his remarks on Dante, Chaucer, and Spenser (5.17f., 25–44) from "Sismondi's Literature of the South" (16.42f., 53ff.).

Moore should not have written *Lalla Rookh* "even for three thousand guineas"; [23] that *The Rape of the Lock* is "the apotheosis of foppery and folly"; [24] that Chaucer "does not affect to shew his power over the reader's mind, but the power which his subject has over his own"; [25] that in *The Way of the World* "the sense of pleasure evaporates in an aspiration after something that seems too exquisite ever to have been realized"; [26] that "Milton's learning has the effect of intuition"; [27] that we sympathize with Shallow and Slender, whereas Tattle and Sparkish "are entitled to no quarter, and receive none"; [28] that *Humphry Clinker* is of all novels the one "which gives the most pleasure with the least effort to the reader"; [29] that "in Ben Jonson, we find ourselves generally in low company, and we see no hope of getting out of it"; [30] that whereas Marlowe's imagination "glows like a furnace, Heywood's is a gentle, lambent flame that purifies without consuming"; [31] that we see Milton's Satan ("the most heroic subject that ever was chosen for a poem") as "gigantic, irregular, portentous, uneasy, and disturbed — but dazzling in its faded splendour, the clouded ruins of a god." [32]

Although he does not deal extensively with theory he often draws upon the notions that he has elsewhere stated systematically, and in this respect his judgments on specific works of art may be regarded as extensions into literature of principles and attitudes that one first encounters in his "metaphysics." Thus *Don Quixote* prompts a comment on the "intuitive perception of the hidden analogies of things, or, as it may be called, this *instinct of the imagination*," [33] and Mrs. Radcliffe's Gothic novels inspire him to a florid meditation on the "poetry of romance" in which the pathos, aspiration, and nostalgia of his Romantic sensibility are brilliantly evoked. [34] No less characteristic are his remarks on Hogarth, Fielding, and other eighteenth-century "realists" whose fidelity to fact is seen as the essence of their art. *Joseph Andrews* is "a perfect piece of statistics," he says in commendation.

In looking into any regular history of that period, into a learned and eloquent charge to a grand jury or the clergy of a diocese, or into a tract on controversial divinity, we should hear only of the ascendancy of the Protestant succession, the horrors of Popery, the triumph of civil and religious liberty, the wisdom and moderation of the sovereign, the happiness of the subject, and the flourishing state of manufactures and commerce. But if we really wish to know what all these fine-sounding names come to, we cannot do better than turn to the works of those, who having no other object than to imitate nature, could only hope for success from the fidelity of their pictures; and were bound (in self-defence) to reduce the boasts of vague theorists and the exaggerations of angry disputants to the mortifying standard of reality. [35]

His most sustained attempts at systematic exposition are in the introductory lectures to each series. There he tries to frame the subject, to set forth his intentions as a critic, and to give an anchor, as it were, to the judgments that will follow in his discussion of specific books and writers. Although the first, "On Poetry in General," is filled with brilliant and often quoted things, it is not an unqualified success. As the *Quarterly Review* observed,[36] he makes poetry mean so much — a certain kind of composition, the talent that produces it, and the subjects that are treated — that he blurs distinctions essential to a definition. None the less, in this lecture he applied to literature the theory of imagination that had been growing in his mind for years, and therefore it retains importance. It proclaims the superiority of imaginative truth to the dry dictates of understanding, the use of "sympathy" as an instrument of knowledge, the transforming moral force of passion, and the futility of restrictive neoclassic rules.

Let the naturalist, if he will, catch the glow-worm, carry it home with him in a box, and find it next morning nothing but a little grey worm; let the poet or the lover of poetry visit it at evening, when beneath the scented hawthorn and the crescent moon it has built itself a palace of emerald light. This is also one part of nature, one appearance which the glow-worm presents, and that not the least interesting; so poetry is one part of the history of the human mind, though it is neither science nor philosophy. It cannot be concealed, however, that the progress of knowledge and refinement has a tendency to circumscribe the limits of the imagination, and to clip the wings of poetry. The province of the imagination is principally visionary, the unknown and undefined: the understanding restores things to their natural boundaries, and strips them of their fanciful pretensions. Hence the history of religious and poetical enthusiasm is much the same; and both have received a sensible shock from the progress of experimental philosophy. It is the undefined and uncommon that gives birth and scope to the imagination; we can only fancy what we do not know.[37]

"On Wit and Humour," which tries to show how the felt distinction "between what things are, and what they ought to be"[38] reveals itself in literature, is a complicated set of variations on themes that Hobbes and Locke had stated long before. Weaving through such concepts as the ludicrous, the comic, the ridiculous, and the humorous, Hazlitt expounds the perennially useful notion that what is unexpected or incongruous is a stimulus to laughter, and that laughter, therefore, is a mark of man's intelligence and ultimately a function of understanding rather than imagination. From his early letters on modern comedy[39] he repeats the cyclic theory that appears so often in his work,[40] and throughout he draws upon the principles that underlie his criticism of the London stage. Moreover, some of his remarks reflect such basic and recurrent themes that they epitomize his whole approach to life and art. Wit, which requires the kind of intellection that is petty, hard, and dry, could not appeal to one who made the culture of the heart the center of his moral and aesthetic theory. "To be indifferent or sceptical, requires no effort," he asserted; "to be enthusiastic and in earnest, requires a strong impulse, and collective power. Wit and humour . . . appeal to our indolence, our vanity, our weakness, and insensibility; serious and impassioned poetry appeals to our strength, our magnanimity, our virtue, and humanity." [41]

The prologue to the Elizabethan lectures shows him at his best. It is on all counts an extraordinary performance, and one of the most stirring and revealing things he ever wrote. As an excursion into *Kulturgeschichte* it presents a panoramic view of sixteenth-century thought and feeling, and as an expression of his own ideals of Protestant individualism and imaginative power it constitutes a vibrant statement of his creed of literature as an instrument of truth. The factors that converged to make the splendors of Elizabethan literature — the Reformation, the translation of the Bible, the growing knowledge of the classics, the impact of "romantic" Mediterranean culture, and colonial expansion — are vividly recalled, and so is that mighty breed of Tudor Englishmen who so greatly stirred his patriotic fervor. "Perhaps the genius of Great Britain (if I may so speak without offence or flattery), never shone out fuller or brighter, or looked more like itself, than at this period." [42] Their work was "Gothic and irregular," as he said, but it was varied, fresh, and bold, and above all it was intensely English. Everything they did was stamped with the imaginative truth that remained the finest legacy of all who speak the language Shakespeare spoke. [43]

Perhaps because his audiences — made up, as Talfourd said, of Dissenters, clerks, and businessmen [44] — had come to be instructed, Hazlitt quoted very freely in his lectures. About celebrities like Milton, Pope, and Johnson he tended to be discursive and expository, but in treating the Elizabethans, who were as new to him, almost, as to his hearers, he threaded his remarks on extremely long quotations. To do "anything like justice" to writers so obscure as Marston, Chapman, and "Deckar," he explained, one must let them be the "vouchers for their own pretensions," [45] and therefore his lectures are miniature anthologies. This technique enabled him, like Lamb, to treat "old authors" not as oddities or relics, but as writers to be read and relished. The fastidious antiquarianism and "awkward" condescension with which the poets of an earlier (and presumably more barbaric) age were usually treated infuriated him, and the deprecation of pert modernity, which runs so strong through all his work, finds a full expression in these lectures. "Pavilioned in the glittering pride of our superficial accomplishments and upstart pretensions," we assume, he said, that "grace, youth, and beauty are things of modern date — as if nature had ever been old, or the sun had first shone on our folly and presumption." [46] Generally his respect for "ancient" writers is matched by his disrespect for their successors, and in his long view of literature the decline from imaginative strength to fancy, and then to wit and "paradox," [47] had ended in a false refinement of "studied elegance and adventitious ornament, which is the result, not of nature, but of art." [48] Consequently the Elizabethan lectures are for him, as Chapman's Homer was for Keats, a voyage of discovery, and his remark that Dekker's characters "raise, revive, and give a new zest to our being" [49] catches his elation. "It is something worth living for," he says on Caesar's speech over the dead Pompey in Fletcher's *False One,* "to write or even read such poetry as this is, or to know that it has been written, or that there have been subjects on which to write it!" [50]

It was not that everything delighted him, or that he treated only authors whom he liked. Not even the Elizabethan age was "all of gold," he said, [51] and as for certain later writers, whose reputations seemed to be secure, there were some, he thought, who required a candid reassessment. Therefore the lectures swing from rapture to a tonic disrespect. No one who cited *Cato* as proof that "a uniform degree of insipidity" preserves a writer from attack [52] could be bound by conventional civilities. Thus we learn that Etherege's plays, except *The Man of Mode,* are "good for nothing," [53] and that Cibber, whom Pope had so artfully maligned, was an able and accomplished writer. [54] Moreover, we are warned to be on guard against orthodox opinion, like that which deprecated Pope and overrated Johnson. Why question Pope's title as a poet when he was obviously so very great a writer? Perhaps his "Muse never wandered with safety, but from his library to his grotto, or from his grotto into his library back again," but there she walked supreme. [55] On the other hand, the disproportion between Johnson's merits and his inflated reputation was proved by the "established rule at present" of praising him extravagantly while dissenting from "almost every one of his critical decisions." [56] His famous style was uniform and pompous, to be sure, but the words did not relate to things, and his intellectual timidity cast a blight on everything he touched.

The structure of his sentences, which was his own invention, and which has been generally imitated since his time, is a species of rhyming in prose, where one clause answers to another in measure and quantity, like the tagging of syllables at the end of a verse; the close of the period follows as mechanically as the oscillation of a pendulum, the sense is balanced with the sound; each sentence, revolving round its centre of gravity, is contained with itself like a couplet, and each paragraph forms itself into a stanza. Dr. Johnson is also a complete balance-master in the topics of morality. He never encourages hope, but he counteracts it by fear; he never elicits a truth, but he suggests some objection in answer to it. He seizes and alternately quits the clue of reason, lest it should involve him in the labyrinths of endless error: he wants confidence in himself and his fellows.*

To say that the most influential writer in recent English literature was "a lazy learned man, who liked to think and talk, better than to read or write" [57] required a valor or bravado that is one of Hazlitt's most out-standing characteristics. Sometimes, of course, it gets him into trouble: he is much too hard on Jonson (for whom, as he confessed, he had no "relish") [58] and most unfair to Sidney (whose *Arcadia* he described as "one of the greatest monuments of the abuse of intellectual power upon record").† He, like everyone, is dull in summarizing plots of plays; he is ill-informed about Donne [59] and hostile to his kind of poetry,‡ and less than fair to Cowper.[60] But when treating books that stir his admiration and thus evoke a strong response he thinks and writes as well as any critic in the language. His lectures on Restoration comedy [61] and the eighteenth-century novel [62] reveal both extraordinary flashes of percep-tion and also a steady driving power that conveys a real *élan*; those on the great quartet of English poets — those few "top-names" usually "cried up for form's sake, and to save the national character" [63] — show him at his brilliant best. The lectures on Chaucer and Spenser, Shake-speare and Milton, are classics of Romantic criticism because they bring into alignment the giants of English literature as exemplars of imagina-tive truth. The poet of "real life," the poet of romance, the poet of nature, and the poet of morality are discriminated very subtly, but all are seen to share one common and defining characteristic that all great artists share: an absorbing interest in their subject, which means that their

---

* 6.102. Hazlitt's comments on Johnson are almost always in the nature of dissent. Elsewhere he attacks his views on Milton (4.36–41), his qualifications as an editor of Shakespeare (4.174–178), the "privileged dulness" of *Rasselas* (19.14), his remarks on *Henry VIII* (4.303), and above all else his style (4.72). It is hardly surprising that a conservative critic in the *New Monthly Magazine* (X [1818], 200) denounced his "idiot raving" against so great a man.

† 6.320; cf. 5.98. In 1823, in the *London Magazine*, Lamb (*Works*, I, 743f.) wrote with unaccustomed heat on "the wantonness (I wish I could treat it by a gentler name) with which W. H. takes every occasion of insulting the memory of Sir Philip Sydney." The remark was no doubt prompted by Hazlitt's recent Table Talk "On Milton's Sonnets," in which he called Sidney's *Astrophel and Stella* "elaborately quaint and intricate, and more like riddles than sonnets" (8.175).

‡ 6.49ff. A few years later Hazlitt said (8.304) that he had "a higher idea of Donne from a rude, half-effaced outline of him prefixed to his poems than from any thing he ever wrote." For his memories of Lamb's defense of Donne at a Wednesday evening party some "twenty years ago" see 17.124f.

commitment to the truth of nature is stronger than their interest in themselves.[64]

It is this that makes them stand so tall above all modern competition. Hazlitt was convinced that his own age — which we regard so highly — had lost the imaginative vigor essential to produce great literature. The fact that science and modern philosophy tended "to circumscribe the limits of the imagination, and to clip the wings of poetry"[65] meant that modern poets did not show the "venturous magnanimity" that their predecessors had in such abundance[66] and that literature itself had sunk to "art," technique, and false refinement.[67] Even in Wordsworth, the greatest of the living English poets, a "devouring egotism" had become the primal force, and therefore poetry, once alive with "imaginative splendour and human passion" was reduced to a narrow, paltry thing — a vent for the poet's self-esteem and a "mere effusion" of his natural sensibility.

Milton and Shakespeare did not so understand poetry. They gave a more liberal interpretation both to nature and art. They did not do all they could to get rid of the one and the other, to fill up the dreary void with the Moods of their own Minds. They owe their power over the human mind to their having had a deeper sense than others of what was grand in the objects of nature, or affecting in the events of human life. But to the men I speak of there is nothing interesting, nothing heroical, but themselves.[68]

In his famous peroration to *Lectures on the English Poets* Hazlitt elaborates this point into a critical tour de force that stands as one of his most notable achievements. Beginning with a deep-toned meditation on the theme of time and fame he reaches the assertion that since "no applause, however loud and violent, can anticipate or over-rule the judgment of posterity" an artist's sole desire should be to state the truth as he has seen it, and not to seek acclaim.

Was Raphael, think you, when he painted his pictures of the Virgin and Child in all their inconceivable truth and beauty of expression, thinking most of his subject or of himself? Do you suppose that Titian, when he painted a landscape, was pluming himself on being thought the finest colourist in the world, or making himself so by looking at nature? Do you imagine that Shakespeare, when he wrote Lear or Othello, was thinking of any thing but Lear and Othello?[69]

Compared with these great men, whose commitment was to "truth and nature" and who annihilated self, the moderns cut a sorry figure. They rely for their effects on shock, technique, and self-expression, and forget that their own wants and needs are not the only source of art. Whereas the work of Rogers "is refined, and frittered away into an appearance of the most evanescent brilliancy and tremulous imbecility,"[70] the fastidious Campbell is so much afraid of doing wrong that he will take no chances

— and "no writer who thinks habitually of the critics, either to tremble at their censures or set them at defiance, can write well." [71] Tom Moore's talent cannot conceal his essential frivolity; Byron's passion is the passion of a mind that preys upon itself, "disgusted with, or indifferent to all other things"; [72] Scott writes "easy, animated verse," but "the Notes to his poems are just as entertaining as the poems themselves, and his poems are only entertaining." [73]

Then he comes to Wordsworth. The only living poet whose work is likely to survive, he raises egotism to the realm of art, says Hazlitt, but it is egotism none the less.

His poetry is not external, but internal; it does not depend upon tradition, or story, or old song; he furnishes it from his own mind, and is his own subject. He is the poet of mere sentiment. Of many of the Lyrical Ballads, it is not possible to speak in terms of too high praise, such as Hart-leap Well, the Banks of the Wye, Poor Susan, parts of the Leech-gatherer, the lines to a Cuckoo, to a Daisy, the Complaint, several of the Sonnets, and a hundred others of inconceivable beauty, of perfect originality and pathos. They open a finer and deeper vein of thought and feeling than any poet in modern times has done, or attempted. [74]

And then, having quoted "Hart-Leap Well" as one of his prime favorites, he interprets Wordsworth and the other so-called Lakists as the products of an age of revolution that they had subsequently betrayed.

There was a mighty ferment in the heads of statesmen and poets, kings and people. According to the prevailing notions, all was to be natural and new. Nothing that was established was to be tolerated. . . . It was a time of promise, a renewal of the world and of letters; and the Deucalions, who were to perform this feat of regeneration, were the present poet-laureat and the two authors of the Lyrical Ballads. . . . They founded the new school on a principle of sheer humanity, on pure nature void of art. [75]

When this "mighty ferment" spent itself, however, the poets were driven back upon themselves, and there they had reposed, with art supplanting nature and their complicated states of mind the "principle of sheer humanity." A studiously terse account of Southey leads to "Mr. Coleridge," who, for all his faults, is described as "the only person I ever knew who answered to the idea of a man of genius," [76] and with a moving valediction to his departed glory Hazlitt closes his account of English poets.

I have thus gone through the task I intended, and have come at last to the level ground. I have felt my subject gradually sinking from under me as I advanced, and have been afraid of ending in nothing. The interest has unavoidably decreased at almost every successive step of the progress, like a play that has its catastrophe in the first or second act. This, however, I could not help. I have done as well as I could. [77]

VII

Politics and Literature

IDEALS

Hazlitt's comment that he was neither a politician nor a party-man, but merely one who hated tyranny, despised its tools, and expressed his feelings "as often and as strongly" as he could [1] provides a theme of sorts for all his sprawling and uneven work on politics. Since this work embraces things so unlike as the *Essay* on benevolence, the *Reply* to Malthus, the savage journalism of his middle years, and the elephantine life of Napoleon — to say nothing of a hundred essays and reviews where his political opinions continually intrude themselves — it would be absurd to claim that it develops and sustains a systematic theory of political behavior. At the start of his career, still throbbing with an ardor for reform, he was intent on finding philosophic sanctions for humanitarian ethics, and at the end, bruised by thirty years of subjection to Toryism, he was mainly concerned with protecting individual rights; but this development represents a shift of emphasis rather than a change of view. There is nothing to suggest that he relinquished the convictions that he adopted as a boy and defended as a man, and if these convictions were not stylish in his later years, as he was fond of saying, they at least were firm.

I have no mind to have my person made a property of, nor my understanding made a dupe of. I deny that liberty and slavery are convertible terms, that right and wrong, truth and falsehood, plenty and famine, the comforts or wretchedness of a people, are matters of perfect indifference. That is all I know of the matter; but on these points I am likely to remain incorrigible, in spite of any arguments I have seen used to the contrary. [2]

This is not very sophisticated, perhaps, but it reminds us that Hazlitt had very little taste — or talent — for theory and abstraction, and a very great regard for "facts" and the "feelings" they inspired. As his *Reply* to Malthus and his journalism show at tedious length, he almost always substituted passion for statistics and rhetoric for logic in treating social problems. If he did not always sound like Elijah calling down destruction on the priests of Baal — as when he described the principle of Legitimacy, or hereditary succession in monarchies, as "absolute, un-ceasing, unerring, fatal, unutterable, abominable, monstrous" [3] — he usually made it clear that his adversaries were bold, bad men who flouted elemental decencies, not merely persons who had fallen into error. When, on rare occasions, he tried to be expository and calm, violence shattered his precarious repose, and he yielded to a moral indignation that often verged on mania. "You would tear out this mighty heart of a nation," he thundered at the Tories in one of his nonstop diatribes,

and lay it bare and bleeding at the foot of despotism: you would slay the mind of a country to fill up the dreary aching void with the old, obscene, drivelling prejudices of superstition and tyranny: you would tread out the eye of Liberty (the light of nations) like "a vile jelly," that mankind may be led about darkling to its endless drudgery, like the Hebrew Sampson (shorn of his strength and blind), by his insulting taskmasters: you would make the throne every thing, and the people nothing, to be yourself less than nothing, a very slave, a reptile, a creeping, cringing sycophant, a court favorite, a pander to Legitimacy — that detestable fiction, which would make you and me and all mankind its slaves or victims . . .

— and so on for two hundred words or so —

and confounds all sense of justice, reason, truth, liberty, humanity, in one low servile deathlike dread of power without limit and without remorse! [4]

Despite a bent for such dithyrambic sentences, which heave and coil with passion, Hazlitt was capable of cool and penetrating comments on England's social problems. He suggested, for example, that the sacred rights of property might be legally restricted; [5] he made sensible pro-posals for revising the barbaric penal code; * he advocated labor unions; [6] he even defended the laborer's right to strike. [7] But for the most part he did not concern himself with specific social and economic questions, and when he did he usually sounded rather foolish. Thus he seriously proposed a tax on hunting dogs and horses as a cure for England's fiscal ailments after Waterloo, [8] and he diagnosed these ailments as a conse-quence of too much "unproductive" labor, [9] without conceding that twenty years of war — with full employment and inflation — had generated problems for which the wicked Tories were not alone responsible. He

---

* Hazlitt's long article on penal reform in the *Edinburgh Review* in 1821 (19.216–255) develops the proposals that he had first advanced in a little piece (19.324–329) commissioned in 1812 by Basil Montagu, president of the Society for the Diffusion of Knowledge upon the Punishment of Death. See page 191n.

tended to regard any attempt to deal objectively with social questions as a case of special pleading for the *status quo,* and therefore he distrusted those like Malthus, Mill, Ricardo, and McCulloch who, in our jargon, might qualify as social scientists. In his view, *An Essay on the Principle of Population* was one of "the poisonous ingredients thrown into the cauldron of Legitimacy 'to make it thick and slab' ";[10] the allegedly "fixed and unalterable" laws by which Malthus and his kind explained the misery of the poor were contrived to gratify the well-to-do;[11] and the so-called "science" of economics was built upon "the caprice, insolence, luxury, prejudices, and insensibility of the rich."[12] His own approach to social problems was somewhat more direct:

It is some difference whether a man has one or two meals a day, whether he has meat for his dinner once a week or not, whether he does or does not lie, coarsely indeed, but warm, whether he is in rags or decently and comfortably clad? All these distinctions are looked down upon from the lofty heights of Political Economy Lecture-Desks, and lost in the cant phrase, *the lowest possible means of subsistence.*[13]

That Hazlitt's career as a political journalist coincided with one of the gravest and most stirring epochs in modern British history is a fact that must be kept in mind. Although as a boy he had merely watched the tumult of the nineties, he came to his professional majority in the years before and after Waterloo; and to recall the main political events between 1812 (when he began reporting Parliamentary speeches) and 1819 (when his *Political Essays* appeared) is to realize that the time was one of crisis. With difficulty the Tories had survived a series of afflictions: in 1809 the Convention of Cintra (which had dashed the hopes of Spanish patriots), the disastrous Walcheren expedition, the charges brought against the Duke of York (for maladministration of the army) and against Castlereagh and Perceval (for Parliamentary corruption) had stirred the gravest discontent; in 1810, after the king went permanently insane, the Regency Bill had exacerbated party strife; in 1811 the Luddite riots in the Midlands had led many men to think that rebellion was at hand; in 1812 the prime minister had been assassinated in the lobby of the House of Commons. By 1813 it was clear that Napoleon's power was waning, and when the Congress of Vienna met the following year — with Castlereagh as head of the English delegation — the long, hard task of restoring European thrones began. Then, in 1815, came Napoleon's escape from Elba and the Allies' triumph at Waterloo, but no sooner was the peace secured than England began to taste the bitter fruits of victory and the consequences — hitherto suppressed — of the Industrial Revolution. The high rents, high taxes, tight money, and

LEIGH HUNT
By Benjamin Robert Haydon
The National Portrait Gallery

JOHN KEATS
By Joseph Severn?
The Harvard Keats Collection

mercantile restrictions required for waging war were continued when the war had ended, and the resulting discontent among the "laboring poor" was a source of terror and dismay to the well-to-do. Agricultural riots in the eastern counties, misery and very vocal disaffection in the manufacturing districts, the Spa Fields riots in London, the suspension of habeas corpus,* acts and proclamations to prevent seditious meetings, repeated rejections of Catholic emancipation and Parliamentary reform, the Peterloo Massacre (in which a charge of cavalry and yeomen was used to suppress a public meeting) † — such events explained but, as many thought, did not justify the repressive Six Acts of 1819, which showed that the Tories were resolved to preserve the *status quo*. It is hardly surprising that between 1815 and 1822 three leading politicians — Whitbread, Romilly, and Castlereagh — committed suicide.

Since it was these events, and many others like them, that Hazlitt wrote about as journalist, we should not be surprised that his journalism has a certain edge. In his own day his opinions were commonly decried as "radical" — a word that carried immense opprobrium in early nineteenth-century England — and ever since it has been customary to regard them as an embarrasing intrusion into his more important work. That they are radical is true, but that they are unrelated to his other work is false, for they represent the extension into politics of the attitudes and values that he held all his life. Apart from expressing this or that opinion, they show the gritty individualism and arrogance of the nonconformist, with the reverence for "principle" and the "captious hostility" to majority opinion that were his defining characteristics. Moreover, they reflect the social and political ideals that had fired the boy at Hackney and that remained his *lares* to the end. In his contempt for the statutory security of the Established Church no less than in his strident disrespect for George III and all his progeny we hear the nonconformist's voice; and beneath the agitated surface of his social commentary we see that he never strayed far from the canon of individual rights, popular sovereignty, and toleration that for Dissenters like his father was a set of assumptions felt as facts.

He did not merely appropriate these notions, but laced them into

---

* It was the suspension of habeas corpus in 1817 that caused Cobbett (whose influence the Tories regarded as malign) to drop his *Political Register* and take his family to America. To think that he would walk in the fields and lie in his bed "merely at the mercy of a Secretary of State" was intolerable, he said (*Autobiography* [ed. William Reitzel, 1947], p. 146), for "neither the song of the birds in spring, nor the well-thatched homestead in winter, could make me forget that I and my family were slaves."

† Peterloo was "an unfortunate business," Southey conceded (*Life and Correspondence*, p. 278), but he regarded the magistrates' use of yeomanry instead of "disciplined troops" as "a natural and pardonable mistake."

the fabric of his thought. Whatever we may think of his "discovery" of benevolence as the "principle of human action," it is clear that his strenuous work in "metaphysics" was, at least in part, an effort to protect his own ideals, and that it led him, later, to his most important theme in criticism. Having showed, or tried to show, that imagination is the liberating faculty by which we project ourselves beyond our narrow needs and identify ourselves with other things and people, he proceeded to explain our creation of and response to art in similar terms, or at any rate as products of the same projectile power; and so ultimately he brought all of man's activities, social and aesthetic, into a rough alignment. Throughout his work the recurrent metaphors are of heart and mind, passion and restraint, imagination and reason; and they express the polarities of those expansive and restrictive impulses that in his view govern our behavior. Although his political writings are mainly staccato commentaries on a species of political privilege that, as he thought, made political morality absurd, they flow from and help to define his moral and philosophic values. Therefore his political pronouncements, though often riddled with invective and coarsely hostile to existing institutions, are not merely the sputterings of a malcontent: they are predicated on the notion that man becomes a truly social creature only when he forgoes reason, prudence, and self-interest to follow the promptings of his heart. Like most political thinkers after Locke — Shaftesbury, Rousseau, Tom Paine, and others — he did not seek theological sanctions for government, but he was much concerned with morals; and as he tried to relate man's behavior as a member of society to the workings of imagination he found a fundamental theme: "passion . . . is the essence, the chief ingredient in moral truth; and the warmth of passion is sure to kindle the light of imagination on the objects around it." [14]

Complementing, and at times almost obscuring, this social and humanitarian strain was his concern for individual rights. This, the clearest sign of his lasting obligation to the ethos of Dissent, deepened as he aged, and by the end of his life it had assumed the status of a ruling passion. Since no man who feeds upon his own emotions can always be consistent, and no man not an idiot can at fifty retain unsullied and unchanged the opinions of his youth, it is not surprising that in Hazlitt's later years the notion of "disinterested" behavior lost something of its bloom. On the other hand, his conviction that each man has the right and duty to assert his "personal identity" suffered no attrition with the passing years. As a young Dissenter he thought that freedom of conscience was a moral absolute; as a fire-breathing journalist he built his politics upon the notion; as an essayist on morals, men, and manners he exemplified and continued to assert the same conviction.

Although one meets the theme everywhere in Hazlitt's work, it is stated with exceptional precision in his "Project for a New Theory of Civil and Criminal Legislation," [15] a piece that he wrote (and failed to publish) a year or so before his death. In a sense completing the unfinished schoolboy essay that he had begun some thirty years before at Hackney, the "Project" does not increase the stock of human wisdom, but it does express in stark and systematic terms one of his fundamental notions. The beginning and the end of civil legislation, we learn, is the protection of each man's right to gratify his own desires. This right needs no support from the "scaly finger" of Hobbes's Leviathan, or Burke's "cloudy sophistry," or Bentham's calculus of pain and pleasure, or Godwin's "omnipotence of reason." It is the expression of an individual's will, and since a thing's being willed "is the most absolute moral reason for its existence," it requires no sanction but itself.[16] It is "the duty which each man owes to himself; or it is that portion of the general good of which (as being principally interested) he is made the special judge, and which is put under his immediate keeping." [17] Although in theory absolute, in fact this right is limited because not all men have the same desires, and therefore governments are formed to adjudicate their claims and control the assertion of their rights. By measuring "the wills of individuals in equal portions" it cushions the shock of man's collision with his fellows, and by enforcing certain minimal restraints it guarantees a maximum of freedom. In the strong tradition of Dissent, Hazlitt conceives of society as an aggregation of discrete entities, and he justifies its "aggregate" coercive power only as the consequence of the separate and "inherent" rights of each of its constituents.

Ignoring questions of administration and finance, Hazlitt proceeds to describe his ideal commonwealth of very rugged individualists. Since "the rage of legislation is the first vice of society," [18] he says (as Dissenters had been saying for a hundred years and more), the proper role of government must be narrowly defined: it is the protection of those liberties — of person, action, property, and opinion — that each man "may especially call his own." Thus a person given to arson, or to the indiscriminate use of daggers, must be curbed because he constitutes a threat to others; but because no man has a right to the products of another's toil, "combinations among labourers for the rise of wages are always just and lawful, as much as those among master manufacturers to keep them down." [19] In everything that pertains to morals and opinion the citizen is of course immune. Drunkenness, gambling, lechery, and Methodism are perhaps unfortunate, but they are not therefore liable to governmental check.

> There should be no secular interference in sacred things; no laws to suppress or establish any church or sect in religion, no religious persecutions, tests, or disqualifications; the different sects should be left to inveigle and hate each other as much as they please; but without the love of exclusive domination and spiritual power there would be little temptation to bigotry and intolerance. [20]

In short, government exists to preserve the individual's freedom by codifying the principle of self-defense or resistance to aggression against his person or his thoughts, and therefore its necessary exactions are only "little *fortalices,* with palisades and outworks about them, for RIGHT to establish and maintain itself in." [21] Its only duty is to protect the independence of its members, and when, "under pretence of the general peace and safety," it neglects that vital function, its becomes the worst of evils. [22]

In Hazlitt's work this theme of individual rights is linked with that of popular sovereignty and its corollary of progressive social change. Although, as we have seen, there were carefully preserved discrepancies between theory and practice, every responsible political theorist from Locke to Burke had reaffirmed, with varying degrees of warmth, the merits of popular sovereignty, representative government, and toleration; and as the abortive efforts of the Stuarts in 1715 and 1745 made clear, the majority of Englishmen were proud of their political arrangements. And with reason: for whereas most Continental nations drifted, or were pushed, deeper and deeper into absolutism throughout the eighteenth century, the English regulated their affairs by the settlement of 1689, and their liberties — a matter of astonishment to Montesquieu and Voltaire and many others — were the envy or the scandal of the age. In such circumstances a demand for real religious toleration and reform in electoral procedures seemed particularly ill-bred, for it was widely feared that such innovations would disturb the *status quo* and perhaps destroy the British constitution. Thus Burke had smitten Price and the Dissenters — the most persistent advocates of continuing reform — on the proposition that the government of England, fixed by the settlement of 1689, required no alteration. Having conceded that the accession of William and Mary had marked "a small and a temporary deviation" from precedent, [23] he would concede no more. He regarded the constitution as a sacred and entailed inheritance,[24] and he thought that any effort to change its fundamental structure should be met with criminal justice.

To this doctrine of social stability the reformers would reply, with Paine, that man has no property in man and no authority over his descendants. This was the line that Priestley took with Burke in 1791, and when he implied that only through revolts — which, when successful, develop into revolutions — do men advance toward social justice, he anticipated Hazlitt's comments on affairs in England after Waterloo. When Canning, paraphrasing Burke, remarked in 1820 that since England for more than a century had enjoyed a liberty "as perfect as ever blessed any country upon the earth" it should resist not only "visionary schemes of ideal perfectibility" but also "doubtful experiments even of possible improvement," Hazlitt was appalled. Has history stopped? he asked. Are all our struggles ended? Is man to believe that whatever is, must be? Is he to turn his back upon the future in order to venerate the past, and assume "that nothing is possible or desirable but what he finds already established to his hand in time worn institutions or inveterate abuses"? Such questions are absurd, he says.

Away then with this miserable cant against fanciful theories, and appeal to acknowledged experience! Men never act against their prejudices but from the spur of their feelings, the necessity of their situations — their theories are adapted to their practical convictions and their varying circumstances. Nature has ordered it so, and Mr. Canning, by shewing off his rhetorical paces, by his "ambling and lisping and nicknaming God's creatures," cannot invert that order, efface the history of the past, or arrest the progress of the future.[25]

Just as the Dissenters of the later eighteenth century described the settlement of 1689 as a limited achievement, not a point of permanent repose but a base for further gains, so Hazlitt tended to regard all English history as a somewhat jerky progress from bigotry and political privilege to the fullest civil and religious toleration. This is a form, perhaps, of the old providential view of history by which all change is seen as serving moral purposes; but whereas St. Augustine and Raleigh referred these purposes to God, and counseled resignation to His secret ways, reformers of Hazlitt's generation explained them otherwise, in terms of natural rights and political advantage, and urged decisive action. With a jibe at Coleridge, Hazlitt jeered at those who use the Bible as a "political palliative." "They would have us learn patience and resignation from the miraculous interpositions of Providence recorded in the Scriptures. 'When the sky falls' — the proverb is somewhat musty." [26] England's proudest hour, said Hazlitt, was when the "detestable" doctrine of divine right "first tottered and fell headless to the ground" with the head of Charles I; [27] and history made it clear that for every revolution against despotic power there should have been a hundred more, all of them successful.[28] Especially after Waterloo, when England's hereditary rulers quoted Burke but relied on the attorney-general, stifled the press, ignored minority opinion, and used its standing army as a tool for retaining un-delegated power, why should "the people" not insist upon their rights? he asked.[29] "Shall we never serve out our apprenticeship to liberty? Must our indentures to slavery bind us for life?" [30]

If in later years he tended to talk less about national resistance to tyranny and more about the slow but steady march of public opinion,[31] there can be no doubt that he preferred the temporary disorders of in-surrection to the lasting ills of despotism.[32] "Liberty must have its festi-vals, its garlands, its altars," he explained in palliation of the Reign of Terror, "and when these fail or are soiled, its tragic stage, its scaffolds, its daggers, and the slider of the guillotine." [33] If a revolution ever came to England, said one who knew him well, he, like Robespierre, would cut off heads by thousands "on a metaphysical principle." [34] His political ideals — individual rights, popular sovereignty, and progressive reform — mark the survival in an age of conservative reaction of the social opti-mism endemic among reformers of the later eighteenth century. Dis-mayed by the failure of reform and galled by the folly of reformers, he was captious about social panaceas, but he was sure that public opinion, which "necessarily tends to the general good," [35] would ulti-mately conquer superstition, error, and oppression.[36] Although a far more violent and embittered man than the pious Dr. Price, as he lay dying he again expressed the hope that Price had voiced in 1789. From the fall of the Bastille Price had inferred the quick beginning of a golden age, whereas Hazlitt, disciplined by forty years of conservative reaction, saw in the abdication of Charles X a timely proof that "the hatred of oppres-sion is 'the unconquerable flame, the worm that dies not.' " [37] However, both were certain that man's proper movement is from darkness into light, and both believed that he would one day reach his goal.

In Napoleon's career Hazlitt found a precedent and inspiration for almost all of his political ideals. Not long before his death he said that he had "staked" — and he might have added "lost" — his "health and wealth, name and fame" on the proposition that "there is a power in the people to change its government and its governors," by peaceful means if possible, but by force if necessary.[38] This conviction shapes a set of letters to the *Times,* where, at the start of his career in journalism, he argued for a nation's right to self-determination and for an easy peace with France. England had waged her "mad, mischievous, and unprincipled" war, he said, not for legitimate political purposes but to demolish an opinion,[39] and when she won the war she was eager only to reinstate the Bourbons, and thus turn back the clock of history. "The serpent's hiss, the assassin's yell, the mowing and chattering of apes, drown the voice of peace; and Vetus [that is, Edward Sterling, a writer for the *Times*], like the solemn owl, joins in the distance, and prolongs the dreary note of death."[40] Such rhetoric should not conceal the fact that for Hazlitt the fall of Napoleon — which he implausibly construed as the destruction of reform — was a personal grief and a public calamity. It meant not only that his hero had been sullied and disgraced, but that the social gains he won were lost.

Apart from a few eccentrics like Byron (who complained that the emperor's abdication meant he would never have the pleasure of seeing Castlereagh's head upon a pole)[41] and Lady Holland (who sent newspapers and fruit to the "poor dear man" on St. Helena),[42] almost everyone in England regarded Napoleon as another Tamerlane and prayed for his destruction. To Wordsworth he was the "barbarian Ravager of Europe" and the "Enemy of mankind";[43] Mackintosh placed him at the head of "the new nobility of dishonour";[44] Southey said that his "acts of perfidy, midnight murder, usurpation, and remorseless tyranny" had consigned him "to universal execration, now and for ever";[45] Shelley damned him as "a hateful and despicable being";[46] Sydney Smith thought that there was no price too great to effect the downfall of "this great disturber of human happiness,"[47] and Jeffrey that his destruction was essential for Europe's preservation;[48] Keats, whose politics were in most respects like Hazlitt's, said that he had done more harm to "the life of Liberty" than all the kings in Christendom, for he had "taught them how to organize their monstrous armies";[49] after the Battle of Leipzig De Quincey, sharing "the fervent joy — the triumph, too noble, too religious, to be boastful," exulted in the universal "rapture";[50] and when Napoleon was sent to Elba, Coleridge, who had been excoriating him for years, designed a great transparency to celebrate the glad event.[51] With Hazlitt it was otherwise. He was so much "confounded" by the emperor's abdication that he was ashamed to show his face,[52] and with the news of Waterloo the following year his grief was deep and bitter. He himself said later that he sat by the waters of Babylon and hung his harp upon the willows,[53] but Haydon, less poetically, recalled that he went about in a "stupor" for weeks, "unwashed, unshaved, hardly sober by day, and always intoxicated by night." * Though dismayed by his behavior, Crabb Robinson no doubt had the proper explanation: of all the men he knew, he recorded in his diary twelve days after Waterloo, only Hazlitt and three others (one of whom was Godwin)

grieve at the late events. Their intentions and motives are respectable, and their sorrow proceeds from mistaken theory, and an inveterate hatred of old names. They anticipate a revival of ancient despotism in France; and they will not acknowledge the radical vices of the French people, by which the peace of Europe is more endangered than the liberties of the French are by the restoration of the Bourbons.†

Robinson's comment anticipates one of the fundamental themes of *The Life of Napoleon Buonaparte,* Hazlitt's last and fullest effort to vindicate the French Revolution as an expression of the people's will. A government that was "an outrage and a burlesque on every principle of common sense or liberty" and that for a century had been "the derision of the gay, the scorn of the wise, and the sorrow of the good" fell before the blasts of public indignation "without one feeling of regret in one worthy and well-informed mind," he said.[54] The French had descended to the use of terror, to be sure, but in Napoleon, the child and champion of the Revolution, they found a spokesman who, in his dizzy rise to power, could satisfy their aspirations. Doing what had to be done if France were to remain "a citadel in which Freedom had hoisted the flag of revolt against the threat of hereditary servitude," he appropriated the dignities and titles of the monarchs whom he crushed, and even though he did "many things wrong and foolish" he left the memory of "one man greater than the throne he sat upon." [55] As history, *The Life of Napoleon Buonaparte,* with its sentimental view of Caesarism, is of course bizarre; but as Hazlitt's paean to the triumphant individualism that he regarded as the consummation of reform it is extremely moving. It enshrines the values and records the aspirations that he had known when young, and it is his memorial to a political idea that, as he thought, his age had almost won, then lost.

Fame, after having slept a thousand years, seemed to have seized her ancient trump; and, as in the early periods of Greece and Rome, freedom smiled on victory. Those who ever felt that dawn of a brighter day, that spring-time of hope and glow of exultation, animate their breasts, cannot easily be taught to forget it,

* *Autobiography,* I, 213. Talfourd (II, 122) was more moderate and probably more accurate in recalling Hazlitt's "stubborn anger" at the time. Elsewhere (II, 170) he says that when he first met Hazlitt in 1815 he was "staggering under the blow of Waterloo."
† *Diary, Reminiscences, and Correspondence of Henry Crabb Robinson* (ed. Thomas Sadlier, 2d ed., 1869), I, 491. For some of the episodes in Robinson's deteriorating friendship with Hazlitt at this time see Robinson, I, 133, 161, 170, 197.

either in the dazzling glare or cheerless gloom that was to succeed it. But it is perhaps enough for great actions to *have been,* and still to be remembered when they have ceased to be; and thus to stir the mind in after-ages with mingled awe, admiration, and regret.[56]

REALITIES

The convictions just rehearsed do not, of course, establish Hazlitt's title as a political theorist of distinction or even of originality, but they do provide a frame for his comments on the politics of early nineteenth-century England. Since he looked upon his country as "a feof held by a junto" committed to "the common cause of despotism,"[1] these comments range from the tart to the vitriolic. He tediously chided the French for their frivolity and vacillation, and just as tediously praised the English for their "sound hearts" and their sturdy love of freedom,* but he refused to be a patriot or to think that England's war with France was just. Sharing the cosmopolitan ideal so common to reformers of the later eighteenth century, he denounced the "prejudices" that Burke, quite properly, had identified with England's ancient way of life as anachronistic evils. True patriotism, he said, is not built upon such "indirect and collateral circumstances" as language and a shared tradition, but on "the love of liberty, of independence, of peace, and social happiness."[2] John Bull had been a manly, honest fellow in 1688, but when, frightened by reform and made servile by his leaders, he "turned bully and coward," it was a matter for disgust. "This is the only politics I know; the only patriotism I feel. The question with me is, whether I and all mankind are born slaves or free. That is the one thing necessary to know and to make good: the rest is *flocci, nauci, nihil, pili.* Secure this point, and all is safe: lose this, and all is lost."[3]

Not unnaturally, therefore, he was disrespectful of such institutions as the Crown, the church, the bar, which conventional patriots, both Whig and Tory, had rallied to support. About the Anglican Establishment, as we have seen,[4] he was witty and abusive; he sneered at lawyers

* 6.191. This point could be documented endlessly. See 4.99, 7.9, 8.306f., 10.29, 162, 14.16f., 189, 15.222, 17.154n. One of Hazlitt's extended comments on the theme is "National Antipathies," an interpolated essay (10.138–147) in his *Notes of a Journey through France and Italy,* and another is chapter xxxii of *The Life of Napoleon Buonaparte* (14.201–212). Ridiculing, in retrospect, the hysteria about a French invasion in 1805, he said that he could not "think so poorly of my countrymen (with all my dissatisfaction with them) as to suppose that even if Buonaparte had made good his landing, it would have been all over with us. He might have levelled London with the dust, but he must have covered the face of the country with heaps and *tumuli* of the slain, before this mixed breed of Norman and Saxon blood would have submitted to a second Norman conquest" (14.210).

as liars by profession, whose business was "to confound truth and false-hood" for a fee; [5] and he hated kings and kingship with a passion that even he must have found fatiguing. Like all Dissenters, he had acquired a wary disrespect for monarchs at a very tender age, and if at the start his antimonarchism was more or less conventional, after Waterloo, when the restoration of the *ancien régime* appeared to be the aim of every European statesman, his aversion to Legitimacy was whipped into a frenzy. It shaped his questionable defense of Napoleon as the hero of reform, it underlay his literary opinions, [6] it led him to denounce as rene-gades and sycophants the poets he had once admired, and it cast a lurid glow on almost all his journalism. By the "doubtful lubricity" of his style, he said, a man like Canning could prove Legitimacy to be a middle term between divine right and popular sovereignty, "compatible with both, and convertible into either"; [7] but he himself regarded it as an unmitigated evil. He called it "the true moral atheism, the equal blas-phemy against God and man, the sin against the Holy Ghost, that lowest deep of debasement and despair to which there is no lower deep." [8] In *Political Essays,* a set of jagged variations on the theme of regal power, he ranges from witty disrespect to maniacal abuse. Through the absurd sanctions of legitimate succession, he said, a person whose natural in-firmities would disqualify him for the duties of a parish beadle could control the lives and fortunes of thirty million people, [9] and it was there-fore clear that hereditary imbecility and native want of talent are all a king requires. [10] Sometimes he identifies Legitimacy with the Bourbons, sometimes with the British royal family (whose power was hardly abso-lute), but it was always a dirty word for him — not the name of a cer-tain kind of government of which he disapproved but a symbol of cor-ruption.

"Look at Norway, look at Italy, look at Spain, look at the Inquisition, look at the Slave Trade," he barked about the Congress of Vienna. [11] Whether his subject is Metternich and Castlereagh (those monsters of deceit), [12] or the Bourbons thrust upon the French at the end of English bayonets, [13] or the Hanoverians seeking, as he thought, to destroy their subjects' freedom, [14] he writes with glittering scorn. The "spirit of mon-archy" is his Duessa, "a foul, ugly witch, drunk with insolence, mad with power, a griping, rapacious wretch, bloody, luxurious, wanton, malicious, not sparing steel, or poison, or gold, to gain her ends." [15] It was impossible for him to treat the subject calmly. When we see a con-temptible creature like Ferdinand VII of Spain, he said,

who can hardly gabble out his words like a human being, more imbecile than a woman, more hypocritical than a priest, decked and dandled in the long robes

and swaddling-clothes of Legitimacy, lullabied to rest with the dreams of superstition, drunk with the patriot-blood of his country, and launching the thunders
of his coward-arm against the rising liberties of a new world, while he claims
the style and title of Image of the Divinity, we may laugh or weep, but there is
nothing to wonder at.*

To recall the inglorious careers of the later Hanoverians is to understand — and perhaps forgive — some of Hazlitt's comments about the
English Crown. It has been said that on every important question in the
first forty years of his reign George III was not only on the wrong side
but proud of being so. He was wrong about Wilkes, Ireland, America,
and France; he systematically subverted the principles of constitutional
monarchy; he resisted all efforts at fiscal or Parliamentary reform; he
opposed the abolition of the slave trade; and he was implacably hostile
to the repeal of the Dissenters' and Catholics' disabilities. Finally, about
the time Hazlitt was beginning his career, the king became insane, and
then his sons stepped forward to sustain the honor of the royal line. We
need not catalogue their offenses against decency and common sense,
but we should remember that the scandals of the Regent and his brothers
— from the Duke of York's sale of military commissions through his
inamorata to the comical vulgarities of Queen Caroline's divorce — made
the royal family an object of contempt and ridicule. Leigh Hunt's costly
attack on the Regent in the *Examiner,* Byron's *Vision of Judgment,* and
Shelley's *Swellfoot the Tyrant* are public records of a wide revulsion,
and the letters of the period are so full of private comments — some
ribald, some scandalized, but nearly all derogatory — about the antics
and the amours of the House of Hanover that Byron may be said to have
expressed a common attitude when he told the Regent's daughter:

> Weep, daughter of a royal line,
>   A Sire's disgrace, a realm's decay;
> Ah! happy if each tear of thine
>   Could wash a father's fault away! [16]

Hazlitt looked upon the royal family as caterpillars of the realm.
Although he usually wrote about the princes' escapades with restrained
contempt,† he roundly called their father one of the villains of the age.

---

* 7.285. The scandal of the Spanish Bourbons' restoration was a topic that always
reduced Hazlitt to sputtering incredulity (11.155, 15.151f., 19.154n), and Southey's
and Coleridge's complacent reaction to the same event — as, for example, in chapter
x of *Biographia Literaria* — was something he could never comprehend.

† Although incensed by the Duke of Cumberland's tossing a half-crown to a Negro
street-sweeper instead of returning his bow (12.219n, 20.197; De Quincey, XI, 438f.),
Hazlitt generally kept his temper in alluding to royal impropriety. Thus he deplored the
fact that the vulgar gewgaws of Carlton House had cost more than ten times the royal
family's and the cabinet's subscription for the relief of starving citizens in 1816 (19.
176), and he suggested that the royal stud, if horses of intelligence, were probably

He thought that George III — a man "with just glimmering of understanding enough to feel that he was a king, but not to comprehend how he could be king of a free people" [17] — had undermined his subjects' freedom when he might have led all Europe into an era of reform. Terrified by the apparition of "popular government," the monarch had begun his reign by trying to undo the very constitution that authorized his power, and he ended it by trying to restore the *ancien régime*.[18] That a Hanoverian "who held his crown in contempt of the Stuarts, and grew old, blind, and crazed in the unsated, undiverted, sacred thirst of Legitimacy is a thing that posterity will wonder at," [19] said Hazlitt, and in his valedictory to the career of George III he achieved a cadenced sorrow more moving than his angry journalism:

Persons who are fond of dwelling on the work of retribution, might perhaps trace its finger here. The Monarch survived the accomplishment of all his wishes, but without knowing that they had been accomplished. To those who long after passed that way, at whatever hour of the night, a light shone from one of the watch-towers of Windsor Castle — it was from the chamber of a King, old, blind, bereft of reason, "with double darkness bound" of body and mind; nor was that film ever removed, nor those eyes or that understanding restored to hail the sacred triumph of Kings over mankind; but the light streamed and streamed (indicating no dawn within) for long years after the celebration of that day which gladdened the hearts of Monarchs and of menial nations, and through that second night of slavery which succeeded — the work of a single breast, which it had dearly accomplished in darkness, in self-oblivion, and in more than kingly solitude! [20]

Despite his antimonarchism Hazlitt was by no means a thorough-paced republican. His comments about representative government — or at least about representative government as it was practiced in his day — are not so savage as those about Legitimacy, but they suggest that he, like many other liberals, did not entirely trust "the people." For one thing, he was made uneasy by the American experiment, which showed that public opinion could be as ruthless as the Inquisition; [21] for another, the loud asserter of individual rights could not accept the fact that democratic government means compromise and trimming, and that personal desires, no matter how intense, must sometimes yield to majority opinion. "Every corporate body, or casual concourse of people," he declared, "is nothing more than a collection of prejudices, and the only arguments current with them, a collection of watch-words." [22] He held

offended by the bizarre architecture of the Regent's pavilion at Brighton (10.90); but for the most part he contented himself with tart allusions to the Duke of York's affair with Mrs. Clarke (7.194, 20.138) and discreet ones to the Regent's corpulence (10.244, 11.174, 12.123, 18.200).

that to be a party man and submit oneself to party discipline means that one is "a concentrated essence, a varnished, powdered representative of the vices, absurdities, hypocrisy, jealousy, pride, and pragmaticalness" of the group to which one owes allegiance.[23] The very fact that Parliament was a corporate body made up of other corporate bodies bearing party labels was proof of its futility. If a mob is a crowd of faceless people in which each man's opinion "is governed by what others say of it, and by what he can get by it," [24] then Parliament is obviously a mob, and a "mere House-of-Commons man" like Canning is one whose sophisms, truisms, and "sorry buffooneries" show that he recognizes the fact.[25] It is not surprising, Hazlitt said, that Burke's colleagues, unlike the beasts from the ark, went out not by twos and threes but by the scores when he began to speak, for in its "corporate capacity" the House of Commons was absurd. "If we were to wait till Noble Lords and Honourable Gentlemen were inspired with a relish for abstruse thinking, and a taste for the loftier flights of fancy, the business of this great nation would shortly be at a stand." [26]

But if all party men were bad, said Hazlitt, Tories were the worst. Whether one accepts Macaulay's definition of Toryism as "the steadying power of the state" [27] or Bagehot's as mere "enjoyment," [28] one must grant that it made for acquiescence — and acquiescence was for Hazlitt a form of moral turpitude. In his old age, Leigh Hunt, his battles far behind, could describe the Tories' love of order as their strength, their weakness as the "love of power for power's sake, and the determination to maintain it in the teeth of all that is reasonable and humane"; [29] but Hazlitt, boy and man, would concede them nothing. The great conservative tradition that they upheld — and in a sense defiled — had a value that he never really understood. He was dedicated to all the things they hated, and the fact that they obstinately or ruthlessly resisted the slightest innovation made them, he thought, the agents of reaction and a "self-centred, well-knit, inseparable phalanx of power and authority." [30] In his view of European history, every great step forward, from the Reformation to the French Revolution, showed that it was not by venerating obsolete tradition that man achieved his gains, but by resisting "the intolerable pressure of long-established, notorious, aggravated, and growing abuses." [31] It was these abuses that the Tories converted into sacred relics. Confronted with any new idea, such as electoral reform or revision of the penal code, they first began to murmur about "licentiousness, confusion, and disorder"; then, more stridently, they talked of "artifice" and "chicanery"; and finally they intoned high-sounding arguments for gradual alteration. But all the while they were resolved, said Hazlitt, to preserve their special status, and to make sure "if any thing in the shape of reform *must* come, to let it come as late, and do as little good as possible." [32] Inertia was their sovereign cure for any social ill.

Tories have never been conspicuous for their suppleness of mind, but those of Hazlitt's day — "when liberal opinions were prohibited and adjudged as contraband of war," as one of his contemporaries recalled [33] — achieved a fossillike rigidity that has earned for them a special place in English history. If one of them had been consulted about the creation of the world, a wag remarked, he would have argued, "No; Chaos is an institution — it is respectable; I would not disturb it." [34] In 1807 Sydney Smith observed that there is not "one single source of human happiness" — turnpike roads, navigable canals, inoculation, hops, tobacco, the Reformation, or the Revolution — that the Tories had not opposed with "the most lugubrious predictions," [35] and half a century later Bagehot, in writing of Lord Eldon, the lord chancellor from 1801 to 1827, made the same complaint:

It is the most difficult thing in the world to believe that there ever was such a man. It only shows how intense historical evidence is, that no one really doubts it. He believed in everything which it is impossible to believe in — in the danger of Parliamentary Reform, the danger of Catholic Emancipation, the danger of altering the Court of Chancery, the danger of altering the Courts of Law, the danger of abolishing capital punishment for trivial thefts, the danger of making landowners pay their debts, the danger of making anything more, the danger of making anything less. [36]

Although Tories like De Quincey (whose ideal was a society built upon "the morals of the gentry, with the manners of the nobility") [37] thought that men like Lord Eldon were essential for sustaining the "anti-popular or timocratic functions" of the British constitution, [38] Hazlitt abominated them. "There has been no stretch of power attempted in his time," he remarked of the lord chancellor, "that he has not seconded: no existing abuse, so odious or so absurd, that he has not sanctioned it. . . . On all the great questions that have divided party opinion or agitated the public mind, the Chancellor has been found uniformly and without a single exception on the side of prerogative and power, and against every proposal for the advancement of freedom." [39] He was equally uncomplimentary about Lord Eldon's colleagues. He thought that Castlereagh ("whose only title to distinction consisted in his desire of and resolution to attain it by an unlimited subserviency to power") [40] was nothing but a ruthless prig, [41] and that Canning was a moral leper who made the worse appear the better reason "with the pertness of a school-boy and the effrontery of a prostitute." [42] It is a relief when, occasionally, he forgoes vituperation to make a joke about the Tories, as when he said of John Cashman's execution for his part in the Spa Fields riots of 1816 that things were getting better all the time, for instead of hanging six hundred citizens the government "only suspended Cashman and the Habeas Corpus." [43] But the jokes are always wry and bitter, and he never modified his views about the party of "corruption and prerogative." [44]

The Tory press and the "hirelings" who conducted it also fanned his wrath, for he thought that they had been the enemies of freedom since 1792, when Burke was pensioned for writing against the French Revolution and Paine was outlawed for supporting it. [45] In this connection his relations with his brother-in-law, John Stoddart, are instructive. The two had never been warm friends, but when Stoddart, early in 1817, founded the *New Times* as a staunchly Tory organ, Hazlitt regarded it as both a duty and a pleasure to expose his error. As a writer for the *Times,* Stoddart — or Dr. Slop, as he was often called by those who disagreed with him — had produced such savagely reactionary attacks upon reform that he had finally been dismissed; [46] but with a paper of his own he did not need to moderate his views, and he expressed them with a candor that even Hazlitt had to recognize. [47] None the less, a man who praised every action of the government — for example, he applauded the suspension of habeas corpus as an admirable device for "rescuing liberty together with morals and religion from the fangs of an insidious and sanguinary democracy" [48] — was obviously fair game for Hazlitt, and he pursued the chase with wicked glee. Among many other things, he called his wife's brother a "virulent and vulgar" apostate to the cause of freedom, [49] a "nondescript person" who mixed "the violence of the bravo with the subtlety of a pettifogging attorney" in his attacks on all reformers, [50] a worshiper at the bloody shrine of Legitimacy, [51] a self-styled "professional *gentleman*" who pulls a "go-cart of slavery and superstition." [52] Even readers who did not agree with Crabb Robinson that this sort of thing was "grossly malignant and offensive" [53] must have found it cloying, but Hazlitt never tired of it. In 1817 he badgered Stoddart for weeks and months on end, and as late as 1823, in the *Edinburgh Review,* he returned to the attack with zest. The man was fascinated, he explained,

with the abstract image of royalty; he has swallowed love-powders from despotism; he is drunk with the spirit of servility; mad with the hatred of liberty; flagrant, obscene in the exposure of the shameful parts of his cause; and his devotion to power amounts to a prostration of all his faculties. It is strange, as well as lamentable, to see this misguided enthusiasm, this preposterous pertinacity in wilful degradation. [54]

Not all the Tory editors came in for such continuous abuse as Hazlitt's own relation, but at one time or another almost all of them — notably William Gifford, of the *Quarterly Review,* and the writers for *Blackwood's Magazine* — were pilloried. Most of them, no doubt, deserved the treatment they received, but when we recall that Hazlitt called the *Courier* (where much of Coleridge's work appeared) "a paper of shifts and expedients, of bare assertions, and thoughtless impudence" [55] and its editor a "sprightly tool" who "rolls and wriggles and crawls about in the rank corruptions of the press like a maggot in a rotten cheese," * we must make a large allowance for the journalistic manners of the day. Hazlitt's malice toward his adversaries was matched, in everything but wit and style, by the brutality of their attacks on him.

He thought the Whigs were little better than their rivals. In 1809 Francis Jeffrey privately conceded that there were only two political parties in England: the Tories ("who are almost for tyranny") and the Democrats or radicals ("who are almost for rebellion"), and between stood the Whigs, "powerless and unpopular." [56] Hazlitt would have probably concurred. As a boy he, like most Dissenters, regarded Fox as England's most enlightened statesman † and his party as the party of reform, but when it became apparent that they were unable or unwilling to resist the war with France he derided them as the "fag-end" of the Tories. [57] Unqualified for the glittering society at Holland House, where so many liberal writers of the age were welcomed, and suspicious of the Whig grandees, he thought that they had grown too sleek and fat to serve a useful purpose. "The sole object of the set is not to stem the tide of prejudice and falsehood, but to get out of the way themselves." [58] Fox — whose life had been deficient at three important points, he said, the beginning, the middle, and the end — had set the pace for them. When, finally, he became prime minister, he was resolved "neither to forfeit his popularity nor to offend power," but he had "hardly nerve for both"; and therefore the politician who started as a Tory, then went over to the opposition, and ended as the colleague of Lord Shelburne

---

* 19.215. Incidentally, a vigorous attack on the *Times* that the *Examiner* printed as one of its "Literary Notices" (1 December 1816, pp. 759ff.) has thus far not been attributed to Hazlitt, but stylistically and otherwise it resembles his acknowledged work and should probably be added to the canon.

† For young Hazlitt's admiration for Fox see pages 160 f. In reprinting his eulogistic piece on him from *The Eloquence of the British Senate* in *Political Essays,* he admitted (7.313n) that it no longer represented his opinion, "but — *what I have written, I have written. So let it pass.*" His later allusions to Fox (for example, 12.274) are for the most part not concerned with politics.

and Lord Grenville was, despite his good intentions, not even master of his own opinions.[59] He was not a "true partisan" but a "political mediator" whose ideal was moderation, and his disciples who survived into the age of Waterloo merely followed his example. So refined and delicate that their reputations, like a woman's, could "bear neither to be blown upon or handled," [60] they had no heart for struggle.

A Whig is properly what is called a Trimmer — that is, a coward to both sides of a question, who dare not be a knave nor an honest man, but is a sort of whiffling, shuffling, cunning, silly, contemptible, unmeaning negation of the two. He is a poor purblind creature, who halts between two opinions, and complains that he cannot get any two people to think alike. He is a cloak for corruption, and a mar-plot to freedom. He will neither do any thing himself, nor let any one else do it. He is on bad terms with the Government, and not on good ones with the people. He is an impertinence and a contradiction in the state.[61]

Although not constituting a "party" like the Whigs and Tories, the radicals and reformers also came in for Hazlitt's strenuous abuse. One might think that with them, committed as they were to electoral and other innovations, he would have been at home, but generally he expressed the same contempt for them as for their adversaries. From time to time, in fact, he even joked about his isolation: the Whigs distrusted him, he said, because his book on Shakespeare had been castigated by the Tories of the *Quarterly Review,* and the reformers, suspecting "an inclination to *belles-lettres,*" never forgave him for writing such a book at all.[62] In any event, he damned all of them impartially. Reformers irritated him because they were so visionary and volatile. Not knowing precisely what they wanted, or even caring very much, they were "governed habitually by a spirit of contradiction," and therefore logic, sense, and facts had no hold on them. "A Reformer never is — but always to be blest, in the accomplishment of his airy hopes and shifting schemes of progressive perfectibility." [63] Moreover, like all men enraptured by their private visions, he tends to be a bigot.[64] Holcroft, whose motives were impeccable, "surrendered his own feelings and better judgment to a set of cant-phrases, called *the modern philosophy*"; [65] Cobbett was a "political humourist" too much taken with himself to distinguish between the possible and the real; [66] Shelley was so much enchanted by his "grand ethical experiment" that in him "the rage of free inquiry and private judgment amounted to a species of madness." [67]

Indeed, Shelley at one extreme and Cobbett at the other were Hazlitt's stock examples of the irresponsible reformers. Greatly to Leigh Hunt's vexation, he described the poet as a man with "a fire in his eye, a fever in his blood, a maggot in his brain, a hectic flutter in his speech, which mark out the philosophic fanatic"; [68] and he cited his "levity of principle" as proof that he and all his kind were self-indulgent visionaries.

Of all people the most tormenting are those who bid you hope in the midst of despair, who, by never caring about any thing but their own sanguine, hair-brained Utopian schemes, have at no time any particular cause for embarrassment and despondency because they have never the least chance of success, and who by including whatever does not hit their idle fancy, kings, priests, religion, government, public abuses or private morals, in the same sweeping clause of ban and anathema, do all they can to combine all parties in a common cause against them, and to prevent every one else from advancing one step farther in the career of practical improvement than they do in that of imaginary and unattainable perfection.[69]

As for Cobbett, Hazlitt's brilliant sketch of him in *Table-Talk* goes beyond mere portraiture to achieve a general truth. A very gifted writer and "a very honest man with a total want of principle,"[70] Cobbett was constant only in his vacillations. "He is like a young and lusty bridegroom that divorces a favourite speculation every morning, and marries a new one every night."[71] Writing as powerfully for reform as in his youth he wrote against it, he was, despite his vehemence, a man without convictions. He gloried only in hostility, and his talent for waging verbal war amounted to a kind of genius.

Wherever power is, there is he against it: he naturally butts at all obstacles, as unicorns are attracted to oak trees, and feels his own strength only by resistance to the opinions and wishes of the rest of the world. To sail with the stream, to agree with the company, is not his humour. If he could bring about a Reform in Parliament, the odds are that he would instantly fall foul of and try to mar his own handy-work; and he quarrels with his own creatures as soon as he has written them into a little vogue — and a prison. I do not think this is vanity or fickleness so much as a pugnacious disposition, that must have an antagonist power to contend with, and only finds itself at ease in systematic opposition.[72]

THE AGING STRIPLING BARDS

So much for Hazlitt's general politics. That they exerted no influence on contemporary affairs is not a matter for surprise, for his brand of liberalism was so self-devouring that it would scarcely call for comment in a history of the period. What he wryly called his "state of perpetual litigation with the community"[1] disqualified him from consideration as a social critic. On the other hand, that his political opinions had a profound effect upon his own career is also not surprising, for they colored — or discolored — his relations with almost everyone he knew. Although, as we have seen, he turned his hand to many things as journalist, for a few years following Waterloo politics were perhaps his main concern.

They crept or thrust themselves into almost all his work, and ultimately they led him to a peak of fury from which his reputation has never quite recovered. To follow all his forays and rebuttals against his adversaries — not all of whom were hidebound Tories — would be an unrewarding task, but his campaign against the poets whom he regarded as apostates to the cause of freedom is significant for early nineteenth-century literature. It meant that one of the greatest critics of the age was, from almost the start of his career in letters, in systematic opposition to some of the greatest writers of the age, and therefore it requires a closer look.

He regarded Wordsworth, like Burke and Scott, as among the first of English writers; and although neither as a friend nor as a man of letters did Southey matter very much to him, he thought that Coleridge had the richest and most stimulating mind that he had ever known. None the less he attacked them all with a virulence almost unmatched in an age of savage journalistic quarrels. Since the attacks presumably did not derive from personal hostility — for Southey was a dim acquaintance of his youth, and apart from the disastrous visit to the Lakes in 1803 he saw virtually nothing of Wordsworth and very little more of Coleridge after 1798 — it would seem that he merely disagreed with their opinions. By 1815, however, these opinions were obstinately Tory and therefore anathema to him, and, in the years that followed, his attack on them was withering and incessant.

It was natural that Southey should have been the first to draw his fire. Except with *The Convention of Cintra* and the short-lived *Friend*, Wordsworth and Coleridge had not ventured into print for several years;[2] but Southey, who in 1809 had helped to organize the *Quarterly Review*, had become an able and insistent spokesman for the Tories, and his accession to the laureateship in 1813 was an earned reward. One of Hazlitt's first political squibs was an ironic congratulation on the appointment,[3] and he took cognizance, a few months later, of Southey's first official publication — the customary New Year's ode — as "a sort of methodistical rhapsody, chaunted by a gentleman-usher."[4] Through the winter, however, he was mainly occupied with other things (including his letters to "Vetus" of the *Times*), and not until the following summer did he give the newly laureled poet the attention he deserved. In July 1814 he reviewed *The Lay of the Laureate* with savage disrespect, calling the poem "a Methodist sermon turned into doggerel verse" and its author a hireling of the Tories. In some ways Southey's mind was much like Hazlitt's. Both were partisans and good haters, and although their views were antithetical, each defended his opinion with brutal disregard of the amenities. It is ironic, therefore, that Hazlitt singled out the laureate's bigotry as his salient characteristic. Whether republican or royalist, "Theophilanthropist" or Anglican, incendiary or courtier, "he not only thinks whatever opinion he may hold for the time infallible, but that no other is even to be tolerated, and that none but knaves and fools can differ with him." * In this review, as in almost all his subsequent attacks on Southey, Hazlitt sports and frolics with his victim. He refused to take him seriously as a poet, and in so far as Toryism was a subject for derision, instead of indignation, he derided it through him. "Many people laugh at him, some may blush for him, but nobody envies him," he said,⁵ and in any event *The Lay of the Laureate* proved at least one thing — that its author, however grossly inconsistent and absurd, was not a hypocrite, for "how should he maintain the same opinion all his life, when he cannot maintain it for two stanzas together?" †

Two months later, when he turned to Wordsworth's latest work, Hazlitt used a different tone. *The Excursion,* which was published in July 1814, a year after Lord Lonsdale had secured for Wordsworth a sinecure as stamp-distributor, gave Hazlitt his first chance to write about the poet whom he regarded as the greatest of the age, and within a month the first installment of his long three-part review appeared in the *Examiner.*‡ Here he was dealing with a man whose politics he hated but whose genius he revered. Renouncing ursine humor, he resolved, it seems, to take a critic's stance, and to treat a serious if imperfect work

---

* 7.86f. This was Macaulay's theme (*Essays*, I, 235) in his famous review of Southey's *Colloquies* fourteen years later: by toleration, he said, the laureate seems to mean "that everybody is to tolerate him, and that he is to tolerate nobody."

† 7.90 f. In a note to this review Hazlitt explains (7.96n) that he has omitted two topics, "the praise of Bonaparte, and the abuse of poetry," at the solicitation of "two poets of our acquaintance." He describes one of them (Leigh Hunt) as a person whose tropical blood "gives a gay, cordial, vinous spirit to his whole character," and the other (Lamb) as a "mad wag . . . equally desperate in his mirth and his gravity, who would laugh at a funeral and weep at a wedding, who talks nonsense to prevent the headache, who would wag his finger at a skeleton, whose jests scald like tears, who makes a joke of a great man, and a hero of a cat's paw."

‡ 19.9–25. The three installments appeared on August 21 and 28 and October 2. One consequence of this review was Lamb's irritation with Hazlitt for having borrowed his copy of the poem (which the *Quarterly*, through Southey's intercession, had asked him to review) and then keeping it too long. On 19 September 1814 Lamb explained to Wordsworth (Lucas, II, 137) the cause of the "detention" and spoke tartly of the "slovenly air of dispatch and disrespect" that Hazlitt had revealed. For Lamb's own review of *The Excursion*, which finally appeared in the October *Quarterly*, see his *Works*, I, 203–216, and for his comments on "those mutilators of collections, spoilers of the symmetry of shelves, and creators of odd volumes" see "The Two Races of Men," *Works*, I, 499–504.

of art with the dignity it deserved. The result was not only a stirring tribute to a poem that in "power of intellect," "lofty conception," and "depth of feeling" he thought had "seldom been surpassed"; [6] it was also his first attempt to explain the workings of the sympathetic imagination in literary creation, and the first assertion of his own old-fashioned but uncompromising politics.

What impresses Hazlitt most about the poem is its "oppressive power," in which it resembles its locale. "Here are no dotted lines, no hedge-row beauties, no box-tree borders, no gravel walks, no square mechanic enclosures. All is left loose and irregular in the rude chaos of aboriginal nature." [7] But *The Excursion* is not a poem on the country so much as on Wordsworth's reaction to the country: everything is subordinated to the poet's brooding and controlling sensibility, for he creates his own materials, and just as "his thoughts are his real subject," his characters — the recluse, the pastor, and the pedlar — are reflections of his mind. At once, then, Hazlitt confronts the salient problem of romantic poetry, its intense subjectivism, and at once he makes his own position clear: Wordsworth is a poet of extraordinary power, he says, but it is a power that "preys upon itself." His mind does not go out to meet experience; it is "the reverse of dramatic," for it is "jealous of all competition," and consequently his "intense intellectual egotism" swallows everything. [8] When we recall Hazlitt's doctrine of benevolence, his theory of imagination as the faculty by which we enlarge and liberate ourselves, and his praise of Shakespeare as the greatest of all poets because he cares more about his subject than himself and so "becomes" the thing he writes about, it is clear that Wordsworth's "repugnance to admit any thing that tells for itself, without the interpretation of the poet" poses fundamental problems. Not only does he reveal "a systematic unwillingness to share the palm with his subject," [9] he imposes on that subject his own reactionary opinions, to which Hazlitt, being Hazlitt, was bound to take exception. "Whatsoever savours of a little, narrow, inquisitorial spirit, does not sit well on a poet and a man of genius," he asserts; and so as he defends *Candide,* his old friend Joseph Fawcett, [10] and the exploded aspirations of reform from Wordsworth's disapproval, his criticism merges into politics. Although Wordsworth had forgotten or repudiated the hopes of that "new and golden era" of his youth, for Hazlitt it retained a splendor "not to be effaced by birth-day odes, or the chaunting of Te Deums in all the churches of Christendom. To those hopes eternal regrets are due; to those who maliciously and wilfully blasted them, in the fear that they might be accomplished, we feel no less what we owe — hatred and scorn as lasting." [11]

POLITICS AND LITERATURE

The third and final part of the review (which was not published till October) contains a tranquil disquisition on imagination and an amusing if irrelevant attack on country people. Poetry of imagination, says Hazlitt, is anchored in its subject and rises from one's "faculties of memory and invention, conversant with the world of external nature," whereas poetry of sentiment is anchored in the poet and draws on his own "moral sensibility." [12] The greatest poets — Chaucer, Spenser, Shakespeare, and Milton — reveal both kinds of strength, but Wordsworth, "whose powers of feeling are of the highest order," is deficient in "fanciful invention." Treating the simplest and the grandest things in nature, he reposes only on his own resources, but since they are so formidable his poetry has uncommon power. "His poems bear a distant resemblance to some of Rembrandt's landscapes, who, more than any other painter, created the medium through which he saw Nature, and out of the stump of an old tree, a break in the sky, and a bit of water, could produce an effect almost miraculous." As the product of "a refined and contemplative mind, conversant only with itself and nature," his work is deeply moving, for he has "described the love of nature better than any other poet." [13] In treating people, on the other hand, he is not successful, partly because he is too much centered in himself to lose himself in others, partly because his people are so dull. "We go along with him, while he is the subject of his own narrative, but we take leave of him when he makes pedlars and ploughmen his heroes and the interpreters of his sentiments. It is, we think, getting into low company, and company, besides, that we do not like." [14] And with this Hazlitt launches on his coda, a sprightly little essay, prophetic of *The Round Table,* on the theme that rustics are "a kind of domesticated savages." However, he closes with a noble valediction. Through Wordsworth's mind, he says, there have passed "about as many fine things" as, with five or six exceptions, have passed "through any human mind whatever." [15]

It is not in our power to add to, or take away from, the pretensions of a poem like the present, but if our opinion or wishes could have the least weight, we would take our leave of it by saying — *Esto perpetua!* [16]

⬦ ⬦ ⬦

Since the critical reception of Wordsworth's work had been, and still was, extremely cold — it was *The Excursion* that prompted Jeffrey's famous "This will never do!" — Hazlitt might have thought he did his former friend a service in writing this review, for, as he said later, it was "the first favourable account that had ever appeared of any work he had ever written." * But Wordsworth was enraged. His sister Dorothy said merely that she was disappointed with Hazlitt's criticism ("for, with all his disagreeable qualities, he is a very clever fellow"),[17] but the poet himself thought that he had been betrayed. In his letters, at least, the chief victim of his wrath was Jeffrey, who was an old offender,[18] but in the "Essay Supplementary to the Preface" of the 1815 *Poems* he turned on all whom he regarded as detractors. His comments there on critics "of palsied imagination and indurated hearts" — "judges, whose censure is auspicious, and whose praise ominous" † — clearly points to Hazlitt as well as to the *Edinburgh* reviewer;[19] and when he came to London, later in the spring of 1815, his irritation was a common topic of discussion with his friends.[20] In fact, he was so much incensed at Hazlitt that he avoided seeing him and requested that Lamb and their other common friends exclude him from their gatherings.[21] As the injured poet said a few months later, Hazlitt was "a man of low propensities, & of bad heart," and as "perverse" a creature as any he had ever known. "His sensations are too corrupt to allow him to understand my Poetry — though his ingenuity might enable him so to write as if he knew something about it."[22]

In the spring of Waterloo politics were being hotly argued among the men of letters, and feelings were intense. Already, in private conversation, Hazlitt had begun to grumble about "the friends of liberty for their apostacy,"[23] but through the spring he printed nothing on the poets. Finally, however, on June 11 — the very week of Waterloo — he expressed himself in print. Reviewing a performance of *Comus* at Covent Garden, he remarked, in closing, that Milton was both a poet and a patriot, and that whatever one might think of his political opinions, they at least were firm and brave.

He did not retract his defence of the people of England; he did not say that his sonnets to Vane or Cromwell were meant ironically; he was not appointed Poet-Laureat to a Court which he had reviled and insulted; he accepted neither place nor pension; nor did he write paltry sonnets upon the "Royal fortitude" of the House of Stuart, by which, however, they really lost something.

* 9.6; cf. 20.68 for another comment on the "thankless office" of trying to please Wordsworth and his friends. Whereas Lamb told Robinson (I, 202) that Hazlitt had wept over his review of *The Excursion* "because he was disappointed, and could not praise it as it deserved," Northcote, many years later, explained to Haydon (Pope, 3 August 1826) that he had "puffed" the poem in order to curry favor with the poet, "but as Wordsworth took no notice of him from contempt, H. immediately upbraided his Poetry, Principles, & Politics. Poor J. Bull read this and enjoyed it, & believed it was done by a Patriot in principle, when it was nothing but pique & disappointment."

† *Prose Works*, II, 231. In his *Letter to a Friend of Robert Burns* (1816) Wordsworth said (*Prose Works*, II, 275f.) that in Jeffrey, as in Robespierre and Napoleon, a professed "reverence for truth," though carried to the "giddiest heights of ostentation," was founded on "the omnipotence of falsehood."

POLITICS AND LITERATURE

In a footnote to this passage he was even more explicit:

> In the last edition of the works of a modern Poet, there is a Sonnet to the King, complimenting him on "his royal fortitude." The story of the Female Vagrant, which very beautifully and affectingly describes the miseries brought on the lower classes by war, in bearing which the said "royal fortitude" is so nobly exercised, is very properly struck out of the collection.[24]

Such perfidy, compounded by the fact that Hazlitt had just joined the corps of *Edinburgh* reviewers, meant that war had been declared. On the very day that Hazlitt's piece on *Comus* appeared in the *Examiner* Wordsworth called on Leigh Hunt (to thank him for his "zeal . . . in advocating the cause of his genius"),[25] and when the host expressed regret for Hazlitt's criticism, the visitor undertook to trace the origin of the critic's malice — whereupon he exhumed the escapade in Keswick.* He had already told the story to Lamb;[26] three days later he repeated it for the benefit of Robinson;[27] and thereafter, presumably, it became a standard piece of gossip, for he was still embroidering on it nine years later.†

So far as we know, Hazlitt made no comment on this gossip — perhaps because there was nothing he could say — but toward the end of summer, in a Round Table paper "On Manner," he testily exhumed and challenged a poem in Wordsworth's 1807 volume in which gypsies had been pointed to as idlers.[28]

> We did not expect this turn from Mr. Wordsworth, whom we had considered as the prince of poetical idlers, and patron of the philosophy of indolence, who formerly insisted on our spending our time "in a wise passiveness." Mr. W. will excuse us if we are not converts to his recantation of his original doctrine; for he who changes his opinion loses his authority. We did not look for this Sunday-school philosophy from him. . . . The gipsies are the only living monuments of the first ages of society. They are an everlasting source of thought and reflection on the advantages and disadvantages of the progress of civilisation: they are a better answer to the cotton manufactories than Mr. W. has given in the *Excursion*.‡

Thereafter Hazlitt was silent on the poets for several months, but by the following spring, when Coleridge, slowly coming back to health after his long and tragic silence, published *Christabel,* he was ready to renew the fray. He had known the poem for years in manuscript[29]

---

* See pages 136ff. Hunt himself does not repeat this part of Wordsworth's conversation, but Robinson's account of the visit (I, 169) supports the inference I have drawn.

† See page 137. That Wordsworth likewise told the story to Haydon is clear from his remark in a letter to John Scott on 11 June 1816 (*TLS*, 27 December 1941, p. 660): "Haydon will tell you something about my quondam connection with Hazlitt, & how it was broken off." John Wilson, Wordsworth's neighbor at the Lakes, was also privy to the ancient scandal, for he raked it up a few years later in *Blackwood's Magazine*. See page 373.

‡ 4.45n. For Keats's comment on this passage, in which he expressed regret at Hazlitt's having "spied an imaginary fault," see Rollins, I, 174f.

and he had once revered its author, but when it fell to his lot to review it for the *Examiner* he apparently decided to throw away the scabbard. Eschewing a long, discursive review like that of *The Excursion* two years earlier, he made the simple point that Coleridge was a person of extraordinary power whose power was poorly used. "Here are two unfinished poems, and a fragment," he observes (for the volume included also "Kubla Khan" and "The Pains of Sleep"), the work of a man of such universal genius "that his mind hangs suspended between poetry and prose, truth and falsehood, and an infinity of other things, and from an excess of capacity, he does little or nothing." He charges Coleridge with "dishonesty" and also "affectation" in his "pretended contempt for the opinion of the public"; he scolds him for concealing the identity of Christabel's companion (and incidentally supplies a missing line from memory); and he takes exception to the theme. "There is something disgusting at the bottom of his subject, which is but ill glossed over by a veil of Della Cruscan sentiment and fine writing — like moonbeams playing on a charnel-house, or flowers strewn on a dead body." But significantly he singles out the passage (lines 402–430) on the decay of friendship as a "genuine outburst of humanity, worthy of the author, when no dream oppresses him, no spell binds him." As for "Kubla Khan," it showed that "Mr. Coleridge can write better *nonsense* verses than any man in England. It is not a poem, but a musical composition." *

❖   ❖   ❖

Within a year of Waterloo, then, Hazlitt was on record with his opinions of the poets. He had said, in effect, that Southey, once an ardent liberal, had become a crusty Tory who abused such talent as he had; that Wordsworth, though a very great writer, was not among the greatest because his "devouring egotism" restricted his imagination; and that Coleridge's genius, which was unsurpassed, exceeded his achievement. Before proceeding to examine Hazlitt's later comments on the poets — which, under mounting political pressures, quickly went beyond the expression of literary opinions — it may be useful to assess these judgments. That his view of Southey's politics and poetry was substantially correct would seem to be the verdict of posterity, and we need not demonstrate the obvious; and although the presumption is

---

* 19.32ff. In 1844 Leigh Hunt (*Essays*, pp. 154f.) recalled this review (of 2 June 1816) with pain. "It was not Mr. Hazlitt's only or most unwarrantable censure, or one which friendship found hardest to forgive," he said. "But peace, and honour too be with his memory!" In his *Lectures on the English Poets* (5.166) Hazlitt cites as the "one fine passage" in *Christabel* the lines on friendship.

that he was wrong about the other two, we should remember that Wordsworth's egotism and Coleridge's chronic inability to use his own uncommon gifts are among the most fully documented facts of literary history.

Wordsworth's egotism may be viewed as a necessary result, or perhaps a cause, of his conception of poetry as a form of self-expression,[30] but its effect on his behavior was noted by almost everyone who knew and wrote about him. When, in 1821, Hazlitt called him "the most original poet of the present day, only because he is the greatest egotist" [31] he gave polite expression to a view that he and many others had elsewhere put in other words. Even if much should be forgiven one who looked upon himself as a "dedicated spirit," [32] those who dealt with Wordsworth had a great deal to forgive: his utter lack of humor, his extreme self-centeredness, his aversion to the slightest criticism, and his reluctance to concede a rival's merit. In a single letter of Lamb's, one of the funniest that he ever wrote, all these points are illustrated. In 1801, several months after Lamb had sent Wordsworth a copy of his play *John Woodvil* (which, because of his "almost insurmountable aversion from Letter-writing," the poet had not even thanked him for), he himself received the second edition of *Lyrical Ballads*. In his letter of acknowledgment Lamb listed several of his favorite passages, he said in describing the event to Thomas Manning, and added,

unfortunately, that no single piece had moved me so forcibly as the *Ancient Mariner, The Mad Mother,* or the *Lines at Tintern Abbey.* The Post did not sleep a moment. I received almost instantaneously a long letter of four sweating pages from my Reluctant Letter-Writer, the purport of which was, that he was sorry his 2d vol. had not given me more pleasure (Devil a hint did I give that it had *not pleased me*) and "was compelled to wish that my range of sensibility was more extended, being obliged to believe that I should receive large influxes of happiness and happy Thoughts" (I suppose from the L.B.) — With a deal of stuff about a certain Union of Tenderness and Imagination, which in the sense he used Imagination was not the characteristic of Shakespeare, but which Milton possessed in a degree far exceeding other Poets: which Union, as the highest species of Poetry, and chiefly deserving that name, "He was most proud to aspire to"; then illustrating the said Union by two quotations from his own 2d vol. (which I had been so unfortunate as to miss.)

The two passages that the poet called to his attention were very well, said Lamb, "but after one has been reading Shakespeare twenty of the best years of one's life, to have a fellow start up, and prate about some unknown quality, which Shakespeare possessed in a degree inferior to Milton and *somebody else*!!" was more than even he could stomach.[33]

De Quincey, a most devout Wordsworthian, tells an amusing story about the poet and his sister's dining with a certain wealthy woman, who, after the meager first course, all alone consumed "a solitary pheasant . . . from alpha to omega" while her hungry guests looked on. Going home, "Miss Wordsworth laughed with undissembled glee; but Wordsworth thought it too grave a matter for laughing — he was thoroughly disgusted, and said repeatedly, 'A person cannot be honest, positively not honest, who is capable of such an act.' " [34] This anecdote, like one that Hazlitt tells, is not without its implications. According to Hazlitt, when "a celebrated lyrical writer" heard, at a party, that the author of *Rob Roy* had used one of his poems for his motto on the title page,

he instantly went to the book-shelf in the next room, took down the volume of his own poems, read the whole of that in question aloud with manifest complacency, replaced it on the shelf, and walked away; taking no more notice of Rob Roy than if there had been no such person, nor of the new novel than if it had not been written by its renowned author. There was no reciprocity in this. But the writer in question does not admit of any merit, second to his own.*

John Rickman, who has not come down to us as a very jovial person, declared that Wordsworth had "neither fun nor common sense in him," [35] but about his gigantic self-esteem there can be no doubt. He and his sister were the "most intensely selfish" people he had ever known, said Southey, and "the one thing to which W. would sacrifice all others is his own reputation, concerning which his anxiety is perfectly childish — like a woman of her beauty." [36] The man who, when asked what he thought of Shelley's work, abruptly answered "Nothing," [37] who told the bankrupt Haydon that he had "too much regard" for him to lend him any money,† who called Keats's hymn to Pan (in *Endymion*) "a pretty piece of

---

* 8.65. Scott took the motto of his novel from Wordsworth's "Rob Roy's Grave," lines 37–40:

> For why? Because the good old rule
> Sufficeth them; the simple plan,
> That they should take who have the power,
> And they should keep who can.

In "On Consistency of Opinion," which appeared in the *London Magazine* in 1821, Hazlitt repeated a story (17.26f.) that he had heard from Charles Lloyd, Wordsworth's former neighbor: although the poet was once so "smit with the love of simplicity and equality" that he would permit only one candle in a room, when Lord Lowther came to dine he was heard to whisper to a servant to put six candles on the table. Hazlitt did not mention any names, but according to Talfourd (Vera Watson, "Thomas Noon Talfourd and His Friends," *TLS*, 20 April 1956, p. 244) Wordsworth was moved to write to Lloyd, "in all the dignity of offended friendship," a letter of "magnanimous self admiration" mixed with anger and contempt. A few months later the poet's wife (*The Letters of Mary Wordsworth* [ed. Mary E. Burton, 1958], pp. 83f.) gave her version of the story to Thomas Monkhouse: when Wordsworth saw only two candles on the table he commanded that the servant bring two more, thus making four and not six, as had been spitefully reported.

† 12.80; cf. L'Estrange, II, 175, where Mary Russell Mitford told Haydon that this "terrible story" about Wordsworth had spoiled his poetry for her. "We clung to him as to Cowper; but now — it will not bear talking of."

Paganism" and left uncut most of the pages in the presentation copy of his *Poems*, [38] must have had an absorbing interest in himself. Although he "spoke freely and praisingly of his own poems," as the aged Robinson recalled of their first meeting, [39] he was as "sceptical" of all poetry but his own, Leigh Hunt recorded in astonishment, as Richardson was of Fielding's novels. [40] In 1830 Hartley Coleridge, reporting that in Wordsworth the poet was yielding to the country squire, remarked that "his weakest points, his extreme irritability of self-approbation and parsimony of praise to contemporary authors are much *in statu quo*"; [41] and in talking to the old man ten years later Carlyle inferred that most English poetry had been vastly overrated: Pope was a partial failure, Milton a writer of narrow limits, Burns an inferior person altogether, and even Shakespeare not without the gravest faults. "Gradually it became apparent to me that of transcendent and unlimited there was, to this Critic, probably but one specimen known, Wordsworth himself!" [42]

All this — and much more that one might add — could be classed as literary gossip, but it reflects the egotism that Hazlitt, Keats, and others regarded as a major flaw in both the man and the poet. "Wordsworth &c should have their due from us," said Keats, "but for the sake of a few fine imaginative or domestic passages, are we to be bullied into a certain Philosophy engendered in the whims of an Egotist?" * In this remark we can almost hear Hazlitt's tone of voice when he proclaimed Wordsworth's "intellectual egotism" to be the "bane of his talents and of his public principles." [43] The "great fault of a modern school of poetry," he said in a lecture of 1818 that Keats most likely heard, is that they tend

to reduce poetry to a mere effusion of natural sensibility; or what is worse, to divest it both of imaginary splendour and human passion, to surround the meanest objects with the morbid feelings and devouring egotism of the writers' own minds. Milton and Shakspeare did not so understand poetry. They gave a more liberal interpretation both to nature and art. They did not do all they could to get rid of the one and the other, to fill up the dreary void with the Moods of their own Minds. They owe their power over the human mind to their having had a deeper sense than others of what was grand in the objects of nature, or affecting in the events of human life. But to the men I speak of there is nothing interesting, nothing heroical, but themselves.†

Although Hazlitt speaks of poets in the plural, "the Moods of their own Minds" echoes one of Wordsworth's phrases, and Wordsworth is the man he means.

⟡   ⟡   ⟡

* Rollins, I, 223. Some two weeks after writing this to Reynolds on 3 February 1818, Keats told his brothers (*ibid.*, I, 237) that Wordsworth's recent stay in London had "left a bad impression where-ever he visited in Town — by his egotism, Vanity and bigotry — yet he is a great Poet if not a Philosopher."
† 5.53. One section of Wordsworth's 1807 *Poems* is called "Moods of my own Mind."

AGING STRIPLING BARDS

Coleridge's galvanic effect on his contemporaries requires no demonstration, for in what Wordsworth called the "strength and plumage" of his youth " his power was overwhelming. To Hazlitt — as to Godwin, Southey, Wordsworth, Lamb, De Quincey, and almost everyone who came within the sound of his enchanting voice — he was, par excellence, the man of genius. Although in his old age he struck Carlyle merely as "a puffy, anxious, obstructed-looking, fattish old man" and something of a bore,⁴⁵ to those who had known him thirty years before he was, in Southey's words, "infinitely and ten thousand-thousand-fold the mightiest of his generation." ⁴⁶ One could assemble a volume of such testimonials, but two will serve to make the point: Godwin, notoriously scanty in his commendations, named Coleridge one of the "principal oral instructors" to whom he felt his mind "indebted for improvement"; ⁴⁷ and the aging Lamb — who wished that his younger friends could have seen Coleridge in "the springtide of his genius" ⁴⁸ — called him, when he died, "the proof and touchstone of all my cogitations." ⁴⁹

This is one of Hazlitt's constant themes. He quotes, remembers, and alludes to Coleridge more often than he mentions any other man but Shakespeare; and even after they were hopelessly estranged he was haunted by the memory of what Coleridge once had been. Invariably, however, this memory is linked with the theme of wasted power, and of genius gone to seed. Of course Hazlitt knew of Coleridge's addiction — though he never refers to it except by implication — and of his fearful, lifelong effort to bring it in control; but he customarily attributes his decline to lassitude or cowardice or to a failure of the will. If Coleridge had had some of his own "irascibility," he said, "then, with his eloquence to paint the wrong, and acuteness to detect it, his country and the cause of liberty might not have fallen without a struggle." ⁵⁰ Sometimes, as we shall see, he was villainously unfair to a great but stricken man,* sometimes nostalgia was his cue, and sometimes moral exhortation, but always there is a trace of anger at the discrepancy between what Coleridge was and what he might have been. "But oh thou!" he cried in 1822,

who didst lend me speech when I was dumb, to whom I owe it that I have not crept on my belly all the days of my life like the serpent, but sometimes lift my forked crest or tread the empyrean, wake thou out of thy mid-day slumbers! Shake off the heavy honey-dew of thy soul, no longer lulled with that Circean cup, drinking thy own thoughts with thy own ears, but start up in thy promised likeness, and shake the pillared rottenness of the world! Leave not thy sounding words in air, write them in marble, and teach the coming age heroic truths! Up,

---

* See, for example, the peroration of a piece on Coleridge's 1818 lectures (19. 210): "You see him now squat like a toad at the ear of the *Courier*; and oh! that we could rouse him up once more into an archangel's shape," etc.

and wake the echoes of Time! Rich in deepest lore, die not the bed-rid churl of knowledge, leaving the survivors unblest! Set, set as thou didst rise in pomp and gladness! [51]

Most often, and especially in his later years, Hazlitt's tone is one of pathos. Coleridge was, as he had said quite simply, the greatest man he ever knew,[52] and because his genius was the triumph of the age, his self-betrayal was a cause for grief and indignation. Coleridge himself sometimes joked about the matter, explaining that he had "laid too many eggs in the hot sands of this wilderness, the world, with ostrich carelessness and ostrich oblivion," * but an aging Hazlitt wrote of it in muted anger and in sorrow. As we see Coleridge in *The Spirit of the Age* he is merely a majestic ruin, though unmatched in taste and erudition and bewitching in his talk. "With an understanding fertile, subtle, expansive, 'quick, forgetive, apprehensive,' beyond all living precedent," he folds up in his mind, "like a rich, but somewhat tattered piece of tapestry," the wisdom of the ages; and when he speaks of men of genius "the critic seems to stand above the author." [53] None the less he had lived for twenty years or more on the sound of his own voice, said Hazlitt, and he would die as he had lived.

Alas! "Frailty, thy name is *Genius!*" — What is become of all this mighty heap of hope, of thought, of learning, and humanity? It has ended in swallowing doses of oblivion and in writing paragraphs in the *Courier.* — Such, and so little is the mind of man! †

In his later comments on the poets, such as those just quoted, Hazlitt seems to be writing for posterity, and posterity has been duly grateful; but it has felt otherwise about the journalism of his middle years, when his theme was post-Napoleonic politics and his frame of reference smaller. If we are to understand this segment of his work we must try to understand the cause of his resentments. As early as 1812 Wordsworth had begun to worry about the "very alarming" rise in benefit societies and journeymen's associations, which he regarded as a prelude to "the horrors of a war between the poor and the rich, a conflict of property with no property," [54] and in 1816 the one-time pacifist, celebrating Napoleon's defeat, reminded the Deity that

* *Biographia Literaria*, I, 32. Coleridge uses this figure, or figures like it, several times in writing of himself. For example, see Griggs, III, 94f.
† 11.34. In his last allusion to Coleridge, which was published posthumously, Hazlitt could still express the hope (17.378) that the "sleep-walker" might, like his own mariner, drop the albatross from round his neck.

AGING STRIPLING BARDS

Thy most dreaded instrument,
In working out a pure intent,
Is Man — arrayed for mutual slaughter,
— Yea, Carnage is thy daughter! *

Thereafter he seemed to think that the oppressive measures of the Tory government were designed to serve the same high purpose. Deeply concerned about the "malady" that reformers and unruly laboring men had brought upon the body politic, by 1817 he was arguing against such luxuries as habeas corpus and disaffected journalists,[55] and already beginning to solidify his hostility to popular education, Catholic emancipation, revision of the penal code, and Parliamentary reform.

As for Southey, although he agreed with Wordsworth as late as 1807 that the Royal Family should be "expatriated," [56] soon thereafter he was busy with the *Quarterly Review*,† and as the years went by his Toryism hardened until it reached a state of petrifaction. When Perceval was assassinated in 1812 he feared a *bellum servile* and urged the immediate suspension of habeas corpus, the free press, and free speech in order to prevent it. The danger was very grave, he said, for one by one the "old principles" that had made England great were falling to the "Romanists, sectarians of every kind, your liberality men, and your philosophers of every kind and every degree of folly and emptiness." ‡ By 1817 he was prophesying "an insurrection of the Yahoos," [57] denouncing Cobbett as a "miscreant" and a "brutal ruffian," [58] and urging deportation for all unruly journalists.[59] If a revolution came, he said, and "were the Hunts and Hazlitt to have the upper hand," his life would be in danger.[60] The "manufacturing populace" are not only discontented with the government, he warned Lord Liverpool; they abhor it with a "deadly hatred," and if the military were withdrawn from London, "four and twenty hours would not elapse before the tricoloured flag would be planted upon Carlton House." [61] Such remarks perhaps explain why Southey thought that Louis XVIII should have celebrated his accession to the throne by executing "some sixteen marshals and great men with-

---

* "Ode 1815," *Poetical Works*, p. 261n. Acknowledging that "many had stumbled" at these lines, Wordsworth softened them in 1845. Hazlitt quotes the phrase "Carnage is thy daughter" in his intensely political discussion of *Coriolanus* (4.214) in *Characters of Shakespear's Plays* and elsewhere, and he refers to it repeatedly (5.348, 7.96n, 142, 9.39n, 12.374).

† It has recently been suggested by Geoffrey Carnall (*Robert Southey and His Age* [1960], p. 99) that Southey's willingness to assist the *Quarterly Review* was perhaps prompted by his resentment against the *Edinburgh*, the first number of which had contained Jeffrey's stern review of *Thalaba*. For a generally sympathetic account of Southey's growing conservatism see Jack Simmons, *Southey* (1948), pp. 151–181.

‡ *Life and Correspondence*, pp. 284f. Although Crabb Robinson (I, 127) was disturbed by Southey's vehemence, he said in 1813, "I cannot but hesitate before I condemn the apprehensions of such men as an idle panic."

out trial or form of judicial inquiry." [62] He continued in this vein until the end. Although by 1825 Sir Walter Scott, one of the sanest of the Tories, was wondering if Southey had not survived his utility for the *Quarterly Review* (especially in matters "where the spirit of the age must be consulted"),[63] the laureate continued and intensified his attacks upon reform.[64] One of our last views of him — in 1839, not long before his mind gave way — is his expounding to Carlyle (a most sympathetic auditor) his "usual" theme of sinister democracy with its "steady decay" of political, social, and personal morality.[65]

Leigh Hunt's remark that Coleridge, before adopting liberal views when young, "should have bethought himself, first, whether he had the courage not to get fat" [66] has a point, but it ignores the fact that his disenchantment with reform was not a product of his middle age. Prompted partly by the excesses of the French and partly by the calamities of the Industrial Revolution, his Toryism had begun to show itself when he was in his twenties. In 1799 he told Southey that "Guillotining is too *republican* a death for such Reptiles" as Sieyès and Bonaparte,[67] and two years later, lamenting "our pestilential commerce" with its social consequences, he said that if Wordsworth and "two or three Farmers" would join him, he would emigrate.[68] In 1802 he was still maintaining, in the columns of the *Morning Post*, that since "all, or the greater part of, the happiness or misery, virtue or vice, of mankind, depends on forms of government," universal suffrage was essential for a people to express its wants and needs;[69] but by 1809, when he came to write *The Friend,* he proclaimed it as an axiom — and moreover, as one that he had always held — that government should rest on property, and that "that government was the best, in which the power or political influence of the individual was in proportion to his property, provided that the free circulation of property was not impeded by any positive law or customs, nor the tendency of wealth to accumulate in abiding masses unduly encouraged." [70]

Not long afterward we find him deploring a bill for the prevention of cruelty to animals as a piece of *"Legislative* Jacobinism," [71] and at the news of Perceval's assassination he went, according to his own account, from numbness to sickness, and then to "a convulsive state of weeping." [72] Thereafter he, like Southey, was terrified by the thought of insurrection. Whereas he had once defined a Jacobin as anyone whose notion of government is built on "personal and natural rights," [73] by 1814 he announced that a Jacobin was anyone who, insisting on his rights but neglectful of his duties, used "terror, secrecy, falsehood, cupidity" in seeking his seditious ends.[74] As a writer for the *Courier,* said Thomas Barnes about this time, Coleridge seemed to have a "shrinking horror lest his thoughts should offend the established orders," [75] and there can be no doubt that fear, or at any rate timidity, played too large a part in his thinking of these years. For him, as for the other poets, the present system represented safety, and so he rationalized its evils. "The ordained and beneficient interdependence of the higher, middle, and lower ranks" was a sacred trust that every Briton should maintain intact, [76] he said, and in his own maturest work on politics — the two *Lay Sermons* and *On the Constitution of Church and State* — he copiously and murkily expounded his hierarchic views. Somewhat less murky, but much more damaging to his reputation as a sage, was his advice to Lord Liverpool in 1817: "It is high time, my Lord," he said in speaking of the current discontents, "that the subjects of Christian Governments should be taught that neither historically or morally, in fact or by right, have men made the State; but that the State, and that alone, makes them men." [77]

ATTACK

It is well to keep these facts in mind in reading Hazlitt's more violent comments on the poets, for they help us understand, if not condone, his rancor and vulgarity. His diatribes of 1816 and 1817, which were simultaneous with *The Round Table, Characters of Shakespear's Plays,* and some of the best theatrical reviews and critical essays in the language, remind us that this gifted but overburdened journalist was capable of the most appalling bad behavior when his temper was aroused. "If any one wishes to see me quite calm," he said, "they may cheat me in a bargain, or tread upon my toes; but a truth repelled, a sophism repeated, totally disconcerts me, and I lose all patience." [1] For reasons not entirely clear, it was Coleridge — needing all the help he got, and more than most of his old friends were willing to supply — whom Hazlitt marked for execution first. In August 1816 he wrote a scathing piece for the *Examiner* on the "Distresses of the Country" in which he pointed out that England's sorry situation was not unrelated to the nine hundred million pounds that it had spent in order to restore "the Pope, the Inquisition, the Bourbons, and the doctrine of Divine Right"; [2] and then in September, learning that Coleridge had elaborately announced a "lay sermon" on the same subject, he proceeded to "review" the advertisement of the book without waiting for the work itself. It was a deplorable performance, for he outlined Coleridge's career, and explained his mental habits, in terms that, valid or not, were grotesquely unfair to a great and greatly troubled man. Not only does he call Coleridge "the Dog in the Manger of literature, an intellectual Mar-Plot, who will neither let any body else come to a conclusion, nor come to one himself," [3] he even ridicules his nose.[*] He charges him with "levity" and vacillation, and deplores his appalling waste of talent; and even the thought of what Coleridge once had been cannot temper his dismay at the thought of what he had become. "Let him talk on for ever in this world and the next; and both worlds will be the better for it," he remarks in closing; "but let him not write, or pretend to write, nonsense." [4]

Such motiveless malignity, which offended even Lamb,[5] of course offended Coleridge. Writing to a friend in mid-September of the "most brutal attack, as unprovoked as it is even to extravagance false," he named Hazlitt as the culprit, said that he had "befriended" him for several years "with the most improvident kindness when he was utterly friendless," and then related his version of the escapade at Keswick thirteen years before.[6] A week later he announced that he would take no notice of Hazlitt or his "libels," at least in so far as they were aimed at him. He was a man of "considerable Talent," Coleridge conceded,

> but it is diseased by a morbid hatred of the Beautiful, and killed by the absence of Imagination, & alas! by a wicked Heart of embruted Appetites. Poor wretch! he is a melancholy instance of the awful Truth — that man cannot be on a level with the Beasts — he must be above them or below them. Almost all the *sparkles* & *originalities* of his Essays are, however, echoes from poor Charles Lamb — and in his last libel the image of the Angel without hands or feet was stolen from a Letter of my own to Charles Lamb, which had been quoted to him.[†]

But if Coleridge had been annoyed by the premature review of his first *Lay Sermon* in the *Examiner* he was outraged by a vicious piece on *Christabel* in the September *Edinburgh*,[7] and under the circumstances it is not surprising that he attributed it to Hazlitt too. Although it is probable that Hazlitt had no hand in it at all,[‡] his attacks on Coleridge, both before and after its appearance, were enough to justify the poet's

[*] 7.381. Hazlitt omitted this passage in reprinting his review in *Political Essays*.

[†] Griggs, IV, 685f. In his anticipatory review of the *Lay Sermon* Hazlitt had said (7.117) that Coleridge's genius had angel's wings, but neither hands nor feet.

[‡] Despite a recent effort to show that Hazlitt wrote at least a part of this *Edinburgh* review (Hoover H. Jordan, "Thomas Moore and the Review of *Christabel*," MP, LIV [1956], 95-105), Howe's conclusion on this moot question (*Life*, pp. 398ff.) seems to me to be substantially correct. Elizabeth Schneider ("The Unknown Reviewer of *Christabel*: Jeffrey, Hazlitt, Tom Moore," PMLA, LXX [1955], 417-432) has suggested that Tom Moore may have been the author. It is perhaps significant that a writer in the *Examiner* (24 November 1816, pp. 743f.) took exception to the harshness of the *Edinburgh* reviewer and at the same time reprinted "Fire, Famine, and Slaughter" as a specimen of Coleridge's work before his political opinions had, like the moon, suffered "total eclipse." This article, which Crabb Robinson noted in his diary (I, 198), appeared on the same page as Hazlitt's "On Common-Place Critics."

bitter irritation. On December 5 Coleridge informed a correspondent that the wretch who had so "grossly calumniated" him in the *Examiner* and the *Edinburgh Review* was one

who owes to me more than to his own parents — for at my own risk I saved perhaps his Life from the Gallows, most certainly his character from blasting Infamy — His reason I give in his own words — "Damn him! *I hate him*: FOR I am under obligations to him." . . . All good I had done him of *every* kind, and never ceased to do him so, till he had done his best to bring down infamy on three families, in which he had been sheltered as a Brother, by vices too disgusting to be named — & since then the only *Wrong,* I have done him, has been to decline his acquaintance.[8]

The year ended in a flurry of abuse. In "On Poetical Versatility," a Round Table paper of December 22, Hazlitt wittily expounded the proposition that since poetry is designed to please, its authors are constitutionally reluctant to defend "unpopular" opinions. "They do not like to be shut out when laurels are to be given away at Court — or places under Government to be disposed of, in romantic situations in the country. They are happy to be reconciled on the first opportunity to prince and people, and to exchange their principles for a pension." [9] Although Coleridge, no doubt to his great regret, was not liable to slurs about his pension, Wordsworth was, and in the same issue of the *Examiner* Hazlitt closed an attack on Stoddart and the *Times* with a passing blow at him:

He hates all greatness, and all pretensions to it but his own. His egotism is in this respect a madness; for he scorns even the admiration of himself, thinking it a presumption in any one to suppose that he has taste or sense enough to understand him. He hates all science and all art; he hates chemistry, he hates conchology; he hates Sir Isaac Newton; he hates logic, he hates metaphysics, which he says are unintelligible, and yet he would be thought to understand them; he hates prose, he hates all poetry but his own. . . . He hates all that others love and admire but himself. He is glad that Bonaparte is sent to St. Helena, and that the Louvre is dispersed for the same reason — to get rid of the idea of any thing greater, or thought greater than himself. The Bourbons, and their processions of the Holy Ghost, give no disturbance to his vanity; and he therefore gives them none.[10]

Crabb Robinson had observed that for such "magnificent & daemonacal" invective Hazlitt deserved "flogging with a golden scourge," [11] but when he encountered him at Basil Montagu's on December 22, the very day of the attack on Wordsworth, he "carefully abstained" from shaking hands with him.[12] The action was symbolic of a wide repudiation.

Meanwhile, the belated appearance of the first *Lay Sermon* — called *The Statesman's Manual* and addressed to "the Higher Classes of Society" — was the cue for new attacks, for in that confused, confusing book Coleridge, protesting that he had been "the object of personal slander, (slander as unprovoked as it was groundless, unless acts of kindness are provocation)," [13] had weightily tried to prove the Bible to be the safest guide in politics and an ample warrant for conservative opinion. Greeting it with derision and contempt in the *Examiner* of December 29, Hazlitt found in it a vindication for his premature review three months before. To argue "that the doctrine of divine right is contained *par excellence* in the Scriptures alone," he said with withering indignation, "is we should suppose, an instance of a power of voluntary self-delusion, and of a delight in exercising it on the most ticklish topics, greater than ever was or ever will be possessed by any other individual that ever did or ever will live upon the face of the earth." * But all of this was prologue to the swelling triumph of invective in the December *Edinburgh* (which did not appear till two months later).† Coleridge's "intended conclusions have always the start of his premises, — and they keep it," he observed, for "he treats his opinions, and his reasons for them, as lawyers do their clients, and will never suffer them to come together lest they should join issue, and so put an end to his business." [14] The Bible does not sanction his absurd beliefs, and he clearly wrote his foolish book for reasons unrelated to religion: "to reprobate that diffusion of free inquiry — that difference of private, and ascendancy of public opinion, which has been the necessary consequence, and the great benefit of the Reformation." [15] It is contemptible, Hazlitt charged, for a presumably pious and disinterested seeker after truth to "impose upon us, by force or fraud, a complete system of superstition without faith, of despotism without loyalty, of error without enthusiasm, and all the evils, without any of the blessings, of ignorance."

Under these circumstances it is astonishing that in a footnote to

---

* 7.123. Another blow of Hazlitt's at this *Lay Sermon*, in a letter to the editor of the *Examiner* (12 January 1817) signed "Semper Ego Auditor" (7.128f.), concerned his meeting with Coleridge in 1798, and from it grew "My First Acquaintance with Poets," which he published in the *Liberal* six years later.

† See Elizabeth Schneider, "The Unknown Reviewer of *Christabel*: Jeffrey, Hazlitt, Tom Moore," *PMLA*, LXX [1955], 421n. On 3 January 1817 Hazlitt wrote to Jeffrey (ALS, National Library of Scotland) that he had been "exceedingly unwell" and therefore unable to complete the two long articles he had planned on "literature and philosophy." In place of these — which were perhaps the reviews of Scott's edition of Swift and of Buhle's history of modern philosophy that he had first proposed two years before (see above, page 213) — he said he would supply a piece, "which you shall have by the twenty-first, on Mr Coleridge's Lay Sermon, if I do not hear from you to the contrary, it will be about a sheet, and enter into the skirts of the Kantean philosophy." Since the review as printed did not deal with Kant we may suppose that Jeffrey exercised his editorial prerogatives, but Hazlitt's ignorant attack on Kant's "monstrous absurdity" in his review, a few months later (16.123f.), of *Biographia Literaria* no doubt represents his thrifty use of the material.

the second *Lay Sermon,* which appeared early in the spring of 1817, Coleridge alluded gracefully (if belatedly) to the "ability and originality" of the author of *An Essay on the Principles of Human Action.*[16] It is less astonishing that simultaneously in *Biographia Literaria* he struck back hard at Hazlitt, the *Edinburgh Review,* and the whole tribe of vituperative critics who had been barking at him for the past six months and more,[17] or that in his letters of this period he expressed a poignant sense of injured innocence.* In the spring of 1817, however, Hazlitt shifted his attack to Southey, for the new year had brought one of the most amusing episodes in this dreary sequence of abuse. On 13 February 1817, in the very week that the *Quarterly Review*[18] appeared with a new demand by Southey for the suppression of reformist agitation, *Wat Tyler,* the crude, seditious little play that he had written as a boy, burst upon the world in its first, unauthorized edition. After the publisher to whom it had been offered in 1794 decided not to print the work, Southey consigned it to oblivion, or at any rate did not retrieve his manuscript, and for more than twenty years it lay forgotten in the custody of one William Winterbotham, a Dissenting preacher who had gone to jail in 1793 for his seditious sermons.[19] Then, in an evil hour, it was resurrected and printed with a scrap of Southey's poetry on the title page. Privately the laureate told a friend that "the sins of my youth are risen against me,"[20] but in a letter to the *Courier* he said that he was unashamed of crude opinions that he had "long outgrown," and denounced the "private malignity" that had been exercised against him.[21]

To Hazlitt and his friends it must have seemed that the Lord had delivered their enemy into their hands. The *Examiner* — which, as Shelley said, had been the laureate's "crown of thorns" for years[22] — had already exhumed and reprinted samples of his early work in an effort to embarrass him,[23] but the hitherto unpublished *Wat Tyler* was a very special find. Hazlitt immediately reviewed both the *Quarterly* article and the little play together with obvious delight,[24] but as if he

* In June 1817, a few months after *Biographia Literaria* appeared, Coleridge informed a correspondent of Hazlitt's bad behavior at the Lakes (Griggs, IV, 735f.), and in the next year he enlarged upon the same old scandal at least twice more (Griggs, IV, 813, 831). In 1819, in a draft of a long letter "To the author of Peter's Letters to his Kinsfolk" (i.e., John Gibson Lockhart) scribbled on the flyleaf of his second *Lay Sermon,* he explained how Jeffrey and Hazlitt had conspired against him, knowing he was "poor, sick, and embarrassed" (Griggs, IV, 972ff.); and in 1820 he cited (*Unpublished Letters,* II, 277) as proof of his unquenchable affection for Lamb his having overlooked the shockingly "friendly connection" that Lamb maintained with Hazlitt. In 1819 Coleridge complained to Southey (Griggs, IV, 918) about Hazlitt's calling Geraldine (in *Christabel*) a man in disguise, and in an undated manuscript jotting of perhaps about this time (Kathleen Coburn, *Inquiring Spirit* [1951], p. 207) he observed that "Mr. H[azlitt?] in his lust of Slander and in the rampancy of his malice first commits a rape upon my words, and then arraigns them as unchaste."

were only warming to the task. A few days later, on March 14, William Smith stood up in Parliament with a copy of the *Quarterly* in one hand and *Wat Tyler* in the other to demand, with heavy irony, that the author of the play be punished. "Now," the *Examiner* remarked, "Mr. Southey's bane and antidote . . . are both before him in one cup — his egotism; and of this, we suppose, he will take a hearty draught, and persuade himself that 'a malignant Renegado' is the most virtuous of mankind." [25] Coleridge, always far more zealous in defense of Southey's reputation than Southey was of his, had just defended the laureate's life and works in *Biographia Literaria,** and when this new attack arose he again put on his armor. Although he conceded to a friend that most of *Wat Tyler* ("a wretched Mess of Pig's meat") was not altogether wrong in its views of social inequality,[26] in the *Courier* he called it "an admirable burlesque on the pompous extravagances" of reformers in the nineties, commented sadly on the wicked glee with which "the Hunts, Hazlitts and Cobbetts" had greeted it, and deplored the "malice prepense" that had inspired its publication.[†] This article in the *Courier* reminded the *Examiner* of a reformed whoremonger who spoke of his old cronies with sorrow and compassion.[27]

Although Leigh Hunt plagued the laureate with such witticisms through the spring,[‡] the main attacks on him in the *Examiner* were clearly Hazlitt's work. Replying to the "maudlin methodistical casuistry" of Coleridge's defense, he remarked on March 30 that whereas Southey's "laurelled Muse" was in such "high court-keeping" that she "tosses up her nose at the very mention of reform," she had not abandoned all her evil ways. "There are, as *The Courier* observes, youthful indiscretions; but there are also riper and more deliberate errors. A woman is more liable to prostitute her person at nineteen — a man is more likely to prostitute his understanding at forty." [28] Then and later it was Hazlitt's

---

* I, 39–49. In his *Edinburgh* review of *Biographia Literaria* (16.120) Hazlitt brusquely answered this defense: "The charge is, that he [Southey] wrote democratical nonsense in his youth; and that he has not only taken to write against democracy in his maturer age, but has abused and reviled those who adhere to his former opinions; and accepted of emoluments from the party which formerly calumniated him, for those good services. Now, what has Mr. Coleridge to oppose to this? Mr. Southey's private character!"

† *Essays*, III, 943f. According to Hoadley (p. 86), Coleridge wrote four letters in all to the *Courier* (March 17, 18, 27, and April 2) in defense of Southey.

‡ For example, he wrote a piece (13 April 1817, pp. 236f.) about the laureate's final illness ("attended with great irritability"), the brave but futile efforts of Dr. Paracelsus Broadnum Coleridge to save him, and his burial by a troop of Jacobins ("with their coats turned"), a deputation from the Inquisition, and a crowd of mourners including Stoddart, Canning, and other "Hirelings on Horse back." A few weeks later (11 May 1817, pp. 300 ff.), after Southey had replied to his tormentors in *A Letter to William Smith,* he described the corpse's rising from his bier to denounce his adversaries.

main contention that Southey's Toryism was as bigoted and unreflecting
as his youthful ardor for reform had been, and as he answers, one by
one, the points of Coleridge's defense he writes so well and wittily that
the "stripling bard" of nineteen is made to look as foolish as the laureate
of forty. "A man may change his opinion. Good. But if he changes his
opinion as his interest or vanity would prompt, if he deserts the weak
to go to the stronger side, the change is a suspicious one! and we shall
have a right to impute it rather to a defect of moral principle than to an
accession of intellectual strength." * (Incidentally, it was shortly after
this appeared that Wordsworth warned Haydon to stay away from
Hazlitt: "Avoid him — hic niger est — And this, I understand, is the
general opinion wherever he is known, in London.") [29]

The comedy of errors grew brisker when Southey, having brought suit
against the publishers, was told by Lord Eldon that his play was so
seditious it was ineligible for copyright. Thereafter, while sales of *Wat
Tyler* soared † its author's prestige drooped. As Byron (who detested
him) remarked, it was no disgrace for Southey to have written his
wretched little play and then his wretched patriotic odes, "but it is something, for which I have no words, for this man to have endeavoured to
bring to the stake (for such he would do) men who think as he thought,
and for no reason but because they think so still, when he has found it
convenient to think otherwise." [30] Under the circumstances the laureate
was almost obliged to take some sort of action, and by the end of April,‡
therefore, he came forward with a *Letter to William Smith* that in certain quarters was regarded as a "triumphant" vindication. [31] Though written with his usual felicity of style, it is not an attractive piece of work.
After a hot attack on Smith for having "grossly and wantonly" insulted
him and on the "skulking scoundrel" who had arranged for the publication of his play, [32] he vigorously defends his current views (including,
among others, censorship, emigration of the poor, and compulsory instruction for the "lower classes" in the tenets of the Church of England), [33]
and he closes by boasting of the "just and memorable severity" with
which he had disposed of his "calumniator." §

* 7.180. This long article of March 30 had been preceded ten days earlier by a
shorter piece (19.196ff.) that Hazlitt wrote at Bristol. The reason for his presence
there does not appear.

† In May Southey told Robinson (I, 206) that there were 36,000 copies of his
play in print, and his son (*Life and Correspondence*, p. 350) later estimated a total
sale of 60,000.

‡ On April 7 Wordsworth told Haydon (*Middle Years*, II, 782) that Southey was
"preparing a rod for Mr Wm Smith," and by April 28 Crabb Robinson — who read
all the newest books at once — recorded in his diary (I, 206) that he was reading
Southey's pamphlet.

§ *Essays, Moral and Political* (1832), II, 31. In a "Postscript" of 1821 to his

POLITICS AND LITERATURE

Hazlitt's extended comment on this *Letter* in his *Examiner* review of May 11 and 18 cannot be said to break new ground, although in both strength of style and rancor it is, as Keats remarked, astonishing.* Hazlitt again rehearses Southey's early ardor for reform, charges him with gross venality, and expatiates upon his bigotry and egotism.

> Poor Doctors Price and Priestley, who were Republicans like Mr. Southey, were religious, moral men; but they were Dissenters, and this excites as much contempt in Mr. Southey, as if they had been atheists and profligates. Others again, among Mr. Southey's political compeers, were atheists and immoral; and for this, Mr. Southey expresses the same abhorrence of them, as if they had been Dissenters! He, indeed, contrives to make the defects of others so many perfections in himself; and by this mode of proceeding, abstracts himself into a *beau ideal* of moral and political egotism — a *Sir Charles Grandison*, calculated for the beginning of the nineteenth, and the latter end of the eighteenth century, upon the true infallible principles of intellectual coxcombry.[34]

He closes with a weary cadence, as if he himself were tired of exposing Southey's errors. He had passed him in the street not many days before, he said, and was sorry not to speak to him; but as he watched him walk away he sighed, *"Alas poor Southey!* 'We saw in him a painful hieroglyphic of humanity; a sad memento of departed independence; a striking instance of the rise and fall of patriot bards!' "* [35]

In March 1817, just as the furor over *Wat Tyler* was coming to a head, Coleridge's *Biographia Literaria* appeared, and Hazlitt's review of that great book in the August *Edinburgh* may be regarded as the final salvo in this phase of his campaign against the patriot bards.† Unlike his *Edinburgh* attack on the first *Lay Sermon* — to say nothing of the wretched piece on *Christabel* that we need not charge against his name

---

Carmen Triumphale (Poetical Works [1838], III, 207) Southey, comparing himself to a "mastiff of the right English breed assailed by a little, impertinent, noisy, meddling cur," said that "by stopping half a minute, and lifting his leg over him" he could quickly and appropriately subdue his adversary. When he reprinted *Wat Tyler* in his *Poetical Works* near the end of his life he asserted (II, 22) that he was no more ashamed of having been a "republican" than of having been a boy.

* Writing to Leigh Hunt on 10 May 1817, Keats (Rollins, I, 137f.) compared one passage in Hazlitt's article (7.194) to "a Whale's back in the Sea of Prose," and three days later he told Haydon (Rollins, I, 144) that he thought the piece "tremendous." Characteristically, however, he deplored Hazlitt's cruel allusion (7.187) to Southey's "withered bay-leaves and a few contemptible grey hairs."

† Although Jeffrey later claimed the authorship of this review (Cockburn, II, 423), its long digression on Burke (16.130–134) — which was printed two years later in *Political Essays* (7.226–229) — as well as ample evidence of style shows that it was mainly Hazlitt's work. Howe (16.425f.) thinks that part of the attack on Southey (16.121) and some of the comments on Wordsworth's theory of poetic diction (16.134f.) were the editor's interpolations.

ATTACK

— his article on *Biographia Literaria* is something more than vulgar and jocose invective. Puzzled by the "multiplicity" of its author's "speculative opinions," Hazlitt — like many other readers since — found it rambling and disorganized, and with certain parts of it he was in strenuous disagreement; but despite occasional lapses into his old bone-crushing style his review is, though derogatory, a solid piece of work.

This is not to say that he had resolved to extend the olive branch, for Coleridge himself had made a truce unlikely. Not only had he devoted an entire chapter of *Biographia Literaria* to the sins of the *Edinburgh* and its "*habit* of malignity*,*" [36] but he had charged that its vile review of *Christabel* was "generally attributed (whether rightly or no I know not) to a man, who both in my presence and in my absence has repeatedly pronounced it the finest poem in the language"; [37] and about the attacks on the first *Lay Sermon* he had been even more explicit:

> it was reviewed . . . by anticipation with a malignity so avowedly and exclusively personal, as is, I believe, unprecedented even in the present contempt of all common humanity that disgraces and endangers the liberty of the press. After its appearance, the author of this lampoon was chosen to review it in the Edinburgh Review; and under the single condition, that he should have written what he himself really thought, and have criticised the work as he would have done had its author been indifferent to him, I should have chosen that man myself, both from the vigor and the originality of his mind, and from his particular acuteness in speculative reasoning, before all others. . . . But I can truly say, that the grief with which I read this rhapsody of predetermined insult, had the rhapsodist himself for its whole and sole object: and that the indignant contempt which it excited in me, was as exclusively confined to his employer and suborner. [38]

In an initialed note affixed to the *Edinburgh* review of *Biographia Literaria* Jeffrey himself undertook to deal with these "averments of a personal and injurious nature," * but Hazlitt, ignoring Coleridge's attack, dealt with the merits of his book. For all kinds of reasons he could not endorse his warm defense of Southey or his praise of German metaphysics; but if he expresses his dissent with a good deal of vulgar witticism at Coleridge's expense, it at least is honest — though, in the case of Kant, ignorant — opposition.

One might wish, however, that about certain major topics he were more explicit. On the subjects that have most attracted later critics —

---

* 16.426f. Jeffrey denied that he had written the review of *Christabel,* that he had ever "employed or suborned any body to abuse or extol" a publication, and that he had any knowledge of the anticipatory review of the first *Lay Sermon.* "Nay, I was not even aware of the existence of the *Lay Sermon* itself, when a review of it was offered me by a gentleman in whose judgment and talents I had great confidence, but whom I certainly never suspected, and do not suspect at this moment, of having any personal or partial feelings of any kind towards its author. I therefore accepted his offer, and printed his review, with some retrenchments and verbal alterations, just as I was setting off, in a great hurry, for London, on professional business, in January last."

Coleridge's theory of imagination and his views of Wordsworth's work
— he professes skepticism, for he resents the elaborate preparation for
a theory never formulated, and he thinks, or seems to think, that Coleridge had nothing of importance to say of Wordsworth's poetical achievement. "The object of this long-winding metaphysical march, which resembles a patriarchal journey, is to point out and settle the true grounds
of Mr. Wordsworth's claim to originality as a poet; which, if we rightly
understand the deduction, turns out to be, that there is nothing peculiar
about him; and that his poetry, in so far as it is good for any thing at
all, is just like any other good poetry." * Similarly with Coleridge's
strictures on Wordsworth's theory of poetic diction: just as there are
various kinds of poetry, Hazlitt says, there are various kinds of language,
each of them of value if it is rightly used. Although the "paste of rich
and honeyed words" that Spenser, Pope, and Gray employ, the "simple
and familiar language" that Shakespeare gives to Lear in his more impassioned utterances, and the heightened "classic" speech of Milton's
Samson are all suited to their subjects, all are in a sense unreal. "Whenever articulation passes naturally into intonation, this is the beginning of
poetry. There is no natural harmony in the ordinary combinations of
significant sounds: the language of prose is not the language of music,
or of *passion*," and it was "to supply this inherent defect in the mechanism of language" that poetry was "invented." [39] A coda on the theme
(already stated in the Round Table paper "On Poetical Versatility")
that poets tend to "oscillate, with a giddy and sickening motion, from
one absurdity to another, and expiate the follies of their youth by the
heartless vices of their advancing age" [40] closes the review. It is not, perhaps, the kind of judgment we would like of a book so great as Coleridge's, but it shows that by 1817 intellectual rapport was no longer
possible between the most important critics of the age.

REPRISAL

For two years Hazlitt, with the *Examiner* as weapon, had been smiting
patriot bards, the party they supported, and the principles they espoused,
and generally he had kept them off their balance in a posture of defense.

---

* 16.121f. Three years later, in the *London Magazine* (18.371), Hazlitt parodied
Coleridge's theory of imagination so knowledgeably that one wishes he had dealt with
it more fully in his review of *Biographia Literaria*: "The principle of the imagination
resembles the emblem of the serpent, by which the ancients typified wisdom and the
universe, with undulating folds, for ever varying and for ever flowing into itself, —
circular, and without beginning or end. The definite, the fixed, is death: the principle
of life is the indefinite, the growing, the moving, the continuous."

But then he wrote a book, and the hour of retribution was at hand. A withering attack on his newly published *Round Table* in the April 1817 *Quarterly Review* made it clear that the Tories had marked him for destruction, and thereafter this ponderous and powerful organ of conservative opinion demolished each successive work of his as it appeared. Meanwhile, beginning in the fall of 1817, the more sprightly *Blackwood's Magazine* began to bombard him and Hunt and other pestilential "Cockneys" with witty and irresponsible abuse. He was not the only victim of the Tory press, of course, but in the hurly-burly of the post-Napoleonic years, when literature and politics were inextricably confused, he had earned a bad distinction; and if, as a friend of his remarked in 1820, some of the attacks on him were "purely brutal and malignant" he himself had helped to set the pattern.[1]

Leigh Hunt's complaint that the *Quarterly* let politics discolor its literary opinions was, to say the least, naive.[2] That celebrated journal had been founded in 1809 as a counterweight to the *Edinburgh Review* — which, as Walter Scott remarked, was doing "incalculable damage" by its attacks upon the government[3] — and the fact, as Southey conceded "in plain English," that "the ministers set it up"[4] meant that its editorial course was clear. Consequently it was hailed, said Hazlitt in mournful retrospect, "as a great relief to all those of his Majesty's subjects who are firmly convinced that the only way to have things remain exactly as they are is to put a stop to all inquiries whether they are right or wrong, and that if you cannot answer a man's arguments, you may at least try to take away his character."[5]

In William Gifford the founders of the *Quarterly* had found an ideal editor for their new review. A poor boy who by hard work — and with the aid of patrons — had scrambled his way to an Oxford education and then to a modest fame for his satires on poetasters and playwrights, he was born, he said,

> To brand obtrusive ignorance with scorn;
> On bloated pedantry to pour my rage,
> And hiss preposterous fustian from the stage.[6]

His couplets in *The Baviad* (1791) and *The Maeviad* (1795) were reinforced with such savage explanatory notes — as when he called Holcroft a "poor stupid wretch, to whom infidelity and disloyalty have given a momentary notoriety" despite his "grovelling and senseless productions"[7] — that he was marked for higher things. His brilliant conduct of the *Anti-Jacobin* (1797–98) and subsequent editions of Juvenal (1802) and Massinger (1805) led to the editorship of the *Quarterly Re-*

view, and there his learning, venom, and implacable hostility to all forms of liberal thought made him one of the most potent figures of the age. He was not, like Jeffrey, the sort of editor who wrote almost as much as his contributors, but he was a man of very firm opinions, and they were stamped so firmly on everything he printed in the *Quarterly* that it was unmistakably his own.* He felt about a Frenchman as certain people feel about a toad, said one of his admirers, and the bare mention of a Whig or liberal politician made him buckle on his armor.⁸ Scott liked Gifford, and shared his politics, of course, but even he admitted that "he flagellated with so little pity, that people lost their sense for the criminal's guilt in dislike of the savage pleasure which the executioner seemd to take in inflicting the punishment." ⁹

As for Gifford's victims, they abominated him. Hazlitt, some of whose best invective he inspired, called him "the invisible link" between literature and the police,¹⁰ pronounced his "despicable eminence in the world of letters" to be a major scandal of the age,¹¹ and said that his review was

a depository for every species of political sophistry and personal calumny. There is no abuse or corruption that does not there find a jesuitical palliation or a bare-faced vindication. There we meet the slime of hypocrisy, the varnish of courts, the cant of pedantry, the cobwebs of the law, the iron hand of power. Its object is as mischievous as the means by which it is pursued are odious. . . . No statement in the *Quarterly Review* is to be trusted: there is no fact that is not misrepresented in it, no quotation that is not garbled, no character that is not slandered, if it can answer the purposes of a party to do so.¹²

Sydney Smith refused to read the *Quarterly* review of a volume of his sermons (which it described as vulgar, heretical, and ungrammatical) ¹³ because its abuse was intended, he explained, not for his correction but his pain.¹⁴ Shelley, whose *Prometheus Unbound* the *Quarterly* described as *"drivelling prose run mad,"* ¹⁵ shared the misconception that its attacks on Keats almost drove that fragile poet mad and brought on his early death.† Macaulay said of John Wilson Croker, the "talking potato" ¹⁶ who, as one of Gifford's favorite contributors, had been assigned to deal with Keats, that he "would go a hundred miles through sleet and snow, on the top of a coach, in a December night, to search a parish register, for the sake of showing that a man is illegitimate, or a woman older than

---

* It has been conjectured that in his fifteen years as editor of the *Quarterly* Gifford himself produced only five reviews and collaborated on three others. See Roy Benjamin Clark, *William Gifford, Tory Satirist, Critic, and Editor* (1930), pp. 187f., 273n.

† *Letters,* II, 828ff. The damage done to Keats was all the greater, said John Scott in the *London Magazine* (I [1820], 387), because the *Quarterly Review* was "read by tens of thousands, nine-tenths of whom are not able to judge for themselves, and half of the other tenth will not take the trouble of doing so."

she says she is." [17] That the *Quarterly* taxed the author of *The Story of Rimini* with "vanity, vulgarity, ignorance, and coarseness" [18] and judged his *Foliage* so unsavory that he would live and die dishonoured and be forgotten by posterity [19] was bad enough, Hunt thought, but its abuse of Shelley's *Revolt of Islam* was so cruel that it moved him to a long rebuttal of the critic, "heavy, and swelling, and soft with venom," who went skulking through its pages like a toad. [20] Later, in *Ultra-Crepidarius* (1823), a satire with Gifford as its subject, he asserted that every one of Gifford's writers was compelled to

> Misdeem, and misconstrue, like miscreant brothers;
> Misquote, and misplace, and mislead, and misstate,
> Misapply, misinterpret, misreckon, misdate,
> Misinform, misconjecture, misargue; in short,
> Miss all that is good, that ye miss not the Court. [21]

In reprinting his *Feast of the Poets* in 1832 Hunt retained a "hostile" sketch of Gifford, partly because Hazlitt had admired it, partly because he himself thought it necessary to protest against "inhumanities which neither age nor suffering do away"; [22] and at the end of his life, when he was mellow and forgiving, he still could not forgive the editor of the *Quarterly Review* — "the only man I ever attacked, respecting whom I have felt no regret." [23]

This, then, was the man who decreed that Hazlitt should be prepared for execution.* The publication of *The Round Table* early in 1817 provided the occasion, and the *Quarterly* made the most of it. That essays by both Hunt and Hazlitt were included in the book was dismissed as of no importance — "we really have not time to discriminate between the productions of the two gentlemen" [24] — but whereas Hunt provided most of the examples of bad writing (including an unfortunate Round Table paper on washerwomen), [25] Hazlitt was most brutally attacked. His work was judged to be beneath contempt, and his faults, including "vulgar descriptions, silly paradoxes, flat truisms, misty sophistry, broken English, ill humour and rancorous abuse," [26] were called the tokens of a "sour Jacobin" who, in his "endeavours to crawl into the light," had left his "slime and filth" on the tombs of the illustrious dead. In short, the critic said, his offensive book would not deserve the honor of review except that it was for the public good to

---

* Although Hazlitt attributed all the *Quarterly* attacks on him to the editor himself (9.18, 11.123), the first three reviews — of *The Round Table* (April 1817), *Characters of Shakespear's Plays* (January 1818), and *Lectures on the English Poets* (July 1818) — were probably the work of James Russell. *Political Essays* was reviewed by Gifford himself (July 1819) and *Table-Talk* by John Matthews (October 1821). See Smiles, II, 44; Clark, *Gifford*, pp. 213–218.

fling him back into the obscurity "in which nature designed that he should grovel." [27] Subsequent *Quarterly* critiques of Hazlitt's works were in the same high strain. Its attack on *Characters of Shakespear's Plays* — which, said Hazlitt, killed the sale of a book that in three months had gone into a second edition and was "fast advancing to a third" * — ended with the comment that the author's knowledge of his subject and of the English language was "exactly on a par with the purity of his morals and the depth of his understanding"; [28] and *Lectures on the English Poets* was dismissed as a work without "a single just observation" on the authors whom it treated, and as an affront to taste and common sense. [29]

Hazlitt's reaction might have been predicted. Soon after the *Quarterly* had attacked his book on Shakespeare he expressed his view of Gifford, in a piece in the *Examiner,* as a "cat's-paw" whose job it was "to keep a strict eye over all writers who differ in opinion with His Majesty's Ministers, and to measure their talents and attainments by the standard of their servility and meanness"; [30] but seven months later, when the review of his *Lectures on the English Poets* belatedly appeared — for Gifford was notoriously unpunctual — he gave himself the pleasure of a full reply. The fact that by then *Blackwood's Magazine* had also turned its fire on him no doubt sharpened his resentment, and as soon as his lectures on the English comic writers were completed he turned on his tormentors. The results were quickly seen: against the "Jackalls of the North" he brought a suit for libel, and then he wrote the famous *Letter to William Gifford, Esq.,* which is both an *apologia pro vita sua* and a triumph of invective. "Sir," he opens coldly, "You have an ugly trick of saying what is not true of any one you do not like; and it will be the object of this letter to cure you of it"; and when he closes, more than forty pages later, Gifford has been tossed and gored with a fury that even Hazlitt rarely equaled. Describing the *Quarterly* as the "receptacle for the scum and sediment of all the prejudice, bigotry, ill-will, ignorance, and rancour, afloat in the kingdom" [31] and its editor as a low-born toady and a liar whose function was to serve "the vilest cabal that ever disgraced this or any other country," [32] Hazlitt proceeds "to fill up the little, mean, crooked, dirty details" by refuting, one by one, the aspersions cast upon his work.

* 9.33; cf. 8.99. Hazlitt later said (8.284) that the *Quarterly* attack even turned his landlord against him, which proves that "the ignorance of the world leaves one at the mercy of its malice."

REPRISAL

Among other things the *Letter* is one of Hazlitt's fullest comments on his own career and on his aspirations as a writer. He rarely thought of style, he says, but only of precision — and "in seeking for truth, I sometimes found beauty." His alleged "facility," a matter of derision to his critics, had been a painful acquisition, for he had started his career "under circumstances of inconceivable and ridiculous discouragement," but even after he had lost his "first dry manner" and found a different "mode," he never used it to gain a quick success.

It is the old story — *that I think what I please, and say what I think.* This accounts, Sir, for the difference between you and me in so many respects. I think only of the argument I am defending; you are only thinking whether you write grammar. My opinions are founded on reasons which I try to give; yours are governed by motives which you keep to yourself. It has been my business all my life to get at the truth as well as I could, merely to satisfy my own mind: it has been yours to suppress the evidence of your senses and the dictates of your understanding, if you ever found them at variance with your convenience or the caprices of others.[33]

And so on point by point, through many bristling pages, until at last he announces that he has done what he set out to do, and Gifford stands exposed as "the head of the literary police"[34] and a man "grown old in the service of corruption."[35] A long coda on the "metaphysical discovery" that he had made when young and set forth in *An Essay on the Principles of Human Action* — "and I have written this Letter partly to introduce it through you to the notice of the reader" — closes this extraordinary work. "I have some love of fame," he says,

of the fame of a Pascal, a Leibnitz, or a Berkeley (none at all of popularity) and would rather that a single inquirer after truth should pronounce my name, after I am dead, with the same feelings that I have thought of theirs, than be puffed in all the newspapers, and praised in all the reviews, while I am living. I myself have been a thinker; and I cannot but believe that there are and will be others, like me. If the few and scattered sparks of truth, which I have been at so much pains to collect, should still be kept alive in the minds of such persons, and not entirely die with me, I shall be satisfied.[36]

Keats was so much stirred by "the force and innate power" with which the *Letter* "yeasts and works itself up" that he transcribed long sections from it for his brother in America.[37] Gifford's own reaction was more muted and delayed, but the following fall, when he descended from the editorial throne to write the *Quarterly* review of *Political Essays*, he showed how deeply he had felt the sting. Dismissing Hazlitt and his "wrath" as unimportant, he professed "unqualified detestation" for the life and work of this "forlorn drudge of the Examiner" who "lays claims to an autocracy of malediction." * He expressed horror at his politics,

* XXII (1819), 159. In his *Diary* (II, 496) Haydon quotes this comment with approval.

369

deplored his disrespectful comments on his betters, and labeled him a slanderer of the human race. Although such an insect could not survive or multiply in England, he remarked in closing, it was well to pin him on a sheet of paper "amongst our other specimens." * Thus having done his duty as an entomologist, Gifford did no more with Hazlitt.†

⬦ ⬦ ⬦

Long before the *Quarterly* attacks subsided, however, the bright young men of *Blackwood's* had stepped briskly forward to save English politics and literature from Cockneys. When, in the fall of 1817, William Blackwood hired John Gibson Lockhart and John Wilson, two young barristers not long out of Oxford, to put some life in his newly founded magazine, it was in the hope that they might save the faltering enterprise. Their success was overwhelming, for despite their youth and inexperience they were clever and unscrupulous, and by combining Toryism with bottomless effrontery they converted a stolid publication into what Mary Russell Mitford called "a very libellous, naughty, wicked, scandalous, story-telling, entertaining work." [38] Established, like the *Quarterly,* as an antidote to the *Edinburgh Review* and other Whiggish publications, it exemplified the proposition that "everything mean or degraded has a tendency to Whiggery, and may be safely classed under that great generic term for everything filthy." [39] Gifford shared these views, of course, but whereas he presided over an austere journal of critical opinion, Blackwood, wishing to meet the competition of Constable's *Edinburgh Magazine,* was not averse to entertainment, and he let his writers have their head. The publication at the start was dull, until the seventh number, when Wilson (who wrote as "Christopher North") and Lockhart were fetched in to make it gay. They never tired of praising Wordsworth or smiting Whigs and *Edinburgh* reviewers, but they also had an eye for fresh, engaging work. They themselves were able men of letters, and they found good writers to assist them, notably

* Page 163. In his Table Talk "On Criticism" (8.226) Hazlitt recalls this comment of Gifford's when he describes those "verbal critics" who "creep, buzz, and fly-blow." Although "the race is almost extinct," he says, "one or two of them are sometimes seen crawling over the pages of the Quarterly Review!"

† Hazlitt had been treated "scurvily," said Robinson (I, 237) on reading this review, "but it is mere retaliation and what he merits." John Matthews' review of *Table-Talk* in 1821 was the last formal attack on Hazlitt in the *Quarterly*. It describes him as a "slang-whanger" and an ass who, like Hunt and William Hone (the publisher and satirist) must be led to the sacrificial altar once again, if only for the benefit of the "younger class of readers." If such creatures were "not more vicious than stupid," the reviewer says (XXVI [1821], 103) "we should almost feel inclined to pity the unconscious levity of the 'beasts' at their fate." John Wilson Croker, one of Gifford's chief contributors, thought that this review was one of the few "good" things in an issue otherwise "abominably bad" (Smiles, II, 54).

James Hogg ("the Ettrick Shepherd") and William Maginn, the alcoholic Irishman with a genius for scurrility whom Thackeray later drew as Captain Shandon in *Pendennis*. As a result, *Blackwood's* — or "Maga," as it was often called — became one of the liveliest publications of the age.

It was also the cruelest and most debonair in its stylized abuse. Wilson's and Lockhart's first number (of October 1817) showed what they could do. To it Hogg contributed his celebrated "Chaldee Manuscript," which amused and scandalized the Scots by insulting half of Edinburgh; * Wilson made brutal sport of Coleridge, jovially declaring that *Biographia Literaria*, "a most execrable" work of staggering conceit, revealed a sense of self-importance unmatched since Joanna Southcote "mistook a complaint in the bowels for the divine afflatus"; [40] and Lockhart, resolved to do his duty by the "Cockney School of Poetry," called Leigh Hunt the leader of a band of vulgar and seditious scribblers. The author of *Rimini* was both ignorant and pretentious, Lockhart said, and his "glittering and rancid obscenities" were a threat to public morals.

His poetry resembles that of a man who has kept company with kept-mistresses. His muse talks indelicately like a tea-sipping milliner girl. Some excuse for her there might have been, had she been hurried away by imagination or passion; but with her, indecency seems a disease, she appears to speak unclean things from perfect inanition. . . . In Rimini a deadly wound is aimed at the dearest confidences of domestic bliss. The author has voluntarily chosen — a subject not of simple seduction alone — one in which his mind seems absolutely to gloat over all the details of adultery and incest.

It was shameful for Jeffrey to have noticed such a work as *Rimini* in the *Edinburgh Review*, said Lockhart (under his pseudonym of "Z"), and all the more so since he had yielded to Hazlitt's "impatient and feverish" solicitations; but it was not too late to strip the Cockneys bare, and in future articles, readers of *Blackwood's Magazine* were promised, they would see them in their naked shame. [41]

With this the "Jackalls of the North," as Hazlitt called them later, were launched on their career of purveying scandal and abuse, and the more their victims howled the greater was the sport. It was "not a question of literary discussion," Hazlitt said, "but of political proscription." [42] While Coleridge contemplated legal action [43] and Hunt indignantly denied to Jeffrey that he had tried to influence Hazlitt's attitude toward *Rimini*, [44] the *Examiner* itself — which is to say John and Leigh

* See Alan Lang Strout, "James Hogg's 'Chaldee Manuscript,'" *PMLA*, LXV (1950), 695–718. It was the "Chaldee Manuscript" that gave the magazine "a lift and a shove" to fame, said the editors three years later (VIII [1820], 80), when they claimed a circulation of 17,000.

Hunt, no doubt with Hazlitt's aid — reprinted "Z's" remarks and demanded that the author show himself. This he could not fail to do, it said, "unless to an utter disregard of all *Truth* and Decency, he adds the height of Meanness and COWARDICE." [45] "Z" of course declined the invitation — "your poem," he told Hunt, "*is* vile, profligate, obscene, indecent, and detestable" [46] — and continued his attacks. Month after month the sorry sport went on, until finally, in April 1818, Hunt announced that because the anonymous libeler had not "come forward" he was prepared to drop the controversy in pity and contempt. [47] This too had no effect. In May "Z" proclaimed that any brother would tear *The Story of Rimini* from his sister's hand, and any husband whose wife enjoyed reading it would "have reason to look with perplexing agony on the countenances of his children"; [48] and two months later, taking leave of Hunt and his vile poem, he boasted that he had been "the first to brand with a burning iron the false face of this kept-mistress of a demoralizing incendiary." [49]

Meanwhile, apart from a few passing blows at "Billy" and at "Bill the painter," *Blackwood's* was strangely kind to Hazlitt. Between February and April Peter George Patmore, a literary entrepreneur who served as secretary of the Russell Institution and also as Blackwood's London correspondent, contributed a string of favorable, factual reports of Hazlitt's current lectures on the English poets, and when he concluded the series by remarking that the lecturer was "among the best, if not the very best, living critic on our national literature" * William Blackwood thanked him for his "admirable" performance.† Then, in June, came an article in which Jeffrey and Hazlitt were described, not without some cautionary strictures, as "at present the two most eminent speculators on literary topics." [50] Simultaneous with these aberrations and amenities, however, were mutterings of the storm to come. Commenting on Patmore's unduly kind remarks about the lectures in the March 1818 issue, Lockhart said that

> Of pimpled Hazlitt's coxcomb lectures writing,
> Our friend with moderate pleasure we peruse, [51]

and thus he hit upon the phrase that infuriated Hazlitt until the day he died. [52] When Patmore, no doubt prompted by Hazlitt himself, com-

---

* *Blackwood's Magazine*, III (1818), 75. In March 1818 Hazlitt wrote to Patmore (*The Hazlitts*, p. 445) to thank him for letting him read the favorable report that was planned for publication in the April *Blackwood's*.
 † Basil Champneys, *Memoirs and Correspondence of Coventry Patmore* (1900), II, 437. When Patmore had requested the assignment of reporting Hazlitt's lectures he was told by Blackwood that although "Z" would be perhaps too "bitter" he himself might be too "panegyrical" (Champneys, II, 433).

plained in his final report about the epithet,[53] his protest was duly printed. It was just a witticism, Blackwood wrote to him, the happy inspiration of "a gentleman of real wit, and perfect good behavior. Some one had told him (it would seem erroneously) that Mr. Hazlitt had a pimpled face, and he accordingly said so, without much meaning." But anyway, he added, why should "the most severe and slashing satyrist of the day" take such unbrage at an "unmeaning *jeu d'esprit*"?[54] It was a cogent question, but Hazlitt was none the less enraged. "Of what use would it be were I publicly to convict them of untruth in this description of me? — of none whatever," he protested to a friend. "They would then persuade their readers, far more to blame than themselves, that in their misrepresentation consisted the very marrow, the excellence of the jest; — nay, that the jest would be nothing if it were true."[55] It was a vile, low blow, he thought, and he promptly wrote an essay on the subject to vent his indignation. "No matter how undeserved the imputation, it will stick; for, though it is sport to the bye-standers to see you bespattered, they will not stop to see you wipe out the stains."[56] Thereafter, nicknames, like Tory politicians and hereditary succession, were among his chief aversions.*

In July, "Z," announcing that he had done with Hunt, warned that "the day is perhaps not far distant" when Hazlitt's turn would come,[57] and the following month his prediction was fulfilled. In the same issue that carried the advice to "Johnny" Keats, the pretentious apothecary, to return to his "plaster, pills, and ointment boxes,"[58] there appeared a letter headed "Hazlitt Cross-Questioned" and signed by "An Old Friend with a New Face." Containing eight questions for the "mere quack" who lounged in third-rate bookshops and wrote third-rate books, it was a savage assault on Hazlitt's morals, talents, and attainments. Had he not sneered at Wordsworth, it inquired, after that great poet had rescued him from an "indignant peasantry" whose ideas of virtue he had flouted? Had he not been "expelled" from the *Edinburgh Review*? Was he not ignorant of the alphabet in Greek, and yet had dared to write of Porson's scholarship? Had he not insinuated that Desdemona was a lewd woman? Had he not attacked the actor William Conway and then published "A Retracting Lie" in order to escape a caning? And finally, did he "know Latin for a goose?"[59] As if this were not enough, other

---

* Nicknames became an *idée fixe* with Hazlitt. The following are typical of dozens of allusions to the subject: 8.222, 263f., 9.197, 10.246, 11.205, 17.308. In an apparently unpublished scrap of manuscript now in the Houghton Library at Harvard, a portion of which is reproduced on page 377, he wrote, "Would I were a Scotchman that I could repeat a nickname whenever I was at a loss for matter, & live upon the poor joke three or four years!"

comments about Hazlitt elsewhere in the number — one about his "perverse and wilful misrepresentation of the truth" in discussing Shakespeare's sonnets [60] and one about Lamb's imprudent friendship with the wretch [61] — made it clear that *Blackwood's* had decreed his ruin.

❖   ❖   ❖

When Hazlitt, at Winterslow, read the August *Blackwood's* his response was prompt and sharp. To retort in kind, he said, would be like making fun of Scott's club foot,[62] and so instead he threatened legal action. On August 27 William Blackwood (who was not unused to litigation) * instructed Patmore to arrange some sort of settlement,[63] but by early September Hazlitt, "very much moved," [64] was back in town and contemplating his next step. "I do not feel tempted to this kind of personal warfare," he told Archibald Constable (for whose *Edinburgh Magazine* he had written several pieces), "& one reason is, if I once entered into it, I should carry the war into the enemy's quarters in a way that I do not wish to do. I have hitherto spared them comparatively. If however you think decidedly otherwise, I will see about it." [65] It was probably on Constable's advice that he decided to proceed. On September 20 Keats reported that he, "excessively vexed," had begun a "prosecution," [66] and on the same day Francis Jeffrey, who was both an editor and barrister, agreed to give him legal counsel. "I know you to be a man of genius," he wrote from Edinburgh, "and I have no reason to doubt that you are a man of integrity and honour, and most certainly my good opinion of you is in no degree affected by the scurrilities of Mr. Blackwood's publication." But since they were not "personal" acquaintances, he said, it was therefore Hazlitt's job to disprove the aspersions on his character.†

Thus it was, no doubt, that he sketched his own defense in the document that we now know as "A Reply to Z." Written probably at a single sitting and then dispatched to Constable for his use and information, it is a bold, unpolished piece of work that burns with indignation.‡

* Earlier, when Blackwood had been disturbed by threats of libel suits, Lockhart and Wilson had tried to give him courage: "All you have to do is to keep up your mind in good fighting condition" and also hire a lawyer, Wilson wrote (Oliphant, I, 140). It has been estimated that during the first five years of *Blackwood's Magazine* the editor paid, in addition to legal expenses, at least £830 in damages. See Alan Lang Strout (ed.), *John Bull's Letter to Lord Byron* (1947), p. 36.

† Constable, II, 220. When news of Hazlitt's suit reached Keswick there was a fear, reported Sara Coleridge, that Southey and Wordsworth might be called upon to give evidence. This would be "very disagreeable," she explained to Tom Poole, "& as Master Hazlitt will cut a very ridiculous figure, I wonder he chuses to make a stir in it" (*Minnow among Tritons* [ed. Stephen Potter, 1934], p. 64).

‡ The manuscript in the British Museum (MS. Egerton 3244) is in Hazlitt's bold

REPRISAL

"If I were in the habit of using the words, Liar, Fool, Coxcomb, Hypocrite, Scoundrel, Blackguard, &c.," he tells "Z," "I should apply them to you, but this would be degrading them still lower unnecessarily, for it is quite as easy to prove you the *things* as to call you the *names*." Although he claims nothing for himself except the honor of having written an *Essay on the Principles of Human Action* ("a book which I daresay you never heard of"), his sense of injured merit plays like lightning on the surface of his prose. Coleridge used to tell him, he recalls, that "if ever I got language for my ideas, the world would hear of it, for that I had guts in my brains. And now that I have got language for *my* ideas, he says they are *his* ideas, that my brains are in his and Mr. Wordsworth's head (I deprecate the last utterly) and he gets such a fellow as Z. (I beg pardon, I forgot that I was writing to you, Sir, you are really below my notice) to say that I am a charlatan." Then, rather like a man denying that he beats his wife, he undertakes to answer the eight questions posed by *Blackwood's Magazine*. He asserts, for instance, that although he considered Wordsworth's egotism to be "the bane of his talents and of his public principles," he had been among the first to recognize his genius; that he had not been fired by the *Edinburgh Review*; that he did indeed know the Greek alphabet; that only Shakespeare could have given "additional elegance and even delicacy" to a woman in Desdemona's painful situation. "Finally, Sir, you call me as a nickname 'pimpled Hazlitt.' And I am *not* pimpled, but remarkably pale and sallow. You were told of this as a false fact, and you repeated and still repeat it, declaring to hundreds of persons individually and to the public that you not only do not care for the distinction between truth and falsehood, but that you are superior to being thought to care about it. . . . Is it answer'd?"

The outcome of this preliminary skirmishing may best be followed in the correspondence between Blackwood and John Murray, his London agent, during the fall of 1818.[67] Murray, a cautious man of business, was made uneasy by the whole affair, but Blackwood professed to be indifferent. It is clear, he wrote on September 22, that "this fellow merely means to make a little bluster, and try if he can pick up a little money." A few days later, when Murray, in a letter running to eleven

---

and fluent hand, with only minor insertions and corrections. A note at the head says that "the following rough sketch of an answer to the queries of an old Friend with a new face (which I wrote with some intention of publishing it) will convey my defence & my notions of the state of the question. The first 4 or 5 pages may be skipped over." In 1918 Charles Whibley printed excerpts from it in "Hazlitt *v.* 'Blackwood's Magazine,'" *Blackwood's Magazine*, CCIV, 388–398, and he followed this in 1923 with an edition of the text. I quote from Howe's transcript, 9.3–10.

quarto pages, warned that the "clamour" against "Maga" was "almost universal," Blackwood tried to comfort him with an apologetic statement by Wilson and Lockhart, in which they deplored the "ferocity" of the attack on Hazlitt, predicted that he would "fret on" but in the end "do nothing," and promised that they would henceforth chasten their abuse.[68] But it was too late for such equivocations. On October 6 Blackwood wrote that he had "this instant received Hazlitt's summons" for £2000 in damages, and although he insisted that "the matter sits very lightly upon me and our friends," he admitted four days later that it would save "a great deal of trouble and botheration" if Hazlitt could be soothed. And then, to Murray's great dismay, Lockhart and Wilson sent challenges to the publisher of *Hypocrisy Unveiled,* a defamatory pamphlet prompted by the "Chaldee Manuscript" of the year before. By this "palpable absurdity," wrote Murray, they had left themselves exposed. "In the name of God," he asked, "why do you seem to think it *indispensable* that each number [of *Blackwood's Magazine*] must give pain to some one or other?" He was angrier still when, in November, he learned that no defense against Hazlitt's suit was ready. "To neglect such a thing as this when three-fourths of the talent of the Bar are in hostility to you, and when any jury will be prejudiced against you, is very reprehensible." It was then, presumably, that he himself took charge of things. By December 7 his agent was in negotiation with Patmore trying to arrange a settlement, and on the sixteenth they had almost come to terms. Hazlitt, through Patmore, had offered to withdraw the suit in return for his expenses and "a small sum for some charity," but Blackwood thought that the money, a hundred pounds, should be paid to Hazlitt "privately," and thus it was finally agreed.[69] By way of epilogue, Murray, a few weeks later, ended his connection with *Blackwood's Magazine,* for it was, he said, a publication that had "involved every one connected with it in alternate anxiety, disgrace, and misery."[70] What Hazlitt thought of this we do not know, but the *Examiner* expressed its satisfaction at the rout of "Mr. Murrain." "Oh! how these fellows might be made to tremble and put to flight in all their quarters, if, as Mr. Hazlitt says, there were not a difficulty in conquering one's contempt for them; — aye, and even one's pity."[71]

Hazlitt's victory did not mean that peace had been secured. Despite a couple of grudging conciliatory remarks by Lockhart and Wilson * the pages of *Blackwood's* were sprinkled for the next few years

* In *Peter's Letters to His Kinsfolk* (1819) Lockhart said that Hazlitt's and John

whenever I was at a loss for matter, & live upon
one poor joke for three or four years! The
want of invention & the pertinacity of purpose
are admirable, & throw one another in a
striking & rational light / point of view.
I wish they had not killed poor K. & yet
I do not like to acknowledge that they did
for it will be a triumph to the only feelings
they have, malice & an insolent hatred of
genius for the impudent hectoring presumption
to & conscious want of any thing more nearly
to it turn the swagger & brutality of a
cudgel-player or bludgeon man. There
is one publication a match for this inflam-
grant impudence & dauntless dulness, which
is the John Bull. This has an Irish, then
a Scotch Editor or Editors. & both my
same they / show what the two nations can
do in this line. Both lie: but the one
tells a different, the other an old / thread-
lie every month. Both are unprincipled

Hazlitt on the Brutality of Reviewers
From an undated MS fragment

with sharp allusions to him and other Cockneys.* Moreover, after 1820 his close connection with the *London Magazine* (whose brilliant editor, John Scott, was killed in 1821 in a duel that followed his attacks on what he called the "Mohocks" of the north) and then with Byron's and Leigh Hunt's *Liberal* led his old tormentors, as he said later, to over-flow "with tenfold gall and bitterness." [72] In August 1822 "Maga" wrote savagely of Hazlitt's *Table-Talk,* and a few months later it urged that its author read with care a piece on vaccination in the *Edinburgh Review* in order to learn about scabs and pus and pimples. [73] He retaliated by recording, in the *Liberal,* his opinion of the "flagrant impudence and dauntless dulness" of *Blackwood's Magazine,* [74] and then, in April, by threatening Thomas Cadell, who had succeeded Murray as Black-wood's London agent, with a suit for libel. [75] But in May the publication of *Liber Amoris,* followed almost immediately by his penetrating appraisal of "The Periodical Press" in the *Edinburgh Review,* [76] was the signal for renewed attacks. Blackwood's writer said that Hazlitt's book about his sordid love affair deserved "the scorn and loathing of every thing that bears the name MAN," [77] and that his aspersions on contemporary journalists were the ravings of a fool. He had written, for example, that the "illiberality" of certain magazines was a cause for real alarm, for "all character, all decency, the plainest matter of fact, or deductions of reason, are made the sport of a nickname, an inuendo, or a bold and direct falsehood." With the *Anti-Jacobin* of an earlier day as precedent, he said, the "Ministerial Press" had learned that slander and abuse could always find a market, for "if you could not reply to your opponent's objections, you might caricature his person; if you were foiled by his wit or learning, you might recover your advantage by stabbing his character." [78] Such comments led *Blackwood's* to sulfurous abuse. By printing such remarks, it said, Jeffrey had destroyed the last fragment of his decaying reputation: he himself was "gone — dished — dead — utterly defunct," and the *Edinburgh Review* was

---

Hamilton Reynolds' contributions to Constable's *Edinburgh Magazine* were the only "enlivening things" in that dreary publication (II, 227f.), and in the first "Noctes Ambrosianae" (*Blackwood's Magazine,* XI [1822], 370) he conceded that Hazlitt was "a real fellow in his small way." Reynolds' work for the *Edinburgh Magazine,* which included some reports of Hazlitt's lectures on the English comic writers (see page 256), impressed William Blackwood so much that he offered him a job. See Alan Lang Strout, "Knights of the Burning Epistle (the *Blackwood* Papers in the National Library of Scotland)," *Studia Neophilologica,* XXVI (1953–54), 85.

* For example, V (1819), 97, where Hunt is called the Cockney Homer, Haydon the Cockney Raphael, and Hazlitt the Cockney Aristotle; VI (1819), 70–76, where all the Cockneys are abused in a review of Leigh Hunt's *Foliage*; X (1821), 556, where Hazlitt's "Stable-Talk" is mentioned; and X, 696–700, where, in a vulgar and jocose review of Shelley's *Adonais,* Keats and all his friends are vilified.

"ruined." As for Hazlitt, he was a "low, vulgar, impudent" manufacturer of filthy books and bad grammar, "a mere ulcer, a sore from head to foot," an "overgrown pimple, sore to the touch." The writer — probably Maginn [79] — went on to vilify Leigh Hunt and "Johnny" Keats, and after many pages of detraction remarked in closing that he had "battered the blood about the brainless heads of these Cockney ragamuffins" so long that he was "weary of the occupation." [80]

And so the dirty work went on, at least sporadically, for the rest of Hazlitt's life. Having chided Thomas Campbell, editor of the *New Monthly Magazine,* for printing such a wretch's work, [81] called him the Priapus of Ludgate Hill, [82] parodied his style,* and had much fun about his pimples, [83] *Blackwood's,* surveying its achievements in 1826, congratulated itself for obliterating Hazlitt and all the "pestilential sect" of Cockneys. "That we did our work *roughly,* we acknowledge; they were not vermin to be crushed by a delicate finger. That we did our work *personally,* we deny; unless their own consciences applied to their persons what we said of their books." [84] Already, however, Hazlitt seems to have wearied of the struggle. Writing at Winterslow in 1823, he said that

my cloudy thoughts draw off, the storm of angry politics has blown over — Mr. Blackwood, I am yours — Mr. Croker, my service to you — Mr. T. Moore, I am alive and well — Really, it is wonderful how little the worse I am for fifteen years' wear and tear, how I come upon my legs again on the ground of truth and nature, and "look abroad into universality," forgetting that there is any such person as myself in the world! [85]

Why challenge "Mr. Blackwood's general candour and veracity," he asked a few years later, when all the world believes him? [86] Once the guardians of the *status quo* did their work by public execution, but now "we arrive at the same end by a politer way of nicknames and anonymous criticism. *Blackwood's Magazine* is the modern version of Fox's *Book of Martyrs.*" † When Hazlitt died, *Blackwood's* duly noted the event, but it did not mention old disputes with this "ingenious author" [87] — a fact that may or may not prove what Wilson later said in praising Hunt: "the Animosities are mortal, but the Humanities live for ever." [88]

---

* XVI (1824), 71ff. When this amusing parody of Hunt and Hazlitt appeared, Maginn told Blackwood that it was "injudicious" to call attention to such men, for they would otherwise remain obscure. See Alan Lang Strout, "Knights of the Burning Epistle (the *Blackwood* Papers in the National Library of Scotland)," *Studia Neophilologica,* XXVI (1953–54), 87.

† 20.309. According to Procter (*New Monthly Magazine,* XXIX [1830], 470), when Hazlitt read in *Blackwood's* something good about Napoleon, "God!" he said, "that's good — that's fine; I forgive 'em all they've said of *me.*"

379

POLITICS AND LITERATURE

As specialists in character assassination Blackwood and his merry men retain a certain morbid fascination. They would be inconceivable today, and judged even by the looser standards of their day they were prodigies of malice. Witty, young, and debonair, they were also deep-dyed Tories who often wrote from real conviction, but just as often, it would seem, they were antic and macabre. They enjoyed their own cruel jokes and frolicked in their killing witticisms. As John Scott said in the *London Magazine,* they never published a "severe" critique that was not also "dirty," for despite their audacity and verve they were "POISON-ERS IN JEST." [89] They themselves, of course, put the matter differently. Their wit, they said, was "clean, clear, bright, sharp, shrewd, biting, bitter, penetrating, sarcastic, and unanswerable"; and every "idiot" who dared to challenge them had been received, "like a flea or a louse, on the point of our pen, and, wriggling, expired." [90] They were gallant knights, said Lockhart, bent on saving English literature and politics; and if they were sometimes too ardent and impulsive, their achievements were none the less impressive; for instance, in their assault on Hunt and Hazlitt and the "conceited knot of superficial coxcombs" whom they had aptly nicknamed Cockneys they performed a public service, for these were "by far the vilest vermin that ever dared to creep upon the hem of the majestic garment of the English muse." [91]

Not even all their friends agreed. Wordsworth refused to have "Maga" in his house,[92] and his sister-in-law, dutifully concurring, said that in spite of "its abuse of the *Ed. Rev.,* & its Toryism" it was "a disgrace to any cause it undertakes." [93] Although he "chuckled" over it, Scott was made uneasy by the "reckless extravagance" of its "juvenile satire" [94] and its predilection for "markedly personal" abuse.[95] However, after Wilson — who could toss off fourteen tumblers of whiskey-punch in five hours [96] — was named professor of moral philosophy in Edinburgh University and Lockhart became Scott's son-in-law and then editor of the *Quarterly Review,* there was a tendency to forgive their youthful indiscretions. Wilson was a man of extraordinary malice, Carlyle said, but it was the malice of a child; [97] and although Scott in 1821 urged Lockhart to withdraw from "Maga" (which was "a snare and temptation" to his "love of satire"),[98] he insisted later that the follies of twenty-three should not be held against a man of thirty.[99] Besides, he said, "to take notice of such men as Hazlitt and Hunt in the *Quarterly* would be to introduce them into a world which is scarce conscious of their existence." [100] Haydon — a kind of regenerated Cockney — came to think that in his later years Lockhart's main desire was "to undo the evil" he had done when young,[101] and Lockhart himself declared that the "jibes and jokes" that, as a "raw boy," he had "inflicted" on his victims was a source of deep regret.[102] But even if he honestly regarded Hunt and Keats and Hazlitt as "cockney and conceited conspirators against the constitution, common sense, and the English language," as his biographer explained,[103] he and his colleagues were guilty of the grossest libels. After they were dead, Henry Cockburn, an aged Whig, said that perhaps their sins should be forgiven, but he added that the "stains" to those "who know the facts can never be effaced." [104] That this was Hazlitt's view is clear, and the opinion he expressed in 1823 was in a sense his valediction to *Blackwood's* bright young men:

Their impudence is extreme, their malice is cold-blooded, covert, crawling, deliberate, without the frailty or excuse of passion. They club their vices and their venality together, and by the help of both together are invincible.[105]

PART THREE

THE LATER YEARS

The Essayist

❖◇

A NEW BEGINNING

Hazlitt's last decade reveals an ironic counterpoint of personal calamity and literary achievement. In 1820 he announced that he was in the sere, the yellow leaf, and the mournful peroration of his Elizabethan lectures records the desolation of a man whose ripest wisdom was the knowledge that life held "nothing worth obtaining." Behind him lay his failure as a painter, his blasted aspirations for reform, the collapse of his unhappy marriage, and the end (as he regarded it) of his career in letters. Before him lay more scribbling of the sort he said he hated, a vulgar and disastrous love affair, another unsuccessful marriage, the failure of his *magnum opus* on Napoleon, and the poverty and isolation that brought him to the sleazy lodging house in Soho where he died at fifty-two. But before him also lay the rich fulfillment of his power in such unquestioned triumphs as *Table-Talk* and *The Spirit of the Age.* It is instructive and amusing to recall that these, and a dozen other things, were tossed off by a man who, at forty-two, hoped only for the strength to "stagger on the few remaining paces" to the grave.[1]

As if to show that providence shapes our ends, it was just when he was winding up the Elizabethan lectures and looking for something else to do that John Scott, his former editor on the *Champion,* returned to England after several years abroad and assumed direction of the newly founded *London Magazine.* Although projected as a counterpart to *Blackwood's,* the new monthly, said its editor, would not be partisan or frivolous or cruel. "The Days are passed when *Vindex* could be suffered to dispute with *Eudosius,* through various successive Numbers, which is most eligible — a married or a single state," he wrote, and he promised that the *London* would address itself to those questions in literature, politics, and manners not noted with enough precision and discernment by conventional newspapers, annual registers, and other monthly magazines, or by the "nominally critical Journals" deeply committed to certain "general principles" of their own.[2] John Scott had courage and acumen, and if he had had more luck he might have lived to reach his high ideals. As one of his contributors — later an illustrious man himself — recalled, he was discriminating, fair, and candid, but above all he had that "which Kent recognised in Lear, which subjects revere in kings, and boys admire in schoolmasters, and contributors should welcome in editors — *authority*; — not manifested in a worrying, teasing, intolerable interference in small matters, but in a judicious and steady superintendence of the whole; with a wise allowance of the occasional excesses of wit and genius."[3] Not the least of his great gifts was a knack for finding able writers. It may be argued that men like Hazlitt, Lamb, and Reynolds would have made any magazine distinguished, but writers must be checked and coaxed and brought along, and this Scott did with extraordinary skill and tact. Although Hazlitt later said that the very excellence of the staff was a certain disadvantage,[*] Scott was able to control his brilliant crew, and the decline of the *London Magazine* after his untimely death in 1821 was itself a testimonial to his editorial sagacity.[4]

That sagacity may be inferred from a letter that he wrote in January 1820, when he was preparing his first issue for the press. There we learn that he had been approached by Hazlitt ("in want of a certain sum of money") with a "specimen" of his work, and that although the editor was prepared to hire him as a critic of the drama he was uncertain of his merits otherwise. "I am sorry to say that I cannot honestly tell you that Mr. Hazlitt's manuscript is likely to suit us in the mag.," he wrote to Robert Baldwin, one of the proprietors.

It falls into all those errors which I know are his besetting ones, but which I hope to keep him clear of when he is directed to particular topics, such as the drama, etc. His talent is undoubted, and his wish to serve us, I believe, at present very sincere. . . . If I could have told you that the Essays, of which a specimen has been forwarded, would surely suit us, the difficulty probably would be small; but although very anxious to find it so, I would not act fairly by you were I to give this as my opinion. At the same time, I will engage for the gentleman, from what I know of his character, that he would be most ready to listen to suggestions,

---

[*] 16.232. In the December 1821 issue, after John Taylor had succeeded Scott as editor, it was noted (IV, 583) "that a greater number of men of talent than the *London Magazine* now unites in its support, were never before combined in furtherance of any undertaking of a similar nature." About this time its writers included, in addition to Hazlitt and Lamb, Thomas De Quincey, Henry Francis Cary (the translator of Dante), John Hamilton Reynolds, John Clare, Thomas Hood, Thomas Carlyle, Bryan Waller Procter ("Barry Cornwall"), and Thomas Griffiths Wainewright ("Janus Weathercock").

and to strain every nerve for us in return for a service. He is naturally grateful, & though an original, is an honest one. I have not spoken to him for several years until Sunday last, but I see that in a very short time I shall be able to influence him to proper subjects and to a proper manner of handling them — I mean *proper* in regard to the magazine, as, generally speaking, I should have little claim to be his judge or guide.*

Although one would like to know what Scott regarded as the applicant's "besetting" errors,† it is clear that he was willing to put him on probation, and so it was that Hazlitt made his debut in the first issue of the *London* (January 1820) with "The Drama: No. I." He surely felt relief at the appointment, for the pay was very good,‡ and the scope and leisure of a monthly magazine, which he regarded as "the flower and cream of periodical literature," ⁵ no doubt seemed to him idyllic after the hurly-burly of writing for the papers. His initial contribution may not have been precisely what the editor had in mind as a monthly survey of the stage, but it was a stunning tour de force, and Scott must have been impressed. Spacious and unhurried, this vivid essay on old actors blends evocation, nostalgia, and criticism in a richly contrapuntal pattern that follows not chronology and facts but the writer's shifting moods. These give texture, shape, and substance to the undulating prose; they provide a base for his digressions; and ultimately they, not the topic he announces, constitute his subject.

We offer our best affections, our highest aspirations after the good and beautiful, on the altar of youth: it is well if, in our after-age, we can sometimes rekindle the almost extinguished flame, and inhale its dying fragrance like the breath of

* *Four Generations*, I, 135ff. Hazlitt had apparently proposed that after their appearance in the *London* his contributions be published as a book by Baldwin and his partners, but on this point too Scott urged caution. "Would it therefore suit you to say to him that, with regard to the Essays, of which one has been sent, you beg leave to think a little farther over the matter," he wrote to Baldwin (*ibid.*, I, 137), "and claim the privilege of suggesting what may occur to you; but that on the general score of dramatic articles, and such other contributions as might hereafter be arranged between himself and you on mutual agreement, you have no objection to treat as for the volume *immediately*. I do not know what he has asked for the vol." These negotiations came to nothing, it would seem, for Hazlitt's *London* essays on the drama were never printed as a book, and when the first volume of *Table-Talk* appeared in 1821 the publisher was John Warren, not the firm of Baldwin, Craddock, and Joy. See Keynes, pp. 54ff.

† "Poor Scott, he was his own assassin, living or dead," wrote Haydon in his *Diary* (II, 315) after the editor had fallen in a duel. "He made Hazlitt tipsey, & got out the secrets & weaknesses of his nature, & then assailed him the very next Sunday in an anonymous letter, touching on these very points! When he met Hazlitt again, his feelings in my room were quite punishment enough." The allusions to Hazlitt's drinking — which he stopped completely in his later years (Procter, pp. 177f.) — and to the weekly paper date the episode during Scott's editorship of the *Champion* (1814–1816).

‡ According to Mary Russell Mitford (L'Estrange, II, 119), by the end of 1820 Hazlitt was getting fifteen guineas a sheet for writing Table Talks, and in 1822 he himself told Sarah Walker (9.112) that by "regularly" turning out ten pages a day he was making thirty guineas a week.

incense, of sweet-smelling flowers and gums, to detain the spirit of life, the ethereal guest, a little longer in its frail abode — to cheer and soothe it with the pleasures of memory, not with those of hope. While we can do this, life is worth living for: when we can do it no longer, its spring will soon go down, and we had better not be! — Who shall give us Mrs. Siddons again, but in a waking dream, a beatific vision of past years, crowned with other hopes and other feelings, whose pomp is also faded, and their glory and their power gone! . . . It is pride and happiness enough for us to have lived at the same time with her, and one person more [that is, Napoleon]! But enough on this subject. Those feelings that we are most anxious to do justice to, are those to which it is impossible we ever should! [6]

As the spring wore on, Hazlitt's contributions to this series — including a salute to Miss O'Neill on her retirement, a vivacious account of London's minor theaters (with a digression on the strolling actors of his youth), and an incisive explanation for the low estate of modern drama * — must have made it clear to Scott that he had found a prize. Later Hazlitt said that in these articles he had only tried to be "exactly dull," [7] and perhaps the comment should be taken as an ironic commentary on Scott's concern about his "errors"; but the doubts of that discerning editor soon were overcome. Already, in reviewing the Elizabethan lectures in the second issue of the *London,* he had acknowledged that, whereas his colleague's politics were something of a bore, he had "a comprehension of innate character, absolutely unequalled by any of his contemporaries, — with a finer and more philosophical taste than any other critic on poetry and art whose name we can cite, — with an intense feeling of the pathetic, the pure, the sublime, in quality, action, and form," [8] and therefore it was not surprising that, a few months later, he resolved to make a wider use of his "undoubted" talents. Thus it was that "On the Qualifications Necessary for Success in Life," the first of many Table Talks, made its appearance in the June issue of the *London Magazine.*

❧ ❧ ❧

This may be regarded as the start of Hazlitt's final phase in letters. He had written essays of a sort for years, but the earlier ones — of which *The Round Table* is, of course, the representative selection — had been mainly tailored for the papers, and they reveal a brevity and shape that set them off at once from the looser and more complex work of his last decade. Something of his later style is apparent in his contributions to the *Edinburgh Magazine* in 1818,[9] after he had left the

---

* 18.280–316. Hazlitt wrote an article on "The Drama" each month from January to September 1821, and then, having prevailed upon a "friend" (probably John Hamilton Reynolds) to relieve him in October and having skipped November altogether (18.369), he closed the series in December. His ten contributions to the series are reprinted by Howe, 18.271–374.

Times, but it was not until Scott had opened up to him the pages of the *London* that he found the voice and manner that have earned his place in English literature. These essays serve another purpose too, for they tell us most of what we know about his doings in these years, when the record otherwise is sparse. We learn, for instance, that in the early months of 1820 he paid a visit to John Hunt near Taunton and lingered in the west of England for a time,[10] that he was back in London by the end of March, when Haydon saw him and Keats together at the exhibition of *Christ's Triumphal Entry,*[11] that presently he went down again to Winterslow, where he stayed, it seems, for several weeks,* that he returned to town in time to report on James Sheridan Knowles's *Virginius,*[12] and that he was there when, in July, he learned about his father's death in Devon.[13] But these movements to and fro are less important than the march of his great essays through successive numbers of the *London Magazine.* There we find not facts and dates, but the man himself revealed. If, for instance, we wonder how he felt about his father's death, or what drew him back to Winterslow, or why he was indifferent to the sort of fame that other writers sought, the answers are at hand in "On the Pleasure of Painting,"[14] "On Living to One's-Self,"[15] and "On the Aristocracy of Letters."[16]

More than ever, it would seem, his life was in his work, and his output in these years was huge. Between June 1820 and December 1821 he wrote thirteen Table Talks, in addition to various articles and reviews, for the *London Magazine,* and after shifting the series to the *New Monthly* in 1822 he wrote eleven more within the next two years. These twenty-four essays were, however, only a fraction of the whole. Of the sixteen pieces in the first volume of *Table-Talk* (1821), fourteen had not appeared in print before, and of the seventeen in Volume II (1822) only three were reprinted from the magazines. He main-

---

* 12.27, 16.196. He was at Winterslow on May 2, when he wrote to Jeffrey (ALS, The Yale University Library) about doing something for the *Edinburgh* and suggested Joseph Farington's life of Reynolds. "The text is in bungling openstitch," he said, "& presents plenty of loop-holes for *apercus* on the subjects of patronage, public taste, portrait painting, & the grand style of art as pursued in this country by Barry, West, Fuseli, Haydon, etc. But I had better do the thing, & then you will judge. I have nearly exhausted my little stock of knowledge on the Age of Elizabeth, but if anything occurs, I will bear in mind your suggestion. I have been reading the Sketch-Book of Geoffrey Crayon, Gent. [Washington Irving], & think something might be made of it in the way of an extract or two, & of a prefatory sketch of the character of American Literature as here exemplified. Southey's Life of Wesley I am half afraid to ask for." By August 11, as Hazlitt informed Haydon (ALS in the possession of Willard Pope), Jeffrey had accepted the piece on Farington "with some corrections," and it was printed in the August *Edinburgh* (16.181–211). Characteristically, Hazlitt salvaged most of these proposals for his later work. He wrote on Irving in *The Spirit of the Age* (11.183f.) and on American literature in an *Edinburgh* review of Channing's *Sermons* (16.318–324).

tained this pace almost until he died. On occasion, to be sure, he turned to other things like *Liber Amoris* and *Characteristics* in 1823, *Select British Poets* in 1824, *Notes of a Journey through France and Italy* in 1826, and the four volumes of his life of Napoleon in 1828 and 1830; but these books punctuated rather than interrupted his endless stream of essays. In 1824 he gathered up a group of them on art (mainly from the *London*) as *The Principal Picture-Galleries in England*; the following year he added to some biographical sketches written for the *New Monthly* to make *The Spirit of the Age* and also published, in Paris, an edition of *Table-Talk* with many new essays; in 1826 he brought together in *The Plain Speaker* another big collection, part of which had not appeared in print before; and there remained, from the *Liberal* and elsewhere, a batch of uncollected essays — including such authentic masterpieces as "My First Acquaintance with Poets," "Merry England," and "The Fight" — big enough to fill a volume in the Centenary Edition.

These statistics underscore the fact that for Hazlitt in his last decade the essay was uniquely suited to his aims and methods as a writer. For one thing, its spatial limitations were ideal for a man who had to write to live and who was never easy with the larger forms of composition. His talent was varied and immense, but he could not sustain the structure that a book with a beginning, a middle, and an end requires. The clumsy patchwork of his first attempt in "metaphysics," the shapeless and undisciplined *Reply* to Malthus, the chunky lectures on philosophy, the episodic structure of his book on Shakespeare, the helter-skelter lectures of his middle years, and, above all, the scraps of journalistic prose that, loosely thrown together, constitute *The Round Table, A View of the English Stage,* and *Political Essays* all exemplify the fragmentation of his work. Without his saying so we would know that he identified the swift, the artless, and the improvised with "truth," and conversely the slow, the stately, and the formal with torpor and stylized deceit. Work that was "struck off at a blow" had its own vitality and vigor," he said, and since the vigor he admired, like the lyric cry in verse, cannot be indefinitely prolonged, it is not surprising that he did not succeed in the larger forms of composition.

Nor is it surprising that his style is so "familiar," for it is shaped and colored by his moods. Not for him the long slow curve of exposition, the neat arrangement of details, the pursuit of facts that, when gathered, must be tested and aligned, the style that subordinates the writer to his craft. He hated sluggish, neutral prose, scorned the merely decorative and elegant, and insisted that a formal style — like Johnson's — could not "impart conviction." [18] Supple and chromatic, his own prose is swift or lush or strident, as he wishes, but it hardly ever sounds contrived. Unchecked by reticence or literary convention, it is the ideal instrument for a writer bent on self-expression.

Indeed, his indifference to structural and stylistic conventions is a function of his urge for self-expression. Despite his deference, as critic, to the humbling power of art and his advocacy, as moralist, of benevolence as a principle of action he was superbly egocentric, and therefore he found the essay, which sprang from introspection and worked toward self-awareness, precisely suited to his needs. As he himself had urged throughout his lectures, the dramatist and novelist are committed to something bigger than themselves; without a "venturous magnanimity" they cannot achieve the self-effacement essential to great art. The essayist, however, is committed only to himself. He works not through narrative and character, but by observing and recording his emotions. He does not suppress, but instead exemplifies, the "devouring egotism" that is fatal to other, nobler forms of art, for if he himself is not his only subject, then his responses are, and ultimately his own judgments and opinions, aversions, memories, and desires, are what he writes about. Hazlitt recognized that "*quicquid agunt homines nostri farrago libelli,* is the general motto of this department of literature," [19] but, as his own performance proved, he thought that the writer's role was central: his mind becomes a prism that refracts the various rays of truth, his "common sense," built on "feeling" and anchored in "experience," constitutes the test of action and opinion. [20] Although he knows that "truth is not one, but many," [21] he none the less asserts his own convictions, and thus records such partial wisdom as he has. Like Montaigne, "who had the courage to say as an author what he felt as a man," [22] he cuts through rhetoric and convention to the rock of self-awareness, and there he takes his stand.

Inevitably Hazlitt idolized Rousseau, and his comments on that towering egotist, whose works he had by heart, illuminate his own performance as a writer. Rousseau's main distinction, he explained, was his "extreme sensibility, or an acute and even morbid feeling of all that related to his own impressions, to the objects and events of his life," and it was this that made him great. To say that "every feeling in his mind became a passion" might not strike everyone as commendation, but for Hazlitt it was the highest accolade, [23] and as we read his own unending colloquies with himself about his own devices and desires we see how he converted the old-fashioned periodical essay, with its Addisonian elegance and stylized restraint, into an instrument of knowledge and a means of self-expression. He was right, of course, in calling his own works "romantic" and "disjointed." [24] They reject decorum and neoclassic form; they subordinate reason to emotion and set up "sentiment" as a moral and aesthetic norm; [25] as "studies in human nature" [26] they show man as comic and sublime, gross and sentimental, but they assert his fundamental goodness; and above all they exemplify and celebrate a rampant individualism. Their candor, their neglect of literary and other kinds of artifice, their disrespect for the conventional civilities, the privileged errors, and the institutions of society enable us to call them the credo of a self-acknowledged egotist.

Although anything and everything could serve him as a subject — Milton's mastery of the sonnet, his own attempts at painting, Cobbett's efforts for reform, a picture by Poussin, Sir Joshua Reynolds' errors as a painter — he usually wrote on general traits of character. Such topics as the ignorance of the learned, people with one idea, genius and common sense, vulgarity and affectation, and egotism enabled him to gratify his bent for speculation, tap his reservoir of memory and allusion, check appearance against the mortifying standard of reality, and apply to men and manners the sovereign test of "feeling." His essays, therefore, rarely show a linear pattern. They trace not the sharp contour of points in ordered exposition but the undulating sequence of his moods. Logic yields to feeling, analysis to introspection and association, and from the polyphonic movement of his pathos, anger, and desire emerge the configurations of his theme. This theme, which confers a unity of sorts on all his later work, may be stated as the need for self-awareness. As he contemplates his own and other people's self-deceptions he responds sometimes with tonic skepticism, sometimes with disapproval, sometimes with acquiescence, often with a flabby pathos; but always he is fascinated by his complicated states of mind and driven by the urge to scrutinize and test his own emotions. No matter what his stated topic, his subject is himself.

That is why he rings so many changes on the theme of time and makes such brilliant use of evocation. "I confess, nothing at present interests me but what has been," he wrote not long before his death,

the recollection of the impressions of my early life, or events long past, of which only the dim traces remain in a smouldering ruin of half-obsolete custom. That *things should be that are now no more,* creates in my mind the most unfeigned astonishment. I cannot solve the mystery of the past, nor exhaust my pleasure in it. [27]

A NEW BEGINNING

A major effort in the essays, therefore, is to salvage and preserve the past — that " 'huge, dumb heap,' of wishes, thoughts, feelings, anxious cares, soothing hopes, loves, joys, friendships" that constitutes one's life.[28] He ranged ceaselessly over his experience, not to reconstruct events in sequence but to isolate and brood upon those moments of elation or despair that, reverberating in his memory, linked the present with the past and thus defined his own "identity." "Later impressions come and go," he said, "and serve to fill up the intervals; but these are my standing resource, my true classics." [29] The poignant moments of experience can last as long as life itself if they are cherished, he explained, for when steeped "in thought and passion" they triumph over time.

Seen in the distance, in the long perspective of waning years, the meanest incidents, enlarged and enriched by countless recollections, become interesting; the most painful, broken and softened by time, soothe. How any object, that unexpectedly brings back to us old scenes and associations, startles the mind! What a yearning it creates within us; what a longing to leap the intermediate space! How fondly we cling to, and try to revive the impression of all that we then were! [30]

Despite his discontent with Hartley he was a master of association, for, as he himself remarked, he had a "morbid interest in things, which makes me equally remember or anticipate by nervous analogy whatever touches it." [31] As we grow older, he observed, time becomes so precious that we hoard it like a miser; [32] and he himself by fusing "feeling" with experience, gathered up the fragments of his life and tried to give to them, through art, a new and richer meaning. Because he, like Lamb, sought verisimilitudes, not verities,[33] his essays are a web of subtly linked associations, each colored by his feelings but spun from facts and things. Sometimes his memories are knit into a sequence of events, and take the form of narrative (as in "My First Acquaintance with Poets"), but generally they represent those spots of time that, embellished by association, are transfigured into vision. Whether these record his moments of exhilaration or his unrealized desires, "durable and delightful even in proportion to the regrets accompanying them," [34] they always have a dazzling clarity. The beauty of Llangollen Vale, as he first entered it "in joy, in youth and gladness," [35] the circumstances of his reading Mrs. Inchbald's *Simple Story*,[36] his discovery of *Tom Jones*,[37] his boyish rapture in the Louvre [38] — these and a thousand other memories could take him back to his lost youth; and the more remote they were in time, the more compelling was their power.[39] Indeed, the last essays he wrote — "The Free Admission," "The Sick Chamber," and "The Letter-Bell" [40] — are so vivid and detailed that they map the whole terrain of his existence.

THE ESSAYIST

One's "eventful" moments should be relished like fine wine, he said,[41] and in the vignettes sprinkled thick throughout his essays he preserved such moments while recording them. Once, in the garden of a little country inn, he began rereading *Love for Love*:

Coffee was brought in in a silver coffee-pot; the cream, the bread and butter, every thing was excellent, and the flavor of Congreve's style prevailed over all. I prolonged the entertainment till a late hour, and relished this divine comedy better even than when I used to see it played by Miss Mellon, as *Miss Prue*; Bob Palmer, as *Tattle*; and Bannister, as honest *Ben*. This circumstance happened just five years ago, and it seems like yesterday. If I count my life by lustres, it will soon glide away; yet I shall not have to repine, if, while it lasts, it is enriched with a few such recollections! [42]

On another occasion he found himself at Burleigh House, "twenty years the worse for *wear and tear*" since his last visit there, and of course he slipped into a sea of recollections.

Oh God! that I could but be for one day, one hour, nay but for an instant, (to feel it in all the plenitude of unconscious bliss, and take one long, last, lingering draught of that full brimming cup of thoughtless freedom,) what then I was — that I might, as in a trance, a waking dream, hear the hoarse murmur of the bargemen, as the Minster tower appeared in the dim twilight, come up from the willowy stream, sounding low and underground like the voice of the bittern — that I might paint that field opposite the window where I lived, and feel that there was a green, dewy moisture in the tone, beyond my pencil's reach, but thus gaining almost a new sense, and watching the birth of new objects without me — that I might stroll down Peterborough bank, (a winter's day,) and see the fresh marshes stretching out in endless level perspective . . .

and so on, wandering through the colonnade of time, until he closes by explaining why he had strayed so far from Burleigh House: "I had some associations about it which I could not well get rid of, without troubling the reader with them." [43]

Although he sometimes thought that the passing years would "snap the brittle threads of memory,"[44] he never lost his power to summon up the past or his delight in gliding back through time to the raptures of his youth, where reality and dream converged and where the present, with its "feverish irritation of pursuit and the certainty of disappointment,"[45] no longer could annoy. Nostalgia is an easy anodyne, and Hazlitt used it to excess, but despite his posturing and rhetoric, his exercises in remembrance enable us to understand what sort of man the writer was. When he tells us, for example, that a single line by Collins — "And bade the lovely scenes at distance hail" — always brought to mind the muddy etchings in his copy of Rousseau's *Confessions,* the book that was the very symbol of his youth, we should be prepared for a torrent of emotion, and the torrent duly comes:

I used to apply this line to the distant range of hills in a paltry landscape, which however had a tender vernal tone and a dewy freshness. I could look at them till my eyes filled with tears, and my heart dissolved in faintness. Why do I recal the circumstance after a lapse of years with so much interest? Because I felt it then. Those feeble outlines were linked in my mind to the purest, fondest yearnings after good, that dim, airy space contained my little all of hope, buoyed up by charming fears; the delight with which I dwelt upon it, enhanced by my ignorances of what was in store for me, was free from mortal grossness, familiarity or disappointment, and I drank pleasure out of the bosom of the silent hills and gleaming vallies as from a cup filled to the brim with love-philtres and poisonous sweetness by the sorceress, Fancy! [46]

The essays were more, however, than a vent for his subjectivism; they also supplied a base and frame for his ideas. If "ideas" is perhaps too sharp a word for the crotchets, values, and opinions so loosely flung together, we may use instead something like "persistent attitudes" or "patterns of emotion," but whatever they are called, they define and organize his work. Here the themes that had informed his "metaphysics," politics, and criticism find their most effective statement. As he himself acknowledged,[47] there is nothing really new in these essays, but they are written with a careless ease and power that transform his old convictions. For example, the progress from *An Essay on the Principles of Human Action* to "Self-Love and Benevolence" [48] is not a progress in ideas — as Hazlitt pointed out, there was at least "a thorough *keeping*" in his work [49] — but the change in style is startling: one is a lumpy piece of bone-dry exposition; the other, which expounds the doctrine of disinterestedness in a witty and ironic dialogue, fuses art and "metaphysics." Similarly, essays like "On the Pleasure of Painting," [50] "On a Portrait of an English Lady," [51] and "English Students at Rome" [52] do not take us far beyond the views expressed in his attacks on Reynolds at the start of his career, but they provide his most accomplished statement of the agony and rewards of art. "Is Genius Conscious of Its Powers?" [53] may be regarded as the apotheosis of "Why the Arts Are Not Progressive," almost his first pronouncement on aesthetics. "On Jealousy and Spleen of Party" [54] is a rich concoction of the thwarted hopes and anger recorded with more violence in *Political Essays*. "On Novelty and Familiarity" [55] and "Madame Pasta and Mademoiselle Mars" [56] distill almost everything he had to say about the art of acting. "On People of Sense" — which he himself described as a "philippic against Bentham" [57] — records his rooted discontent with the "poverty and nakedness" [58] of a mechanistic social science. "Of Corporate Bodies" [59] and "On Personal Identity" [60] assert in different ways his lifelong indignation at "the formal crust of circumstances and the mechanism of society." [61] "On Reason and Imagination," [62] which superbly brings into alignment his commitment to "individual facts and feelings," to the moral force of passion, and to imagination as the *associating* principle," constitutes the finest single statement of his values as a critic.

Indeed, the theme of "feeling" versus "reason" runs so strong through all the late essays that it constitutes their leitmotif. It would be absurd, of course, to claim the theme as Hazlitt's own. The recoil from eighteenth-century mechanism found expression in the work of so many men, and different kinds of men, that Burke's attack on those who construe all things in terms of quantity and substance [63] could be regarded as the war cry of the age. Rousseau's dictum, "Si c'est la raison qui fait l'homme, c'est le sentiment qui le conduit," became the watchword for a generation that saw nature as something more than a set of mechanistic forces, feeling as the source of man's best knowledge, and art as the product of imaginative vision. When, at Haydon's immortal dinner in December 1817, the tipsy Lamb reproved his host for putting Newton's head in *Christ's Triumphal Entry* — a fellow "who believed nothing unless it was as clear as three sides of a triangle" — and then jovially led the group in drinking Newton's health and confusion to mathematics, [64] he gave one kind of statement to the theme that is treated variously in *The Prelude* and *Biographia Literaria* and "Lamia." It is also treated, in a hundred different ways, throughout the work of Hazlitt.

As early as his preface to Tucker's *Light of Nature* he had denounced the "modern sophists" (by which he meant the heirs of Locke and Newton), and against them he opposed the race of men who base their thought on feeling. [65] On this conviction — which would have been the theme of the history of modern philosophy that he aspired and failed to write — he built his early lectures, and then, as journalist and critic, he gave it such importance that almost everything he has to say on ethics, art, and politics must be referred to it. "In art, in taste, in life, in speech," he remarked, "you decide from feeling, and not from reason." [66] It is not surprising, then, that the essays so often deal with "passion" as a form of knowledge, or that they are built upon the wisdom of the "heart." He was not a transcendentalist, of course: what he called "fact, concrete existences" were for him the base of all cognition; [67] but unless they were transformed through passion and emotion, as he thought, they had no moral or intellectual value.

Whatever interests, is interesting. I know of no way of estimating the real value of objects in all their bearings and consequences, but I can tell at once their intellectual value by the degree of passion or sentiment the very idea and mention of them excites in the mind. To judge of things by reason or the calculations of positive utility is a slow, cold, uncertain, and barren process — their power of appealing to and affecting the imagination as subjects of thought and feeling is best measured by the habitual impression they leave upon the mind, and it is with this only we have to do in expressing our delight or admiration of them, or in setting a just mental value upon them. They ought to excite all the emotion which they do excite; for this is the instinctive and unerring result of the constant experience we have had of their power of affecting us, and of the associations that cling unconsciously to them. Fancy, feeling may be very inadequate tests of truth; but truth itself operates chiefly on the human mind through them.[68]

Although he recognized no absolutes, moral or scientific, he held that common sense and feeling, custom and experience, supply our deepest needs. With their cumulative power, which mocks the frail dictates of "reason," they are the safest guides to action and the largest reservoir of value. "He is indeed a poor creature who does not *feel* the truth of more than he *knows* or can explain satisfactorily to others." [69] It is through sympathy and imagination that we assimilate experience, identify ourselves with what we know, and distinguish right from wrong, he said, and where "the heart reposes almost entirely upon itself" our judgments rarely err.[70] "Reason may play the critic, and correct certain errors afterwards; but if we were to wait for its formal and absolute decisions in the shifting and multifarious combinations of human affairs, the world would stand still. . . . Science after a certain time becomes presumption; and learning reposes in ignorance." *

To rely only on our reason is to join that "dry and husky" class of men who divorce their moral constructs from reality and resolve our sadly human problems by ignoring them.[71] Such a man was Bentham, who, like all the "self-conceited wise," thought his own particular dogmatism superior to its rivals. He and his disciples — for "utility" was the modern shibboleth, said Hazlitt — would "make a man with a quadrant, as the tailors at Laputa made a suit of clothes."

They put the mind into a machine, as the potter puts a lump of clay into a mould, and out it comes in any clumsy or disagreeable shape that they would have it. They hate all grace, ornament, elegance. They are addicted to abstruse science, but sworn enemies to the fine arts. They are a kind of puritans in morals. Do you suppose that the race of the Iconoclasts is dead with the dispute in Laud's time about image-worship? We have the same set of moon-eyed philosophers in our days, who cannot bear to be dazzled with the sun of beauty. They are only half-alive. They can distinguish the hard edges and determinate outlines of things; but are alike insensible to the stronger impulses of passion, to the finer essences of thought. Their intellectual food does not assimilate with the juices of the mind,

* 20.327; cf. 8.103, 17.309. In his later years Hazlitt used the celebrated phrenologist Johann Spurzheim as a stock example of the learned fool who deceived himself and others with the jargon of a pseudo science. See 12.137–156, 20.248–255.

or turn to subtle spirit, but lies a crude, undigested heap of material substance, begetting only the windy impertinence of words. . . . Such enlightened geniuses would pull down Stonehenge to build pig-sties, and would convert Westminster Abbey into a central House of Correction.[72]

His aversion to such "modern sophists" reinforces his contempt for their Utopias. The Utilitarians were "prosaical visionaries," he said, who cared for nothing but their "grim, bare idols." [73] They were zealots bent on their exclusive method of salvation,[74] but with their hedonistic calculus they were open, as he thought, to two unanswerable objections: they were ignorant of man's complex nature and they waged a "clownish war" on art.[75] What could such theorists know about "the drudgery, the struggles, the poverty, the disease or anguish" that are the common lot of man? [76] Like Godwin in the nineties or Bentham in the post-Napoleonic era,[77] they would convert law into a system and men's minds into machines, not knowing — or perhaps not caring — that we act through "habit, imagination, sense, passion, prejudice" and do not govern our behavior by "the cool calculation of consequences." [78] This is the burden of "The New School of Reform" (subtitled "A Dialogue between a Rationalist and a Sentimentalist"), where Hazlitt wittily explores "the extremes of practical wrong and impractical right" and reasserts his old contempt for reason as the gauge of human action. "I place the heart in the centre of my moral system," the Sentimentalist says,

and the senses and the understanding are its two extremities. You leave nothing but gross, material objects as the ends of pursuit, and the dry, formal calculations of the understanding as the means of ensuring them. Is this enough? Is man a mere animal, or a mere machine for philosophical experiments? . . . Can you divest the mind of habit, memory, imagination, foresight, will? Can you make it go on physical sensations, or on abstract reason alone? Not without making it over again. . . . To deprive man of sentiment, is to deprive him of all that is interesting to himself or others, except the present object and a routine of cant-phrases, and to turn him into a savage, an automaton, or a Political Economist.

The Rationalist is of course appalled by such remarks, but when he closes the dispute by saying that "the poets have spoiled you for all rational and sober views of men and society," it is clear to whom the victory falls.[79]

Also, and inevitably, the essays are strewn with literary opinions and allusions. Usually these are cryptic, terse, and undeveloped — half-remembered lines and fragments dredged up from his reading as a boy and worked into the fabric of associations with which he drapes his themes; but they often take the form of judgments on his favorite books and writers. "On the Prose-Style of Poets," for example, contains a stunning piece on Burke; [80] "Sir Walter Scott, Racine, and Shakespear" [81] — which says almost nothing of Racine — discriminates Scott, the inspired compiler and transcriber, from Shakespeare, the Proteus of the human intellect, with extraordinary precision; "Why the Heroes of Romance Are Insipid" [82] is one of Hazlitt's ripest comments on the English novel; "Of Persons One Would Wish to Have Seen," * which brilliantly recalls, after twenty years or more, Lamb's Wednesday evening parties, ranges over all of English literature; "My First Acquaintance with Poets" [83] is, of course, a major document in the history of Romanticism; "On Reading Old Books" [84] is a rich annotated catalogue of Hazlitt's favorite reading.

Another steady theme is politics. His old attachments and resentments intrude themselves continually, but here they seem, if not more mellow, more solid and secure, as if they had grown with incremental repetition and gathered weight with years. He still despised the Tory politicians [85] and praised the child and champion of the Revolution, [86] and from time to time he lashed out against the poets; [87] but for the most part the heat and anger of *Political Essays* have yielded to the recognition that things are as they are. For this reason, "Arguing in a Circle," [88] which deals with Burke and his successors, has extraordinary weight and power. From time to time, of course, he broke out in his old strain. Twice, he said, he had seen "the dastard, vaunting, venal crew" march forth to trample human rights — once at the beginning of the war with France and again at its conclusion — and the memory seared his soul. "Yet I have endured all this marching and counter-marching of poets, philosophers, and politicians over my head as well as I could, like 'the camomoil that thrives, the more 'tis trod upon.' By Heavens, I think, I'll endure it no longer!" [89] Usually, however, he showed not wrath but bitter sorrow at man's persistent folly. "Oh, Reason! when will thy long minority expire? It is not now the fashion to make Gods of wood and stone and brass, but we make kings of common men, and are proud of our own handy-work." [90]

The fact is that in his later years he could see these things in deep perspective. It was not that the Tories were less wicked than before or that the solemn frauds of church and state had ceased to vex his soul, but merely that he could take a longer view of them. [91] It was in these

---

* 17.122–134. Although Howe, in his edition of this famous essay, restored from Hazlitt's manuscript the initials of the speakers that Thomas Campbell, the editor of the *New Monthly,* had altered when he printed it in 1826, the textual problems have stirred a lively correspondence in *TLS.* See the issues of 27 February 1953 (p. 137), 6 March 1953 (p. 153), 13 March 1953 (p. 169), 8 May 1953 (p. 301), 5 June 1953 (p. 365), 12 June 1953 (p. 381).

later essays that he began to write so much about his father and the tradition of Dissent, to recall his own "first perilous and staggering search" for truth,[92] and to trace the rise and progress of his own ideals; and this continuing exploration of the past gave a new dimension to the present. Embedded in and shored up by the recollections of his youth, his convictions seem to gain in depth[93] and to appear almost as traits of character rather than assertions. Moreover, there is a persistent, if somewhat muted, optimism. He could not persuade himself, he said, that the rotten structure of society, "propped and patched-up by the sword and hireling pens," was about to tumble, yet he did not despair. "I do not see how institutions can for ever exist at war with opinions; and no one will, I should think, maintain that existing institutions are the growth of existing opinions."[94] In spite of folly and imposture, men move, however slowly, toward the good, he said. He did not always sheathe his old asperities or blunt his cutting scorn, but in such essays as "On Paradox and Common-Place"[95] and "On the Spirit of Monarchy"[96] his accustomed wit and anger are instrumental to a larger end, which is to understand, not merely to protest, man's behavior as a social animal.

In earlier chapters we have drawn extensively on the essays; here a few examples will serve to illustrate their range. In "On Novelty and Familiarity" he shapes the simple theme that "practice makes perfect — experience makes us wise"[97] into a dark-hued meditation on illusion as a solace for the ills of life. In "Why Distant Objects Please" he unlocks "the casket of memory" and draws back "the warders of the brain"[98] to show how time, the great destroyer, does not destroy everything. In "On the Disadvantages of Intellectual Superiority"[99] he wittily seeks a reason for his evil reputation. In "On Coffee-House Politicians"[100] he evokes, with affection and precision, the only kind of talk he liked, and in "Of Persons One Would Wish to Have Seen"[101] he recaptures the exhilaration of those nights in Mitre Court when he and Lamb were young. "On Paradox and Common-Place"[102] — the essay that includes, among many other things, the sketch of Shelley that enraged Leigh Hunt — opens quietly by discussing intellectual independence and ends with a sulfurous account of modern Toryism. "The Fight" is a triumph of journalistic prose and also an extended metaphor of his delight in life and action. "How matter presses on me," he exclaims. "What stubborn things are facts! How inexhaustible is nature and art!"[103] "On Personal Identity"[104] is the full assertion of the theme that runs through all his work, and in "On Going a Journey" [105] he invests a little inn at St. Neot's and Llangollen Vale with memories that give to them the magic of romance. On the other hand, there is nothing mellow in "On the Pleasure of Hating," where his anger with the world recoils upon himself in self-destructive malice:

Seeing all this as I do, and unravelling the web of human life into its various threads of meanness, spite, cowardice, want of feeling, and want of understanding, of indifference towards others and ignorance of ourselves — seeing custom prevail over all excellence, itself giving way to infamy — mistaken as I have been in my public and private hopes, calculating others from myself, and calculating wrong; always disappointed where I placed most reliance; the dupe of friendship, and the fool of love; have I not reason to hate and to despise myself? Indeed I do; and chiefly for not having hated and despised the world enough. [106]

Some of these essays are so loose in structure that they defy analysis. For example, he opens "On Great and Little Things" by discussing, very flatly, certain minor irritations, advances to the statement of a seeming paradox — that "to great evils we submit, we resent little provocations" — and then expands the theme with a set of richly orchestrated memories of Lamb's fiasco as a playwright, his own addiction to the game of rackets, his unrequited love for Sarah Walker, his contempt for ladies with literary pretensions, his metaphysical "discovery," and his copies from the Louvre. And then, just as he is sinking in melodious despair at the thought of his repeated failures, he thinks about his love, and spiraling through the linked associations of art and sex and politics he surrenders to intoxicating revery.

A purple light hovers round my head. The air of love is in the room. As I look at my long-neglected copy of the Death of Clorinda, golden gleams play upon the canvas, as they used when I painted it. The flowers of Hope and Joy spring up in my mind, recal the time when they first bloomed there. The years that are fled knock at the door and enter. I am in the Louvre once more. The sun of Austerlitz has not set. It still shines here — in my heart; and he, the son of glory, is not dead, nor ever shall, to me. I am as when my life began. The rainbow is in the sky again. I see the skirts of the departed years. All that I have thought and felt has not been in vain. I am not utterly worthless, unregarded; nor shall I die and wither of pure scorn. Now could I sit on the tomb of Liberty, and write a Hymn to Love. Oh! if I am deceived, let me be deceived still. Let me live in the Elysium of those soft looks; poison me with kisses, kill me with smiles; but still mock me with thy love! [107]

For Hazlitt to explain, in an antiseptic note, that this "specimen of the mock-heroic style" has "nothing to do with any real facts or feelings" cannot conceal its fervor, and its neglect of syntax, logic, and propriety stamps it as authentic.

Authentic in a different way is the splendid "Indian Jugglers." [108]

THE ESSAYIST

Here instead of pathos and gesticulations we find tonic self-appraisal, and instead of querulous complaint a steady current of ideas. The whole is bathed in "feeling," to be sure, but it fuses reminiscence, speculation, and reporting to achieve the statement of a general proposition secured by deep emotion. Like "On the Pleasure of Painting" and "On Genius and Common Sense," it is one of those essays that illuminate our knowledge of the man by showing how and why he reached his values. When, at a lecture on anatomy at the Royal Academy,[109] he watched some jugglers do their tricks, he marveled at the "skill surpassing difficulty, and beauty triumphing over skill," but he was troubled too.

I ask what there is that I can do as well as this? Nothing. What have I been doing all my life? . . . Is there no one thing in which I can challenge competition, that I can bring as an instance of exact perfection, in which others cannot find a flaw? . . . What abortions are these Essays! What errors, what ill-pieced transitions, what crooked reasons, what lame conclusions! How little is made out, and that little how ill! Yet they are the best I can do.

And thus he starts to speculate on different kinds of power, and works into his theme. Was Richer, the "matchless" rope-dancer whom he had seen "a great many years" ago at Sadler's Wells, a better man than Reynolds? The acrobat "added to his extraordinary skill exquisite ease, and unaffected natural grace"; the painter was "slovenly" at best. And yet Reynolds was a greater man, he says, because, "happen how it will, there have been more people in the world who could dance on a rope like the one than who could paint like Sir Joshua."

The reason is that Reynolds was an artist, Richer a mere "mechanical performer," and therefore they were not to be compared. Working through "human skill and industry," a dancer or a juggler has only to emulate himself each time he does his tricks, but an artist, whose work begins where mechanical skill leaves off, has an immensely harder task.

The soft suffusion of the soul, the speechless breathing eloquence, the looks "commercing with the skies," the ever-shifting forms of an eternal principle, that which is seen but for a moment, but dwells in the heart always, and is only seized as it passes by strong and secret sympathy, must be taught by nature and genius, not by rules or study. . . . The more ethereal, evanescent, more refined and sublime part of art is the seeing nature through the medium of sentiment and passion, as each object is a symbol of the affections and a link in the chain of our endless being.

In short, Reynolds was an artist because he had this "involuntary" power. It is not to be confused with skill like Richer's, which must be learned by trial and error, or with talent like Leigh Hunt's, which is merely "voluntary." It does not yield to "abstract rules," nor can it be "verified" by mechanical experiment. It is sporadic and uncertain, and yet, imperfect as it is, it is man's true splendor. In that "enchanted ground" where skill and reason fail, it serves him as a guide and enables him — sometimes — to escape with "half a triumph." Such power never spends its force, for unlike mechanical exertions it is known by its effects — "great results spring from great inherent energy" — that are stamped upon "the page of history." Because Shakespeare, Newton, Bacon, Milton, and Cromwell, like all great men, had "an idea of something greater" than themselves, their power may be felt, and in a manner shared, by everyone who feels, whereas a lord mayor or a rope-dancer or a master chess-player leaves the world as he found it, and "no act terminating in itself constitutes greatness." *

The coda to this great essay is one of Hazlitt's triumphs. Indolence or bravado, perhaps, led him to reprint from the *Examiner* his vivid sketch of Cavanagh, "the famous hand fives-player," but it exemplifies the kind of "feeling" that he himself identified with genius.

When a person dies, who does any one thing better than any one else in the world, which so many others are trying to do well, it leaves a gap in society. It is not likely that any one will now see the game of fives played in its perfection for many years to come — for Cavanagh is dead, and has not left his peer behind him.

A humble, unpretentious man, Cavanagh was none the less an artist, and therefore one of the elect: "he could do what he pleased, and he always knew exactly what to do."

His blows were not undecided and ineffectual — lumbering like Mr. Wordsworth's epic poetry, nor wavering like Mr. Coleridge's lyric prose, nor short of the mark like Mr. Brougham's speeches, nor wide of it like Mr. Canning's wit, nor foul like the *Quarterly,* not *let* balls like the *Edinburgh Review.* Cobbett and Junius together would have made a Cavanagh.

"The Indian Jugglers" ends as it began, by celebrating merit. Cavanagh's was not the excellence of a Cromwell or Cervantes, to be sure, but it was incontestably his own, and a consequence of his own power. Thus as Hazlitt eulogizes his old friend he reaffirms the theme on which his essay rests: "greatness is great power, producing great effects."

THE DEATH OF SCOTT

Lacking any record to the contrary, we must assume that during most of 1820 Hazlitt was engaged — sometimes in London, sometimes at the Hut in Winterslow — in writing monthly essays on "The Drama"

* Elsewhere (8.162f.) Hazlitt says that to be a king, an alderman, or a member of the Royal Society is a "vulgar distinction," but to be a Vergil, a Milton, or a Raphael "is what fell to the lot of humanity but once."

and in turning out his Table Talks, but events already taking place would soon shatter his repose.* These events began in May, when, in an article on the English press, John Scott had protested the slanders on the so-called Cockneys in *Blackwood's Magazine*.¹ For several months, it seems, his rivals made no answer, but finally, in October, they acknowledged his complaints in a long and sometimes witty explanation of their journalistic ways. Since their sale had grown "prodigious," so that "even in Cockaigne" their name and fame were overwhelming, the charge that they had converted criticism into personal abuse was, they said, absurd.

When a person publishes a book, in prose or verse, encouraging, upon principle, all kind of licentiousness, or seeking to undermine the foundation of religious belief, is it an attack on his private character, to say that such an author deserves the hatred and scorn of all good men? If a poet recommends incest — is it an attack on private character to call him incestuous?

As for "Baldwin's new bang-up concern" — that is, the *London Magazine* — they "civilly" requested "the Jehu, John Scott, to keep on his own side of the road — not to be so fond of running races — and not to abuse passengers who prefer going by another conveyance. He drives rather stylishly, but not steadily — he blows his tits too much in going up hill — and before he makes the end of his stage, why, they are all in a lather." † Such condescension, coupled with some fresh abuse of Keats and Haydon, infuriated Scott, and in November he reopened his attack, not, as he explained because he himself was hurt by the *Blackwood's* libels but because "the dignity of literature, and the order and peace of society" were imperiled. His protest was *au fond* against "sectarians and egotists" in modern literature, but since it was *Blackwood's*

---

* In a note, probably of September 1820, to Robert Baldwin (ALS, Berg Collection, New York Public Library) he wrote from Winterslow that he was "busy transcribing," for a projected collection of Table Talks, "On the Present State of Parliamentary Eloquence" (17.5–21), "On the Pleasure of Painting" (8.5–21), "on reading old authors" (i.e., "On Reading Old Books," 12.220–229), "On Vulgarity and Affectation" (8.156–168), and "On the Look of a Gentleman" (12.209–220), adding that if he thought they would all "be regularly inserted" he "would finish the whole 40 nos. out of hand." In a postscript he explained that he was "anxious to contribute my full share to determine the question which is the best, Baldwin's or Blackwood's Magazine." About the same time he wrote to Haydon (ALS, 11 August 1820, in the possession of Willard Pope) that Jeffrey had accepted "with some corrections" his review of Farington's *Reynolds* for the *Edinburgh* (16.181–211). On the strength of a comment (in his December essay on "The Drama") about his contributions "to the stock of literary amusement and scientific intelligence" (18.367f.), it has been suggested that he perhaps had been assigned to "Literary and Scientific Intelligence," a monthly feature in the *London Magazine*. See E. L. Brooks, "Was William Hazlitt a News Reporter?" *Notes & Queries*, New Series I (1954), 355f.

† *Blackwood's Magazine*, VIII (1820), 83, 99, 105. The allusion to an incestuous poet was, of course, a thrust at Leigh Hunt and *The Story of Rimini*.

Magazine, as he thought, that most ominously exemplified the "diseased, false, affected, profligate, whining, and hypocritical character" of contemporary letters, he said that it should be "abated," and he closed his "branding" article by declaring open war.² Although *Blackwood's* professed to find such "drivelry" amusing,³ Scott continued his attack, in the November issue of the *London,* with his famous disquisition on "the Mohock Magazine." When principle yields to "the flippancies of personal allusion" all is lost, he said.

Insensibility, insincerity, and spite, are necessarily engendered by them; and when the poisonous stimulus exercises its full strength, treachery and malignity darken the aspect, and corrupt the influence of what may be termed the literary pleasures of general society. The infamous distinction of industriously and selfishly pandering to these unlawful desires, and systematically contriving seductions addressed to them, belongs to Blackwood's Magazine. Its present management set out with offering gross captivations to the coarsest appetites in this way; — and Iscariot treachery, and Iago malice, took for auxiliaries the levity and folly of a tea-table gossip, and the saucy freedoms of an intermeddling buffoon.⁴

Finally, in January, Scott announced — prematurely, as it happened — that we would have no more to do with Blackwood's gang. "We are now willing to put up the instrument of justice, and inflict no more stripes," he wrote in taking leave of them,

— that is to say, provided they keep to their good behaviour. They must not continue to drag forth *real names,* without authority. . . . Irony may be permitted them, — but not *forgeries* and *fabrications,* intended to justify their own crimes, by sacrificing the interests and character of the guiltless. We give them notice, that this must be done by them for the future, — or else —.⁵

But things had gone too far for such a quick solution. Just about the time that Hazlitt, still in Winterslow, was advising Scott not to "hold out your hand to Blackwoods yet, after having knocked those blackguards down," * the quarrel took a new and deadly turn with John Lockhart's announcement that his honor was impugned. The details of the ensuing fracas are too complicated for a full discussion here, but its consequences may be quickly summarized. When Lockhart, through his friend J. H. Christie, demanded a dictated apology or satisfaction in a duel, Scott in turn insisted that Lockhart disclose his true connection with *Blackwood's Magazine.* Their subsequent negotiations, inept beyond belief, would have been amusing in a comic opera, but there was nothing comic in the denouement, for Christie, thinking that he himself had been insulted, finally jockeyed Scott into a challenge. When the

* *Four Generations,* I, 140. W. C. Hazlitt implausibly dates this letter 12 April 1820, but its allusions to the contents of the latest issue of the *London Magazine* show that it was written early in 1821.

two men met on February 16 at Chalk Hill Farm in Hampstead, Patmore, acting as Scott's second, apparently bungled the arrangements; Scott fell badly wounded, and on February 27, after great torments, he died.* At the inquest a week later Christie, his second James Traill, and Patmore were charged with "Wilful Murder," ° but at their trial in April — where Christie and Traill appeared "dressed in deep mourning" and Patmore did not appear at all — the judge recommended that in "a case of doubt" the jury should "take the side of mercy," and all three men were found not guilty.†

The uproar caused by these events was very great. Lamb, who, as "Elia," had been writing for the *London* since the previous summer, was deeply moved.⁷ The author of Waverley, whose tacit endorsement of the scurrilities in *Blackwood's* had been sharply criticized by Scott, told Lockhart that their adversary had got "exactly what he was long fishing for." ⁸ Haydon, and many others too, it seems, thought that the "Reptile" Patmore — "a fellow who ought to be stamped on like a worm & grated to powder by the angry tread of the public" — was the villain of the piece.‡ Although during most of the excitement Hazlitt had apparently been at Winterslow writing on the charms of solitude, Thomas Campbell was certain that he had urged on Scott his fatal course of action.§ Haz-

---

* For several days following the duel it was thought that Scott was convalescent, but when the *Times* announced on Wednesday, February 28, that he was "still living, but in such intense suffering as much speedily exhaust what remains of existence" he had in fact already died the night before.

† *Examiner*, 15 April 1821, p. 239. For accounts of the Scott-Christie duel see Andrew Lang, *The Life and Letters of John Gibson Lockhart* (1897), I, 236–283; Bauer, *The London Magazine*, pp. 75–80; Marion Lockhead, *John Gibson Lockhart* (1954), pp. 82–85; Alan Lang Strout, "John Scott and Maga," *TLS*, 29 August 1936, p. 697. In the February 1821 issue of the *London* Scott stitched in (following p. 124) a torturously involved account of the abortive negotiations with Lockhart and Christie.

‡ *Diary*, II, 315; cf. L'Estrange, II, 128. There survives an undated "manifesto" (Basil Champneys, *Memoirs and Correspondence of Coventry Patmore* [1900], II, 426–429) in which Patmore tried to explain his part in the affair.

§ Cyrus Redding, *Past Celebrities Whom I Have Known* (1866), I, 85f. Elsewhere (*Fifty Years' Recollections* [1858], II, 225) Redding wrote that Horatio Smith (who had briefly served as John Scott's second during the protracted negotiations with Christie) did not share this view: Campbell was too prone to believe whatever he might hear in disparagement of Hazlitt, said Smith, "and in this instance I have reason to think he was misinformed." Although Campbell, as editor of the *New Monthly Magazine*, printed much of Hazlitt's work after 1822, the two were never friends. Indeed, after the critic, in his lectures on the English poets in 1818, pointed out (5.150) that the line "Like angels' visits, few, and far between" in The Pleasures of Hope — a work in which "the decomposition of prose is substituted for the composition of poetry" — had been pilfered from Hugh Blair, the poet always bore a grudge

litt himself made no comment that survives, but by mid-February he was back in town, and a few weeks later Robert Baldwin, the owner of the *London,* had accepted his "kind offer to assist in filling up the chasm" left by John Scott's death.⁹ As a result, he at once stepped up his contributions, and for a month or so, perhaps, he even served as editor.* It must have been a busy spring for him. While preparing for the press a collection of his Table Talks (most of which were new) he most likely carried on "The Lion's Head," a feature of the *London* that Scott had made his own; for the May issue he supplied, in addition to the customary Table Talk,¹⁰ a cool review of Byron's *Marino Faliero,*¹¹ an even cooler piece on Crabbe,¹² and an article on *Christ's Agony in the Garden,* Haydon's newest picture.¹³ He followed these, in June, with a long review-essay on Bowles's and Byron's controversy over Pope, one of his most elaborate efforts as a critic.†

Sandwiched in among these heavy duties there were fresh distractions. In April *Table-Talk* appeared, and provoked the quarrel with Hunt that we have noted earlier.¹⁴ Something of Hazlitt's exacerbated state of mind is shown in his long list of grievances that he itemized for Hunt on this occasion. "I pique myself on doing what I can for others," he remarked,

but I can not say that I have found any suitable returns for this, and hence perhaps my outrageousness of stomach! For instance, I praised you in the *Edinburgh Review,* and when in a case of life and death I tried to lecture, you refused to go near the place, and gave this as a reason, saying it would seem a collusion, if you said any thing in my favour after what I had said of you. 2. I got Reynolds to write in the *Edinburgh Review,* at a time when I had a great reluctance to ask any favour of Jeffrey, and from that time I never set eyes on him for a year and a half after. 3. I wrote a book [the *Reply* to Malthus] in defence of Godwin some years ago, one half of which he has since stolen without acknowledgment, without even mentioning my name, and yet he comes to me to review the very work and I write to Jeffrey to ask his consent, thinking myself, which you do not, the most

(Redding, *Fifty Years' Recollections,* II, 277; 8.210). In 1826 he felt obliged to apologize to Leigh Hunt for Hazlitt's comments (11.188f.) on Shelley in one of the Northcote "Conversations" that had appeared in the *New Monthly* (see below, page 454), and soon he stopped the series altogether (*Memoirs,* II, 210 ff.). When, in 1830, he printed Procter's eulogistic obituary sketch of Hazlitt in his magazine, he did so with misgivings, as he ostentatiously explained (*New Monthly Magazine,* XXIX [1830], 482). For his part, Hazlitt thought that Campbell, both as poet (5.149) and editor (16.232), was too fastidious and prim, but in *The Spirit of the Age* (11.159f.) he praised him as an almost faultless craftsman.

* On 31 March 1821 Charles Armitage Brown reported to Joseph Severn in Rome (Jack C. Stillinger, "The Letters of Charles Armitage Brown" [Harvard dissertation, 1958], I, 176) that Hazlitt was to be the "chief man" of the *London Magazine.*

† 19.62–84. On May 9 Robert Baldwin, writing to arrange a meeting between Hazlitt and John Taylor (*Memoirs,* II, 8), asked that "the article on Pope" be sent as soon as possible.

magnanimous person in the world in the defence of a cause. 4. I have taken all opportunities of praising Lamb, and I never got a good word from him in return, big or little, till the other day. He seemed struck all of a heap, if I ever hinted at the possibility of his giving me a lift at any time. 5. It was but the other day that two friends did all they could to intercept an article about me from appearing in the said *E. R.*, saying "it would be too late," "that the Editor had been sounded at a distance, and was averse," with twenty other excuses, and at last I was obliged to send it myself, *graciously* and by main force, as it were, when it appeared just in time to save me from drowning. Coulson had been backwards and forwards between my house and Bentham's for between three or four years, and when the latter philosophically put an execution in my house, the plea was he had never heard of my name; and when I theorized on this the other day as bad policy, and *felo de se* on the part of the Radicals, your nephew [Henry Leigh Hunt] and that set said: "Oh, it was an understood thing — the execution, you know!" My God, it is enough to drive one mad. . . . I want to know why everybody has such a dislike to me.[15]

Meanwhile James Hessey and John Taylor, who were in negotiation for the purchase of the *London Magazine* and were looking for an editor, made cautious overtures to him.* He no doubt rebuffed them, for he regarded editors with a suspicion based on hard-earned knowledge, and, as he must have realized, he would have made a wretched one himself. "A prodigious look of business, an air of suspicion which passes for sagacity, and an air of deliberation which passes for judgment"[16] were clearly not within his power, and since he did not aspire to correct another's grammar and arrange his paragraphs † he continued as a writer, turning out his Table Talks, playing whist at Lamb's,[17] and living

---

* *Memoirs,* II, 8f. On 16 April 1821 Talfourd told Mary Russell Mitford (Vera Watson, "Thomas Noon Talfourd and His Friends," *TLS,* 20 April 1956, p. 244) that he had been offered the editorship of the *London* "provided some unknown person in the country does not accept it, but I think I shall withstand the temptation — indeed I have, in my own mind, determined to refuse it. I do not think it would be compatible with my professional pursuits [as a barrister]."

† 17.362. On 23 May 1821 Talfourd told Miss Mitford (*TLS,* 20 April 1956, p. 244) that Scott, whose salary had been £600 a year, had not only edited the *London* but had also written half of it, "and as the Publishers did not wish any individual to do this in future, they would have made proportionate deductions. I understand there is to be no Editor — now — but that Taylor & Hessey will conduct the mechanism of the work & leave the rest to regular Correspondents who will furnish certain portions." In the June 1821 issue (IV, 591) the new publishers announced that "arrangements have been completed for the future Editorship of the London Magazine," and for the next four years John Taylor was in charge of it. See Bauer, pp. 119–144.

Something of the proprietors' difficulties with the *London* after Scott's untimely death may be inferred from the thirty-one letters (recently acquired by Harvard) that Procter wrote to them between 1822 and 1824. In one of them, for instance — a withering comment on their irresponsible editorial procedures that was probably written at the start of 1822 — Procter protests the cuts and alterations to which his work has been subjected. "Not only I, but, I may say, four of your *principal* contributors feel that this system is not the best. If there be any thing contrary to morals or good feeling strike it out — If a man makes [?] his papers too long tell him in plain terms — He will, if he has any sense, fashion his labours accordingly."

the free, disordered life described in "On Coffee-House Politicians." [18] All this while, however, the crisis of his life was fast approaching, as a note to Talfourd in December 1821 makes clear. "Driven almost into a corner" by his needs, he wrote, he had thought to print another set of essays, and to this end he requested Talfourd's help with Henry Colburn, a "little bookselling Buonaparte" [19] who listed with his other assets the *New Monthly Magazine*. For £200 he would sell to Colburn twenty essays ("all *virgins* but one"), or for £400 he would add to these another twenty (on subjects "not at all blown upon"), which might be used in the *New Monthly* and then reprinted as a book. The important thing, as he implied, was to lay hands upon a sum of money. "The truth is, I seem to have been hurt in my mind lately, and continual effort to no purpose is too much for any patience, & mine is nearly exhausted. My dear Talfourd, if you have a girl that loves you & that you have a regard for, lose no time in marrying, & think yourself happy, whatever else may happen." *

---

* *Life,* pp. 304f. A note to Jeffrey on 26 November 1821 (ALS, The Yale University Library) shows that negotiations with Colburn were already well advanced:

Winterslow Hut
near Salisbury

Dear Sir,

I am got down here to try my hand on Lady Morgan. Would you send me word when will be the latest time for forwarding the article if I can succeed in it? I sent you some proof sheets of the new volume of Table-talk. Might I hope (when you have looked at them) for a notice in the next number? The work will I understand be transferred to Colburn to publish. I am, Dear Sir, always your truly obliged & obedient servant.

W. Hazlitt.

Novr 26, 1821.
I had forgot to say what I ought to have acknowledged long ago that I received your kind remittance in due course.

Hazlitt may have written, or at least begun, his review of Lady Morgan's *Life and Times of Salvator Rosa* at this time, but three years later, while at Melrose following his second marriage, he told Jeffrey that he hoped to make "something better" of the piece (Keynes, facing p. 83), and it was finally published in the July 1824 issue of the *Edinburgh* (16.284–318). Jeffrey's "kind remittance" was no doubt in payment for the article "Capital Punishments," which had been printed in the July 1821 issue (19.216–255).

"On Going a Journey" (8.181–189), which appeared in the *New Monthly* for January 1822, was followed by "On Great and Little Things" (8.226–242) in February and by "On Milton's Sonnets" (8.174–181) in March. For the circumstances under which "The Fight" (17.72–86) appeared in the February *New Monthly* see Stewart C. Wilcox, *Hazlitt in the Workshop: The Manuscript of* The Fight (1943), pp. 1–8. Despite his affiliation with the *New Monthly* Hazlitt did not cut his ties entirely with the *London*. To the January 1822 issue he contributed a review of Scott's *Pirate* (19.85–94), and he followed this in February and May with an important two-part essay on the Elgin Marbles (18.145–166). After his return from Scotland he resumed his contributions in the fall of 1822 with a piece on Fonthill Abbey (18.173–180).

THE ESSAYIST

Thus it was that as the new year opened his Table Talks were moved to the *New Monthly Magazine*, and his affair with Sarah Walker entered its disastrous final phase.

A MIND DISEASED

This episode with Sarah Walker, which has always given pain to Hazlitt's admirers and satisfaction to the prurient, is, ironically, the most fully documented in his life. He himself recorded it with Rousseauistic frenzy in *Liber Amoris* (1823), an extraordinary compilation of the lovers' "conversations" and of his own correspondence.* In addition, there survives Sarah Hazlitt's "Journal of My Trip to Scotland," in which that blunt, long-suffering woman gave her version of the facts relating to the dissolution of her marriage.† With the aid of these documents, which enable us to follow, sometimes too close for comfort, the workings of a mind diseased, we can understand, perhaps, Hazlitt's own remark about himself:

I am not mad, but my heart is so; and raves within me, fierce and untameable, like a panther in its den, and tries to get loose to its lost mate, and fawn on her hand, and bend lowly at her feet.[1]

The shabby liaison began in August 1820 when he returned from Winterslow to his old lair in Southampton Buildings, took lodgings with a tailor by the name of Walker, and first saw his landlord's daughter Sarah.‡ As certain cryptic comments in his later essays seem to indicate,[2] he perhaps had already had what Howe delicately describes as an "emotional relationship" at Winterslow after parting from his wife, but the effect that Sarah Walker had on him was prompt and overwhelming. "The idol we fall down and worship is an image familiar to our minds," he wrote in retrospect:

---

    * Part I, comprising seven reconstructed "conversations" and two letters that Hazlitt sent to Sarah Walker while on his way to Scotland in the spring of 1822, describes the start of the affair; Part II, comprising thirteen letters to P. G. Patmore (who was, after his strange fashion, keeping watch on Sarah while Hazlitt was away), one note to Sarah herself, a letter from Patmore to Hazlitt, and various essay-like interpolations, concerns the absent lover's torments; Part III, in the form of a long three-part letter addressed to James Sheridan Knowles (but most likely never sent), constitutes a kind of epilogue. Hesketh Pearson's lurid *Fool of Love* (1934) is largely based on this material.
    † This journal was included by Richard Le Gallienne and W. C. Hazlitt in their "privately printed" edition of *Liber Amoris* in 1894. Recently Willard Hallam Bonner, in his edition of *The Journals of Sarah and William Hazlitt 1822–1831* (1959), has made available, from materials in the Lockwood Memorial Library at the University of Buffalo, more reliable texts of Sarah Hazlitt's Scottish journal, several of her letters, and some chaotic "Journal-Notes" jotted down by Hazlitt in the spring of 1823.
    ‡ 9.120, where he dates his first sight of the "sweet apparition" as 16 August 1820.

A MIND DISEASED

It has been present to our waking thoughts, it has haunted us in our dreams, like some fairy vision. Oh! thou, who, the first time I ever beheld thee, didst draw my soul into the circle of thy heavenly looks, and wave enchantment round me, do not think thy conquest less complete because it was instantaneous; for in that gentle form (as if another Imogen had entered) I saw all that I had ever loved of female grace, modesty, and sweetness! [3]

Although it was not strange that a footloose man of forty-two should be attracted by a girl of half his age, it was disastrous that he fell in love with her. A born coquette, she did not yield to him completely, but neither did she resist the fumbling overtures that later he described in print. The details, which one could almost reconstruct in the absence of his masochistic revelations, need not be rehearsed. Despite what Haydon called Sarah's "palpable selfishness, her dowdy trolloping, her passionless, icy, cold blooded art," [4] within five months he was making veiled allusions to the situation in his Table Talks, [5] and then, as his infatuation grew, his love and lust became obsessive. Mrs. Hazlitt, a woman noted for her candor, thought that Sarah Walker "was as thin and bony as the scrag end of a neck of mutton," [6] and even the more romantic Procter conceded that she was a very ordinary girl; [7] but Hazlitt, whose "heart" had "filled up the moulds of the imagination," [8] saw in her a goddess. "I want an eye to cheer me, a hand to guide me, a breast to lean on," he explained; "all of which I shall never have, but shall stagger into my grave without them, old before my time, unloved and unlovely, unless —. I would have some creature love me before I die. Oh! for the parting hand to ease the fall!" [9] He had wasted all his life in "one long sigh," he said, but it was not too late for her to bring him peace and joy — "not too late, if that face, pure, modest, downcast, tender, with angel sweetness, not only gladdens the prospect of the future, but sheds its radiance on the past, smiling in tears. A purple light hovers round my head. The air of love is in the room." [10]

This vision of ecstatic joy in his Table Talks is more appealing than the reality described in *Liber Amoris,* where we see Hazlitt hold his "Infelice" on his lap and fumble with her clothing, [11] but in his disordered state of mind the two were indistinct. He lived through most of 1821, it seems, in a state of suspended but erotic animation, hoping he might marry Sarah Walker [12] and trying to forget that he already had a wife. By December, when he wrote the letter to Talfourd about his need of money, he had hit upon a plan: to go to Edinburgh with Sarah Hazlitt and there, where the law was more accommodating than in England, to secure a Scottish divorce.* After a stormy parting from his

---

* Under English law (which was not changed until 1857) the Hazlitts would have been obliged to secure from the Spiritual Court, on proof of "certain matrimonial offences," a decree of separation *a mensa et thoro* and then have it ratified by a special

Infelice — for he feared he had a rival[13] — he set forth the following month, and at Stamford, feeling "dull" and lonely, he began to reconstruct the "conversations" that already, it would seem, he had planned to make into a book.* He then pushed on to Renton, in Berwickshire, where he stayed for several weeks in order to establish a legal Scottish residence,† and where, as he wrote Sarah Walker, he "regularly" did ten pages a day for the new volume of Table Talks that he had promised Colburn.[14] Having finished this assignment ("magnificently," as he himself told Patmore) ‡ by early March, he promptly sent the news to Colburn:

> Renton-Inn, Berwickshire, Scotland.
> Sunday, March 3.
>
> My Dear Sir,
> By the time you receive this, the New Volume will be done, & ready, if you desire it, to go to press with, or to send up in lumps of 50 pages at a time for the Magazine. It contains, I hope, better things than any I have done. I thank God for my escape, & have now done with essay-writing for ever. I do wish you would send me 30£ by return of post, or I shall be obliged to write to Jeffrey for money to get away from here, which I wish to do immediately after my task is done. I have worked at it, I assure you, without ceasing & like a tyger. I am on the whole better in health, & hope to take a trip into the Highlands before I return. Has Mr. Patmore called on you in my behalf? I remain, Dear Sir,
> Your obliged & very humble servant,
> W. Hazlitt.§

He then went on to Edinburgh, and there, while waiting for his wife to come and start negotiations for divorce, he was prey to all the doubts that afflict an aging lover parted from his love. He was in "a sort of purgatory," Patmore was informed.

---

act of Parliament. In Scotland, on the other hand, proven infidelity on the part of either spouse was held sufficient cause for the annulment of a marriage. See Augustine Birrell, *William Hazlitt* (1902), pp. 170 f.

* 9.117. On March 30 he wrote to Patmore from Edinburgh (*Memoirs*, II, 32) that he had "finished the book of my conversations with her, which I call 'Liber Amoris'."

† Under Scots law a residence of forty days was required for an action for divorce. Since, as Birrell points out (p. 171n) this residential requirement was never recognized in English law, Hazlitt's second marriage was bigamous in England.

‡ *Memoirs*, II, 68, where he lists the essays he had done or was about to do: "On the Knowledge of Character" (8.303–317), "Advice to a School-boy" (17.86–100), "On Patronage and Puffing" (8.289–302), "On Spurzheim's Theory" (12.137–156), "On the Disadvantages of Intellectual Superiority" (8.279–289), "On the Fear of Death" (8.321–330), "Burleigh House" (10.62–69), "Why Actors should not sit in the Boxes" (8.272–279), "On Dreams" (12.17–24), and "On Individuality" (which can be identified with none of Hazlitt's published work).

§ 9.261. The critical response to the second volume of *Table-Talk*, which Colburn published in June (Keynes, p. 57), was what one might expect. Although the *Quarterly*, as we have noted (see page 370 n), reviewed it very harshly, the *Examiner* (8 September 1822, pp. 569ff.) predicted that it would be a great success, and the *London* (VII [1823], 689–693) praised Hazlitt highly for his style and intellectual independence.

If I knew she was a mere abandoned creature, I should try to forget her; but till I do know this, nothing can tear me from her, I have drank in poison from her lips too long — alas! mine do not poison again. I sit and indulge my grief by the hour together; my weakness grows upon me; and I have no hope left, unless I could lose my senses quite. Do you know I think I should like this? To forget, ah! to forget — there would be something in that — to change to an ideot for some few years, and then to wake up a poor wretched old man, to recollect my misery as past, and die! [15]

But when these black moods passed he would lose himself in dreams of bliss. "It is not what she says or what she does," he wrote a few days later,

it is herself that I love. To be with her is to be at peace. I have no other wish or desire. The air about her is serene, blissful; and he who breathes it is like one of the Gods! So that I can but have her with me always, I care for nothing more. I never could tire of her sweetness; I feel that I could grow to her, body and soul. My heart, my heart is her's. [16]

Although there were lucid moments too — for at long last he met Jeffrey, who not only made him welcome but, as so often in the past, aided him financially * — it was Sarah who haunted his imagination. " 'Stony-hearted' Edinburgh! What art thou to me? The dust of thy streets mingles with my tears and blinds me. . . . The air is too thin for me, that has not the breath of Love in it; that is not embalmed by her sighs!" [17]

On April 22 Sarah Hazlitt came, and thereafter the factual entries in her journal provide an amusing counterpoint to her husband's wild ejaculations. While the sordid preparations for divorce were going forward (for Sarah had to certify that her husband had had "carnal and adulterous intercourse and dealings") † and the financial arrangements were being hammered out, [18] the Hazlitts fretted at the law's delay. "So here I am," wrote Sarah after she had been in Edinburgh a month, "lonely, in a strange place, my quarter's money and the four pounds all gone, and obliged to borrow; instead of having the £37-10-0 repaid me to lay by, and money in my pocket for present expences, as Mr. Hazlitt repeatedly promised: and can neither see or hear from my boy, who is my dearest comfort!" [19] In early May Hazlitt moved on to Glasgow to

---

* *Memoirs*, II, 32, 48; 9.126, 154. For some of the details of Hazlitt's conversation with Jeffrey see Patmore, III, 20 ff. Part of the money that he got from Jeffrey at the time may have been in payment for a review of Byron's *Sardanapalus*, which, although accepted for publication in the *Edinburgh* (*Memoirs*, II, 32) and duly printed in the February 1822 issue, was later claimed by Jeffrey as his own. See 16.421; *Life*, pp. 310 f.; Douady, pp. 30 f.

† Bonner, p. 190. One cause for anxiety and delay, as far as Sarah was concerned, was the taking of the oath *de calumnia*, which required a solemn affirmation that there had been no collusion between man and wife in securing evidence of marital infidelity. For Sarah's doubts upon this subject — which, of course, were justified — see Bonner, pp. 185, 189, 223, 224f., 246; cf. Birrell, p. 172.

give a pair of lectures,* after which he tramped with Knowles into the Highlands;[20] but then, in a frenzy of despair, he took the boat to London, where he had a string of frantic, inconclusive scenes with Sarah Walker.† Meanwhile his wife beguiled the time with prodigious walking tours, a visit to the north of Ireland, and endless legal consultations. Toward the end of May Hazlitt, maddened by the fear that he had been betrayed, returned to Edinburgh for the final act of this bizarre affair. "The sky is marble to my thoughts," he wrote;

> nature is dead around me, as hope is within me; no object can give me one gleam of satisfaction now, nor the prospect of it in time to come. I wander by the seaside; and the eternal ocean and lasting despair and her face are before me. Slighted by her, on whom my heart by its last fibre hung, where shall I turn? I wake with her by my side, not as my sweet bedfellow, but as the corpse of my love, without a heart in her bosom, cold, insensible, or struggling from me; and the worm gnaws me, and the sting of unrequited love, and the canker of a hopeless, endless sorrow.‡

But, as he told Patmore, he would do it all again. Even though his mind was "half-disordered" it was clear enough for him to understand his situation. "Wretched being that I am! I have thrown away my heart and soul upon an unfeeling girl; and my life (that might have been so happy, had she been what I thought her) will soon follow either voluntarily, or by the force of grief, remorse, and disappointment."[21]

In June, fortified by a hundred pounds advanced to him by Jeffrey,§ he went again to Renton to see if he could do a little work, but a few weeks later he was back in Edinburgh,[22] and there he stayed, it seems, until the action for divorce was finished on July 17. That very afternoon he and Sarah took a friendly cup of tea and, in the waning of a cold and "drizzly" day, rehearsed their life together. It was an extraordinary conversation, and Sarah recorded it in extraordinary detail. They

---

* *Memoirs*, II, 41f.; Bonner, p. 198; Charles Gibbon, *The Life of George Combe* (1878), I, 151f. According to his wife (Bonner, p. 223), Hazlitt made £56 from these Glasgow lectures.

† 9.122f., 142–154. It was on this flying trip to London, according to Patmore (III, 20), that Hazlitt, on May 21, paid a visit to John Hunt in Coldbath Fields Prison, where he was serving out his term for an alleged libel on the House of Commons.

‡ 9.125. In an addition (8.305) made in proof to "On the Knowledge of Character" about this time he expressed the same anxiety: "The greatest hypocrite I ever knew was a little, demure, pretty, modest-looking girl, with eyes timidly cast upon the ground, and an air soft as enchantment; the only circumstances that could lead to a suspicion of her true character was a cold, sullen, watery, glazed look about the eyes, which she bent on vacancy, as if determined to avoid all explanation with yours. I might have spied in their glittering, motionless surface, the rocks and quicksands that awaited me below!"

§ 9.129ff.; *Memoirs*, II, 48ff.; Bonner, p. 224. Sarah Hazlitt recorded tartly (Bonner, p. 236) that her husband "had squeezed £100 out of Jeffrey, like so many drops of blood."

talked about their son,* of course, and about financial problems, but mainly they talked, with clinical precision, about Hazlitt's odd behavior. He had acted badly, he admitted, but his wife had had her "intrigues" too, and as for Sarah Walker, her conduct baffled comprehension. He said

> that she professed the greatest fondness, affection and esteem for him & for the last year and an half, had made a constant practice of coming up and sitting on his knee for two or three hours every day of her life, with her arms round his neck, kissing him and expressing the greatest love and attachment. and that he had done every thing but go to bed to her. yet though he made the warmest love to her. she either had no passions, and her fondness was all deceit. or she had the most astonishing controul over them. for there she stopped short. and declared that all this fondling was only friendship and the story she told was that there was a courtship and affection subsisting between herself and a young man who lodged in their house about three years ago, but that some obstacles arising to the match it was broken off by mutual consent, and she would never have any body.[23]

And so they talked the afternoon away, not with any real affection, to be sure, but with perfect ease and candor. The next day Hazlitt abruptly left for London, and as Sarah's journal closes we see her making tidy preparations for her own departure.

Although Haydon's moral judgments sometime ring a little false, his account of this bizarre affair may serve us as a summary. Hazlitt had disgraced his "character & reputation," he recorded in his diary.

> The Genius of this day really all seem to have a wrong feeling as to duty. Hazlitt married some years ago; his wife had property, she produced him a child, a fine boy. As he got into Society, the manner of his wife appeared unpleasant. The poor woman, irritated by neglect, irritated him in return. At last he got so in love with a young coquette, young enough to be his daughter; his wife is a bar to his success. He remembers adultery in a man can procure divorce in Scotland. He advises his wife to let him go down & commit adultery, & then for her to come down & proceed against him. Down he goes, sleeps in a brothel, with a strumpet one *eyed from disease*! (his own acct.), his wife brings her action, & he [is] divorced! By heavens! There is something so disgusting in this that it makes the gorge rise. The Scotch, who are a moral people, hear of this, & he comes away with a fixed hatred from their remark on it. The bawd & the strumpet come into court. The Judge says, "did you ever see this Gentleman?" "Yes, Sir," said the girl, looking at him with one eye! "How long?" "Three hours at a time, may it

---

* Having put his son to school "at a Mr. Dawson's, in Hunter Street, London," just before setting forth for Scotland (*Memoirs*, II, 16; Bonner, p. 237), at Renton a few weeks later (*Memoirs*, II, 68) Hazlitt wrote the parental "On the Conduct of Life; or, Advice to a Schoolboy" (17.86–100) that was included in the Paris *Table-Talk* in 1825. The child — whom Crabb Robinson (I, 265) thought "troublesome and forward" — is frequently alluded to in *Liber Amoris* (9.123, 125, 139, 143) and also in Sarah Hazlitt's journal (Bonner, pp. 187, 196, 209, 237, 239), always with affection. After the divorce Hazlitt may have taken him to Winterslow, as he had planned to do (Bonner, p. 239), but presently the boy was sent to a school conducted by the Rev. William Evans at Tavistock (*Christian Reformer*, New Series, III [1847], 631ff., 679). Several of his mother's letters to him there survive (Bonner, pp. 255–261).

please your Lordship." "Then you have known this gentleman carnally?" "Yes, Sir, & please your Lordship."

Upon my honor, as Hazlitt was telling this, I felt my cheek redden at his wilful moral degradation.

One has heard of people being caught in adultery, & few are proud of it, but here is a man who goes 500 miles to break a commandment of God, & brazenly enters a brothel — it is no use writing about it.*

There was one more scene in this sad farce, and it sustained the note of frenzy. Encouraged by Patmore (whose interest in Sarah Walker, Mrs. Hazlitt said, was open to suspicion),[24] on his return to London Hazlitt prepared to make one final plea. "How ought I to behave when I go back," he asked. "Advise a fool, who had nearly lost a Goddess by his folly."[25] Things at first were calm when he returned to his old lodgings with the Walkers, but Sarah, who turned equivocation into art, still would not commit herself. Finally, when, after several days of indecisive conversations, she went out one evening for a stroll, Hazlitt followed her. When he came upon her walking with a tall, good-looking man, at last he knew the truth. "I turned and looked," he said, "they also turned and looked — and as if by mutual consent, we both retrod our steps and passed again, in the same way. I went home. I was stifled."[26] As he had long suspected, Sarah was playing with her current beau, who was also one of Mr. Walker's lodgers, the "same game" that she had played with him, and so, "groveling, stunned, stupefied," he faced the fearful fact that she, a "wanton" and a "practised, callous jilt," had made a fool of him.[27] Later, after he had left Southampton Buildings,† he saw her in the street one day and was hardly stirred at all. "I am afraid she will soon grow common to my imagination, as well as worthless in herself," he said in closing *Liber Amoris*. "Her image seems fast 'going into the wastes of time,' like a weed that the wave bears farther and farther from me. Alas! thou poor hapless weed, when I entirely lose sight of thee, and for ever, no flower will ever bloom on earth to glad my heart again!"

❖   ❖   ❖

The aftermath of this affair was as painful as the rest of it. Although he had been forced to face the truth, he had not learned to live

* *Diary*, II, 373. When Hazlitt told this story, or one much like it, to Landor in Florence in 1825, the poet laughed with "irrepressible delight" (John Forster, *Walter Savage Landor* [1869], p. 438).
† 9.162. When Hazlitt wrote to Jeffrey toward the end of August (ALS, postmark 24 August 1822, The Yale University Library) he was still living at 9 Southampton Buildings, but by October 2 (ALS, The Yale University Library) he had moved to 4 Chapel Street West, Curzon Street, Piccadilly.

with it, and for several months he felt, as he told Jeffrey, "like a man who has been thrown from the top of a house." [28] To Procter, on the other hand, he called himself "a cursed fool."

I saw J— going into Wills' Coffee-house yesterday morning; he spoke to me. I followed him into the house; and whilst he lunched I told him the whole story. "Then" (said he) "I wandered into the Regent's Park, where I met one of M—'s sons. I walked with him some time, and on his using some civil expression, by God! sir, I told him the whole story." [Here he mentioned another instance, which I forget.] "Well, sir" (he went on), "I then went and called on Haydon; but he was out. There was only his man, Salmon, there; but, by God! I could not help myself. It all came out; the whole cursed story! Afterwards I went to look at some lodgings at Pimlico. The landlady at one place, after some explanations as to rent, etc., said to me very kindly, 'I am afraid you are not well, sir?' — 'No, ma'am,' said I, 'I am not well;' and on inquiring further, the devil take me if I did not let out the whole story, from beginning to end!" [29]

In early August, shortly after his return from Scotland, he was, said Haydon, "in a state of absolute insanity," [30] and six weeks later he still was "full of his Sally Walker"; [31] but meanwhile he had found catharsis of a sort by working on *Liber Amoris*. "He has written down all the conversations without colour," Haydon reported to Mary Russell Mitford on September 8, "literal as they happened; he has preserved all the love-letters, many of which are equal to anything of the sort, and really affecting; and I believe, in order to ease his soul of this burden, means, with certain arrangements, to publish it as a tale of character. He will sink into idiotcy if he does not get rid of it." [32] Until he did "get rid of it" he was like a man demented — "crying like an infant! cursing like a fury! loving like a dotard! and anticipating revenge like a Demon!" [33] Under the circumstances it is not surprising that, according to Crabb Robinson, no one made him welcome when he called * or that he himself declared we learn about "the folly and the malice of mankind" from the "impertinence" of our so-called friends. [34]

THE SLOW RECOVERY

For twelve months or so after his return from Scotland — that is, until the fall of 1823 — he lived a kind of double life, part of it devoted to his work, part to seeking his revenge on Sarah Walker. A note to Jeffrey in the fall of 1822 shows him struggling to his feet but still uncertain where to go:

* Robinson, I, 286. Recalling Mrs. Basil Montagu's "most singular social and spiritual *ménagerie*" about this time, Carlyle (*Reminiscences*, p. 252) said that Hazlitt was "not now 'of the admitted' (such was the hint); at any rate, kept strictly away." For Hazlitt's former high opinion of the lady's conversation see 12.41f.

THE ESSAYIST

Dear Sir,

I understand the Memoirs of Napoleon by Count Montholon are forthcoming. Might I in that case try my hand upon them? I have been thinking, at your suggestion, of doing an article on the Newspaper & Periodical Press, taking in the Times, Chronicle, Magazines, Reviews, etc. The abuses of the Ministerial press might come into this, but I am afraid I know too little of them in detail to make a separate article on that subject. I could make something of the general subject, I know, for it has been some time in my head. I am better than I was, & able to work. If you could lay your hand on the metaphysical article on Bühle [sic], I should take it as a great favour if you would forward it by the Mail to No. 4 Chapel Street West, Curzon Street. You see by this I have moved. I have come away *alive*, which in all the circumstances is a great deal. I believe I did very wrong in not calling on you while in Edinburgh, but the truth is, *I hated the sight of myself* & fancied every body else did the same. Otherwise, I do assure you it would have been the greatest relief my mind was just then capable of. I remain
Dear Sir,
your much obliged & faithful servant, W. Hazlitt.*

Oct. 2

No doubt encouraged by Jeffrey, Hazlitt wrote the brilliant essay on the press that appeared the following summer in the *Edinburgh Review*,[†] and meanwhile he resumed his contributions to the magazines. Among the other things that he had done at Renton while on his way to Edinburgh was a moving essay on the pictures at Burleigh House that had been printed as a Table Talk in the *New Monthly Magazine* for April 1822,[1] and the following fall he resumed his contributions to the *London* with a matching piece on Fonthill Abbey.[2] It is significant that in this time of crisis he turned again to art, not only as a way of making money but as a solace for his grief. There was no "greater treat," he said, than to be admitted freely to a great collection,

where the mind reposes with full confidence in its feelings of admiration, and finds that idea and love of conceivable beauty, which it has cherished perhaps for a whole life, reflected from every object around it. It is a cure (for the time at least) for low-thoughted cares and uneasy passions. We are abstracted to another sphere: we breathe empyrean air; we enter into the minds of Raphael, of Titian, of Poussin, of the Caracci, and look at nature with their eyes; we live in time past, and seem identified with the permanent forms of things. The business of

---

* ALS, The Yale University Library. Although Hazlitt was not entrusted with the review of *Mémoires pour servir à l'histoire de France sous Napoléon* (1823) by Charles Tristan, Marquis de Montholon, he made good use of it later in his own life of Napoleon. See 13.37n; Robert E. Robinson, *William Hazlitt's Life of Napoleon Buonaparte* (1959), pp. 70–75.

† 16.211–239. This essay had been finished and dispatched to Edinburgh by December 23, when Hazlitt wrote to Jeffrey (ALS, The Yale University Library) that he "should be very sorry indeed if you do not think it good enough for the Review, but in that case you would perhaps let me have it again." Leigh Hunt took notice of it in the *Literary Examiner* (9 August 1823, p. 95) and predicted that it would surely cause a stir. "The public will not be at a loss to attribute it to the right author, — one who 'knows all the qualities' of the journals he describes 'with a learned spirit.' "

the world at large, and even its pleasures, appear like a vanity and an impertinence. What signify the hubbub, the shifting scenery, the fantoccini figures, the
folly, the idle fashions without, when compared with the solitude, the silence, the
speaking looks, the unfading forms within? — Here is the mind's true home. The
contemplation of truth and beauty is the proper object for which we were created,
which calls forth the most intense desires of the soul, and of which it never tires.[3]

It was in this mood that he wrote the highly charged essays — "Mr.
Angerstein's Collection," "The Dulwich Gallery," "The Marquis of Staf-
ford's Gallery," "The Pictures at Windsor Castle," "The Pictures at
Hampton Court," and "Pictures at Oxford and Blenheim" — that were
printed in the *London* during 1822 and 1823 and that in 1824 were
brought together as *Sketches of the Principal Picture-Galleries in England.**

In the fall of 1822 he also began his contributions to the *Liberal,*
the short-lived magazine made famous by the famous names associated
with it.[4] Of the three prime movers in this abortive undertaking —
Byron, Shelley, and Leigh Hunt — two were expatriates in Italy and
the third was ill and out of funds; and so it seemed a good idea, as
Shelley wrote to Hunt from Pisa in August 1821, for them to pool
their talents. The proposal was not without its merits: Byron, vexed at
John Murray's squeamish reservations about the later cantos of *Don
Juan,* would secure an outlet for his work,[5] and Hunt's health and fortunes would, he hoped, improve if he left England. Since one of them
was well equipped with money and the other with experience, there
would "be no doubt," Shelley prophesied to Hunt naively, "that the
profits of any scheme in which you and Lord Byron engage, must from
various, yet co-operating reasons, be very great. As for myself, I am, for
the present, only a sort of link between you and him, until you can
know each other, and effectuate the arrangements."[6] But no sooner had
Hunt agreed to join the other two in Italy than their troubles started.
For one thing, there was only the dimmest understanding as to what
sort of magazine they wanted. With typical insouciance Hunt told

* 10.7–81. The book also included the essay on Burleigh House that he wrote at
Renton in 1822 (*Memoirs*, II, 68) and his old *Round Table* paper on Hogarth (4.25–
31). It would seem that he conceived these sketches of the great collections in 1821,
for on June 9 of that year he wrote to Hessey and Taylor from Winterslow that he
would "send the British Gallery in a day or two" (ALS, The Yale University Library).
Two weeks later, however, he acknowledged (ALS, 22 June [1821], The Yale University Library) that he had "not done the article on the Gallery, & it is too late now. I
have been but indifferent since I came here, & after labouring a long article to no
purpose, did not feel myself in spirits to begin a new one." The abandoned article was
probably on the pictures of Windsor Castle or Hampton Court.

Byron that almost anything would do. "Suppose, for instance," he wrote in January 1822, "we made a monthly or two-monthly publication, entirely of Pisan origin, that is to say, written by ourselves & friends there . . . we might have essays, stories, poetry, poetical translation, especially from the Italian, — in short, any thing we chose to blurt out or to be inspired with." [7]

While these fuzzy plans were going forward, most of Byron's friends in England — Moore, Hobhouse, Murray, and Kinnaird — professed to be appalled by the low-bred company he kept; the Tory press began to rumble at the alliance of a knot of rogues and atheists; Wordsworth ominously predicted that such a raffish set of writers would attack "everything in religion, in morals and probably in government and literature, which our Forefathers have been accustomed to reverence"; [*] and the nameless author of a sleazy satire called *The Press* remarked, with obvious disapproval, that "the morality of Childe Harold, and the politics of the Examiner will be well met." [8] Even the weather was adverse, for the emigration of the Hunts, which had started in November 1821 and was then delayed by storms, was not completed until June. Then, a few weeks after they arrived in Genoa, there fell the fearful blow of Shelley's death at sea in July 1822. When the Hunts — man and wife and their six children — were finally installed in Byron's unconventional establishment at Pisa the sparks began to fly. Whereas Byron found his new associate foolish and ill-bred, Hunt thought Byron rude and overbearing. Moreover, the domestic complications were bizarre. Byron, although not fastidious himself, complained that the children were "dirtier and more mischievous than Yahoos," [9] and the ailing Mrs. Hunt, ruffled by Teresa Guiccioli, expressed herself with feeling about Byron's way of life. When he remarked to her, for instance, that Trelawny had objected to his morals she sniffed and said that she had never heard of them before. [10] Amid such irritations and distractions Hunt spent the next few months "sweating articles for his new Journal" [11] and sending them to his brother John in London, who had been entrusted with the printing. Although he professed to be untroubled by their problems, [12] Byron, on the eve of publication, wrote disingenuously to Murray that he had martyrized himself.

I am afraid the Journal *is* a *bad* business, and won't do; but in it I am sacrificing *myself* for others — *I* can have no advantage in it. I believe the *brothers H.* to be honest men; I am sure that they are poor ones. They have not a rap: they

* *Later Years*, I, 69. In the "Preface" to the *Liberal* (I, [v]) Hunt ironically acknowledged that he and his associates, said to be intent upon the "dilapidation of all the outworks of civilised society," were supposed to "cut up religion, morals, and everything that is legitimate; — a pretty carving."

pressed me to engage in this work, and in an evil hour I consented: still I shall not repent, if I can do them the least service. I have done all I can for Leigh Hunt since he came here; but it is almost useless: his wife is ill, his six children not very tractable, and in the affairs of this world he himself is a child. The death of Shelley left them totally aground; and I could not see them in such a state without using the common feelings of humanity, and what means were in my power, to set them afloat again.[13]

For the first number (October 1822) the three chief sponsors supplied all the contributions, one of which — "The Vision of Judgment" — has gained a place in English literature. In addition to Byron's great poem (the preface of which Murray had spitefully withheld) it contained Shelley's version of the Walpurgisnacht scene from *Faust* and no less than eight pieces, in prose and verse, by Hunt. Apart from the *Examiner,* which of course was laudatory, the response in England, both public and private, was almost uniformly hostile. Privately, Southey said that the contents of the *Liberal* were "as disgusting as brutality and impiety can make them";[14] Crabb Robinson predicted that such a "worthless" publication would "scarcely reach a second, certainly not a third number";[15] and Murray assured Byron that never had he heard "such a universal outcry as this work has occasioned."[16] Publicly, William Jerdan, of the *Literary Gazette,* pronounced that "the union of wickedness, folly, and imbecility" was perfect;[17] Theodore Hook, in *John Bull,* wondered if Leigh Hunt's children had not written most of the first number;[18] and *Blackwood's,* as usual, was jaunty and abusive.[19] To add to everybody's joy, in December John Hunt was indicted for printing "The Vision of Judgment," which, the Crown asserted, was a libel on the late monarch. Later, after the *Liberal* had expired, Hazlitt recalled this furor with disgust. When Byron leagued himself with Hunt and Shelley, he wrote in 1825,

Blackwood's Magazine overflowed, as might be expected, with tenfold gall and bitterness; the John Bull was outrageous; and Mr. Jerdan black in the face at this unheard-of and disgraceful union. But who would have supposed that Mr. Thomas Moore and Mr. Hobhouse, those staunch friends and partisans of the people, should also be thrown into almost hysterical agonies of well-bred horror at the coalition between their noble and ignoble acquaintance, between the Patrician and "the Newspaper-Man?" Mr. Moore darted backwards and forwards from Cold-Bath Fields' Prison [where John Hunt was serving out his sentence for a libel on the House of Commons] to the Examiner-Office, from Mr. Longman's to Mr. Murray's shop, in a state of ridiculous trepidation, to see what was to be done to prevent this degradation of the aristocracy of letters, this indecent encroachment of plebeian pretensions, this undue extension of patronage and compromise of privilege.[20]

In the fall of 1822, when, as Hunt said later, "alarm as well as envy" was rising to a peak,[21] Hazlitt joined the fray. Although William Jerdan had reported that Byron was fetching Hazlitt down to Pisa to "throw a little spirit into future Numbers, and prevent their being so inhumanly disgraced by Lordly spleen and sycophantic, even if congenial, prostitution," [22] it was probably at John Hunt's invitation that Hazlitt started writing for the "obnoxious publication." [23] Leigh Hunt professed to be delighted at the news of his forthcoming contributions, but Byron must have been annoyed to be associated with a man who had baited him for years. Reviewing the fourth canto of *Childe Harold's Pilgrimage* in 1818 Hazlitt had said that he was weary of his lordship's griefs, "of which we can perceive neither beginning nor end"; [24] in his lectures on the English poets he had complained about his "unaccommodating selfishness" and his inconsistent comments on Napoleon; [*] in discussing *Marino Faliero* in the *London Magazine* in 1821 he had suggested that its author was incapable of writing plays because of his excessive interest in himself; [25] and, a little later, in his *London* essay on the Bowles and Byron controversy over Pope he had been extremely tart about Byron's "pribble-prabble" and his affectations. "An Irish servant," he remarked, "with a little whiskey in his head, would not fall upon more blunders, contradictions, and defective conclusions" than this patrician man of letters. [26] It is therefore not surprising that by 1821 Byron, in the style of *Blackwood's,* was describing Hazlitt as a pimple [27] or, according to Leigh Hunt, that he assented to his writing for the *Liberal* because he was afraid of him. [†]

At least one of Hazlitt's contributions to the ill-starred magazine must be ranked among the great essays in English, and all are in his most accomplished style. For the second issue (January 1823) he supplied "On the Scotch Character" [‡] and "On the Spirit of Monarchy," [28]

---

[*] 5.153. Byron had been so much nettled by these comments that in a note designed for *Mazeppa* but actually printed with *Don Juan* (I.ii) he tried to justify himself. "I tell Mr. Hazlitt that I never flattered Napoleon on the throne, nor maligned him since his fall," he said (*Poetical Works* [ed. Ernest Hartley Coleridge], VI [1903], 12n). "I wrote what I think are the incredible antitheses of his character." Murray (Prothero, IV, 282n) urged Byron not to answer Hazlitt by name, but to refer to him as "a certain lecturer." On the audience's unfavorable reception of Hazlitt's disrespectful comments on Byron in his lectures see Landseer, I, 147f.

[†] *Lord Byron and Some of His Contemporaries,* I, 108. Although Leigh Hunt, in October 1822, told his brother that "Lord B. admires Hazlitt's writings" (Luther A. Brewer, *My Leigh Hunt Library: The Holograph Letters* [1938], p. 155) and Procter, after Hazlitt's death, recalled that it was Byron who had "invited" him to join the *Liberal* (*New Monthly Magazine,* XXIX [1830], 475), the evidence hardly supports either assertion.

[‡] 17.100–106. Like Lamb, who all his life tried to like the Scots but was finally "obliged to desist from the experiment in despair" (*Works,* I, 545), Hazlitt had a very low opinion of almost everyone who lived beyond the Tweed. "They hate every appearance of comfort themselves, and refuse it to others," he remarked (17.236). "Their climate, their religion, and their habits are equally averse to pleasure." As for

one an unflattering reassessment of the Scots' alleged distinction (with, of course, a glancing blow at *Blackwood's*) and the other an assertion of his republican convictions. For the third issue (April 1823) he worked up, from a little piece in the *Examiner* of several years before,[29] "My First Acquaintance with Poets,"[30] his most revealing comment on his youth. To the fourth and final issue (July 1823) he contributed "Pulpit Oratory — Dr. Chalmers and Mr. Irving,"[31] an analysis of theological pretension, and "Arguing in a Circle,"[32] a superb lament on political apostasy.

Not even such brilliant work as this could save the sinking *Liberal*. Although the third issue carried things by Mary Shelley, Charles Armitage Brown, Thomas Jefferson Hogg, and Horace Smith, in addition to those by Byron, Hunt, and Hazlitt, by the spring of 1823 it was clear that the magazine was doomed; for its critics, though less virulent and noisy with each successive issue, were still intent on its destruction, its sale was falling off, and — worst of all — Byron was eager to be free of it. By the time the fourth issue appeared he was already on his way to Greece, and the Hunts, their seventh child just born, were preparing their departure. "The eternal laws of gravitation held their course," said a writer in the *Quarterly* in gleeful retrospect. "Messrs. Hunt, Hazlitt, and Co. furnished the principal part of the cargo; and the 'Liberal' sunk to the bottom of the waters of oblivion almost as rapidly as the *Table-Talk*, or the *Foliage*, or the *Endymion*." * As a sort of epilogue John Hunt was brought to trial and found guilty of libeling George III, and in June 1824 he was fined a hundred pounds. Byron, who said that he would bear the costs, had died two months before, and although Hazlitt was dismayed by the poet's seeming desertion of his friends he was glad, as he said later, that he had "died a martyr to his zeal in the cause of freedom, for the last, best hopes of man. Let that be his excuse and his epitaph." †

⋄ ⋄ ⋄

Another product of this period was a set of maxims that, though intended for the *Liberal*, were worked up into a little book and published

---

Jeffrey, who seemed to be an exception to the rule, he said (11.133) that "he ought to have belonged to us!" For some other characteristic comments of this kind see 9.214f., 20.113.

* XXXVII (1828), 419. For a similar post-mortem see *Blackwood's Magazine* (XXIII [1828], 386), where it was asserted that the *Liberal* died because Byron was disgusted with it, Hunt was driveling, Shelley dead, and Hazlitt "worse than dead."

† 11.78. Elsewhere (12.319) Hazlitt explained Byron's death in different and less exalted terms.

anonymously in 1823.* *Characteristics: In the Manner of Rochefou-cault's Maxims* is one of Hazlitt's most acerb productions. Like "On the Spirit of Obligations" [33] and "On the Pleasure of Hating," [34] which reflect the same atrabiliar state of mind, it records his anger at a world that made him "sick." [35] In writing it, he said, he had no theory to maintain, and at first glance it appears to be a shapeless set of disconnected jot-tings. In point of fact, however, the 434 apothegms it comprises — some of them a line or so in length, some of them long paragraphs — tend to fall in groups that have such common themes as envy, friendship, pride, hypocrisy, and love. The result is a catalogue of man's besetting sins and follies, and on the whole it makes grim reading. Sometimes, to be sure, we get an echo of his earlier and more optimistic views, and even an oblique assertion of his theory of benevolence, [36] but he gives a saw-tooth edge to almost everything he says, as if he hopes to cut his reader free from self-deception and unexamined error. None the less, he is sometimes astonishingly banal [37] and sometimes merely repetitious, espe-cially when he writes about the Scots [38] or nicknames [39] or women's men-tal prowess. [40] Occasionally he indulges in a kind of sour wit, as when he says that the world, if good for nothing else, is good to speculate about, [41] and that one should fear a fool because he might also be a knave. [42]

Mainly, however, the maxims gloss his love-affair with Sarah Walker, and so they show how hurt and bruised he was. Some of them are Swiftian in their black despair. "Mankind are a herd of knaves and fools," he says. "It is necessary to join the crowd, or get out of their way, in order not to be trampled to death by them." [43] We are told that envy is the universal passion, [44] that friendship is a form of "quackery" [45] and exhausts itself with use, [46] that "vice is man's nature: virtue is a habit — or a mask," [47] that any woman can be had by any man. [48] Most caustic and recurrent are the epigrams that deal with love, and even if he did not cite a gull of his acquaintance who "divorced his wife to marry a wench at a lodging-house, who refused him, and whose cruelty and charms are the torment of his own life, and that of all his friends," [49] we would know that his most painful maxims are pointed to himself. Although he announces that "it is better to desire than to enjoy — to love than to be loved," [50] within a page or so he talks of unrequited pas-

---

* See the unpublished letter of 25 February 1823 from John to Leigh Hunt that is quoted by William H. Marshall in his *Byron, Shelley, Hunt, and The Liberal* (1960), p. 174. *Characteristics* was probably published in the early summer of 1823, not long after *Liber Amoris*. See Douady, p. 34; Keynes, p. 68. In the *Literary Examiner* (12 July 1823, p. 29) Hunt said that any reader would recognize the little book as Hazlitt's. "His vinous spirit is certainly not so highly rectified as that of Rochefoucault, and the flavour of the stalk is too frequently perceptible; but what it loses in concentration and unity, it gains in raciness and variety, and will be proportionably attractive."

sion as a "poison" in the mind,[51] and calls "the contempt of a wanton for a man who is determined to think her virtuous" the "strongest" contempt of all.[52]

An accomplished coquet excites the passions of others, in proportion as she feels none herself. Her forwardness allures, her indifference irritates desire. She fans the flame that does not scorch her own bosom; plays with men's feelings, and studies the effect of her several arts at leisure and unmoved.[53]

Here as elsewhere in the *Characteristics* Sarah Walker's shadow falls across the page.

Our few glimpses of Hazlitt in the spring of 1823 show that her shadow fell across his actions too. Almost every time we see him he is in a posture of defiance or despair. In February, for instance, his debts had landed him in jail. "I have been arrested this morning, and am at a loss what to do," he wrote to Talfourd on the twelfth. "Would you give me a call to talk the matter over, and see if your influence could procure me any terms of accommodation?"[54] Talfourd came to his assistance, it would seem, but Hazlitt was so much upset, as he explained a few days later, that he was quite unfit for work.[55] One indication of his disturbance at this time was, perhaps, his threat to bring another suit for libel on *Blackwood's Magazine* (a threat, so far as we can tell, that was never executed),[56] but a clearer one is found in the scrappy journal that he kept between March 4 and 16.*

This astonishing and dismaying document, which concerns his belated effort to prove that Sarah Walker was a "whore," records the experiences of a friend of his — probably Patmore, but called "F." in Hazlitt's messy scrawl — who had taken lodgings with the Walkers in order to seduce their daughter. On F.'s first meeting with the girl on March 5, Hazlitt noted in his diary, she gave him "one of her set looks";[57] the next day, when she came to light his fire, she "gently" blocked his efforts at a kiss;[58] but two days later there was progress to report:

Mr. F. got a paper & lent it to the Father to read. Saw Miss several times. In the evening pressed her to stay tea which she declined, but he followed her to the door, & kissed her several times on the stair case, at which she laughed. While this passed he had hold of one hand, & the other was at liberty, but she did not once attempt to raise it so as to make even a show of resistance. This is what she calls "being determined to keep every lodger at a proper distance."[59]

By March 9, when Sarah put on her "best ruff" to bring F.'s breakfast

* This journal, a highly garbled form of which appeared in W. C. Hazlitt's *Lamb and Hazlitt* (1899), pp. 119–133, has been printed in its entirety from the manuscript in the Lockwood Memorial Library at the University of Buffalo by Bonner, pp. 269–277.

to his room, Hazlitt had reached a peak of fury. "Decoy! Damned, treble damned ideot," he burst out in recording the event.

Yet I like to hear about her — that she had her bedgown or her ruff on, that she stood or sat, or made some insipid remark, is to be in Heaven — to know that she is a whore or an idiot is better than nothing. Were I in Hell, my only consolation would be to learn of her. In Heaven to see her would be my own reward.[60]

Although he goes on, in morbid fascination, with each successive episode of the tawdry boudoir game, we need follow him no further. The journal stops abruptly on March 16, just when it seems likely that Sarah will bestow on F. the final favor that she had never granted to his friend. "Let her be to hell with her tongue," Hazlitt wrote in taking leave of them. "She is as true as heaven wished her heart & lips [to] be." [61]

The appearance, in May, of *Liber Amoris* was the most flamboyant demonstration of his madness over Sarah Walker. Although his behavior was a scandal throughout the whole affair, the publication of this book (which, though anonymous, was promptly recognized as his) seemed to seal his reputation as a lecher and a fool. In June *Blackwood's* fell upon it with delight, declaring that "nothing so disgusting" had ever come its way before and calling down on Hazlitt's head "the scorn and loathing of every thing that bears the name of MAN." [62] This reaction may be said to represent the common view. To be sure, a few eccentrics and admirers professed half-hearted approbation: Charles Armitage Brown equivocally remarked, before the book appeared, that he would rather read the "Lodging-house Romance" than its author's other work; [63] and Mary Russell Mitford, while acknowledging his "desperation and folly," thought that he revealed "fine passion." [64] Generally, however, almost everyone agreed that, as Hazlitt had acknowledged, there was something "discordant to honest ears" [65] in the tortured little book. What Charles Ollier called his "slobbering courtship of the tailor's daughter" [66] had been such common knowledge that Mrs. Basil Montagu closed her drawing room to him, [67] and even Charles and Mary Lamb, his friends for twenty years, maintained a deafening silence. *Liber Amoris,* said Crabb Robinson, was "nauseous and revolting" proof that its author was a wretch, [68] and the *Literary Gazette* announced that whoever wrote "this matchless conjunction of vulgar sensuality and Cockney affectation" (which had been "cruelly ascribed by some malignant enemy to Mr. Hazlitt") had made himself an "ass in the face of a despising and hissing public." [69] Mary Shelley joked about the "love-sick youth" who had been jilted by his "Infelice," [70] and George Crabbe gravely told his son that whereas it was "strange" for any man to write a book like this, it was "marvelous" for him to publicize "his own Weakness, Vice and Gullibility." [71] At the start of the affair, when Hazlitt poured his troubles out to Haydon, the painter thought that the sight of his "old, hard, weather-beaten, saturnine, metaphysical face," twitching with passion, was enough "to provoke a saint to laughter," [72] but when these troubles were recorded for all the world to read it was a different, and less amusing, matter.* Even Procter, who always had a sane and hearty admiration for Hazlitt and his work, decided that on this one point, at least, he was "substantially insane," [73] and so did Hazlitt's son when he came to deal with the "regretted publication" in his father's *Literary Remains*. [74] When De Quincey, a generation later, recalled the ancient scandal, he said that in *Liber Amoris* Hazlitt

threw out his clamorous anguish to the clouds, and to the winds, and to the air, caring not *who* might listen, *who* might sympathise, or *who* might sneer. Pity was no demand of his; laughter was no wrong: the sole necessity for *him* was to empty his overburdened spirit. [75]

Ignorant, vulgar, and ill-tempered, Hazlitt was a horrid man at best, De Quincey always thought, but at this crisis of his life he added to his other charms "the nympholepsy of some fond despair." [76]

Liber Amoris, however regrettable, was no doubt a necessary cathartic, and in the months that followed its appearance we see Hazlitt slowly coming back to health. In July he wrote to Thomas Hood from Winterslow that he still was smarting from his wounds. "I used to think she read and perhaps approved these articles," he said about his current series on the picture galleries. "But whatever I can do, implying an idea of taste or elegance, only makes me more odious to myself, and tantalises me with feelings which I can never hope to excite in others — wretch that I am, and am to be, till I am nothing!" [77] However, the things he did that summer — more *London* essays on great pictures and more Table Talks for the *New Monthly* † — show few traces of this mortuary mood, and therefore, although he, as usual, deprecated them, they point to his recovery. "If what I write at present is worth nothing," he said about this time,

at least it costs me nothing. But it cost me a great deal twenty years ago. I have added little to my stock since then, and taken little from it. I "unfold the book and volume of the brain," and transcribe the characters I see there as mechanically as any one might copy the letters in a sampler. I do not say they came there

---

* According to Mary Russell Mitford (*Letters*, I, 126), Haydon and his wife "did all they could to prevent his publishing, but it was in vain."

† For the *London* he produced his essays on the pictures at Blenheim, Oxford, Wilton House, and Longford Castle; for the *New Monthly* "On the Old Age of Artists" (12.88–97), "On Sitting for One's Picture" (12.107–116), and "On Application to Study" (12.55–66). See Douady, pp. 34f.

mechanically — I transfer them to the paper mechanically. After eight or ten years' hard study, an author (at least) may go to sleep.[78]

That he returned to London in September "for a night or two, and passed nearly the whole of each in watching Sally's door," according to Haydon,[*] is less important than that he had finally put aside his grief and flung himself into his work. Significantly, in October there appeared, in the *London Magazine*, Lamb's bold defense of his old friend as "one of the wisest and finest spirits breathing" when in his "natural and healthy state," [†] and Hazlitt's response to this "magnanimous" assertion — "I think I must be friends with Lamb again" [‡] — may be regarded, with appropriate relief, as the end of his derangement.

THE SPIRIT OF THE AGE

As Hazlitt worked throughout the fall of 1823 at his former steady pace his spirits were revived. "I look out of my window and see that a shower has just fallen," he wrote from Winterslow;

the fields look green after it, and a rosy cloud hangs over the brow of the hill; a lily expands its petals in the moisture, dressed in its lovely green and white; a shepherd-boy has just brought some pieces of turf with daisies and grass for his young mistress to make a bed for her sky-lark, not doomed to dip his wings in the dappled dawn — my cloudy thoughts draw off, the storm of angry politics has blown over — Mr. Blackwood, I am yours, Mr. Croker, my service to you — Mr. T. Moore, I am alive and well — Really, it is wonderful how little the worse I am for fifteen years' wear and tear, how I come upon my legs again on the ground of truth and nature, and "look abroad into universality," forgetting there is any such person as myself in the world! [1]

Between September and December he contributed a string of "Common Places" to Leigh Hunt's short-lived *Literary Examiner*;[2] in October, in a letter to the *London Magazine*, he protested De Quincey's unacknowl-

---

* *Correspondence and Table-Talk*, II, 79. "He had another flame," adds Haydon, "who is at Hampton: down he went to tempt her for Gretna, but her brother, an officer in the Navy, happened to be with her; and 'officers,' said Hazlitt, 'you know, are awkward fellows to deal with!' Oh, the gallant, gay Lothario!"

† *Works*, I, 298f. Lamb's letter was prompted by Southey's *Quarterly* review of M. Grégoire's *Histoire de la Théophilanthropie*, in which he referred (XXVIII [1823], 524) to *Elia* as "a book which wants only a sounder religious feeling to be as delightful as it is original." On the resulting fracas see E. V. Lucas, *The Life of Charles Lamb* (1907), II, 151–159.

‡ 12.132. See Lucas, II, 406. A few months earlier, in "My First Acquaintance with Poets" (17.122), Hazlitt had alluded to his introduction to Lamb in 1803, when, at one of Godwin's parties, the guests "were disputing fiercely which was the best — Man as he was, or man as he is to be. 'Give me,' says Lamb, 'man as he is *not* to be.' This saying was the beginning of a friendship between us, which I believe still continues."

edged use of his ideas on Malthus;[3] he continued writing Table Talks for the *New Monthly,** as well as other things that he reserved for future publication.[†] But, most important, it was in the fall of 1823 that he composed the famous sketch of Bentham from which *The Spirit of the Age* was born.[4] His return to London at the start of 1824[5] hardly broke his stride, for he had half a dozen things in hand that spring. In addition to a group of sketches for inclusion in *The Spirit of the Age* he turned out a pair of *Edinburgh* reviews,[‡] prepared his essays on the picture galleries for publication as a book,[§] and set about completing an anthology of his favorite English poets that apparently had been started and abandoned several years before.

Select British Poets, or New Elegant Extracts from Chaucer to the Present Time, with Critical Remarks poses many problems that, unless new data are discovered, will probably never be resolved. It is clear that the book as published in the summer of 1824 had been projected, and in part completed, long before. For one thing, the sheets of more than half the book bear a watermark of 1817, and nearly all the rest a watermark of 1820.[6] For another, although both Shelley and Keats are included in a section on the "Living Poets" in the "Critical List of Authors" that serves as an introduction, Hazlitt speaks of Shelley (who was drowned in 1821) as having died "since the commencement of this publication" and of Keats as "also dead."[7] We do not know the circumstances under which he launched the work (perhaps in 1819–20 as a by-product of his recent lectures), or why he left the job unfinished while it was going through the press, or why he picked it up again after several years had passed. Indeed, the little that we know is what we learn from Mary Shelley, who on 9 September 1823 wrote to Hunt about a recent visit with the Lambs:

L[amb] said one thing which I am sure will give you pleasure. He corrected for Hazlitt a new edition of Elegant Extracts, in which the Living Poets are included. He said he was much pleased with many of your things, with a little of Montgomery and a little of Crabbe — Scott he found tiresome — Byron had many fine things but was tiresome but yours appeared to him the freshest and best of all. These Extracts have never been published — they have been offered to Mr.

---

* "On Sitting for One's Picture" (12.107–116), "On Application to Study" (12. 55–66), "On the Spirit of Obligations" (12.78–87).

† "Whether Genius Is Conscious of Its Powers" (12.117–127), "On the Pleasure of Hating" (12.127–136).

‡ "Landor's Imaginary Conversations" (16.240–264), "Shelley's Posthumous Poems" (16.265–284). In the July *Edinburgh* appeared "Lady Morgan's Life of Salvator" (16.284–318), which he had started working on in the fall of 1821 (see above, page 409n). It was the last review he wrote for Jeffrey.

§ After various delays (see Keynes, p. 72), *Sketches of the Principal Picture-Galleries in England* appeared in the summer of 1824.

Hunter and seeing the book at his house, I had the curiosity to look at what the extracts were that pleased L[amb].[8]

We hear no more of Rowland Hunter, but no sooner did the ill-starred work appear in 1824 (from the shop of William Hall) than it had to be withdrawn because the section on the "Living Poets" infringed the law of copyright. The following year it was published once again — this time by William Tegg — with its type set up anew and the section on the "Living Poets" deleted.

Despite its casual texts and insubstantial apparatus, Hazlitt's big anthology is, of course, a useful index to his taste, for as an adjunct to his lectures it exemplifies his judgments as a critic. Designed to supply the deficiencies of (and usurp the steady market for) Vicesimus Knox's *Elegant Extracts in Verse* (1789), the book, the editor explained, tried to represent that branch of literature in which the English were supreme, and thus it gave, instead of "shreds and patches," big samples of the most important poems by the most important poets. "By leaving out a great deal of uninteresting and common-place poetry, room has been obtained for nearly all that was emphatically excellent." [9] Running to more than eight hundred double-column pages in the 1824 edition, it is arranged, in roughly chronological order, into "Poets from Chaucer to the Present Time," "Living Poets," and "Miscellaneous" pieces "chiefly from the ancient dramatic authors."

By way of introduction the reader is supplied with "A Critical List of Authors," with commentary, in which we recognize, in capsule form, the judgments that Hazlitt had expounded in his lectures. Thus Chaucer is presented as a "natural" poet who excels in wit and "manly sense"; Spenser as "the poet of romance" who "describes things as in a splendid and voluptuous dream"; Sidney as "affected"; Milton as a writer of "preternatural grandeur and unavoidable interest"; Prior as "not a very moral poet, but the most arch, piquant, and equivocal of those that have been admitted into this collection"; Dryden and Pope as the two great masters of "the second class of poets, *viz.* the describers of artificial life and manners"; Thomson as one whose work, though often "barbarous" in style, shows "great descriptive power"; Young as overrated; Gray as a poet whose merits match his "great pretensions"; Goldsmith as "nearly faultless" in everything he tried to do; Burns, the last of the "illustrious dead," as one requiring elegy instead of criticism. As for the living poets, of whom Hazlitt promised to "speak freely, but candidly," Rogers, we are told, is "an elegant and highly polished writer, but without much originality or power"; Crabbe sings "a sort of funeral dirge over human life, but without pity, without hope"; Coleridge, despite the "great wildness of conception in his *Ancient Mariner,*" has written "nothing equal to his powers"; Wordsworth is "sublime without the Muse's aid, pathetic in the contemplation of his own and man's nature"; Byron is a gifted but uneven poet who "*wills* to be sublime or pathetic"; "the late Mr. Shelley (for he is dead since the commencement of this publication)" had "spirit and genius, but his eagerness to give effect and produce conviction often defeated his object, and bewildered himself and his readers"; Keats gave "the greatest promise of genius of any poet of his day." [10]

The "elegant excerpts" are substantial for the major poets, but there are odd omissions and also odd inclusions. It is not surprising, for example, that Hazlitt prints, as Chaucer's work, "The Floure and the Leafe" — a work that he associated with the Lambs' first trip to Winterslow [11] and that he had praised for years,[12] but one wonders at the absence of *Troilus and Criseyde. The Faerie Queene* is richly tapped, of course, but except for the February eclogue from *The Shepheardes Calender* and the *Epithalamion* Spenser's minor work is not disturbed. Since he thought Sidney's sonnets "jejune, far-fetched and frigid," [13] the eight that he includes may be regarded as a sop to Lamb, who had challenged his opinion.[14] Drayton supplies some heroical epistles, two songs from *Poly-Olbion,* and — inevitably — the ode on Agincourt, Wither only an eclogue from *The Shepherd's Hunting.* Milton comes off very well, *Samson Agonistes* being the only conspicuous omission. Although Marvell — "a writer almost forgotten: but undeservedly so" [15] — and Cowley are given several pages, Donne finds no place at all; Butler's *Hudibras,* "the greatest single production of wit" in the golden age of witty writers,[16] is copiously represented; Dryden and Pope get almost seventy pages each.

Although Johnson is ignored, in general the minor eighteenth-century poets are represented by the works that keep their names alive (like John Philips' *Splendid Shilling,* Blair's *Grave,* Dyer's *Grongar Hill,* and Akenside's *Pleasures of Imagination*); and the more generous selections from Gay and Swift, Thomson and Collins, Gray and Goldsmith, are those that, by and large, still have a place in English literature, or at least in the anthologies. Thomas Warton's sonnets are included because Hazlitt inexplicably rated them among the finest in the language; [17] and if thirty pages of Cowper seems to be excessive it is not, perhaps, too much for one who, despite his "elegant trifling," was declared worthy of his reputation.[18] The offensive section devoted to the "Living Poets" reflects Hazlitt's judgments in his lecture on that touchy subject. It gives us, among others, Rogers, Campbell, Crabbe, Scott, Lamb, Moore, Leigh Hunt, and Milman, a bit of Robert Bloomfield's *Farmer's Boy* and also Bowles and Southey; but its main attractions lie in its selections from the bigger men. We get all of *The Rime of the Ancient Mariner* as well as some of Coleridge's shorter poems (but none of *Christabel*); a splendid retrospective survey of Wordsworth's major works; a sample of *Childe Harold* as well as lesser things (including *Manfred*), but nothing from *Don Juan*; a short but excellent offering of works by Shelley, including "Ode to the West Wind" and "To a Skylark"; and, from Keats, excerpts from *Endymion* and the first *Hyperion,* "The Eve of St. Agnes," and "Ode to a Nightingale." Under the rubric of "Miscellaneous" pieces in the third section of the book are gathered a few of Shakespeare's sonnets (which Hazlitt always deprecated),[19] some lovely songs from Elizabethan and Jacobean drama, and some shorter poems by such men as Raleigh, Herrick, Carew, King, and Walton.

The *Elegant Extracts* is at best a sort of epilogue to Hazlitt's strictly belletristic work, and as such its imperfections are apparent. For example, its omission of dramatic poetry was, as he himself conceded, a matter for regret, and its comments on the poets represented are, though terse and candid, hardly contributions to the literature of criticism. But, casual as it is, the book contains a splendid roll of poets who, said Hazlitt in misquoting Wordsworth,

> on the steady breeze of honour sail
> In long possession, calm and beautiful.*

He explained that he had tried to glean enough "to make a 'perpetual feast of nectar'd sweets, where no crude surfeit reigns.' Such at least has been my ardent wish; and if this volume is not pregnant with matter both 'rich and rare,' it has been the fault of the compiler, and not of the poverty or niggardliness of the ENGLISH MUSE." [20] With that remark, at least, no one could disagree.

❖ ❖ ❖

Although Hazlitt told Landor that he had written parts of *The Spirit of the Age* in a "depression of body and mind" hard to be imagined,[21] the work shows nothing of fatigue. Indeed, in its verve and sweep and power it constitutes a major triumph. As with almost everything he did,

---

* See *The Excursion,* VII.1012–1016:
> A memorable age!
> Which did to him assign a pensive lot —
> To linger 'mid the last of those bright clouds
> That, on the steady breeze of honour, sailed
> In long procession calm and beautiful.

except the life of Napoleon, what started as a journalistic chore accidentally grew into a book, and achieved its final form through a process of accretion. Of the twenty-five essays ultimately included in the three editions that he himself prepared, seven were reprinted or adapted from other publications.[22] "Mr. Crabbe" was written for the "Living Authors" series in the *London* after John Scott's death in 1821, and the "Character of Cobbett" made its first appearance in Volume I of *Table-Talk*; but no doubt the real beginning of the book was the sketch of Bentham that he wrote at Winterslow in the fall of 1823 and printed in the *New Monthly* at the start of 1824. This launched a string of essays for the magazine — "Rev. Mr. Irving" in February, "The Late Mr. Horne Tooke" in March, "Sir Walter Scott" in April, and "Lord Eldon" in July — which, with "Mr. Canning" from the *Examiner* of 11 July 1824, formed the matrix of the work. Well before the last of these appeared, however, he had written seventeen other pieces for inclusion in the book. A *terminus ad quem* for their composition is provided by his elegiac coda to "Lord Byron," [23] which he composed on learning of the poet's death in April of that year, and the book itself was in print in the fall.*

The Spirit of the Age is therefore journalism of a sort, but if, as we are told, literature is that which we read more than once, it is literature too, with the sheen and poise of art. Written, as it were, in one creative burst, and flowing from a steady source of power, it has a logic all its own, for its sweeping arc of structure binds the separate but related parts into a whole not contrived or accidental, but generated by the theme: that despite their energies and triumphs the men of Hazlitt's generation had not fulfilled their promise. The age then coming to a close had failed, he thought, and therefore through his valediction there runs a melancholy strain: alive with promise at the start but thwarted by a false refinement or by the forces of reaction, the age had spent its best resources and was sputtering out in contradictions. His assertion that "it was a misfortune to any man of talent to be born in the latter end of the last century" is clearly open to debate, and his renewed complaints about the power of kings grow tedious to the most attentive reader.

Genius stopped the way of Legitimacy, and therefore it was to be abated, crushed, or set aside as a nuisance. The spirit of the monarchy was at variance with the spirit of the age. The flame of liberty, the light of intellect was to be extinguished

---

* That the book, despite the date 1825 on the title page, was in print by the end of 1824 is proved by a note that Godwin wrote to Colburn on 22 November 1824 (ALS, Victoria and Albert Museum). Godwin said that he was regretfully returning his copy of *The Spirit of the Age*, which he had read with pleasure, "& the more so, as it appears to me to be written with admirable temper & fairness, except perhaps the article on Gifford." I am indebted to Professor H. M. Sikes for his transcript of this letter.

with the sword — or with slander, whose edge was sharper than the sword. The war between power and reason was carried on by the first of these abroad — by the last at home.[24]

But as he traces the careers of Godwin, Coleridge, Wordsworth, Malthus, and the rest his theme becomes less doctrinaire and simple, for these men of genius force him, as it were, to modify his own convictions. Finally, therefore, his book becomes a subtle exploration of the central problem of the age: the reciprocal relations of convention and revolt, of freedom and restraint.

Recording, as it does, the pressures of his place and time and also his response to them, *The Spirit of the Age* is Hazlitt's *Prelude*, in a sense, for it shows the shaping of his mind. In it he surveys the men, the values, and the books that had stirred his generation, and while his panoramic view of early nineteenth-century England enabled him, as it enables us, to take one final look at the terrain that he and his contemporaries had crossed, it also shows the critic and the writer at the apex of his power. Inevitably, his assessment of the age is in terms of people, not of abstract notions. They include eleven writers (Coleridge, Scott, Byron, Southey, Wordsworth, Campbell, Crabbe, Moore, Hunt, Lamb, and — curiously — Washington Irving), eight politicians (Tooke, Mackintosh, Brougham, Cobbett, Burdett, Lord Eldon, Wilberforce, and Canning), three speculative thinkers (Bentham, Godwin, and Malthus), two influential editors (Jeffrey and Gifford), and one rabble-rousing preacher (Edward Irving). By and large these men were ending their careers by 1824, and so Hazlitt could assess in retrospect the work that they had done and gauge their impact on their time. Some of them, of course, were of extraordinary power; some had not deserved their fame; and some, as he believed, were evil; but they all had won a measure of success, or at any rate renown, and taken altogether they formed a profile of the age.

He traces this profile with an unerring sense of style. *The Spirit of the Age,* like the late essays, carries on his exploration of the past, but because his subject here is something other than himself, we get, instead of introspection and self-indulgent pity, criticism and controlled emotion. For all its supple play his prose is never soft or insecure. Without the sometimes tinny brilliance of *The Round Table,* the convolutions of *Political Essays,* the mawkish sentiment of *Table-Talk,* it has a strength and tawny splendor of its own. As he himself remarked of Burke, it is forked and playful as the lightning, crested like the serpent. He modulates his style, of course, to accommodate the different things he wants to do; but whether depicting, in Hogarthian detail, the aged

Bentham walking in his garden,[25] or recording Southey's heaving anger at reform,[26] or expounding Malthus' theory,[27] or plumbing Gifford's malice,[28] or recapturing the magic that Sir Walter worked upon his readers,[29] he never loses his own voice. There is an enormous range between the jaunty sketch of Canning as the brisk, accomplished politician [30] and the dirge for Godwin's fallen fame,[31] but despite the variations — in tempo, tone, and coloration — both rest upon a common base, and both reveal the same presiding mind. In literature as in music, style serves as signature — any scrap of *Tristan*, any song of Schubert, any Mozart serenade identifies its maker; and thus it is with Hazlitt's writing in *The Spirit of the Age*.

No book lives by style alone, however, and *The Spirit of the Age* would be as dead as Southey's *Colloquies,* another peak of English prose with a not dissimilar scope and theme, if technique were all it had. Hazlitt's work has kept its place in English literature because it teaches us so much. If in some unimaginable holocaust all the other literary artifacts of early nineteenth-century England were destroyed, it would help us gauge our loss, for hardly any other book delineates with such precision and perception the contour of the age. One might wish to make some substitutions among the men discussed, of course: Wellington and Castlereagh, for instance, could well replace Burdett and Brougham; and Campbell, Moore, and the two Irvings have lost their former luster. But in general Hazlitt chose to write on men who, important in and for themselves, were also emblematic of the time. Thus Godwin stood for those Utopians who thought "too nobly" of their fellows,[32] Malthus for the sophists who turned politics into a science,[33] Bentham for the devotees of theory who ignored the facts of life.[34] Coleridge, who would have been the "finest writer" of his generation if he had not talked his life away, epitomized the eclectic erudition of the age.[35] The young Wordsworth, seeing "nothing loftier than human hopes" and "nothing deeper than the human heart," gave literary expression to the major innovation of the time: the rejection of the artificial. His "levelling" muse, distinguished by a "proud humility," found poetry in the feelings that common things excite, and although his later "philosophic" work departed from and in a sense betrayed his first ideals, he was none the less without a peer.* On the other hand, Gifford, like Lord Eldon, was the agent of reaction, inclining

---

* 11.86f., 90 f. *Laodamia*, which has the "smoothness and solidity of marble," was one of Hazlitt's favorite works. "It is a poem that might be read aloud in Elysium," he said (11.90), "and the spirits of departed heroes and sages would gather round to listen to it!" See 16.253, where he makes the same remark in his *Edinburgh* review of Landor's *Imaginary Conversations*.

by a natural and deliberate bias, to the traditional in laws and government; to the orthodox in religion; to the safe in opinion; to the trite in imagination; to the technical in style; to whatever implies a surrender of individual judgment into the hands of authority, and a subjection of individual feeling to mechanic rules.[36]

Cobbett was the hot reformer who really had no interest in reform, but merely thrived on opposition,[37] and Wilberforce the well-bred friend of all good causes so long as they did not disturb the *status quo*.[38]

The essays are marvels of compression. For instance, the account of Coleridge's intellectual quest — a dazzling conspectus of *Biographia Literaria* — suggests within a page or so the brilliance, charm, and vacillation of that extraordinary man. Bewitched by Hartley in his youth, he "busied himself for a year or two with vibrations and vibratiuncles and the great law of association that binds all things in its mystic chain"; was briefly trapped by Priestley's materialism, from which he escaped by means of Berkeley's "fairy-world" to Malebranche, Cudworth, Butler, and Leibniz; "fell plump, ten thousand fathoms down (but his wings saved him harmless) into the *hortus siccus* of Dissent"; journeyed on to Spinoza, the Neoplatonists, and the Schoolmen; "walked hand in hand with Swedenborg through the pavilions of the New Jerusalem" and then descended from that dizzy height to Milton and other English poets; dabbled in Italian art; and finally

wandered into Germany and lost himself in the labyrinths of the Hartz Forest and of the Kantean philosophy, and amongst the cabalistic names of Fichtè and Schelling, and Lessing, and God knows who — this was long after, but all the former while, he had nerved his heart and filled his eyes with tears, as he hailed the rising orb of liberty, since quenched in darkness and in blood, and had kindled his affections at the blaze of the French Revolution, and sang for joy when the towers of the Bastile and the proud places of the insolent and the oppressor fell, and would have floated his bark, freighted with fondest fancies, across the Atlantic wave with Southey and others to seek for peace and freedom —

"In Philarmonia's undivided dale!"

Alas! "Frailty, thy name is *Genius!*" — What is become of all this mighty heap of hope, of thought, of learning, and humanity? It has ended in swallowing doses of oblivion and in writing paragraphs in the *Courier*. — Such, and so little is the mind of man! [39]

As sketches, instead of formal portraits, these essays in *The Spirit of the Age* reveal the quick, incisive line and the meaningful detail that imply immediate perception, not research and erudition; and even when, as in the case of Scott and Malthus, his knowledge came from books, he shows uncanny skill in catching essential traits of mind. Except for Burke — who, of course, was of another generation and had to be excluded — almost every friend and writer who had played a vital part in his career is represented in his book, and his intuition, together with his instinct for the telling phrase, makes them come alive. We are told, for instance, that Bentham's "quick and lively" eye darts from thought to thought, not from one thing to another;[40] that Scott "dotes on all well-authenticated superstitions" but "shudders at the shadow of innovation";[41] that by shuttling between the misanthrope and the voluptuary Byron "makes out everlasting centos of himself";[42] that Gifford's "happy combination of defects, natural and acquired," enable him to be the perfect editor for the *Quarterly Review*;[43] that Lamb "*blurts* out the finest wit and sense in the world";[44] that Mackintosh "belongs to a class (common in Scotland and elsewhere) who get up school-exercises on any given subject in a masterly manner at twenty, and who at forty are either where they were — or retrograde, if they are men of sense and modesty";[45] that Southey, who had lost his way in Utopia and found it in Old Sarum, "is ever in extremes, and ever in the wrong";[46] that if Tom Moore's *Irish Melodies* "do indeed express the soul of impassioned feeling in his countrymen," then Ireland's case is hopeless.[47]

Despite such tart pronouncements *The Spirit of the Age* is Hazlitt's wisest, gentlest, and most mellow book. By no means acquiescent or complacent, he still despises Gifford, reproaches Canning and the Tory politicians, and refuses to concede that power justifies established wrong. But he seems to be above the smoke and din of battle, and to watch the struggle from afar. Serenity, not sputtering indignation, is the keynote of the book. He laments, instead of ridiculing, Coleridge's dissipation of his powers,[48] and overwhelmed by Wordsworth's genius, he forgives his faults of character.[49] He even finds a few good things to say of Malthus.[50] Southey, once the victim of his vulgar and jocose abuse, is here depicted as an amiable eccentric — foolish and unstable, to be sure, but not a wicked man:

In all those questions, where the spirit of contradiction does not interfere, on which he is not sore from old bruises, or sick from the extravagance of youthful intoxication, as from a last night's debauch, our "laureate" is still bold, free, candid, open to conviction, a reformist without knowing it. He does not advocate the slave-trade, he does not arm Mr. Malthus's revolting ratios with his authority, he does not strain hard to deluge Ireland with blood. On such points, where humanity has not become obnoxious, where liberty has not passed into a by-word, Mr. Southey is still liberal and humane. The elasticity of his spirit is unbroken: the bow recoils to its old position. He still stands convicted of his early passion for inquiry and improvement. He was not regularly articled as a Government-tool! *

* 11.83. Although it is not surprising that Hazlitt was very much impressed by Southey's prose, it is gratifying to observe that in his later years he rarely missed a chance to praise it (11.84, 12.16, 20.107, 261).

THE ESSAYIST

The sketch of Scott provides perhaps the best example of his attempt to comprehend, rather than denounce, those with whom he disagreed. For years, Scott had posed a problem for him. He had long "held out" against the Wizard of the North, he said, because he did not like to read new books, but finally he succumbed, and admitted him to the "scanty library" of twenty or thirty works that made up his pantheon.[51] Thereafter Scott, like Burke, had teased him out of thought: how could so black a Tory be so great a writer? In his lectures he had not excluded the author of *Marmion* and *The Lady of the Lake* from his strictures on contemporary poets — "he has just hit the town between the romantic and the fashionable"[52] — but he had saluted the author of *Waverley* as that rarest thing among the moderns, a writer who does not use or tamper with his characters, but "leaves them as he found them."[53] Whereas Byron came to rival Wordsworth as Hazlitt's stock example of the egotistic artist, each new book of Scott's — even so bad a novel as *The Pirate* — showed him to be the only modern author who ranked his subject higher than himself.[54] For example, Hazlitt, like the rest of us, was not enraptured by *Redgauntlet,* but even there he found the mark of genius: when Blind Willie and his wife and son, in the hollow of the heath, sing their little catch, "there is more mirth and heart's ease," he said, than in *Don Juan* or all the facile lyrics by Tom Moore. "And why? Because the author is thinking of beggars and a beggar's brat, and not of himself while he writes it. . . . This is the great secret of his writings — a perfect indifference to self."[55]

This, of course, is one of Hazlitt's favorite themes, and it is ironical that he found it best exemplified by a man whose values he abhorred. He told Jeffrey, in 1822, that he would not accept an introduction to Sir Walter because although he was willing to kneel before him he could not shake his hand; * and the following year, in reviewing *Peveril of the Peak,* he marveled that an artist of such "magnanimity" should also be

a professed toad-eater, a sturdy hack, a pitiful retailer or suborner of infamous slanders, a literary Jack Ketch, who would greedily sacrifice any one of another way of thinking as a victim to prejudice and power, and yet would do it by other hands, rather than appear in it himself. Can this be all true of the author of Waverley; and does he deal out such fine and heaped justice to all sects and parties in time past? †

* Patmore, III, 22; cf. Landseer, I, 172. When Northcote told Hazlitt that a meeting with Scott might help to "rub off" some of his "asperities," he replied (11. 275f.) that he already admired the man "this side of idolatry and Toryism." The aging Procter's recollection (p. 157) of a dinner at Haydon's that included, among "various other people," Scott and Hazlitt is almost certainly confused. So far as we can tell, the two men never met.

† 19.95. I quote from that part of the review that John Taylor, then editor of the

Lest all this seem too hard on Scott we should remember that he endorsed the hatchet-work of Gifford, flattered and hobnobbed with the Regent, helped to subsidize the *Beacon* (a Tory scandal-sheet of exceptional scurrility),* and supported with his prestige and his money the most grotesque abuses. In Hazlitt's estimation, not to disapprove of such a man would be infamous, but not to venerate the author of the Scottish novels would be to hate ourselves and human nature.[56]

In *The Spirit of the Age* Hazlitt makes his fullest effort to accommodate both the artist and the Tory. Sir Walter knows and loves the past, he says, as much as he distrusts the present and the future, and because he "thinks that nothing *is* but what *has been*" he is deficient in invention. His poetry shows "no voluntary power of combination," for his associations are "those of habit or of tradition. He is a mere narrative and descriptive poet, garrulous of the old time. The definition of his poetry is a pleasing superficiality." [57] The fiction is, of course, another matter. The author of *Waverley* does not need to tag his rhymes or seek the proper word; he has merely to surrender to his subject. He shows that "facts are better than fiction; that there is no romance like the romance of real life; and that if we can but arrive at what men feel, do, and say in striking and singular situations, the result will be 'more lively, audible, and full of vent,' than the fine-spun cobwebs of the brain." To praise the work of such a man, he says, is like praising nature, and then he documents the point with an overwhelming survey of Scott's great scenes and people. This annotated catalogue, written *con amore,* is a virtuoso flight, and it spirals to a string of exclamations that express unbounded admiration: "What a list of names! What a host of associations! What a thing is human life! What a power is that of genius! What a world of thought and feeling is thus rescued from oblivion! How many hours of heartfelt satisfaction has our author given to the gay and thoughtless! How many sad hearts has he soothed in pain and solitude!" [58]

Even in their "political bearing" the novels merit praise, he says, for by the "candour" of his pen Scott reconciles "all the diversities of human nature to the reader" and presents all sects and parties fairly. It is all the more regrettable, therefore, when, relinquishing the role of author, he tries to shape the present by the standards of the "good old times."

London Magazine, suppressed after only a few copies had been issued and that *Blackwood's* subsequently reprinted and attributed to him. See 19.343.

    * For Hazlitt's comments on the *Beacon* see 17.106, 19.91f. On Scott's connection with the publication see Constable, II, 370, and III, 162; *Examiner,* 7 October 1821, p. 629, and 18 November 1821, p. 725. Lockhart's guarded conclusion (III, 613) that from this "lamentable" undertaking Scott and his associates "did not escape in any very consolatory plight" may be regarded as an understatement.

Is he infatuated enough, or does he so dote and drivel over his own slothful and self-willed prejudices, as to believe that he will make a single convert to the beauty of Legitimacy, that is, of lawless power and savage bigotry, when he himself is obliged to apologise for the horrors he describes, and even render his descriptions credible to the modern reader by referring to the authentic history of these delectable times? . . . This is what he "calls backing his friends" — it is thus he administers charms and philtres to our love of Legitimacy, makes us conceive a horror of all reform, civil, political, or religious, and would fain put down the *Spirit of the Age.*[59]

It is on this note that Hazlitt closes, not resolving the antinomy but citing it — in a coiling, nonstop sentence — to show the contradictions of the time. Viewing the inexplicable union of the most expansive and accommodating talent with the most restrictive party spirit, of private liberality and public venom, of tolerance and bigotry, he concludes "there is no other age or country of the world (but ours), in which such genius could have been so degraded!" [60]

Hazlitt's second marriage, under circumstances so obscure that neither place nor date is known, probably occurred about the time that he was winding up *The Spirit of the Age.* Mrs. Isabella Bridgewater, perhaps the dimmest figure of all those who played a part in his career, was said by Hazlitt's son to be the widow of a lieutenant-colonel; [61] W. C. Hazlitt — who changed the spelling of her name — promoted her first husband to a colonelcy and fixed her income at £300 a year; [62] John Hunt described her as "a very pleasant and ladylike person" and the widow of a barrister; [63] and one who knew her as a girl recalled (in 1866) that she had been married to a "Planter" in some "West India" island.[64] And there our ignorance rests. How Hazlitt wooed her is unknown, but despite his contempt for ladies who professed to like his books [65] it is easier to accept the rumor, spread by one who might have known the facts, that "she fell in love with him on account of his writings" [66] than to think he won her with his charm. Howe's guess that the marriage was performed in Edinburgh [67] is lent a certain credence by the record of their stay at Melrose while on their wedding trip in 1824.[68] In the summer of that year Haydon happened to encounter Hazlitt's little boy — "better drest, cleaner, more modest & more respectable than I had ever seen him before" — and from him learned that the family was installed in Down Street, Picadilly.[69] It was there, no doubt, as Mary Shelley reported with evident astonishment, that Sarah Stoddart Hazlitt paid a formal call and found the bride attractive.[70] With no new work in hand Hazlitt occupied himself, it seems, in cleaning up unfinished business. After various delays, *Sketches of the Principal Picture-Galleries in England* was published in the summer,[71] and *The Spirit of the Age* was no doubt being readied for the press. In the July *Edinburgh* "Lady Morgan's Life of Salvator"[72] (begun three years before)[73] made its long-postponed appearance, together with "Shelley's Posthumous Poems."[74] These were Hazlitt's last reviews for Jeffrey. Not unnaturally, Mary Shelley was offended by his comments on her husband, but she could not be angry, she explained, in view of his condition.

I never was so shocked in my life — gaunt and thin, his hair scattered, his cheek bones projecting — but for his voice and smile I sh[oul]d not have known him — his smile brought tears into my eyes, it was like a sun beam illuminating the most melancholy of ruins — lightning that assured you in a dark night of the identity of a friend's ruined and deserted abode.[75]

By the end of August the Hazlitts had set forth for France on an extended Continental tour.* He did not know it at the time, of course, but the departure marked another, and indeed the final, phase of his career. Battered by the force of circumstance no less than by his own emotions, and old before his time, he had six more years to live; but his important work was done, and what remained for him to do was in the nature of an epilogue.

* 10.91. On 24 August 1824 John Hunt informed his brother Leigh (ALS, British Museum Add. MS. 38,108) that "Mr Hazlitt and his new Bride have departed for France. . . . *This* Mrs. Hazlitt seems a very pleasant and ladylike person. She was the widow of a Barrister, and possesses an independence of nearly 300 l. a year."

IX

Epilogue

❖◇❖❖

THE CONTINENTAL TOUR

Although the second Mrs. Hazlitt's little fortune no doubt eased her husband's situation, it did not enable him to be a man of leisure, and so we have his *Notes of a Journey through France and Italy*, a compilation of the articles commissioned by his friend John Black and published serially in the *Morning Chronicle* between September 1824 and November 1825.* As a record of his travels it rests upon a base of facts and therefore has a sharper line and firmer texture than his Table Talks; but as a string of meditations prompted by those facts — for example, digressions on the "Popish religion" as "a convenient cloak for crime, an embroidered robe for virtue," [1] the characteristics of the French, [2] the pictures in the Louvre, [3] the ruins of Tivoli [4] — it is a potpourri of little essays in his ripest style and manner. Without the depth and resonance of *The Spirit of the Age*, it is none the less a complex piece of work in its fusion of soliloquy and narrative, topography and literary association, social comment and aesthetic judgments; and in addition it enables us to trace his movements for twelve months or so with extraordinary precision.

The Hazlitts' route was one well worn by generations of the English: from Brighton to Dieppe, and then Rouen ("an immense, stately mass of dark grey stone") [5] and Paris, where they stayed for several months. The

* These articles — for which, according to his former wife (Bonner, p. 255), Hazlitt was paid £300 — appeared at irregular intervals between 14 September 1824 and 16 November 1825. It would seem that most of them were written during the Hazlitts' extended stays in Paris, Florence, and Vevey. Chapter XX, a sort of Table Talk entitled "English and Foreign Manners," was printed in the *Examiner* on 1 May 1825. According to Sarah Hazlitt (Bonner, p. 260) Taylor and Hessey had planned to do the book, but when Hazlitt failed to come to terms with them he resolved to "sell" it to the highest bidder, and so it was finally published in May 1826, some six months after his return, by the new firm of Hunt and Clarke (Henry Leigh Hunt, the son of Hazlitt's old friend John, and young Charles Cowden Clarke).

first thing Hazlitt did on reaching there, of course, was to wander through the Louvre.

Here Genius and Fame dwell together; "*School* calleth unto *School*," and mighty names answer to each other; that old gallery points to the long, dim perspective of waning years, and the shadow of Glory and of Liberty is seen afar off. In pacing its echoing floors, I hear the sound of the footsteps of my youth, and the dead start from their slumbers! . . . In all the time that I had been away from thee, and amidst all the changes that had happened in it, did I ever forget, did I ever profane thee? Never for a moment or in thought have I swerved from thee, or from the cause of which thou wert the pledge and the crown. Often have I sought thee in sleep, and cried myself awake to find thee, with the heart-felt yearnings of intolerable affection. Still didst thou haunt me, like a passionate dream — like some proud beauty, the queen and mistress of my thoughts.[6]

Not all the sights of Paris were so exhilarating. Although he conceded Mademoiselle Mars's talent for Molière,[7] he was puzzled by the universal veneration for Racine,[8] found the glossy, artificial brilliance of the modern pictures in the Luxembourg offensive,* and tried, without success, to see the merit in French sculpture.[9] Moreover, although he does not say so in the *Notes*, he encountered his first wife (who had been in Paris since July),[10] arranged with the firm of Galignani for new editions of *Table-Talk* and *The Spirit of the Age*, and wrote a string of essays, some for immediate publication in the *New Monthly Magazine* and some for *The Plain Speaker*, a new collection put together after he returned to England.† He also met Stendhal, who, on his trip to England seven years before, had come to know and like his work enough to borrow sections of the Holcroft *Memoirs* and the *Edinburgh* review of Schlegel and to urge a French translation of his book on Shakespeare. These extraordinary men, though different in so many ways, shared so many views — contempt for the frigid classicism of David and Ingres, immense respect for Shakespeare, veneration for Napoleon — that it is easy to believe, with M. Vigneron, that such essays as "Madame Pasta and Mademoiselle Mars" and "Sir Walter Scott, Racine, and Shakespear" are distillations of their talks. Hazlitt's subsequent allusions to and citations from "my friend Mr. Beyle"[11] and "the celebrated Count Stendhal"[12] are a welcome indication that he could still find pleasure in the warmth of human intercourse.

* 10.129–138. Four years later, in a piece for the *Examiner* (18.379), Hazlitt put his views more tersely: "*Imprimis*, we abhor French pictures. In the second place, we tolerate French tragedy. Thirdly, we adore French comedy."

† Three of these Parisian essays — "On Old English Writers and Speakers" (12.311–324), "Madame Pasta and Mademoiselle Mars" (12.324–335), and "On Novelty and Familiarity" (12.294–311) — were printed in the *New Monthly Magazine* at the start of 1825. These and two others written at the time — "On a Portrait of an English Lady, by Vandyke" (12.280–294) and "Sir Walter Scott, Racine, and Shakespear" (12.336–346) — were included in *The Plain Speaker*.

EPILOGUE

Their three-month stay in Paris ended, they continued on their tour. It was mid-January 1825 when they set forth for Italy, and their journey, via Lyons ("a fine, dirty town") [13] and the "humbler passage" of Mont Cenis rather than the arduous Simplon, [14] produced enough mendacious inn-keepers and rascally postilions to supply a book by Smollett. At Pont Beau-Voisin, where there was trouble with the customs about a chest of books, [15] he first saw the Alps. It was, he said, a "new sensation," and as they climbed the pass and approached the Grande Chartreuse it seemed that the ideal and the real converged. "Between those four crystal peaks stood the ancient monastery of that name, hid from the sight, revealed to thought, half-way between earth and heaven, enshrined in its cerulean atmosphere, lifting the soul to its native home, and purifying it from mortal grossness. I cannot wonder at the pilgrimages that are made to it, its calm repose, its vows monastic. Life must there seem a noiseless dream: — Death a near translation to the skies!" [16]

At first Turin appeared to him to be a city of enchantment, but the magic did not last.

A Monk was walking in a solitary grove at a little distance from the common path. The air was soft and balmy, and I felt transported to another climate — another earth — another sky. The winter was suddenly changed to spring. It was as if I had to begin my life anew. Several young Italian women were walking on the terrace, in English dresses, and with graceful downcast looks, in which you might fancy that you read the soul of the Decameron. It was a fine, serious grace, equally remote from French levity and English sullenness, but it was the last I saw of it. I have run the gauntlet of vulgar shapes and horrid faces ever since. The women in Italy (so far as I have seen hitherto) are detestably ugly. They are not even dark and swarthy, but a mixture of brown and red, coarse, marked with the small pox, with pug-features, awkward, ill-made, fierce, dirty, lazy, neither attempting nor hoping to please. [17]

The endless plain of Lombardy was so bleak, he said, that "Mr. Crabbe should travel post to Italy on purpose to describe it, and to add it to his list of prosaic horrors." [18] Going on through Parma and Bologna, and then across the "unqualified desolation" [19] of the Apennines, they finally came to Florence, which was "like a town that has survived itself." [20] There they stayed for several weeks, perhaps because Leigh Hunt, who had lingered on in Italy after the debacle of the *Liberal*, was living in the suburb of Maiano. [21] Looking from his house, said Hazlitt, one could feel the weight of time.

You see at one view the village of Setiniano, belonging to Michael Angelo's family, he house in which Machiavel lived, and that where Boccaccio wrote, two ruined castles, in which the rival families of the Gerardeschi and the Visconti carried on the most deadly strife, and which seem as they might still rear their

444

mouldering heads against each other; and not far from this the *Valley of Ladies* (the scene of *The Decameron*), and Fesole, with the mountains of Perugia beyond. With a view like this, one may think one's sight "enriched," in Burns's phrase. On the ascent toward Fesole is the house where Galileo lived, and where he was imprisoned after his release from the Inquisition, at the time Milton saw him. In the town itself are Michael Angelo's house, the Baptistery, the gates of which he thought worthy to be the gates of Paradise, the Duomo, older than St. Peter's, the ancient Palace of the Medici family, the Palace Pitti, and here also stands the statue that "enchants the world." [22]

Another of the sights of Florence was the irascible Walter Savage Landor. The year before, in reviewing the *Imaginary Conversations* for the *Edinburgh*, Hazlitt had complained that Landor, though an "excellent" writer "whenever excellence is compatible with singularity," was too much at the mercy of his own headstrong opinions. To write about Tiberius as "a *man of sentiment*, who retired to Capri merely to indulge a tender melancholy on the death of a beloved wife," describe Nero as "a most humane, amiable, and deservedly popular character," follow Milton's anachronistic spelling, and call Locke "the most *elegant* of English prose writers" was, he said, to indulge in the kind of "Literary Jacobinism" that had vitiated much of Southey's work. "To agree with it is an impertinence: to differ from it a crime." [23] These critical pronouncements were not, perhaps, the soundest basis for friendship with a man like Landor, but Hazlitt, for reasons not entirely clear, was intent on meeting him. Refusing Charles Armitage Brown's proffered introduction — for he said that "he would beard the lion in his den" — he attired himself in nankeen shorts and white stockings, rapped on Landor's door, and, to everyone's surprise, received a cordial welcome. [24] It may be, as Landor later told Crabb Robinson, that he came ready with an "awkward" explanation for his "scurrilous" *Edinburgh* review,[*] but in writing of a new installment of the *Conversations* in 1828 he once more qualified his praise, calling Landor a combination of Nestor and Thersites, and complaining that his splendid style was sometimes "deformed" by passion. [25] Landor may have been offended by such views in 1824, yet the two became great friends — perhaps, as John Forster suggested later, because each enjoyed the other's "wilfulness and caprice." For no other reason, surely, would his host have shown "delight" at Hazlitt's vulgar circumstantial story about securing his divorce. [26]

By the end of March, the travelers had gone on to Rome,[†] where, as

---

[*] Robinson, I, 390f. In sending this review to Jeffrey the year before (while on his honeymoon at Melrose) Hazlitt had expressed his discontent with parts of it. See Keynes, opposite p. 83; 16.435.

[†] Early in the spring Charles Armitage Brown wrote to Joseph Severn about Hazlitt's plans to get in touch with him when he reached Rome (William Sharp, *The Life and Letters of Joseph Severn* [1892], p. 149). He had arrived by March 28, when

EPILOGUE

Landor was informed, everything was "very bad and dear."[27] There he saw the pope ("a harmless, infirm fretful old man")[28] and, of course, as many pictures as he could, but nothing pleased him very much in the city that he later called "the very tomb of ancient greatness, the grave of modern presumption."[29] There is a species of malaria in Rome, he wrote, that infects both mind and body, for although the city swarmed with dilettantes and connoisseurs, it seemed to stifle true creation.

A common stone-mason or sign-painter, who understands the use of his tools and sticks close to his business, has more resemblance to Raphael or Michael Angelo, and stands a better chance of achieving something great, than those who visit the Corridors of the Vatican of St. Peter's once a day, return home, spend the evening in extolling what they have witnessed, begin a sketch or a plan and lay it aside, and saunter out again the next day in search of fresh objects to dissipate *ennui* and kill the time without being obliged to draw for one instance on their own resources or resolution.[30]

Even St. Peter's, "illuminated to the very top" for Easter, was a disappointment to one who saw in the ruins of Melrose Abbey a better token of the faith that once had been the splendor of the Roman church.[31] With summer coming on, he thought of going to Albano for a while, or perhaps of pushing on to Venice. "I should be glad, if I settle at Albino, if you could manage to come over and stop a little," he wrote on April 9 to Landor.

I have done what I was obliged to write for the Papers, and am now a leisure man, I hope, for the rest of the summer. I am much gratified that you are pleased with the *Spirit of the Age*. Somebody ought to like it, for I am sure there will be plenty to cry out against it. I hope you did not find any sad blunders in the second volume; but you can hardly suppose the depression of body and mind under which I wrote some of these articles. I bought a little Florentine edition of Petrarch and Dante the other day, and have made out one page.[32]

As it happened, they returned to Florence and then went on to Venice. Hazlitt found Ferrara to be the jewel of all Italian cities.

You are in a dream, in the heart of a romance; you enjoy the most perfect solitude, that of a city which was once filled with "the busy hum of men," and of which the tremulous fragments at every step strike the sense, and call up reflection. In short, nothing is to be seen of Ferrara, but the remains, graceful and romantic, of what it was — no sordid object intercepts or sullies the retrospect of the past — it is not degraded and patched up like Rome, with upstart improvements, with earthenware and oilshops; it is a classic vestige of antiquity, drooping into peaceful decay, a sylvan suburb. . . . Here Ariosto lived — here Tasso occupied first a palace, and then a dungeon.[33]

---

he wrote to Landor from 33 Via Gregoriana — the former house of Salvator Rosa that he alludes to in his *Notes* (10.231f.) — to inquire about a copy of the Paris *Table-Talk* that he had ordered to be sent to him (ALS, The Historical Society of Pennsylvania).

THE CONTINENTAL TOUR

Leaving Venice with its Titians and its palaces, they crossed the fertile valley of the Po, through Padua and Verona, to Milan, where, unfortunately, he "did not see the great picture of the Last Supper by Lionardo nor the little Luini . . . which my friend Mr. Beyle charged me particularly to see."[34] The Simplon, though startling in its "sudden and terrific contrasts," was, he thought, inferior to the "simple expansive grandeur" of Mont Cenis, "blending and growing into one vast accumulated impression."[35]

Their goal was now Vevey, on Lake Geneva, rich in its associations with Rousseau, and there, in a farmhouse a mile outside the town, they stayed until September. Among other things he wrote that summer was the famous "Merry England," his most stirring tribute to the land he loved despite its politicians. Work was not his main concern, however.[36]

We breakfasted at the same hour and the tea-kettle was always boiling (an excellent thing in housewifery) — a *lounge* in the orchard for an hour or two, and twice a week we could see the steam-boat creeping like a spider over the surface of the lake; a volume of the Scotch novels (to be had in every library on the Continent, in English, French, German, or Italian, as the reader pleases), or M. Galignani's Paris and London *Observer*, amused us till dinner time; then tea and a walk till the moon unveiled itself, "apparent queen of night," or the brook, swoln with a transient shower, was heard more distinctly in the darkness, mingling with the soft, rustling breeze; and the next morning the song of peasants broke upon refreshing sleep, as the sun glanced among the clustering vine-leaves, or the shadowy hills, as the mists retired from their summits, looked in at our windows.[37]

It was here that Thomas Medwin, Shelley's friend and future biographer, called on him and recorded fragments of his conversation. Short, ill-shaved, and slovenly, he was anything but "striking" in appearance, Medwin later wrote, but "there was an habitual melancholy in the expression, as though he had been chewing on the end of past miseries, or brooding on bitter anticipations of the future." They talked of travel, literature, and common friends, and on everything they touched Hazlitt had pronounced opinions. He expressed his disapproval of the mountains, spoke acidly of Byron's failings as a poet and a man, praised Southey's *Thalaba*, and deplored the low estate of modern drama. Scott, "the high priest of legitimacy," had "done more to put back the age than any writer of the day," he said, "the political economists and Malthus only excepted." They talked about Napoleon and about the book that Hazlitt hoped to write on him one day (for it was still "too early" to see him "in his true proportions"), about the trouble poets had in writing decent prose, and — most of all — about the "bitter persecution" that he himself had suffered from the Tory critics. "Working himself up, at last, into a fury, he poured forth the venom of a tongue, that was never equalled but by the gall of his pen," and the conversation became so "painful and distressing" that Medwin was glad to get away.[38]

Following an excursion late in August to Chamonix and Geneva — not the most impressive town that they had seen, "but very well for a Calvinistic capital"[39] — they left Vevey in September, went down the Rhine to Holland ("the only country you gain nothing by seeing" because it is precisely like its pictures),[40] took passage at Calais, and, after thirteen months abroad, returned to England in October. "I confess," he wrote in conclusion to the readers of his *Notes,*

London looked to me on my return like a long, straggling, dirty country-town; nor do the names of Liverpool, Manchester, Birmingham, Leeds, or Coventry, sound like a trumpet in the ears, or invite our pilgrim steps like those of Sienna, of Cortona, Perugia, Arezzo, Pisa and Ferrara. I am not sorry, however, that I have got back. . . . It is well to see foreign countries to enlarge one's speculative knowledge, and dispel false prejudices and libellous views of human nature; but our affections must settle at home.*

THE LATER WORKS

Hazlitt's final years need not detain us long, for his life from 1826 to 1830 is almost completely unrecorded, and it is vain to speculate about events concerning which we have no certain information. His later works, moreover, do not require extended treatment. Following the example set by his contemporaries, posterity has willingly let die *The Life of Napoleon Buonaparte* (which he himself regarded as his magnum opus), and although the other products of this period — the so-called "conversations" with the painter James Northcote and the last essays — exhibit all his customary skills, they do not materially affect his reputation. Without them the canon would of course be smaller, but his place in English literature would no doubt be the same. Therefore we shall take our cue from Hazlitt's comment in his essay "On the Fear of Death":

The pleasures of our existence have worn themselves out, are "gone into the wastes of time," or have turned their indifferent side to us: the pains by their repeated blows have worn us out, and have left us neither spirit or inclination to

* 10.302f. "Travelling Abroad" (17.332–344), which appeared in the *New Monthly Magazine* in 1828, may be regarded as Hazlitt's retrospective comment on his Continental tour. "I am one of those who do not think that much is to be gained in point either of temper or understanding by travelling abroad," he says (17.332). "Give me the true, stubborn, unimpaired John Bull feeling, that keeps fast hold of the good things it fancies in its exclusive possession, nor ever relaxes in its contempt for foreign frippery and finery."

encounter them again in retrospect. . . . We shut up the book and close the account once for all! [1]

To follow him through his last four years of life is to trace a shadow through the deepening gloom. We get a glimpse of him from time to time — as when Haydon, in November 1825, reported that although he still looked sick his trip had done him good, and that under the watchful eye of his "present wife" he was even keeping clean* — but the record is so sparse that his last years, like his first, are mainly a subject for conjecture. Leigh Hunt's cordial letter that we have quoted earlier [2] permits the pleasant inference that the two old friends perhaps saw something of each other at this time, but all we really know is the dates and contents of his publications. Thus, although the winter of 1825–26 yields no certain information, the appearance, in May, of *The Plain Speaker* (at the same time as his *Notes of a Journey*) suggests that he had not been idle since his return to England.

This big two-volume work may be regarded as the last installment of his Table Talks. Ranging from his first attempts in the *Edinburgh Magazine* in 1818 through his essays in the early issues of the *London* and the *New Monthly* to his most recent (and hitherto unpublished) work, it is a retrospective survey of his contributions to the form that he had made his own. In the absence of other information we could almost trace the main events of his career, or at any rate the sequence of his moods, from this representative collection. "On Respectable People," the first in point of time, reflects his anger and dismay with "the conventional hypocrisy of the world" [3] and with the pressures making for political conformity in post-Napoleonic England. Such early *London* essays as "On the Conversation of Authors," "On Reading Old Books," and "On Antiquity" show him turning to the past in an effort to explore the forces that had shaped his own "identity." "On the Spirit of Obligations" and "On the Pleasure of Hating," which were written in his madness over Sarah Walker, express the savage disaffection of a man who felt himself betrayed. ("We hate old friends," he had said in 1823; "we hate old books; we hate old opinions; and at last we come to hate ourselves.")[4] "On Sitting for One's Picture" and "On the Portrait of an English Lady, by Vandyke" are among his many testimonials to the healing power of art. In "On the Prose-Style of Poets," "Sir Walter Scott, Racine, and Shakespear," and "Whether Genius is Conscious of Its Powers" we see the critic and man of letters speculating, with immense

---

* *Correspondence and Table-Talk*, II, 99. About this time Haydon recorded in his diary (Pope, 10 November 1825) that he had paid a three-hour call on Hazlitt "with great pleasure."

effect, on the mysteries of his craft. In "On Reason and Imagination" and "The New School of Reform" the critic merges with the moralist to assert his trust in "feeling" as the source of knowledge and in passion as the "essence" of our "moral truth." *

◇　◇　◇

The Plain Speaker, then, was mainly a collection of things already done, but one of its new pieces was a dialogue "On Envy," and this, the first of Hazlitt's "conversations" with his old friend James Northcote, pointed to the future. Northcote was already something of a legend when he and Hazlitt (then in his early twenties) had met almost thirty years before.[5] The son of a humble watchmaker of Plymouth who became a student and assistant of Sir Joshua Reynolds, a royal academician, and a painter of the celebrated and the well-to-do, he had won his way to wealth and fame; but he was born with his sardonic wit, and this, together with his years — for he lived to eighty-five — made him a sort of Nestor to the younger generation. When Haydon, resolved to rescue English art from academic hucksters, had called on him in 1804, the "diminutive wizened figure in an old blue-striped dressing gown, his spectacles pushed up on his forehead," predicted, in his broad Devonian dialect, that as a "heestoricaul peinter" he would surely starve,[†] and when Sir Walter Scott — by no means a young Turk himself — was sitting for his portrait a quarter-century later, he looked upon the "Wizzard" as an "animated mummy."[6] To talk with him, said Hazlitt when he himself was middle-aged, was "like conversing with the dead,"[7] for when he spoke of Burke and Reynolds and "that set of persons" he obliterated time. "All you have to do is to sit and listen; and it is like hearing one of Titian's faces speak."[8]

Age had withered him, of course, but it could not make him mellow. Too old to be impressed by what was merely new, too busy to repose on his past triumphs, he had a tonic disrespect for modern errors and pretensions, even when they were his own. He was derisive of the

---

* 12.46. Of the thirty-two essays in *The Plain Speaker* one had first appeared in the *Edinburgh Magazine*, nine in the *London*, nine in the *New Monthly*, and one ("On Egotism") in the Paris *Table-Talk*. The remaining twelve, which had been written between 1822 and 1826, had not appeared in print before.

† *Autobiography*, I, 19. As late as 1823 Haydon (*Diary*, II, 418) was still seething over Northcote's rude remark: "The instant I entered his room in 1804, my face, as if prophetic of my power, attracted the piercing viper glitter of his contracting little eyes. He darted a look into me that pricked my feelings as a needle does the skin, and when he read the letter of introduction from his Brother, his 'What, be a come to starve!' proved my anticipations to be conclusive. From that moment to the present hour I have been on his fears, his hopes, his reputation like a dim shadow that pursued him!"

commonplace, said Hazlitt, and he always set himself "to prop the falling cause," [9] not to seem magnanimous but to tease the self-complacent, and when he found his own enthusiasms shared he backed away from them. Witty, haughty, and acerb, he had what Haydon called "a habit of perpetual malice," [10] for he laughed or snarled at almost everyone, and especially at all earnest, dedicated people. He and Hazlitt disagreed on many things, of course, but since they thrived on opposition, each honed his mind upon the other's, and found mutual stimulation better than affection. "Why, I very often say things behind peoples' backs because I delight to think how they will be mortified when it is told them again," the gossipy old painter said, "and when I see them, and they don't seem to know what I have said, I say it to their faces, & they look so! Oh, it is quite delightful." [11] Whatever one might think of Northcote, a visit to his studio (which Hazlitt said he entered with the most delight and quitted with the most regret) [12] was bound to be amusing.

His thoughts bubble up and sparkle, like beads on old wine. The fund of anecdote, the collection of curious particulars, is enough to set up any common retailer of jests, that dines out every day; but these are not strung together like a row of galley-slaves, but are always introduced to illustrate some argument or bring out some fine distinction of character. The mixture of spleen adds to the sharpness of the point, like poisoned arrows. [13]

It is not surprising, then, that despite the difference in their ages and their views the writer and the painter maintained sporadic intercourse for almost thirty years. When Northcote, in his eighties, was preparing for the press his *One Hundred Fables, Original and Selected* (1828) Hazlitt helped him with the "editing" — "I may say writing them," he explained [14] — and he also had a hand in the old man's life of Titian (1830).* It is touching that the aged Northcote bequeathed a hundred pounds to him "as a memento of their intimacy," [15] and appropriately ironical that he survived him by a year.

As early as 1820 Hazlitt said that any tête-à-tête with Northcote could be turned into an essay if its "diverging rays" were focused, [16] and six years later the dialogue "On Envy" showed that he was right. It has a theme of sorts, or at any rate a topic, but it has no formal structure. As the two men talk about themselves and art and human nature they indulge in gossip, anecdote, and even dialectic, but their conversation follows no set course and reaches no conclusion. It merely shows what happens

---

* *Memoirs*, II, 212f.; Allan Cunningham, *The Lives of the Most Eminent British Painters* (Bohn's Standard Library, 1879), II, 428. In a note to Basil Montagu, written from his bed only a week or so before he died (ALS in the possession of Sir Geoffrey Keynes), Hazlitt said that "the second vol. of the Titian is at p. 304, & I will be done this week."

when two active minds collide. Although "On Envy" is as shapeless as a Table Talk, it uses dialogue instead of introspection, and the presence of two speakers gives it thrust and tension. Northcote sometimes serves almost as monologist (a role he dearly loved), but sometimes he appears to be an alter ego for the writer, a persona who expresses Hazlitt's own self-doubts and contradictions. When the writer, for example, says that envy is foreign to his nature, the painter charges him with self-deception. "You start off with an idea as usual," he remarks,

and torture the plain state of the case into a paradox. There may be some truth in what you suppose; but malice or selfishness is at the bottom of the severity of your criticism, not the love of truth or justice, though you may make it the pretext. You are more angry at Sir W***** S****'s success than at his servility. You would give yourself no trouble about his poverty of spirit, if he had not made a hundred thousand pounds by his writings. The sting lies there, though you may try to conceal it from yourself.

And he continues in this vein until at last he asks, "Why do you so constantly let your temper get the better of your reason?" This question is the peg on which Hazlitt hangs his own self-portrait — and, incidentally, explains his strength and weakness as a critic:

Because I hate a hypocrite, a time-server, and a slave. . . . I do not think that, except in circumstances of peculiar aggravation, or of extraordinary ill-temper and moroseness of disposition, any one who has a thorough feeling of excellence has a delight in gainsaying it. The excellence that we feel, we participate in as if it were our own — it becomes ours by transfusion of mind — it is instilled into our hearts — it mingles with our blood. We are unwilling to allow merit, because we are unable to perceive it. But to be convinced of it, is to be ready to acknowledge and pay homage to it. Illiberality or narrowness of feeling is a narrowness of taste, a want of proper *tact*. A bigotted and exclusive spirit is real blindness to all excellence but our own, or that of some particular school or sect.[17]

This dialogue provided Hazlitt with the model for a series of such conversations that, written in the early months of 1826 before he went abroad again, were published serially in the *New Monthly Magazine* under the title "Boswell Redivivus" between August 1826 and March 1827.* Even looser and therefore in a sense more realistic than the

* From such internal evidence as allusions to recent pieces in the paper (11.238) and disrespectful comments about Zachariah Mudge (11.367), Howe (11.351) has plausibly conjectured that Hazlitt wrote some fifteen conversations for the *New Monthly* in the early months of 1826 before he went to Paris in the summer. When Thomas Campbell, editor of the magazine, abruptly stopped the series in March 1827, after No. vi appeared, the unprinted conversations must have been returned to Hazlitt, for when he resumed the enterprise two years later (under the title "Real Conversations") in the *London Weekly Review* he drew upon this old material. Following the failure of the *London Weekly Review* he moved the series (now called "Conversations as Good as Real" to the *Atlas* in the spring of 1829, and then, in 1830, he shifted it again (as "Conversations with an Eminent Living Artist") to the *Court Journal*. For the circumstances under which he brought all this scattered work to-

dialogue "On Envy," they do not progress from theme to theme, or even point to point; they merely ripple on, through allusion, anecdote, and repartee, until the speakers stop. Anything could set them going — a piece about Lord Byron in the paper,[18] a picture standing on the easel,[19] the publication of a recent book [20] — but since a single conversation might touch upon, among other things, Northcote's defects as a painter, Raphael's unapproachable perfection, the art of portraiture, Northcote's memories of Sir Joshua Reynolds, the secret of good acting, "the common sense of mankind" as the ultimate criterion, James Boaden (the biographer of Sarah Siddons), Kemble, Master Betty (the famous boy actor), Garrick, Romney, Opie, and Dr. John Mudge (who married his housemaid),[21] it is clear that they were anything but tightly built. None the less, in his introduction to the series Hazlitt was careful to explain that they had been composed, and not transcribed.

I differ from my great original and predecessor (James Boswell, Esq., of Auchlinleck), in this, that whereas he is supposed to have invented nothing, I have feigned whatever I pleased. I have forgotten, mistaken, mis-stated, altered, transposed a number of things. All that can be relied upon for certain is a striking anecdote or a sterling remark or two in each page. These belong as a matter of right to my principal speaker: the rest I have made for him by interpolating or paraphrasing what he said. . . . In a word, Mr. N— is only answerable for the wit, sense, and spirit there may be in these papers: I take all the dulness, impertinence, and malice upon myself. He has furnished the text — I fear I have often spoiled it by the commentary.[22]

Whatever its attractions, this procedure had its perils. Whether works of art or not, the conversations dealt so freely with persons still alive that they were bound to give offense, and to assign responsibility for their tart and even libelous opinions proved to be a problem from the start. The fact that Hazlitt went abroad before the first of them appeared, and so was out of reach, whereas Northcote (who doted on publicity) professed to be as much surprised by them as any other disaffected reader compounded the confusion.* When, shortly after the appearance of "Boswell Redivivus, No. I," Northcote and Haydon — who detested one another — gave themselves the pleasure of raking over Hazlitt's old and new offenses and of analyzing his defects of character, Haydon asked Northcote how he could "tolerate" the wretch. " 'Why, to be sure,' said he, 'because I fear him. He is now publishing

gether as *Conversations of James Northcote, Esq., R.A.* just before he died see pages 465f. The twenty-two conversations included in that book were made up of some twenty-nine pieces that he had printed earlier as well as two (Nos. 13 and 14) that had not appeared before.

 * According to Hazlitt (11.228) Northcote had in fact given the project a kind of retroactive endorsement, adding characteristically that the writer did not know enough about society to be a "judge" of civil conversation.

conversations with me that never took place, and he will vent his spite on those he has any cause for disliking because he is too great a coward to do it himself, and by flattering my vanity, he makes me say what I never said, so that he may escape all responsibility.' " [23] When Leigh Hunt complained to Thomas Campbell about remarks [24] ascribed to him in the very first installment, the editor agreed that the passage was "detestable," and he called his failure to delete it an "oversight" that he would not be guilty of again. "If I can say or write anything that can make you a shadow of satisfaction," he assured the angry Hunt, "I am willing to do so; but I suppose you will despise this devil's aspersions, even though they have come from the quarter from which they ought least to have come." He at least had learned, he said, "to keep a better look-out" in the future, and he was certain he would not be caught again in such a "painful" situation. [25]

Thereafter all went well, it seems, until the appearance of the March *New Monthly Magazine* raised another and a much more violent storm. The offensive passage there concerned the Reverend Zachariah Mudge (1694–1769), late prebendary of Exeter and vicar of St. Andrew's, Plymouth, whom no less a man than Samuel Johnson had honored with a visit and later eulogized for his "virtues and abilities."* Since it was this eminent divine who, many years before, had introduced young Northcote to their fellow-townsman Reynolds and thus had started him on his career, there had always been a tender tie between the painter and the family of his early benefactor. Not unnaturally, then, when Hazlitt, in "Boswell Redivivus, No. VI," reported Northcote as having said that in his salad days Mudge ran away from school because a housemaid had rejected his advances and, after various discreditable adventures, abandoned the Dissenters to join the Church of England "because the former would not give him some situation that he wanted," [26] all the tribe of Mudge, which still continued strong in Plymouth, rose in righteous indignation. [27]

Their spokesman, one Richard Rosdew, a son-in-law of Zachariah Mudge's son, promptly paid a call on Northcote to protest his ingratitude and slander, but he found, to his surprise, that the painter, full of "rage and passion," thought that he himself had been abused. "He called Hazlitt an assassin, a wretch, a viper," Rosdew reported in delight,

* Boswell, p. 1125. According to Hazlitt (11.220), Northcote thought Johnson's "pompous" character of Mudge was "proper only for a tomb-stone — it was like one of Kneller's portraits, — it would do for anybody." Incidentally, it was while visiting Plymouth with Sir Joshua Reynolds in 1762, when Dr. Mudge preached a special sermon for the benefit of his distinguished guest, that Johnson attributed his wrong definition of *pastern* to "Ignorance, Madam, pure ignorance." See Boswell, pp. 211, 267f.

"whom he would stab if he could get at him. He said, when he first read the article he thought for three days it would have killed him: in short, he said so much, and so warmly, that I pitied him, and left him with as warm feelings of regard as before." Thus the crafty Northcote (who, as the subeditor of the *New Monthly* recalled, had really been "delighted" with the conversations)* deflected the attack. Since the old man liked to gossip the way a drunkard likes to drink, he may very well have slandered Zachariah Mudge, but by shifting all the blame to Hazlitt and acting like a man bowed down with grief he could assume the role of martyr. Hazlitt was the villain, he declared to Thomas Campbell, he himself the victim of his own good nature; and if he had let "the devil" visit him because he liked his conversation, he had learned, to his deep sorrow, that such imprudence had a price.

I thought no more of what was said by either of us afterwards, concluding that it had passed off in air; but I now find to my sorrow, that this despicable and worthless trash has been treasured up, and is proclaimed at the market cross, where my family connections and dearest friends are brought forward to public inspection, with their names at full length, properly spelt, in order to prevent any possible mistake being made; and things uttered in idle merriment now stamped in everlasting print, not as I represented them, but as speeches of cold, dry, and hateful malignity, and grossly different from my meaning; and I am now kept in perpetual torture, not knowing what each new month may bring forth. Good God; do you not think such a situation terrible?

Campbell, declaring himself "afflicted beyond measure" that through his "inattention" he had helped to wound "the feelings of a venerable man of genius," promptly fell in line. Northcote could dictate the "form and manner" of "atonement," he asserted, and as for "the *infernal* Hazlitt," he would never again be permitted to write for the *New Monthly Magazine*. If "Boswell Redivivus" ended midway in its career, however, the controversy sputtered on. Although Northcote expressed his gratitude to Campbell for his swift and simple justice to the "viper" who had brought them so much trouble, the "mischief" was already done, he said, and he himself could only "suffer" for having been too kind to such a wretch. Meanwhile Rosdew, mollified by this exchange of letters ("exact copies" of which had been supplied to him by Northcote), was urging Campbell to repair the damage done the Mudges by reprinting Dr. Johnson's eulogistic sketch of Zachariah when he learned, to his dis-

* Cyrus Redding, "Life and Reminiscences of Thomas Campbell," *New Monthly Magazine*, LXXXI (1847), 336. When, in 1830, the *Conversations* were brought together in a book, Haydon was indignant. "One talks & the other writes," he recorded in his journal (Pope, 18 June 1830). "If you accuse Northcote, he swears Hazlitt has put down what he [did] not say, and if you go to Hazlitt, he says, 'Am I answerable for what Northcote says?'"

may, that he had been betrayed: far from stabbing Hazlitt ("if he could get at him") the sly old painter had continued to receive his visits, had remained his "bosom" friend, and had even put him in his will. It was then that Rosdew's patience snapped. Declining further intercourse with such a hypocrite as Northcote, he asked "a mutual friend of both" to protest his strange behavior. When Northcote flippantly replied, however, that it was impossible "to explain this nonsense, therefore pray torment me no more, as, at present, my great age and load of infirmities render me unfit for such silly matters," Rosdew, with awful finality, removed his portrait from the wall. "Ingratitude, envy, meanness, and inordinate self-conceit, together with falsehood, have marked the painter's conduct respecting the Mudges," Rosdew said in valediction, and he would have no more to do with him. Thus the matter ended, for the time at least.

Meanwhile Hazlitt had returned to France, and his part, if any, in all this comic agitation is, like almost everything about him after 1826, obscure. In particular, his stay of fourteen months in Paris, from July 1826 to October 1827, is barren of detail. We must assume that he was busy doing what he had gone to do, which was to write a book about Napoleon, because when he returned to London he had half of that gigantic undertaking finished; but our only certain information is that provided by a note of August 1826:

My dear Patmore,
    I am damnably off here for money, as I have taken a house & garden (No. 58, Rue Mont-Blanc) and have been disappointed in two remittances which I ought to have received. If you could by any possibility raise 20£, I will send you back Manuscript to that amount by return of post, written on the spot since I have been here. My best remembrances at home, & believe me ever truly yours,
W. Hazlitt.

I have made a rough copy of the Titian, & get into nothing but rows & squabbles. I shall be glad to hear from you *tandem-wise*.[28]

Patmore came to his assistance, it would seem, for in January the *Monthly*, a magazine that he had not written for before, published "On the Want of Money," a piece from which we may infer that Mrs. Hazlitt's income, which no doubt helped provide the house and garden, was not enough to keep the family going. ("Poverty is the test of sincerity, the touchstone of civility," he said. "Even abroad, they treat you scurvily if your remittances do not arrive regularly, and though you have hitherto lived like a *Milord Anglais*.")[29] This essay is one of Hazlitt's most excoriating comments on the writer's hard condition, and like its companion pieces — "On the Feeling of Immortality in Youth," "On Reading New Books," "On Disagreeable People," "On Ends and Means" [30] — it shows him "gathering up the fragments of my early recollection, and putting them into a form that might live." [31] Although in style as rich and polyphonic as anything he ever wrote, these essays have a dark, autumnal coloration, and they seem to sound a note of valediction. "We do not in the regular course of nature die all at once," he said; "we have mouldered away gradually long before; faculty after faculty, attachment after attachment, we are torn from ourselves piece-meal while living; year after year takes something from us; and death only consigns the last remnant of what we were to the grave. The revulsion is not so great, and a quiet *euthanasia* is a winding-up of the plot, that is not out of reason or nature." [32]

His return to England in October 1827 apparently coincided with the break-up of his marriage, but all we know of that event (to which he himself makes no allusion in his published work) is Brown's remark, a few years later, that Isabella Hazlitt parted from her husband "on account of the ill-conduct of the boy." [*] While the second Mrs. Hazlitt left his life, as she had entered it, under circumstances so obscure that she almost seems to be a ghost, he himself went back to Winterslow, where he could "listen to the silence" [33] and meditate on "what has been." More and more he was turning to the past, he said, and that is why he liked to hear the curfew, which told a tale of other times.

The days that are past, the generations that are gone, the tangled forest glades and hamlets brown of my native country, the woodman's art, the Norman warrior armed for the battle or in his festive hall, the conqueror's iron rule and peasant's lamp extinguished, all start up at the clamorous peal, and fill my mind with fear and wonder. I confess, nothing at present interests me but what has been — the recollection of the impressions of my early life, or events long past, of which only the dim traces remain in a smouldering ruin or half-obsolete custom. That *things should be that are now no more*, creates in my mind the most unfeigned astonishment. I cannot solve the mystery of the past, nor exhaust my pleasure in it. [34]

It was in this tranquil, retrospective mood that he resumed his essays, some of them for the *New Monthly* [†] (for Campbell, despite his anger

---

[*] Robinson, I, 387. The account that "the boy" himself presumably gave to his own son a generation later (*Memoirs*, II, 196) is, as Howe has shown (*Life*, pp. 355ff.), hopelessly confused.

[†] "On a Sun-Dial" (October 1827), 17.238–245; "Why the Heroes of Romance Are Insipid" (November 1827), 17.246–254; "The Shyness of Scholars" (December 1827), 17.254–264; "The Main Chance" (February 1828), 17.275–290. About the same time the *New Monthly* printed two essays that derived from Hazlitt's stay in Rome in 1825: "English Students at Rome" (October 1827), 17.134–143; "The Vatican" (November 1827), 17.144–151.

over "Boswell Redivivus," had relaxed his interdiction,) some for the *London Weekly Review,** and one, at least, for the *Examiner.*†

Most of these are built upon the theme of isolation. Earlier — in "On the Spirit of Obligations," for example — he had railed against a world where all is "prostituted, degraded, vile," [35] but here he writes with poise and self-control. "Do not begin to quarrel with the world too soon," he had told his son, "for, bad as it may be, it is the best we have to live in — here," and if it really is, as it often seems to be, "incorrigible," it should make a wise man sad, not angry.[36] Such mellow wisdom shines throughout these essays of his later years, which represent his last sustained attempt to show what sort of man he was, and why he was not otherwise. Conceding that he failed in almost everything he tried to do, and that he was ending his career alone, he accepts these facts without complaint. Men "mounted on an abstract proposition," he explains, with obvious reference to himself, are almost always unattractive and unloved:

they trample on every courtesy and decency of behaviour; and though, perhaps, they do not intend the gross personalities they are guilty of, yet they cannot be acquitted of a want of due consideration for others, and of an intolerable egotism in the support of truth and justice. You may hear one of these Quixotic declaimers pleading the cause of humanity in a voice of thunder, or expatiating on the beauty of a Guido with features distorted with rage and scorn. This is not a very amiable or edifying spectacle.[37]

It is hard, he says, to "have all the world against us," [38] for it "unhinges" our opinion of our "motives and intentions," [39] but when we learn to trust ourselves and to rely on our emotions, we find that there are compensations. Who would "wear the livery of the world" if he has resources of his own? [40] He himself had learned the cost of independence, but he at least was his own man, and if his works were dull and misinformed and repetitious, as his urbane critics charged, they at least were honest, and his own.

To a want of general reading, I plead guilty, and am sorry for it; but perhaps if I had read more, I might have thought less. As to my barrenness of invention, I

* "On the Knowledge of the World" (1, 8, 15 December 1827), 17.290–303; "On Public Opinion" (19 January 1828), 17.303–308; "On the Causes of Popular Opinion" (16 February 1828), 17.308–313; "A Farewell to Essay-Writing" (29 March 1828), 313–320.
† "The Dandy School" (18 November 1827), 20.143–149. The tone of this review of Disraeli's *Vivian Grey* is suggested by the following passage (20.148): "At present, it should seem that a seat on Parnassus conveys a title to a box at the Opera, and that Helicon no longer runs water but champagne. Literature, so far from supplying us with intellectual resources to counterbalance immediate privations, is made an instrument to add to our impatience and irritability under them, and to nourish our feverish, childish admiration of external show and grandeur."

have at least glanced over a number of subjects — painting, poetry, prose, plays, politics, parliamentary speakers, metaphysical lore, books, men, and things. There is some point, some fancy, some feeling, some taste shown in treating of these. Which of my conclusions has been reversed? Is it what I said ten years ago of the Bourbons which raised the war-whoop against me? Surely all the world are of that opinion now. I have, then, given proofs of some talent, and of more honesty: if there is haste or want of method, there is no common-place, nor a line that licks the dust; and if I do not appear to more advantage, I at least appear such as I am."[41]

These excogitations find their most affecting statement in the superb "Farewell to Essay-Writing," which, if he had written nothing else, would secure his place in English letters. This apologia for a life then drawing to its close presents the man and writer at his best, for it enables us to feel, and even understand, his valor, taste, and skill. Its vignette of Charles and Mary Lamb when they first came to Winterslow and its softly cadenced peroration, where pathos rests on common sense, is one of Hazlitt's triumphs.[42]

With these and other things contrived to bring him a little money he was no doubt busy through the fall and early winter of 1827–28, but also, as he informed Charles Cowden Clarke early in December, he was "nearly in the other world" with illness. "I got a violent spasm by walking fifteen miles in the mud, and getting into a coach with an old lady who would have the window open," he explained. "Delicacy, moderation, complaisance, the *sauviter in modo*, whisper it about, my dear Clarke, these are my faults and have been my ruin."[43] His convalescence was occupied, if not sweetened, by the composition of a set of dry, expository "outlines" on such topics as morals, law, and intellection. Of these the most important was the "Project for a New Theory of Civil and Criminal Legislation,"[44] which brought to its completion the schoolboy essay that he had started working on at Hackney more than thirty years before. None of these, it seems, was published in his lifetime.*

❖ ❖ ❖

What was mainly on his mind that fall, however, was the preparation of his magnum opus for the press. The publication, in January 1828,

---

* In a letter to David Constable on 10 January 1828 (*Life*, pp. 360f.) Hazlitt listed his topics as law, morals, the human mind, taste, political economy, and grammar. In 1836 the first of these (19.302–320) was published, in an abridged form, by Hazlitt's son as "Project for a New Theory of Civil and Criminal Legislation" in *Literary Remains*, and expanded fourteen years later for a collection of his father's works called *Winterslow*. All the others, with the exception of the piece on grammar (which has apparently not survived), have been printed by Howe from manuscript as follows: "Outline of Morals," 20.376–386; "Outlines of the Human Mind," 20.442–447; "Outlines of Taste," 20.386–391; "Outlines of Political Economy," 19.294–302. See *Memoirs*, I, xxxii.

of the first two volumes of *The Life of Napoleon Buonaparte* by the firm of Hunt and Clarke was the chief event of Hazlitt's later years, and indeed, in his opinion, the chief event of his career. When he was forty-four he had said that he would "like to leave some sterling work" behind him; [45] by 1825, as he implied to Medwin at Vevey, he had settled on a topic; [46] and thereafter, despite the hard hack work he did to make a living, it was his main concern almost until he died. Apart from Hazlitt's high intentions, virtually everything about the writing and the publication of this big, ambitious work is a matter of conjecture, but the few details we have show that there was trouble from the start. Even while the first two volumes were going through the press, for instance, the publishers, "in deference to advice," [47] decided to delete the preface. "I thought all the world agreed with me at present that Buonaparte was better than the Bourbons," Hazlitt wrote to Clarke in protest,

or that a tyrant was better than tyranny. In my opinion, no one of an understanding above the rank of a lady's waiting-maid could ever have doubted this, though I alone said it ten years ago. It might be impolicy then and now for what I know, for the world stick to an opinion in appearance long after they have given it up in reality. I should like to know whether the preface is thought impolitic by some one who agrees with me in the main point, or by some one who differs with me and makes this excuse not to have his opinion contradicted? In Paris (jubes regina renovare dolorem) the preface was thought a masterpiece, the best and only possible defence of Buonaparte, and quite new *there*! It would be an impertinence in me to write a Life of Buonaparte after Sir W[alter Scott] without some such object as that expressed in the preface. After all, I do not care a *damn* about the preface. It will get me on four pages somewhere else. Shall I retract my opinion altogether, and foreswear my own book? *

From Lamb's terse but penetrating comment — "Hazlitt's speculative episodes are capital; I skip the Battles" [48] — we know that he read, or read at, the first installment of the work, and so did Hunt and Robinson; † but otherwise, it seems, the publication went almost unnoticed. This fact is not surprising, for even stripped of its offensive preface *The Life of Napoleon Buonaparte* is Hazlitt's paean to the hopes that had inspired his youth, and it could not have pleased the British public that, the year before, had welcomed Scott's nine-volume demonstration

---

* *Memoirs*, II, 217. For Hazlitt's two other extant letters to Clarke about his book while it was going through the press at the start of 1828 see *Four Generations*, II, 188ff. "Do not suppose that I am vexed," the second of them closes; "I am only frightened." Although his publishers refused to yield about the preface, it was subsequently printed as a sort of prologue to the opening chapter (xxxi) of Volume III in 1830. In the Centenary Edition Howe returns it to its proper place.

† For Hunt's opinion see the *Companion*, 20 February 1828, p. 78. After "several" mornings spent in reading Hazlitt's work, Robinson (I, 356) decided that "as a narrative writer he is worthless, but his powers of thought are admirable. . . . I have had infinitely more pleasure in this book than in Walter Scott's *Life of Napoleon*."

of Napoleon as the bogey-man of Europe.* "The success of the great cause, to which I had vowed myself," he wrote in 1828, "was to me more than all the world," and it was not until he saw "the axe laid to the root" of his ideals that he knew how much he had to lose and suffer. "But my conviction of the right was only established by the triumph of the wrong; and my earliest hopes will be my last regrets." [49] Such valor — or forlorn defiance — helps us understand why Hazlitt pushed his work to its completion despite its poor reception and the failure of his publishers, by which he lost £200 and landed in the debtors' prison.†
After various delays, concerning which we have no certain knowledge, Volumes III and IV, together with the unsold stock of Volumes I and II, were published under the imprint of Effingham Wilson and Chapman and Hall in the year of Hazlitt's death, and if, as he had said, "the last pleasure of life is the sense of discharging our duty" [50] he no doubt died content.‡

Perhaps the kindest thing to say about such a monumental failure as *The Life of Napoleon Buonaparte* is that it deserves its reputation. There are splendors here and there, of course: the preface is a vibrant presentation of Napoleon as the child and champion of the Revolution, which itself is shown to be the clear assertion of a people's right to self-respect and freedom; Chapter III, from which we quoted often in the early pages of this book, is a brilliant evocation of reformers' hopes and fears as they were caught in the convulsive test of their ideals; the lurid treatment of the Terror [51] and of the horrors of the Russian winter [52] are proof of Hazlitt's skill with words. But these are not enough to save the elephantine work. Any modern reader would concede that Lamb did

---

* Five days after the appearance of Scott's *Napoleon* — for which Longman's had offered him 10,500 guineas (Scott, p. 241) — the publisher wrote a "grumbling" letter (Scott, p. 369) because he still had 700 unsold copies out of an edition of 5,000. "What would they have?" the author asked.

† In August 1829 Hazlitt, asking payment in advance for an *Edinburgh* review, explained to Macvey Napier that he would "not thus early appear in *forma pauperis*, but the loss of £200 on my life of Napoleon through the failure of Messrs. Hunt & Clarke has driven me to great straits at the present moment" (P. P. Howe, "Unpublished Letters of William Hazlitt," *Athenaeum*, 15 August 1919, p. 743). On Hazlitt's subsequent arrest for debt see below, page 467, and on the failure of the firm of Hunt and Clarke in April 1829 see Richard D. Altick, *The Cowden Clarkes* (1948), pp. 63f. See *Memoirs*, II, 235.

‡ The tangled bibliographical history of *The Life of Napoleon Buonaparte*, like so many other things about that massive work, requires a more extended treatment than it can be given here. Keynes (pp. 94–98) poses some of the outstanding problems. From a notice in the *Atlas* on 2 May 1830 (which Hazlitt may have written, for he had been working for that paper) it has been supposed that the completed work was published in the spring of 1830. However, all the extant copies that are dated 1830 contain a preface (13.353f.) and an index that are not the author's work, and so it is entirely possible that although he saw the book through proof he did not live to see its publication.

EPILOGUE

well to skip the battles, which are relentlessly detailed, and unless he shared the author's hero-worship he would even be unhappy with the "speculative episodes." Since, as a recent survey shows,* the work was to a large extent compiled instead of written — for of some thousand pages in the Centenary Edition almost eight hundred are paraphrased, translated, or transcribed — one should look for Hazlitt's contribution in those sections where he gives, or tries to give, the meaning of events. Most of these display the strength that he could always summon when his passions were involved, but anyone who knows his early work can see that they repeat, with damnable iteration, the convictions he had been expressing for twenty years or more. Thus he gives us, time and time again, his defense of revolution as a people's last defense against the usurpation of their natural rights,[53] his attacks upon the French as a vacillating nation unworthy of their champion,[54] his detestation of the Tories for waging war against reform,[55] and, most insistently and tediously, his foolish veneration of the god of his idolatry.† In short, *The Life of Napoleon Buonaparte*, though partisan and ill-informed, is Hazlitt's most mature assertion of opinions that, as he believed, were "in the nature of realities." [56] No reader can accept as fact, for instance, his bitter comment on the field of Waterloo — the sun that rose that day, he said, would set upon "the triumph of the despot and the slave throughout the world, and as long as it shall continue to roll round this orb of ours" [57] — but it conveys his version of the truth, and truth, as he had wisely said, "is not one, but many." [58]

THE END

Perhaps because he came to think that "a man should study to get through the world as he gets through St. Giles's — with as little annoyance and interruption as possible from the shabbiness around him," [1] Hazlitt's final years, between the appearance of Volumes I and II of his *Napoleon* and his death in 1830, are almost entirely unrecorded.

* Robert E. Robinson, *William Hazlitt's Life of Napoleon Buonaparte* (1959), pp. 15f. Mr. Robinson's careful and conclusive study of the sources (pp. 43–93) — which supersedes Howe's note (13.356) upon the subject — shows Hazlitt's heavy use and sometimes "virtual plagiarism" of the work of Antommachi, Bausset, Constant, Fain, Gourgaud, Hobhouse, Las Cases, Mignet, Montholon, O'Meara, Savary, Scott, Ségur, Southey, Thibaudeau, and Young.

† For example, 13.ix–x, 38, 317f., 14.181, 198 (on Napoleon's invasion of Switzerland), 224 (on the execution of the Duc d'Enghien), 236ff., 241, 15.21, 72n, 320. Only rarely does Hazlitt permit himself the kind of criticism that he made about Napoleon's Spanish policy (14.305) or about his refusal to emancipate the Russian serfs (15.45f.).

THE END

It was not that he was idle — for until the last few months he was working at his usual steady pace — but merely that he seemed to fade from view. "He lived alone in the midst of the metropolis," one of his acquaintances recalled, "a hermit, among two or three millions of living men." [2] In his essay "On the Fear of Death," which he wrote in 1822, he had said that he would like to see his shattered hopes "re-edified," produce one "sterling work," and have "some friendly helping hand" consign him to the grave, for he would then be "ready, if not willing to depart" and could write upon his tomb "GRATEFUL AND CONTENTED." [3] We may hope, and from his works we may infer, that some, at least, of these desires he thought he had attained before he died, but the record is too skimpy to be sure. Even in 1831, as Carlyle complained, one could not discover "how it really stood with him" as he ended his career,[4] and a century and a half have not dispelled the shadows where he flitted, like a shadow, as he approached the end.

The scrappy facts we have are quickly told. He was still at Winterslow when he dated his "Farewell to Essay-Writing" on 20 February 1828,[5] but he soon returned to London, where he served throughout the spring as drama critic for the *Examiner*.[6] The nature of his work, which was as much concerned with his "golden" memories of the stage as with the plays that he reviewed, is suggested by this flight on Mrs. Siddons:

Her person was made to contain her spirit; her soul to fill and animate her person. Her eye answered to her voice. She wore a crown. She looked as if descended from a higher sphere, and walked the earth in majesty and pride. She sounded the full diapason, touched all chords of passion, they thrilled through her, and yet she preserved an elevation of thought and character above them, like the tall cliff round which the tempest roars, but its head reposes in the blue serene! [7]

This was not entirely relevant to the drama of the day (for Mrs. Siddons had ended her career some twenty years before), but, as he himself remarked in apologizing for a long digression, "without sometimes going out of our way, we should hardly get to the end of our task." [8] By June he was again in Paris,[9] and no doubt busy with the second part of his *Napoleon*, but he turned up again at Winterslow that fall,[10] and there, it seems, he stayed until the task was done.

Although his major work, as he himself conceived of it, was finished, still he had to live, and so he scribbled on. "An author by profession," as he remarked about this time, knows nothing of repose.

He must write on, and if he had the strength of Hercules and the wit of Mercury, he must in the end write himself down:

EPILOGUE

And like a gallant horse, fallen in first rank,
Lies there for pavement to the abject rear,
O'er-run and trampled on.

He cannot let well done alone. He cannot take his stand on what he has already achieved, and say, Let it be a durable monument to me and mine, and a covenant between me and the world for ever! He is called upon for perpetual new exertions, and urged forward by ever-craving necessities. The *wolf* must be kept from the door: the *printer's devil* must not go empty-handed away.[11]

In addition to a solid contribution to the *New Monthly Magazine* in the fall of 1828 — the splendid two-part dialogue on "Self-Love and Benevolence" [12] — his "new exertions" at the time comprised a string of patchy little pieces for the *Atlas,* a weekly that was willing to accept, it seems, almost anything he wrote. He found his subjects — or his topics, rather — everywhere: in Cobbett's recent criticism of the Quakers,[13] the nefarious enterprise of Burke and Hare ("the resurrection men" of Edinburgh),[14] the richness of the English language [15] and the problems of its grammar,[16] the pretensions of phrenologists,[17] his scattered recollections of some famous men whom he had known,[18] whatever popped into his mind. His own opinion of this sorry stuff perhaps may be inferred from his remark that whereas "there is some dignity in a contest with power and acknowledged reputation," a conquest of "the sordid and the mean is itself a mortification, while a defeat is intolerable." [19] But if much of what he wrote was trash, among his bagatelles one finds a pair of knotty essays on aesthetics,[20] a little piece on logic,[21] and a set of meditations — mainly on a man's commitment to his own ideals [22] — that seem to shine with mellow wisdom. "The best way to prevent our running into the wildest excesses of prejudice and the most dangerous aberrations from reason," he said in one of them,

is, not to represent the two things as having a great gulph between them, which it is impossible to pass without a violent effort, but to show that we are constantly (even when we think ourselves most secure) treading on the brink of a precipice; that custom, passion, imagination, insinuate themselves into and influence almost every judgment we pass or sentiment we indulge, and are a necessary help (as well as hindrance) to the human understanding; and that, to attempt to refer every question to abstract truth and precise definition, without allowing for the frailty of prejudice, which is the unavoidable consequence of the frailty and imperfection of reason, would be to unravel the whole web and texture of human understanding and society.[23]

Also he revived, first for the *London Weekly Review* and then for the *Atlas,* the Northcote conversations that Campbell had abruptly dropped from the *New Monthly Magazine* in 1827 in deference to the Mudges.[24] Here he once again employs his old friend, the painter, as a spokesman for "the world" that he had long defied and that, as he himself believed, had taken its revenge. "You turn your back on the world, and fancy that they turn their backs on you," says Northcote. "This is a very dangerous principle. You become reckless of consequences. It leads to an abandonment of character. By setting the opinion of others at defiance, you lose your self-respect." Hazlitt answers that it may be so, and yet he stands his ground:

Taking one thing with another, I have no great cause to complain. If I had been a merchant, a bookseller, or the proprietor of a newspaper, instead of what I am, I might have had more money or possessed a town and country-house, instead of lodging in a first or second floor, as it may happen. But what then? . . . I rise when I please, breakfast *at length*, write what comes into my head, and after taking a mutton-chop and a dish of strong tea, go to the play, and thus my time passes.[25]

These conversations were a source of trouble to the end. When, in the last year of his life, Hazlitt set about collecting them — both the "Boswell Redivivus" series of 1826–27 and those of recent vintage — for publication as a book, the protests were renewed. Richard Rosdew, still smarting from the earlier altercation, warned Northcote that if any "*false* and *libellous* accounts of the Mudge family" were included in the work "the parties" would be brought to justice at the bar, whereupon Northcote, dissociating himself from the "Cursed papers" that caused him so much woe,* took the precaution of looking through the book, then already printed, to delete whatever was offensive. The fact that certain extant copies show some cancellations that were clearly made to please the Mudges explains this note that Hazlitt sent to Northcote two months before he died:

My dear Sir,
     I heard of the letter you sent me yesterday a week ago. The subject of complaint in it is one that occurred four years ago [in the "Boswell Redivivus" series], & is entirely & sedulously removed in the forth-coming work. What cause of alarm there is from the evil of passages that are struck out, I can not well comprehend. If there is to be the same outcry about these obnoxious expressions after they have been cancelled as before, they might as well have remained to

---

* Stewart C. Wilcox, "Hazlitt and Northcote," *ELH*, VII (1940), 326, quoting letters found in a copy of the *Conversations* owned by D. Nichol Smith. On 4 May 1833 the *Athenaeum* (pp. 279f.) printed a letter signed "Veritas" in strong defense of Hazlitt and the *Conversations*. There was no question of Hazlitt's violating Northcote's confidence, the writer says, for "there was no confidence. On the contrary, when one of the Conversations appeared in print, he [Northcote] said — 'It's beautiful! It's beautiful! My God! It brought me to life. I was in bed. I was almost dead. But when it was brought to me, it revived me. I read it six times over. It's beautiful,' &c. — and this was the case more than once. You will observe that, as Northcote knew all along that the Conversations were in a course of publication, *he must have talked for the purpose of having his sayings repeated.*" See 11.351f.

afford some rational ground for your fears & reproaches. At present, the first appear to me as entirely gratuitous as the others are (in what concerns the papers in their corrected state) unmerited on my part. I cannot pretend to say what the character you have drawn of me is in your letter to Mr Campbell, but I almost regret that the present subdued tone of the *Conversations* may be the means of depriving the world of another master-piece. I remain

> Dear Sir,
> with much respect
> and some little
> disappointment,
>> your obliged very
>> humble servant,
>>> W. Hazlitt.

Frith Street,
July 29th 1830.[26]

The publication, in September, of the book itself almost coincided with its author's death.

The last important product of these final years was a set of *Edinburgh* reviews.[27] When Macvey Napier, perhaps prompted by a graceful little essay in the *Atlas* on 21 June 1829 about Jeffrey's resignation,[28] invited him to re-establish the connection that had lapsed since 1824, Hazlitt said he would be "happy" to oblige.[29] Thus he set to work at once on Channing's *Sermons,* even though, as he explained to Napier, he feared he would not like the book. He followed this review, which was finished by the end of August, with a piece on Flaxman's *Lectures* for the October *Edinburgh,* and then, three months later, with one on Walter Wilson's massive *Memoirs* of Defoe — a book in which he was "*au fait,*" he said, and one that he would like to treat.[30] Finally, in March 1830, just before his weekly contributions to the *Atlas* ended, he asked for Godwin's *Cloudesley* if he could have a certain "latitude" of style, and the next month the review itself appeared. Thus ending his career as he had started it, as an *Edinburgh* reviewer, he used these final contributions to reassert the values that had informed his first reviews some fifteen years before. Channing, a man "full of pretensions, and void of offence," [31] represents to him the dangers of conformity, whereas Flaxman shows the baleful influences of an art tied down to "rules." His essay on Defoe, whom he interprets as a hero of Dissent, expresses his commitment to the "republicanism and puritanism" that, as he said elsewhere at the time, were his by "education and conviction"; [32] and his valedictory piece on Godwin is his last full-breathed repudiation of "reason" as the key to man's behavior. If we were other than we are, then Godwin's ethics might apply, he says, but when measured by the facts of life they are seen to be absurd. "To refuse to avail ourselves of mixed motives and imperfect obligations, in a creature like man, whose

THE END

'very name is frailty,' and who is a compound of contradictions, is to lose the substance in catching at the shadow." [33]

When Hazlitt said about Defoe that "to the last, when on the brink of death, he was on the verge of a jail" [34] he perhaps was thinking of himself. By the failure of the firm of Hunt and Clarke he not only lost the money that had been promised for *Napoleon*, [35] but also, it would seem, was held responsible for their other obligations. Whatever the details of these transactions, the brutal fact is clear that in the last year of his life he had to go to jail because he could not pay his debts. He had been arrested, Talfourd wrote to Mary Russell Mitford on 18 February 1830,

on one of those detestable Bills of that detestable firm of Hunt & Clarke for £150, all honestly earned by him, & is at a Lock-up House; — but I have endeavoured with the aid of Procter, who is a good fellow in spite of his verses, to induce Basil Montague to procure Bail for him, & I hope have succeeded. [36]

The lurid tale of Hazlitt's asking an acquaintance for a shilling because he had not eaten for two days was perhaps invented, [37] but his own bitter comments, made not long before he died, about the "littleness, uncertainty, suspicion, and mortification" that one encounters in his progress through the world were no doubt based on hard experience. [38] For the author of *An Essay on the Principles of Human Action* to say that he believed in "the theoretical benevolence, and the practical malignity of man" would otherwise be hard to understand. [39]

It was perhaps a matter of relief to him that his race was nearly run. "If we merely wish to continue on the scene to indulge our headstrong humours and tormenting passions," he had written years before, "we had better begone at once: and if we only cherish a fondness for existence according to the benefits we reap from it, the pang we feel at parting with it will not be very severe!" [40] Although we do not know why his contributions to the *Atlas* stopped in April 1830, it is likely that his "weak digestion" — a matter of complaint for several years * — was finally recognized as fatal. "All other things but our disorder and its cure seem less than nothing and vanity," he wrote about this time.

It assumes a palpable form; it becomes a demon, a spectre, an incubus hovering over and oppressing us: we grapple with it: it strikes its fangs into us, spreads its arms round us, infects us with its breath, glares upon us with its hideous aspect; we feel it take possession of every fibre and of every faculty; and we are at length so absorbed and fascinated by it, that we cannot divert our reflections from it for an instant, for all other things but pain (and that which we suffer

* See 10.286n, 12.354; Bonner, p. 260. Although Hazlitt's son described his father's disease as "a species of cholera" (*Literary Remains*, I, lxvi), it was probably cancer of the stomach.

most acutely,) appear to have lost their pith and power to interest. They are turned to dust and stubble.[41]

In the essays that he wrote that summer for the *New Monthly Magazine* one can almost feel the presence of the dying man. "The Free Admission," which shows the magic that the stage retained for him almost until the end, is a poignant farewell to the plays and players he had known.[42] "The Sick Chamber," which, like Donne's *Devotions,* turns illness into art, is an extraordinary attempt to record the consequences, psychological and other, of his own disease.[43] "The Letter-Bell," his last, most brilliant exercise in reminiscence, subtly interweaves his memories of the Revolution with his first staggering steps toward art, and it closes with a reference to the latest turn in French affairs — the expulsion of the Bourbons — which shows that he could still rejoice.[44] The "Three Glorious Days" that led to Charles X's abdication was like "a resurrection from the dead," he wrote in laying down his pen forever, for it proved that "liberty too has a spirit of life in it; and that the hatred of oppression is 'the unquenchable flame, the worm that dies not.' " [45]

Death at last laid hold of him with the customary indignities. In August he suffered another "violent attack" of the old "disorder" that had plagued him through the summer,[46] but from this one he did not recover. George Darling, the doctor who had taken care of Keats,[47] was called into attendance, and so was Carlyle's brother John,[48] but by mid-September it was clear, at least to James Hessey, that Hazlitt was a dying man.[49] None the less, his "pecuniary circumstances," to use his son's resounding phrase,[50] were so shaky that he worked, or tried to work, almost until the end. A note to Basil Montagu, which he wrote a week or so before he died, provides a melancholy gloss upon his own remark that "learning unconsecrated, unincorporated, unendowed, is no match for the importunate demands and thoughtless ingratitude of the reading public": [51]

September 1830

My Dear Sir,
    I am confined to my bed with illness, or I would have come out. The second vol. of the Titian is at p. 304, & I will be done this week. Could you in the course of today let me have 15£ on account to prevent law expences, which I dread? Ceci devient trop longue.
    I remain, Dear Sir, your truly obliged humble servt.,

W. Hazlitt

[In another hand:] I believe the Mackintosh has been of service to me.*

* ALS in the possession of Sir Geoffrey Keynes. For the transcription of this letter, which was probably written on September 6, I am indebted to Professor H. M. Sikes. The "Titian" was no doubt Northcote's book about that artist (see page 451), and the "law expences" those resulting from the failure of the firm of Hunt and Clarke.

THE END

He was so "ghastly, shrunk, and helpless" when Procter went to see him in his Frith Street lodgings that he could hardly speak, even in a whisper. "I never was so sensible of the power of Death before," the visitor recalled.[52] On Saturday, September 18, at four-thirty in the afternoon, Hazlitt's struggle ended. His son was with him when he died, and so were Hessey and one Edward White, but it was no doubt Lamb who most fully understood his dying words: "Well, I've had a happy life."[53]

He was buried five days later in the nearby churchyard of St. Anne's, with Lamb and Patmore as the only mourners.* Busy, brawling Wardour Street was a fitting place for Hazlitt's grave, Leigh Hunt reflected when he happened to be passing through it not long after, for "love, hate, business, pleasure, books or no books, laughter and tears, — nothing was indifferent to him that affected mankind."[54]

IN RETROSPECT

There were times, toward the end, when Hazlitt liked to think that he had lived his life "in a dream or trance on the side of the hill of knowledge," where he "fed on books, on thoughts, on pictures, and only heard in half-murmurs the trampling of busy feet, or the noises of the throng below."[1] Although probably as true as most attempts at self-appraisal, this pastoral fiction seems particularly inappropriate for one whose efforts and achievements were so great, and whose works fill twenty volumes. Despite the difficulty, as he put it, of inferring what people are from what they write,[2] it is clear that he was not a languid man. "To do any thing," he said, "to dig a hole in the ground, to plant a cabbage, to hit a mark, to move a shuttle, to work a pattern, — in a word, to attempt to produce any effect, and to *succeed*, has something in it that gratifies the love of power, and carries off the restless activity of the mind of man."[3] His own career exemplified this dictum. No one can read him long without responding to the vigor of his thought and style, for he wrote with a steady, throbbing power that seems to generate a torrent of ideas and then to shape them, with easy authority, into the

---

* In his annotated copy of Talfourd's *Final Memorials of Charles Lamb*, where it is said (II, 178) that "Lamb joined a few friends" in attending Hazlitt's funeral, Patmore wrote: "Not 'a few' — only *one* — myself. This is the third or fourth time that this error has been repeated — as if in consciousness of the shame attending the fact. P. G. P. He (C.L.) gave all orders about the funeral." See Joanna Richardson, "P. G. Patmore on Lamb and Hazlitt," *TLS*, 19 June 1953, p. 397.

ordonnance of prose. Often sentimental but never flaccid, copious but never thin, he worked from great reserves of strength. He had a "demon," Keats explained,[4] and he epitomized the "gusto" which he himself defined as "power."[5]

His work is marked by careless ease, which means that it tends to be uneven. There is a certain bravado in everything he did. "He who stops to reflect, to balance one thing against another, is a coward," he asserted. "The better part of valour is indiscretion."[6] In life and art and books he liked fervor, color, and intensity. "Downright passion," he said at the start of his career, "unconquerable prejudice, and unaffected enthusiasm, are always justifiable; they follow a blind, but sure instinct; they flow from a real cause; they are uniform and consistent with themselves."[7] Because he was incapable of detachment, humor (except for savage irony) lay beyond his reach, and to elegance he refused to stoop; yet he had a giant command of language, and he used it with a giant's power. Mere style, he told a hostile critic, did not greatly interest him: his only goal was truth, and in seeking it he "sometimes found beauty."[8] Trusting only in his own emotions and assuming that what was deeply felt was also likely to be "true," he built his passions into an ethic and aesthetic where reason, prudence, and constraint could find no place. Sometimes, when he luxuriates in sentiment or, shrill with rage, leaps upon his prey, he soils his own great gifts, but he is usually saved by his intelligence and taste; and at its best his work reposes on what Leigh Hunt called his intellectual tact.[9] He is a strange, disreputable creature, Coleridge said in 1803, but "He sends well-headed & well-feathered Thoughts straight forwards to the mark with a Twang of the Bowstring."[10] Fifteen years later, when Hazlitt was no less strange but much more famous, Keats announced that his "depth of Taste" was one of the glories of the age.[11] Indeed, for him taste and feeling were almost everything. His predominant ideas — political, philosophical, and literary — can startle no one with their freshness, yet few men have a surer claim to intellectual independence. Lacking a real creative mind, he found a certain compensation in arrogant integrity, and he earned the right to his opinions with an effort that greater men (like Coleridge) and lesser but more facile men (like Jeffrey) were not obliged to make. Having hacked his way to his convictions, he expressed them with an exhilaration all his own. His energy was ultimately a function of character.

Except to a heroic few like Procter and the Lambs — and even they were sometimes overtaxed — his friendship was an exercise in patience. Dissenting from almost all received opinions, and too maladroit or proud to face the petty compromises that more prudent people meet with smiles or sighs, he nurtured his convictions until, sometimes, they grew into fixations. Without the gift of humor, the greatest of the unbought graces, he was unarmed against his own absurdities, and consequently in combatting knaves and fools he relied too much on moral indignation. His adversaries — an immense majority — might call his manners horrid, his education thin, his reading meager, his politics outrageous, and his morals contemptible; but they were obliged to grant him a devotion to his own ideals. On this point, at least, he himself concurred. "If my opinions are not right," he said in 1821, "at any rate they are the best I have been able to form, and better than any others I could take up at random, or out of perversity, now." [12] In a world of slippery men and "mechanical" beliefs, he knew, such constancy might cost a heavy price, but he would not be "brow-beat or wheedled" out of the convictions that he had made his own. "Opinion to opinion," he would challenge anyone, he said, for "where the pursuit of truth has been the habitual study of any man's life, the love of truth will be his ruling passion." [13]

If we are made uneasy by such cocksure talk of "truth" we should remember that a truculent probity served Hazlitt as a kind of signature. "An honest man," he said, "is one whose sense of right and wrong is stronger than his anxiety that others should think or speak well of him." [14] At its best this candor is his most engaging characteristic; at its worst it hardens into bigotry. No man can resist him when he writes on his deathbed that he has never given the lie to his own soul or changed his beliefs for the sake of profit or convenience. "There is at least a thorough *keeping* in what I write — not a line that betrays a principle or disguises a feeling. If my wealth is small, it all goes to enrich the same heap; and trifles in this way accumulate to a tolerable sum." [15] It is less attractive to hear him praise Guy Fawkes — admittedly a "cruel, bloody-minded" bigot — because "downright, rooted, rancorous prejudices are honest, hearty, wholesome things," [16] or to watch him lash in fury the physical and moral infirmities of those with whom he disagreed.

Since journalism rarely makes for the wholeness, harmony, and radiance of art, no one who writes as much for publication as he did can always write his best; but allowing for the pressures under which he wrote some three million words of copy in twenty years, we must concede that to his own emotions he was never false. It is as Diderot somewhere says: our truest opinions are not those we have never changed, but those to which we most often return. Brooding over an idea until it became "a kind of substance" in his brain, [17] he nurtured his aversions and desires until, as many thought, he became a freak. But

EPILOGUE

Hazlitt would not wish it otherwise: "If I have had few real pleasures or advantages, my ideas, from their sinewy texture, have been to me in the nature of realities; and if I should not be able to add to the stock, I can live by husbanding the interest." [18] For him, as for Rousseau, revery was an intoxicating instrument of self-knowledge, introspection a narcotic for soothing or evading ills of life, and memory a retreat to that distance in space and time where enchantment lay. Without the learning, the tranquillity, and the solvency that would, in other men, make for systematic thought and ordered exposition, he could at least rejoice in the depth and force of his emotions; and it was these, as his admirers knew, that made him great. To his dismay Coleridge and Wordsworth had shown that men might change their minds — "a thing unsightly and indecent!" [19] — but the ideas, books, and pictures that had thrilled him as a boy thrilled him as a man, and he boasted that they would last him to the end. "This continuity of impression is the only thing on which I pride myself," [20] he said.

The most egregious and expensive of his loyalties was to the French Revolution. In an age of triumphant Toryism most prudent men had abandoned libertarian ideals with the other follies of their youth, but Hazlitt found it unnecessary, as he said, to collate his opinions with received prejudices. [21] His political ideas, rooted in the Dissenting commonplaces of his boyhood and focused on the Revolution as the symbol of a golden age, were his penates, and he himself was the keeper of the sacred flame. He had set out in life with the Revolution, and for him it had a luster and a rapture that time could not destroy. "It was the dawn of a new era, a new impulse had been given to men's minds, and the sun of Liberty rose upon the sun of Life in the same day, and both were proud to run their race together." [22] The fact that the race had failed was obliterated by the glory of its start, for its hopes, its vision, and its hero inspired him to the end. He defiantly worshiped Napoleon when the name of the Corsican tyrant was used to frighten children and the effort to destroy him had united all Europe against a monstrous peril. The child and champion of the Revolution became for him the symbol of reform, and the last great effort of his pen was to venerate his fallen god. "My conviction of the right was only established by the triumph of the wrong; and my earliest hopes will be my last regrets." [23]

When Hazlitt told Coleridge that he had not changed any of his opinions since he was sixteen, "Why then," answered Coleridge, "you are no wiser now than you were then!" [24] Hazlitt did not concede the inference. He was a man of "principle," he said, and principle he defined as "a passion for truth; an incorrigible attachment to a general proposition." [25] Despite his proud allegiance to such abstractions as liberty and benevolence, however, his principles were rooted in his own emotional response to facts rather than in facts themselves or in inferences logically derived from them. Like most men, he lived by feeling, not by thought. The vital center was himself, and his acute awareness of and respect for his personal identity were the focus of his values in morals, art, and politics. Probity, consistency, and even egotism help to define his notion of personal identity, and so does an occasional maudlin obsession with his own exacerbated states of feeling; but whatever form it takes, it lies at the center of his work. His aggressive individualism stamps itself on everything he wrote. It is seen in his profound, and profoundly English, respect for "facts," sensation, and experience, and conversely in his contempt for the "general truths" of reason and analysis. It informs his recurrent metaphors of heart and mind as the mutually exclusive principles of human action. It explains his extraordinary capacity for dredging up and reworking the data of sensation. It gives tonality to the echoing reverberations of revery in his later essays. It inspires his contempt for "corporate bodies" — academic, political, and ecclesiastical — and it helps us understand his dogged and often uncritical advocacy of lost causes. No matter where we open Hazlitt's work we feel the presence of the man and hear his tone of voice.

Therefore he retains his hold on our affections. "We leave it to others to be shrewd, ingenious, witty and wise," he once remarked in his offhand manner; "to think deeply, and write finely; it is enough for us to be exactly dull." [26] Perhaps because he always deprecated his own work, perhaps because, as one much vilified in his own time, he doubted that posterity, which tends to rest upon the verdict of a man's contemporaries, would take the pains to try the same case twice, [27] he did not expect to be remembered. The event has proved him wrong, of course; but if two collected editions and a small library of critical and biographical studies disqualify him as the prophet of his own oblivion, at any rate they underscore another of his favorite notions: that only time, whose judgment cannot be wooed or bought, decides a writer's reputation. "Genius is the heir of fame," he said, "but the hard condition on which the bright reversion must be earned is the loss of life." He warned those eager for a quick renown that fame is not to be confused with temporary success. It is not

the idle buzz of fashion, the venal puff, the soothing flattery of favour or of friendship; but it is the spirit of a man surviving himself in the minds and thoughts of other men, undying and imperishable. It is the power which the intellect exercises over the intellect, and the lasting homage which is paid to it,

EPILOGUE

as such, independently of time and circumstances, purified from partiality and evil-speaking. Fame is the sound which the stream of high thoughts, carried down to future ages, makes as it flows — deep, distant, murmuring evermore like the waters of the mighty ocean.[28]

Perhaps because he dared not look for such a guerdon, he has found it after all.

SHORT FORMS OF CITATION

NOTES ❖ ❖ ❖ INDEX

SHORT FORMS OF CITATION

All references to Hazlitt's works are to the Centenary Edition (21 vols., 1930–1934) by P. P. Howe, and are given thus, 18.305, the first number referring to the volume and the second to the page. Substantive references are printed as footnotes, but all others (which are indicated by superscript numbers) are brought together at the end.

For works frequently cited these short forms are used throughout:

BONNER	*The Journals of Sarah and William Hazlitt 1822–1831,* ed. Willard Hallam Bonner, The University of Buffalo Studies, Vol. XXIV, No. 23, 1959
BOSWELL	James Boswell, *Life of Johnson,* Oxford Standard Authors, 1957
BURKE	*The Works of the Right Honorable Edmund Burke,* 9th ed., 12 vols., 1889
BYRON, *Correspondence*	*Lord Byron's Correspondence,* ed. John Murray, 2 vols., 1922
CLARKE	Charles and Mary Cowden Clarke, *Recollections of Writers,* 1878
COCKBURN	Henry Thomas, Lord Cockburn, *Life of Lord Jeffrey,* 2 vols., 1852
COLERIDGE, *Biographia Literaria*	*Biographia Literaria,* ed. John Shawcross, 2 vols., 1907
—— *Essays*	*Essays on His Own Times,* 3 vols., 1850
—— *The Friend*	*The Friend: A Series of Essays to Aid in the Formation of Fixed Principles, in Politics, Morals, and Religion, with Literary Amusements Interspersed,* Bohn's Standard Library, 1899
—— *Letters*	*Letters of Samuel Taylor Coleridge,* ed. Ernest Hartley Coleridge, 2 vols., 1895
—— *Notebooks*	*The Notebooks of Samuel Taylor Coleridge,* ed. Kathleen Coburn, 1957 —
—— *Poems*	*The Poems of Samuel Taylor Coleridge,* ed. Ernest Hartley Coleridge, Oxford Standard Authors, 1912
—— *Table Talk*	*The Table Talk and Omniana of Samuel Taylor Coleridge,* Oxford Edition, 1917
—— *Unpublished Letters*	*Unpublished Letters of Samuel Taylor Coleridge,* ed. Earl Leslie Griggs, 2 vols., 1932
CONSTABLE	Thomas Constable, *Archibald Constable and His Literary Correspondents,* 3 vols., 1873
COTTLE	Joseph Cottle, *Reminiscences of Samuel Taylor Coleridge and Robert Southey,* 1847
DE QUINCEY	*The Collected Writings of Thomas De Quincey,* ed. David Massion, 14 vols., 1889–1890
DOUADY	Jules Douady, *Liste Chronologique des Oeuvres de William Hazlitt,* 1906

SHORT FORMS OF CITATION

ELH	[*Journal of English Literary History*]
Four Generations	W. C. Hazlitt, *Four Generations of a Literary Family*, 2 vols., 1897
GODWIN'S DIARY	The manuscript diary of William Godwin, Abinger Collection, Duke University
GODWIN, *Political Justice*	William Godwin, *Enquiry Concerning Political Justice and Its Influence on Morals and Happiness*, 3d ed., 1798
GRIGGS	*Collected Letters of Samuel Taylor Coleridge*, ed. Earl Leslie Griggs, 1956 —
HAYDON, *Autobiography*	*The Autobiography and Memoirs of Benjamin Robert Haydon*, A New Edition with an Introduction by Aldous Huxley, 2 vols. [1926]
—— *Correspondence and Table-Talk*	*Benjamin Robert Haydon: Correspondence and Table-Talk. With a Memoir by His Son, Frederic Wordsworth Haydon*, 2 vols., 1876
—— *Diary*	*The Diary of Benjamin Robert Haydon*, ed. Willard Bissell Pope, 1960 —
Hazlitts, The	W. C. Hazlitt, *The Hazlitts: An Account of Their Origin and Descent*, 1911
HUNT, *Autobiography*	*The Autobiography of Leigh Hunt*, With an Introduction by Edmund Blunden, Oxford World's Classics, 1928
—— *Correspondence*	*The Correspondence of Leigh Hunt. Edited by His Eldest Son* [Thornton Hunt], 2 vols., 1862
—— *Essays*	*Essays of Leigh Hunt*, ed. Reginald Brimley Johnson, The Temple Library, 1891
—— *Poetical Works*	*The Poetical Works of Leigh Hunt*, ed. H. S. Milford, 1923
JEFFREY, *Contributions*	Francis Jeffrey, *Contributions to the Edinburgh Review*, 1854
JEGP	*Journal of English and Germanic Philology*
JOHNSON, *Works*	*The Works of Samuel Johnson, LL.D.*, 9 vols., 1825
Keats Circle, The	*The Keats Circle: Letters and Papers 1816–1878*, ed. Hyder Edward Rollins, 2 vols., 1948
KEYNES	Geoffrey Keynes, *Bibliography of William Hazlitt*, 1931
LAMB, *Works*	*The Works in Prose and Verse of Charles and Mary Lamb*, ed. Thomas Hutchinson, 2 vols., Oxford Edition, n.d.
LANDSEER	Thomas Landseer, *Life and Letters of William Bewick*, 2 vols., 1871
L'ESTRANGE	*The Life of Mary Russell Mitford . . . Related in a Selection from Her Letters to Her Friends*, ed. A. G. L'Estrange, 3 vols., 1870
Life	P. P. Howe, *The Life of William Hazlitt*, New edition with an Introduction by Frank Swinnerton, 1947
Literary Remains	*Literary Remains of the Late William Hazlitt*, ed. William Hazlitt, 2 vols., 1836

SHORT FORMS OF CITATION

LOCKHART	John Gibson Lockhart, *Memoirs of the Life of Sir Walter Scott*, 5 vols., 1902
LUCAS	*The Letters of Charles Lamb to Which Are Added Those of His Sister Mary Lamb*, ed. E. V. Lucas, 3 vols., 1935
MACAULAY, *Essays*	*Critical and Historical Essays Contributed to the Edinburgh Review by Lord Macaulay*, ed. F. C. Montague, 3 vols., 1903
MACKINTOSH	Robert James Mackintosh, *Memoirs of the Life of the Right Honourable Sir James Mackintosh*, 2d ed., 2 vols., 1836
MACLEAN	Catherine Macdonald Maclean, *Born under Saturn: A Biography of William Hazlitt*, 1943
MEDWIN	Thomas Medwin, "Hazlitt in Switzerland: A Conversation, *Fraser's Magazine*, XIX (1839), 278–283
Memoirs	W. C. Hazlitt, *Memoirs of William Hazlitt. With Portions of His Correspondence*, 2 vols., 1867
MLN	*Modern Language Notes*
MLQ	*Modern Language Quarterly*
MLR	*Modern Language Review*
MOORE	Thomas Moore, *Memoirs, Journal, and Correspondence*, ed. Lord John Russell, 8 vols., 1853–1856
MP	*Modern Philology*
NAPIER	*Selection from the Correspondence of the Late Macvey Napier, Esq.*, ed. Macvey Napier, 1879
OLIPHANT	M. O. Oliphant, *Annals of a Publishing House: William Blackwood and His Sons*, 3 vols., 1897
PAINE	*Thomas Paine: Representative Selections*, ed. Harry Hayden Clark, American Writers Series, 1944
PARTINGTON	*The Private Letter-Books of Sir Walter Scott*, ed. Wilfred Partington, 1930
PAUL	C. Kegan Paul, *William Godwin: His Friends and Contemporaries*, 2 vols., 1876
PATMORE	P. G. Patmore, *My Friends and Acquaintance*, 3 vols., 1854
PMLA	[*Publications of the Modern Language Association of America*]
POPE	The manuscript diary of Benjamin Robert Haydon, now in the possession of Willard Bissell Pope of Burlington, Vermont
PROCTER	Bryan Waller Procter, *An Autobiographical Fragment and Biographical Notes*, 1877
PROTHERO	*The Works of Lord Byron . . . Letters and Journals*, ed. Rowland E. Prothero, 6 vols., 1898–1901
RES	*Review of English Studies*
ROBINSON	*Henry Crabb Robinson on Books and Their Writers*, ed. Edith J. Morley, 3 vols., 1938

SHORT FORMS OF CITATION

ROGERS	*Recollections of the Table-Talk of Samuel Rogers. To Which Is Added Porsoniana,* ed. Alexander Dyce, 1856
ROLLINS	*The Letters of John Keats 1814–1821,* ed. Hyder Edward Rollins, 2 vols., 1958
SCHNEIDER	Elisabeth Schneider, *The Aesthetics of William Hazlitt,* 1933
SCOTT	*The Journal of Sir Walter Scott,* 1950
SHELLEY, *Letters*	*The Letters of Percy Bysshe Shelley,* ed. Roger Ingpen, 2 vols., 1914
SMILES	Samuel Smiles, *A Publisher and His Friends: Memoir and Correspondence of the Late John Murray,* 2 vols., 1891
SMITH, *Essays*	Sydney Smith, *Essays Social and Political,* n.d.
SMITH, *Letters*	*The Letters of Sydney Smith,* ed. Nowell C. Smith, 2 vols., 1953
SOUTHEY, *Life and Correspondence*	*The Life and Correspondence of Robert Southey,* ed. Charles Cuthbert Southey, 1851
TALFOURD	Thomas Noon Talfourd, *Final Memorials of Charles Lamb,* 2 vols., 1848
TLS	(London) *Times Literary Supplement*
WARTER	*Selections from the Letters of Robert Southey,* ed. John Wood Warter, 4 vols., 1856
WILLIAMS	Orlo Williams, *Lamb's Friend the Census-Taker: Life and Letters of John Rickman,* 1911
WORDSWORTH, *Early Letters*	*The Early Letters of William and Dorothy Wordsworth (1787–1805),* ed. Ernest de Selincourt, 1935
—— *Later Years*	*The Letters of William and Dorothy Wordsworth: The Later Years,* ed. Ernest de Selincourt, 3 vols., 1939
—— *Middle Years*	*The Letters of William and Dorothy Wordsworth: The Middle Years,* ed. Ernest de Selincourt, 2 vols., 1937
—— *Poetical Works*	*The Poetical Works of Wordsworth,* ed. Thomas Hutchinson, revised by Ernest de Selincourt, Oxford Standard Authors, 1953
—— *Prose Works*	*Prose Works of William Wordsworth,* ed. William Knight, 2 vols., 1896

NOTES

PART ONE

BEGINNINGS

I

Prologue

THE TRADITION OF DISSENT

1. *Christian Reformer*, V (1838), 701.
2. W. C. Hazlitt included excerpts from his great-aunt Margaret's diary in *Four Generations*, I, 9–61. The manuscript, now at the University of Delaware, is being edited by Ernest J. Moyne.
3. On the elder Hazlitt's later years see "Joseph Hunter on the Hazlitts," *Notes & Queries*, New Series IV (1957), 265f.
4. *Christian Reformer*, V (1838), 763.
5. 8.92.
6. 9.30.
7. 9.3.
8. 17.312.
9. 17.114.
10. 12.258, 17.116f.
11. 4.71, 8.258.
12. 12.61f.; cf. 17.197f.
13. Joseph Priestley, *An Essay on the First Principles of Government* (2d ed., 1771), p. 76; cf. p. 115.
14. Smith, *Essays*, p. 429; cf. pp. 501, 532.
15. Macaulay, *Essays*, II, 104.
16. Smith, *Essays*, p. 503; cf. Griggs, II, 806f.
17. 7.239.
18. 20.283.
19. Coleridge, *Table Talk*, p. 311.
20. Boswell, p. 441.
21. Priestley, *A Letter to the Right Honourable William Pitt* (1787), p. 17.
22. 13.48.
23. Rogers, p. 4.
24. 20.237.
25. Lucas, I, 11.
26. Jeffrey, *Contributions*, p. 492.
27. Rogers, p. 122.
28. Griggs, I, 372.
29. Richard Price, *Observations on the Nature of Civil Liberty* (5th ed., 1776), p. 6.
30. Price, *A Review of the Principal Questions and Difficulties in Morals* (1758), p. 190.
31. Price, *Observations on the Nature of Civil Liberty*, p. 32.
32. Price, *A Discourse on the Love of Our Country* (3d ed., 1790), p. 23.
33. David Bogue and James Bennett, *History of Dissenters from the Revolution in 1688, to the Year 1808* (1808–1812), IV, 424.
34. Priestley, *A Discourse on Occasion of the Death of Dr. Price* (1791), p. 9. In his diary (1 May 1791) Godwin records that he heard this sermon.
35. Priestley, *An Essay on the First Principles of Government*, p. 124.
36. *Ibid.*, p. 139.
37. *Ibid.*, p. 52.
38. *Boswell's Journal of A Tour to the Hebrides with Samuel Johnson, LL.D.* (ed. Frederick A. Pottle and Charles H. Bennett, 1936), p. 37.
39. Bogue-Bennett, *History of Dissenters*, III, 333f.
40. Paine, p. 106.
41. Smith, *Letters*, I, 374.
42. See John R. H. Moorman, *A History of the Church in England* (1954), pp. 276f.
43. William Warburton, *The Alliance between Church and State, or, the Necessity and Equity of an Established Religion and a Test-Law Demonstrated* (1736), pp. 121, 132, 154.
44. Leslie Stephen, *The English Utilitarians* (1900), I, 38f.
45. A. E. Rodway (ed.), *Godwin and the Age of Transition* (1952), p. 16.
46. D. C. Somervell, *English Thought in the Nineteenth Century* (1947), p. 17.
47. Mary Wollstonecraft, *A Vindication of the Rights of Man* (2d ed., 1790), p. 82.
48. Wordsworth, *Prose Works*, I, 4.
49. Coleridge, *Essays*, I, 46.
50. Coleridge, *Table Talk*, pp. 125f.; cf. p. 205.
51. Godwin, *Political Justice*, II, 234.
52. 7.251.
53. 17.114.
54. 19.323.

55. 12.315.
56. 19.319.
57. 17.325.
58. Priestley, *Letters to the Right Honourable Edmund Burke, Occasioned by His Reflections on the Revolution in France, &c.* (3d ed., 1791), p. 39.
59. Priestley, *The Doctrine of Philosophical Necessity Illustrated* (1777), p. 126; cf. p. 112.
60. Godwin, *Political Justice*, I, 123; Price, *A Discourse on the Love of Our Country*, p. 33.
61. John Williams, *Memoirs of the Late Reverend Thomas Belsham* (1833), p. 428.
62. Priestley, *An Essay on the First Principles of Government*, pp. 4f.
63. Priestley, *Letters to the Right Honourable Edmund Burke*, p. 155.
64. Price, *A Discourse on the Love of Our Country*, pp. 49ff.
65. 6.182.
66. 12.322.
67. 20.309; cf. 16.375.
68. 7.240.
69. 13.46f.; cf. 7.9.
70. 13.47.
71. 17.329.
72. 16.371.
73. 8.208.
74. 8.176, 181.
75. 12.322; cf. 9.191.
76. 17.88; cf. 20.266.
77. 20.308f.
78. 20.333f.
79. 4.47-51.
80. De Quincey, XI, 342; cf. Procter, p. 213.
81. James Mackintosh, *Miscellaneous Works* (1854), p. 455; cf. Godwin's attack on compulsory tests in *Political Justice*, II, 253-261, and Lamb's complaint to Southey, *Works*, I, 299f.
82. 7.273.
83. 19.303.

THE YOUNG DISSENTER

1. 12.230.
2. For the early letters, which are variously reproduced by W. C. Hazlitt in his works about his family, I follow the texts in *Memoirs*, I, 10-24, and *Four Generations*, I, 67ff.
3. William Hazlitt, Sr., *Human Authority, in Matters of Faith, Repugnant to Christianity* (1774), p. xi.
4. The remark, which Hazlitt himself

recalls (8.288f.), is perhaps based on an event recorded in one of his boyish letters from Liverpool in 1790 (*Four Generations*, I, 69).
5. *Four Generations*, I, 24.
6. Hazlitt, Sr., *Human Authority, in Matters of Faith, Repugnant to Christianity*, p. 52.
7. *Letters to and from Richard Price, D.D., F.R.S., 1767-1790* (1903), p. 64.
8. *A Thanksgiving Discourse, Preached at Hallowell, 15 December, 1785* (1786), p. 12. On the elder Hazlitt's other published sermons, the prose of which his son did not greatly like (17.111n), see *Memoirs*, I, 266n.
9. 6.182-185.
10. 7.241f.; 17.110.
11. 12.316.
12. 8.12f; cf. 12.108.
13. *Letters of Robert Southey: A Selection* (ed. Maurice H. Fitzgerald, 1912), p. 67.
14. Robinson, I, 7.
15. 7.241f.; cf. 17.245.
16. *London Magazine*, I (1820), 38.
17. 17.110.
18. 19.302.
19. Bogue-Bennett, *History of Dissenters*, IV, 309.
20. Boswell, p. 540.
21. Priestley, *A Letter to the Right Honourable William Pitt*, p. 38.
22. Griggs, I, 578. There is a useful account of Dissenting academies in Anthony Lincoln, *Some Political & Social Ideas of English Dissent, 1763-1800* (1938), pp. 66-100.
23. See Bogue-Bennett, *History of Dissenters*, II, 1-89, IV, 258-310.
24. Thomas Belsham, *Memoirs of the Late Reverend Theophilus Lindsey, M.A.* (1873), p. 186.
25. Daniel Lyson, *Environs of London* (1792-1811), III, 633f.
26. H. W. Stephenson, *William Hazlitt and Hackney College* (1930), p. 8.
27. *Gentleman's Magazine*, LXI (1791), 1023f.
28. Griggs, I, 577.
29. Belsham, *Memoirs of the Late Reverend Theophilus Lindsey*, pp. 186f.
30. Williams, *Belsham*, p. 446.
31. *Gentleman's Magazine*, LXVI (1796), 555f.; cf. Bogue-Bennett, *History of Dissenters*, IV, 266.
32. *Gentleman's Magazine*, LXVI (1796), 458f.
33. For example, *ibid.*, LX (1790), 793;

LXI (1791), 509f., 621f., 984; LXIII (1793), 396, 409, 618.

34. *Ibid.*, LXVI (1796), 519.

35. *Ibid.*, LXVI (1796), 955f. Further details about the melancholy end of Hackney College may be found in Lyson, *Environs of London*, IV, 628; VI, 169.

36. I follow the texts (but not the questionable dating and arrangement) of the letters as printed in *The Hazlitts*, pp. 398–408.

37. 19.302f.

38. 12.307.

39. Robinson, I, 6.

40. 8.312; cf. 12.224.

41. *Christian Reformer*, V (1838), 508, 763.

WINDS OF DOCTRINE

1. Williams, *Belsham*, p. 461.

2. Alan Lang Strout, "Knights of the Burning Epistle (the *Blackwood* Papers in the National Library of Scotland)," *Studia Neophilologica*, XXVI (1953–54), 90f.

3. Haydon, *Autobiography*, I, 255.

4. Luther A. Brewer (ed.), *My Leigh Hunt Library: The Holograph Letters* (1938), p. 169.

5. 8.76.

6. 4.128f.

7. 20.348.

8. 19.321.

9. 10.235f.

10. 11.232.

11. 14.130.

12. 12.177.

13. 14.130f.

14. 16.159; cf. 17.206f.

15. 7.270, 11.146, 19.174, 221, 323, 20.293f.

16. 14.130.

17. 10.215.

18. 14.132.

19. 12.177.

20. 14.132.

21. 17.261.

22. 7.258.

23. Burke, III, 368.

24. 7.243.

25. 7.245.

26. 7.246.

27. Burke, III, 246f.

28. 11.46.

29. 20.118; cf. 16.108.

30. 4.48; cf. 20.266.

31. 4.59.

32. 4.58.

33. 12.351.

34. 4.60.

35. 4.58.

36. 4.60.

37. 9.189.

38. 12.129.

39. 20.113; cf. 11.41.

40. 20.238.

41. 20.238.

42. 20.120.

43. 20.224.

44. 12.129f.

45. 20.224f.

46. 9.226.

47. 9.220.

48. Brewer, *My Leigh Hunt Library: The Holograph Letters*, p. 169.

49. 20.266.

50. 6.183ff.

51. 8.322–325.

52. 12.261.

53. Haydon, *Autobiography*, I, 253.

54. 17.110.

II

The Currents of Reform

THE PRESENT DISCONTENTS

1. Southey, *Poetical Works* (1838), I, xxix f.

2. Bogue-Bennett, *History of Dissenters*, IV, 197.

3. Priestley, *Letters to the Right Honourable Edmund Burke*, pp. 143f., 145.

4. *Christian Reformer*, V (1838), 510.

5. *The New Annual Register . . . for the Year 1793* (1794), "British and Foreign History," pp. 3ff.

6. Thomas Moore, *Memoirs of the Life of the Right Honourable Richard Brinsley Sheridan* (5th ed., 1827), II, 92.

7. Joel Barlow, *Political Writings* (1796), pp. iii, xvi.

8. Wordsworth, *The Prelude*, x.257–262.

9. Paul, I, 69.

10. 3.134.

11. See Patrick Colquhoun, *A Treatise on the Police of the Metropolis* (1797), pp. 30–46; cf. Ford K. Brown, *The Life of William Godwin* (1926), p. 19.

12. Godwin, *Political Justice*, I, 19.

13. Barlow, *Advice to the Privileged Orders* (1792) in *Political Writings*, p. xi.

14. Burke, V, 181.

15. James Mackintosh, *Vindiciae Gallicae*, in *Miscellaneous Works* (1854), p. 448.

16. Burke, II, 136.
17. Burke, II, 423.
18. Burke, II, 73.
19. Burke, II, 140.
20. Burke, I, 440f.
21. Burke, VI, 334.
22. Burke, VI, 340.
23. 13.50.
24. Burke, III, 422.
25. Burke, III, 397.
26. Burke, I, 526.
27. Burke, IV, 7f.
28. Burke, III, 281.
29. Burke, III, 344.
30. Burke, III, 336.
31. Burke, IV, 169.
32. Burke, II, 271.
33. Burke, II, 442.
34. Burke, VII, 71.
35. Burke, II, 357.
36. Wordsworth, *The Prelude*, vii.523–530.
37. Burke, V, 216.
38. Burke, I, 477.
39. Burke, V, 187.
40. Burke, III, 259.
41. Burke, III, 275.
42. Burke, II, 180.
43. Burke, II, 156.
44. Burke, III, 296.
45. Burke, IV, 322.
46. Burke, I, 437.
47. Burke, III, 416.

THE ADVOCATES OF CHANGE

1. Wordsworth, *Prose Works*, I, 25.
2. Mary Wollstonecraft, *A Vindication of the Rights of Man*, p. 74.
3. *Ibid.*, p. 144.
4. Sydney Smith, *Letters*, I, 63.
5. Mackintosh, I, 83.
6. Mackintosh, *Vindiciae Gallicae*, in *Miscellaneous Works*, p. 437.
7. *Ibid.*, p. 405.
8. *Ibid.*, p. 448.
9. *Ibid.*, p. 423.
10. *Ibid.*, p. 430.
11. *Ibid.*, p. 424.
12. 13.52.
13. Burke, III, 335.
14. Paine, p. 95.
15. Paine, p. 184; cf. pp. 61f.
16. Paine, p. 14.
17. Paine, pp. 16f.
18. Paine, p. 4.
19. Paine, p. 163.
20. Paine, p. 231.
21. Paine, p. 55. The phrase occurs in the preface to the French edition.

BURKE AND HAZLITT

1. 17.111.
2. 12.228.
3. 8.51.
4. *Four Generations*, I, 98.
5. 7.301n.
6. 12.52.
7. One of Hazlitt's most effective statements of this basic theme is "The New School of Reform," 12.179–195.
8. 16.268.
9. 11.141.
10. 11.137.
11. For a sampling of Hazlitt's many later statements of this theme — which has both literary and political implications — see 8.192, 11.28f., 12.235, 318, 17.209, 20.282, 311, 342.
12. 8.148.
13. 8.154.
14. 7.301.
15. 17.111.
16. 7.305.
17. 7.307.
18. 7.308.
19. 7.309.
20. 7.310.
21. 7.310.
22. 7.312f.
23. 7.227.
24. 7.228.
25. 7.229.
26. 7.229.
27. 19.167.
28. 4.105n.
29. 7.231.
30. 19.271f. These views also find expression in "Arguing in a Circle" (19.267–278), which, written for the *Liberal* in 1823, is one of Hazlitt's most moving essays on political apostasy.
31. 7.269.
32. 13.51.
33. 5.350.
34. 6.107.
35. 19.182–196.
36. 19.196.
37. 17.321.
38. 19.268.
39. 13.51f.
40. 12.10.
41. 12.100.
42. 6.280.
43. 12.10.

FRIENDS OF LIBERTY

1. 7.99.
2. *New Annual Register . . . for the*

Year 1793 (1794), "Domestic Literature," pp. 218f.

3. Robinson, I, 72.

4. *Christian Reformer*, V (1838), 510, 756; *Four Generations*, I, 99f.

5. Alexander Gilchrist, *Life of William Blake* (Everyman's Library, 1945), p. 79.

6. Griggs, I, 139. On Holcroft's atheism see Cottle, pp. 330f.

7. Coleridge, *Poems*, pp. 350ff.; Griggs, I, 589.

8. Griggs, I, 563.

9. Robinson, I, 5.

10. 17.133, 203n; 20.162.

11. Paul, I, 17.

12. Robert Bloomfield, *The Farmer's Boy* (4th ed., 1801), p. ix.

13. Joseph Fawcett, *Sermons Delivered at the Sunday-Evening Lecture, for the Winter Season, at the Old Jewry* (2d ed., 1801), I, 161–183.

14. *Ibid.*, I, 225–243.

15. *Ibid.*, II, 101–125.

16. 8.225. For a more favorable estimate of "an original, and very impressive poet" see the *New Annual Register . . . for the Year 1795* (1796), "Domestic Literature," pp. 279f.

17. *Gentleman's Magazine*, LXXIV (1804), 185.

18. 3.171n; 8.224f.

19. See Lucas, I, 417.

20. 8.224f.

21. Wordsworth, *The Excursion*, ii.221f., 263–266.

22. George McLean Harper, *William Wordsworth* (1916), I, 261; cf. M. Ray Adams, *Studies in the Literary Backgrounds of English Radicalism*, Franklin and Marshall Studies, No. 5 (1947), 191–226; Arthur Beatty, *Joseph Fawcett, The Art of War, Its Relation to the Early Development of William Wordsworth*, University of Wisconsin Studies in Languages and Literature, No. 2 (1918), *passim*.

23. Quoted by Adams, *Studies in the Literary Backgrounds of English Radicalism*, p. 224.

24. 4.116.

STRIPLING BARDS

1. De Quincey, II, 274.

2. Southey, *Life and Correspondence*, p. 72.

3. James Gillman, *The Life of Samuel Taylor Coleridge* (1838), p. 23.

4. Coleridge, *Essays*, I, 103.

5. Coleridge, *Poems*, p. 10.

6. Griggs, I, 152f.

7. Southey, *Life and Correspondence*, p. 334.

8. *Ibid.*, p. 70.

9. Griggs, I, 122; cf. Coleridge, *Poems*, pp. 72f.

10. Griggs, I, 114.

11. Griggs, I, 163.

12. Coleridge, *Poems*, pp. 68f. On the details of Pantisocracy see Mrs. Henry Sandford, *Thomas Poole and His Friends* (1888), I, 96–99; Southey, *Life and Correspondence*, p. 72; Griggs, I, 114; William Haller, *The Early Life of Robert Southey, 1774–1803* (1917), pp. 127–172.

13. Griggs, I, 103.

14. Griggs, I, 99.

15. Cottle, p. 22.

16. Coleridge, *Poems*, p. 75.

17. *Ibid.*, pp. 80, 81, 83f., 86.

18. Griggs, I, 121.

19. Tom Poole's nephew John, as quoted by James Dykes Campbell (ed.), *The Poetical Works of Samuel Taylor Coleridge* (1895), p. xxi n.

20. Griggs, III, 510.

21. Southey, *Joan of Arc*, iii.496–502 (*Poetical Works* [1838], I, 47f.) On Southey's enthusiasm for Rousseau at this period see his letter to G. C. Bedford, 16 March 1793 (*Life and Correspondence*, p. 64).

22. See pages 359–362.

23. Southey, *Poetical Works*, II, 25f., 54.

24. Southey, *Life and Correspondence*, p. 78; Cottle, pp. 13–19.

25. Griggs, I, 152.

26. Southey, *Life and Correspondence*, p. 80.

27. Griggs, I, 163.

28. Griggs, I, 216.

29. Coleridge, *Biographia Literaria*, I, 123.

30. Wordsworth, *Poetical Works*, p. 14.

31. Wordsworth, *The Prelude*, xi.235–244.

32. Wordsworth, "Guilt and Sorrow," *Poetical Works* (ed. Ernest de Selincourt, I [1940], 340f.) Another product of the same mood and period is "The Convict," which Wordsworth included in the first edition of *Lyrical Ballads* and never reprinted.

GODWIN

1. 11.16.

2. 20.259.

3. Bogue-Bennett, *History of Dissenters*, IV, 114.

4. 11.27.

5. See Jack W. Marken, "William Godwin's Writings for the *New Annual Register*," *MLN*, LXVIII (1953), 477ff.; "The Canon and Chronology of William Godwin's Early Works," *MLN*, LXIX (1954), 176–180.

6. Robinson, I, 14; Edward John Trelawny, *Records of Shelley, Byron, and the Author* (1878), II, 13; Lucas, I, 273, 304, 317.

7. Ford K. Brown, *The Life of William Godwin* (1926), p. 198.

8. 11.235.

9. Paul, I, 359.

10. Paul, II, 269.

11. Brown, *Godwin*, pp. 98f.

12. Robinson, I, 135.

13. Clarke, pp. 36f.

14. Lucas, I, 334.

15. Godwin, *Political Justice*, I, vii–xii.

16. Paul, I, 118.

17. Brown, *Godwin*, p. 17.

18. This general view of Godwin's system is derived from the "Summary of Principles" (I, [xxiii]–xxvii).

19. Godwin, *The Enquirer. Reflections on Education, Manners, and Literature. In a Series of Essays* (1797), pp. [v] f.; cf. *Political Justice*, I, 26.

20. Godwin, *Political Justice*, I, 55.

21. *Ibid.*, II, 453.

22. *Ibid.*, I, 14.

23. *Ibid.*, II, 233.

24. *Ibid.*, I, 86.

25. *Ibid.*, I, 422; cf. I, 56, 67f.

26. *Ibid.*, I, 68.

27. *Ibid.*, I, 433.

28. *Ibid.*, I, 430.

29. *Ibid.*, I, 238.

30. *Ibid.*, II, 35–47.

31. *Ibid.*, I, 245.

32. *Ibid.*, II, 2.

33. *Ibid.*, II, 508.

34. *Ibid.*, II, 510f.

35. *Ibid.*, II, 431–453.

36. *Ibid.*, I, 129.

37. *Ibid.*, II, 455.

38. *Ibid.*, I, 42f.

39. *Ibid.*, I, 49f.

40. *Ibid.*, I, 43. For Hazlitt's most sympathetic statement of the Godwinian ideal see his life of Holcroft, 3.134ff.

THE NATURAL MAN

1. Scott, p. 14.

2. Lamb, *Works*, I, 296.

3. Wordsworth, *The Prelude*, xi.139–144.

4. Godwin, *Political Justice*, I, 6, 12.

5. Coleridge, *Essays*, I, 17. For a similar statement by Southey long after he had turned against reform see *The Life of Horatio Lord Nelson* (Everyman's Library, 1906), pp. 133f.

6. 3.155.

7. Boswell, p. 359; cf. pp. 310ff.

8. 4.89n.

9. Godwin, *Political Justice*, I, 93.

10. 11.18.

11. 17.209; cf. 7.97ff.

12. 17.196f.; cf. 4.119f.

13. 3.132ff.

III

The Assault upon Reform

THE CONSERVATIVE REACTION

1. Scott, *Poetical Works* (ed. J. Logie Robertson, 1916), p. 90.

2. See Crane Brinton, *A Decade of Revolution, 1789–1799* (1934), pp. 167–174; W. T. Laprade, *England and the French Revolution, 1789–97* (1909), p. 125.

3. Coleridge, *Biographia Literaria*, I, 121.

4. Coleridge, *Essays*, I, 39f.

5. For example, see his comments (Griggs, I, 573) on Pitt as a "*stupid insipid Charlatan.*"

6. Robinson, I, 22. For Hazlitt's similar opinion see 7.75.

7. De Quincey, II, 169.

8. Williams, pp. 24f.

9. Wordsworth, *Early Letters*, p. 120.

10. Wordsworth, *Prose Works*, I, 116f. See Wordsworth's comments on Pitt's death in *Middle Years*, I, 7; *The Prelude*, x.300–314.

11. Smith, *Letters*, I, 112; cf. II, 778.

12. Paul, II, 155. See *Four Generations*, I, 98, for Hazlitt's comments on Godwin's sketch of Pitt.

13. 1.113.

14. 14.137.

15. *New Annual Register . . . for the Year 1792* (1793), "Public Papers," p. 60.

16. Jeffrey, *Contributions*, p. 210.

17. Macaulay, *Essays*, II, 61.

18. Boswell, p. 7.

19. 3.141.

20. Coleridge, *Essays*, I, 118.

21. Southey, *Letters from England* (ed. Jack Simmons, 1951), p. 34.

22. Rogers, p. 141.

23. Smith, *Letters*, I, 205.
24. William Blake, *Letters* (ed. Geoffrey Keynes, 1956), p. 94.
25. Thomas Mathias, *Pursuits of Literature* (13th ed., 1805), pp. 20, 62. For Mathias' comments on the reformers of the nineties see pp. 370ff., and for his coarse attack on Godwin, pp. 387–396.
26. *Poetry of the Anti-Jacobin* (ed. L. Rice-Oxley, 1924), p. 77.
27. *Anti-Jacobin* (5th ed., 1803), I, 7.
28. *Ibid.*, II, 228, 264.
29. *Poetry of the Anti-Jacobin*, p. 175.
30. Coleridge, *Biographia Literaria*, I, 49n.
31. Griggs, I, 552.
32. E. K. Chambers, *Samuel Taylor Coleridge: A Biographical Study* (1938), p. 121.

THE TREASON TRIALS

1. Burke, V, 285.
2. W. P. Hall, *British Radicalism 1781–1797* (1912), pp. 160f.
3. *Memoirs of Thomas Hardy . . . Written by Himself* (1832), p. 13.
4. Thomas Moore, *Memoirs of the Life of the Right Honourable Richard Brinsley Sheridan* (5th ed., 1827), II, 222f. Sheridan's comments are underscored by William Hone's account of his induction into the Corresponding Society as a youth of sixteen. See Frederick W. Hackwood, *William Hone: His Life and Times* (1912), p. 53.
5. Hall, *British Radicalism*, pp. 178–181.
6. Hardy, *Memoirs*, p. 10.
7. Robert Birley, *The English Jacobins from 1789 to 1802* (1924), pp. 49f.
8. Hardy, *Memoirs*, p. vii.
9. *Ibid.*, pp. 14ff., 21.
10. Paul, I, 127.
11. James Grant, *Cassell's Old and New Edinburgh* (1883), II, 107.
12. Paul, I, 137.
13. 3.142.
14. Rogers, p. 127.
15. Godwin, *Cursory Strictures on the Charge of Chief-Justice Eyre* (1794), pp. 13, 20.
16. 11.26.
17. Paul, I, 119.
18. Hardy, *Memoirs*, p. 46.
19. 11.27n. Godwin himself records the anecdote in his diary (29 January 1809) and more elaborately in a note reprinted by Paul, I, 147. For a full contemporary account of the treason trials of 1794, including the preliminary debates in Parliament, see the *New Annual Register . . . for the Year 1794* (1795), "British and Foreign History," pp. 187–287.
20. George Macaulay Trevelyan, *British History in the Nineteenth Century and After (1782–1919)* (1937), p. 71.
21. Kenneth Neil Cameron, *The Young Shelley* (1950), p. 46.
22. 8.109; cf. 9.27.
23. *Anti-Jacobin*, I, 466.
24. Godwin, *Thoughts Occasioned by the Perusal of Dr. Parr's Spital Sermon* (1801), p. 7.

THE POETICAL APOSTATES

1. Godwin, *Thoughts Occasioned by the Perusal of Dr. Parr's Spital Sermon*, p. 2.
2. 11.17.
3. *Anti-Jacobin*, I, 195–199.
4. Mackintosh, I, 149f.
5. De Quincey, XI, 327f.
6. Godwin, *Thoughts*, pp. 21f.
7. Coleridge, *Poems*, p. 86.
8. Griggs, I, 141n.
9. For example, see Godwin, *Memoirs of the Author of a Vindication of the Rights of Woman* (1798), pp. 120f.
10. Southey, *Life and Correspondence*, p. 67.
11. *Ibid.*, p. 81; cf. p. 84.
12. Coleridge, *Notebooks*, no. 1658.
13. Coleridge, *Essays*, I, 135f.
14. *Ibid.*, I, 163f.
15. Griggs, I, 267.
16. Griggs, I, 138.
17. Griggs, I, 215.
18. Griggs, I, 549.
19. Griggs, I, 221.
20. Coleridge, *Table Talk*, p. 189.
21. Coleridge, *Poems*, p. 119.
22. *Ibid.*, pp. 121f.
23. Wordsworth, *Early Letters*, pp. 115f.
24. 11.17.
25. Wordsworth, *The Prelude*, ix.288–552.
26. *Ibid.*, x.270.
27. Wordsworth, *Early Letters*, p. 121.
28. *Ibid.*, pp. 121f.
29. *Ibid.*, pp. 119f.
30. *The Prelude*, x.583–589.
31. On the complicated revisions of "Guilt and Sorrow," one version of which was printed in *Lyrical Ballads* as "The Female Vagrant," see *Poetical Works* (ed. Ernest de Selincourt), I (1940), 330–335; cf. De Selincourt's discussion of Godwin's

influence on Wordsworth in his edition of *The Prelude* (1926), pp. 603–606.

32. *The Prelude*, xi.279–282.
33. *Ibid.*, xi.294f.
34. *Ibid.*, xi.304f.
35. Wordsworth, *Poetical Works*, p. 699.
36. Quoted by Bateson, *Wordsworth*, p. 185, from a manuscript presumably written at Goslar in the winter of 1799 and now preserved at Grasmere.
37. Wordsworth, *Poetical Works*, p. 377.

MACKINTOSH AND PARR AND MALTHUS

1. Quoted by Brown, *Godwin*, pp. 154f.
2. Paul, I, 378.
3. Mackintosh, I, 87–90.
4. 11.100.
5. Robinson, III, 842.
6. Mackintosh, *Miscellaneous Works*, pp. 41, 43, 35.
7. Mackintosh, I, 125. Although the "Discourse" is reprinted in *Miscellaneous Works* (pp. 27–43), only fragments of the famous lectures are preserved in the *Memoirs* (for example, I, 110–115). The series was repeated "with some variations" in 1800.
8. 1.67n; 1.63, 64, 76. In his diary Godwin records that he saw Hazlitt at the lecture of 20 February 1799.
9. 11.98; cf. 7.62, 102.
10. 11.98.
11. Smith, *Essays*, p. 251.
12. Cyrus Redding, *Past Celebrities Whom I Have Known* (1866), I, 145f.
13. De Quincey, V, 66. On Parr's efforts for reform see M. Ray Adams, *Studies in the Literary Backgrounds of English Radicalism* (1947), pp. 281–292.
14. Paul, I, 384.
15. Paul, I, 376.
16. Samuel Parr, *Works* (1828), II, 365.
17. Smith, *Essays*, p. 253.
18. Paul, I, 378.
19. Paul, I, 378–383.
20. Paul, I, 386.
21. Godwin, *St. Leon* (1799), I, viiif.
22. Smith, *Essays*, p. 261.
23. Godwin, *Enquirer* (1797), p. 176. For Malthus' formal analysis of this notion see his *Essay on the Principle of Population* (1798), pp. 279–302.
24. Malthus, *Essay* (1798), pp. 2f.
25. *Ibid.*, pp. 11–17.
26. *Ibid.*, p. 73.
27. *Ibid.*, pp. 176f.
28. Godwin, *Thoughts*, pp. 56, 70, 76.
29. *Ibid.*, pp. 69, 74f.

30. Paul, I, 323f.
31. G. R. Potter, "Unpublished Marginalia in Coleridge's Copy of Malthus' *Essay on Population*," PMLA, LI (1936), 1062.
32. Southey, *Life and Correspondence*, p. 171. For a discussion of Southey's review see Geoffrey Carnall, *Robert Southey and His Age* (1960), pp. 62–65.
33. Griggs, II, 1039.
34. 1.227; cf. 1.208n.

THE FAILURE OF REFORM

1. 8.150.
2. 12.241.
3. 11.14.
4. 8.67.
5. Shelley, *Complete Poetical Works* (ed. Thomas Hutchinson, 1904), p. 408; cf. the fragment (presumably of 1817) in which Shelley addressed Godwin as a "Mighty eagle" that "defiest/The embattled tempests' warning" (*ibid.*, p. 595).
6. Godwin, *Enquirer* (1823), p. vii.
7. 11.17, 23, 20f., 18; cf. 20.259.
8. 19.304.
9. 11.18ff.
10. 5.161f.
11. 5.167.
12. 17.297.
13. Griggs, I, 397.
14. Coleridge, *The Friend*, p. 116.
15. Wordsworth, *Prose Works*, II, 230.
16. See page 127.
17. Wordsworth, *Prose Works*, I, 52.
18. *The Prelude*, ix.300 ff.; cf. David Perkins, *The Quest for Permanence: The Symbolism of Wordsworth, Shelley, and Keats* (1959), p. 49.
19. Wordsworth, *Poetical Works*, p. 403.
20. Wordsworth, *Prose Works*, I, 52.
21. 19.269. For a recent statement of the same opinion see Albert Guérard, *Napoleon I* (1956), pp. 63f.
22. Wordsworth, *Prose Works*, I, 117.
23. Southey, *The Life of Horatio Lord Nelson*, p. 134; cf. p. 44.
24. Henry Cockburn, *Memorials of His Time* (1856), p. 92.
25. Sydney Smith, *Works* (1854), I, viiif.
26. 7.102f. For the mature Hazlitt's disrespectful opinion of Parr and Mackintosh see 7.62.
27. 12.375; cf. 14.273ff.

IV

The Long Apprenticeship

BOOKS

1. 8.71.
2. *Four Generations*, I, 51.
3. *Memoirs*, I, 9.
4. 11.316.
5. De Quincey, II, 166f., 265.
6. Griggs, I, 260.
7. 17.313.
8. 4.84.
9. 10.69.
10. 4.4; cf. 17.206.
11. 17.92f.
12. 11.237.
13. 8.56.
14. 4.4ff., 80–88.
15. 20.296.
16. 8.268; cf. 6.179f.
17. 8.72. See his comments on Mackintosh, 11.103.
18. 8.73.
19. 17.203n.
20. 12.43.
21. 16.68.
22. 11.209.
23. 8.206f.
24. 12.25.
25. 5.90, 147; 8.294.
26. 6.99; 8.294.
27. 12.222.
28. 12.231; cf. 17.94 on the use of standard novels and essays as an antidote to "the dreams of poets and moralists."
29. 12.220f.
30. 17.98.
31. 12.223.
32. 17.91.
33. 12.224.
34. 4.88.
35. Leigh Hunt, *The Indicator, and the Companion; A Miscellany for the Fields and the Fireside* (1840), Pt. II, p. 50.
36. 12.224.
37. 6.362.
38. 12.226; cf. 16.98.
39. 6.363.
40. 12.313.
41. *Memoirs*, I, 13.
42. 4.331f.; 6.108.
43. 17.168.
44. John Forster, *Walter Savage Landor* (1869), p. 440.
45. 12.312f.
46. Leigh Hunt, *The Indicator, and the Companion*, Pt. II, p. 50.
47. Rollins, I, 143.
48. 12.227.
49. 12.226.
50. 12.227.
51. 12.126; cf. 6.247, 13.40, 17.376.

THE MEETING WITH THE POETS

1. Griggs, I, 192.
2. Griggs, I, 375.
3. For another account of Coleridge's walking and talking see 8.183.
4. See *The Poetical Works of William Wordsworth* (ed. Ernest de Selincourt and Helen Darbishire), IV (1947), 411.
5. 8.203.

PICTURES

1. 12.226.
2. 17.121n.
3. *Memoirs*, I, 9.
4. *Four Generations*, I, 98.
5. 8.5.
6. 8.122.
7. 10.7f.
8. 10.58f.
9. 17.99.
10. 10.64.
11. 7.133.
12. 7.183n.
13. 8.14.
14. 10.63f.
15. *Memoirs*, I, 84–102.
16. 8.15.
17. 17.144.
18. 13.212.
19. 18.102.
20. 6.148f., 8.15f., 10.106f., 13.212.
21. 10.106.
22. 10.246f.
23. Patmore, III, 105; see pages 242ff.
24. *Memoirs*, I, 87.
25. 10.225. For some of Hazlitt's many other tributes to this famous portrait see 8.16; 12.286; 18.76, 120, 163.
26. Clarke, p. 60.
27. Griggs, II, 990.
28. Griggs, II, 949f.
29. De Quincey, II, 236.
30. 17.115f.

31. Wordsworth, *Later Years*, III, 1349f.
32. De Quincey, II, 294.
33. 17.139. See Coleridge, *Notebooks*, no. 1619.
34. Southey, *Life and Correspondence*, p. 164.
35. Southey, *Life and Correspondence*, p. 167.
36. *Ibid.*, p. 181.
37. Wordsworth, *Early Letters*, pp. 496f.
38. *Ibid.*, p. 503. For further mention of this portrait see Griggs, II, 958, 1004, 1024f., 1058.
39. Southey, *Life and Correspondence*, p. 167.
40. Coleridge, *Notebooks*, no. 1618.
41. Griggs, II, 1004.
42. Griggs, II, 990f.
43. Coleridge, *Notebooks*, no. 1616.
44. Griggs. IV, 669f.
45. Griggs, IV, 735.
46. *Minnow among Tritons: Mrs. S. T. Coleridge's Letters to Thomas Poole, 1799-1834* (ed. Stephen Potter, 1934), p. 64.
47. Haydon, *Diary*, II, 470.
48. Robinson, I, 6; cf. Lucas, II, 15.
49. Griggs, IV, 735.
50. Wordsworth, *Later Years*, III, 1349f.
51. ALS, postmark 6 August 1807, Abinger Collection. See page 166.
52. Wordsworth, *Middle Years*, I, 196f.
53. Partington, p. 174.
54. 17.139.

THE ESSAY

1. *Memoirs*, I, 154.
2. Griggs, II, 949f.
3. ALS, Hazlitt to Crabb Robinson, 26 February [1810], Dr. Williams's Library.
4. 11.102.
5. Lucas, I, 420.
6. 11.102.
7. 9.4; cf. 17.114.
8. *On the Constitution of Church and State . . . Lay Sermons* (ed. Henry Nelson Coleridge, 1839), p. 379n.
9. 9.4
10. 12.29.
11. 12.28.
12. 9.58.
13. 20.369.
14. 17.312.
15. 1.46-49.
16. 20.183.
17. 1.130-134.
18. 2.215-245.
19. 9.51-58.
20. 20.162-186.

21. See page 127.
22. See page 136.
23. 1.113f.
24. 4.91.
25. 2.127.
26. 2.219.
27. Fawcett, *Sermons Delivered at the Sunday-Evening Lectures, for the Winter Season, at the Old Jewry* (2d ed., 1801), II, 124.
28. Godwin, *Political Justice*, I, 421-438.
29. *Ibid.*, I, 430.
30. Hazlitt, *An Abridgment of the Light of Nature Pursued, by Abraham Tucker, Esq.* (1807), p. 148.
31. 1.61.
32. 1.19n.
33. 1.1f.
34. 1.40f.
35. See W. J. Bate, "The Sympathetic Imagination in Eighteenth-Century Criticism," *ELH*, XII (1945), 144-164.
36. 12.55; cf. 12.193.
37. 5.347.
38. 12.51; cf. 13.51n.
39. 20.365. For an admirable discussion of this and cognate matters see John M. Bullitt, "Hazlitt and the Romantic Conception of the Imagination," *PQ*, XXIV (1945), 343-361.
40. 16.63; cf. 5.54, 12.245f.
41. 6.23.
42. 8.42. See 19.10f., 19f., where Hazlitt applies this notion to Wordsworth.
43. 20.369.
44. 8.8f.
45. 11.71f.
46. 4.346f.
47. Rollins, I, 387.
48. 9.5.
49. 18.308. For a softer statement of this theme see 8.53ff.
50. 19.15.
51. 16.401.
52. 8.42f.
53. 20.170.
54. 12.101.
55. Rollins, I, 186.
56. Griggs, I, 137.
57. Coleridge, *Poems*, p. 123.
58. See page 28.
59. 17.121.
60. Griggs, II, 949.
61. 1.50.
62. 1.51.
63. 8.35, 12.51. See Bullitt, p. 351.
64. 1.56.
65. 1.67; cf. 1.71.
66. 1.66f.

67. 1.70.
68. 1.56.
69. 1.61.
70. 1.72.
71. 1.76.
72. 1.77.
73. 1.80.
74. 1.83.
75. 1.83.
76. 1.91. For a sampling of Hazlitt's later strictures on Hartley see 1.128n, 4.250, 20.43, 376.
77. 1.46.

THE BUSY HACK

1. Lucas, I, 380.
2. 12.35.
3. 17.133.
4. 8.194; cf. 12.126, 390n.
5. See page 211.
6. 12.43; cf. 17.203n.
7. Lucas, II, 59.
8. Lucas, II, 59.
9. Lucas, I, 176. For Hazlitt's views of Lamb's political detachment see 7.96n.
10. 11.180f.; cf. 17.318.
11. See pages 280n, 304.
12. Lucas, II, 137.
13. Wordsworth, *Poetical Works*, p. 458.
14. ALS, Crabb Robinson to Wordsworth, 1816, Dr. Williams's Library.
15. Lucas, II, 195f.
16. Lamb, *Works*, I, 298f.
17. 12.132.
18. 17.189; cf. 8.324.
19. Lucas, I, 409.
20. Lucas, II, 15.
21. *Four Generations*, I, 98.
22. 12.157.
23. See page 83.
24. Griggs, II, 950.
25. 1.123.
26. *An Abridgment of the Light of Nature Pursued*, p. xli.
27. 1.122.
28. *Four Generations*, I, 96.
29. 1.123.
30. Robinson, III, 844.
31. 1.129.
32. 1.141.
33. 1.169f.
34. 1.165.
35. 1.148.
36. 1.162f.
37. 1.156.
38. 1.147f.
39. 1.140.
40. 7.297f.
41. 7.314.

42. 7.317.
43. 1.183.
44. 1.181f.
45. 7.350n.
46. *Edinburgh Review*, X (1807), 386.
47. 1.179.
48. Robinson, III, 844.
49. 14.212.
50. 1.188.
51. 1.197.
52. 1.212.
53. 1.207.
54. 1.214; cf. 1.249, 17.209.
55. 1.243.
56. 1.339.
57. 11.103.
58. 1.247.
59. 1.211.
60. 1.212.
61. 1.340n.
62. See page 171.

THE EARLY YEARS OF MARRIAGE

1. Lucas, I, 417.
2. Lucas, II, 10.
3. Lucas, II, 15.
4. Lucas, II, 37ff.
5. Lucas, II, 39f.
6. *Memoirs*, I, 154f.
7. *Memoirs*, I, 115.
8. Lucas, I, 20.
9. 12.34.
10. Lucas, II, 46.
11. *Life*, pp. 106-116; Maclean, pp. 256-275.
12. Lucas, II, 111.
13. 10.55.
14. 12.121.
15. 17.245.
16. 4.19. This remark is found in "On the Love of the Country," an essay written for the *Examiner* in 1814 and included three years later in *The Round Table*. It is one of Hazlitt's most Wordsworthian pieces.
17. 4.124.
18. 20.134.
19. Rollins, II, 130; cf. 10.89.
20. 20.132.
21. *Biographia Literaria*, II, 32.
22. 17.319f.; Lucas, II, 85ff., 102.
23. ALS [1810], The Houghton Library, Harvard. This letter is reprinted, with many errors of transcription, by W. C. Hazlitt in *Lamb and Hazlitt* (1899), pp. 105-108.
24. 2.113.
25. Lucas, II, 112.

26. ALS, [?fall 1809], Abinger Collection. This letter is inaccurately reprinted by Paul, II, 175.

27. I quote from an undated draft in the Abinger Collection. The full text of Godwin's letter, dated 23 November 1809, is printed by Constable, II, 52ff.

28. 16.408.

29. 2.21.

30. 2.5f.

31. 1.128n.

32. 2.270–284.

33. 11.47–57.

34. 11.53.

35. Minnie Clare Yarborough, *John Horne Tooke* (1926), p. 110.

36. ΕΠΕΑ ΠΤΕΡΟΕΝΤΑ [*Winged Words*], *or the Diversions of Purley. By John Horne Tooke . . . to Which Is Annexed His Letter to John Dunning, Esq.* (ed. Richard Taylor, 1860), p. 697.

37. *Ibid.*, p. 220.

38. *Ibid.*, p. 692.

39. 11.54.

40. 2.6f.

41. See 2.6n.

42. 1.128n.

43. *Diversions of Purley*, p. 306.

44. *Ibid.*, p. 600.

45. *Ibid.*, p. 723.

46. 1.128n.

47. 2.270f.

48. 2.271.

49. 2.274.

50. Griggs, II, 709.

51. 2.280.

52. 2.283.

53. 2.283f.

THE HOLCROFT MEMOIRS

1. Lucas, II, 68; cf. Brown, *Godwin*, p. 247.

2. Paul, II, 238f.

3. Lucas, II, 87.

4. ALS, Hazlitt to Crabb Robinson, undated but endorsed by the recipient 4 December 1809, Dr. Williams's Library.

5. *Ibid.*

6. For example, see 3.104n.

7. 3.125.

8. 3.81.

9. The inadequacy of Hazlitt's information is suggested by the interpolations and revisions in Elbridge Colby's edition of the *Life* (1925).

10. 3.127–158.

11. ALS, Abinger Collection.

12. Lucas, II, 98.

13. 3.169.

14. *Memoirs*, I, 179.

THE LECTURES ON PHILOSOPHY

1. ALS, 26 February [1810], Dr. Williams's Library.

2. Paul, II, 226; Griggs, III, 317.

3. Robinson, I, 24f.

4. 14.159n. See 7.115, 135, 12.374, 16.102, 263, 19.188.

5. Williams, p. 157; Griggs, III, 340.

6. See page 101.

7. ALS, 15 May 1811, Dr. Williams's Library.

8. ALS, 3 May 1811, Dr. Williams's Library.

9. See page 170n.

10. Lucas, II, 117f.

11. ALS, 29 October 1811, Dr. Williams's Library; see *Life*, pp. 124f.

12. ALS, 30 October 1811, Dr. Williams's Library.

13. ALS, 13 December 1811, Dr. Williams's Library.

14. ALS, 14 December 1811, Dr. Williams's Library.

15. Lucas, II, 51.

16. De Quincey, II, 188.

17. William Beattie, *Life and Letters of Thomas Campbell* (1850), I, 540; cf. Smiles, I, 331.

18. I, 57–70.

19. *Literary Remains*, I, 115n.

20. Robinson, I, 57f.

21. ALS, 26 February [1810], Dr. Williams's Library. See *Life*, pp. 113f.

22. 2.113.

23. 2.114.

24. 2.116.

25. 2.114.

26. 2.116.

27. 2.117.

28. 2.118.

29. 2.118.

30. 2.127.

31. 2.149f.

32. 2.180.

33. 2.160.

34. 2.218.

35. 2.147.

36. 2.151.

37. 2.210.

38. Robinson, I, 28. See 2.207 for Hazlitt's early statement of this theme and "On the Pleasure of Painting" (8.5–21) for his richest treatment of the subject.

39. 2.197.

40. 2.220.
41. 2.256.
42. 17.203n.
43. 20.18–22.
44. 2.198f.
45. 2.163.
46. 20.21; cf. 16.123f.
47. 8.31.
48. 12.46.
49. 10.243n.
50. 12.52.
51. 12.46.

V

The Trade of Letters

THE RISING JOURNALIST

1. 17.186f.
2. Coleridge, *Biographia Literaria*, I, 145.
3. Robinson, I, 104.
4. Robinson, I, 110.
5. Robinson, I, 116.
6. 16.222.
7. James Bain, *James Mill* (1882), p. 72; cf. p. 108.
8. 12.271.
9. Robinson, I, 128.
10. 16.223.
11. 17.312.
12. 11.288.
13. Griggs, III, 441.
14. 5.179–196, 18.191–196.
15. 19.5–9.
16. 7.24–72.
17. 18.5–24.
18. 20.12–36.
19. L'Estrange, II, 48.
20. 18.18; cf. L'Estrange, II, 48.
21. For example, 7.64ff.
22. Robinson, I, 153f.
23. 12.204f.
24. 16.223.
25. Robinson, I, 154.
26. 5.174.
27. "On the Late War," *Champion*, 3 April 1814 (7.72–77).
28. 18.24–100.
29. 5.196–211, 18.196–200.
30. Hunt, *Autobiography*, p. 297.
31. *Examiner*, 25 December 1814, p. 820.
32. Robinson, I, 153.
33. Robinson, I, 161.
34. *Examiner*, 21 and 28 August and 2 October 1814 (19.9–25).

35. Wordsworth, *Middle Years*, II, 781f.; Robinson, I, 169f.
36. Robinson, I, 164.
37. Lucas, II, 195f.
38. Quoted from the *Champion* by Howe, *Life*, p. 162. On John Scott's politics see Jacob Zeitlin, "The Editor of the *London Magazine*," JEGP, XX (1921), 328–354.
39. *Champion*, 28 August, 11 September, and 2 October 1814 (18.37–51).

THE EXAMINER

1. Hunt, *Autobiography*, p. 214.
2. *Examiner*, 7 November 1819, p. 714.
3. 16.229f.
4. Hunt, *Correspondence*, I, 40.
5. Bain, *James Mill*, p. 123.
6. Edmund Blunden, *Leigh Hunt and His Circle* (1930), p. 146.
7. Leigh Hunt, *Correspondence*, I, 167; cf. George Dumas Stout, *The Political History of Leigh Hunt's Examiner* (Washington University Studies — New Series, Language and Literature, No. 19, 1949), pp. 5, 37f.; William H. Marshall, *Byron, Shelley, Hunt, and The Liberal* (1960), 203ff.
8. Clarke, p. 16.
9. Rollins, II, 11, 180, 218.
10. Landseer, I, 23.
11. Clarke, p. 26.
12. Clarke, p. 210.
13. See Stout, *Political History of Leigh Hunt's Examiner*, p. 17.
14. Lucas, II, 195f.
15. 10.244.
16. Daniel Stuart, *Letters from the Lake Poets* (1889), p. 364.
17. Charles Duke Yonge, *The Life and Administration of Robert Banks, Second Earl of Liverpool, K.G.* (1868), II, 299.
18. Robinson, I, 189.
19. See H. R. Fox Bourne, *English Newspapers* (1887), I, 341–347; Blunden, *Leigh Hunt and His Circle*, pp. 47–63; Carl Woodring, "The Hunt Trials: Informations and Manoeuvres," *Keats-Shelley Memorial Bulletin*, X (1959), 10–13.
20. Hunt, *Autobiography*, p. 280.
21. *Autobiography*, p. 246; cf. p. 281.
22. *Examiner*, 25 December 1814, p. 819.
23. *Lord Byron and Some of His Contemporaries* (2d ed., 1828), I, 49f.
24. Stout, *Political History of Leigh Hunt's Examiner*, pp. 38–42.
25. *Examiner*, 25 December 1814, p. 820.

26. *Examiner*, 1 January 1815, p. 12. On Barnes see Talfourd, II, 179–186.
27. *Examiner*, 8 January 1815, p. 28.
28. See pages 193, 200n.
29. *Examiner*, 16 April 1815, p. 255.
30. 6.94, 99, 100, 104.
31. 6.95, 92.
32. 9.29.
33. 4.88–93.
34. 4.140–151.
35. 4.80, 132f.
36. 4.51–57.
37. 4.100–105.
38. 4.152.
39. 4.36–41.
40. 4.128–131.
41. 4.77–80.
42. 4.57.
43. 4.371.
44. 4.63.
45. 4.78, 79f.
46. See pages 210–213.
47. 5.174.
48. See page 126.

THE EDINBURGH REVIEW

1. See Constable, I, 48f.; Cockburn, I, 294; *The Life and Times of Henry Lord Brougham Written by Himself* (1871), I, 253.
2. Smith, *Works* (1854), I, ix.
3. Jeffrey, *Contributions*, p. viii.
4. James A. Grieg, *Francis Jeffrey of the Edinburgh Review* (1948), p. 87.
5. *Westminster Review*, I (1824), 505.
6. John Gibson Lockhart, *Peter's Letters to His Kinsfolk* (2d ed., 1819), p. 138.
7. Smiles, I, 97.
8. Smith, *Letters*, I, 152.
9. *Blackwood's Magazine*, X (1821), 668f.
10. 8.216f.
11. Quoted by Grieg, *Jeffrey*, p. 64.
12. Jeffrey, *Contributions*, p. 336.
13. Jeffrey's famous essay on beauty, which was built on his *Edinburgh* review (May 1811) of Archibald Alison's *Essays on the Nature and Principles of Taste*, appeared in the supplement to the sixth (1824) and subsequent editions of *The Encyclopaedia Britannica*.
14. *Edinburgh Review*, I (1802), 63; cf. Grieg, *Jeffrey*, p. 76.
15. Jeffrey, *Contributions*, p. 478.
16. Southey, *Life and Correspondence*, pp. 229f.; cf. Warter, I, 346.
17. Smiles, I, 97; cf. Constable, II, 19f. On Scott's early contributions to the *Edin-*burgh (which, as a Scottish publication, he encouraged despite its Whiggish leanings) see Lockhart, I, 356.
18. Partington, p. 65.
19. Smith, *Letters*, I, 152; cf. Wordsworth, *Middle Years*, I, 295.
20. Lockhart, *John Bull's Letter to Lord Byron* (ed. Alan Lang Strout, 1947), p. 73.
21. Southey, *Life and Correspondence*, p. 159.
22. Griggs, II, 936.
23. Smith, *Letters*, I, 95f.
24. 20.189.
25. Lockhart, II, 36n; cf. Scott, p. 298.
26. Smith, *Letters*, I, 121.
27. Cockburn, II, 86.
28. Thomas Carlyle, *Reminiscences* (Everyman's Library, 1932), p. 339.
29. Shelley, *Letters*, II, 920f.
30. De Quincey, II, 371.
31. Byron, *Correspondence*, I, 37; cf. I, 248; Prothero, II, 322.
32. Cockburn, II, 159.
33. Cockburn, II, 139.
34. Cockburn, I, 302.
35. Bain, *James Mill*, p. 110. On Jeffrey's editorial behavior see John Clive, *Scotch Reviewers* (1947), pp. 57ff.
36. ALS, 20 April 1815, The Yale University Library.
37. ALS, The Yale University Library.
38. ALS, The Yale University Library. The translator was John Black (1783–1855), a former colleague of Hazlitt's on the *Morning Chronicle* who in 1817 succeeded James Perry as editor of the paper.
39. 16.5.
40. 16.19f.
41. Carlyle, *Early Letters* (ed. Charles Eliot Norton, 1886), I, 147.
42. 16.25.
43. 5.17f. Hazlitt read and quoted from the *Inferno* in Henry Boyd's translation (1785).
44. 16.41.
45. 5.25–42.
46. See pages 270f.
47. 16.58; cf. 19.5.
48. 16.60–66.
49. 16.63.
50. 16.68.
51. 16.59.
52. *London Mercury*, XII (1925), 411.
53. ALS, The Yale University Library.
54. ALS, postmark 12 August 1817, The Yale University Library.
55. Jeffrey, *Contributions*, p. 314.
56. Robinson, I, 210.

57. *New Monthly Magazine*, X (1818), 299.
58. Constable, II, 219.
59. ALS, Hazlitt to B. R. Haydon, 11 August 1820, in the possession of Professor Willard Pope.
60. Constable, II, 218f.
61. Bonner, pp. 209, 236.
62. 11.129.
63. 11.127.
64. 11.130. For a somewhat sharper judgment of "the most admired of our Reviews" see 8.216.
65. *Edinburgh Review*, XLII (1825), 254–260.
66. Procter, p. 261.
67. 20.245f.
68. Napier, p. 70.

THE RELUCTANT MAN OF LETTERS

1. Griggs, II, 990.
2. Cyrus Redding, *Past Celebrities Whom I Have Known* (1866), I, 93; cf. *The Prose of John Clare* (ed. J. W. and Anne Tibble, 1951), p. 88.
3. Patmore, II, 305.
4. 17.317; cf. 12.214.
5. Talfourd, II, 170f.
6. Leigh Hunt, *The Indicator* (1840), II, 10. For Hazlitt's own comment on his way of shaking hands — which Hunt had no doubt talked about to him — see 8. 306.
7. 8.306.
8. Landseer, I, 107.
9. 9.176; cf. 9.194, 197.
10. 8.193.
11. 12.42.
12. 8.236.
13. 12.31.
14. 12.30.
15. L'Estrange, II, 48.
16. Robinson, I, 151.
17. 12.24–44.
18. 8.189–204.
19. George Ticknor, *Life, Letters and Journals* (1909), I, 293f.
20. *New Monthly Magazine*, XXIX (1830), 473.
21. ALS, John Hamilton Reynolds to Mary Pearse Leigh, 28 April 1817, Leigh Browne-Lockyer Collections at the Keats House, Hampstead. I am indebted to Professor Jack Stillinger for his transcript of this letter.
22. *Tatler*, 28 September 1830, p. 81.
23. Talfourd, I, 171.
24. Rollins, I, 203, 205; II, 76.
25. Clarke, p. 61.

26. Richard Brinsley Knowles, *The Life of James Sheridan Knowles* (1872), pp. 11f.; cf. p. 89.
27. Lucas, II, 196.
28. Lamb, *Works*, I, 298f.
29. Procter, p. 169.
30. Haydon, *Diary*, II, 376.
31. 17.313.
32. 17.274.
33. 11.311.
34. 9.189.
35. 9.195.
36. 8.161.
37. 8.324.
38. 17.268.
39. Rollins, II, 76.
40. Haydon, *Autobiography*, I, 161.
41. 8.203.
42. Robinson, I, 170.
43. Clarke, pp. 128f.
44. Hunt, *Autobiography*, p. 338.
45. *Ibid*, p. 297.
46. 12.274.
47. 5.146.
48. 9.208.
49. Rollins, II, 43.
50. 4.131–136.
51. 4.151ff.
52. 4.132f.
53. 16.218; cf. 12.323n.
54. 18.308.
55. 6.175–192.
56. 5.233.
57. 16.20f.; cf. 11.37.
58. 12.364f.
59. 16.213; cf. 8.102.
60. 18.46; cf. 5.96, 8.97, 17.207, 20. 386.
61. 17.201; cf. 4.95, 6.319, 16.212f.
62. 10.222; cf. 8.214–226.
63. 8.217.
64. 17.311.
65. 12.409.
66. Patmore, III, 5.
67. 16.396; cf. 12.274.
68. 8.292.
69. 17.171f.
70. 12.121ff.
71. 12.168.
72. 17.268.
73. 8.6f., 12.125f.
74. 8.79.
75. 12.61f.; cf. 17.197f.
76. 16.222n.
77. Scott, p. 105.
78. 12.58.
79. 6.214.
80. Procter, pp. 172f.
81. 9.112f.

82. 5.106, 12.7.
83. 12.250.
84. 8.244; cf. 9.21, 12.250.
85. 8.243.
86. 12.336f.
87. 8.247.
88. 12.11.
89. 8.244.
90. 8.247.
91. 7.310; cf. 5.105, 8.243, 12.6.
92. 11.15; cf. 12.250.
93. 12.15.
94. 12.17.
95. 12.16.
96. 12.16; cf. 11.84.
97. 12.11.
98. 1.[179]; cf. 17.311f., 19.303, 20. 238.

THE HUNTS

1. Byron, *Correspondence*, II, 238.
2. Hunt, *Autobiography*, p. 215.
3. Edmund Blunden, *Leigh Hunt and His Circle*, p. 301.
4. Prothero, VI, 183, 158. For Byron's relations with John Hunt as publisher of his later works see Leslie Marchand, "John Hunt as Byron's Publisher," *Keats-Shelley Journal*, VIII (1959), 119–132.
5. Cyrus Redding, *Fifty Years' Recollections, Literary and Personal* (1858), II, 226.
6. Haydon, *Autobiography*, I, 109.
7. Patmore, III, 98.
8. W. C. Hazlitt, *Lamb and Hazlitt* (1899), p. xli.
9. Oliphant, I, 189.
10. Clarke, p. 18.
11. Prothero, II, 357.
12. Prothero, IV, 237, 239.
13. Rollins, I, 113.
14. Rollins, I, 143.
15. Rollins, II, 11.
16. Haydon, *Diary*, I, 288.
17. *Ibid.*, II, 82.
18. *Ibid.*, II, 101.
19. Procter, p. 200.
20. Lamb, *Works*, I, 297.
21. 8.202.
22. 20.160; cf. 12.16f.
23. 18.381.
24. 12.38.
25. 11.177.
26. Hunt, *Poetical Works*, p. xxix.
27. Bonner, pp. 228, 237.
28. *Memoirs*, I, 108n.; cf. 8.8f., 17.313; Patmore, III, 102f.
29. "To William Hazlitt" (Hunt, *Poetical Works*, pp. 228ff.) was reprinted in *Foli-*

age (1818) from the *Examiner* of 14 July 1816.
30. *Memoirs*, I, 255.
31. W. C. Hazlitt, *Lamb and Hazlitt*, p. 152.
32. 8.69.
33. 8.150.
34. Clarke, p. 26; cf. *Mary Shelley's Journal* (ed. Frederick L. Jones, 1957), p. 77.
35. *Mary Shelley's Journal*, p. 77.
36. *Four Generations*, I, 131.
37. Hunt, *Essays*, p. 188.
38. *Memoirs*, II, 304; cf. 17.317 for Hazlitt's allusion to the incident.
39. 11.188f.
40. Hunt, *Correspondence*, I, 251f.; cf. *Life*, pp. 401f.
41. Hunt, *Lord Byron and Some of His Contemporaries* (1828), I, x (note).
42. 17.317.
43. 17.313.
44. *Tatler*, 28 September 1830, p. [81].
45. *Ibid.*

HAYDON

1. Haydon, *Autobiography*, I, 160.
2. Talfourd, II, 186ff.
3. Haydon, *Autobiography*, I, 41.
4. *Ibid.*, I, 90.
5. Talfourd, II, 189.
6. Haydon, *Diary*, I, 15.
7. Haydon, *Autobiography*, I, 237.
8. Byron, *Poetical Works* (Oxford Standard Authors, 1946), p. 143.
9. Haydon, *Autobiography*, I, 208.
10. *Ibid.*, I, 238. For the text of Haydon's famous letter on the Elgin Marbles, see I, 233–238.
11. *Ibid.*, I, 232; cf. Eric George, *The Life and Death of Benjamin Robert Haydon* (1948), pp. 79–90.
12. Haydon, *Autobiography*, I, 293.
13. Coleridge, *Table Talk*, p. 458.
14. Rollins, I, 114f.
15. Rollins, I, 117; cf. Haydon, *Autobiography*, I, 252.
16. Rollins, I, 124.
17. Haydon, *Autobiography*, I, 280.
18. *Ibid.*, I, 282.
19. Talfourd, II, 191; cf. Haydon, *Diary*, II, 265.
20. Amy Lowell, *John Keats* (1925), I, 193.
21. Haydon, *Correspondence and Table-Talk*, II, 107.
22. Haydon, *Autobiography*, I, 166.
23. *Ibid.*, I, 171.
24. 18.19ff.

25. Haydon, *Diary*, II, 65. There is an inaccurate transcript of this entry, misdated 1817, in *Correspondence and Table-Talk*, II, 301f.
26. For Hazlitt's articles on the Catalogue Raisonné see page 269.
27. For example, see his notice of the 1814 exhibitions of the British Institution and the Royal Academy, 18.10–19; cf. below, pages 269f.
28. 10.164.
29. 18.100–103. A sequel to this article in the *Examiner* was worked into an important pair of essays on the Elgin Marbles that Hazlitt wrote for the *London Magazine* in 1822 (18.145–166).
30. Haydon, *Diary*, II, 213. For Hazlitt's opinion of Wilkie see 6.139ff., 18.96–100.
31. Haydon, *Diary*, I, 386f.
32. *Ibid.*, II, 64f.; cf. Landseer, I, 122f.
33. Haydon, *Autobiography*, I, 159; Landseer, I, 41; Rollins, I, 206, 214, 288.
34. For Haydon's account of Hazlitt's sitting for his portrait see *Diary*, II, 110. On the heads in *Christ's Triumphal Entry* see Rollins, I, 129n.
35. Haydon, *Autobiography*, I, 171.
36. Haydon, *Diary*, I, 466 (where Hazlitt, though not named, is obviously the critic Haydon had in mind). See *Autobiography*, I, 160.
37. Haydon, *Correspondence and Table-Talk*, II, 33f.
38. Haydon, *Diary*, II, 495.
39. 16.209f.
40. Haydon, *Autobiography*, I, 204.
41. ALS, [?1819], in the possession of Professor Willard Pope.
42. Haydon, *Autobiography*, I, 288.
43. Haydon, *Diary*, II, 376.
44. *Ibid.*, II, 440.
45. *Ibid.*, II, 417.
46. Haydon, *Autobiography*, I, 375.
47. Haydon, *Diary*, II, 433.
48. *Ibid.*, II, 493f.
49. *Ibid.*, II, 495f.
50. Haydon, *Correspondence and Table-Talk*, II, 319.
51. Pope, 30 September 1827; cf. Haydon, *Correspondence and Table-Talk*, II, 338.
52. Partington, p. 172.
53. Pope, 18 September 1830.

KEATS

1. Haydon, *Correspondence and Table-Talk*, II, 80.

2. *Examiner*, 1 December 1816, pp. 761f.
3. Leigh Hunt, *Lord Byron and Some of His Contemporaries*, I, 410.
4. Amy Lowell, *John Keats*, II, 587. Miss Lowell (II, 587–590) reproduces all of Keats's annotations in his copy of *Characters of Shakespear's Plays*.
5. Rollins, I, 137, 144; cf. page 362n.
6. Rollins, I, 173f.; cf. page 346.
7. Rollins, I, 138.
8. Rollins, II, 69; cf. II, 203, 205.
9. Rollins, I, 166.
10. Rollins, I, 206, 214, 288, 368, 402, II, 8, 173; Landseer, I, 41f.; Haydon, *Autobiography*, I, 282.
11. Rollins, II, 227.
12. See Rollins, I, 124n., 147n., 192n., 223n., 237n., 239n., 265n., 280n., II, 156n., 192n.
13. Rollins, II, 76.
14. Rollins, II, 24.
15. Rollins, II, 76.
16. Rollins, I, 252.
17. Rollins, I, 203, 205.
18. "Sleep and Poetry," ll. 186f.; cf. 4.40.
19. "Lamia," ii.234; cf. 5.9.
20. Rollins, I, 223; cf. 5.233, 19.10f. See page 350.
21. Rollins, I, 193f.; cf. 16.137.
22. Rollins, I, 192.
23. 4.77–80, 271f. For Keats's comments on this passage see Lowell, *John Keats*, II, 589f.
24. Rollins, I, 184.
25. Rollins, I, 387.
26. 5.47–50. See page 307.
27. Rollins, I, 237.
28. 5.123–126.
29. 6.189, 18.368.
30. Haydon, *Autobiography*, I, 282.
31. 18.368n.
32. 8.99.
33. 8.211; cf. 16.269.
34. 10.247.
35. 16.237.
36. 12.123; cf. 11.118, 12.208.
37. 8.254f.
38. 9.244f.
39. 12.225.

THE LECTURER

1. 8.99, 9.33.
2. See pages 214f.
3. *Edinburgh Magazine*, I (1817), 354.
4. See pages 367f.
5. See pages 371ff.

6. *Memoirs*, I, 241f.; cf. pages 202n, 232n.

7. Patmore, II, 250f. On the Surrey Institution, which was in Blackfriars Road, see Henry B. Wheatley, *London Past and Present* (1891), III, 336.

8. *Literary Gazette*, 7 March 1818, p. 158.

9. Talfourd, II, 174; cf. *Literary Remains*, I, cxxvii f.

10. Landseer, I, 143f.; cf. *Examiner*, 18 January 1818, p. 39.

11. Landseer, I, 41f.

12. Rollins, I, 214.

13. Rollins, I, 237; cf. I, 227.

14. See page 249.

15. Lucas, II, 227.

16. *Keats Circle*, I, 13.

17. *Ibid.*, I, 27; cf. Robinson, I, 222.

18. Constable, II, 218f.

19. See page 372.

20. 9.43–49.

21. *Keats Circle*, I, 101.

22. ALS, The Yale University Library.

23. 19.210ff.

24. See pages 374f.

25. Rollins, II, 19, 24f.

26. Robinson, I, 225f.

27. *Edinburgh Magazine*, III (1818), 540–548, IV (1819), 12ff., 143–149.

28. *Blackwood's Magazine*, V (1819), 97.

29. Frederick W. Hackwood, *William Hone: His Life and Times* (1912), p. 212.

30. 8.86–89.

31. 12.409, 17.318. See Patmore, III, 130; *New Monthly Magazine*, XXIX (1830), 479; Landseer, I, 136–140; Rollins, I, 402.

32. Griggs, II, 888.

33. 20.41.

34. Haydon, *Diary*, II, 373.

35. 20.339.

36. Landseer, I, 118f.; Patmore, II, 261f.

37. Rollins, II, 59.

38. Landseer, I, 118.

39. 6.385f.

40. Procter, p. 173.

41. 6.247.

42. *Memoirs*, I, 253ff.

43. ALS, The Yale University Library. On Jeffrey's previous advance of a hundred pounds see above, page 215.

44. Talfourd, II, 174.

45. Rollins, II, 227.

46. Rollins, II, 228n.

47. *Edinburgh Review*, XXXIV (1820), 438f.; *London Magazine*, I (1820), 187.

48. *Examiner*, 19 March 1820, p. 190.

49. 6.363f.

VI

The Making of a Critic

THE LURE OF ART

1. 18.182.

2. 8.5.

3. 8.16f.

4. Haydon, *Diary*, II, 65.

5. 17.219.

6. 18.5–24.

7. 18.24–37, 84–100.

8. I, 146.

9. 18.37–84.

10. 4.25–31. It was printed on 5 June 1814.

11. 4.77–80.

12. 18.104–111; 4.140–151.

13. 18.100–103.

14. 18.111–124.

15. Carlyle, *Early Letters* (ed. Charles Eliot Norton, 1886), I, 147.

16. 18.135–140.

17. 8.5–21.

18. 8.168–174.

19. 8.31–50.

20. 8.122–145.

21. 12.44–55.

22. 12.117–127.

23. 12.88–97.

24. 12.107–116.

25. 17.134–143.

26. 8.14.

27. 10.9.

28. 8.17.

29. 10.21.

30. 8.14ff.; 10.17f., 62ff.

31. 10.65.

32. 10.7f.

33. 8.8f.

34. 17.139f., 219f.

35. 11.223.

36. 20.302.

37. 4.28.

38. 4.77.

39. 10.225.

40. 10.112.

41. 10.44.

42. 10.49.

43. 12.291.

44. 10.179.

45. For example, 10.129–138.

46. 10.57.

47. 18.105; cf. 16.204ff., 217.

48. 18.10.

49. Haydon, *Autobiography*, I, 160.

50. 16.193.

51. 16.197; cf. 18.137.

52. 17.223f.; cf. 18.74.

53. 17.226.
54. Sir Joshua Reynolds, *Discourses*, no. iv (ed. Helen Zimmern [1887], p. 43). For Hazlitt's version of this definition see 18.161.
55. 16.208.
56. 18.155.
57. 8.219.
58. 8.269.
59. 18.52.
60. 18.13.
61. 18.14.
62. 18.92.
63. 10.41.
64. *Memoirs*, I, 8.
65. Reynolds, *Discourses*, no. xiii (ed. Zimmern, p. 225).
66. 18.51–62.
67. For general discussions of Hazlitt's art criticism see Stanley P. Chase, "Hazlitt as a Critic of Art," *PMLA*, XXXIX (1924), 179–202; Schneider, pp. 43–83; G. M. Sargeaunt, "Hazlitt as a Critic of Painting" in *The Classical Spirit* (1936), pp. 206–223.
68. Johnson, "Pope," in *The Lives of the English Poets, Works*, VIII, 324.
69. Johnson, "Butler," *ibid.*, VII, 151.
70. Quoted by Joseph Wood Krutch, *Samuel Johnson* (1944), p. 552.
71. Reynolds, *Discourses*, no. vi (ed. Zimmern, p. 79).
72. *Ibid.*, no. vi (p. 81).
73. Hobbes, "Answer to Davenant's Preface to *Gondibert*," in *Critical Essays of the Seventeenth Century* (ed. J. E. Spingarn, 1908), II, 59.
74. Reynolds, *Discourses*, no. iii (ed. Zimmern, p. 31).
75. Addison, *The Spectator*, no. 160 (Everyman's Library, I, 283, 285).
76. Pope, *Essay on Criticism*, line 144; *Shakespeare Criticism: A Selection* (ed. D. Nichol Smith, 1946), p. 42.
77. Krutch, *Samuel Johnson*, p. 293.
78. *Boswell's Journal of A Tour to the Hebrides* (ed. Frederick A. Pottle and Charles H. Bennett, 1936), p. 234.
79. Maurice Morgann, *An Essay on the Dramatic Character of Sir John Falstaff*, in *Shakespeare Criticism: A Selection*, p. 176.
80. Reynolds, *Discourses*, no. xiii (ed. Zimmern, p. 214).
81. *Ibid.*, no. ii (pp. 21f.).
82. 18.66.
83. 18.68.
84. 18.69; cf. 6.187, 8.47.
85. 12.117–127; cf. 6.109.

86. 18.41.
87. 8.46, 84, 16.186.
88. 12.118.
89. 11.225.
90. 10.110.
91. 12.305.
92. 18.69.
93. 18.70.
94. 4.72–77.
95. 18.111.
96. Reynolds, *Discourses*, no. vi (ed. Zimmern, p. 76).
97. *Ibid.* (p. 84).
98. 18.66.
99. 12.239.
100. 6.187. For some of Hazlitt's typical strictures on Neoclassic formalism see 8.217f. (on Dryden) and 12.311 (on La Harpe).
101. Johnson, "Preface to Shakespeare," *Works*, V, 105.
102. Johnson, *The History of Rasselas, Prince of Abissinia, Works*, I, 222.
103. Johnson, "Preface to Shakespeare," *Works*, V, 109.
104. Reynolds, *Discourses*, no. iii (ed. Zimmern, pp. 28f.).
105. Wordsworth, *Prose Works*, I, 61ff.; cf. I, 72, where Wordsworth cites Reynolds on the necessity of "long-continued intercourse with the best models of composition."
106. 8.144.
107. 19.74.
108. 9.189.
109. 20.298; cf. 20.373, where Hazlitt criticizes Bacon's methodology because it seems to set a "trap for truth."
110. 9.228.
111. 8.46.
112. 12.291.
113. 8.46.
114. 20.300.
115. 18.154.
116. 20.298.
117. 11.229.
118. 8.84.
119. 8.145.
120. 4.75.
121. 18.71.
122. Reynolds, *Discourses*, no. iv (ed. Zimmern, p. 41).
123. 8.140.
124. 8.132.
125. 18.150.
126. Reynolds, *Discourses*, no. iii (ed. Zimmern, p. 37).
127. 16.145; cf. 6.133, 139.
128. 18.60; cf. 10.26, 55.

129. 18.118.
130. 18.106f.
131. 16.207.
132. 18.114. Hazlitt, who uses this illustration several times (for example, 16. 199, 18.82), in 1822 attributed it to Coleridge (18.157).
133. 8.39f., cf. 18.78.
134. 8.241.
135. 12.285f.
136. 8.141.
137. 20.303.
138. 8.31.
139. 16.63.
140. Rollins, I, 192.
141. 16.320.
142. 19.52f.
143. 6.146. See 11.201, 246, 268, where Hazlitt attributes to Northcote similar remarks about Hogarth's tedious fidelity to low details.
144. 16.273.
145. 12.246; cf. 8.148f., 9.244, 16.265f.
146. 20.299.
147. 18.164.
148. 19.25.
149. 8.169.
150. 9.199.
151. 12.341.
152. Coleridge, "Dejection: An Ode," *Poems*, p. 365.
153. Wordsworth, *Prose Works*, II, 209.
154. 8.42.

PLAYS AND PLAYERS

1. 8.292.
2. Notably "The Free Admission" (17. 365–370).
3. 17.367.
4. 18.392.
5. 5.272; cf. 4.153.
6. Rollins, II, 68, where Keats describes Richard Lalor Sheil's *Evadne*. For a similar comment by Coleridge see *Biographia Literaria*, II, 181, where he attacks the vogue for German drama.
7. *The Reflector, A Quarterly Magazine, on Subjects of Philosophy, Politics, and the Liberal Arts*, I (1811), 467.
8. *Blackwood's Magazine*, XXIII (1828), 33.
9. 18.302.
10. 18.369.
11. 18.210.
12. 5.258.
13. 5.366.
14. 5.225.
15. 5.323.
16. 5.299.

17. 18.221.
18. 18.361f.
19. 5.203, 247, 299.
20. 18.303.
21. 18.327.
22. 18.356.
23. 18.366.
24. 18.409.
25. 4.367, 5.366.
26. 5.334f.
27. 5.253.
28. 5.275.
29. 12.297; cf. 5.189.
30. 18.281.
31. 8.279; cf. 12.299. For Hazlitt's comments on illusion as a principal ingredient of drama see 9.209, 18.297.
32. 5.229f.
33. 18.274–277; cf. 18.392.
34. 18.278.
35. 18.227.
36. 5.199.
37. 12.301f.
38. 5.313.
39. 5.198.
40. 4.189.
41. 8.50; cf. 5.199.
42. 5.312.
43. 18.232; cf. 5.373.
44. 5.345.
45. 5.374.
46. 5.314; cf. 18.341f.
47. Hunt, *Autobiography*, p. 193.
48. 18.198; cf. 5.376.
49. 5.350.
50. 18.388f.
51. 5.346.
52. See 5.174f.
53. 8.293.
54. 5.179.
55. 18.377.
56. L'Estrange, II, 47n.
57. 5.179.
58. 5.181.
59. 5.188.
60. 5.189.
61. 5.190.
62. 5.175.
63. 5.208.
64. 5.175.
65. L'Estrange, I, 288.
66. 5.184.
67. 18.263; cf. 5.189, 357.
68. 18.205; cf. 18.283f.
69. Prothero, II, 385f.
70. Keats, *The Poetical Works and Other Writings* (ed. Harry Buxton Forman, 1883), III, 5; cf. Rollins, I, 191. On Keats's drama criticism in the *Champion*

(which was much in Hazlitt's style) see
page 248n.
71. Haydon, *Diary*, I, 397.
72. Clarke, p. 15.
73. 19.257.
74. 5.354f.
75. 5.180; cf. 5.190.
76. 5.355.
77. 5.292ff.
78. 5.181f.
79. 5.187f.
80. 5.190.
81. 5.203f.
82. 5.207.
83. 5.227f.
84. 5.179.
85. 5.203.
86. 5.205f.
87. 5.209.
88. 5.223.
89. 5.223.
90. Coleridge, *Table Talk*, p. 44.
91. 5.189, 271f.
92. 5.188.
93. 5.207; cf. 18.342.
94. 5.209f.; cf. 18.278.
95. 5.202.
96. 5.208-211.
97. 5.221-224.
98. 5.290f.
99. 5.307.
100. 18.225, 227f.
101. 18.290.
102. 18.331ff.
103. 5.184.
104. 18.278f.
105. 5.199.
106. 5.291; cf. 18.212.
107. 5.261. For a more favorable, and more characteristic, appraisal of Miss O'Neill's Belvidera see 18.265f.
108. 18.283.
109. 18.280-286.
110. 5.339f.
111. 5.334.
112. 5.338.
113. 18.340f. Perhaps Macready remembered some of these comments when, much later, he expressed his low opinion of Hazlitt's book on Shakespeare (*Diaries*, I, 55).
114. 5.235.
115. 5.334.
116. 18.355; 20.285.
117. 5.224.
118. 5.236.
119. 5.278.
120. 5.252.
121. 5.300.

122. 5.299.
123. 5.340.
124. 5.177.
125. 5.331.
126. For example, 5.296, 18.338.
127. Lamb, *Works*, I, 520.
128. 5.296.
129. 18.404.
130. 18.244.
131. 5.296.
132. 20.93; cf. 11.170, where Tom Moore's poetry is compared to opera.
133. 20.94.
134. 18.339.
135. 5.196.
136. 18.353f.
137. 20.95.
138. 12.336f.
139. 5.250.
140. 5.268f.
141. 18.254.
142. 9.91f.
143. 9.93. See Hazlitt's comments on Cumberland's *West Indian*, 9.69, Mrs. Centliver's *Busy Body*, 9.79, and Farquhar's two great comedies, 9.84, 88.
144. See W. T. Albrecht, "Hazlitt's Preference for Tragedy," *PMLA*, LXXI (1956), 1042-1051.
145. 6.5.
146. 6.7.
147. 20.362.
148. 20.357.
149. 4.338.
150. 4.338.
151. 6.33ff.
152. 6.38.
153. 20.353.
154. 6.35.
155. 6.18.
156. 5.347.
157. 20.356.
158. 5.347.
159. 4.311.
160. 6.149. For Hazlitt's two letters on the decline of modern comedy see page 194n; cf. 4.313, 6.149-154.
161. 4.12.
162. 20.4, 6.150.
163. 4.12.
164. 6.36f.
165. 6.89f.
166. 9.68f.
167. 4.13.
168. 5.213; cf. 6.272. See Sylvan Barnet, "More on Hazlitt's Preference for Tragedy," *PMLA*, LXXIII (1958), 443f.
169. 20.274; cf. 6.272.
170. 5.58.

171. 12.46.
172. 5.51f.
173. 18.345; cf. 11.184.
174. 16.76.
175. 16.57–99.
176. 6.347f.
177. Rollins, I, 264f.
178. 18.305; cf. 8.29.
179. 5.48, 50.
180. 19.44f.
181. 18.307–310. This point received its first impressive statement in Hazlitt's *Examiner* review of *The Excursion* (19.10f.); see pages 342ff.
182. 12.53.

SHAKESPEARE

1. Rollins, I, 143; cf. I, 280.
2. 4.174.
3. De Quincey, V, 236ff.
4. 4.171.
5. 16.57–99; see pages 212f.
6. 4.175.
7. 8.77.
8. 4.357.
9. 4.245.
10. Lamb, *Works*, I, 135.
11. 4.237; cf. Hazlitt's admiring citation of Lamb at 4.270f.
12. 5.221.
13. 9.91.
14. 18.255; cf. 5.222, 234. See the comments on the acting versions of *Comus* (5.231) and *A Midsummer Night's Dream* (5.276).
15. 5.198.
16. 18.343.
17. 4.258.
18. *Johnson on Shakespeare* (ed. Walter Raleigh, 1908), p. 158.
19. 4.188.
20. 4.258.
21. 4.285.
22. 4.322.
23. 4.180.
24. 4.273.
25. 4.286.
26. 4.299.
27. 4.230f.
28. 4.228.
29. 4.254.
30. 4.246.
31. 4.257.
32. For example, 4.198 (on Brutus as a disappointed liberal), 4.216 (on Coriolanus as an aristocrat), 4.285 (on Henry V as a militarist), 4.305 (on Henry VIII as a despot).
33. 4.271.

34. 4.294.
35. 4.226.
36. 4.226.
37. 4.233.
38. 4.186.
39. 4.284.
40. 4.232.
41. 4.345f.
42. Johnson, "Preface to Shakespeare," *Works*, V, 115.
43. 4.346f.
44. 6.33.
45. 4.341.
46. 4.253f.
47. 4.235.
48. 4.293f.
49. 4.77.
50. 5.211–221.
51. 4.233.
52. 4.324.
53. 4.249.
54. 4.180.
55. 4.192f.
56. 4.333.
57. 4.314.
58. 4.200.
59. 4.257.
60. 4.224.
61. 4.229.
62. Rollins, II, 24.

THE LITERATURE OF ENGLAND

1. 6.247.
2. 12.256f., 17.140.
3. 5.144; cf. 10.27.
4. 8.107.
5. 6.247.
6. 18.10.
7. 11.78.
8. 4.86, 95, 12.157, 187, 276f., 297, 16.66, 170, 211.
9. 5.143f.; cf. 9.223.
10. 16.214f.
11. 5.120ff. See page 249.
12. 5.98.
13. 5.111.
14. 5.98.
15. 6.311.
16. 6.302.
17. 6.176.
18. 6.301f.
19. 6.73ff.
20. 6.121.
21. 6.243.
22. 5.97.
23. 5.152.
24. 5.72.
25. 5.22.

26. 6.72.
27. 5.58f.
28. 6.36.
29. 6.117.
30. 6.40.
31. 6.211f.
32. 5.63, 64f.
33. 6.109.
34. 6.125f.
35. 6.106.
36. *Quarterly Review*, XIX (1818), 424–434. For Hazlitt's rebuttal of this charge see 9.44f.
37. 5.9.
38. 6.5.
39. See page 194n.
40. See page 300.
41. 6.23.
42. 6.175.
43. 6.192.
44. Talfourd, II, 174.
45. 6.224.
46. 6.177.
47. 5.82.
48. 5.96.
49. 6.235.
50. 6.254; cf. 6.193.
51. 6.197.
52. 6.356.
53. 6.68.
54. 6.162.
55. 5.70. See W. P. Albrecht, "Hazlitt on the Poetry of Wit," *PMLA*, LXXV (1960), 245–249.
56. 6.30.
57. 5.105.
58. 6.39.
59. 5.82f., 6.51ff.
60. 5.91f.
61. 6.70-91.
62. 6.106–132. See Charles I. Patterson, "William Hazlitt as a Critic of Prose Fiction" *PMLA*, LXVIII (1953), 1001–1016.
63. 6.180.
64. 5.46f.
65. 5.9.
66. 18.308.
67. 6.151ff., 16.211–221.
68. 5.53.
69. 5.144f.
70. 5.148.
71. 5.150.
72. 5.153.
73. 5.155.
74. 5.156.
75. 5.161f.
76. 5.167.
77. 5.168.

VII

Politics and Literature

IDEALS

1. 7.7.
2. 7.7.
3. 7.12.
4. 7.259f.
5. 19.317f.
6. 19.309.
7. 1.313.
8. 19.156.
9. 15.219; cf. 7.107f., 223.
10. 11.112.
11. 19.282.
12. 19.284.
13. 19.298f.
14. 12.46.
15. 19.302–320.
16. 19.303.
17. 19.305.
18. 19.315.
19. 19.309.
20. 19.317.
21. 19.312.
22. 19.320.
23. Burke, *Works*, III, 253.
24. *Ibid.*, III, 274.
25. 8.153ff.; cf. 1.288.
26. 7.273.
27. 19.140; cf. 19.180.
28. 7.278; cf. 8.155, 13.51n.
29. 7.270.
30. 7.273.
31. 17.325; cf. 19.223.
32. 7.192; cf. 8.164.
33. 13.120.
34. Pope, 12 November 1832.
35. 7.267.
36. 19.324; cf. 17.327.
37. 19.334n; cf. 17.382.
38. 14.236f.
39. 7.73f.
40. 7.34; cf. 19.125ff., where, in an article written for the *Morning Chronicle* in March 1814, Hazlitt argued that the treasures gathered by Napoleon for the Louvre should not be scattered by his vindictive conquerors. See 13.213, 20.59.
41. Leslie Marchand, *Byron* (1957), II, 533; cf. Byron's comment in his journal in *Byron: A Self-Portrait* (ed. Peter Quennell, 1950), I, 316.
42. Hesketh Pearson, *The Smith of Smiths* (1934), p. 109.
43. Wordsworth, *Prose Works*, I, 206, 237.
44. Mackintosh, I, 125.

45. Southey, *The Life of Horatio Lord Nelson* (Everyman's Library, 1906), p. 108.
46. Shelley, *Letters*, I, 375.
47. Smith, *Letters*, I, 245; cf. I, 29 for Smith's prophetic comment in 1798, on the war with France.
48. Cockburn, II, 158; cf. II, 183f. for Jeffrey's prediction of the ultimate consequences of the Napoleonic wars.
49. Rollins, I, 397.
50. De Quincey, III, 60. For a similar comment see William Jerdan, *The Autobiography* (1852–53), I, 204f.
51. Cottle, pp. 355f.
52. Robinson, I, 142, where Robinson is quoting Lamb.
53. 12.122.
54. 13.42f.
55. 13.ix f.
56. 13.317f.

REALITIES

1. 9.32.
2. 4.68.
3. 7.9.
4. 7.259f.
5. 7.139f.
6. For example, 4.286, 306.
7. 11.157.
8. 7.10.
9. 7.274.
10. Hazlitt's most notorious statements of his antimonarchism are "On the Regal Character" (7.281–287) and "On the Spirit of Monarchy" (19.255–267).
11. 7.82.
12. 7.289; 19.270; 20.133.
13. 7.93.
14. 16.20, 19.263.
15. 7.193.
16. Byron, *Poetical Works* (Oxford Standard Authors, 1956), p. 66.
17. 12.136.
18. 13.48; cf. 6.122f.
19. 19.270; cf. 13.48ff.
20. 14.200f.
21. 16.325, 18.363, 20.283.
22. 7.14.
23. 8.267.
24. 7.13.
25. 11.151f.
26. 12.267.
27. Macaulay, *Essays*, III, 398.
28. Bagehot, quoted by John Buchan, *Scott* (1932), p. 369.
29. Hunt, *Autobiography*, p. 269.
30. 7.17.
31. 8.155.

32. 19.217.
33. Edward John Trelawny, *Records of Shelley, Byron, and the Author* (1878), II, 26.
34. Constable, II, 47.
35. Smith, *Essays*, p. 519.
36. Bagehot, *Literary Studies* (1895), I, 150.
37. De Quincey, I, 20.
38. De Quincey, IX, 373.
39. 11.145f.
40. 15.156.
41. 7.79; 17.14.
42. 17.20.
43. 19.186; cf. Hazlitt's remarks on Castlereagh, Burke, and Wellington, 7.162n.
44. 7.17.
45. 7.145. See 7.269f. for Hazlitt's views about the liberal press and its "incredible struggles" in behalf of English freedom.
46. 7.151, 19.186, 188. See W. C. Hazlitt, *Lamb and Hazlitt* (1899), pp. xlix f.; Derek Hudson, *Thomas Barnes of The Times* (1943), pp. 27f.
47. 16.228.
48. Quoted by H. R. Fox Bourne, *English Newspapers* (1887), I, 360.
49. 7.136.
50. 7.141.
51. 7.150.
52. 7.289.
53. Robinson, I, 199.
54. 16.227.
55. 16.228.
56. Cockburn, II, 127.
57. 7.19.
58. 12.380.
59. 14.274f.; cf. 7.313n.
60. 12.378.
61. 7.21.
62. 12.381.
63. 7.14f.; cf. 20.139.
64. 11.192, 230f., 20.264.
65. 11.311.
66. 17.294; cf. 17.41.
67. 16.267.
68. 8.148.
69. 8.150.
70. 8.55.
71. 8.57.
72. 8.54.

THE AGING STRIPLING BARDS

1. 7.237.
2. For some of Hazlitt's later comments on these works see 7.115, 11.35, 12.374, 19.161, 198.
3. 7.24f.; cf. 19.115ff.

4. 7.25.
5. 7.89.
6. 19.9.
7. 19.9.
8. 19.10f.
9. 19.12f.
10. See page 61.
11. 19.18.
12. 19.18.
13. 19.19f.
14. 19.20. For Mary Wordsworth's comment on Hazlitt's attitude toward country people see page 137n.
15. 19.24.
16. 19.25.
17. Wordsworth, *Middle Years*, II, 602; cf. II, 606f.
18. See Partington, p. 65; *Middle Years*, II, 620, 633, 642.
19. See George McLean Harper, *William Wordsworth* (1916), II, 252f.
20. Robinson, I, 166.
21. Robinson, I, 169f.
22. Wordsworth to John Scott, 11 June 1816, *TLS*, 27 December 1941, p. 660.
23. Robinson, I, 161.
24. 5.233; cf. 8.176. For Wordsworth's sonnet (which in its final version has "regal fortitude") see his *Poetical Works*, p. 256.
25. Hunt, *Autobiography*, pp. 304f.; cf. Edmund Blunden, *Leigh Hunt and His Circle* (1930), pp. 90ff.
26. Lucas, II, 146.
27. Robinson, I, 169f.
28. Wordsworth, *Poetical Works*, pp. 152f.
29. See page 192n.
30. See M. H. Abrams, *The Mirror and the Lamp* (1953), p. 98.
31. 8.44.
32. Wordsworth, *The Prelude*, iv.337.
33. Lucas, I, 245ff.
34. De Quincey, II, 349.
35. Williams, p. 151.
36. Quoted, from an unpublished letter, by Earl Leslie Griggs, "Robert Southey's Estimate of Samuel Taylor Coleridge: A Study in Human Relations," *Huntington Library Quarterly*, IX (1945), 74f.
37. Trelawny, *Records of Shelley, Byron, and the Author*, I, 7.
38. Amy Lowell, *John Keats* (1925), I, 345, 544.
39. Robinson, I, 10.
40. Hunt, *Autobiography*, pp. 305f.
41. Hartley Coleridge, *Letters* (ed. Grace Evelyn Griggs and Earl Leslie Griggs, 1937), p. 111.

42. Carlyle, *Reminiscences*, p. 360.
43. 9.5.
44. Wordsworth, *The Prelude*, vi.296.
45. Carlyle, *Reminiscences*, p. 251.
46. Southey, *Letters* (ed. Maurice H. Fitzgerald, 1912), p. 68.
47. Paul, I, 17.
48. Talfourd, II, 196.
49. Lamb, *Works*, I, 454.
50. 12.347.
51. 8.251.
52. 5.167.
53. 11.29f.
54. Robinson, I, 90.
55. Wordsworth, *Middle Years*, II, 782; Daniel Stuart, *Letters from the Lake Poets* (1889), pp. 364f.
56. De Quincey, II, 323.
57. ALS, Southey to Crabb Robinson, 13 March 1817, Dr. Williams's Library.
58. Southey, *Essays, Moral and Political* (1832), II, 100ff.
59. See page 198.
60. Southey, *Life and Correspondence*, p. 340; cf. Procter, p. 139.
61. Charles Duke Yonge, *The Life and Administration of Robert Banks, Second Earl of Liverpool, K.G.* (1868), II, 298.
62. Robinson, I, 239.
63. Scott, p. 22; cf. pp. 33f.
64. See Partington, p. 82; Hartley Coleridge, *Letters*, p. 190.
65. Carlyle, *Reminiscences*, p. 355.
66. Hunt, *Autobiography*, p. 343.
67. Griggs, I, 554.
68. Griggs, II, 710.
69. Coleridge, *Essays*, II, 544f., 546f.
70. Coleridge, *The Friend*, p. 140.
71. Griggs, III, 537.
72. Griggs, III, 410.
73. Coleridge, *Essays*, II, 548.
74. *Ibid.*, III, 689f.
75. Derek Hudson, *Thomas Barnes* of The Times (1943), p. 177.
76. Coleridge, *Essays*, II, 699f.
77. Yonge, *Liverpool*, II, 305.

ATTACK

1. 12.347.
2. 7.106.
3. 7.115.
4. 7.118.
5. Lucas, II, 195f.; cf. Robinson, I, 197.
6. Griggs, IV, 669f.
7. *Edinburgh Review*, XXVII (1816), 58-67.
8. Griggs, IV, 692f.
9. 4.152.

10. 7.144f.
11. ALS, Crabb Robinson to Thomas Robinson, 16 December 1816, Dr. Williams's Library; cf. Robinson, I, 199.
12. Robinson, I, 201.
13. Coleridge, *On the Constitution of Church and State . . . Lay Sermons* (ed. Henry Nelson Coleridge, 1839), pp. 275f.
14. 16.100.
15. 16.105.
16. Coleridge, *On the Constitution of Church and State . . . Lay Sermons*, p. 379n. On Hazlitt's retort (9.4) to this long-delayed acknowledgment see above, page 141.
17. See below, pages 362ff.
18. *Quarterly Review*, XVI (1816–17), 225–278.
19. See above, page 85.
20. Warter, III, 62.
21. Southey, *Life and Correspondence*, p. 351. For a good account of the episode see Frank Taliaferro Hoadley, "The Controversy over Southey's *Wat Tyler*," SP, XXXVIII (1941), 81–96.
22. Shelley, *Letters*, II, 649.
23. Geoffrey Carnall, *Robert Southey and His Age* (1960), p. 162; cf. 7.179.
24. 7.176ff.
25. *Examiner*, 16 March 1817, p. 172.
26. Griggs, IV, 713.
27. *Examiner*, 6 April 1817, pp. 211f.
28. 7.178.
29. Wordsworth, *Middle Years*, II, 781f.
30. Prothero, IV, 117f.; cf. IV, 483.
31. Sir Walter Scott, *The Letters* (ed. H. J. C. Grierson), IV (1933), 444; cf. Edward Bulwer-Lytton, *England and the English* (1833), II, 60.
32. Southey, *Essays, Moral and Political* (1832), II, 8f.
33. *Ibid.*, II, 25.
34. 7.201f.
35. 7.208.
36. Coleridge, *Biographia Literaria*, II, 86. Coleridge's main attacks on the *Edinburgh* are in chapters iii and xxi.
37. *Ibid.*, II, 211.
38. *Ibid.*, II, 214.
39. 16.136.
40. 16.137.

REPRISAL

1. *Edinburgh Review*, XXXIV (1820), 438.
2. *Examiner*, 9 June 1822, p. 356.
3. Smiles, I, 100f.; cf. Warter, II, 110.
4. Warter, II, 107.

5. 11.127.
6. William Gifford, *The Baviad, and Maeviad* (8th ed., 1811), p. 13.
7. *Ibid.*, p. 25.
8. Smiles, II, 178f.
9. Scott, p. 305.
10. 9.13.
11. 9.15.
12. 11.124.
13. *Quarterly Review*, I (1809), 387–398.
14. Smith, *Letters*, I, 163.
15. *Quarterly Review*, XXVI (1821), 179.
16. 20.113n.
17. Harriet Martineau, *Biographical Sketches* (1869), p. 62.
18. *Quarterly Review*, XIV (1816), 481.
19. *Ibid.*, XVIII (1818), 335.
20. *Examiner*, 26 September 1819, p. 620.
21. Hunt, *Poetical Works*, p. 166.
22. *Ibid.*, p. xxvii.
23. Hunt, *Autobiography*, p. 263.
24. *Quarterly Review*, XVII (1817), 159.
25. *Examiner*, 15 September 1816, pp. 587ff.
26. *Quarterly Review*, XVII (1817), 155.
27. *Ibid.*, XVII (1817), 155, 157, 159.
28. *Ibid.*, XVIII (1818), 466.
29. *Ibid.*, XIX (1818), 424–434.
30. 19.210f. This article on Gifford appeared in the *Examiner* on 14 June 1818.
31. 9.14.
32. 9.15.
33. 9.30f.
34. 9.33.
35. 9.17.
36. 9.58f.
37. Rollins, II, 71–76.
38. L'Estrange, II, 42. Of great importance to any student of *Blackwood's* is Alan Lang Strout's *Bibliography of Articles in Blackwood's Magazine: Volumes I through XVIII 1817–1825*, Texas Technological College Library Bulletin, No. 5, 1959.
39. *Blackwood's Magazine*, XVI (1824), 179. For the depth of Lockhart's Toryism see Alan Lang Strout, "Some Unpublished Letters of John Gibson Lockhart to John Wilson Croker," *Notes & Queries*, CLXXXV (1943), 156.
40. *Blackwood's Magazine*, II (1817), 6.
41. *Ibid.*, pp. 40f.
42. 8.221.
43. Griggs, IV, 785ff.; Robinson, I, 213.
44. Hunt, *Correspondence*, I, 103.
45. *Examiner*, 16 November 1817, p. 729.

46. *Blackwood's Magazine*, II (1818), 416.

47. *Examiner*, 12 April 1818, p. 233.

48. *Blackwood's Magazine*, III (1818), 200.

49. *Ibid.*, p. 453.

50. *Ibid.*, p. 303.

51. *Ibid.*, II (1818), unpaged "Notices" preceding the body of the issue.

52. Alan Lang Strout, "Hunt, Hazlitt, and Maga," *ELH*, IV (1937), 151–159, has traced the history of "pimpled Hazlitt" through *Blackwood's Magazine*.

53. *Blackwood's Magazine*, III (1818), 75.

54. Basil Champneys, *Memoirs and Correspondence of Coventry Patmore* (1900), II, 437.

55. Charles Armitage Brown, "Life of John Keats," *Keats Circle*, II, 58f.

56. 17.48.

57. *Blackwood's Magazine*, III (1818), 456. Lockhart's forthcoming attack on Hazlitt had been strongly hinted in the May *Blackwood's* (III [1818], 200).

58. *Ibid.*, p. 524.

59. *Ibid.*, pp. 550ff.

60. *Ibid.*, p. 587.

61. *Ibid.*, p. 599.

62. Clarke, p. 147.

63. Champneys, *Patmore*, II, 439ff.

64. J. A. Hessey to John Taylor, *Keats Circle*, I, 37.

65. *TLS*, 21 March 1936, p. 244.

66. Rollins, I, 368.

67. Smiles, I, 482–493.

68. For the text of this letter by Wilson and Lockhart see Oliphant, I, 164–167.

69. Some of the details of this settlement are given in a letter of 1823 from Blackwood to Thomas Cadell, when Hazlitt was threatening to bring another suit for libel. See Theodore Besterman, *The Publishing Firm of Cadell & Davis* (1938), pp. 67f.

70. Oliphant, I, 173.

71. *Examiner*, 7 May 1819, p. 156.

72. 12.378. For the attacks in *Blackwood's Magazine* on the *Liberal* see William H. Marshall, *Byron, Shelley, Hunt, and* The Liberal (1960), pp. 45–48, 114ff., 183n, 199.

73. *Blackwood's Magazine*, XII (1822), 786f.

74. 17.106.

75. *Four Generations*, I, 142; cf. Theodore Besterman, *The Publishing Firm of Cadell & Davis*, pp. xviii ff., 67f.; *Life*, pp. 324f.

76. 16.211–239.

77. *Blackwood's Magazine*, XIII (1823), 640–646.

78. 16.232f.

79. See Ralph Wardle, "Outwitting Hazlitt," *MLN*, LVII (1942), 459–462.

80. *Blackwood's Magazine*, XIV (1823), 219, 221, 231.

81. *Ibid.*, p. 309.

82. John Wilson, *Noctes Ambrosianae* (ed. R. Shelton Mackenzie, 1875), I, 366.

83. Wilson, *Noctes Ambrosianae*, II, 125.

84. *Blackwood's Magazine*, XIX (1826), xvi f.

85. 12.123.

86. 17.308; cf. 20.129, 150.

87. *Blackwood's Magazine*, XXVIII (1830), 862.

88. Wilson, *Noctes Ambrosianae*, V, 290.

89. *London Magazine*, II (1820), 513.

90. *Blackwood's Magazine*, XI (1822), vi.

91. John Gibson Lockhart, *Peter's Letters to His Kinsfolk* (1819), II, 222f.

92. Wordsworth, *Middle Years*, II, 841.

93. *The Letters of Sara Hutchinson* (ed. Kathleen Coburn, 1954), p. 194; cf. p. 155; *Minnow among Tritons: Mrs. S. T. Coleridge's Letters to Thomas Poole, 1799–1834* (ed. Stephen Potter, 1934), pp. 82f.

94. Lockhart, III, 158; cf. Constable, II, 348f.

95. Oliphant, I, 151f.

96. Carlyle, *Reminiscences*, pp. 376f.

97. *Ibid.*, p. 380.

98. Sir Walter Scott, *Letters* (ed. H. J. C. Grierson), VI (1934), 363.

99. Smiles, II, 221.

100. Scott, p. 19.

101. Haydon, *Autobiography*, I, 266.

102. Andrew Lang, *The Life and Letters of John Gibson Lockhart* (1897), I, 127ff.

103. *Ibid.*, I, 203.

104. *Some Letters of Lord Cockburn* (ed. Harry A. Cockburn, 1932), p. 93.

105. 17.105.

VIII

The Essayist

A NEW BEGINNING

1. 6.364.
2. *London Magazine*, I (1820), iv f.; cf. Josephine Bauer, *The London Magazine 1820–29* (1953), pp. 57–74.
3. Talfourd, II, 2f.
4. On the decline of the *London* after 1821 see Bauer, pp. 80–89.
5. 16.231.
6. 18.273f.
7. 18.367.
8. *London Magazine*, I (1820), 187.
9. See page 255n.
10. 18.368.
11. Haydon, *Autobiography*, I, 282; see above, page 238.
12. 18.345, 368. Another product of his stay in London was a review of Macready's Macbeth that he supplied for the *Examiner* on June 25 (18.340–343).
13. *Memoirs*, I, 261ff.
14. 8.12f.
15. 8.90–101.
16. 8.205–214.
17. 16.222n; 12.62f.
18. 8.247, 12.11.
19. 6.91.
20. 8.37.
21. 9.228.
22. 6.92.
23. 4.88.
24. 17.268; cf. 8.8f., 79, 12.61f., 409, 17.197.
25. 17.272.
26. 17.219.
27. 17.242.
28. 8.28.
29. 17.320.
30. 8.256; cf. 20.51.
31. 12.347.
32. 17.198.
33. Lamb, *Works*, I, 584.
34. 12.308.
35. 8.186f.
36. 12.303f.
37. 12.222f.
38. 12.24.
39. 17.376f.
40. 17.365–382.
41. 8.184.
42. 12.127; cf. 8.185f.
43. 10.63f.
44. 17.314.
45. 8.29.
46. 12.304f.
47. 12.61f., 17.197f.
48. 20.162–186.
49. 17.378.
50. 8.5–21.
51. 12.280–294.
52. 17.134–143.
53. 12.117–127.
54. 12.365–382.
55. 12.294–311.
56. 12.324–335.
57. *Four Generations*, I, 140.
58. 12.247.
59. 8.264–272.
60. 17.264–275.
61. 17.272.
62. 12.44–55.
63. Burke, III, 478.
64. Haydon, *Autobiography*, I, 269.
65. 1.127ff.
66. 8.31.
67. 12.50; cf. 8.73ff., 10.243n.
68. 12.161f.
69. 9.189.
70. 16.48; cf. 12.78.
71. 12.45f.; cf. 10.222, 20.29.
72. 12.247ff.; cf. 8.105, 11.13f.
73. 12.382n.
74. 12.159–162, 180.
75. 20.374.
76. 8.249.
77. 12.251f.; cf. 11.19f., 19.304.
78. 17.275.
79. 12.193ff.
80. 12.10–13.
81. 12.336–346.
82. 17.246–254.
83. 17.106–122.
84. 12.220–229.
85. 8.150–156.
86. 8.196, 17.197, 316.
87. 8.65, 68, 251, 12.15f., 29, 241.
88. 19.267–278.
89. 8.152n.
90. 19.259f.
91. 8.62f., 12.243f.
92. 12.307.
93. 12.259, 17.22, 34, 320.

94. 17.324f.; cf. 8.153ff., 12.315, 19.223.
95. 8.146–156.
96. 19.255–267.
97. 12.295.
98. 8.257.
99. 8.279–289.
100. 8.189–204.
101. 17.122–134.
102. 8.146–156.
103. 17.75.
104. 17.264–275.
105. 8.181–189.
106. 12.136; cf. 12.87.
107. 8.237f.
108. 8.77–89.
109. See Landseer, I, 141f.

THE DEATH OF SCOTT

1. *London Magazine*, I (1820), 495f.
2. *London Magazine*, II (1820), 509–521.
3. *Blackwood's Magazine*, VIII (1820), 207f.
4. *London Magazine*, II (1820), 677.
5. *Ibid.*, III (1821), 2f.
6. *Examiner*, 4 March 1821, p. 143.
7. Robinson, I, 262.
8. Sir Walter Scott, *Letters* (ed. H. J. C. Grierson), VI (1934), 374.
9. *Memoirs*, II, 6.
10. "On Antiquity," 12.252–261.
11. 19.44–51.
12. 19.51–62.
13. 18.140–145.
14. See pages 233f.
15. *Four Generations*, I, 133ff.
16. 8.213.
17. Robinson, I, 264, 265, 278.
18. 8.189–204.
19. 18.411. A few years later Sir Walter Scott (p. 476) called Colburn "a puffing quack."

A MIND DISEASED

1. 9.127.
2. 8.24, 259, 12.122, 259, 17.269. For Howe's assessment of the evidence on this point see 9.262f.
3. 8.311; cf. 20.349.
4. Haydon, *Diary*, II, 441.
5. 8.95f.
6. Bonner, p. 247.
7. Procter, p. 181.
8. 9.134.
9. *Memoirs*, II, 11. On this passage, which, though not printed by Hazlitt himself, Hazlitt's grandson said was in the manuscript of "On the Fear of Death,"

see Stewart C. Wilcox, "A Manuscript Addition to Hazlitt's Essay 'On the Fear of Death'," *MLN*, LV (1940), 45ff.
10. 8.237.
11. 9.106; cf. Bonner, p. 246.
12. 8.235, 9.111.
13. 9.116, 122.
14. 9.112.
15. 9.118f.
16. 9.121. (Howe's text carries a question mark after the word "soul.")
17. 9.126.
18. Bonner, pp. 191f., 195.
19. Bonner, p. 209.
20. 9.140ff.
21. 9.128f.
22. Bonner, p. 227.
23. Bonner, p. 246.
24. Bonner, pp. 245f.
25. 9.138.
26. 9.157.
27. 9.160.
28. ALS, postmark 24 August 1822, The Yale University Library.
29. Procter, pp. 180f.
30. Haydon, *Diary*, II, 375.
31. *Ibid.*, II, 382.
32. Haydon, *Correspondence and Table-Talk*, II, 75.
33. Haydon, *Diary*, II, 440.
34. 12.78.

THE SLOW RECOVERY

1. 10.62–69.
2. 18.173–180.
3. 10.7.
4. The history of the *Liberal* has been admirably recorded by William H. Marshall in his *Byron, Shelley, Hunt, and The Liberal* (1960).
5. Leigh Hunt, *Lord Byron and Some of His Contemporaries* (2d ed., 1828), I, 87.
6. Shelley, *Letters*, II, 909.
7. Quoted from a letter of 27 January 1822 in the Berg Collection of the New York Public Library by Marshall, p. 52.
8. *The Press, or Literary Chit-Chat, A Satire* (1822), p. 48.
9. Prothero, VI, 119.
10. Hunt, *Lord Byron and Some of His Contemporaries*, I, 45.
11. Prothero, VI, 109.
12. Hunt, *Lord Byron and Some of His Contemporaries*, I, 79f., 84–89.
13. Prothero, VI, 122–125.
14. Warter, III, 340.
15. Robinson, I, 286.
16. Quoted from a letter of 29 October 1822 in the Murray archives by Leslie A.

Marchand, *Byron* (1957), III, 1040.

17. *Literary Gazette*, 2 November 1822, p. 694.

18. Quoted by Marshall, p. 104.

19. See Marshall, pp. 114ff.

20. 12.378; cf. 11.175f. For Hunt's acerb discussion of the situation see *Lord Byron and Some of His Contemporaries*, I, 80–84.

21. *Lord Byron and Some of His Contemporaries*, I, 91.

22. *Literary Gazette*, 26 October 1822, p. 678.

23. See William H. Marshall, "Three New Leigh Hunt Letters," *Keats-Shelley Journal*, IX (1960), 118, 121.

24. 19.35.

25. 19.44f.

26. 19.67.

27. *Byron: A Self-Portrait* (ed. Peter Quennell, 1950), II, 577.

28. 19.255–267.

29. "Mr. Coleridge's Lay-Sermon," 7. 128f.

30. 17.106–122.

31. 20.113–122.

32. 19.267–278. In the *Literary Examiner* (2 August 1823, pp. 76ff.) Leigh Hunt reprinted from "Arguing in a Circle" the passage on Burke.

33. 12.78–87.

34. 12.127–136.

35. 12.87.

36. Nos. 106, 119 (9.185, 187f.).

37. For example, nos. 161, 378 (9.192, 222).

38. No. 331 (9.215).

39. No. 195 (9.197).

40. Nos. 314–320 (9.212f.).

41. No. 302 (9.210).

42. No. 225 (9.201).

43. No. 239 (9.202).

44. No. 22 (9.169).

45. No. 60 (9.176).

46. No. 230 (9.201).

47. No. 417 (9.226).

48. No. 426 (9.227).

49. No. 278 (9.207).

50. No. 205 (9.198).

51. No. 251 (9.204).

52. No. 254 (9.204).

53. No. 351 (9.219).

54. *Life*, p. 322.

55. Hazlitt to Taylor and Hessey, ?February 1823, P. P. Howe, "New Hazlitt Letters," *London Mercury*, VII (1923), 498.

56. See above, page 378.

57. Bonner, p. 269.

58. Bonner, p. 269.

59. Bonner, p. 270.

60. Bonner, p. 272.

61. Bonner, p. 277.

62. *Blackwood's Magazine*, XIII (1823), 646.

63. *Some Letters & Miscellanea of Charles Brown* (ed. Maurice Buxton Forman, 1937), p. 18.

64. Mary Russell Mitford, *Letters* (Second Series, ed. Henry Chorley, 1872), I, 126.

65. 9.154.

66. W. M. Parker, "Charles Ollier to William Blackwood," *TLS*, 7 June 1947, p. 288.

67. Robinson, I, 286.

68. Robinson, I, 296.

69. *Literary Gazette*, 31 May 1823, pp. 339f.

70. *The Letters of Mary W. Shelley* (ed. Frederick L. Jones, 1944), I, 255.

71. ALS, George Crabbe to the Rev. George Crabbe, 2 December 1824, The Yale University Library.

72. Haydon, *Correspondence and Table-Talk*, II, 76.

73. Procter, p. 182.

74. *Literary Remains*, I, lxiii.

75. De Quincey, XI, 346.

76. *Ibid.*, III, 81. For a bibliographical account of *Liber Amoris* see *TLS*, 14 August 1943, p. 396.

77. *Life*, p. 327.

78. 12.61f.

THE SPIRIT OF THE AGE

1. 12.123.

2. 20.122–142.

3. See above, page 166n.

4. 11.5–16.

5. Robinson, I, 301.

6. Keynes, p. 74.

7. 9.244f.

8. *The Letters of Mary W. Shelley* (ed. Frederick L. Jones, 1944), I, 260.

9. 9.233ff.

10. 9.236–245.

11. 17.319f.

12. 4.162, 5.27f., 82, 18.9, 20.53–56.

13. 6.326; cf. 8.175.

14. See page 317n.

15. 9.238.

16. 6.62.

17. 5.120f., 9.242, 12.317f.

18. 5.92.

19. 4.36of., 8.175, 12.120.

20. 9.234f.

21. *Four Generations*, I, 184.

22. On the changes in the three editions that appeared in 1825 — two published by Colburn and one by the Parisian firm of Galignani — see Keynes, pp. 83ff.
23. 11.77f.
24. 11.37.
25. 11.6f.
26. 11.79f.
27. 11.108-111.
28. 11.125f.
29. 11.63f.
30. 11.150-158.
31. 11.16ff.
32. 11.18.
33. 11.103ff.
34. 11.7ff.
35. 11.28ff.
36. 11.117.
37. 8.55f.
38. 11.147f.
39. 11.32ff.
40. 11.6.
41. 11.58.
42. 11.71.
43. 11.114.
44. 11.182.
45. 11.103.
46. 11.79.
47. 11.174.
48. 11.29f.
49. 11.93f.
50. 11.114.
51. 12.220.
52. 5.155.
53. 6.128f.
54. 19.93.
55. 12.319f.; cf. 11.276, 16.401.
56. 12.180; cf. 10.254f., 12.99, 105, 18.407.
57. 11.58, 60f.
58. 11.62, 64.
59. 11.65f.
60. 11.68.
61. *Literary Remains*, I, lxiv; cf. *Memoirs*, II, 106f.
62. *Four Generations*, I, 182.
63. ALS, John to Leigh Hunt, 31 August 1824, British Museum Add. MS. 38,108.
64. ALS, G. Huntley Gordon to W. C. Hazlitt, 15 February [1866], British Museum Add. MS. 28,899.
65. 8.236.
66. Robinson, I, 387.
67. *Life*, p. 335.
68. Landseer, I, 157-173.
69. ALS, Mary Russell Mitford to Thomas Noon Talfourd, [?July or August 1824], Rylands Collection, The University of Manchester. I follow the conjectural

dating of Mr. William A. Coles, to whom I am indebted for his transcript of this letter.
70. Mary Shelley, *Letters*, I, 303.
71. See Keynes, p. 72.
72. 16.284-318. This review gave great offense to Haydon (*Diary*, II, 494f.).
73. See page 409n.
74. 16.265-284.
75. Mary Shelley, *Letters*, I, 307.

IX

Epilogue

THE CONTINENTAL TOUR

1. 10.214.
2. 10.102ff., 113f., 120f., 138-147.
3. 10.106-113.
4. 10.256f.
5. 10.98.
6. 10.106f.
7. 10.147-151.
8. 10.114-118.
9. 10.162-168.
10. Bonner, pp. 253-261.
11. 10.278, 20.162n.
12. 8.285; cf. the long quotation from *De l'amour*, 10.251f. This subject has been ably treated by Robert Vigneron in his "Stendhal et Hazlitt," *MP*, XXXV (1938), 375-414.
13. 10.182.
14. 10.182.
15. 10.186f. On the eventual disposition of these books see page 257n.
16. 10.188f.
17. 10.196.
18. 10.200.
19. 10.210.
20. 10.212.
21. See Edmund Blunden, *Leigh Hunt and His Circle* (1930), pp. 218-223.
22. 10.211f.
23. 16.240-244.
24. John Forster, *Walter Savage Landor* (1869), p. 434, quoting a letter of the artist Seymour Kirkup. For a somewhat different account see the reminiscences of Charles Armitage Brown's son, *Keats Circle*, I, lviii.
25. 19.107.
26. Forster, pp. 437f.
27. *Four Generations*, I, 183.
28. 10.235.
29. 17.140.
30. 17.136.
31. 10.235f.

32. *Four Generations*, I, 183f.
33. 10.265f.
34. 10.278.
35. 10.280.
36. 17.152–162.
37. 10.287.
38. Medwin, pp. 278–283.
39. 10.294.
40. 10.301.

THE LATER WORKS

1. 8.325.
2. See page 235.
3. 12.361.
4. 12.130.
5. *Memoirs*, I, 87, 95; II, 198.
6. Scott, p. 538.
7. *New Monthly Magazine*, XXXIX (1830), 481f.
8. 11.202; 12.86.
9. 17.30.
10. Haydon, *Diary*, II, 418.
11. Pope, 3 August 1826.
12. 12.85.
13. 12.39; cf. 11.317, 12.39f., 85f., 91ff.
14. Landseer, II, 122; cf. 11.269f.
15. Cyrus Redding, *Fifty Years' Recollections*, II, 299.
16. 12.40.
17. 12.99ff.
18. 11.187.
19. 11.193.
20. 11.206.
21. 11.193–198.
22. 11.350.
23. Pope, 3 August 1826.
24. 11.188f.
25. Hunt, *Correspondence*, I, 251f.
26. 11.357f.
27. My account of Northcote's controversy with the Mudges is drawn mainly from Allan Cunningham, *The Lives of the Most Eminent British Painters*, II, 422–428; cf. Stewart C. Wilcox, "Hazlitt and Northcote," *ELH*, VII (1940), 325–332.
28. 13.354. On his attempt to copy Titian see 17.219.
29. 17.185.
30. 17.189–237.
31. 17.197.
32. 17.198f.
33. 17.245.
34. 17.242.
35. 12.87.
36. 17.89.
37. 17.234; cf. 12.256.
38. 17.298.
39. 17.311.
40. 17.293.

41. 17.313.
42. 17.319f.
43. *Memoirs*, II, 217f.
44. 19.302–320. See pages 325f.
45. 8.325f.
46. Medwin, p. 282.
47. Clarke, p. 61.
48. Lucas, III, 151f.
49. 17.316.
50. 12.310; cf. 9.225.
51. 13.150–154.
52. 15.71–88.
53. For example, 13.37–60, 91–94, 14.235ff.
54. For example, 13.119f., 187f., 14.5, 277, 15.169, 200f., 221.
55. For example, 13.26, 47–52, 14.194, 273ff., 332, 352f. (on Scott as a Tory historian).
56. 17.320.
57. 15.259.
58. 9.228.

THE END

1. 20.331.
2. Cyrus Redding, *Past Celebrities Whom I Have Known* (1866), I, 97.
3. 8.325f.
4. James Anthony Froude, *Thomas Carlyle: A History of the First Forty Years of His Life* (1910), II, 169.
5. 17.313n.
6. 18.374–417. The first of these reviews was printed on 16 March 1828, the last on June 15.
7. 18.408.
8. 18.403f.
9. The last of his reviews for the *Examiner* (15 June 1828) concerns Kean's recent appearance in Paris.
10. On 6 October 1828 he wrote sternly to the postmaster at Salisbury about his "impertinence and collusion" in overcharging for the post (*Four Generations*, I, 195).
11. 16.395f.
12. 20.162–186. See page 395.
13. 20.187ff.
14. 20.191–194.
15. 20.196f.
16. 20.212–215.
17. 20.200–204, 248–253, 254f.
18. 20.215–218, 236–239.
19. 20.316.
20. 20.296–306.
21. 20.227–230.
22. "The Spirit of Controversy," 20.306–311; "Prejudice," 20.316–321; "Party Spirit," 20.321–324.

23. 20.321.
24. See page 455.
25. 11.318ff.
26. ALS, Cornell University Library. On the concellations in certain copies of the *Conversations* see Keynes, pp. 100ff.
27. 16.318–408.
28. 20.243–246; see page 217.
29. For the texts of Hazlitt's six letters to Napier between 13 July 1829 and 19 March 1830 see P. P. Howe, "Unpublished Letters of William Hazlitt," *Athenaeum*, 15 August 1919, pp. 742ff.
30. For other comments on Hazlitt's eagerness to review this book see Frederick W. Hackwood, *William Hone: His Life and Times* (1912), p. 293; Lucas, III, 233.
31. 16.324.
32. 20.283.
33. 16.405f.
34. 16.391.
35. *Athenaeum*, 15 August 1919, p. 743.
36. Vera Watson, "Thomas Noon Talfourd and His Friends," *TLS*, 27 April 1956, p. 260.
37. George Gilfillan, *A Third Gallery of Portraits* (1855), p. 178.
38. 20.332.
39. 20.343.
40. 8.330.
41. 17.372f.
42. 17.365–370.
43. 17.371–376.
44. 17.376–382.
45. 19.334n.
46. *Literary Remains*, I, lxvi.
47. *Ibid.*; cf. *Keats Circle*, I, lxxiv f.
48. Thomas Carlyle, *Letters . . . 1826–1836* (ed. Charles Eliot Norton, 1889), p. 171.
49. Edmund Blunden, "New Sidelights on Keats, Lamb, and Others from Letters to J. Clare," *London Mercury*, IV (1921), 149.
50. *Literary Remains*, I, lxvi.
51. 16.396.
52. *New Monthly Magazine*, XXIX (1830), 478; cf. Clarke, p. 63; *Gentleman's Magazine*, C (1830), 372f.
53. *Memoirs*, II, 238. Sarah Hazlitt's memorandum of her former husband's death and burial, from which some of these details are taken, is preserved in British Museum Add. MS. 38,898.
54. *Tatler*, 28 September 1831, p. [81].

IN RETROSPECT

1. 8.326; cf. 17.116.
2. 16.154.
3. 8.11.
4. Rollins, II, 76.
5. 4.77.
6. 20.105.
7. 1.153.
8. 9.30.
9. Hunt, *Poetical Works*, p. 228.
10. Griggs, II, 991.
11. Rollins, I, 203, 205.
12. 17.34.
13. 17.22.
14. 7.230f.
15. 17.378.
16. 20.97, 102.
17. 17.317.
18. 17.320.
19. 17.297.
20. 17.318.
21. 17.316.
22. 17.197.
23. 17.316.
24. 17.22f.; cf. 12.259.
25. 4.102.
26. 18.367.
27. 11.191.
28. 5.144.

INDEX

INDEX

INDEX

INDEX

INDEX

INDEX

INDEX

INDEX

INDEX

338; and Wordsworth, 344f.; and
Leigh Hunt, 209, 371
Jerdan, William, 421f.
Joan of Arc (Southey), 64f., 87
Johnson, Joseph, 56f., 85; and WH, 140,
156, 158
Johnson, Samuel: on Priestley, 7; on Parliament, 11; WH on, 35n, 200, 201,
229, 279, 303f., 316f.; critical theory
of 273ff., 277f.; on Shakespeare, 304,
305, 307f.; cited, 309f.; and Zachariah Mudge, 454
Jonson, Ben, WH on, 299, 313, 317
Jordan, Dorothea Bland, 288
Joseph Andrews (Fielding), 55, 313
Journalism, WH's career in, 140, 191–
197. See also *The Champion, The
Examiner, The Morning Chronicle,
The Times, The Yellow Dwarf*
Judgment of Soloman, The (Haydon), WH
on, 239, 241f.
Julian (Mitford), 215n

Kant, Immanuel, 189, 358n
Kean, Edmund, WH on, 194, 290–295
Keats, John: on Charles Dilke, 112n; and
Wordsworth, 148, 249, 349f.; on tourists, 170; and WH, 123, 148f., 221,
238, 247–251, 253, 254, 256, 262,
303, 346n, 362, 369, 374, 389, 431f.,
470; and the *Examiner*, 198, 247f.;
and the *Edinburgh Review*, 207; on literary men, 224; and Leigh Hunt, 231;
and Haydon, 238; on Coleridge, 249;
and Shakespeare, 123, 249, 283, 303;
on Benjamin West, 283; on contemporary drama, 286; on beauty, 302; on
Napoleon, 329; and the *Quarterly Review*, 366, 423; and *Blackwood's Magazine*, 378n, 379
Kemble, John Philip, 285n, 289f., 292
Kemble, Stephen, 296
Keswick, Cumberland, WH at, 134–139
Keynes, Sir Geoffrey, 468n
King Lear (Shakespeare), 249, 283, 301n,
305, 306
Kippis, Andrew, 22n, 25, 28n, 29
Knowles, James Sheridan, 221, 301, 389,
410n, 413
Knox, Vicesimus, 430
"Kubla Khan" (Coleridge), 347

Labor Unions, WH on, 321
Lalla Rookh (Moore), 312f.
Lamb, Charles: and WH, 135n, 136,
139n, 152–156, 165n, 167f., 170,
181, 183, 192, 196, 221, 223f., 233n,
258, 260, 262, 280n, 304, 317n,
343n, 407, 408, 426, 428, 437, 459,

460, 469; and Godwin, 71f., 171n;
on Holcroft, 76; on Mrs. Godwin, 171;
on politics, 224; and Leigh Hunt, 224,
231; and Haydon, 238; and Wordsworth, 238, 348; on lectures, 253f.; on
Hogarth, 280n; on oratorios, 297; on
Shakespeare, 304; on Sir Philip Sidney,
317n; on Donne, 317n; and *The Excursion*, 342n, 345n; on Coleridge,
351; and the *London Magazine*, 386n,
406; on science, 396; and John Scott,
406; on the Scots, 422n
Lamb, John, 219n
Lamb, Mary, 152–156 *passim*, 167f., 177,
180
"Lamia" (Keats), 396
Landor, Walter Savage, and WH, 123,
416n, 432, 445f.
Laodamia (Wordsworth), 435n
Lawrence, Sir Thomas, 270
Lawyers, WH on, 331f.
Lay of the Last Minstrel (Scott), 192n
Lay of the Laureate (Southey), 341f.
Lay Sermon (Coleridge): first, 355–358
passim, 363; second, 141, 358f.
Lectures: WH's on philosophy, 139, 142,
183–190; on English poets, 252ff.; on
English comic writers, 254 ff.; on Elizabethan literature, 260–263; at Glasgow,
413f.; on literature of England, 310–
319; Coleridge's, 184, 253, 351n
Lectures on History and General Policy
(Priestley), 15
Lectures on Rhetoric and Belles Lettres
(Blair), 146
Legitimacy, WH on, 331–334. See also
Monarchy
Leibniz, Baron Gottfried Wilhelm von,
154n
Letters on Chivalry and Romance (Hurd),
271
*Letters to the Right Honourable Edmund
Burke* (Priestley), 47, 327
Letter to a Friend of Robert Burns (Wordsworth), 253, 345n
Letter to a Noble Lord (Burke), 46n, 51
Letter to John Dunning, Esq., A (Tooke),
174
Letter to the Bishop of Llandaff, A (Wordsworth), 68f.
Letter to William Smith, A (Southey),
202n, 361
Lewis, William Thomas ("Gentleman"),
288
Liberal, The, 233, 419–423
Life of John Buncle, Esq. (Amory), 201
Life of Titian, The (Northcote), 451, 456,
468
Lindsey, Theophilus, 22n, 24

524

INDEX

INDEX

INDEX

INDEX

Robinson, Mary ("Perdita"), 57, 77
Robinson, Thomas, WH's portrait of, 182ff., 191
Rob Roy (Scott), 349
Rogers, Samuel: on the treason trials, 91; on Godwin and Mackintosh, 102n; and Godwin, 104n; and Jeffrey, 206; and Haydon, 239; WH on, 318, 430
Roman Catholic Church: disabilities of, 5; WH on, 30f., 33, 204, 442
Rome, WH's visit to, 445f.
Romilly, Sir Samuel, 323
Rosa, Salvator, 446n
Rosdew, Richard, and Northcote, 454ff.
"Round Table, The" (in the *Examiner*), 165n, 196n, 199–202
Rouen, 442
Rousseau, Jean Jacques: political thought of, 78f.; the *Anti-Jacobin* on, 87; WH on, 42n, 78, 122, 143, 200, 209, 391f., 472; on feeling, 396
Rowe, Nicholas, 298
Royal Society, the, 269. *See also* Academic art
Russell, James, 367n
Russell Institution, the, 184n

St. Andrews, Holborn, WH's marriage at, 168
St. Anne's, Soho, WH's burial at, 469
St. Leon (Godwin), 102f., 131
St. Neot's, Huntingtonshire, 268n, 401
St. Peter's, Rome, 446
"Salisbury Plain" (Wordsworth), 97
Sardanapalus (Byron), WH's alleged review of, 208n, 216n, 413n
Schiller, Johann Christoph Friedrich von: Coleridge on, 63; WH on, 122f.
Schlegel, August Wilhelm von, WH on, 120, 209, 210, 212f., 301, 303
Scholarship, WH on, 303f., 312
School for Scandal, The (Sheridan), 298
Science, WH on, 271, 300
Scots, the, WH on, 422f.
Scott, John, First Earl of Eldon, 336, 361, 435f.
Scott, John (editor), 195f., 223, 262, 346n, 366n, 380, 385–388, 403–409
Scott, Sir Walter: WH on, 55, 121, 148, 209, 283n, 284f., 302, 319, 374, 399, 435, 437, 438ff., 447; on reformers, 76; on Pitt, 81; and Coleridge's *Christabel*, 192n; and the *Edinburgh Review*, 205, 206, 207; and *The Encyclopaedia Britannica*, 217n; and Haydon, 244n, 245; on Southey, 354; and the *Quarterly Review*, 365; on Gifford, 366; and Lockhart, 380f.; on John

Scott, 406; on Northcote, 350; life of Napoleon, 460f.
Sculpture, WH on, 239f., 443
Seasons, The (Thomson), 127f.
Seditious Meetings Bill, the, 92
Sensationalism, WH on, 145, 187–190. *See also* Modern philosophy
Severn, Joseph, 445n
Shaftesbury, Third Earl of, *see* Cooper, Anthony Ashley
Shakespeare, William: WH on, 123, 148, 152, 154, 201, 212f., 284f., 297, 299f., 302–310, 317, 375, 399; WH on performances of, 285–310 *passim*
Shelley, Mary Wollstonecraft, 71, 423, 426, 429f., 440f.
Shelley, Percy Bysshe: and WH, 30n, 110f., 233, 284, 339f., 431, 432; irreligion of, 36; and Malthus, 109n; and Godwin, 111; and the *Examiner*, 198, 359; and the *Edinburgh Review*, 206, 207; WH's and Leigh Hunt's quarrel over, 233f.; on Napoleon, 329; and Southey, 359; and Gifford, 366f.; and *Blackwood's Magazine*, 378n; and the *Liberal*, 419–423 *passim*
Shepherd, Sally, and WH, 132n
Sheridan, Richard Brinsley: on political agitation, 88; comedies of, 298, 300
Shrewsbury, 3, 20, 123, 124, 257n
Siddons, Sarah, 179, 238; WH on, 288f., 388, 463
Sidney, Sir Philip, 147; WH on, 311, 317, 430f.
Sieyès, Emmanuel Joseph, 354
Sikes, H. M., 193n, 433n, 468n
"Simon Lee" (Wordsworth), 97
Simple Story, A (Inchbald), 132n, 393
Simplon pass, the, 447
Sismondi, J. C. L. de, WH on, 211f.
Six Acts, the, 323
Slavery, WH on, 19
Smith, Adam, WH on, 144, 151f.
Smith, Charlotte, 78
Smith, Horatio ("Horace"), 230, 406, 423
Smith, Sydney: on Dissenters, 5f.; on Parliament, 11f.; on Methodists, 33; on Pitt, 82, 115; on Parr, 102f.; on Malthus, 104f.; and the *Edinburgh Review*, 204–207 *passim*; on Napoleon, 329; on Tories, 336; on Gifford, 366
Smith, William, and Southey, 360f.
Social progress, WH on, 38, 110f., 326ff., 400
Southampton Buildings, Holburn, WH's residence in, 168n, 181, 410, 416
Southey, Robert: on Dissenting ministers, 22; and Priestley, 25n; on his youthful indiscretions, 37, 361n; as a young re-

INDEX

INDEX

Date Due